1 MONTH OF
FREE
READING

at

www.ForgottenBooks.com

By purchasing this book you are eligible for one month membership to ForgottenBooks.com, giving you unlimited access to our entire collection of over 1,000,000 titles via our web site and mobile apps.

To claim your free month visit:
www.forgottenbooks.com/free966231

ISBN 978-0-260-71992-8
PIBN 10966231

REPORTS

OF

CASES

ARGUED AND DETERMINED

IN

The Court of King's Bench.

VOL. III.

REPORTS

OF

CASES

ARGUED AND DETERMINED

IN

The Court of King's Bench.

WITH TABLES OF THE NAMES OF THE CASES
AND THE PRINCIPAL MATTERS.

BY

RICHARD VAUGHAN BARNEWALL, of Lincoln's Inn,

AND

CRESSWELL CRESSWELL, of the Inner Temple, Esqrs.

BARRISTERS AT LAW.

VOL. III.

Containing the Cases of TRINITY, MICHAELMAS, and HILARY Terms,
in the 5th and 6th Years of GEO. IV. 1824, 1825.

LONDON:

PRINTED BY A. STRAHAN,
LAW-PRINTER TO THE KING'S MOST EXCELLENT MAJESTY;

FOR J. BUTTERWORTH AND SON, LAW-BOOKSELLERS, 43. FLEET-STREET;
AND J. COOKE, ORMOND-QUAY, DUBLIN.
1825.

JUDGES

COURT OF KING's BENCH,

During the Period of these REPORTS.

Sir CHARLES ABBOTT, Knt. C. J.
Sir JOHN BAYLEY, Knt.
Sir GEORGE SOWLEY HOLROYD, Knt.
Sir JOSEPH LITTLEDALE, Knt.

ATTORNEY-GENERAL.

Sir JOHN SINGLETON COPLEY, Knt.

SOLICITOR-GENERAL.

Sir CHARLES WETHERALL, Knt.

A

TABLE

OF THE

NAMES OF THE CASES

REPORTED IN THIS VOLUME.

a   Middleton,

TABLE OF CASES REPORTED.

18

ERRATUM.

In p. 750. l. 23. dele the words " and then," and insert the words " From the other facts of this case."

CASES

ARGUED AND DETERMINED

IN THE

Court of KING's BENCH,

IN

Trinity Term,

In the Fifth Year of the Reign of GEORGE IV.

THOMPSON *against* MACERONI.

THE defendant had been held to bail, upon an affi-davit of debt for goods sold and delivered. Bail above were put in and justified. After issue was joined, a special count for not delivering a bill of exchange was added. At the trial evidence was given of an order for the goods, and of their having been made pursuant to the order; and that the goods remained in the plaintiff's pos-session, at the request of the defendant, and were of the value of 144*l.*; that the defendant took away a small part, of the value of 2*l.* 10*s.* No bill was given, and the plaintiff, at the trial, obtained a verdict for 144*l.*, on the count for not delivering the bill. A rule nisi had been obtained by *Scarlett* for entering an exoneretur on the

Where goods of the value of 144*l.* were made to order and remained in the posses-sion of the ven-dor at the re-quest of the vendee, with the exception of a small part which the latter took away: Held, that there was no acceptance of the residue of the goods with-in the statute of frauds, sect. 17.

VOL. III.   B   bail-

bail-piece, on the ground that the plaintiff had recovered
on the special count for not delivering the bill.

Marryat shewed cause, and contended, first, that there
was sufficient evidence to entitle the plaintiff to recover
on the count for goods sold and delivered.(*a*) They were
made to the defendant's order, and he took away some
of the articles; and the rest remained in the plaintiff's
shop, at the request of the defendant. The plaintiff
had put it inthe vendee's power to take away the goods,
and that, according to the opinion of *Holroyd* J. in
Smith v. *Chance* (*b*), was sufficient to maintain the action.

But the Court were clearly of opinion, that there was
no actual acceptance of these goods by the buyer within
the 17th section of the statute of frauds, and that the
plaintiff was not entitled to recover on the count for goods
sold and delivered, and the rule was made absolute.

Rule absolute.

(*a*) It was agreed, that the question should be considered on this motion,
in order to save the expence of a cross motion for a new trial.
(*b*) 2 *B. & A.* 755.

STODDART against PALMER.

Where in an
action for a
false return to
a fieri facias,
the declaration
stated that the
plaintiff in *T.*
term, 2 *G.* 4.,
ACTION against the defendant, as late sheriff of
       Surry, for a false return of nulla bona to a writ of
fieri facias. The declaration stated that the plaintiff, in
Trinity term, in the second year of our lord the now

by the judgment recovered, &c. " as appears by the record," and the proof was of a judgment in *Easter* term, 3 *G.* 4. : Held that this was no variance: for that the averment, " as
appears by the record," was surplusage, and might be rejected, inasmuch as the judgment
was not the foundation of, but mere inducement to the action.

king,

king, in the Court of King's Bench, by the consideration and judgment of the Court, recovered &c., as by
the record remaining in the Court of King's Bench appears. Plea, general issue. At the trial it appeared,
upon the production of the record of the judgment, that
the costs were taxed on the postea in *Easter* term, the
3 G. 4.; and the Lord Chief Justice was of opinion that
this was a variance, and the plaintiff was nonsuited. A
rule nisi had been obtained for setting aside this nonsuit,
against which .

Marryat now shewed cause. The plaintiff having set
out a judgment in his declaration, and concluded prout
patet per recordum, was bound to prove a judgment
precisely the same in all its circumstances as that alleged. *Pope* v. *Foster* (a) is in point; and although the
decision in that case was overruled by that of *Purcell* v.
Macnamara (b), yet in the latter case Lord *Ellenborough*
expressly took the distinction, that if the plaintiff had
stated the record, and then alleged prout patet per recordum, that it would not have been an allegation of
substance but of description. This, therefore, falls
within that distinction. In the subsequent case of *Phillips* v. *Shaw* (c) this averment was omitted in the count
on which the verdict was taken. Besides, it was impossible to maintain this action without shewing a writ
founded upon that judgment. The judgment, therefore,
is the very foundation of the action, and it was necessary to set it out precisely.

Scarlett contrà. The averment of prout patet per
recordum is unnecessary. It may be therefore rejected,

(a) 4 *T. R.* 590. (b) 9 *East,* 157. (c) 4 *B. & A.* 435. and 5 *B. & A.* 964.

as surplusage, for the distinction is, as laid down in
Co. Litt. 303., and recognised and acted upon in *Wate*
v. *Briggs* (a), " that when the record is the ground of
the plaintiff's action, he ought to conclude prout patet
per recordum; but where it is matter of inducement
only, that is unnecessary." That was an action of debt
for an escape. The commitment was held to be mere
inducement, and the prout patet per recordum to be
unnecessary. So in this case the judgment is mere
inducement, the foundation of the action being the false
return. The allegation, therefore, was unnecessary. It
may be rejected altogether, and the plaintiff will still
have a sufficient cause of action disclosed in his declaration. That being so, it was not necessary for him to
give evidence of a judgment, in all its circumstances
precisely the same as that set out in the declaration.

Abbott C. J. We are all of opinion that this rule
ought to be made absolute. Whatever may have been
the rule upon this subject in ancient times, a distinction
is now established between allegations of matter of substance and allegations of matter of description. The
former require to be substantially proved; the latter
must be literally proved. That distinction was laid
down by the Court in *Purcell* v. *Macnamara*, and has
since been acted upon in the case of *Phillips* v. *Shaw*.
If, therefore, the allegation that the plaintiff by judgment recovered, &c., be an allegation of substance only,
it was sufficient to prove any judgment to warrant the
writ. If, on the other hand, it be an allegation of description, it was necessary to prove a judgment, corre-

(a) 1 *Ld. Raym.* 35. 3 *Salk.* 565.

sponding

sponding in time and in all other circumstances with that stated in the declaration. Now it is contended, that this is a descriptive allegation, because the plaintiff has alleged a judgment "prout patet per recordum." The declaration in *Purcell* v. *Macnamara*, and the count on which the verdict was taken in *Phillips* v. *Shaw*, did not contain any such averment, and Lord *Ellenborough*, in the former case, intimated an opinion, that if there had been such an averment, it might have been considered as descriptive of the record, and that the variance would have been fatal. But, upon consideration, it appears to us that that opinion is not correct, and that the introduction of the averment in this case is wholly immaterial. It is an unnecessary allegation, and may be rejected as surplusage; and if it can be altogether struck out of the declaration, without injuring the plaintiff's cause of action, it is quite clear, that the proof necessary to support such an allegation (when material) need not be given. Now it is fully established, by the passage referred to in *Co. Litt.* 303 *a.*, and the case of *Wate* v. *Briggs*, that where a matter of record is insisted upon only by way of inducement, and not as the very foundation of the action, the party insisting upon it need not conclude prout patet per recordum. That being so, the averment in this case was unnecessary, and may be rejected as surplusage; and if it be rejected, then the case is precisely similar to those of *Purcell* v. *Macnamara* and *Phillips* v. *Shaw*. For these reasons we are of opinion, that the rule for setting aside the nonsuit must be made absolute.

Rule absolute.

Saturday,
June 19th.

SKINNER *against* BUCKEE.

By statute
55 G. 3. c. 137.
s. 6. no church-
warden or over-
seer of the
poor, either in
his own name
or in the name
of any other
person, shall
supply *for his
own profit* any
goods, materi-
als, or provi-
sions for the
use of any
workhouse, or
otherwise for
the support or
maintenance of
the poor in any
place for which
he shall be ap-
pointed over-
seer, during the
time he shall
retain such ap-
pointment, nor
shall be con-
cerned directly
or indirectly in
supplying the
same, or in any
contract or con-
tracts relating
thereto, under
the penalty of
100*l.*: Held,
that an over-
seer who sup-
plied coals in-
directly for the
use of the poor,
was not liable
to any penalty,
unless he did
it with a view
to his own
profit.

THIS was a penal action, founded on the 55 *G. 3.* *c.* 137. *s.* 6. The first count of the declaration charged, that the defendant, on, &c., was overseer of the poor of the liberty of *Saffron-hill*, *Hatton-garden*, and *Ely-rents*, in the county of *Middlesex*, duly appointed in that behalf, to wit, at, &c., and that during the time he retained such appointment as aforesaid, to wit, on, &c., did, in his own name, provide, furnish, and supply certain goods, to wit, coals for the use of a workhouse belonging to the said liberty for which he was appointed, to wit, at, &c., contrary to the form of the statute, by reason whereof, &c. Another count stated, that the defendant did, in the name of a certain other person, provide, furnish, and supply, for his, defendant's, own profit, coals for the use of a certain workhouse, &c. The third count stated, that he was concerned indirectly in supplying, for his own profit, coals, &c.. The fourth stated, that he was concerned directly in supplying, coals, for the use of the workhouse, (omitting the words, " for his own profit.") The fifth count was, that he was concerned indirectly in supplying coals for the use of the workhouse. The sixth count, that he was concerned in a certain contract relating to the providing, furnishing, and supplying goods, materials, and provisions for the use of the workhouse. At the trial before *Abbott* C. J., at the sittings after *Michaelmas* term, it appeared that the defendant was a coal-merchant, and that he was duly appointed overseer of the

16   liberty

liberty of *Saffron-hill*, *Hatton-Garden*, and *Ely-rents*, and during the time that he was overseer, a quantity of coals were provided for the workhouse, nominally by one *Gaubert*, who was the brother-in-law of the defendant, but that the latter had an interest in the coals. It was doubtful upon the evidence, however, whether either he or *Gaubert* made any profit by them. The Lord Chief Justice was of opinion, that unless the defendant acted with a view to profit, it was not a case within the 55 G. 3. c. 137. s. 6.; and he told the jury to find for the defendant, if they were of opinion, upon the evidence, that the defendant did not send in the coals with a view of making a profit. The jury having found for the defendant, a rule nisi for a new trial had been obtained in last *Hilary* term.

Scarlett now shewed cause. It is quite clear, that if the defendant had, in his own name, or in the name of another, supplied the coals for the use of the poor at prime cost, he would not have been within the words of the act of parliament, because they would not be supplied for his own profit. The words, *for his own profit*, over-ride the whole clause; for the legislature cannot have intended to subject a party to a penalty, concerned directly or indirectly in furnishing and supplying provisions for the poor, or in any contract relating thereto, when the very same party does not incur any penalty by supplying the same provisions in his own name, provided it be not done for his own profit.

Gurney contrà. The act creates two distinct species of offences. The first is the supplying of provisions, either in the name of the overseer, or in that of another

B 4   person,

person, and that must be for his own profit. The second offence is the being concerned directly or indirectly in supplying provisions, or in any contract relating thereto, and there the words, *for his own profit*, are omitted. A party who, in his own name, or even in that of another person, supplied the provisions openly, might do so, provided it were not done for his own profit; but the being concerned secretly in supplying the same, or in any contract relating thereto, is a suspicious circumstance, and the legislature may intentionally have made that an offence, although it were not done with a view to profit.

Abbott C. J.   We are all of opinion that this rule must be discharged. The question, in this case, arises upon the construction of the 55 G. 3. c. 137. s. 6.; the words are, that " no churchwarden or overseer of the poor, either in his own name, or in the name of any other person or persons, shall provide, furnish, or supply, *for his or their own profit*, any goods, materials, or provisions, for the use of any workhouse, or otherwise, for the support or maintenance of the poor in any parish or place for which he shall be appointed such overseer, during the time which he shall retain such appointment, nor shall be concerned directly or indirectly in furnishing or supplying the same, ·or in any contract or contracts relating thereto, under the penalty of 100*l*."   Now, if the overseer himself, in this case, had supplied all the provisions required for the support of the poor, at prime cost, and not with a view to his own profit, it is quite clear that he would not have committed any offence within the words of this part of the act of parliament: that was laid down by *Gibbs* C. J. in

Pope

Pope v. *Backhouse.* (a) Inasmuch, therefore, as an overseer providing, in his own name, the poor of his parish with all the provisions and goods required for their support, would not be liable to any penalty, provided he made no profit, it cannot be supposed that the legislature intended that the same overseer who is concerned directly or indirectly in any contract for supplying any part of the provisions, however small, should be liable to a penalty, although he derived no profit from it. That would involve a manifest contradiction. I think, therefore, that the words, *for his own profit*, must be taken to over-ride the whole clause, and that the legislature intended that no overseer for his own *profit*, either in his own name or in that of any other person, should supply the poor with provisions, nor be concerned, directly or indirectly, in any contract relating to it.

Rule discharged.

(a) 8 *Taunt.* 248.

Martin v. Daws 11. M. Neil. 754

STANWAY *against* HESLOP.

A RULE having been made to change the venue,

The Court will
not change the
venue in an
action on an
award.

Park obtained a rule to discharge the former rule, on an affidavit that the action was brought upon an award.

Patteson shewed cause. It is true that in *Whitburn* v. *Staines* (a) the Court of Common Pleas refused to

(a) 2 B. & P. 355.

change

1824.

Stanway
against
Healor.

change the venue, the action being on an award, but in *Greenway* v. *Carrington* (a) *Wood* B. expressed considerable doubt of that, as a general proposition, and it has never been held in this court that the venue may not be changed in such an action.

Abbott C. J.   There is not any case deciding that the venue may be changed in an action on an award, and as the contrary has been held in the Court of Common Pleas, we think it best that the practice of this court should be conformable to that decision.

Rule absolute. (b)

(a) 7 *Price*, 564.   (b) See *Morice* v. *Hurry*, 7 *Taunt.* 506.

LONG *against* GREVILLE.

*Monday,
June 21st.*

Assumpsit for goods sold and delivered, and on the money counts. Pleas, general issue, and the statute of limitations. Defendant paid money into court generally: Held, that such payment did not take the case out of the statute.

ASSUMPSIT for goods sold and delivered, and on the common money counts. Pleas, non assumpsit, and the statute of limitations. At the trial before *Abbott* C. J., at the *Westminster* sittings after last *Michaelmas* term, the plaintiff's witnesses swore, that in 1813 the defendant dined several times at plaintiff's hotel, together with other persons; that each person was to pay for his own share of the dinners; that the bill for that and for small sums expended on account of the defendant amounted to 13*l.* In 1822 a bill was delivered to the defendant, who refused to pay it, saying, that he had never dined at plaintiff's hotel unless invited. He afterwards paid 2*l.* 12*s.* 6*d.* into court generally. The Lord Chief Justice thought that the case

was

was not taken out of the statute of limitations, but left it to the jury to say whether the defendant had, at the time when he dined at the plaintiff's hotel, consented to pay for his share of the dinners, and gave the defendant leave to move to enter a nonsuit. The jury found for the plaintiff, and in *Hilary* term a rule for a nonsuit was obtained, against which

Gurney and *Claridge* shewed cause, and contended, that by paying money into court generally, without confining it to any one item of the bill, the defendant had admitted that something was due to the plaintiff. The amount alone remained in dispute. *Stoveld* v. *Brewin* (a), *Dyer* v. *Ashton*. (b) Now, unless the case were taken out of the statute nothing could have been due, the whole demand having arisen ten years ago.

Denman, contrà, was stopped by the Court.

Per Curiam. If we were to hold, that by the payment of money into court, in this case, the defendant had excluded himself from the benefit of the statute of limitations, we should certainly give to such a payment an effect never before contemplated. Where money is paid in upon a declaration, setting forth a special contract, that is admitted as alleged. But in no case has the effect gone beyond admitting that the sum paid in is due. Here no special contract was set out; the declaration only stated that so much money was due. The payment into court was equivalent to saying so much is due and no more. You cannot, from such a

(a) 2 B. & A. 116.   (b) 1 B. & C. 8.

negative,

negative, imply an affirmative. The plaintiff, therefore,
with respect to the rest of his demand, was in precisely.
the same situation as if that sum had not been paid in;
and the rule for a nonsuit must be made absolute.

Rule absolute.

; SIDAWAY *against* HAY.

A debt con-
tracted in *Eng-
land* by a trader
residing in
Scotland is
barred by a
discharge under
a sequestration
issued in con-
formity to the
54 *G.3; c. 137.*,
in like manner
as debts con-
tracted in *Scot-
land.*

DEBT for goods sold and delivered, with the common
money counts. Pleas, first, nil debet; second, the
statute of limitations; third, actio non; because defendant before and on *January* 1st, 1814, and thence continually until the sequestration of the estate, heritable
and moveable, real and personal, of defendant thereinafter mentioned, was a merchant and trader in gross and
by retail, to wit, an ironmonger, residing and carrying
on his said trade at *Edinburgh,* in that part of the United
Kingdom called *Scotland;* and during all that time
sought his living by buying and selling; and that defendant on the day and year aforesaid became indebted
to *C.* and Co. in the sum of 186*l.* 15*s.* 2*d.* for a just and
true debt, and was also indebted to divers other persons
in divers large sums of money; and being so indebted,
and being insolvent and unable to pay the said debt due
to *C.* and Co., and the said other debts, afterwards, on,
&c., at *Edinburgh* aforesaid, became and was under
legal diligence by horning and caption against him for
the debt due to *C.* and Co.; and having fled for his personal safety from such diligence, did afterwards, and
within four months of the last step of the said diligence,
with concurrence of the said *C.* and Co. to whom he

13

was

was so indebted as aforesaid, apply, by summary petition
to the lords in council and session of the first division of
the Court of Session in *Scotland*, for the sequestration
of the whole real and personal estate of him the defendant. The plea then stated that a sequestration was
granted, and meetings fixed and advertised, as required
by section 16. of the *54 G. 3. c.* 137., and that the petition was registered as required by section 22. It then
stated that the meetings were holden; that at the first,
an interim factor, and at the second, a trustee was
chosen. That meetings for the examination of the
bankrupt were appointed and advertised, as required
by section 32. It then set out the amount of debts
proved, and of the debts of those creditors who consented to the bankrupt's discharge, shewing that the
number required by sections 61. and 64. gave such consent. A petition for the discharge was then set out in
the terms of the sixty-first section, and that the court on
the 11th day of *March* 1818, did find defendant entitled
to be finally discharged of all his debts contracted before
the said application to sequestrate his estate, and did
grant commission to the sheriff-depute of the county of
Edinburgh to take the oath of the defendant. Averment,
that the defendant did make oath that he had complied
with all the requisites of the *54 G. 3. c.* 137.; and that
afterwards, to wit, on 2d day of *June* 1820, the court by
their decree did find that defendant had complied with
all the requisites of the statute, and therefore found him
freed and discharged of all debts contracted by him
before the 21st day of *May* 1816. Averment, that the
several supposed debts and causes of action in the declaration mentioned accrued to the plaintiff before the
21st day of *May* 1816, and were proveable under the
said

said sequestration. Issue on the first two pleas and to the third, replication, that the said causes of action accrued to the plaintiff in *England*. Demurrer and joinder.

Scarlett in support of the demurrer. The claim of the plaintiff was barred by the discharge under the sequestration, although the debt was contracted in *England*. The proceedings under the sequestration are calculated to give notice to creditors wherever they are resident; and the 54 G. 3. c. 137. s. 61., which gives the discharge to the bankrupt, is general in its terms, and makes no distinction between debts contracted in *Scotland* and in other places. But the question does not depend upon the statute alone; for in *The Royal Bank of Scotland* v. *Cuthbert and Others* (a), it was decided by the *Scotch* court, that a certificate obtained under an *English* bankruptcy discharged *Scotch* debts contracted before the date of the commission. The jus domicilii is to govern the distribution of the estate, and the principle is known to our law, that a discharge in a foreign country is a discharge here.

Campbell contrà. If the 54 G. 3. c. 137. had been an act of the *Scotch* parliament, it is clear that it could not have operated as a discharge of this debt. If the debt had been contracted in *Scotland*, a discharge there would have been a discharge every where (b); but it is otherwise when the debt is contracted in a foreign country. It has

(a) 1 *Rose*, 462.
(b) See *Ballantyne* v. *Golding*, Co. Bkpt. Laws, 464.   *Pedder* v. *M'Master*, 8 T. R. 609.   *Potter* v. *Brown*, 5 East, 124.

frequently

frequently been decided that a foreign bankruptcy is no bar to the demand of a debt contracted here; *Quin* v. *Keefe* (a), *Smith* v. *Buchanan*. (b)   But it must be admitted, that the 54 G. 3. c. 137., being an act of the parliament of the United Kingdom, was made by an authority capable of saying that the *Scotch* sequestration shall operate as a discharge here.   The question then is, what was the intention of the legislature.   Since the Union, all the judicial regulations of the courts have remained the same, and the judgments of *Irish* and *Scotch* courts are still treated as foreign judgments.   The title of the act is not immaterial : it is, " An act for rendering the payment of creditors more equal and expeditious in *Scotland*."   Now where an act is made relating expressly to one particular part of the United Kingdom, primâ facie as least, it applies to that alone, and it cannot have a larger operation, unless such an intention on the part of the legislature is clearly made out.   The notices which are required to be given in the *London Gazette* might be for the information of *Scotch* creditors resident in *England*.   If this plea be a bar to the action, then all *English* creditors must, in similar cases, go down to *Scotland*, in order to prove their debts there.   So, also, an *Englishman*, being insolvent, might go down into *Scotland*, and become domiciled there by a short residence, and then take the benefit of a *Scotch* sequestration, under which the distribution of the estate is very different from that which is made under an *English* commission. (c)   An *English* creditor certainly might prove under a *Scotch* sequestration, but a trustee under such a

(a) 2 H. Bl. 553.   (b) 1 East, 6.
(c) Per Lord Eldon, in *Selkrig* v. *Davis*, 2 Rose, 314.

seques-

sequestration could not sue in *England* for a debt due here. *Jaffrey* v. *M'Taggart.* (a)   The creditor, therefore, proving in *Scotland*, would not have the same advantage as under an *English* commission of bankruptcy. The same difference arises as to the real property.   If the *Scotch* sequestration bars an *English* commission, the *English* real property cannot be touched. *Selkrig* v. *Davis*, In the face of these difficulties the Court will not hold that the debt is barred by the sequestration, unless the intention of the legislature that it should be so is plainly expressed.   In the case of the *Bank of Scotland* v. *Cuthbert* an opinion was thrown out, that a certificate under the 5 *G*. 2. *c*. 30. barred a debt in *Scotland*; but that was not the point decided.   [*Bayley* J. It appears to me, that some of the difficulties which you mention apply equally to *English* commissions and *Scotch* sequestrations. Is there any clause in the 49 *G*. 3. *c*. 121. which transfers the bankrupt's real property in *Scotland* and *Ireland?*] The only case which can be cited in favor of the defendant is *Odwin* v. *Forbes* (b), where a suit in *Demerara* was held to be barred by a certificate under an *English* commission: but there the debt arose in *England*; for although the goods were shipped from *Demerara*, yet the order was given, the goods were delivered, and the bills for the price were accepted in *England*.   That it was to be considered as a debt arising in *England* is therefore plain, from *Lewis* v. *Owen* (c), which is also important in another point of view; for there the Court said, that a certificate under a commission of bankruptcy in *Ireland*, since the union with that country, could have no greater operation than a certificate under a *Scotch* sequestration,

(a) K. B. *Hil.* 57 *G.* 3.   (b) 1 *Buck.* 57.   (c) 4 *B.* & *A.* 654.

which

which was never thought to discharge a debt contracted in *England*.

1824.

SIDAWAY
against
HAY.

· *Scarlett* in reply. [*Abbott* C. J. You have this difficulty to contend with. Supposing a debt contracted in *England* to be discharged by the certificate under a sequestration, the bankrupt may enjoy real property in *England* without discharging his debts.] In the cases of the *Bank of Scotland* v. *Cuthbert* and *Selkrig* v. *Davis*, it appears to have been considered that the creditors might compel the bankrupt to assign his real property, by withholding his certificate until he consented to do so. Besides the 29th section of the 54 G. 3, c. 137. appears to have contemplated the passing of real estates in *England* as well as *Scotland*. As to the title of the act, that relates merely to the residence of the debtor, not of the creditors, and the sixty-first section gives the discharge from *all debts* contracted before the application for sequestration, without reference to the place where they were contracted.

Cur. adv. vult.

The judgment of the Court was now delivered by

ABBOTT C. J. This case was argued in *Easter* term in the last year, when the present Lord Chief Justice *Best* was one of the Judges of this Court. It stood over for some time in order that an amendment might be made in the defendant's special plea, and afterwards for the consideration of the Court; the judgment which I am now about to deliver, is to be considered as the opinion only of my Brothers *Bayley* and *Holroyd*, and myself. We are of opinion that judgment must be given for the defendant.

VOL. III.   C   The

The action is for goods sold and delivered and on the common money counts, the venue being laid in *London*. The defendant has pleaded the general issue and the statute of limitations upon which no question arises. He has also pleaded, that before and at the time of the accruing of the several causes of action in the declaration mentioned, and also before and on the first of January 1816 and from thence continually until the sequestration of his estate in the plea after mentioned, he was a merchant and trader in gross and by retail, residing and carrying on his trade at *Edinburgh*, in *Scotland ;* and then has proceeded to allege, with all due formalties, a sequestration and a decree of the lords of council and session, discharging him from all debts contracted before the 21st of *May* 1816, being the date of. the application for sequestration, and has averred that the plaintiff's several causes of action accrued before that day, and were proveable under the sequestration. To this plea the plaintiff has replied, that the several causes of action accrued in *England*. The defendant has demurred. to the replication, and the plaintiff has joined in demurrer.

The plea is framed upon the statute 54 G. 3. c. 137, of which statute the sixty-first section gives the discharge. The statute is entitled " an act for rendering the payment of creditors more equal and expeditious in *Scotland*." And the question is whether a trader residing in *Scotland*, and during such residence contracting a debt in *England*, can be discharged from it under a sequestration issued in *Scotland* in conformity to that statute, in like manner as from a debt contracted in *Scotland*. The statute is an act of the parliament of the United Kingdom, competent to legislate for every part of the kingdom, and to. bind the rights of all persons residing in *England*,

..   equally

equally with those of persons residing in *Scotland*. There
is therefore no question as to the authority of the power
by which the statute was passed, and the question must
turn entirely upon the construction and effect of the
statute. By the sixty-first section, the bankrupt is
enabled, with the concurrence of the persons therein
mentioned, to apply to the Court of Session by petition,
praying that he may be held as finally discharged of all
his debts contracted before the application for sequestration; and the Court is authorised, under the circumstances therein mentioned, to pronounce an act or order
in terms of the prayer of the petition. The expression
here is "all debts," and it is used without any reference or regard to the place where the debts may have
been contracted. It must be admitted, however, that
notwithstanding this generality of expression, it is possible that debts contracted in *England* may be out of the
general operation and view of the statute, and, therefore,
not to be comprehended within the terms, "all debts."
But there is not a single expression in the statute im-
porting that debts contracted in *England* are to be
excluded from its operation; and there are many provisions manifestly shewing the contrary.

By section 15. *Any* creditor, without reference to
his country or residence, or the place at which the debt
was contracted, may petition for a sequestration, the
deposition being made before any judge ordinary or
justice of the peace, and the sequestration is to be of
the debtor's whole estate and effects, heritable and
moveable, real and personal, for the benefit of his whole,
just, and lawful creditors,

By sect. 17. The interim manager is to take possession of the bankrupt's whole estate and effects, and of

the

the title deeds and instructions of his estate; and the bankrupt must, if required, grant powers of attorney, or other deeds necessary or proper for the recovery of his estate and effects situate in foreign parts.

By sect. 25. The bankrupt is required to exhibit a state of his affairs, specifying the whole estate and effects, heritable and moveable, real and personal, wherever situate.

By sect. 29. When the nomination of a trustee has been approved, the court shall ordain the bankrupt to execute proper deeds of conveyance, making over to the trustee his whole estate and effects, heritable and moveable, real and personal, wherever situate, with full powers of recovery and sale for behoof of the creditors, and on refusal to do so, may be punished by imprisonment; and whether such deeds be executed or not, the whole estate and effects, of whatever kind, and wherever situate, (in so far as may be consistent with the laws of other countries when the effects are out of *Scotland*,) shall be deemed to be vested in the trustee for behoof of the creditors.

By sect. 33. The bankrupt is to make oath, that the state of his affairs contains a full and true account of all his estate and effects, heritable and moveable, real and personal.

By sect. 41. The trustee is to proceed to recover and convert into money the whole estate under his management or power, whether at home or in foreign parts.

By sect. 43. Oaths of verity upon debts may be taken before any judge ordinary or justice of the peace: and where any creditor is out of the kingdom of *Great Britain* and *Ireland*, an oath of credulity by his agent, taken in the same manner, shall be sufficient.

Upon

1824.

SIDAWAY
against
HAY.

Upon the view of these clauses it is manifest, that all the property of the bankrupt of every kind and wherever situate, is to be taken from him for payment of his debts; and that creditors, wherever resident, may prove their debts and receive their share of the estate.

But this is not all: notices are required to be given in the *London Gazette*, as well as in the *Edinburgh Gazette*, on important occasions: as of the meetings to choose an interim manager and a trustee, sect. 16.: of the appointment of the trustee, and the two days appointed for the public examination of the bankrupt upon the state of his affairs, sect. 32.: of meetings of creditors for directing a sale of remaining effects, and of the time of the sale, sect. 56.: of the bankrupt's petition for his discharge, of which the court is to resume the consideration at a distance of not less than three months, sect. 61.: and of a meeting after the expiration of three years for the disposal of outstanding effects, sect. 75.

Now it appears to us, that the legislature would not have required these notices unless it had been intended that the discharge should operate upon *English* as well as *Scotch* creditors. No sufficient reason has occurred to us for giving the opportunity of inquiring into the affairs and conduct of the bankrupt, and of objecting to his discharge, to persons against whom the discharge would be inoperative with reference to a proceeding in an *English* court. If it be said, that it was intended only to enable *English* creditors to take the benefit of the sequestration if they should so think fit, and to object to the discharge for the purpose of retaining their right of suit in *Scotland,* this argument will contain an acknowledgment that *English* creditors may have the

    benefit

benefit of the sequestration; and then, it being clear that the bankrupt is deprived of all his property for the benefit of all his creditors who choose to partake of the distribution of it, by an act of a legislature having authority over all parts of the United Kingdom, justice seems manifestly to require that no one who may partake of the benefit, should be allowed to sue the debtor, whose all has been thus given up, if by accident he may happen to meet with him in *England*. And, therefore, we think we ought not to narrow the effect of the language of the sixty-first section, but to give to the phrase, " all his debts," the meaning usually and ordinarily belonging to those words.

Several cases were quoted in the argument at the bar, which I will now proceed to notice. The cases of *Smith* v. *Buchanan* (a) and *Potter* v. *Brown* (b) arose upon discharges under the authority of *American* states, that is, of legislatures not competent to bind the subjects of this country. *Pedder* v. *M'Master* (c) arose on a discharge at *Hamburgh*, and came before the court on an application to discharge the bail and enter an exoneretur on the bail-piece, which of course would not be done if the effect of the discharge was doubtful. *Quin* v. *Keefe* (d) came before the court first in the same way, and afterwards upon a plea which was badly pleaded, and there was no decision on the merits. It was the case of an *Irish* certificate, and of a debt contracted in *England* while the defendant was residing here. The case of *Jeffery* v. *M'Taggart*, which was before this Court in *February* 1817, on a motion for a new trial, arose, indeed, upon this act of the 54 *G. 3. c.* 137.,

(a) 1 *East*, 6,   (b) 5 *East*, 124.
(c) 8 *T. R.* 609,   (d) 2 *H. Bl.* 553.

but

but the question was entirely different from the present. It was an action of assumpsit brought by the trustee under a *Scotch* sequestration in his own name. The demand had vested in the trustee under this statute, so far as by the law of this country it could do, but as the assignee of a chose in action cannot, by the common law of this country, sue in his own name but must sue in the name of the assignor, and as this statute gives no express power to the trustee to sue in his own name, and the statute 1 *Jac. c.* 15. *s.* 13. does expressly give such a power to the assignees under an *English* commission, it was decided that the action was not well brought in the name of the trustee.

Upon this view of the cases, it appears that no one of them contains a decision contrary to our present opinion, which is founded not upon any general principle, but upon the effect of the particular statute on which the defendant's plea is framed. And for the reasons already mentioned, the judgment of the Court is to be entered for the defendant.

Judgment for the defendant.

M'GREGOR *against* THWAITES and Another.

Declaration for
a libel purport-
ing to contain
an account of
a proceeding
which had
taken place be-
fore a magis-
trate respecting
a matter in
which he was
merely asked
for advice, and
not called upon
to act in his
magisterial ca-
pacity. The
libel itself al-
leged that *A.B.*
and *C. D.*
stated the mat-
ter charged to
the magistrate,
a great part of
which was
not action-
able when
spoken, but be-
came so when
written. Plea,
that *A. B.* and

DECLARATION charged, that the defendant published the following libel in the *Morning Herald*
newspaper, in the shape of a report of certain proceedings in the city of *London.* " *Mansion-house.* Yesterday Mr. *Prince*, a common councilman, with Captain *Antrim*, of the ship *Lloyd's*, waited upon the
lord mayor elect (who sat for the lord mayor) to
request his lordship's advice as to the disposal of
three orphan children who had been brought on shore
under the following melancholy circumstances. Captain *John Antrim* stated, that on the 31st of *July* last
he sailed from *Honduras*. Before he departed from
that settlement he consented to receive on board one of
the families of the unfortunate *Poyais'* settlers, the rem-
nant of whom had sought the protection of the *British*
authorities at *Honduras*, and had received all the suc-

C. D. did go before the magistrate and make the statement set forth in the libel, and that
it contained a correct account of the proceedings before the magistrate, and that the facts
charged in it were true. The jury found that the matters contained in the libel were not
true, but that it contained a correct account of the proceedings which had taken place before
the magistrate: Held, first, that, as the matter brought before the magistrate was not
brought before him in his judicial character, or in the discharge of his magisterial functions,
the defendant could not justify the publication on the ground of its being a correct report
of the proceedings which had taken place before the magistrate.
Held, secondly, that it was no justification that the defendants, when they published the
libel, mentioned the names of the parties who stated the matter of the libel to the magistrate, because as to part of the slanderous matter no action would lie against the party who
stated it to the magistrate; it had become actionable merely from its having been published
by the defendants in print, and therefore, by stating the names of the persons from whom
they heard it, they gave the plaintiff no right of action against them.
Held, thirdly, that, in order to justify the repeating of slander, it was necessary that the
party repeating it should, at the time of repeating it, offer himself as a witness to prove the
uttering of the slander, and therefore that, as the defendants did not state that they themselves heard the slander uttered by *A. B.* and *C. D.*, but merely stated that *A. B.* and *C. D.*
had said so and so, the plea was bad.

cour which the governor had it in his power to give them. The unfortunate creatures who had survived the effects of their short residence at the desert swamp to which they had been taken, were sent back by the different vessels which sailed from *Honduras*. The family which Captain *Antrim* consented to receive, consisted of *Thomas Chalmers*, his wife and three children. The husband and wife when received on board were both ill with the fever, and died in the course of the passage. The captain said he had landed the three orphans, who were utterly destitute, at *Poplar*, and he now requested his lordship's advice as to the best means of getting them provided for. The captain then handed in the following certificate to his lordship." The libel then set out a certificate of the governor of *Honduras*, that the persons in question were received on board from motives of charity. It then stated some questions put by the lord mayor elect and the answers given to them, and the final advice of the lord mayor, that application should be made to the parish officers to relieve the children. It then proceeded as follows. Mr. *Prince* observed, that the captain, in consequence of his charity in receiving the poor emigrants, had himself caught the fever, and had narrowly escaped. He stated, that above 200 of the victims of delusion had returned from the *Mosquito* shore to *Honduras* in a state of utter destitution and of disease, which terminated the sufferings of a great part of them soon after. They must have all died, but for the charity of the people, and the authorities of *Honduras*. The poor creatures had been led by *M'Gregor* to expect a land where they would live in the greatest plenty, where every thing was flourishing, and but little labour would be required; it was mentioned to them, as a mark of the improvement of

the

the place, that a fine theatre had been established,
and other establishments formed, indicative, not merely
of civilization and comfort, but of luxury. Captain
Antrim mentioned a charge which the poor creatures
had preferred to him against *M'Gregor*. Most of those
who sailed from *Leith* were poor people, who had by
their frugality saved small sums of money of from
15*l.* to 30*l.* *M'Gregor* learned the property which
the settlers had with them, and telling them that *Scotch*
money would not pass at the settlement, persuaded
them to give it all up to him, and take his draughts for
the amount upon his bankers at *Poyais*. The savings
were all given up to him, and it is perhaps unnecessary
to add, that the settlers on their arrival at the houseless
wilds of *Poyais* found that no such thing as a banking-
house was in existence. Captain *Antrim* regretted that he
had not arrived sooner, as another ship had sailed, with
settlers for the same place just before his arrival, who he
feared would also fall a sacrifice. He had thought it his
duty to make the statement publicly, that the poor might
be put on their guard." The second count stated, as
inducement, that certain persons had emigrated from
Great Britain to *Poyais*, on the *Mosquito Shore* in
America, with the intention of forming a settlement there,
and on their arrival at *Poyais*, the emigrants had under-
gone great sufferings from sickness, disease, and other
accidents, whereof some of the emigrants had died, and
many others had been thereby compelled to remove to
Honduras, and from thence had returned to *Great Britain;* and that shortly before the committing of the
grievances by the defendants, in that and the following
count mentioned, an application was made to the lord
mayor elect of the city of *London*, at the *Mansion-house*,

9   in

in the said city, by certain persons, to wit, one Mr. Prince and one Captain *Antrim*, relative to certain children of certain of the said emigrants; yet the defendants, further contriving and maliciously intending, &c. The count then set out, that part of the libel contained in the first count, beginning with the words, " Mr. *Prince* observed, that the captain, in consequence of his charity, &c." The third count was similar to the last, and set out that part of the libel beginning with the words " Captain *Antrim* mentioned a charge," &c. Plea, first, not guilty; secondly, to the whole declaration, that on the 13th *October* 1823, at the *Mansion-house*, &c., one Mr. *Prince*, a common councilman, with Captain *Joshua Antrim*, of the ship *Lloyds'*, did wait upon the lord mayor of the said city of *London* elect, who sat for the lord mayor, to request his lordship's advice as to the disposal of three orphan children, who had been brought on shore, as stated in the said supposed libels; and the said *Joshua*, on that occasion, then and there did make such statements, and mention such charge, circumstances, matters, and things, and hand to his lordship such certificate as in the said supposed libels are respectively mentioned; and the said lord mayor elect did then and there ask such questions, and made such statements, as in the said supposed libels are also in that behalf mentioned, to which questions such answer was given as therein is mentioned; and the said Mr. *Prince* did also make such observations as therein are mentioned; and the said report in the said newspaper was and is a true, fair, and correct account of the said proceedings before the said lord mayor elect, and what took place on that occasion, and the several facts and circumstances therein detailed and adverted to are

likewise

likewise true; and the said report contains no false or untrue statement or allegation whatever, wherefore the defendant published, &c. Third plea, that the report, or account in the said newspaper, of the said proceedings at the said *Mansion-house*, whereof the said supposed libels in the declaration mentioned were and are composed, was and is a true, fair, and correct report and account of the said proceedings, and which proceedings did actually take place at the said *Mansion-house*, as is stated in the said supposed libels, to wit, at, &c. Fourth plea, that the several matters and things in the libels contained were and are true in fact. There then followed pleas similar to the two last, pleaded separately, to the first and second counts of the declaration; and replication, &c. de injuriâ suâ.

At the trial before *Abbott* C. J., at the *London* sittings after last *Michaelmas* term, the jury found that the libel did contain a true, fair, and correct report of the proceedings which had taken place before the lord mayor elect, but that the facts stated in the libels were not true. In last *Hilary* term the plaintiff had obtained a rule nisi for liberty to enter up judgment, notwithstanding the verdict found for the defendant upon those pleas, which alleged that the libel contained a true account of the proceedings before the lord mayor.

Scarlet and *E. Lawes* now shewed cause against the rule. The circumstance disclosed in the plea found for the defendants, that the publication was a correct account of proceedings which took place before a magistrate, is an answer to the action. It rebuts the presumption of malice, which, in ordinary cases, arises from the publication of any matter injurious to the reputation of another, and, upon that ground it has been

held

held lawful to publish the proceedings of courts of justice, even though they contain matter injurious to the feelings of individuals. *Rex* v. *Wright* (a), *Currie* v. *Walter*. (b) Assuming that the magistrate had no jurisdiction over the subject-matter brought before him, and that the question is to be considered as if the matter had been communicated to the lord mayor elect in his private character in the presence of the defendants; still this publication is justifiable within the rule laid down in Lord *Northampton's* case (c), because the defendants, at the time of publishing the slander, mentioned the name of the person from whom they heard it.

Denman, F. Pollock, and *R. V. Richards* contrà. The question as to the right of publishing judicial proceedings does not arise. The lord mayor elect was not sitting in a judicial capacity, or enquiring into any matter over which he had jurisdiction as a magistrate. But even if the matter had been within his jurisdiction, the defendants would not have been justified in publishing what passed; as it was a mere ex parte proceeding, *Rex* v. *Fisher*. (d) And if this is to be considered as a case where the slanderous matter was first stated in the presence of the defendants to the lord mayor elect in his private character, then the defendants were not justified in publishing it in writing or print, although at the time of the publication they stated the name of the person from whom they heard it; because, with respect to a great part of the matter published by them, they give the plaintiff no right of action against any other person. With respect to all that

(a) 8 *T. R.* 293.   (b) 1 *Bos. & Pul.* 525.
(c) 12 *Rep.* 133.   (d) 2 *Campb.* 563.

part

part which charges the plaintiff with having deluded the persons who emigrated, no action would lie against the person who merely uttered it; but it became actionable when reduced into writing or print, and that was the act of the defendants. It may even be questionable, whether any action would be maintainable against the original utterer of the other words, which charges the plaintiff with having, by false pretences, got possession of the money of the emigrants; for unless they import that the fraud was committed in this country they do not charge an offence within the statute 30 *G. 2. c. 24.* It is quite clear, however, that as to the other part of the slander no action would be maintainable against the parties who uttered it. Now, in Lord *Northampton's* case, the naming of the original author of the slander is considered a justification for the person who repeats it, because the party repeating it thereby gives the party slandered a right of action against another person. That reason does not apply here, and therefore this case does not fall within that rule: besides, it is quite clear that an action is maintainable against a person who maliciously repeats slander, although he names his author at the time. *Maitland* v. *Goldney.* (a) The jury, by their verdict, have found that the defendants published maliciously. Besides, here the libel does not profess to give the evidence verbatim, but a mere summary of the case. That is not a justifiable publication. *Lewis* v. *Waller.* (b.)

ABBOTT C. J. I am of opinion, that the rule for entering the judgment for the plaintiff, notwithstanding

(a) 2 *East*, 426.　　　(b) 4 *B. & A.* 605.

the

the verdict found for the defendants on some of the issues, ought to be made absolute. My judgment in this case is founded entirely upon the matters stated upon the record. It does not appear by the record that the libel gives an account of any thing which took place before the magistrate, whilst he was acting in his judicial character, or even in the discharge of his magisterial functions. The question, therefore, does not necessarily arise in this case, whether it be lawful to publish a correct report of proceedings which take place in the course of a judicial enquiry, or even of any enquiry before a magistrate acting in the discharge of his official duty. The allegation in the libel is, that an application was made to the magistrate, sitting for the lord mayor, for his advice as to the disposal of some orphan children; but the libel itself proceeds to state matter which goes far beyond what any application of that kind would warrant. It charges the plaintiff with having deceived the persons whom he had induced to emigrate, and with having, by false pretences, got possession of all their money. Assuming that the parties who originally uttered this slander might be justified by the occasion and purpose with respect to which it was uttered, it by no means follows that these defendants would be justified in republishing the slander so unnecessarily uttered, on the ground that their publication was only a true, fair, and correct report of what had taken place; for it is by no means true that the publication of every matter which passes even in a court of justice, however truly represented, is, under all circumstances and with whatever motive published, justifiable. It has been said, however, that this is a privileged publication; because the defendants only professed to repeat that which they heard another person say, and they name that person at the time when they repeat

repeat it, and that this case falls within the rule laid down in Lord *Northampton*'s case. Now it is to be observed that that was a case of oral slander: this is the case of slander reduced into writing or print by the act of the defendants. It is thereby rendered more injurious, and part of it has thereby become actionable, which before was not so. There may, therefore, be a material distinction in this respect between merely repeating slander and publishing it in writing or print. I do not mean, however, to pronounce any decided opinion upon that point, because, admitting the law to be correct, as laid down in Lord *Northampton*'s case, in its fullest extent, and assuming that it applies to written as well as to oral slander, I think that this case does not fall within it. The rule there stated is this: " If *I. S.* publish that he hath heard *J. N.* say that *I. G.* was a traitor or thief, in an action on the case, if the truth be so, he may justify. But if *J. S.* publish that he hath heard generally, without a certain author, that *J. G.* was a traitor or thief, there an action on the case lieth against *J. S.*, for this, that he hath not given to the party aggrieved *any cause of action against any but against himself who published the words.*" Now, this case falls short of the rule there laid down in two particulars; the first is, that with respect to a considerable part of the matter published no action would be maintainable against the party who uttered it. I allude to that part which charges the plaintiff with having, by false representations, induced the persons alluded to to emigrate. It is perfectly clear, that if the words published by the defendants had only been spoken no action would be maintainable in respect of them, unless the plaintiff could shew that he had thereby sustained a special damage. The other particular in which this case falls short of the rule laid down in Lord *North-*

ampton's

ampton's case is, that here the defendants do not offer themselves as witnesses to prove the uttering of the words. The rule is, that "if *J. S.* publish that *he* heard *J. N.* say." In that case *J. S.* offers himself as a witness to prove that *J. N.* did utter the slander; but here the defendants do not say that they heard Captain *Antrim* repeat the slander, and, therefore, they do not offer themselves as witnesses, and do not bring themselves within the rule laid down in Lord *Northampton*'s case. I am of opinion, therefore, that it is no answer to the action that the matter published by the defendants was a correct report of what actually took place in the presence of the magistrate, inasmuch as it appears that he was not then called upon to act either in a judicial or magisterial capacity; and, secondly, that this is not a privileged publication, on the ground that the defendants, at the time of publication, named the party who originally uttered the slander. The rule for entering judgment for the plaintiff, non-obstante veredicto, must be made absolute.

BAYLEY J. There is a great distinction between oral and written slander. No action is maintainable for words spoken, unless they impute to a man a crime for which he is punishable by law, or that he has an infectious disorder; or unless they are spoken of him in his office, profession, or business. But an action is maintainable for slander either written or printed, provided the tendency of it be to bring a man into hatred, contempt, or ridicule. Now, here, the report of the matter stated by Captain *Antrim* is calculated to bring the plaintiff into hatred; it is, therefore, actionable when reduced into writing. The greater part of the matter

VOL. III.　　　　　D　　　　　charged,

charged, if merely spoken, would give no cause of action to the plaintiff; and it may be questionable whether any action could be maintainable even in respect of that part which charges the plaintiff with having obtained the money of the emigrants, under false pretences, for unless they were defrauded of the money in this kingdom it would not be a case within the statute of the 30 G. 2. c. 24.; and there being no false token, it would not be an offence at common law. This, therefore, may be considered as a case where either wholly or in part the matter charged became actionable, from the circumstance of its having been written or printed by the act of the defendants, and, therefore, if the plaintiff cannot maintain this action against the defendants he has no remedy whatever. According to the rule laid down in Lord *Northampton*'s case the party is excused, because, by naming the person from whom he heard the slander, he gives the party slandered an action against another; but here the defendants gave the plaintiff no action against any other person. The reason of the rule does not apply to the present case. This being a case, therefore, where the matter published by the defendants is actionable, and no action can be maintained in respect of a part, if not in respect of the whole, against any other person, it follows that it must be maintainable against the defendants, or otherwise the plaintiff would be without any remedy.

Holroyd J. I am also of opinion that the plaintiff is entitled to judgment, notwithstanding the verdict found for the defendant on some of the issues, for that finding does not afford any answer to the action. The count alleges that the defendants, *maliciously* in-

tending

tending to injure the character of the plaintiff, published the libel. The pleas state, that that libel contains a true account of some proceedings which took place before the lord mayor elect. But it appears by the libel, that those proceedings were not in any way connected with the judicial or magisterial character of the lord mayor elect. The jury have found by their verdict on the other issues, that the facts stated in the libel were untrue. The question therefore is, whether a person falsely and maliciously publishing matter, (for after verdict it must be taken to have been done maliciously,) is justified in so doing because it is a correct account of what was said by others. I am of opinion that such a plea is no answer to the action. It gives no ground of action against any other person. It does not state who heard the slander repeated. It therefore gives the plaintiff no means of establishing by evidence his right of action against another. Part of the matter alleged would not be actionable at all if the words were only spoken, unless there were special damage. It comes to this, if Mr. *Prince* and Captain *Antrim* had, themselves, caused the matter to be printed, an action might be maintained against them; but they only made an oral statement before the lord mayor, and that is not actionable. But it has been printed by another, and he says, that he is not liable to an action, because at the time that he printed it he disclosed in the publication itself the name of the person from whom he heard it; but if the action be not maintainable against him, the party of whom the slander has been published in a manner which the law considers injurious, will have no remedy against any person. In *Maitland* v. *Goldney*, the declaration contained a charge against the defendants, that they published the slander with the

D 2　　　　　　knowledge

knowledge

knowledge that the person who had originally uttered it was satisfied that it was untrue. The defendants justified, by shewing that they had named the original author at the time when they published the slander; and Lord *Ellenborough* said, " that the fact of such previous uttering was merely used by the defendants as a pretence for publishing the same slander; that shews *malice* in the defendants, and an injury to the plaintiffs." The opinion of that learned Judge was, that an action would lie against a person who *maliciously* repeated slander, even though he named his author at the time. Now, in this case the jury by their verdict found that the defendants published the slander maliciously; and, therefore, our decision in this case accords with the opinion of Lord *Ellenborough*. For these reasons, I am of opinion that the plaintiff is entitled to recover in this action.

LITTLEDALE J. I am of the same opinion. I think that the lord mayor elect had no legal authority to inquire into the matter brought before him by Captain *Antrim ;* that he was not then exercising his office of a magistrate; and that this case is to be considered in the same light as if the communication had been made to him in his private room. It is unnecessary, therefore, to decide in this case, whether the defendants would have been justified in publishing this matter in a newspaper, if it had contained a correct report of a proceeding which had taken place before a magistrate acting in a judicial capacity. But the question is, whether a person hearing slanderous matter uttered in private company, may cause that matter to be written, printed, and published, provided that he, at the same time,

time, state the name of the person from whom he heard
it. Now, if the law as to the repetition of oral slander
were to be propounded for the first time to day, the
propriety of the rule laid down in Lord *Northampton's*
case might perhaps admit of some doubt. It is sufficient, however, to say that this case does not fall within
that rule. If the slanderous matter published constitute a civil injury, either from the nature of the matter
charged, or from the manner in which it is published,
it is quite clear that the party injured must have an
action against some person. If, therefore, the plaintiff
in this action cannot have an action against the relator
of the slander, he must have one against the person who
subsequently printed and published it. Now, here it is
evident, that in respect of part of the slanderous matter
charged, no action would lie against the relator, because
the words themselves were not actionable. As to the
other part, it may be doubtful whether any action could
be maintained. It being clear, however, that no action
would lie against the original relator as to part, it follows
as a necessary consequence, that as to that part it must
lie against the party who printed and published it, for
otherwise the party injured will be without any remedy.

Rule absolute.

1824.

Tuesday,
June 22d.

DYER and Another *against* PEARSON, PRICE, and
CLAY.

*A. employed
B., his agent,
to import goods
from a foreign
country. Upon
the arrival of
the goods B.,
who resided in
London, trans-
mitted to A.,
who resided in
the country, the
invoice, but de-
livered the bill
of lading to a
warehouse-
keeper in order
to get the goods
entered and
warehoused.
In the ware-
house-keeper's
books they were
described as the
property of B.
By the bill of
lading the
goods were to
be delivered to
the order of the
shipper or his
assigns, and it
was indorsed
by the shipper
in blank. B.
had no autho-
rity from A. to
sell the goods,
but after they
had been stand-
ing in his name
in the ware-
house-keeper's*

TROVER for ten bags of wool. Plea, not guilty. At
the trial before *Abbott* C. J., at the *London* sittings
after last *Michaelmas* term, the following appeared to be
the facts of the case: The plaintiffs resided at *Wootton
under Edge, Gloucestershire.* The defendants, *Pearson*
and *Price*, were warehouse-keepers, and the defendant
Clay was a woollen draper, and all the defendants resided
in *London.* In *November* 1823, the plaintiffs directed one
Smith, who also resided in *London*, to import for them
from *Germany*, thirty bags of wool. *Smith* ordered the
same from *Van Smissen* and Co. merchants in that country,
who required, that before the bills of lading should be delivered to *Smith*, bills drawn by them for the amount of the
wools should be accepted by a banker in *London.* In
consequence of this the plaintiffs procured *Esdaile* and
Co., bankers in *London*, to accept bills for the amount.
The thirty bags of wool arrived in *December* 1823,
accompanied with a letter of advice, covering the bill of
lading and invoice. *Smith* transmitted the invoice to
the plaintiffs. By the bill of lading, the wool was made
deliverable to order or assigns, and it was indorsed by
Van Smissen and Co. in blank. *Smith* delivered it to
the defendants, *Pearson* and *Price*, to enable them to

*books nearly five months, B. sold them: Held, in an action of trover brought by A. against
the purchasers, that upon these facts the jury ought to have been directed that A. was entitled to recover, inasmuch as B. had no authority to sell, or at least that it ought to have
been submitted as a question of fact to the jury, whether A. had by his conduct enabled B.
to hold himself out to the world, as having the property as well as the possession of the goods.*

enter

enter and warehouse the wool. *Smith* had no authority from the plaintiffs to sell the wools, but he procured the defendants, *Pearson* and *Price*, to advance the sums payable for the duties, and afterwards at their request, one *Squires* advanced a further sum of 200*l.* on the security of the wool. The wool was entered in the books of *Pearson* and *Price* as the property of *Smith*, and he transmitted twenty bags to the plaintiffs. In *May* 1823, *Clay* purchased the ten bags in question, of *Smith*, for 579*l.* At that time the bill of lading remained in the possession of *Pearson* and *Price*, and the sum due to them in respect of the duties and other charges amounted to 328*l.* 11*s.* 4*d.*, which, with the sum of 200*l.* due to *Squires*, amounted altogether to 528*l.* 11*s.* 4*d.*; and that sum *Clay*, by order of *Smith*, paid to *Pearson* and *Price*, and the remaining 51*l.* he paid to *Smith*. In *August*, the plaintiffs claimed the ten bags of wool of *Pearson* and *Price*, and they, after notice of the plaintiff's claim, delivered the same to the defendant *Clay*. Before the commencement of the action, the plaintiffs tendered to *Pearson* and *Price* the amount of the charges due to them, and demanded the wool from all the defendants, which they refused to deliver. Upon these facts the Lord Chief Justice told the jury, that if a man takes upon himself to purchase from another under circumstances which ought to excite his suspicion, and to have induced him to distrust the authority of the person selling, such a purchaser could not hold the property if it afterwards turned out that the person from whom he bought had no authority to sell; and he left it to the jury to say, whether *Clay* had purchased under circumstances which would induce a reasonable, prudent, and cautious man to believe that *Smith*, of whom he purchased, had

D 4 authority

authority to sell. · If they thought that he had purchased under such circumstances, they were to find for the plaintiffs; if otherwise, for the defendants. A verdict having been found the defendants, in *Hilary* term last the present Attorney-General (then Solicitor-General) obtained a rule nisi for a new trial. He contended that the true question which ought to have been submitted to the jury was, whether the purchaser was led by any negligence on the part of the plaintiffs to suppose that *Smith* was the real owner of the goods; for the general principle was, that an agent could not bind his principal beyond the scope of his authority, and for that reason, a factor having authority to sell, could not bind his principal by a pledge. Therefore, the true question in this case was, whether *Smith* had any authority, express or implied, to sell. It was clear that he had no express authority, and then the only question was, whether the Plaintiff had left the property in the possession of *Smith,* under circumstances from which the law would imply that he had authourity to sell. Thus in *Pickering* v. *Busk* (a), the law did imply such authority. There the purchaser of hemp, lying at wharfs in *London,* had, at the time of his purchase, the hemp transferred in the wharfinger's books in the name of the broker who effected the purchase for him, and whose ordinary business was to buy and sell hemp: and this was held to give the broker an implied authority to sell it. Here, there were no circumstances from which such an authority could be implied; the original invoice was in the hands of the plaintiffs. There was no evidence that *Smith* was in the habit of buying and selling wool, and all the circumstances were con-

(a) 15 *East,* 38.

sistent

sistent with the fact of his being a mere agent, having authority to receive and transmit the goods to the country. An authority to sell, was not to be implied from his possession of the bill of lading; that gave him no title, for, by it the goods were to be delivered unto the order of the shipper or his assigns, and it was indorsed in blank by the shipper. Besides, it was necessary that the bill of lading should remain in his possession; for the purpose of enabling him to get possession of the goods, and to have them warehoused.

Scarlett and *F. Pollock* now shewed cause. It may be conceded, as a general proposition, that a principal is bound by his agent only when he acts within the scope of his authority, but the case of *Pickering* v. *Busk* shews that such an authority may be implied from circumstances. Now here, there are circumstances from which such an implication arises; for the plaintiffs suffered *Smith* to import the goods in his own name, and to appear to the world as the owner, from the month of *December* until the month of *May*, for during that time they were entered in the books of *Pearson* and *Price* as the property of *Smith*, and the bill of lading remained in the possession of him or his agent; and although his name did not appear upon the face of it, yet, as the goods were to be delivered to the order of the shipper or his assigns, and as the indorsement was in blank, they were deliverable to *Smith*, who was the bearer. The plaintiffs, therefore, enabled *Smith* to appear to the world as the owner of the wool, and that being so, they were bound by the sale.

The

The *Attorney-General*, contrà, was stopped by the Court.

Abbott C. J. We all think there ought to be a new trial in this case. The question which I left to the consideration of the jury does not appear to me to have embraced the whole case. The general rule of the law of *England* is, that a man who has no authority to sell, cannot, by making a sale, transfer the property to another. There is one exception to that rule, viz. the case of sales in market overt. This was not a sale in market overt, and therefore does not fall within the exception. Now this being the rule of law, I ought either to have told the jury, that even if there was an unsuspicious purchase by the defendants, yet as *Smith* had no authority to sell, they should find their verdict for the plaintiffs; or I should have left it to the jury to say, whether the plaintiffs had by their own conduct enabled *Smith* to hold himself forth to the world as having not the possession only, but the property; for if the real owner of goods suffer another to have possession of his property, and of those documents which are the indicia of property, then perhaps a sale by such a person would bind the true owner. That would be the most favorable way of putting the case for the defendant; and that question, if it arises upon the evidence, ought to have been submitted to the jury. It is unnecessary to consider what would be the effect of the evidence upon that question. The rule for a new trial must be made absolute.

                                      Rule absolute.

1824.

BURWOOD *against* FELTON.

Tuesday,
June 22d.

ASSUMPSIT for work and labour, money had and received, money paid, &c. Plea, general issue. At the trial before *Abbott* C. J., at the sittings after last *Michaelmas* term, it appeared that the plaintiff was a messenger, under a commission of bankruptcy, issued against one *Farquharson*, and that the defendant was the sole assignee under that commission. The plaintiff claimed 113*l.*, being 85*l.* for fees due to the plaintiff as messenger, before the choice of the assignee, and 28*l.* for similar fees, which had accrued due subsequent to the appointment of the assignee. The latter sum the defendant paid into court. A letter by the defendant's attorney to the attorney of the plaintiff was given in evidence, and it was contended, that it contained an express promise to pay the sum due to the plaintiffs, when sufficient funds should be collected. The Court were ultimately of opinion that it did not amount to such a promise. As the question turned entirely on the terms of the letter, it is unnecessary to state the argument or decision upon it. But it was further objected, first, that the assignee of a bankrupt was not liable to the messenger for any costs incurred before the choice of assignees; because, by the 5 *G.* 2. *c.* 30. *s.* 25., the petitioning creditor is to pay all costs and expences of suing forth and prosecuting a commission until the assignees are chosen; he is, therefore, personally bound to pay the messenger. The Lord Chief Justice reserved the point, and a verdict was taken for the plaintiff, with liberty to the

The assignee of a bankrupt is not liable to the messenger under the commission for fees due to him before the choice of the assignee.

the defendant to move to enter a nonsuit. A rule nisi for that purpose having been obtained by *Marryat* in last *Hilary* term,

Archbold now shewed cause, and contended, that as the assignee had money in his hands, applicable to the payment of the debt due, he was responsible in the present action. The petitioning creditor was liable, at all events, to pay the messenger; but if he were to abscond, surely the messenger might recover against the assignee who has in his hands the funds applicable to the payment of the debt. Here, too, the defendant, after his appointment as assignee, continued to employ the plaintiff, and therefore he is personally liable for the work done. *Tarn* v. *Heys.* (a)

Abbott C. J. I am of opinion that the rule for a nonsuit ought to be made absolute. By the stat. 5 G. 2. c. 30. s. 25. it is enacted, " that the creditor who shall petition for and obtain any commission of bankrupt, shall be and is hereby obliged, at his own costs and expences, to sue forth and prosecute the same, until an assignee shall be chosen of such bankrupt's effects," and then the commissioners are directed, at the meeting for the choice of the assignees, to ascertain the costs, and to order the assignees to pay the petitioning creditor such costs out of the bankrupt's estate. It is clear, therefore, that an assignee is not liable by law to the messenger, in respect of fees due to him antecedent to the choice of the assignee. But the petitioning creditor is personally liable for such fees, and the statute points

(a) 1 *Starkie*, 278.

out

out the mode in which his expences are to be paid. That being so, we are of opinion that the defendant is not liable to pay to the messenger any fees due to him before the former was chosen assignee; and therefore, the rule for entering a nonsuit must be made absolute.

Rule absolute.

GORGIER *against* MIEVILLE and Another.

TROVER for a *Prussian* bond. Plea, not guilty. At the trial before *Abbott* C. J., at the *London* sittings after last *Michaelmas* term, it appeared, that the bond in question had been deposited by the plaintiff in the hands of Messrs. *Agassiz* and Co., to hold for the benefit of the plaintiff, and receive the interest upon it. *Agassiz* and Co. being in want of money, pledged the bond to the defendants. By the bond, the King of *Prussia* declared himself and his successors bound *to every person who should for the time being be the holder of the bond,* for the payment of the principal and interest, in the manner there pointed out. It was further proved, that bonds of this description were sold in the market, and passed from hand to hand daily, like exchequer bills, at a variable price, according to the state of the market. Upon these facts the Lord C. J. was clearly of opinion, that this bond might be pledged to any person who did not know that the person pledging it was not the real owner, and he directed the jury to find a verdict for the defendants, unless they thought that the defendants knew son who did not know that the party pledging was not the real owner.

Where a foreign prince gave bonds, whereby he declared himself and his successors bound to every person who should for the time being be the holders of the bonds for the payment of the principal and interest in a certain manner: Held, that the property in those instruments passed by delivery as the property in bank notes, exchequer bills, or bills of exchange, payable to bearer; and that, consequently, an agent in whose hands such a bond was placed for a special purpose, might confer a good title by pledging it to a per-

that

1824.

Gassiz
against
Mirville.

that Messrs. *Agassiz* and Co. were not the owners of the bond at the time when they deposited it in their hands. The jury having found a verdict for the defendants, a rule nisi for a new trial was obtained in last *Hilary* term, and now

. *Scarlett, Marryat, Gurney,* and *F. Pollock* shewed cause, and contended, that a bond of this description being payable to bearer, and the subject of sale like exchequer bills, the property in it passed by delivery, and therefore, like bank notes or bills of exchange indorsed in blank, might be pledged by any person holding it in character of agent; and they cited *Miller* v. *Race* (a), *Grant* v. *Vaughan* (b), *Peacock* v. *Rhodes* (c), *Collins* v. *Martin* (d), *Wookey* v. *Pole.* (e)

The *Attorney-General* and *D. F. Jones*, contrà. This case falls rather within *Glyn* v. *Baker* (f), in which it was held, that the property in an *India* bond did not pass by delivery. The principal ground upon which bank notes, bills of exchange indorsed in blank, and exchequer bills have been held to pass by delivery, is, that such instruments constitute a part of the circulating medium of the country, which would be materially impeded if they could be followed. That reason does not apply to a security of a foreign state.

ABBOTT C. J. I think that this rule must be discharged. This instrument, in its form, is an acknowledgment by the King of *Prussia*, that the sum men-

---

(a) 1 *Burr.* 452.   (b) 3 *Burr.* 1516.
(c) *Doug.* 633.   (d) 1 *Bos. & Pul.* 648.
(e) 4 *Barn. & A.* 1.   (f) 13 *East,* 509.

tioned in the bond is due to every person who shall for the time being be the holder of it; and the principal and interest is payable in a certain mode, and at certain periods mentioned in the bond. It is, therefore, in its nature precisely analogous to a bank note payable to bearer, or to a bill of exchange indorsed in blank. Being an instrument, therefore, of the same description, it must be subject to the same rule of law, that whoever is the holder of it, has power to give title to any person honestly acquiring it. It is distinguishable from the case of *Glyn* v. *Baker*, because there it did not appear that *India* bonds were negotiable, and no other person could have sued on them but the obligee. Here, on the contrary, the bond is payable to the bearer, and it was proved at the trial that bonds of this description were negotiated like exchequer bills.

Rule discharged.

The KING *against* The Bishop of PETERBOROUGH.

THIS was a rule calling upon the bishop of *Peterborough* to shew cause why a writ of prohibition should not issue, to prohibit him from proceeding to issue a sequestration upon a monition issued by him against *Charles Wetherell*, clerk, on behalf of *S. S. Paris*, clerk. Cause was shewn against the rule in last *Michaelmas* term by *Littledale*, and at the sittings after *Easter* term by *Alderson* and *C. E. Law*, and the rule was supported by *Denman* and *Twiss*. The facts and arguments are so fully stated and commented on in the judgment, that it has been thought expedient to omit them here.

A curate cannot have the benefit of a proceeding by monition for the recovery of a salary assigned by a bishop without the consent of the incumbent, the incumbent being resident on his benefice, and discharging the duties generally, but desirous of the assistance of a curate.

The

1824.

The King
against
The Bishop of
Peter-
borough.

The judgment of the Court was delivered in the course of this term by

ABBOTT C. J. This was an application for a prohibition to stay the proceedings on a monition issued by the bishop to the Rev. Mr. *Wetherell*, the rector of *Byfield*, for payment of his curate's salary. The case has been very elaborately argued on the construction of the statute 57 *G.* 3. *c.* 99. The facts upon which the question has arisen are shortly these: Mr. *Wetherell* being generally resident on his benefice and discharging his duties, but desirous of having some assistance, and particularly with reference to a school established by himself, and with a view to occasional absence, engaged Mr. *Paris* to become his curate at a yearly stipend of 100*l.*, with power to either party to put an end to the contract on three months' notice, and having so done, applied to the bishop of *Peterborough* to license Mr. *Paris*. The bishop approved of the person nominated, but thought he could not, under the statute, allow a less salary than 120*l.* a year; and he communicated this to Mr. *Wetherell* who remonstrated against the salary, and insisted that the bishop might allow less than 120*l.* A licence, however, issued fixing the salary at 120*l.*, but Mr. *Wetherell* asserts, that Mr. *Paris* declared to him that he should not demand more than 100*l.*, but this fact does not appear to have been communicated to the bishop; and if the salary of 120*l.* was well assigned, an agreement to receive less would be void by the statute. Differences arose between Mr. *Wetherell* and the curate, who refused to quit the curacy, and claimed his salary at the rate of 120*l.* a year. The curate then applied to the bishop, who, at his instance, issued a monition for payment of the curate's salary, but without specifying the amount. Soon after this Mr. *Wetherell* received from the church-

9   warden,

1824.

The KING
against
The Bishop of
PETER-
BOROUGH.

warden, a copy of a licence similar to the original licence, but having a memorandum, stating, that "the 120*l.* was assigned by mistake, and that the bishop, therefore, thought proper to reduce it to 100*l.*, the stipend assigned on the nomination." Mr. *Wetherell* then applied to this Court for a prohibition. The alteration of the salary thus made comes too late to give to the case the character of a curate licensed at the nomination and request of an incumbent, with an assignment of salary by the incumbent's consent. And, therefore, the question is, whether a curate can have the benefit of a proceeding by monition for the recovery of a salary assigned by a bishop, without the consent of the incumbent, the incumbent being resident on his benefice, and discharging the duties generally, but desirous of the assistance of a curate.

The proceeding by monition is not according to the general course of the Ecclesiastical law in cases of a curate's claim to his salary, and can be resorted to only where it is given by act of parliament; and it has been argued against the prohibition, and in support of the proceeding, that this proceeding is given generally for the recovery of the curate's salary, by the 53d section of the stat. 57 *G.* 3. *c.* 99. By this section it is enacted, "that it shall be lawful for the bishop, and he is thereby required, subject to the several provisions and restrictions contained in the act, to appoint to every curate such salary as is allowed and specified in the act; and every licence to be granted to a stipendiary curate under the act, shall contain and specify the amount of the salary allowed by the bishop to the curate; and in case any difference shall arise between any rector, &c. and his curate, touching *such* stipend or allowance, or the pay-

VOL. III.   E   ment

1824.

The King
against
The Bishop of
Peter-
borough.

ment thereof, or of the arrears thereof, the bishop, on
complaint to him made, may and shall summarily hear
and determine the same; and in case of wilful neglect
or refusal to pay *such* stipend, salary, or allowance, or
the arrears thereof, he is empowered to proceed by sequestration or monition." We think this section relates
only to licences granted, and salaries assigned in some
way in conformity to the act; and we are, therefore, to
enquire, whether the salary in question has been so assigned. It has been assigned to the curate of a resident
incumbent, and to an amount to which the incumbent
did not consent; and this proceeding by monition cannot
be within the act, unless in every case of a resident incumbent desirous of the assistance of a licensed curate, the
bishop has authority to assign a salary of greater amount
than the incumbent is willing to pay. Upon a careful
review of this act, and of the several statutes that
preceded it, we are of opinion that the bishop has not
such a power. The authority of the bishop to refuse a
licence, if he considers the proposed stipend to be in-
adequate, is very different from an authority to increase
the proposed stipend according to his discretion, limited
only by reference to the statutable allowance in other
cases. In the argument at the bar reference was made
to the preceding statutes.

The first statute upon this subject is the act of the
12 *Anne*, stat. 2. *c.* 12. This statute gives a summary
remedy to the curate for his stipend, but it is evidently confined to a curate nominated by a rector or
vicar to the bishop, to serve the cure *in the absence*
of the rector or vicar. The maximum of the stipend
to be appointed by the bishop under this act is 50*l.*
a year.

                                              The

The next statute on the subject is the act of the 36 *G. 3. c.* 83. This act begins by reciting at length the provision of the statute of Queen *Anne,* and further reciting, that in many places the provision made by that statute for the maintenance of the curate is become insufficient; and it then proceeds to enact, in the first section, that it shall be lawful for the bishop to appoint any stipend or allowance for any curate theretofore nominated or employed, or thereafter to be nominated or employed, not exceeding 75*l.* a year, over and besides, on livings where the rector or vicar does not personally reside for four months in the year at least, the use of the house, or, under certain circumstances, an additional stipend of 15*l.* in lieu thereof. The words of this section are, " any curate;" but, nevertheless, connecting the enactment with the preamble, and with the subsequent provision as to the use of the house, this enactment appears to be confined in its operation to the curates of non-resident incumbents. It however not only increases the stipend, but gives the authority in the case of a curate employed, as well as of a curate nominated by the incumbent, whereas the statute of Queen *Anne* mentions only curates nominated. The only other section of the statute on this subject is the sixth, which, after reciting it to be expedient that the authority of ordinaries to license curates and to remove licensed curates, should be further explained, enlarged, and confirmed, enacts, that it shall be lawful for the ordinary to license any curate who is or shall be actually employed by an incumbent, although no express nomination of such curate be made to the ordinary by the incumbent, and that the ordinary may summarily revoke any licence granted to any curate, and remove him, on reasonable cause, subject to appeal,

1824.

The King
against
The Bishop of
Peter-
borough.

1824.

The King
against
The Bishop of
Peter-
borough.

as well in the case of a licence to a curate not nominated, as in the revocation of a licence granted to a
curate. Construing this section of the statute, with
reference to the first section, which (as before observed)
has introduced the word "employed," it appears that
this section also respects only the curates of non-resident
incumbents; and even if it extends to others, it contains
nothing as to the allowance of stipend. The next
statute is the 53 *G. 3. c.* 149. This begins by a recital
of the titles, but not the enactments of the two preceding statutes, a recital of one of the canons of 1603,
(which contains nothing as to the assignment of stipend
to a curate,) and of the insufficiency of the provisions of
those statutes and canon, and of the laws in force respecting curates, and of the necessity of making a more
effectual provision to secure a competent maintenance
to curates, in order to ensure the due performance of
the service of the church, in parishes where incumbents
do not reside. It then enacts, that an incumbent *not
duly residing* (unless he shall do the duty of the church,
having an exemption from or licence for non-residence)
and who shall, for six months after the passing of the
act, or after his appointment, or after the death or removal of a former curate, neglect to nominate a curate,
to be licensed by the bishop to serve his church, or who
shall, for three months after the death or resignation of
any curate who has served his church, neglect to notify
the death or resignation to the bishop, shall forfeit all
benefit of dispensation or exemption from residence, or
licence for non-residence; and in every case in which
no curate shall be nominated to the bishop, for the purpose of being licensed within such period as aforesaid,
the bishop may appoint and license a proper curate,

with

with such salary as is by this act allowed and directed, to serve the church of the place in respect of which such neglect or default shall have occurred. This first section, therefore, plainly relates only to curates licensed for non-resident incumbents. The second section of this act, from which the 53d section of the 57 G. 3. c. 99. is admitted to have been taken, enacts, that it shall be lawful for the bishop, subject to the several provisions thereinafter contained, to appoint to every curate *so licensed*, such sufficient salary as is allowed and specified in this act, and that the licence to be granted as aforesaid shall specify the amount of the salary allowed; and it then proceeds to give the summary remedy in cases of difference between the curate and incumbent, and for the recovery of arrears of the stipend. This section is an addition to the first, and plainly refers to it by the words " so licensed," and therefore cannot be applied to any cases except those mentioned in the first section, unless by some subsequent part of the act it shall clearly appear to be extended to such cases. The third, fourth, and fifth sections certainly contain no such extension, for they relate to the parsonage-house and its enjoyment by the curate. The sixth section relates only to the registering of the grant and revocation of licences under the act. The seventh section gives a scale of salary, according to the population of the parish, but never exceeding the value of the living, nor 150*l.* to be appointed to a curate licensed *to serve the benefice of* an incumbent appointed after the passing of the act, who shall not duly reside, (unless, &c. in the very words of the first section,) in the absence of such non-resident incumbents. According to the scale thus given, the salary may, in many cases, amount to the whole value

1824.

The King
against
The Bishop of
PETER-
BOROUGH.

E 3   of

1824.

The King
against
The Bishop of
Peter-
borough.

of the benefice; and therefore the eighth section enacts
that in such cases the salary shall be subject to the legal
charges on the benefice. The ninth section relates to
the case of an incumbent of one parish serving the cure
of one or two adjoining parishes, and in those cases the
salary is regulated by a diminution from the salary
which, in the several cases before mentioned, the bishop
is required to appoint; the cases before mentioned are
those of non-resident incumbents only, and this section
can only apply to cases of that description. .

The tenth section introduces, for the first time, the
case of an incumbent who may be resident, but this
is done incidentally rather than directly; for it provides
and enacts, that in case it shall be made appear to the
satisfaction of the bishop that the incumbent of a benefice is or has become non-resident, *or incapable of performing the duties* thereof, from age, sickness, or other
unavoidable cause, and that from those or other special
circumstances great hardship would arise if the full
amount of the salary specified in the act should be
allowed to the curate, the bishop may assign to the
curate a salary less than such full amount. This provision is very suitable to the case of non-resident incumbents, for whose curates the act had previously fixed
the amount of salary, leaving nothing to the discretion
of the bishop; but it is wholly unnecessary and inoperative in the case of resident incumbents disabled from
the performance of their duties, because as to their
curates no amount of salary had been previously specified in the act. And it is obvious that the incapacity
of performing the duties must have been introduced into
this section by way of caution, and without that strict

attention

attention to the other parts of the act, by which it would have been found to be unnecessary.

1824.

The KING
against
The Bishop of
PETER-
BOROUGH.

The eleventh section contains a further provision in relief of the incumbent of a benefice, of which the whole profit shall be allowed to the curate, which manifestly relates to the scale given by the seventh section, and consequently to the curate of a non-resident incumbent.

The twelfth section also clearly relates to the scale given by the seventh section, and the occupation of the parsonage-house under the first section; and so also to the case of a non-resident incumbent.

The thirteenth section, in the case of benefices exceeding 400*l.* a year, authorizes the assignment of a salary to a curate, being resident in the parish, greater than is allowed by the seventh section, and must, therefore, be construed with reference to the seventh section, and be applied to such curates only as are therein mentioned.

The fourteenth section, upon which much stress was laid in the argument at the bar, is a restraining and not an enabling clause. It enacts, that nothing in the act contained shall authorise a bishop to assign to a curate a greater stipend than is allowed by the statutes in force before the passing of this act, unless with the consent of the incumbent in three several instances; first, to the curate of an incumbent holding his benefice before the passing of the act, and on which he shall be non-resident by licence or exemption; secondly, to the curate of any incumbent who shall duly reside on his benefice; thirdly, to the curate of an incumbent of a benefice who shall himself do the duty of the same, having a legal exemption from residence, or a licence to reside out of his benefice, or out of the parsonage house.

E 4   A clause

1824.

The King
against
The Bishop of
Peter-
borough.

A clause so framed cannot, according to any rule of construction, be deemed to give any power to a bishop ; neither can any inference be reasonably drawn from it, that a bishop possessed any antecedent authority to fix the salary of the curate of a resident incumbent, because in the two other instances mentioned in this section this statute had given no power to the bishop which he did not possess before this act was passed, as will appear by a reference to the seventh and first sections of this act. And this clause also seems to have been introduced only by way of caution, and like many other clauses of the same character, is introduced where caution was not required.

The seventeenth section provides for the salary of the curate of an incumbent, having two or more benefices, and residing part of the year on one, and part on another, and employing a curate from time to time, upon such of the same from which he shall be absent during his residence on the other; which is, in effect, a provision for the curate of a non-resident incumbent.

The eighteenth section relates to the particulars to be stated by an incumbent applying for a licence for non-residence, and requires him to state the salary he proposes to give to his curate; and the nineteenth requires the same particulars to be stated, on an application for a curate by an incumbent exempt from residence.

Upon this view of these statutes it is plain that they do not authorise the bishop to fix the salary of a curate of a resident incumbent, without the consent of such incumbent.

These statutes were all repealed by the 57 G. 3. c. 99. for the purpose of explaining some of their provisions,

and

and of adding others, and they are now to be referred
to, not as law, but for the purpose only of explanation
and construction of the last-mentioned act. This act
embraces several other subjects as well as the licensing
of curates and assignment of their salaries; and upon
an attentive perusal it appears that almost every clause
on this subject is taken from some clause in one of the
former acts, with some variations and improvements, but
without any alteration important to the present question.
The only clause on this subject entirely new is the
fiftieth section, which empowers the bishop to appoint
a curate, with such stipend as is therein mentioned,
when it shall be made appear to him that by reason of
the number of churches or chapels belonging to any
benefice, or their distance from each other, or the distance of the incumbent's residence from any of them,
or the negligence of the incumbent, the ecclesiastical
duties of the benefice are inadequately performed. The
case now before the court is not of this description.
And having detailed and commented so minutely on the
clauses in the former acts, it is wholly unnecessary to
refer particularly to the corresponding clauses in the
new act. It is sufficient to say, that we find nothing in
the new act that can authorise the court to consider the
case now before us as falling within the scope of the fifty-
third section. It is no part of our duty to pronounce
an opinion upon the expediency of giving to the ordinary a direct authority to appoint a salary to the curate of a resident incumbent. We learn from these
acts that the legislature has thought it expedient to give
to the ordinary a power of fixing a curate's stipend in
certain cases, and within certain restrictions. If the
power is not given in other cases, we ought to infer that
the

1824.

The KING
against
The Bishop of
PETER-
BOROUGH.

1824.

The King
against
The Bishop of
Peter-
borough.

the legislature has not hitherto thought it expedient to give the power: whether from an apprehension that resident incumbents might be thereby deterred from taking an assistant to the performance of their duties, or for what other cause, it is not our business to inquire. Our judgment on the present case is given with reference to its own peculiar circumstances, viz. the assignment of a salary to the curate of a resident incumbent, greater in amount than the incumbent had proposed or consented to. Our judgment, therefore, is not a decision upon the general question as to the effect of a salary assigned to a curate of a resident incumbent in conformity to his own proposal, nor upon the authority of the bishop to entertain, in any case, a suit for a curate's salary in a formal manner, according to the course and usage of the ecclesiastical law; but I cannot abstain from remarking, that the power to proceed by monition in any case regarding the stipend of the curate of a resident incumbent is so questionable, that it may be a fit subject for the consideration of the legislature. One of the objects of these statutes appears to be the maintenance and protection of curates. We cannot doubt that the reverend prelate against whom this application was made thought that he was acting in pursuance of this object, and discharging a duty according to the provisions of the statute; but we think he has been mistaken in the application of the statute to this particular case, and are, therefore, of opinion that the rule for a prohibition must be made absolute.

Rule absolute.

1824.

. .. The King .. v. The Inhabitants of Thackhill & Bradbury

The KING *against* The Inhabitants of NEWARK-UPON-TRENT.

UPON appeal against an order of two justices for the removal of *W. Hales,* his wife and child, from the parish of *Newark-upon-Trent,* in the county of *Nottingham,* to the township of *North Collingham,* in the same county, the sessions discharged the order of removal, subject to the opinion of this Court on the following case:

The pauper, *W. Hales,* a poor boy, of and then legally settled in the parish of *North Collingham,* in the county of *Nottingham,* was on the 18th day of *June* 1817, pursuant to an order of two justices of that county, bound apprentice by the churchwardens and overseers of the poor of the said parish to *Edward Sutton,* of the parish of *Newark-upon-Trent,* in the borough of *Newark-upon-Trent,* in the county of *Nottingham,* by indenture, for a term therein mentioned. A premium of 10*l.* was given with the apprentice to the master by the said churchwardens and overseers, although only 5*l.* was set forth in the indenture as the sum paid. The two justices who signed the aforesaid order afterwards signed and sealed their allowance of the indenture of apprenticeship before the same was executed by any of the other parties thereto. The parishes of *North Collingham* and *Newark-upon-Trent* are distant from each other about six miles, and in the same county. *No notice whatever was given to the over-*

A pauper, settled in the parish of N. C., in the county of Nottingham, was, pursuant to an order of two justices of the county, bound apprentice by the churchwardens and overseers of that parish to A. B. of another parish, in a borough situate in the same county, but having justices who had exclusive jurisdiction therein. The indenture was allowed by the two county justices, but no notice was given to the overseers of the poor of the parish in the borough of the intention to bind such apprentice, nor did they or any of them attend before the county justices who allowed the indenture, and admit such notice: Held, by three justices, Abbott C. J. dissen-

tiente, that by 56 G. 3. c. 319. the indenture was void for want of such notice, and that the pauper did not gain any settlement by serving under it.

seers

1824.

The KING
against
The Inhabit-
ants of
NEWARK-UPON-
TRENT.

seers *of the poor of the parish* of *Newark-upon-Trent,* or
to any of them, of the intention to bind out such apprentice, nor did they or any of them attend before the
justices who signed the order and allowed the indenture,
nor was any such notice alleged or attempted to be
proved to have been given, but the said justices allowed
the said indenture without any such proof of service or
admission of notice. *Newark* is a borough situate in the
county of *Nottingham,* having justices who have exclusive jurisdiction therein. The pauper resided under this
indenture in *Newark-upon-Trent* more than forty days.
This case was argued in last term by *Chitty* in support
of the order of sessions, and *Scarlett* and *Balguy* contrà.
The arguments are so fully commented on by the learned
judges, that it is unnecessary to state them here. There
being a difference of opinion on the bench, the Court
now delivered their judgments seriatim.

LITTLEDALE J. I am of opinion the indenture of
apprenticeship is invalid, because no notice was given to
the overseers of *Newark-upon-Trent,* and that no settlement was gained under it. The question depends entirely on the construction of the statute 56 *G.* 3. *c.* 139.,
which recites that inconveniences had been felt from
binding poor children apprentices to improper persons,
and to persons residing at a distance from the parishes
to which such children belong.

Sect. 1. directs, that before any child shall be bound
apprentice by the overseers of the poor of any parish,
&c., such child shall be carried before two justices of
the county, &c. in which such parish shall be situate,
who shall enquire into the propriety of binding such
child apprentice to the person proposed; and such justices shall particularly enquire whether the person proposed

posed reside or carry on his business within a reasonable distance from the place, &c. to which such child shall belong, or whether circumstances make it advisable that the child shall be bound at a greater distance. The justices are directed to examine the father and mother, and inquire into the circumstances of the person proposed as the master, and if the justices upon such examination and enquiry think it right the child should be bound, they shall make an order that the overseer shall be at liberty to bind the child apprentice, the order to be delivered to the overseer as the warrant for binding the child, and the indenture shall refer to the order, and the justices shall sign their allowance of the indenture before it is executed by any of the parties. Provided that no such child shall be bound to any person residing or having an establishment in trade in which the child shall be employed out of the county at a greater distance than forty miles from the place to which the child shall belong, unless it belong to a parish above forty miles from *London*.

Sect. 2. enacts, that in all cases where the residence or establishment of business of the person to whom any child shall be bound shall be within *a different county or jurisdiction of the peace* from that within which the place by the officers whereof such child shall be bound shall be situate; and in all other cases where the justices of the peace for the district or place within which the place by the officers whereof such child shall be bound shall be situated, and who shall sign the allowance of the indenture by which such child shall be bound, shall not have jurisdiction, every indenture by which such child shall be bound shall be allowed, as well by two justices of the peace for the county or district

1824.

The KING
against
The Inhabitants of
NEWARK-UPON-TRENT.

1824.

The King
against
The Inhabit-
ants of
Newark-upon-
Trent.

district within which the place by the officers of which such child shall be bound shall be situated, as by *two justices of the peace for* the county or district within which the place shall be situated wherein such child shall be intended to serve.

Provided always, that no indenture shall be allowed by any justice of the peace for the county into which such child shall be bound, who shall be engaged in the same business, employment, or manufacture in which the person to whom such child shall be bound is engaged. And notice shall be given to the overseers of the poor of the parish or place in which such child shall be intended to serve an apprenticeship, before any justice of the peace for the county or district within which such parish or place shall be shall allow such indenture, and such notice shall be proved before such justice shall sign such indenture, unless one of such overseers shall attend such justice and admit such notice.

Sect. 3. Provided that the allowance of two justices of the peace for the county within which the place in which such child shall be intended to serve an apprenticeship shall be situated shall be valid and effectual, although such place may be situate within a town or liberty within which any other justices of the peace may in other respects have an exclusive jurisdiction. Sect. 5. No settlement shall be gained by any child who shall be bound by the officers of any parish, &c. by reason of such apprenticeship, unless such order shall be made, and such allowance of such indenture of apprenticeship shall be signed as hereinbefore directed.

In the present case I think it is not necessary to consider whether notice must, in all cases, be given to the overseers of the parish into which the child is to be

bound

1824.

The King
against
The Inhabit-
ants of
NEWARK-UPON-
TRENT.

bound, whether such parish be in the county to which the child shall belong, or in the district into which it is to be bound, or whether the necessity of the notice to the overseers is to be confined to the cases where the child is to be bound into a different jurisdiction from that to which it belonged.   There seems to be one reason why notice should not be necessary in the same county, because the justices have more power and better means of information as to the points to which they are to direct their inquiries before binding an apprentice, and, therefore, there is not the same necessity for notice to the overseers that there is in a foreign county, in which the justices are less acquainted, where they have not the same communication with the overseers, nor the same means of inquiry that they have in their own county; and, therefore, it may appear reasonable that notice should be given to the overseers of a parish in a foreign county into which the child shall be bound, so that between the justices of the county where the binding parish is, and the overseers of the parish into which the child is to be bound, a full investigation may be made as to those points on which the statute directs inquiries to be made. Another reason may be given why notice should not be required, viz. that the second section of the act in which this enactment is contained begins with making provisions in cases where the binding is to be into a different county, and that, therefore, all the provisions in that section ought to be so confined; this last reason, however, does not appear sufficient, because the division of an act of parliament into sections is a mere arbitrary thing, forming no part of the act, and ought not to furnish any rule for interpreting any clause. The only proper way to interpret any sentence is to look

at

1824.

The King
against
The Inhabit-
ants of
NEWARK-UPON-
TRENT.

at the language of the sentence itself, and the connection it has with the other enactments, without any reference to a division into sections. Much may be said on both sides of the question arising out of the way in which the different sections are worded. There is nothing about notice in the first section, it only comes in the second section. Many comments may be made on the phraseology of that clause, as with reference to different parts of the same clause, and also with reference to the language of the first section. But, without considering that point, it is quite clear that in a binding into a *foreign* district, which this is, notice is requisite in general, unless it can be said,

First, that the clause as to the notice to the overseers is merely directory: or, secondly, that the clause in section 3., that the allowance of two justices of the peace for the county within which the place in which such child shall be intended to serve an apprenticeship shall be situated shall be valid and effectual, although such place may be situated within a town or liberty within which any other justices of the peace may, in other respects, have an exclusive jurisdiction, supersedes the necessity of giving notice, where the power so given to the county justices is exercised by them.

I think the clause of notice to the overseers is not merely directory.

The object of the clause seems to be, that the overseers of the parish, in the foreign county, shall assist the justices of the binding county with such information as they can, as to the points which the act has directed to be investigated, and, therefore, the notice to these overseers seems an essential thing to be attended to, in order to get at all the preliminary information; it must, how-

ever,

1824.

The King
against
The Inhabit-
ants of
NEWARK-UPON-
TRENT.

ever, be observed, that in the fifth clause, which says, that no settlement shall be gained unless certain things are done, there is no mention of notice to the overseers.

The clause is, " that no settlement shall be gained by any child who shall be bound by the officers of any parish, &c., by reason of such apprenticeship, unless such order shall be made, and such allowance of such indenture of apprenticeship shall be signed, as hereinbefore is directed ;" and therefore it appears to be tantamount to saying, that if the order be made, and such allowance signed, the binding shall be effectual, though no notice be given ; but inasmuch as the latter part of the second section directs, that the justices of a foreign district are not to allow the indenture till the notice be given to the overseers, and that, therefore, the notice to the overseers must precede the allowance by the foreign justices : the clause in section 5., which requires the allowance of two justices, means an allowance after notice to the overseers, and embodies that as part of the allowance.

Then comes the question, whether, if justices of the county exercise the powers given by the third section, the notice to the overseers is dispensed with ? The third section does not, in terms, dispense with it, and one cannot see any ground for dispensing with it, merely because the county justices put themselves in the place of the foreign district justices. They can have no more power than the foreign district justices have ; but by the second section the foreign district justices are not to sign the allowance till notice has been given to the overseers, and, therefore, if the county justices are to represent the foreign district justices, they should do so in every thing, and therefore only have a conditional power to allow the indenture ; that is, after notice to the overseers.

VOL. III.   F   It

1824.

The KING
against
The Inhabit-
ants of
NEWARK UPON-
TRENT.

It may be contended, that by this third section the separate jurisdictions are all swallowed up and made to form part of the county, for the purposes of this act, and that the powers given to the county justices put them exactly in the same situation as if the particular district was part of their own jurisdiction, and that they may act as if it originally was so : and if that were so it would become necessary to consider whether the act requires notice in all cases, including those of binding into the same county.

But the act has not, in express terms, given the county justices any such power, and it does not appear likely it should be meant ; for if the reason of notice to the overseers be, that the justices in the county where the binding parish is have not the same means of communication, and the same facility of getting information in a foreign county or district that they have in their own, they may, by these means, bind the child into a county or district where they have not full means of getting information.

The third section is not compulsory on the county justices, but the foreign district justices may still allow the indenture, but they can only do it after notice to the overseers, and therefore, there may be two children bound from the same parish into the same foreign district by different means, viz. one by county justices only (I do not speak of the binding overseers) and the other by county justices, followed up by notice to the overseers, and by the allowance of the foreign district justices, and which last would probably be after a fuller inquiry as to the circumstances directed to be inquired about, than the first, and therefore the two bindings would be accompanied by different degrees of information as to the propriety of the binding. It may be said there will be a want

of

1824.

The King
against
The Inhabit-
ants of
NEWARK-UPON-
TRENT.

of full inquiry if the county justices allow the indenture, where the binding is into a foreign district, and
yet the act expressly permits it. But there will be very
nearly the same information as if the district justices
allow the indenture, because if notice be given to the
overseers they will collect all the information they can,
which they will communicate to the county justices
before the latter allow the indenture. Upon the whole,
I think the want of notice to the overseers invalidates
the indenture; and as I think the indenture is invalidated, it follows, if I am right, that no settlement was
gained.

HOLROYD J. This is a case arising upon the binding of a parish apprentice, and the question is, whether
it is a valid binding, pursuant to the statute 56 G. 3.
c. 139., so as to enable the apprentice by service and
residence under the same, to gain a settlement in the
parish of *Newark-upon-Trent*, the parish into which the
apprentice was bound.

It is a binding by the churchwardens and overseers
of the poor of a parish within the county of *Nottingham*,
made under the order and allowance of two justices of
the peace for that county, to a master resident in the
parish and borough of *Newark-upon-Trent*, which is a
borough and parish within the same county of *Nottingham*, but wherein other persons have an *exclusive* jurisdiction as justices of the peace. But by section 3. of
the statute it is provided, that the allowance of two justices of the peace for the county within which the place
in which such child shall be intended to serve an apprenticeship shall be situated, shall be valid and effectual,
although such place shall be situated in a town or
liberty within which any other justices of the peace may

F 2　　　　　　　　　　　　　　in

1824.

The King
against
The Inhabit-
ants of
Newark-upon-
Trent.

in other respects have an exclusive jurisdiction. The objection however is, that notice was not given to the overseers of the poor of the parish of *Newark-upon-Trent*, the parish in which the child was intended to serve the apprenticeship, nor was any such notice proved or admitted before the above magistrates, pursuant to the proviso, which is printed as part of sect. 2. of the statute. And the question then is, whether this case, which is the case of a binding by one parish in a particular county into another parish within the same county, but in a town where other justices of the peace have in other respects an exclusive jurisdiction, is within that branch of the proviso which requires such notice or proof or admission thereof, before the allowance of the indenture, or whether that would only have been requisite in case this binding had been into a different county. I am of opinion, that this case is within that branch of the proviso; and if so, then I think, that for want of such notice and proof, or admission thereof, before the justices allowed the indenture, the binding was so invalid as to prevent the apprentice from gaining a settlement under it in the parish of *Newark-upon-Trent*.

The proviso as to notice, or the proof or admission thereof, in cases where the same is required, appears to me not to be directory merely, but the want thereof, I think, goes to affect the settlement itself. The fifth section of the statute, enacts that no settlement shall be gained by any child who shall be bound by the officers of any parish by reason of such apprenticeship, unless such order shall be made and *such* allowance of such indenture of apprenticeship shall be signed as directed by the statute. It is true, the statute does not also say "the settlement shall not be gained unless such notice

be

1824.

The King
against
The Inhabit-
ants of
NEWARK-UPON-
TRENT.

be given," but (in cases where by the statute that notice was required), unless the notice had been previously
given, the allowance would not have been *such* as the
statute directed. The allowance itself, in such a case,
would therefore be null and void for want of the notice;
for where a special authority is given to magistrates or
others by statute, their acts are null and void, unless
they proceed in the manner and under the restrictions
which the statute itself imposes.

In requiring the notice the legislature may be considered as having in view two objects, the benefit and
welfare of the apprentice and the protection of the
parish into which it is intended he should be bound.
For both purposes the notice to and attendance of an
overseer from that parish may be useful before the binding has become conclusive, both with regard to the information he may be able to give the magistrates of
the character, circumstances, conduct, and habits of the
intended master, and of the state in that parish of the
particular trade, and the number of apprentices to it,
and to the probability of the child's being able in future
to maintain himself by his trade there, after the expiration of his apprenticeship, or instead thereof of his
becoming a burden upon the parish. This seems to be
equally important, whether the binding be into a parish
in the same or in a different county; and the parish,
whether in the one case or in the other, may become
equally aggrieved by the binding, and equally aggrieved,
for want of previous notice of the intended binding, from
such parish losing thereby their right of appeal, which
by the seventeenth section is given (but it can be exercised within a limited time only) to any person or

F 3   persons

1824.

The King
against
The Inhabit-
ants of
Newark-upon-
Trent.

persons who shall be dissatisfied with any act done by any justice of the peace in the execution of the statute.

In order to remedy the grievances recited in the preamble, which recites, amongst others, that many grievances had arisen from the binding of poor children as apprentices by parish officers to *improper persons*, and to carry into effect the objects of the statute, the first section, (which applies to parish bindings whether into a parish within the same or within a different county,) enacts, that before any child shall be bound apprentice by the overseers of the poor of any parish, such child shall be carried before two justices of the peace of the county, &c. wherein such parish shall be situate, who shall make certain enquiries there specified; those enquiries particularly regard the fitness, circumstances, and character of the intended master, and appear to be equally material to be enquired into, both with a view to the well doing of the apprentice and to the considerations of justice that are due to the parish into which he is to be bound, whether the intended binding be into a parish in the same county, or into a parish in a different county, and with a view to that enquiry, as well as with a view that the parish into which he is to be bound may obtain justice by an appeal, in case the child ought not to be so bound; and in case such binding will probably be injurious to such parish, the notice to the overseers of that parish appears to be equally important, whether the binding is to be into the same or a different county. And if the binding is to be into the same county, those justices are the only justices who are to make those enquiries, and to sign the allowance; but by sect. 2. there is also to be, where the binding is into a different county or jurisdiction of the peace, a further

allowance

1824.

The King
against
The Inhabit-
ants of
NEWARK-UPON-
TRENT.

allowance by two justices also of the county or district within which the place shall be situated wherein such child shall be intended to serve.

Then follows the proviso upon which the present question arises, and which is printed as part of the second section; but whether it be printed as part of the second section, or had been separated from it by the printer, and made into a third section, can make no difference in the construction of the statute; for in the construction of a statute, the question whether a proviso in the whole or in part relates to, and qualifies, restrains, or operates upon the *immediately* preceding provisions only of the statute, or whether it must be taken to extend in the whole or in part to *all* the preceding matters contained in the statute, must depend, I think, upon its words and import, and not upon the divisions into sections that may be made, for convenience of reference in the printed copies of the statute. The same construction must prevail, I apprehend, in this case, as if the proviso, which has been printed as if incorporated in the second section, had been, as I think it might with as much or more propriety have been, separated therefrom and made into a different section.

The proviso in question is as follows: " Provided always, that no indenture shall be allowed by any justice of the peace for the county *into which such child shall be bound,* who shall be engaged in the same business, employment, or manufacture, in which the person to whom such child shall be bound is engaged." This part of the proviso, I think, is *confined* to an allowance by a magistrate of the second county, and to cases where there is a binding from one county into another, and

the

1824.

The King
against
The Inhabit-
ants of
Newark-upon-
Trent.

the expression appears to me to be most correct and
apt to mark it to be the intent of the legislature that
the construction should here be so confined; the expression, "the county *into which* such child shall be
bound," appearing to me to imply another county *out of*
which he is bound. The same proviso then immediately further proceeds thus: "and notice shall be given
to the overseers of the poor of *the parish or place in*
which such child shall be intended to serve an apprenticeship, before any justice of the peace *for the county or*
district within which such parish or place shall be, shall
allow such indenture, and such notice shall be proved
before such justice shall sign such indenture, unless one
of such overseers shall attend such justice and admit
such notice." Here the expression "justice of the
peace for the county into which such child shall be
bound," which immediately before, as I conceive, confined the first part of the proviso to a binding into a different county, is changed into expressions, both as to
overseers and justices, which let in both descriptions of
bindings, in requiring notice to be given, not to the overseers of "the parish or place in the county into which
such child shall be bound," but "to the overseers of
the poor of the parish or place in which such child
shall be intended to serve an apprenticeship, before any
justice of the peace for the county or district within
which *such* parish or place" (that is, the parish or place
in which he is intended to serve, whether it be in the
same or a different county,) "shall be, shall allow such
indenture." The legislature, as it intends, as I think,
to restrain the first part of the proviso to cases of bindings into a different county, adopts the correct expression

for

1824.

The King
against
The Inhabit-
ants of
NEWARK-UPON-
TRENT.

for that very purpose; and again, where it has not, as I think, such intent of restraint, it abandons that restraining expression which it had just adopted, and uses the more enlarged expression, which here will embrace the whole object and subject matter of the legislature's care, and regulations, namely, parish apprentices and parish bindings in general, and not merely parish apprentices bound into a different county. These circumstances shew that the legislature in this very part of the statute, where it plainly, as I think, intends restraint, uses a corresponding restraining expression, when such restraining expression is either necessary or useful for that purpose, and it recurs again to the more enlarged one, when the expression can, according to the legislature's intent, be more extensively applied. This proviso in sect. 2. is immediately followed by the proviso, printed as sect. 3. " Provided always and it is hereby declared, that the allowance of two justices of the peace for the county *within which the place in which such child shall be intended to serve an apprenticeship shall be situated,* shall be valid and effectual, although such place may be situated in a town or liberty within which any other justices of the peace may in other respects have an exclusive jurisdiction." This section, it is not only admitted, (but which, in order to gain a settlement in *Newark-upon-Trent,* must be contended and established,) does extend to and embrace parish apprentices in general and parish bindings, whether into a different county or not, and yet the expression in this section is the same as those in question which are contained in the proviso in the second section. For unless this third section extends to parish apprentices bound to serve in a parish in the same

1824.

The King
against
The Inhabit-
ants of
Newark-upon-
Trent.

same county, the want of an allowance of the indenture
by two justices of the exclusive town or liberty of *Newark-upon-Trent* would be fatal to the claim of the apprentice's settlement being established there. And if
this section does so extend, then, I ask, upon what
principle of construction is it that a different interpretation is to be given to the same expression in the proviso
in the second section from that which is to be given to
it in the third section? And, if the same interpretation
be to be given to both, then no settlement is gained in
Newark whether that interpretation be according to the
restrained or according to the extended construction.
In either case the indenture is ineffectual for that purpose; in the former case for want of an allowance of
the indenture by two magistrates of *Newark*, and in the
latter case for want of notice to the overseers of the
parish of *Newark*. The expression, " such child," in
the proviso in the second section, includes, I think,
parish apprentices in general, and is not confined to
" parish apprentices bound into a different county."
And the relative expressions, " such parish or place,"
and " such indenture," and " such justice" in that section, and " such place" in the third section, must, I
think, be taken to mean (according to their grammatical
construction with reference to the context) the parish or
place in which the child is intended to serve, and the
indenture by which he is so bound, whether it be into
a parish in the same or a different county. This, I
think, will more distinctly appear by having, in the construction of the first expression " such child," regard to
the first section as well as to the second section, and by
considering that a different and more restrained construction

1824.

The King
against
The Inhabit-
ants of
NEWARK-UPON-
TRENT.

struction cannot be given to the expressions in the second section, without getting into this dilemma, either of giving a different interpretation to the like expressions in the proviso in the third section, or else, by narrowing their construction, of invalidating the apprentice's settlement in the parish of *Newark*, by reason that a binding into a parish in the same county would not in that case come within the third section.

In the present case, the overseers of the poor of the parish of *Newark* are the overseers of the poor of the parish within which the child was intended to serve the apprenticeship; and, therefore, within the description of the persons entitled to notice, or proof, or admission thereof, within the words of this proviso, though their parish is within the same county with the binding parish. No such notice, or proof, or admission thereof, has been given or made. As they are within the *words* of the proviso, they must, I think, be construed to be within its operation, more especially as such notice might be of importance to the protection both of the apprentice and of themselves, unless a different intent can clearly be collected from the context, or from the scope and objects of the statute. No such different intent can, as it appears to me, be so collected; but in my opinion, an inference to the contrary of such a different intent is to be drawn, the intent being, as far as I can collect it, that notice should be given to the overseers of the parish in which it is intended the child should serve, in all cases, whether the binding be into the same or into a different county.

I have considered this case in a great measure without regard to the circumstance of the binding being into a different

1824.

The King
against
The Inhabit-
ants of
Newark-upon-
Trent.

different exclusive jurisdiction, treating it only as a binding into the same county, and as if the third section had the effect of rendering that circumstance of another local exclusive jurisdiction immaterial, though it may be questioned whether the third section by its making a binding by the county magistrates valid, so as to dispense with the allowance of the local magistrates, would have the effect also of dispensing with notice to the overseers in such a case if such notice would otherwise be requisite. But in the view I have taken of the case, it has become unnecessary for me to consider that point.

For the above reasons, I think that a settlement in this case has not been gained in the parish of *Newark upon Trent*.

Bayley J. I agree in opinion with my two learned Brothers. It is unnecessary for me to discuss the question at any length after the judgments delivered by them. The first section of the statute applies generally to all cases, and directs the duties the justices are in *all* cases to perform. It imposes no qualification as to the justices, and contains no restrictions except as to the distance of the master's residence or business. The second section introduces two provisions, one to exclude justices who may be interested, the other to require a notice to the overseers of the parish in which the service is to be, but whether these provisions, or either of them, are general, applicable to all cases, or confined to particular cases contemplated by the earlier part of the section, admits of doubt. The nature of the provisions has a tendency to shew that they are general, their position in the act the contrary. But whether they are

general

1824.

The King
against
The Inhabit-
ants of
NEWARK-UPON-
TRENT.

general or not, if this case is within the earlier part of
the second section, and not taken out of it by the third
section, they apply to this case. The earlier part of the
second section contemplates two cases, first, where the
master's residence or business is in a different *county or
jurisdiction* from that of the binding parish; and,
secondly, other cases where the justices for the *district
or place* in which the binding parish is, shall not have
jurisdiction; and in either of those cases it provides,
that the indenture shall be allowed as well by two
justices for the *county or district* in which the binding
parish is, as by two justices of the *county or district* within
which such child shall be intended to serve. The binding parish here is in the county of *Nottingham;* the parish
in which the service is to be in the town of *Newark,*
where the county magistrates have no jurisdiction. The
master's business, therefore, is in a different jurisdiction
from that of the binding parish, so as to bring this case
in words within the first class of cases mentioned in the
second section, and the justices of the place in which
the binding parish is, have not jurisdiction, so as to
bring it also in words within the second class of cases in
the second section. And there is nothing, as far as I
can judge, in principle or in the other provisions of this
act to exclude it. The provisions to exclude interested
magistrates, and to obtain the information which the
overseers may be enabled to give, are calculated to promote the object of the act to secure proper, disinterested, and unexceptionable bindings, and to place
magistrates in the place of the parent, and to put them
in possession of whatever knowledge may be desirable
to influence their discretion; and the greater the number
of

1824.

The KING
against
The Inhabit-
ants of
NEWARK-UPON-
TRENT.

of cases to which these provisions are extended, the
more the object of the act will be advanced. Is there
any thing then, upon principle, which should exclude
this case from the protection of the second section, or
are there any words in that clause which shew with
such certainty as to furnish a ground for judicial decisions, it was not intended to include it? As the object
of the whole act is to give protection to the helpless,
and to introduce guards to prevent abuse, such a construction should, upon principle, be given to the act as
will extend that protection to every object to which the
words would extend it, and to introduce those guards
as extensively as the words will allow, and the exclusion
of interested judges; and the chance of obtaining useful
information should be applied to every case to which
the words of the provision will warrant its application.
Are there any words then in this clause which will
justify us in saying, it was not intended to include this
case? The only ground upon which, as it seems to me,
any question can be raised upon this point, is this: the
variation of phrase with regard to the justices: section 1.,
speaking of justices of peace for the "county, riding,
division, or place;" and section 2., in one instance, of justices of the "district or place," in others, of the justices
of the "county or district," and in one, of justices of the
"county" only; but whether this variation is intentional
or accidental I cannot discover, and the language appears
to me to be too loose to be a foundation upon which a
court of justice can act. I therefore conclude, that this
case will fall within the second section, unless it is taken
out of it by the third section. That section provides,
that an allowance of two justices for the "county," drop-

9   ping

ping the words "district or place," in which the place
of service is situate, shall be valid, though that place is
within a town or liberty of exclusive jurisdiction. It
does not state that such a town or liberty shall, for the
purposes of this act, be deemed part of the county in
which such town or liberty is situate, but that the
allowance of two justices of the binding county shall
be valid. It does not supersede in words the excluding
restriction, that the justices shall not be of the same
business, nor does it in terms dispense with the notice
to the overseers, and it seems to me, the true construction
of section 3. is, that in cases like the present, to which
sections 2. and 3. both apply, the allowance by the
original magistrates, according to section 1., shall not
alone be sufficient unless they are exempt from the exclusion of section 2., as being magistrates of the same
business with the intended master, and unless notice has
been given to the overseers of the poor of the place in
which the service is to be. If the service is to be in
the county from which the binding is to be, the justices
of that county may, from the business which comes before them as magistrates, be supposed to be sufficiently
acquainted with the circumstances of every part of their
own county to make information by overseers unnecessary; but this may not be the case in places of exclusive
jurisdiction, though within their own county, because, in
their character of magistrates, they can have no knowledge of the local circumstances of such places. I am
therefore of opinion, that in this case there ought to
have been a notice to the overseers of the parish in
which the service was to be, and that for want thereof,
no settlement was gained under these indentures.

ABBOTT

1824.

The King
against
The Inhabit-
ants of
NEWARK-UPON-
TRENT.

1824.

The King
against
The Inhabit-
ants of
Newark-upon-
Trent.

ABBOTT C. J. I have the misfortune to differ from my learned Brothers on the present occasion; and not-- withstanding my great and unfeigned reverence for their opinions, I still think that a settlement was gained in *Newark* under the circumstances of this case. It is not necessary to repeat the facts. The case arises upon the statute 56 *G.* 3. *c.* 139. It is enacted by the fifth section of that statute, that no settlement shall be gained by the apprentice unless such order shall be made and such allowances of the indenture signed as are directed by the statute. As to some of the directions, the statute is introductive of a new law: and as a non-compliance with its directions will prevent the gaining of a settle- ment, I apprehend that, according to general principles, the construction of the statute must not be carried be- yond the plain and obvious meaning of the language of the directions, upon any supposition that a case, not within such meaning, may be within the mischief in- tended to be remedied, or within the reason upon which the direction may be supposed to have been enacted. Those directions may, in my opinion, properly be con- sidered as divided into two classes; those of the first class applying to every case of the binding of a parish apprentice; and those of the second class confined to certain particular bindings, with reference to the local authority of the justices of the peace. I consider all the directions of the first class to be placed together in order, and printed as the first section of the statute; and those of the second class to be in like manner placed together in order, and printed as the second section of the statute. And I consider the third section as ex- planatory only of the jurisdiction of the justices.

The

The directions of the first class are three-fold; first, the duty of the justices to enquire into the particulars of distance and other matters wherein the interest of the apprentice is concerned; secondly, if the justices upon enquiry approve of the binding proposed by the parish officers, to make an order authorising the officers to bind the apprentice as proposed: this order is, by the statute, made the warrant to the officers for the binding, and it must be referred to in the indenture by its date and the names of the justices; thirdly, the signature of the allowance of the indenture by the justices after the order made, and before the execution of the indenture by any of the other parties thereto. These directions apply to every case of every binding, without regard to the jurisdiction within which the master's parish may be situate; and they are followed by a proviso applicable to them, not containing any general regulation as to the binding of an apprentice to be employed in another county; but prohibiting a binding for employment in another county at a greater distance than forty miles from the parish to which the apprentice belongs, unless such parish be more than forty miles from *London;* in which latter case the justices, on a binding to a distance exceeding forty miles, are to make a special order specifying the grounds on which they think fit to allow a binding to the greater distance. Thus far, all the enactments regard only the justices of the county to which the apprentice belongs; and whether we attend to the comprising of the whole in one numbered section, or disregard that circumstance and attend only to the order and disposition of the sentences, which is the more correct mode of reading an act of parliament, the effect will be the same.

1824.

The King
against
The Inhabitants of
Newark-upon-Trent.

  I come

1824.

The King
against
The Inhabit-
ants of
Newark-upon-
Trent.

I come now to the second class, which, as before observed, I consider to be placed together and printed as the second section of the act. By this section it is further enacted, " that in all cases where the residence or establishment of business of the person to whom any child shall be bound, shall be within a different county or jurisdiction of the peace from that within which the place by the officers whereof such child shall be bound, shall be situate; and in all other cases, where the justices of the peace for the district or place within which the place, by the officers whereof such child shall be bound, shall be situate, and who shall sign the allowance of the indenture by which such child shall be bound, shall not have jurisdiction, every indenture by which such child shall be bound, at any time after the said first day of *October*, shall be allowed as well by two justices of the peace for the county or district within which the place, by the officers of which such child shall be bound, shall be situate, as by two justices of the peace for the county or district within which the place shall be situate wherein such child shall be intended to serve." This is an *enactment*, the sentence that immediately follows begins with the word " provided," a word properly applicable to qualify some antecedent matter. I think the enactment plainly requires a two-fold allowance, and by two distinct authorities. The words, " who shall sign the allowance of the indenture by which such child shall be bound," considering the place in which they are here introduced, convince my mind that the things required by this enactment are to be done after the allowance required, in the first instance, for the binding, and by different persons. The enactment applies to the binding into a " different county or jurisdiction

jurisdiction of the peace;" it seems to have been thought, that if those words had stood alone, a doubt might be raised whether the word "jurisdiction" would apply to a town or place, parcel of a county, but whose justices have a jurisdiction, excluding the authority of the justices of the county wherein it is situate; and to prevent this, there is mention, as it were, of another class of cases, viz. those wherein the justices who shall sign the allowance shall not have jurisdiction. It is to be observed, that bindings under this act are not of that class which is compulsory upon the master, so that, as far as regards him and his place of residence, the allowance of the binding in the first instance by the justices is not properly the exercise of a local authority. By this enactment, if it be not afterwards controlled, a two-fold allowance will be requisite whensoever the master's parish and the parish of the apprentice happen to be under the general jurisdiction of different justices; and the second allowance must be by the justices of the local district within which the master's parish is situate, whether that parish be in the same county as the parish of the apprentice, or in a different county: if the two parishes happen to be in the same county, and the parish of the apprentice is in a local district, and that of the master in the county at large, the second allowance must be by the justices of the county. It is clear, however, that some qualification is introduced as to this matter by the third section; but before I notice that more particularly, it is fit to advert again to the second section. The part of that section following the enactment before detailed, begins, as I have observed, with the word "provided." It runs thus, " Provided always that no indenture shall be allowed by any justice of the peace

1824.

The KING
against
The Inhabit-
ants of
NEWARK-UPON-
TRENT.

G 2   for

1824.

The King
against
The Inhabit-
ants of
Newark-upon-
Trent.

for the county into which such child shall be bound, who shall be engaged in the same business, employment, or manufacture, in which the person to whom such child shall be bound, shall be employed." This proviso appears to me to relate only to those cases which form the subject of the enactment immediately preceding, as well by reason of its position in the statute, as of the expression, " into which such child shall be bound," which I consider to denote plainly a county different from that to which the child belongs, and *in which* the binding by the discretion of the justices is made. The following words are introduced by the conjunction " and," which is properly applicable to connect them with the preceding words, and so connecting to confine them to the cases mentioned immediately before: the following words are, " And notice shall be given to the overseers of the poor of the parish or place in which such child shall be intended to serve an apprenticeship, before any justice of the peace for the county or district within which such parish or place shall be, shall allow such indenture; and such notice shall be proved before such justice shall sign such indenture, unless one of such overseers shall attend such justice and admit such notice." If the act had nothing further on the subject of the jurisdiction of justices, I cannot satisfy my mind that it would have been ever thought that the whole matter of this second section of the act was not confined to those cases in which an allowance of the indenture by justices of two distinct jurisdictions was required. And it seems to me, that the doubt has arisen from the matter contained in the third section of the act. This section begins also with the word " provided," and it appears to

18   me

me a continuation of the second section, and a further qualification of those cases and those alone, which form the first part of the section, viz. the cases of different jurisdictions of justices. It is in these words, " Provided always, and it is hereby declared, that the allowance of two justices of the peace for the county within which the place *in which* such child shall be intended to serve an apprenticeship shall be situate, shall be valid and effectual, although such place may be situate in a town or liberty within which any other justices of the peace may, in other respects, have an exclusive jurisdiction." I consider this section to give the jurisdiction to the county justices, whether the town or liberty be within the county to which the master alone belongs, or the county to which both the master and the apprentice belong, but to give it only as it regards the master's parish ; so that if a child belonging to a town or liberty is to be bound to a master residing out of the town or liberty, the inquiry in the first instance as to the fitness of the proposed master and the order for the binding, and the first allowance of the indenture, must be by the justices of the town or liberty : and applying this section to the case now before the Court, I think the question is the same as it would be if the town of *Newark* had no local justices. And then the question will be, whether upon a binding to a master residing in the county to which the child belongs, notice of the binding must be given to the overseers of the master's parish.

I have already observed upon the order in which this clause requiring notice stands in the act, and its connection by the copulative " and" with the sentence next before it, and have said, that I consider that sentence,

1824.

The KING
against
The Inhabitants of
NEWARK-UPON-
TRENT.

1824.

The KING
against
The Inhabit-
ants of
NEWARK-UPON-
TRENT.

tence, also, as relating only to the justices of what I may call the second jurisdiction. If it had been intended that notice should be given to the overseers of the master's parish in all cases, I cannot forbear thinking, that this would have been effected by some distinct enactment, and not by words immediately following and connected in language with an enactment regarding certain cases only. I cannot say that I have found any reason for thus expressly requiring the notice to the parish officers, where the binding is into another county, which may not be urged with almost equal force to a binding in the same county. But it is to be observed, that the legislature has, in the first section, expressly directed the justices of the apprentice's county to enquire into the fitness of the proposed master and the distance of his residence; and I presume it was thought, that where the discharge of this prescribed duty should appear to the justices to require a notice to the officers of the master's parish, they would require such notice to be given, whereas no special duty is imposed by the act on the justices of the master's county; and, as I construe the act, there is a special qualification respecting those justices in regard to their business or manufacture; and the notice may therefore have been required in this case, as well for the purpose of supplying the place of that enquiry which is enjoined in the other, as for security against the allowance of the indenture by any justice of the same business as the master. I think, also, that if such an intention had been entertained by the legislature, the sentence requiring notice would have contained some words denoting that the notice was to be given, whether the master's parish was in the same county as the apprentice's, or in a different county; and if the master's parish was in the

same

1824.

The King
against
The Inhabit-
ants of
NEWARK-UPON-
TRENT.

same county, then that the notice should be given before making the order for the binding, which is the important act, and not merely before the allowance of the indenture, which is only a ministerial act, as it respects the justices who have made the order; for I think it cannot have been intended that the same justices should make an enquiry and then an order for the binding, and afterwards give an opportunity for the officers of another parish to attend before them, who might induce them to rescind their order. If notice to such officers and proof thereof were to be required, I think they ought to be required in the first instance, and before making the order. If the notice is confined to the allowance of the indenture by the justices of another county, it is required before any act is to be done by them. The notice is certainly required only with reference to an allowance of the indenture by the justices of the master's county. If it is required where that county happens to be the same as the county of the apprentice, then, as I have before observed, it will be required before an allowance by the binding justices in some cases and not in others, and this will not be distinctly shewn by the statute; whereas, according to my construction of the statute, the several matters required of the justices of the two distinct jurisdictions will be detailed in a plain and intelligible order, without any confusion of arrangement or perplexity of language. For these reasons, I am of opinion that the notice is not required where the apprentice and his master reside in the same county. The statute upon which the question has arisen is certainly not free from ambiguity. I have already noticed, that if its requisitions are not complied with, a settlement cannot be gained, under

G 4   circum-

1824.

The King
against
The Inhabit-
ants of
NEWARK-UPON-
TRENT.

circumstances in which it might have been gained before the passing of the act; and I have thought myself bound to decide upon that which I deem to be the true sense and meaning of the words of the statute, regard being had to the order and arrangement of its matter; and I have the satisfaction of knowing, that if my construction be erroneous, the error is of no practical importance, because the opinion of my learned Brothers must prevail, and the rule for quashing the order of sessions must be made absolute.

Order of sessions quashed.

WILSON against ABBOTT.

A. let apart-
ments in his
dwelling-house
to B., at a
rent payable
half yearly.
B. took pos-
session at
Michaelmas
1822, and at
Lady-day 1823
paid half a
year's rent. In
June of that
year, B. left
the apartments
without giving
any notice to
quit, but at Mi-
chaelmas 1823
he paid half a
year's rent.
At Lady-day
1824, A. de-
manded an-
other half
year's rent,
which B. re-
fused to pay:
Held, that from these facts the law would not imply a taking from a year to year.

ASSUMPSIT for use and occupation. Plea, non-assumpsit. At the trial before *Abbott* C. J., at the *London* sittings after last term, it appeared upon the examination of the plaintiff's witnesses, that the plaintiff, at *Michaelmas* 1822, let apartments in his dwelling-house to the defendant, at the rent of 45*l.* payable half-yearly. The defendant took possession at *Michaelmas* 1822, and at *Lady-day* 1823 paid half a year's rent. On the 23d *June* 1823 the defendant left the apartments without giving any notice to quit, and tendered to the landlord one quarter's rent to the then *Midsummer*; this was refused by the plaintiff, and when *Michaelmas* 1823 arrived he demanded half a year's rent, which the defendant paid. At *Lady-day* 1824 the plaintiff demanded another half year's rent, which the defendant refused

to

1824.

WILSON
against
ABBOTT.

to pay, upon which the present action was brought. The plaintiff gave no evidence of what passed at the time of taking the apartments, so as to shew whether there was a taking from year to year, or only for one year. Upon this the Lord Chief Justice held, that a taking from year to year could not be inferred from the facts proved. If the defendant had continued in possession after the commencement of a second year, that might have been evidence of a yearly taking, but not having done so he was not liable for rent during the second year. The plaintiff was nonsuited.

Chitty now moved for a new trial. A contract for a tenancy from year to year ought to have been implied from the facts proved in this case, for it was holden as long ago as the reign of *Henry* VIII. that a general occupation should be considered to be an occupation from year to year; and that a person so holding should not be ejected from his lands without half a year's notice from his landlord to relinquish the possession. Here the plaintiff proved a general occupation of the premises by the defendant at a yearly rent. It lay on the latter, therefore, to rebut the presumption arising from such a state of things, by shewing a specific contract creating less than a yearly tenancy. The landlord could not have maintained any ejectment against the tenant, without having given a notice to quit, and if that be so the tenant ought not to be at liberty to determine the tenancy without a similar notice. *Adams on Eject-ment*, 97. *Right* v. *Darby*. (a)

(a) 1 *T. R.* 162:

ABBOTT

ABBOTT C. J. I am of opinion that a tenancy for more than a year ought not to have been inferred from the facts proved in this case. According to the ordinary practice lodgings are not usually let even for so long a period as a year, and we are now called upon to infer the existence of a contract continuing for two years at least, contrary to the general usage. If the defendant had continued to occupy the apartments after the commencement of a second year, there would have been ground for inferring a contract for a tenancy continuing from year to year, for it might reasonably be supposed that he continued in possession in pursuance of the contract made. But here the tenant quits during the current year, having, in the first instance, paid half a year's rent, and offered to pay rent for the current quarter, during which he quitted; and he afterwards consents to pay the rent to the end of the current year, but refuses to pay it for a longer period. The inference arising from these facts is, that the defendant considered himself a tenant for one year and no longer, and there being no evidence of any express contract creating a tenancy for a longer period than a year, I think that such a contract, which is certainly contrary to the general usage which prevails in letting lodgings, ought not to be inferred. That being so, I think that the nonsuit was right, and that there should be no rule.

Rule refused. (a)

(a) See *Thompson* v. *Maberly*, 2 Campb. 573.

1824.

Since Hull & Selby Railway 5 m. With 827.

The KING *against* The Right Hon. CHARLES ANDERSON PELHAM, Lord YARBOROUGH.

THIS was a record transmitted from the petty bag office into the Court of King's Bench, which sets forth an inquisition taken at *Cleathorps*, in the county of *Lincoln*, on the 12th day of *November* 1818, by which, amongst other things, it was found that there is a certain piece of land, being salt-marsh, lying near or adjoining to the parish or lordship of *North Cotes* in the said county, which piece of land is bounded towards the south and south-west by the sea-wall or sea-bank of the said lordship of *North Cotes*, and towards the north-west by part of the sea-wall or sea-bank of certain lands in the lordship of *Titney*, and on all other parts by the sea, and contains by estimation 453 acres or thereabouts, and is of the annual value of 4s. an acre, and was in times past covered with the water of the sea, but is now, and has been for several years past by the sea *left*, and is not covered with water, except at high tides, when the sea doth flow to the said sea-walls or sea banks; which said piece of land, from the time of such *dereliction*,

Where an inquisition found that a piece of land had in times past been covered with the water of the sea, but was then and had been for several years past by the sea left, and the commissioners caused the same to be seised into the king's hands. The defendant filed a traverse, stating that he was seised in fee of the manor of North Thoresby cum North Cotes and the demesne lands thereof; and that the same piece of land mentioned in the inquisition, by the slow, gradual, and imperceptible projection, allu-

vion, subsidence, and accretion of ooze, soil, sand, and other matter, being slowly, gradually, and by imperceptible increase, in long time cast up, deposited, and settled by and from the flux and reflux of the tide upon and against the extremity of the said manor, hath been formed, &c., and thereby became parcel of the demesne lands of the manor; without this, that the land was *left* by the sea, as found by the inquisition. The replication by the Attorney-General traversed that the land was formed as alleged in the inducement to the defendant's traverse, and joined issue on the traverse taken by the defendant. Issue was also joined on the traverse taken by the Attorney-General. It appeared by the evidence that the land in question had been formed gradually by ooze and soil deposited by the sea, and that the increase could not be observed when actually going on, although a visible increase took place every year, and in the course of fifty years a large piece of land had been thus formed: Held, first, that upon this evidence the land could not be said to have been *left* by the sea; secondly, that it was formed by the slow, gradual, and imperceptible projection, &c., of ooze, soil, and sand, as alleged in the inducement to the defendant's traverse, and that both issues were properly found for him.

hitherto

hitherto has been, and still is unoccupied, but the herb-age thereof has been from time to time eaten and consumed by the cattle and sheep belonging to divers tenants or occupiers of lands situate within the said parish or lordship of *North Cotes.* And the inquisition then stated that the said piece of land, together with other lands therein specified, the commissioners had taken and caused to be seized into the hands of our said lord the king. To this inquisition the defendant filed a traverse, which, after craving oyer of the commissioner's return and inquisition, and admitting the boundaries, quantity, and value of the land in question, and that the same piece of land is now, and has been for several years past not covered with water, except at high tides, when the sea doth flow to the said sea-wall or sea-bank, states, that " from time whereof the memory of man runneth not to the contrary, there hath been, and still is a certain ancient manor called or known by the name of the manor of *North Thoresby* cum *North Cotes,* situate within the parish of *North Cotes* aforesaid, in the said county of *Lincoln,* and that the defendant, long before the respective days of issuing the commission and finding the inquisition, to wit, on, &c., was seized in his demesne as of fee, of and in the manor of *North Thoresby* cum *North Cotes,* and the demesne lands thereof, and that the same piece of land heretofore, to wit, on the 1st day of *January* 1300, and on divers other days and times between that day and the day of the finding the inquisition, by the slow, gradual, and imperceptible projection, alluvion, subsidence, and accretion of ooze, soil, sand, and matter, being slowly, gradually, and by imperceptible increase in long time cast up, deposited, and settled by and from the flux and reflux of the tide and

waves

waves of the sea, in, upon, and against the outside and
extremity of the demesne lands of the same manor, hath
been formed, and hath settled, grown, and accrued upon
and against and unto the said demesne lands of the
same manor, and the same and every portion thereof,
when and as the same hath so there been formed, settled, grown, and accrued, hath thereupon and thereby
at those times respectively in that behalf above mentioned, forthwith become and been, and from the same
several times respectively have and hath continued to be,
and still are and is part and parcel of the said demesne
lands of the same manor, and the several owners and
proprietors of the same manor for the time being during
all the time aforesaid, until the time of the seisin of the
defendant as aforesaid, and defendant during the time
he hath been so as aforesaid seised of and in the said
manor, from the time of the formation and accretion of
the same piece of land and every part thereof respectively, continually until the time of the finding of the
inquisition respectively were and was seised in their and
his demesne as of fee, of and in the same piece of land
and every part thereof, when and as the same hath so
been formed and accrued as aforesaid, as and for part
and parcel of the demesne lands of the same manor.
Without this, that the said piece of land in the plea
mentioned and in the inquisition last above mentioned,
or any part or parcel thereof, was or now is by the sea
left in manner and form as in the inquisition is above
supposed and found.   The replication of the Attorney-
General traversed part of the inducement to the defendant's traverse, as follows: " without this, that the said
piece of land in the inquisition lastly mentioned, being
the piece of land before described at the times in the
                                                      said

The King
against
Lord
Yarborough.

said plea mentioned, by the slow, gradual, and imperceptible projection, alluvion, subsidence, and accretion of ooze, soil, sand, and other matter being slowly, gradually, and by imperceptible increase in long time, cast up, deposited, and settled by and from the flux and reflux of the tide and waves of the sea in, upon, and against the outside and extremity of the demesne land of the same manor, hath been formed, and hath settled, grown, and accrued upon and against and unto the said demesne lands of the same manor in manner and form as the defendant hath above in his plea in that behalf alleged;" and the defendant in his rejoinder took issue upon that fact. The replication then took issue on the defendant's traverse, " that the said piece of land in the plea of defendant mentioned, was and now is by the sea *left*, in manner and form as in the inquisition 'is above supposed and found;" and thereupon also the defendant joined issue. These issues were tried at the last assizes for the county of *Derby* before *Park* J., and a verdict found for the defendant. A rule nisi having been obtained to shew cause why a new trial should not be had, the Court directed, at the time of shewing cause against the rule, that the facts proved at the trial should be stated in a special case for the opinion of the Court, and that if judgment should be given for the king upon such case, the verdict obtained for the defendant should be set aside and a new trial had; and if judgment should be given for the defendant upon such case, judgment should be entered for the defendant upon the verdict. The case was as follows :

The land in question consists of 450 acres of saltmarsh called fittees, being the land covered with herbage, which, at the time of taking the inquisition set forth in

15   the

the pleadings, lay between the sea-wall and the sea opposite to *North Cotes*, in the county of *Lincoln.* It was proved that this land had been formed in the course of time by means of ooze, warp, silt, sludge, and soil carried down by the *Humber*, and deposited and cast up by the flux and reflux of the sea upon and against the adjacent land, whereby the land has been enlarged and increased, and the sea has receded. The matter thus deposited is at first soft and sludgy, but in the course of five or six years grows firm, and then produces herbage. With respect to the degree or rate of growth and increase of the land, the evidence produced on the part of the crown was as follows : the first witness proved that the sea had receded in parts 140 or 150 yards within twenty-six or twenty-seven years; and that within the last four years he could see that it had receded much in parts, but could not say how much; and in parts he believed that it had not receded at all. The alteration, he said, had been slow and gradual, and he could not perceive the growth as it went on, though he could see there had been an increase in twenty-six or twenty-seven years of 140 or 150 yards, and that it had certainly receded since he measured the land the year before. The second witness proved that in fifteen years there had been an increase of the fittees on the outside of the sea-wall; in some parts from 100 to 150 yards; that it grows a little from year to year. That within the last five years there had been a visible increase in some parts during that period, of from thirty to fifty yards; that the gradual increase is not perceptible to the eye at the moment. The third witness said there had been some small increase in every year; and the fourth witness said the swarth increased every year very gradually, and that

perhaps

1824.

The King
against
Lord
YARBOROUGH.

perhaps it had gathered a quarter of a mile in breadth in some places within his recollection, or during the last fifty-four or fifty-five years, and in some places it had gathered nothing. It was proved that the ground between the sea-wall above mentioned and another sea-wall still more remote from the sea, appeared to have been covered over with the sea formerly.

Goulburn for the crown. The principles of law which govern the rights of the crown to maritime accretions are laid down with great precision, by Lord *Hale,* in his treatise *De Jure Maris.* He states that " the king hath a title to maritime increments, or increase of the land by the sea, and this is of three kinds, viz. first, increase per projectionem vel alluvionem; second, increase per relictionem vel desertionem; third, per insulæ productionem," (a) and he gives a description of each. The increase per alluvionem is now in question, and that he describes as follows: " The increase per alluvionem is when the sea, by casting up sand and earth, doth by degrees increase the land, and shut itself out further than the ancient bounds went. The reason why this belongs to the crown is, because, in truth, the soil where there is now dry land was formerly part of the very fundus maris, and consequently belonged to the king. But, indeed, if such alluvion be so insensible that it cannot be by any means found that the sea was there, idem est non esse et non apparere, the land thus increased belongs, as a perquisite, to the owner of the land adjacent." In page 28 Lord *Hale* again describes the jus alluvionis in nearly the same words, and then

(a) Pt. 1, c. 4, p. 14.

cites

cites the following passage from *Bracton*, lib. 2. c. 2.
" Item quod per alluvionem agro tuo flumen adjecit
jure gentium tibi acquiritur. Est autem alluvio latens
incrementum. Et per alluvionem adjici dicitur quod
ita paulatim adjicitur, quod intelligere non possis quo
momento temporis adjiciatur, &c. Si autem non sit
latens incrementum contrarium erit, ut vis fluminis
partem aliquam ex tuo prædio detraxit et vicini prædio
appulit, certum est eam tuum permanere, &c.," and
then he observes, " but *Bracton* follows the civil law in
this and some other following places;" and soon after
he adds, " This jus alluvionis, as I have before said, is,
de jure communi, by the law of *England* the king's."
With respect to the increase per relictionem, or recess
of the sea, Lord *Hale* says, " This doth de jure communi
belong to the king" (*a*), and he assigns the same reason as
before, that the sea is part of the waste of the crown, and,
therefore, that which lies under it belongs to the king;
and he cites the case of an information against *Oldsworth*
and others " for intruding into 300 acres of land which
was relictum per mare, and now called *Sutton Marsh* ;
the defendants pleaded specially, and entitled themselves
by prescription to the lands *project* by the sea; and
upon demurrer adjudged against them, that, first, by
the prescription or title made to lands project, which is
jus alluvionis, no answer is given to the information for
lands *relict*, for these were of several natures. Second,
it was held that it lies not in prescription to claim lands
relict per mare." This case proves two things; first,
that it is necessary to plead specially a title to lands
gained per alluvionem; and, secondly, that custom cannot give a right to lands per relictionem. In the case

1824.

The KING
against
Lord
YARBOROUGH.

(*a*) P. 14.

of the Abbot of *Peterborough* (a), he pleaded and proved a title by custom to lands formed per alluvionem, and judgment was given for him. It is not contended that the defendant, in the present case, might not have shewn a title to the lands in dispute if he had alleged and proved a custom, but he has not done so. In the Abbot of *Ramsay's* case (b), where the Crown demanded sixty acres of land which the abbot had appropriated to himself; he pleaded that he held the manor of *Brancaster*, situate near the sea, and that there was there a certain marsh sometimes diminished and sometimes increased by the flux and reflux of the sea, and traversed the appropriation; and upon issue joined a verdict was found for the abbot, and judgment given quod eat sine die. This case is cited by Lord *Hale* (c), who observes upon it, " Here is no custom at all alleged, but it seems he relied upon the common right of his case, as that he suffered the loss, so he should enjoy the benefit, even by the bare common law, in case of alluvion." Upon that authority it must be conceded that a subject may be entitled to accretions by alluvion, if he pleads and proves that he has been subject to loss by the sea in the same place. At the commencement of that case *Dyer* puts a quære, " whether lands left by the sea shall belong to the prince or the owner of the adjoining land," which is answered in a note supposed to be by *Treby* C. J. " The prince shall have all lands left by or gained from the sea." There is another way also in which the subject may be entitled to increase by alluvion, viz. if the alluvion is so insensible that it cannot be known that the sea ever was

(a) *Hale, De Jure Mar.* 29.   (b) *Dyer*, 326. b.   (c) P. 29.

there.

there. To this right *Callis* (*a*) applies the principle " de minimis non curat lex." It is unnecessary to notice the increase per insulæ productionem. The right of the king to lands formed by alluvion, or left by the sea, is therefore clear. It is also admitted that where the land of a subject is overwhelmed by the sea, and again left dry, the right of the subject revives. *Roll. Abr.* 168. *Prerog. du Roy*, B. pl. 2. The crown, therefore, in claiming maritime increments takes nothing from the subject: it merely claims to retain, in a dry state, that which clearly belonged to it when covered with water. In the present instance the subject seeks to take something from the crown. Probably the passage cited from *Bracton* by Lord *Hale* may be relied on by the other side; but Lord *Hale* observes, that the passage in question follows the civil law, and in various other works *Bracton* is spoken of as not being entitled to much weight as an authority in our law. See *Fitz. Abr. Gard.* pl. 71. *Stowell* v. *Zouch* (*b*), *Ball* v. *Herbert.* (*c*) Another authority relied upon by the defendant at the trial was 2 *Bl. Com.* p. 261., but that is plainly a very loose passage, for no distinction is made between the increment by alluvion and by dereliction: it cannot be contended that all increase by alluvion belongs to the subject if it be imperceptible to the eye whilst going on, for then the increase by alluvion must always belong to the subject for the actual formation of the land can never be observable at the moment. The right of the subject really depends on the principle, " de minimis non curat lex." Here the whole increase was 460 acres, and it went on at the rate of eight or nine yards in width every year. The

(*a*) *On Sewers,* p. 51.   (*b*) 1 *Plowd.* 357.
(*c*) 3 *T. R.* 263. But see a different opinion of *Bracton,* in Pref. to 9 *Co,* p. 13., and *Doddridge's Eng. Lawyer,* 41.

     principle

principle before mentioned is here inapplicable; no customary or prescriptive right was pleaded, nor was the defendant's case made to depend upon the liability to loss by the encroachment of the sea, the first issue should, therefore, have been found for the crown. On the second issue the only question was, whether the land had been left in the manner stated in the inquisition. Now, the only object of the inquisition was to find whether land which had originally been covered with the sea had been left dry. No technical distinction was made by the commissioners between lands formed by alluvion and those derelict by the sea. Their finding was in substance that the sea had receded from the lands in question, and that was supported by the evidence.

Phillipps, contrà. The word "imperceptible," in the first issue, must be understood in the sense which the term commonly bears. It has not any legal or technical meaning in contradistinction from the sense which it bears in common parlance. The same meaning will be collected from the context. The issue is, whether the piece of land in dispute has been formed upon the demesne lands of the manor by the "slow, gradual, and imperceptible projection, alluvion, subsidence, and accretion of ooze, soil, and other matter being slowly, gradually, and imperceptibly deposited by the flux and reflux of the tides." The words "slow, gradual, and imperceptible accretion and alluvion," must be understood to describe an alluvion so gradual as not to be observed at the time, as not to be perceived in its progress. The deposition being thus imperceptible, the increase must be the same. By the operation of the tides, then, a small increment has been deposited from

14   day

day *to* day, until, in the course of time, a considerable piece of land has been formed; still, however, composed of minute increments, each part being to the whole as the fluxion to the fluent. If the words of the issue are to be understood in their ordinary sense, the evidence completely established the defendant's allegation, and the jury could only find their verdict for him. One witness stated, that the alteration had been slow and gradual, and he could not perceive the growth as it went on. Another said, that the land grows a little from year to year, and that the gradual increase is not perceptible to the eye at the moment. If there be in rerum naturâ, such a thing as imperceptible alluvion, it was that which the witnesses in this case proved to have taken place. It exactly corresponds with *Bracton's* definition of alluvion : " Latens incrementum quod ita paulatim adjicitur ut intelligere non possis quo momento temporis adjiciatur." The jury, therefore, could not do otherwise than find the first issue for the defendant, and if so, all question as to the second is at once disposed of; for that describes the lands as *left* by the sea. Now Lord *Hale* and *Callis,* in a variety of passages, speak of lands formed by alluvion and those *left* by the sea, as totally different in nature, and subject to different rules of law. If, therefore, the first issue was properly found for the defendant, the jury could not have done right had they found the second for the crown. The principle point made on the other side, was, that even supposing the land in question to have been deposited by imperceptible degrees, still the defendant cannot be entitled to the judgment of the Court, inasmuch as he has not stated on the record any custom or prescription, or other legal title to it. But, upon a careful examination of the authorities, it will be

H 3　　　　　　　　　　found,

found, that the subject is entitled to such lands of common right. There is little to be found touching the point in the old books. Neither *Brooke's* or *Fitzherbert's Abr.* contains any trace of such a prerogative as that now claimed, nor is it mentioned in *Staunford de Prerog. Regis.* *Dyer* C. J. puts it as a doubtful question, whether a great quantity of land *relinquished* by the sea shall belong to the prince by his prerogative, or to the owner of the adjoining land, as a perquisite (a); and, after referring to several text writers, he cites the *Abbot of Ramsay's* case, and afterwards *Digges* v. *Hammond* as a like case. In both judgment was given for the subject against the crown, although the record did not contain any allegation of a customary or prescriptive title; and it appears by *Callis*, pp. 50. and 53., that the lands were formed by alluvion. With respect to the note by *Treby* C. J., it is plain, that if it was meant as a solution of C. J. *Dyer's* doubt, it applies to derelict lands only; but if it is to be taken in a larger sense, still it can only apply to derelict lands, and those from which the sea has been excluded by artificial means. It cannot be supposed to include lands formed by alluvion; that is contrary to the natural meaning of the words, and in opposition to the two cases reported immediately after the quære put in the text: now it is not probable that *Treby* C. J. would have expressed an opinion inconsistent with those cases, without making some observation upon them. In 2 *Roll. Abr. Prerog. B.* pl. 9, 10., the cases cited by *Dyer* are adopted, and then follows pl. 11. " If the salt water leave *a great quantity* of land on the shore, the king shall have the land by his prerogative,

(a) *Dyer*, 326. b.

and

and the owner of the adjoining soil shall not have it as a perquisite." Whence it may be inferred, that *Rolle* thought, land formed gradually by alluvion, would go to the owner of the adjoining land, of common right, as a perquisite; and it has been so understood; *Com. Dig. Prerog.* (D. 61.) and 2 *Bl. Com.* 261. Lord *Hale*, in his treatise *De Jure Maris*, manifestly speaks of two different kinds of gain by alluvion; the one where a considerable increase takes place at one time, the other where it is gradual and by insensible degrees. In the former case it belongs to the crown, in the latter to the subject; and he does not cite any case to shew, that, under such circumstances, the right of the subject depends on custom or prescription. In the *Abbot of Peterborough's* case a custom was certainly alleged, but it is not stated that his right could not have been established without it; and in the *Abbot of Ramsay's* case no such title was stated on the record. Lord *Hale* cannot be taken to mean that the increment belongs to the subject only when it is so inconsiderable as to be scarcely perceptible; for in the *Abbot of Ramsay's* case, which he cites, the dispute was for sixty acres; and unless the land is, after the lapse of many years, clearly discernible, a dispute respecting it can hardly arise. The true and only sensible meaning is, that where the increase is imperceptible in its progress, there the land becomes the property of the subject as it is formed; it is then vested in him de die in diem; and what is once vested in him cannot be devested by the circumstance of a still further increase afterwards taking place. This agrees with the case cited in *Callis* (a), from the 22 *Lib. ass,* pl. 93.

(a) 51.

H 4

" The

" The case was, that a river of water did run between two lordships, and the soil of one side, together with the river of water, did wholly belong to one of the said lordships, and the river, by little and little, did gather upon the soil of the other lord, but so slowly, that if one had fixed his eye a whole day thereon together, it could not be perceived. By this petty and imperceptible increase the increasement was got to the owner of the river; but if the river, by a sudden and an unusual flood, had gained hastily a great parcel of the other lord's ground, he should not thereby have lost the same; and so of petty and imperceivable increasements from the sea, the king gains no property for " de minimis non curat lex." The case of the river clearly explains the mode in which *Callis* intends to apply the maxim, viz. that the king has no claim to the land where the increase is by imperceptible degrees, however large it may ultimately become. There is not, then, either upon authority or principle, any ground for disturbing the verdict found for the defendant.

Cur. adv. vult.

The judgment of the Court was now delivered by

ABBOTT C. J. Upon this case the only question for the judgment of the Court is, whether the evidence given at the trial was such as to justify the verdict of the jury upon the issues joined. Whether the pleadings have been correctly framed on either side, or what may be the legal consequence and effect of the verdict, supposing it to stand, are points not now before us. I notice this, because some part of the argument at the bar was more properly applicable to a matter of law upon admitted facts, than to the question whether par-

ticular

ticular issues are maintained by the evidence; or in other words, whether particular facts are found to exist.

The second issue upon the record arises upon a traverse of the matter found by the inquisition. The matter thus found, is, that the land now claimed by the crown was in times past covered with the water of the sea, but is now, and has been for several years, *left* by the sea. Now, the distinction between land derelict, or left by the sea, acquiring a new character in consequence - of the mere subsidence and absence of the salt water; and land gained by alluvion or projection of extraneous matter, whereby the sea is excluded and prevented from overflowing it, is easily intelligible in fact, and recognised as law by all the authorities on the subject. Upon the evidence it is very plain, that the land in question is of the latter description, and therefore the issue joined upon this point was properly found for the defendant.

The principal question arose upon the first issue and it is, as I have before intimated, merely a question of fact. The defendant has pleaded, that the land in question, by the slow, gradual, and imperceptible projection, alluvion, subsidence, and accretion of ooze, soil, sand, and other matter, being slowly, gradually, and by imperceptible increase, in long time cast up, deposited, and settled by and from the flux and reflux of the tide and water of the sea in upon and against the outside and extremity of the demesne lands of the manor, hath been formed, and hath settled grown and accrued upon against and unto the said demesne lands. This allegation has been denied on the part of the crown, and an issue taken upon it. The allegation regards only the manner in which the land has been formed: it contains nothing as to the result of its formation, nothing

as

as to the practicability of ascertaining, after its form—ation, by any marks or limits or quantity previously existing and known, or by measure to commence and be taken from such marks, or with reference to such quantity, how much is now land, that once was sea. It is clear upon the evidence, that the land has been formed slowly and gradually in the way mentioned in the plea. The argument was upon the word "im-perceptibly;" and for the crown, two passages were cited from Sir *Matthew Hale's* treatise, *De Jure Maris,* wherein that very learned writer speaks of land gained by alluvion, as belonging generally to the crown, unless the gain be so insensible that it cannot be *by any means,* according to the words of one of the passages, or *by any limits or marks,* according to the words of the other passage, found that the sea was there; idem est non esse et non apparere. In these passages, however, Sir *Matthew Hale* is speaking of the legal consequence of such an accretion, and does not explain what ought to be considered as accretion insensible or imperceptible in itself, but considers that as being insensible, of which it cannot be said with certainty that the sea ever was there. An accretion extremely minute, so minute as to be imperceptible even by known antecedent marks or limits at the end of four or five years, may become, by gradual increase, perceptible by such marks or limits at the end of a century, or even of forty or fifty years. For it is to be remembered that if the limit on one side be land, or something growing or placed thereon, as a tree, a house, or a bank, the limit on the other side will be the sea, which rises to a height varying almost at every tide, and of which the variations do not depend merely upon the ordinary course of nature at fixed and ascertained periods, but in part also, upon the strength and direction of the wind, which are different almost from day to day. And, therefore, these passages from the work of Sir *Matthew Hale* are not properly applicable to this question. And considering the word " imperceptible" in this issue, as connected with the words " slow and gradual," we think it must be understood as expressive only of the manner of the accretion, as the other words undoubtedly are, and as meaning imperceptible in its progress, not imperceptible after a long lapse of time. And taking this to be the meaning of the word " imperceptible," the only remaining point is, whether the accretion of this land might properly upon the evidence be considered by the jury as imperceptible. No one witness has said that it could be perceived, either in its progress, or at the end of a week or a month. One witness, who appears twice to have measured the land, says, that within the last four years he could see that the sea had receded, but he could not say how much; the same witness said, that it certainly had receded since he measured it last year, but he did not say how much; and, according to his evidence, the gain in a period of twenty-six or twenty-seven years, was on the average about five yards and a half in a year. Another witness speaks of a gain of from 100 to 150 yards in fifteen years; a much greater increase than that mentioned by the first witness; and this second witness adds, that during the last five years there had been a visible increase in some parts of from thirty to fifty yards. Upon the evidence of this witness, it is to be observed that he speaks very loosely, the difference between 100 and 150 in fifteen years, and between thirty and fifty in five years, being very great. The third witness said there had been some small increase in every year. The fourth

.witness

witness said, the swarth increases every year very gradually, and *perhaps* it had gathered a quarter of a mile in breadth in some places within his recollection, or during the last fifty-four or fifty-five years, and in some places it had gathered nothing. And this was the whole evidence on the subject. We think the jury might, from this evidence, very reasonably find that the increase had not only been slow and gradual, but also imperceptible, according to the sense in which, as I have before said, we think that word ought to be understood. And, consequently, we are of opinion, that a new trial ought not to be granted, and the rule therefore must be discharged.

Rule discharged.

Aspinall *against* Stamp and Another.

Where a defendant was by a Judge's order allowed to go to trial upon certain terms, upon payment to the plaintiff of a certain sum of money and the costs incurred up to the date of the order; and the plaintiff consented to the trial proceeding on those terms before the costs had been paid: Held, that the defendant having obtained a verdict, was bound to pay those costs, and could not set them off against those afterwards taxed for him on the postea.

THIS was an action for an alleged trespass in seizing certain goods and chattels alleged to be the property of the plaintiff. The venue was laid in *Yorkshire*. The defendants justified under the 13 *Eliz. c.*7. and 1 *J.* 1. *c.* 15., as assignees of one *James Shaw*, a bankrupt. But afterwards defendants entertaining doubts as to whether all the goods were the bankrupt's, made an application at a judge's chambers, whereupon the Lord Chief Justice made an order, " That upon payment of the sum of 20*l.*, together with the costs of the cause up to the date of the order, the defendants should be entitled to a verdict in their favour, unless the plaintiff should, at the

trial,

trial, prove that the value of the goods enumerated on the back of the order, exceeded the sum of 20*l.*, or should prove a trespass as to entering the dwelling-house or taking some of the other goods mentioned in the declaration." This order was served on the plaintiff's attorney, on the 19th of *March* last. The commission day at *York* was the 20th. About half an hour after the order was served the defendant's attorney tendered the sum of 20*l.* to the plaintiff's attorney, and at the same time observed, that the amount of the costs could not then be known, but that he would pay them as soon as it was ascertained. The cause was tried at the *York* assizes, and the plaintiff failing to give the proof mentioned in the order, a verdict was found for the defendants. On the 17th of *April* the costs payable to the plaintiff were taxed at 46*l.* 13*s.*, and the costs for the defendants were taxed at 132*l.* 10*s.*

Parke moved that the defendants might be at liberty to deduct the interlocutory costs from those which were taxed for them, instead of paying them to the plaintiff, and cited *Howell* v. *Harding.* (*a*) The plaintiff's attorney might have insisted upon having them paid before the cause was tried; but as he did not insist upon his right then, he cannot now resist this application.

Alderson shewed cause in the first instance, and contended that the payment of the costs mentioned in the order was a condition precedent to the defendants' being entitled to go to trial on the advantageous terms which the order gave them.

(*a*) 3 *East*, 362.

Per

Per Curiam. These costs were payable on a special order, and the payment was certainly a condition precedent, which ought to have been performed before the defendants could have the benefit of the order.

Rule refused.

---

*Wednesday,
June 30th.*

HUNTER *against* SIMPSON and Another.

In K. B. a defendant served with a copy of process by original, has eight days from the quarto die post of the return of the process to enter an appearance.

A RULE was obtained, calling upon the attorney for the defendants to shew cause why he should not enter an appearance for the defendants, pursuant to his undertaking. On the 14th of *June* the defendants' attorney received copies of a special capias against the defendants, returnable on that day, and gave an undertaking to appear for them. This rule was obtained on the 23d of *June.*

Chitty shewed cause, and contended that it was not necessary to enter an appearance until the 26th of *June,* and cited the rule laid down in *Tidd's Prac.* (a) that the appearance is to be entered within eight days after the quarto die post of the return of the process.

Archbold., contrà. The practice adopted in this court is correctly stated, but that practice is wrong: the writ was returnable on the 14th of *June,* and the time allowed for the entering of appearances by *5 G. 2. c. 27. s. 1.* is eight days from the return, not from the day of appappearance. That day, usually called the quarto die

(a) 246., sixth edit.

post,

post, was, at common law, a day granted ex gratia curiæ.
The statute 12 G. 1. c. 29. first gave the common appearance, and that enacted that it should be entered
within four days from the *return*. The same expression
is adopted in the 5 G. 2. c. 27. s. 1. Had the legislature
intended to give the longer time contended for on the
other side, they would have directed that the compu-
tation should be made from the quarto die post, and not
from the return. The court of C. P. have put that
construction on the act which the plaintiff now con-
tends for.

ABBOTT C. J. The whole question is, what is meant
by the expression, " return of the writ." The court of
C. P. have held it to mean the very day; we have held it
to be, the quarto die post. Which construction is best I
do not now pretend to decide; but we cannot make this
rule absolute against a person who has not yet neglected
to perform his undertaking according to the rule of
practice prevailing in this court. The motion was
made too soon, and the rule must be discharged, but
without costs.

Rule discharged without costs.

1824.

*Wednesday,
June 30th.*

THORNE and Others *against* R. HUTCHINSON and
Another, Bail of J. HUTCHINSON.

Where a defendant was
duly rendered
after judgment
in discharge of
his bail, but
notice thereof
was not given
until after execution had
been regularly
issued and executed against
the bail, the
Court set aside
the execution,
and entered an
exoneretur on
the bail-piece
on payment of
costs.

*C*ROWDER had obtained a rule to set aside the
execution issued and executed against the defendants, and enter an exoneretur on the bail-piece, on the
ground that the defendant, in the original action was
rendered in time in discharge of the bail.

Archbold shewed cause, and contended, that the application was too late, execution having been executed, and
notice of the render not having been given until after
that time. His affidavit stated, that final judgment was
signed in the original action on the 11th of *June*, 1823.
On the 30th of *March*, 1824, a ca. sa. into *Middlesex* was
issued against the defendant, and returned non est invent.
In *Easter* term, which commenced on the 16th of *April*,
writs of sci. fa., and alias sci. fa. against the bail were
lodged with the sheriff of *Middlesex*, and returned. On
the 28th of *May*, a *non omit. test. fi. fa.* was issued into
Surrey, under which the goods of *R. Hutchinson* were
seized. Two days after the seizure the attorney for defendants gave notice (and the fact was so) that the defendant in the original action was surrendered in discharge of his bail on the 17th of *April* preceding.

Per Curiam. The defendant in the original action
having been rendered in time, the execution against the
bail must be set aside, and an exoneretur entered. But
as they neglected to give notice of the render, they must
pay the costs which have been incurred.

Rule absolute on payment of costs.

DECLARATION stated that the Plaintiff, before the publication of the libel thereinafter mentioned, had long been an attorney, and in that profession had been employed by the parishioners as vestry clerk in the parish of *St. Matthew, Bethnal Green*, and that, whilst the plaintiff was such véstry clerk as aforesaid, certain prosecutions were preferred and carried on against one *Joseph Merceron*, for certain misdemeanors before then alleged to have been committed by him; and *in furtherance of such proceedings*, and *to bring the same to a successful issue*, certain sums of money belonging to the parishioners of the parish of *St. Matthew, Bethnal Green*, were appropriated and applied to the discharge of the said expences and law charges incurred on account of the said proceedings, to wit at, &c.; yet the defendant, well knowing, &c., but contriving, &c. to injure plaintiff in his said business and profession of an attorney, and to cause him to be esteemed and taken to be a dishonest, corrupt, and fraudulent practiser in his said profession, and in his office and situation as vestry clerk as

In an action for a libel, the defendant cannot, either in bar of the action or in mitigation of damages, give in evidence other libels published of him by the plaintiff not distinctly relating to the same subject.

Declaration stated that plaintiff was an attorney, and had been employed as vestry clerk in the parish of *A.*, and that whilst he was such vestry clerk, certain prosecutions were carried on against *B.* for certain misdemeanors, and in furtherance of such proceedings, and *to bring the same to a successful issue,*

certain sums of money belonging to the parishioners were appropriated and applied to the discharge of the expences incurred on account of the said proceedings, yet defendant intending, &c. to injure the plaintiff in his profession of an attorney, and to cause him to be esteemed a fraudulent practiser in his said profession and in his office as vestry clerk, and to cause it to be suspected that the plaintiff had fraudulently applied money belonging to the parishioners, on, &c., at, &c., falsely and maliciously published of and concerning the plaintiff, and of and concerning his conduct in his office as vestry clerk, and of and concerning *the matters aforesaid*, the libel. &c. It appeared on the production of the libel at the trial, that the imputation was, that the plaintiff had applied the parish money in payment of the expences of the prosecution *after* it had terminated: Held, that this was no variance, because it did not alter the character of the libel, the fraud imputed to the plaintiff being the same, whether the money was misapplied before or after the proceedings had terminated; and that the allegation, that the libel was published of and concerning *the matters aforesaid*, did not make it necessary to prove precisely that the libel did relate to every part of the matter previously stated.

aforesaid,

aforesaid, and to be a person not fit to be trusted therein, and to deprive him of the same, and to cause it to be suspected and believed, that the plaintiff had fraudulently and clandestinely appropriated and applied certain sums of money, of and belonging to the said parishioners, theretofore, to wit, on, &c., at, &c., falsely, wickedly, and maliciously did compose, write, and publish in a newspaper called the *Sunday Monitor*, of and concerning the plaintiff, and of and concerning his conduct in his office as vestry clerk as aforesaid, and of and concerning *the matters aforesaid*, a certain malicious and defamatory libel, containing, amongst other things, the defamatory matters following, of and concerning the plaintiff, and of and concerning his conduct as such vestry clerk as aforesaid, and of and concerning *the matters aforesaid*, that is to say : " *St. Matthew, Bethnal Green.* At a vestry meeting held in the parish of *St. Matthew, Bethnal Green*, on *Wednesday*, the 29th of *March* last, the following resolutions were confirmed, and ordered to be printed in the *Sunday Monitor*. It is worthy of remark, that the circumstances to which the resolutions here inserted relate, took place shortly after the trial of Mr. *Merceron* (meaning the aforesaid *Joseph Merceron*), though only very recently discovered ; and the present Lord Chief Justice on that occasion, in his charge to the jury, expressly declared, that although notice had been given in the church, and although the vestry voted the payment of Mr. *Merceron*'s law expences, yet, if the jury thought that he had not given all the publicity to the transaction which it was in his power to give, then the charge of clandestinity was established. Mr. *May*, (meaning the plaintiff), the vestry clerk, and Mr. *Wrightson*, were then present as principal witnesses against Mr. *Merceron*, as

were

were also Mr. *Bumford* and Mr. *Talbot*, two of the committee of his prosecutors." And in a certain other part of which libel were contained the false, scandalous, malicious, and defamatory matters following of and concerning the plaintiff, and of and concerning nis said duty and office of vestry clerk, and of and concerning other his legal and professional duties, and of and concerning *the matters aforesaid*, that is to say: " Resolved, that a committee having been appointed on the 29th day of *April* 1818, to proceed with certain prosecutions against Mr. *Merceron*, (meaning the said *Joseph Merceron*,) and to raise by subscription a fund to defray the future law expences consequent thereupon, the said committee did, on the 20th day of *August* following, make a report in writing to the vestry, which stated *that they had not raised any money by subscription to defray* the future law expences which they had nevertheless incurred ; and that the said law charges consisted of two bills of Messrs. *Knight* and *Freeman*, viz. one amounting to 313*l.* 19*s.* 7*d.*, and the other to 314*l.* 3*s.*, making together 628*l.* 2*s.* 7*d.* In consequence of such report several persons (specified by name in the declaration) and *May* the vestry clerk (meaning the plaintiff) were appointed to examine into the identity and accuracy of the said bills; and the aforesaid persons (thereby meaning the said persons so appointed as aforesaid, including the plaintiff,) did pass the amount of the said bills in three specific sums for payment, notwithstanding they well knew at the time that the real and true amount of the law and other expences which the committee had altogether incurred amounted to no more than 503*l.* 2*s.* 7*d.*, instead of 628*l.* 2*s.* 7*d.*, of which only 243*l.* 2*s.* 8*d.* ought to have been taken out of the poor-rate fund, whereas 628*l.* 2*s.* 7*d.* was actually

I 2   taken.

taken. This vestry, therefore, deem the conduct of the aforesaid persons highly censurable, and they, in the most unqualified terms, censure them accordingly; but as respects the conduct of Mr. *James May,* the vestry clerk (meaning the plaintiff) and legal adviser of this parish, who not only concurred in this transaction, but actually furnished a bill, paid before the vestry knew of the prosecutions, and incorporated it in his own hand writing with the unpaid law expences of the committee; he also signed his name, as testifying to the truth of the printed receipts and disbursements of the parish in which were inserted the two fictitious bills under the denomination of Messrs. *Knight* and *Freeman's* bills; as also a charge of upwards of 630*l.* for weekly payments to outdoor poor, when they never received a farthing of it, and of which 113*l.* 9*s.* 3*d.* was expended by himself (meaning the plaintiff) and other persons, called constituted authorities, in eating and drinking; this vestry, therefore, consider Mr. *James May,* meaning the plaintiff, as most unworthy of their future confidence and support" (meaning thereby, that the plaintiff, in the examination and allowance of, and in his conduct and proceeding with respect to the said bills and accounts, supposed to have been incurred for and on behalf of the said parishioners of the said parish of *St. Matthew, Bethnal Green,* acted corruptly and fraudulently as a vestry clerk of the said parish.) Plea, first, not guilty; secondly, that the matters contained in the libel were true. At the trial before *Abbott* C. J., at the sittings after *Easter* term, 1823, the libel set out in the declaration was produced in evidence, and it was objected, on the part of the defendant, that there was a variance between the libel proved and that described in the declaration, inasmuch as it was averred

in

in the declaration, that the prosecutions were preferred
against *Merceron*, and that *in furtherance of such pro-*
ceedings, and to bring the same to a successful issue,
certain sums of money belonging to the parishoners were
appropriated and applied to the discharge of the expences, and that it appeared by the proof, that the libel
charged this money to have been applied to discharge
the expences, *after* the proceedings had terminated. The
Lord Chief Justice overruled the objection, but reserved
liberty to the defendant to move to enter a nonsuit. In
the course of the trial the defendant offered in evidence
other libels published of him by the plaintiff, but not relating to the same subject as that on which this action
was brought. The Lord Chief Justice refused to receive
this evidence of particular libels, but he did receive general evidence, that before the publication of the libel in
question, the plaintiff had published other libels of the
defendant. The plaintiff having obtained a verdict on
both issues, a rule nisi for a nonsuit or a new trial was
obtained, upon the grounds taken at the trial.

Scarlett, Gurney, and *Holt* now shewed cause. There
is no variance in this case. The averment that the libel
relates to certain introductory matters before stated,
does not form any part of the description of the libel.
It is matter of inducement introduced to explain the
libel; and if so, it is quite clear that it need not be
proved precisely as it is alleged. *Yarley* v. *Turnock.* (a)
Rickets v. *Salwey.* (b) *Figgins* v. *Coggswell.* (c) Lord
Churchill v. *Hunt.* (d) It is sufficient in an action of tort

1824.

MAY
against
BROWN.

(a) *Palmer*, 259.   (b) 2 *B. & A.* 360.
(c) 3 *M. & S.* 369.   (d) 2 *B. & A.* 585.

I 3   to

to prove the same ground of action as that which is laid
in the declaration, and it is not necessary to prove the
whole of the charge laid.   Here the allegation was divisible, and it was sufficient to prove part of it.   *Rex* v.
Hunt. (a)   *Rex* v. *Sutton.* (b)   Assuming the allegation
to be descriptive of the libel, still if it be descriptive of a
circumstance wholly immaterial to the defamatory character of the libel, it need not be proved.   Now here the
defamatory character of the libel consists in the imputation that the parish money was improperly applied, with
the plaintiff's concurrence, to defray expences incurred
in a prosecution against *Merceron.*   That is the gist of
the fraud and dishonesty charged upon the plaintiff.
The fraud imputed is the same, and the imputation is
equally injurious to the character of the plaintiff; and
the damages which he will be entitled to recover will be
the same, whether the fraud is charged to have been
consummated before or after the proceedings against
Merceron were at an end.   That circumstance, therefore, does not alter the character of the libel. ·Now
even with respect to written, instruments, it is sufficient
to produce instruments corresponding in all material
circumstances with those set out on the record.   In
Draper v. *Garratt* (c), the declaration on a replevin bond
stated, that the party replevying levied his plaint at the
next county court, to wit, at the county court holden
before *A. B. C.* and *D.*, suitors of the said court, which
suit was afterwards removed, &c.   By the record · produced in evidence, it appeared that the plaint was levied
at a court holden before *E., F., G.,* and *H.* ; and it was
contended that the plaintiff in his declaration had affected

(a) 2 *Campbell,* 583.   (b) 4 *M. & S.* 532.
(c) 2 *B. & C.* 2.

to

to describe the record, and that the variance therefore was fatal; but the Court held it to be immaterial, because it was unnecessary to state or prove the names of the suitors, and therefore that allegation might be rejected as surplusage. So here it was wholly unnecessary to allege that the libel predicated any particular time when the money was misapplied. The case of *The King* v. *Horne* (a) is distinguishable from the present, because the allegation there, that the libellous matter was " of and concerning the king's government and the employment of his troops," with reference to the libel then under prosecution, constituted one entire proposition, for unless the libel related to troops employed by the government, it could not be a libel concerning the king's government. But here the proposition that the libel was published " of and concerning the matters aforesaid," is a proposition consisting of several distinct parts, and it is sufficient to prove a libel published relating to so many of those previous matters as were essential to give it the particular defamatory character so described. Secondly, the evidence of particular libels published by the plaintiff of the defendant was not admissible, either in answer to the action or in mitigation of damages. Such evidence would lead to great inconvenience if admitted in trials at Nisi Prius. The jury are summoned to try the issue joined between the parties. Instead of trying that issue only, they would be called upon to try matter which ought rather to be the subject of separate actions. It would be productive also of great injustice; for the plaintiff would not have notice of the libels intended to be produced against him, and

(a) *Cowper*, 72.

I 4   could

could not be prepared to defend himself against the charge of having published them.

The Attorney-General, Brougham, and *Kelly,* contra. It may be conceded as a general proposition, that in an action of tort, or in an indictment, it is sufficient to prove substantially the same ground of action, or the same offence as that which is alleged on the record; but here the plaintiff has made it necessary, by the form of the declaration, to prove a libel precisely similar to that which he has described; for the allegation that it was " of and concerning the matters aforesaid," is descriptive of the libel itself. The plaintiff has therefore undertaken to prove a libel relating to *all* the matters before specified; one of the matters previously recited being, that parish money had been applied to defray the expences of *Merceron's* prosecution in order *to bring the same to a successful termination.* It was necessary, therefore, for the plaintiff to prove a libel charging that the money had been misapplied before the prosecution against *Merceron* had terminated. In *The King* v. *Horn,* it was laid down both by Lord *Mansfield* and Lord C. J. *De Grey,* that the allegation, " of and concerning the king's government and the employment of his troops," made it necessary to prove that a libel had been published relating both to his majesty's government and the employment of his troops. It would have been an answer to the indictment if it had appeared that the libel published was not relating to the king's government or to the employment of his troops. In *Teesdale* v. *Clement* (*a*), the declaration was for a libel, stating that the plaintiff, a constable, had apprehended persons

(*a*) 1 *Chitty's Rep.* 603.

stealing

stealing a dead body, and had carried the body to Surgeons'-hall, and that defendant published the libel of and concerning plaintiff's said conduct; second count, that defendant published a certain other libel of and concerning the conduct of the plaintiff respecting the said dead body: and it was held necessary, in support of both counts, to prove that the plaintiff had carried the body to Surgeons'-hall. That case is precisely in point. So in *Shepherd* v. *Bliss* (a); the declaration alleged that the words were spoken of and concerning certain soap, alleged by *A. B.* to have been stolen: it was held that the declaration was not supported by evidence, that the words were spoken concerning certain soap alleged by *A.B.* to have been taken out of his yard. Secondly, the libels distributed by the plaintiff concerning the defendant ought to have been received in evidence, either in bar of the action, or in mitigation of damages. In *Anthony Pasquin's* (b) case, Lord *Kenyon* held that they were admissible even in bar of the action. In *Finnerty* v. *Tipper* (c), Lord C. J. *Mansfield* allowed other libels, published by the plaintiff of the defendant to be received in mitigation of damages. It is true that these were only nisi prius cases. It seems however to be more reasonable to allow the libels themselves to be produced in evidence than to receive general evidence of the plaintiff having libelled the defendant. In that case, the witness is suffered to give parol evidence of a matter reduced into writing, and his judgment as to the nature of the publication is conclusive upon the parties, whereas if the particular evidence be received, the papers contain-

1824.

MAY
against
BROWN.

(a) 2 *Stark.* 510.
(b) Cited in *Finnerty* v. *Tipper*, 2 *Campb.* 76.; and in *Tabert* v. *Tipper*, 1 *Campb.* 350.
(c) 2 *Campb.* 76.

ing

ing the matter itself are produced, and the jury then have an opportunity of judging whether they amount to a libel or not.

Abbott C. J. I am of opinion, that neither of the objections which have been taken in the present case on the part of the defendant ought to prevail. The first objection is on the ground of variance. The supposed variance is between matter of fact alleged in the declaration, and matter of fact proved. It is not a variance between the contents of a written instrument described on the record, and a written instrument proved in evidence. Now it is a general rule, that a variance between the allegation and the proof will not defeat a party, unless it be in respect of matter which, if pleaded, would be material. If the variance be in respect of matter not essential to maintain the action or the plea, it is of no importance. Then the question to be considered is, whether the matter, with respect to which the variance is alleged to exist, with reference to the libel itself, was in any degree essential to support the action? The matter of fact alleged is, that certain prosecutions had been instituted against *Merceron* ; and that, in furtherance of those proceedings, and *to bring the same to a successful issue*, certain sums of money belonging to the inhabitants of the parish of *Bethnal Green* were appropriated and applied to discharge the expences. Now, it is quite immaterial with regard to the defamatory character of the libel, whether the money of the parishioners appropriated and applied to the discharge of law expences incurred in the prosecutions, was so appropriated and applied before the prosecutions had arrived at their termination by the judgment of the Court or afterwards.
                                        Then,

Then, according to the general rule, this variation between the allegation and the proof will not be material, unless the plaintiff has, by some other matter on the record, rendered it necessary for him to prove the allegation precisely as he has made it. It was contended that the plaintiff had, by the form of his declaration, rendered it necessary for him to prove (though otherwise it would have been unnecessary,) that the libel does relate to all the matter previously alleged; that by the averment, that the defendant published a libel " of and concerning the matters aforesaid," he has rendered it necessary for him to prove *all* the matters aforesaid, to be matters to which the supposed libel relates. I am, however, of opinion, that the allegation does not compel the plaintiff to prove formally and precisely that the libel relates to every part and particular of the matter so previously stated, but that it satisfies all he has taken on himself to prove, if he shews that the libel relates *substantially* to the matters previously alleged by way of introduction, in such a manner as that the defamation contained in the libel is of the character and effect which the plaintiff has described. It is true, that in the case of the *King* v. *Horne*, the words " of and concerning the king's government and the employment of his troops," were held to connect the libel with the king's government and the employment of his troops; and most undoubtedly in that case they did, and it was therefore essential that it should in some way appear on the record, that the libel was a libel concerning the king's government and the employment of his troops; or otherwise the matter which was said to be a libel, might have been innocent in itself, at least innocent as against the crown in the way alleged. It
would

would not have had that defamatory character which the
information had given to it in the introductory averment.
In the case of *Teesdale* v. *Clement*, the decision proceeded
on this ground, that the fact on which the plaintiff failed in
proof, was material to the defamatory character of the libel
itself. Now, here, the fact which the plaintiff has failed in
proving (viz. the object for which, and the time when, the
money of the parishioners was appropriated) is wholly immaterial. As to the other cases referred to in the course of
the argument, I think the utmost effect that can be given
to them is this, that the judges before whom those cases
occurred, were inclined to think that that which followed
the words " of and concerning" must be precisely proved.
It has at times certainly been the inclination of my own
opinion, and I believe in one case I ruled accordingly.
But that was an opinion delivered at Nisi Prius (a) on the
best attention I could give to the case then, but I think
since, on reviewing the former decisions, more weight
has been given to them, than on grave consideration and
attention they are fairly entitled to. For the reasons
already given, I think the plaintiff did prove so much of
his allegation as was necessary to maintain his action,
notwithstanding the reference to introductory matter by
means of the words " of and concerning" which occurs
in the subsequent part of the allegation.

The other objection is, that I rejected evidence which
it is contended ought to have been received. The evidence offered at the trial was of particular libels alleged
to have been published and distributed by the plaintiff.
It was not contended that any one of those libels could
be said to be the provocation to the particular libel of

(a) *Lewis* v. *Walter.*

which

which the plaintiff complains. I thought that unless it could be made to appear that the libels offered in evidence related to the same subject as the libel on which the action was brought, I ought not to receive them as evidence. It is not contended that they do distinctly relate to the same subject as the libel on which the action is brought. It must now be taken that they did not. Then it comes to this single question, whether when one man brings an action against another for libelling him, it is competent for that other to shew, that, as to other subjects, the plaintiff has published libels on him. The inconvenience of allowing such evidence has been adverted to in argument, and no one who is acquainted with the nature and course of a trial by a jury, who are summoned to try the issue joined between the parties, can doubt that it would be most inconvenient. That, however, is not of itself a decisive ground for the exclusion of evidence; but, in considering the question, whether evidence ought to be received, it is important to look at the inconvenience to which its reception would lead. If I had received the evidence in this case, the effect of it would have been, that the attention of the jury would have been distracted with a multiplicity of questions and issues, not raised upon the record, but raised on a sudden at Nisi Prius, of which the party against whom the proof was offered could have no previous notice, and which he could not come prepared in any degree to meet. It is said, that to be consistent with myself, I ought to have received the particular libels in evidence, and that it would have been better to have done so, than to have admitted general evidence that the plaintiff had distributed papers defamatory of the defendant. The question is not now whether general evidence was properly allowed. If that was so,

I should

I should pause before I gave an opinion upon it sitting in this place. For the reasons I have already given, as they did not properly form part of the matter in issue in this cause, I am of opinion that they could not be received in evidence, either in bar of the action, or in mitigation of damages. It seems to me, that it is not a just ground for mitigating damages in an action brought for one libel, that on other occasions the plaintiff has written libels on the defendant, on some other matter unconnected with that which is the subject of the action. It would be a set-off of one libel against another. I am, therefore, of opinion, that I certainly did right in refusing to receive the particular libels in evidence. I give no opinion whether I did right or wrong in admitting the general evidence; it is unnecessary to do so, the verdict having been found for the plaintiff. For these reasons, I think that this rule ought to be discharged.

BAYLEY J. It appears to me quite clear, that the evidence which my Lord Chief Justice rejected was rightly rejected, and that he went quite as far as the law allowed him, when he received general evidence to prove that the plaintiff had, before that period of time, been libelling the defendant. In deciding whether particular matter is evidence or not, it is necessary to consider what is the issue joined between the parties; for evidence of particular facts not relating to that issue is not admissible. In some instances general evidence is admissible, where evidence of a particular fact is not. Thus, when the credit of a witness is objected to, general evidence that he is not to be believed on oath is admissible; but specific evidence that at some period he had committed a particular crime is not admis-

sible.

sible. Here, the issues were, did the defendant publish the libel in question, and was the libel true? Upon those two points only, as it seems to me, particular evidence, as distinguished from general evidence, could be received. The reason of the distinction is, that the admission of evidence of particular facts would be calculated not only to produce general inconvenience, but would operate as a surprise upon the party against whom it is offered. When a party knows what the issue is, he knows on what points to prepare himself. He may also be prepared upon general points, not connected with the issue; but he certainly would not be prepared upon particular points. Suppose, in answer to an action for a libel, the defendant gives in evidence that the plaintiff, at another time, published a libel of the defendant. There might be first a question, whether the plaintiff did or did not publish; secondly, whether it was or was not true; and then in this action for one libel, the matter tried would be that which ought to be the issue in another action brought for another libel. Besides, if the defendant might give in evidence one libel, he might give in evidence twenty; and so, instead of trying one point and one issue joined, twenty different issues would be tried at once, the inconvenience of which would be incalculable.

The next question is whether there is a variance or not? That depends on the effect of the words " of and concerning," following the different introductory matters stated in the declaration. The libel is stated to be " of and concerning" those different matters, and if it is therefore necessary to prove a libel relating specifically to every one of those matters, then there has been a failure of proof in this particular case, and there ought to be a nonsuit. But I take the words " of and

and concerning" not to have that effect; but that they only make it necessary on the part of the plaintiff to prove a libel relating to those matters, so far as they are connected with the libel in respect either of the particular defamatory character ascribed to it in the declaration, or of the manner in which it is afterwards set out. If, for instance, the plaintiff in stating the libel had connected it by innuendo with a particular allegation, then he would be bound to prove a libel relating to the matter contained in that allegation. At first I thought that the case of the *King* v. *Horne* went to an extent to which I was afterwards satisfied it did not go. There it is stated by Lord C. J. *De Grey*, that the words "of and concerning" tied the prosecutor down to prove that it was " of and concerning his majesty's government, and of and concerning the employment of his troops;" and that if the prosecutor's proof failed in either branch of that proposition, the prosecutor must have failed in toto. But that was one entire indivisible proposition, and not a proposition containing two distinct and separate branches. If there had been two distinct and separate branches of the proposition, then that case would have been an authority to shew that the allegation, which was " of and concerning" two things, would, at all events, make it necessary to prove that it was " of and concerning" each. But there the libellous matter was of and concerning one entire proposition, and therefore the consequence does not follow. The information there charged, that the defendant intended to create dissatisfaction towards his majesty's government, and published the libel of and concerning his majesty's government, and the employment of his troops. The employment of them is understood by Lord C. J. *De Grey* to mean employment by his majesty's government. The libel

did

did not say a syllable about his majesty's government at all; all that was stated was, that some of the subjects were inhumanly murdered by the king's troops. Unless those troops were acting under the employment of government, there was no libel on his majesty's government, therefore the allegation, that the libel was " of and concerning his majesty's government, and of and concerning the employment of his troops," was one entire indivisible proposition, both branches of which it was necessary to prove. And so it was considered by Lord C. J. *De Grey*, in delivering the 'opinion of the judges, for he says, " The natural import of the words seems to be this, I am speaking of the king's administration of government relative to his troops." That case, therefore, being out of the question, there is not any other which establishes that the averment that the libel is " of and concerning the matters aforesaid," makes it necessary to prove a libel relating to every part of the introductory statement in the declaration. That part of the introductory statement in this case which is supposed not to have been warranted by the language of the libel, is not connected by any innuendo with the libel itself, nor has it, as it seems to me, any material connection with it. It states, " that certain prosecutions were preferred and carried on against *Merceron*, and in furtherance of such proceedings, and to bring the same to a successful issue, money belonging to the parishioners was applied in discharge of the said expences and law charges incurred on account of the said proceedings." The words " said expences" are improperly introduced, for they are not previously mentioned ; it must be considered, therefore, to allege, that the money was applied to the discharge of expences and law charges incurred on account of the proceedings. But then it is said,

that the allegation that these monies were appropriated
in furtherance and for the purpose of bringing the prosecution to a successful termination implies, that the
money was appropriated while the cause was in progress, whereas, in point of fact, it was appropriated
after the cause had terminated; but the period of
time at which that appropriation took place had nothing to do with the character of the libel. The
charge against Mr. *May* is, that he suffered to be
brought forward a sum of 628*l.* at a period of time when
503*l.* was all that was due, and 243*l.* was all that ought
to have been charged against the parish. It is equally
a libel, and the fraud imputed to him is precisely the
same, whether the money was misappropriated in the
progress of the prosecution, or after it came to its termination. This circumstance, introduced in the declaration, and concerning which the libel is said to have
been published, is wholly immaterial to the defamatory
character of the libel. Another part of the libel is
entirely unconnected with that previous allegation, viz.
that part which insinuates that another sum of 600*l.*
and upwards, pretended to have been applied to the
payment of out-door paupers, had, in point of fact,
never been so applied, but that Mr. *May* and others had
appropriated a considerable part of it to the expences
of eating and drinking in taverns. For these reasons I
am of opinion that the evidence was properly rejected,
and that there was not any variance.

HOLROYD J. I am of opinion, that neither of the objections which have been made in this case ought to prevail.
First, I think that the evidence tendered was properly rejected. It certainly would be pregnant with the greatest
inconvenience, if, in an action for a libel, evidence of other
                                                    specific

specific libels published by the plaintiff of the defendant were to be admitted. The issue to be tried was, whether the defendant was guilty of publishing the libel with which he was charged. It was wholly immaterial to that issue whether the plaintiff had published other specific libels of the defendant or not. It has been said that the evidence ought to have been received in mitigation of damages. It would be very strange, however, if, when the plaintiff is seeking damages for an injury done to him by an act of the defendant, the latter should be permitted to avail himself of the law to recover damages against the plaintiff for another libel produced at a time when the plaintiff could not be expected to be prepared with evidence to justify or excuse it; for that would be the effect of allowing him to give other libels in evidence to diminish the damages which the plaintiff would otherwise receive in consequence of the act which the defendant had done. I think the plaintiff is entitled to recover the damages which he really has sustained from the act of the defendant, whether he has injured the defendant on other occasions or not. If that evidence is not admitted, no injury can be done to the defendant, for he may resort to his remedy and recover damages for the injury he has sustained; and by the plaintiff then becoming defendant, he will have an opportunity of justifying, excusing, or denying that which is alleged. The argument ab inconvenienti is of importance in considering what the law is, and there cannot be any doubt that the reception of this evidence would tend to great inconvenience and injustice.

I am also of opinion, that there is no variance. It cannot be contended that there is any valid objection on this ground, unless it amounts to a misdescription of the

K 2   libel;

libel; that is, that one libel is charged in the declaration, and that another libel of a different nature is proved. It is stated to be a libel " of and concerning the matters aforesaid." That is a general allegation, which is not to be considered as extending to all and every the matters aforesaid. In the case of *The King* v. *Horne* the libel was alleged to be " of and concerning" the government. That was considered not to import that it was of and concerning every branch of the government; but that it was of and concerning some one branch of the government. But there it was also alleged to be of and concerning the employment of the king's troops: that was held not to import that it was " of and concerning the general employment of all troops;" but it was held that the allegation was sustained by proof of a libel of and concerning any part of the king's troops. The introductory part of the declaration here says, that the plaintiff was vestry clerk appointed by the parishioners: that has been proved. It is stated, that while he was vestry clerk proceedings were carried on against Mr. *Merceron* for something alleged to have been committed by him. Then it goes on to state, that certain sums of money belonging to the parishioners of *St. Matthew, Bethnal Green*, were appropriated and applied to discharge the expences incurred in the said proceedings, in furtherance of such proceedings, and in order to bring them to a successful issue. The injurious character of the libel is precisely the same, whether the money was applied with the particular motive and at the particular time mentioned in the introductory part of the declaration or not. It seems to me, therefore, that that allegation was wholly immaterial to the character of the libel itself, and being

immaterial,

immaterial, it was unnecessary to prove it. In an action
upon a bill of exchange (a), where the declaration stated
the bill to have been accepted and indorsed before it
became due, and the proof was, that it was indorsed
after it became due, the court held it to be no variance,
because it was immaterial, whether the bill was indorsed
before or after it became due; and, therefore, it was
unnecessary to prove the indorsement precisely at the
time when it was alleged. So here, it is wholly immaterial, with respect to the character of the slanderous
matter imputed by this libel, whether the charge be,
that the money was applied before or after the prosecution was terminated. For these reasons I am of opinion, that the present rule must be discharged.

LITTLEDALE J. I think that the evidence was properly rejected. Upon the plea of not guilty the only
question was, whether the defendant had published the
libel in question. Upon that issue, therefore, it was not
competent to the defendant to give in evidence other
libels published of him by the plaintiff. That was no
part of the issue raised upon this record. I think that
they could not be received as evidence to mitigate the
damages. If they were received in evidence to mitigate
damages, see what the situation of the plaintiff would
be; he has no notice that the libels will be offered in
evidence; he has no means, therefore, of disproving
the fact of having published them. The defendant may
come prepared to prove that the plaintiff did in fact
publish them. If the plaintiff had notice that such
proof was intended to be given, he might be prepared

(a) *Young v. Wright,* 1 *Campb.* 139.

K 3   with

with evidence either to shew that he never published them at all, or that he was justified in publishing them. The plaintiff, by whom they are alleged to have been published, ought to be in as good a situation as if he himself was a defendant in an action brought against him on those libels. That, however, is not the only inconvenience. For this would not only be a set-off of libels, but a great deal more; for in a common set-off the debt is extinguished. If the defendant, by a set-off, reduce the debt claimed of him, that demand so proved, and of which the defendant has had the benefit, can never be claimed again. But in this case, the libels which were offered in evidence, as published by the plaintiff, would go to reduce the damages, and yet the defendant might afterwards bring an action against the plaintiff for publishing those very libels; and although the plaintiff, in consequence of those libels having been received in evidence against him, has been prevented from getting more than 10l. damages, when he otherwise would have been entitled to 100l., still that would not operate to estop the defendant from bringing an action, as in the case of a common set-off. At common law, a set-off is not allowable at all; and even where it is allowable by the act of parliament, the plaintiff always has previous knowledge of what the set-off is to be, either by plea or by notice. So that if the evidence were admitted in this case, the party would be in a worse situation in that respect than the defendant in a common case of set-off of a debt. If this evidence were admissible, the defendant in an action for an assault, would, upon the same principle, be entitled to give in evidence that, two or three months before, the plaintiff had assaulted him. I think, therefore, that this evidence was properly

rejected,

rejected, both on the ground that a plaintiff in such a case has no notice of the intended defence, and that it would produce great inconvenience, by leading to a multiplicity of enquiries.

I am of opinion, also, that there is no variance. In an action for a libel it is necessary in the declaration to shew the libel, the time at which it was published, and that it relates to the plaintiff. If, on the face of the libel the plaintiff is mentioned by name, or is described as filling a particular character, it is not necessary to shew by averment that the libel relates to him individually, or in that particular character. In this case, therefore, in order to maintain this action, no averment was necessary, because the plaintiff was described in the libel as Mr. *May*, vestry clerk. But, if a party bringing an action for a libel wishes to shew that he sustained additional injury in respect of a particular character which he filled, or in respect of other circumstances entitling him to damages, then it is necessary to shew by averment those circumstances, or that he filled that character, in order to entitle himself to greater damages, upon account of the discredit thrown on him in that character. Now here the plaintiff does claim damages in respect of the injurious imputation cast upon him in his character of vestry clerk; for the declaration states, that whilst the plaintiff was such vestry clerk as aforesaid, prosecutions were carried on against *Merceron;* and in furtherance of such proceedings, and to bring the same to a successful issue, monies were appropriated and applied to the discharge of the expences and law charges incurred on account of the proceedings. He makes this averment to connect himself in his character of vestry clerk with some part of the libel, and if he

K 4   seeks

seeks to recover damages in respect of his character as
vestry clerk, he must prove that allegation, but if he does
not prove it, it does not prevent him from recovering
damages in respect of the injury sustained in his individual capacity.   The declaration then goes on to describe the tendency of the libel, or the intention with
which the defendant published it.   It states, that the defendant, " intending to deprive the plaintiff of his good
name, and to injure him in his business and profession
of an attorney, and in his office of vestry clerk, and to
cause him to be esteemed a fraudulent practiser in his
said profession of an attorney, and in his said office as
vestry clerk, and to be a person not fit to be trusted
therein, and to deprive him of the same, and to cause it
to be suspected and believed that the plaintiff had fraudulently and clandestinely appropriated and applied certain
sums of money belonging to the parishioners, published
the libel ;" the character of the libel, therefore, of which
the plaintiff complains, is one the tendency of which is
to injure him in his individual character, in his character
of attorney and vestry clerk, and to cause it to be suspected that he had fraudulently applied money belonging to the parish.   The declaration then goes on to say,
that the defendant published the libel of and concerning
the plaintiff, and of and concerning his conduct in his
office as vestry clerk, and of and concerning the matters
aforesaid.   Now these latter words, " of and concerning
the matters aforesaid," connect the libel afterward set
out with the previous averments, so far as they are calculated to shew that the libel is of the particular defamatory character.   I think that the plaintiff, therefore, was
only bound to allege and prove a libel of that character,
viz. a libel charging him with having fraudulently applied

money

money belonging to the parishioners. It has been urged, that it was necessary in this case to prove every word contained in the previous averments, because the allegation that the libel was " of and concerning" such and such things amounted to a specific description of the libel; but I think that it does not amount to a specific description of the libel, but to a description of the nature of the injury the plaintiff has sustained. It seems to me, that when the declaration alleges the libel to be published " of and concerning the plaintiff and of and concerning his conduct as vestry clerk, and of and concerning *the matters aforesaid,*" that, reddendo singulo singulis, it may be considered in the same light as if the words " of and concerning" had followed each of the previous averments. If, therefore, the declaration had stated that certain prosecutions had been preferred against *Merceron,* and in furtherance of the proceedings, and to bring the same to a successful issue, money belonging to the parishioners had been applied in discharge of the expences, and it had then been averred that the libel was published of and concerning the matters aforesaid; I think that the latter words would not be applicable to all the subject-matter recited in the previous averment, but only to so much of it as was material to shew the libel to bear the defamatory character ascribed to it in the declaration. The charge in the libel is, that parish money was improperly applied. It is wholly immaterial whether it was applied while the proceedings were in progress or after they had terminated. That term does not form any ingredient in the quality of the slander, nor can it in any degree alter the nature of the injury sustained by the plaintiff. In *The King* v. *Horne* the averment was, that the libel was published " of and concerning the king's government and
the

1824.

MAY
against
Brown.

the employment of his troops;" that was one entire proposition, for the libel was not of and concerning the
government, except so far as it related to the act of government exercised by the troops. It was not of and
concerning the king's troops individually, but as acting
on behalf of the government, it was, therefore, an entire
proposition, and the allegations were not divisible; but
here they are perfectly distinct. In *Peppin* v. *Solomons* (*a*),
which was an action on a policy of insurance, the declaration stated, that *after* the making of the policy the ship
sailed. The evidence was, that she sailed *before;* but it
was held to be no variance, because it was quite immaterial whether she sailed before or after the making of
the policy. So here, it was quite immaterial whether
the money was appropriated whilst the proceedings were
in progress against Mr. *Merceron* or after they had terminated. I am, therefore, of opinion, that the averment
did not require proof applicable to the whole of the allegation; and, secondly, that if such proof was necessary,
it has been given upon the only material point upon
which the question arose.

Rule discharged. (*b*)

(*a*) 5 T. R. 496.

(*b*) *Lewis* v. *Walter.* — In this case the declaration alleged that the
plaintiff was an attorney, and that the defendant, intending to injure him
in his good name, and also in his business of an attorney, published the
libel of and concerning the plaintiff, and of and concerning him in his
said business or profession. At the trial before *Abbott* C. J. at the *London*
sittings after *Michaelmas* term 1822, the plaintiff merely proved that he
was admitted an attorney on the 5th *July* 1813. He failed in proving
that he had either taken out a certificate in the year 1819, (the libel having
been published in that year,) or that he had, during that time, practised as

Declaration for
a libel stated
that the plain-
tiff was an at-
torney, and
that the defend-
ant, intending
to injure him
in his good
name, and in
his said profes-
sion of an at-
torney, pub-

lished a libel of and concerning the plaintiff, and of and concerning him in his said profession. At the trial, the plaintiff failed in proving that at the time of the publication of
the libel he was an attorney: Held, that this was not a fatal variance between the allegation and the proof, the words of the libel being actionable, although not used with
reference to the professional character of the plaintiff.

an

an attorney. The Lord Chief Justice was of opinion, that as the allegation in the declaration was not merely that the plaintiff had been admitted as an attorney, but that the matter published of him by the defendant was of and concerning him in his business and profession of an attorney, it was necessary for him to prove that he was an attorney at the time of the publication; and the plaintiff was nonsuited. A rule nisi for setting aside the nonsuit was obtained in the following term, upon the ground that the allegation in the declaration was divisible, and that it was sufficient for the plaintiff to prove that the libel was published of and concerning him in his individual capacity, the words being actionable, although not used with reference to his professional character. The point was fully discussed in *Trinity* term 1823; and it was contended by the defendant's counsel that the allegation was descriptive of the libel itself, and that there was consequently a variance between the allegation and the proof. No judgment was pronounced at that time; but in the course of this term *Abbott* C. J., after stating the facts of the case, said that it must be governed by the decision in *May* v. *Brown*, and that the rule for setting aside the nonsuit must therefore be made absolute.

1824.
——
MAY
against
BROWN.

AUSTIN *against* DEBNAM.

CASE for a malicious arrest. The declaration alleged, that defendant, on, &c. at, &c. not then having any reasonable or probable cause of action whatsoever against the plaintiff, to the amount of the sum of money for which he maliciously caused him to be arrested as thereinafter mentioned, maliciously caused and procured a bill of *Middlesex* to be issued out of the Court of King's Bench, commanding the sheriff of *Middlesex* to arrest the plaintiff, and falsely, and without having any reasonable or probable cause of action whatever against the plaintiff, to the amount of 15*l.* or upwards, caused and procured the said bill of *Middlesex* to be, and the same was indorsed for bail for 23*l.* And the said defendant afterwards, to wit, on, &c. at, &c. without any reasonable or probable cause of action what-

Where there are mutual dealings between two parties, and items known to be due on each side of the account, an arrest for the amount of one side of the account, without deducting what is due on the other, is malicious, and without probable cause.

whatsoever against the said plaintiff, to the amount of
15*l.* or upwards, maliciously caused the plaintiff to be
arrested, and kept imprisoned until he gave a bail bond;
and plaintiff did afterwards, to wit, on, &c. at, &c. pay to
the defendant the sum of 5*l.* 5*s.*, and also the sum of
3*l.* 13*s.* 6*d.* in full discharge of the said suit; which said
sum of 5*l.* 5*s.* defendant accepted of and from the plaintiff as the amount of the debt in the suit, and the sum
of 3*l.* 13*s.* 6*d.* for the costs.   And such proceedings
were thereupon had in the said suit, that it was ordered
by *Bayley* J. that all proceedings in the said suit should
be stayed, which order was afterwards made a rule of
Court; and the said action was, and is by means of
the said premises, and according to the course and
practice of the Court, wholly discharged, ended, and
determined.   By means of which said premises plaintiff was injured, &c. (in the usual form.)   Plea, general
issue.   At the trial before *Abbott* C. J. at the *London*
sittings after last *Trinity* term, the affidavit to hold
to bail and the bill of *Middlesex* indorsed for bail for
23*l.* were proved, also the arrest and the execution of
the bail bond for which the plaintiff paid 1*l.* 9*s.*   It also
appeared in evidence, that the plaintiff was a baker and
the defendant a carpenter; the latter did work for the
plaintiff, and bought bread of him.   They had a dispute,
and the plaintiff desired the defendant to send him his
bill; and on the following day, defendant said he had
reckoned up his book and there was 5*l.* coming to him.
A letter from the defendant's attorney, demanding of
plaintiff payment of the *balance* due to defendant, was
proved.   The whole account for carpenter's work, not
allowing for bread furnished by the plaintiff, was 20*l.*;
plaintiff tendered that sum; defendant refused it at first,
                                              saying,

saying, that it was more than was due, then that he had employed an attorney and could not settle it. After the plaintiff was arrested, defendant being asked why he arrested him for 23*l.*, replied that there had been obstinacy on both sides; and in reply to a question whether he had cast up his books, answered that he had, and that 5*l.* was due to him. The payment of 5*l.* 5*s.* for the debt, and 3*l.* 13*s.* 6*d.* costs, was also proved, and a receipt was put in, given by the defendant for the first-mentioned sum as being the balance due to him. The rule of Court for staying proceedings was then put in. *Gurney*, for the defendant, contended, first, that the rule could not be considered as a termination of the suit; and, secondly, that although the plaintiff might have a right of set-off, yet still 20*l.* and upwards was a debt due to the defendant; and he cited and relied on *Brown* v. *Pigeon.* (a) *Scarlett*, contrà, as to this point, mentioned Dr. *Turlington's* case (b), and *Dronefield* v. *Archer* (c); thirdly, it was objected, that the plaintiff was not at liberty on this declaration to give evidence of the set-off, the special circumstances not being stated. The Lord Chief Justice overruled all the objections, and left it to the jury to say, whether the plaintiff had been maliciously arrested, but gave the defendant leave to move for a nonsuit. A verdict being found for the plaintiff with 5*l.* damages: in *Michaelmas* term, a rule to enter a nonsuit or for a new trial was obtained on the points urged for the defendant at the trial.

Scarlett and *Archbold* now shewed cause. All the transactions between the plaintiff and defendant shew

(a) 2 *Campb.* 594.   (b) 4 *Burr.* 1996.   (c) 5 *B. & A.* 513.

a plain

a plain understanding, that the balance of the accounts was to be considered as the debt existing between them. The defendant, soon after the quarrel, said, he had cast up his book, and 5*l.* was due; the attorney wrote, and demanded the *balance* due to the defendant, and the latter, when 20*l.* was tendered, at first refused to accept it on the ground that so much was not due. But admitting that this evidence did not shew an understanding that the balance was to be considered as the real debt, still, where there is a running account, an arrest cannot be lawfully made for more than the balance. Since the statute of set-off, the just debt is to be taken as the ground of arrest. This was held in Dr. *Turlington's* case, cited with approbation by Lord *Mansfield* in *Barclay* v. *Hunt* (a); and again, expressly in *Dronefield* v. *Archer,* where the Court said, that the reasonable and probable cause for arrest is the obtaining security for that which is fairly due, and that is the balance.

Gurney and *Chitty,* contrà. The first question is, whether the defendant had a probable cause for arresting the plaintiff. The case of *Brown* v. *Pigeon* clearly shews that he had; there was no evidence, that the defendant had agreed that the balance of the accounts should be considered as the existing debt, nor does the statute authorising a set-off expressly direct that it shall be made. It is very different in that respect from the 5 G. 2. c. 30. as to mutual credits. The plaintiff might not have chosen to insist upon his set-off. But, even supposing that in strict law the balance only is the debt, it by no means follows that the arrest was malicious. Secondly,

(a) 4 *Burr.* 1996.

the

1824.

AUSTIN
against
DERHAM.

the declaration is insufficient to let in evidence of the cross demand. It does not apprize the defendant of the ' real cause of complaint, but says, generally, that the defendant had. no cause of action against the plaintiff, whereas the special circumstances should have been set forth.

ABBOTT C. J. It is not clear that the general question arises upon the evidence given in this case, which certainly tends to shew an understanding between the parties, that the balance only was to be considered as the existing debt. But I am of opinion upon the construction of the statute of set-off, that where there are mutual accounts, the balance only is to be considered as the existing debt for the purpose of arrest. Notwithstanding the great respect which I feel for every decision by Lord *Ellenborough,* I cannot forbear observing that the case of *Brown* v. *Pigeon* was only a *Nisi Prius* decision, and the termination of the suit was such (a juror being withdrawn) as to give no opportunity of revising the opinion there expressed. Since that time the case of *Dronefield* v. *Archer* was before the Court, and the former case was. cited, yet the arrest being on one side of the account only was held to be malicious. That decision appears to me consistent with justice and common sense. Then an objection has been made to the declaration: it does not, as stated in argument, allege that the defendant had no cause of action against the plaintiff, but that he had no reasonable or probable cause of action to the amount for which the plaintiff was arrested. It is certainly rather loosely framed, but still. I think it was sufficient to let in evidence of the real justice of the case, and that shews that the plaintiff was

entitled

entitled to maintain the present action; this rule must, therefore, be discharged.

HOLROYD and LITTLEDALE Js. concurred.

Rule discharged. (a)

(a) *Bayley* J. was in the Bail Court.

TYLER *against* JONES, Gent., One, &c.

By an order of reference, the award was to be delivered to the parties, or if they or either of them were dead before the making of the award to their respective personal representatives, on or before a given day, with liberty to the arbitrator to enlarge the time for making his award. The plaintiff died before the award was made, and after his death, the arbitrator enlarged the time for making the award: Held, that the award made within the enlarged time was good.

Rose . on . Coffe 4 *Bing: 448 .*

'THIS was an action against the defendant, an attorney, for negligence in not investigating the title to an annuity. At the trial, at the sittings before *Hilary* term, 1823, a verdict was found for the plaintiff, subject to the award of an arbitrator. By the order of nisi prius, which was afterwards made a rule of court, the award was to be delivered to the parties, or any of them requiring the same, *or if they or either of them should be dead before the making of the award*, to their respective personal representatives requiring the same, on or before the first day of *Hilary* term then next, with liberty to the arbitrator to enlarge the time for making his award. The plaintiff in the action died before any award was made, and after his death the arbitrator enlarged the time for making the award. By his award he found that the plaintiff had a good cause of action against the defendant to the amount of 500*l.*, and ordered the verdict to be finally entered for the plaintiff for that sum, and directed that the executors of the plaintiff should assign the annuity to the defendants, and allow their names or that of the plaintiff to be

used

used in an action on the bond of indemnity. A rule nisi having been obtained for setting aside the award, on the ground that the death of the plaintiff was a revocation of the arbitrator's authority. A cross rule had been obtained to enter up judgment on the verdict, as of *Hilary* term, 1823, the executors of the plaintiff undertaking to assign the annuity.

Marryat now shewed cause and admitted, that in ordinary cases the death of a party was a revocation of the authority of an arbitrator, but contended, that that event was expressly provided for by the terms of the rule of reference.

Nolan and *Abraham*, contrà. The arbitrator had no power to enlarge the time for making his award after the death of the plaintiff, and, consequently, the award not being made within the time limited by the order of reference is void. Secondly, the death of the party must necessarily operate as a revocation of the arbitrator's authority, because the executors cannot be compelled to assign the annuity, according to the terms of the award, and that annuity was the consideration for which the 500*l.* was paid. It is clear that an attachment would not be granted against the executors, because they are not parties to the rule of reference.

Per Curiam. The death of a party, generally speaking, operates as a revocation of an arbitrator's authority. This rule, however, has provided in express terms for that event; and an award made under such a rule after the death of a party, in ordinary cases, would clearly be valid. It is said, however, that in this case the award

VOL. III.   L   is

is void, because it was not made on or before the day mentioned in the order of reference, and that there was no express power given to the arbitrator to enlarge the time for making his award after the death of any of the parties; but, as the order of reference gave him express power to make his award after the death of any of the parties, it must be intended to give him incidentally the same power of enlarging the time after that event as he had before; and, therefore, the award made within the enlarged time is good. It is said further, that this award cannot be enforced against the executors; and, consequently, it ought not against the defendant. It is true, that it cannot be enforced by attachment; but an action would lie against the executors, upon the undertaking of their testator to perform the award. They therefore might be compelled to perform it. Circumstances might possibly exist, under which it might be improper to allow such an award to be enforced, but there are no such circumstances in the present case; and, therefore, this rule for setting aside the award must be discharged; the executor to be at liberty to enter up judgment of the term when the distringas was returnable, upon his undertaking to assign the annuity, and in other respects to perform his part of the award.

Rule discharged.

The KING *against* The Justices of KING's LYNN.

A RULE had been obtained, calling upon two of the justices of *Kings Lynn* to show cause why a mandamus should not issue directed to them, commanding them to cause a taxation to be made and levied for raising and paying the taxed costs of defending two actions brought on the 57 *G.* 3. *c.* 19. *s.* 38., against the applicants for the recovery of certain damages found to have been sustained by the plaintiffs in those actions, in consequence of certain tumultuous assemblages of persons within the borough. The rule was obtained on an affidavit by one of the defendants in those actions, stating that *Lynn* is a town not within any hundred; that the costs incurred by them amounted to the sum of 111*l.*; that they had been duly taxed, and that they had requested two of the justices of the town to make a rate to reimburse them that sum. The justices refused to interfere, thinking that they had not authority to do so.

The inhabitants of a town not within any hundred are not entitled to be reimbursed the expences which they incur in defending actions brought against them on the 57 G. 3. c. 19. s. 38. to recover the damages done by tumultuous assemblies.

Nolan and *Tindal* shewed cause. There are two answers to this application. First, that no statute has provided for reimbursing the expences incurred by inhabitants of towns, in defending actions on this or the other statutes relating to similar matters. Secondly, even if they are entitled to be reimbursed the application should have been made to the justices at sessions, and not to two magistrates out of sessions. Until the 8 *G.* 2. *c.* 16. persons against whom actions on the statutes of 13 *Edw.* 1. *st.* 2. *c.* 1., and 27 *Eliz. c.* 13., were

L 2   brought

brought had not any means of recovering the costs of their defence. The fourth section of that act provided, that the high constable of the *hundred* should be sued, and if he were cast, that two justices might cause taxation to be made and levied for the payment of his costs incurred in defending the action, over and above the damages recovered: but that act was confined to *hundreds*. The 22 G. 2. c. 46. s. 34. extended the relief given, as last mentioned, to all defendants in actions against a *hundred*, but makes no mention of actions against the inhabitants of a *town*. Perhaps the 1 G. 1. st. 2. c. 5. s. 6. may be relied on, but that only provides for reimbursing the persons on whom the damages recovered by the plaintiff have been levied, and says nothing about the costs of the defence; and besides, in the case of a town, the application for relief is to be made to the justices at the quarter sessions, which direction has not been complied with in this case. *Dibben* v. *Cooke* (a), *Ingle* v. *Wordsworth* (b), *Cone* v. *Bowles* (c), and *Rex* v. *Glastonby* (d) shew that statutes giving costs are to be construed strictly.

Scarlett, Pryme, and *Parke,* contrà. The true question is, whether this case falls within the meaning of the 22 G. 2. c. 46. s. 34. The word *town* certainly is not found in that section, but the statute is remedial, *hundred* is made use of as the largest word, and must be taken to include all districts that may be sued for damages under any act of parliament; they are all within the same mischief, and ought to have the same remedy.

(a) 2 *Str.* 1005.　　　(b) 3 *Burr.* 1284.
(c) 1 *Salk.* 205.　　　(d) *Cas. temp. Hardw.* 355.

Again.

Again, it may fairly be contended that a town not within a hundred is, for this purpose, to be considered as a hundred in itself. In 2 *Inst.* 110. and 150. two instances are given where a liberal construction is put upon the statute of *Marlebrige,* in order to remedy the mischief contemplated, and there is no reason why the same should not be done here. In some of the statutes giving remedies to persons injured by robbery or riots the word *town* is introduced, in others omitted ; but as they are all made in pari materiâ, it must be supposed that remedies against the same divisions of the county were intended to be given by them all.

Cur. adv. vult.

The judgment of the Court was now delivered by

ABBOTT C. J.   This was an application for a mandamus to be directed to two justices of *King's Lynn,* commanding them to raise the costs incurred by two persons in defending actions brought against them on the statute 57 G. 3. c. 19. s. 38., for recovery of the damages sustained by riotous assemblies. *Lynn* is a town corporate, not within any hundred, nor a county of itself.

Two objections were made in shewing cause against the rule: first, that this case was not in any manner provided for by any statute: second, that if it was in any manner provided for, the mode of relief was by application to the quarter sessions.

The thirty-eighth section of the statute 57 G. 3. c. 19., on which the actions were brought, is as follows: " And be it further enacted, that in every case where any house, shop, or other building whatever, or any part thereof, shall be destroyed, or shall be in any manner damaged or injured, or where any fixtures thereto attached, or any furniture, goods, or commodities what-

L 3   ever

ever which shall be therein, shall be destroyed, **taken**
away, or damaged by the act or acts of any riotous
or tumultuous assembly of persons, or by the act or
acts of any person or persons engaged in, or making
part of, such riotous or tumultuous assembly, the inhabitants of the city or town in which such house,
shop, or building, shall be situate, if such city or town
be a county of itself, or is not within any hundred, or
otherwise the inhabitants of the hundred in which such
damage shall be done, shall be liable to yield full compensation in damages to the person or persons injured
and damnified by such destruction, taking away, or
damage; and such damages shall and may be demanded, sued for, and recovered by the same means,
and under the same provisions as are provided in and
by the 1 *G.* 1. *c.* 5., with respect to persons injured and
damnified by the demolishing or pulling down of any
dwelling-house by persons unlawfully, riotously, and
tumultuously assembled." It is to be observed that this
act speaks only of the damages sustained by the party
injured, and is silent as to the costs of a defence. The
stat. 1 *G.* 1. *st.* 2. *c.* 5. also mentions only the damages
to be recovered by the plaintiff, and directs, that at the
plaintiffs' request, made to the justices of the town, at
any quarter sessions, the damages shall be raised and
levied on the inhabitants of the town, and paid to the
plaintiff in the manner directed by the stat: 27 *Eliz.* for
reimbursing the persons on whom money recovered
against any hundred, by any party robbed, shall be levied.
The stat. 27 *Eliz. c.* 13. *s.* 4. and 5. provides only for
relief of the particular inhabitants of a hundred upon
whom the damages recovered against the hundred may
have been levied, and directs that, upon complaint made
by the parties so charged, two justices of the county

shall

shall tax the hundred. This statute, therefore, has made no provision for the costs of the defence; it is confined to hundreds, and though it gives the power to two justices, and is referred to by the stat. 1 *G*. 1. *st*. 2. *c*. 5., yet by the express words of that statute the power is given to the quarter sessions in the case of a town: so that unless there be some other statute that can be embodied into and made a part of the legislative provision of the statute 57 *G*. 3., there is clearly no foundation for the present application to the court. In support of the application it was contended, that the statute 8 *G*. 2. *c*. 16. and 22 *G*. 2. *c*. 46. were to be so considered.

The 8 *G*. 2. *c*. 16. relates only *to the statutes of hue and cry*. It directs that in actions against the hundred the process shall be served on the high constable, who is to defend, and if the plaintiff obtains judgment the sheriff is to produce the writ of execution to *two justices* of the county, who are to make an assessment as directed by the statute of queen *Elizabeth*, and are to include therein, in addition to the damages and costs recovered by the plaintiff, the necessary expences of the high constable in defending the action.

The 22 *G*. 2. *c*. 46. *s*. 34. extends the remedy given by the 8 *G*. 2. (which, as before observed, was confined to the statute of hue and cry,) to all actions against the inhabitants of any hundred, and directs the sheriff to produce the writ of execution to two justices of the peace of the county, as directed by the 8 *G*. 2., and thereupon requires the justices to raise, by taxation, as well the costs and damages recovered, as the expence incurred by any inhabitant in defending the action.

These are the only statutes upon the subject, and of these the only one that mentions the inhabitants of a

town

town is the 1 G. 1. c. 5. and this statute makes a distinction between the inhabitants of a hundred and those of a town ; and as to the first directs the assessment to be according to the 27 *Eliz.*, that is by two justices of the county ; but as to the latter, that is, the inhabitants of a town, gives the authority to the justices at the quarter sessions. If, therefore, we were to grant the writ in the present case, we should be giving relief for costs to a defendant, in a case in which no statute has, in terms, given such relief, and should also order the relief to be administered by two justices, although the only statute providing for the case of a town has given the power of relief to the justices at quarter sessions. To do this would be to ordain and make a new law, which we have as little inclination as authority to do. For these reasons the rule for the mandamus must be discharged.

Rule discharged.

The King *against* The Mayor and Aldermen of the Borough of Portsmouth.

Where a charter does not require the members of a corporation to be resident, the Court will not grant a mandamus commanding the corporation to meet and consider of the propriety of removing from their offices non-resident corporators, unless their absence has been productive of some serious inconvenience.

An alderman is not bound to reside within the borough, unless that is necessary to the discharge of the duties of his office, or required by the charter.

THIS was a rule calling upon the mayor and aldermen of the borough of *Portsmouth,* to shew cause why a writ of mandamus should not issue, directed to them, commanding them to assemble themselves together within the said borough, and consider of the propriety of removing certain persons (naming them)

aldermen

aldermen of the borough, from their respective offices of
aldermen. *Portsmouth* is a borough by prescription;
but by a charter of the 3 *Car.* 1., that king granted that
they should be a corporation, by the name of " mayor,
aldermen, and burgesses"; that there should be within
the borough one alderman elected mayor, and that there
should be likewise within the borough twelve other burgesses, to be elected as therein mentioned, who should
be aldermen, and that the aldermen for the time being
should be called the council of the borough, and should
be from time to time aiding and assisting the mayor in all
causes and matters touching or concerning the borough;
that whensoever any of the aldermen for the time being
should die or be removed from that office, (which aldermen or any of them the said king willed should be re-
moveable for any offence or default, or reasonable cause,
at the discretion of the mayor, and the rest of the aldermen of the said borough for the time being, or the
greater part of them;) then it should be lawful for the
mayor, and the rest of the aldermen for the time being,
or the greater part of them, to elect one other or more
of the burgesses of the borough to supply the place of
the alderman or aldermen happening to die or be removed; that any person elected mayor or alderman, refusing to accept the office after notice, should be subject
to such fines and amerciaments as should seem reasonable to the mayor and aldermen, or the major part of
them; that there should be a recorder elected by the
mayor and aldermen, and that the mayor, aldermen, and
burgesses might have a court of record, to be holden
before the mayor, recorder, and aldermen, or any four
of them, of whom the mayor or recorder should be one,
on every *Tuesday*; that the mayor and recorder, and
every

1824.

The King
against
The Mayor,
&c. of
PORTSMOUTH.

1824.

The King
against
The Mayor,
&c. of
Portsmouth.

every mayor, for one year, after serving the office of
mayor, and three other aldermen should be justices of
the peace for the borough, to be elected annually by the
mayor, aldermen, and burgesses.; and in case of death
or vacating the office of alderman, another to be elected
in his room. It appeared by the affidavits, that the
aldermen mentioned in the rule had not for several years
resided within the borough; one of them had, during
that time, been elected one of the justices of the peace
for the borough; he resided five miles from *Portsmouth*, and always attended when justice business was
going on. It did not appear that any obstruction of
justice or *serious* inconvenience to the inhabitants of
the borough had resulted from the absence of the parties
named.

Scarlett, *Adam*, *Selwyn*, and *Erskine* shewed cause
against the rule. This rule was granted upon the authority of *Rex* v. *Truro* (a), but that case has no application to the present, for there residence was made
necessary by the charter. But there is not a single
syllable in the charter now before the court which makes
the residence of aldermen necessary. In *Rex* v. *Monday* (b), which was a case on the same charter, it seems
to have been taken for granted that the aldermen were
bound to reside; but that rests on the statement of
counsel; the charter itself contains no provision respecting it. There is no case in which it has been held
that mere non-residence vacates the office of an alderman, the mayor and the rest of the aldermen have a
discretionary power to remove him, for any cause which
appears to them sufficient, but that must be where some

(a) *H. T.* 1821.   (b) *Cowp.* 530.

incon-

1824.

The King
against
The Mayor,
&c. of
Portsmouth.

inconvenience results from his absence. In the present case, nothing of that kind is shewn. Five of the aldermen, viz. the mayor, the ex-mayor, and three other aldermen are to act as justices; four of those have always been resident, and the fifth so near as to be able to attend whenever it was necessary. The administration of justice has, therefore, never been impeded, and no inconvenience to the inhabitants of the borough, sufficient to call for the interference of this court, has been made out.

The *Attorney-General, Gaselee,* and *Merewether,* contrà. It has been declared, in a variety of cases, that where a charter expressly makes the residence of an alderman necessary, that is merely declaratory of the common law. The duty of residence is incident to the office; *Vaughan* v. *Lewis* (a), *City of Exeter* v. *Glyde.* (b) It is therefore immaterial whether residence be mentioned in the charter or not; and here the aldermen have duties to perform which cannot but be neglected during their absence; they form the council of the borough, and must be at hand, to assist the mayor in all corporation business. The only question is, with respect to the mode of proceeding where aldermen absent themselves. Now the writ prayed for is connected with the administration of justice, and to enforce performance of that which is virtually if not actually made necessary by the king's charter. The subject is, therefore, entitled to it, according to *Bull. N. P.* p. 199. This is not by any means the first application of the kind: before the case of *Rex* v. *Truro*, it had been laid down by *Ashurst* J., in *Rex* v. *Heaven* (c), " when a corporator

(a) *Carth.* 227.   (b) 4 *Mod.* 33.   *Holt,* 435.   (c) 2 *T. R.* 772.

neglects

1824.

The King
against
The Mayor,
&c. of
Portsmouth.

neglects the duties of his office, the corporation should first take cognizance of it, and deprive him, and then it may be properly brought before this court. And there is no inconvenience in this mode of proceeding; for if any persons find themselves injured by the non-residence of a corporator, and the corporation refuse to interfere and to do their duty, such persons may apply to this court for a mandamus, directed to the corporation to enforce a performance of their duty." In *Regina* v. *Truebody* (a) *Rex* v. *Mayor of Shrewsbury* (b), *Rex* v. *Ponsonby* (c), non-residence was considered as a fault, for which a corporator might be removed. It is, therefore, very reasonable, that, in the present instance, the mayor and aldermen of *Portsmouth* should at least meet and consider of the propriety of exercising the power which they have to remove the aldermen who have, for a long period, ceased to reside within or near the borough.

ABBOTT C. J. Applications of this nature are of modern introduction, and have probably grown out of the dictum of *Ashurst* J. in *Rex* v. *Heaven*, which has been cited. But that observation is confined to instances where persons find themselves aggrieved by the non-residence of corporate officers. An alderman, when he accepts that office, takes upon himself the burthen of giving such attention to his office, as is made necessary by the public duties which he has to discharge. If residence within the borough is necessary for that purpose, it follows that he must reside there. But we should open a fruitful source of litigation if we were to listen too readily to applications of this nature. Public justice and public convenience should be the grounds of

(a) 2 Ld. Raym. 1275.   (b) Cas. temp. Hardw. 147.   (c) 1 Ves. jun. 1.

17

the

1824.

The King
against
The Mayor,
&c. of
PORTSMOUTH.

the application; and this Court ought not to interfere, unless for the purpose of redressing some serious inconvenience. No case of that nature is established by the affidavits before the court. The non-residence of some aldermen rather has the effect of casting an additional burthen upon the others, than of causing an injury to the public; and it does not appear that those who are resident think it necessary to make any complaint. Those who have had to discharge the office of justices of the peace have always been actually or virtually resident; the administration of justice has not, therefore, been impeded. For these reasons, and considering also the great and manifest inconvenience that would result from a too ready interposition, I think that we ought not to grant a mandamus in this case.

Rule discharged.

WILSON, Gent., One, &c. *against* GUTTERIDGE.

TAUNTON shewed cause against a rule obtained by *Brodrick* for referring to the master for taxation the plaintiff's bill of costs, to recover which this action was brought. All the items in the bill, except three, relating to a warrant of attorney, were agreed to be out of the statute 2 G. 2. c. 33. Those charges were for drawing the warrant of attorney and attending the defendant respecting it, but it never was engrossed or executed. Against this rule he cited the recent case of *Burton* v. *Chatterton* (a), wherein all the former authorities were reviewed, and it

The Court will order an attorney's bill to be taxed, though it consists merely of a charge for drawing a warrant of attorney and attending a defendant respecting it.

(a) 3 B. & A. 486.

was decided that a charge for drawing an affidavit of a petitioning creditor's debt and bond to the chancellor in order to the striking of a docquet was not within the statute.

But *Per Curiam.* The point there occurred on the statute as to the necessity of delivering a bill. But we have a paramount jurisdiction, independently of the statute, to refer an attorney's bill for taxation.

Rule absolute.

— Harrison. v. Bray. N. M. Will. Off

STORER *against* RAYSON.

*Friday,
July 2d.*

The Court will not set aside the service of a latitat served in a wrong county, without an affidavit that the place where it was served is not on the confines of the county into which it issued.

LANGSLOW moved to set aside the service of a latitat directed to the sheriff of *Leicestershire* upon an affidavit of defendant, that he was served at his house situate in the county of *Northampton,* and not in the county of *Leicester,* and that there was no doubt or dispute about the same. [*Abbott* C. J. Is the place where the defendant was served on the confines of the county of *Leicester?*] The affidavit is silent as to that, but the statement is rendered unnecessary by the distinct allegation, that there was no doubt or dispute about the place being in the county of *Northampton, Chase* v. *Joyce* (a), *Hammond* v. *Taylor.* (b) If this service be good, a sheriff may, in all cases, execute a writ beyond the limits of his county, although the boundary is perfectly well known.

(a) 4 M. & S. 412.   (b) 3 B. & A. 408.

Per

Per Curiam. In several recent cases it has been held, that to support such a motion as the present, the affidavit must state that the place where the writ was served is not upon the confines of the county into which it is issued.

Rule refused. (*a*)

(*a*) See 1 *Chitt. Rep.* 15.

NESTOR *against* NEWCOME and Another.

TRESPASS for an act done by *Newcome* in his office of magistrate; the other defendant acted by his orders. Pleas, general issue and a justification. After issue joined and notice of trial given, a rule was obtained for defendant, *Newcome*, to be at liberty to withdraw his pleas, pay money into court by way of amends, and plead the general issue de novo.

In trespass against a magistrate for an act done in execution of his office, the Court, after issue joined, and notice of trial given, allowed the defendant to withdraw his pleas, pay money into court under the 24 G. 2. c. 44. s. 4., and plead the general issue de novo.

Chitty shewed cause, and contended, that the statute 24 *G.* 2. *c.* 44. *s.* 4. merely authorised the payment of money into court *before* issue joined. The defendant in this case is therefore clearly too late, notice of trial having been given.

Brodrick, contrà, cited *Devaynes* v. *Boyes.* (*a*)

Per Curiam. That is a direct authority, the point having been expressly brought under the consideration

(*a*) 7 *Taunt.* 85.

of

of the court. It is very common under the statute of set-off, to allow the general issue to be withdrawn and pleaded de novo with notice of set-off. The sum to be paid in must be mentioned in the rule, as the whole is done by the leave of the Court.

Rule absolute.

---

*Wednesday,
July 7th.*

The KING *against* JOSEPH TURNER.

If a defendant remove an indictment here by certiorari, giving the usual recognisance under stat. *5 W. & M. c. 11.,* and be found guilty, and die before the day in bank, his bail are liable to pay the costs.

AN indictment found against the defendant, at the quarter sessions for the borough of *Doncaster,* in the West Riding of the county of *York,* for an assault, was removed into this court by certiorari, and recognizances were given in pursuance of the statute *5 W. & M. c. 11. s. 3.* The indictment came on to be tried at the *York Lent* assizes, 1824, when the defendant was convicted, but he died before the day in bank. The master of the crown office taxed the costs of the prosecution, which not being paid, a rule had been obtained by *Brandt,* calling upon the defendant's bail to shew cause why the recognizances should not be estreated, and an affidavit was filed, shewing that *Charles Lister,* the husband of *Ann Lister,* was the party grieved.

D. F. Jones now shewed cause. This application is probably founded upon the authority of *Rex* v. *Finmore.* (a) But that case seems to be deserving of further consideration. The statute of *William* and *Mary* in terms applies only to cases of " conviction," which

(a) 8 T. R. 409.

ought

ought to be construed to mean a conviction by *judgment*, and not merely by verdict; otherwise, though the conviction might be set aside, upon a motion in arrest of judgment, or upon a writ of error, the defendant's bail might be charged with the costs of a defective prosecution. But if *conviction* under this act means a conviction by verdict, then the prosecutor ought to have taxed his costs immediately after the verdict, and endeavoured to obtain them from the defendant, which might have exonerated the bail. At all events, the prosecutor should have demanded the costs of the *representatives* of the defendant, before making this application to the bail, who stand in the situation of sureties. In the case of *Rex* v. *Lyon* (a), which is cited in *Rex* v. *Finmore*, there was a forfeiture of the recognizance, for the defendant did not proceed to trial according to notice. Here the bail did every thing that it was possible for them to do, in pursuance of their recognizance. The defendant appeared, pleaded, and was tried, and that he did not appear to receive judgment arose from the act of God.

ABBOTT C. J. The case of the *King* v. *Finmore* cannot be distinguished from the present, and we see no reason to disturb it. The third section of the stat. of the 5 & 6 *W. & M. c.*11. is express that the recognizance shall not be discharged till the costs, when taxed, are paid. Though it be true that the failure arose from the act of God, the expence to the prosecutor is nearly the same as though the defendant had received judgment. As to the alleged necessity of first making a demand upon

(a) 3 *Burr.* 1461.

the

1824.

The King
against
Townes.

the representatives of the defendant, the bail do not
now show, by affidavit, that there is an executor or administrator upon whom such a demand could be made.

Rule absolute

Wednesday,
July 7th.

Harrison and Another *against* Williams.

In an action
for the breach
of a bye-law
restraining per-
sons from ex-
ercising trades
within the
limits of a cor-
porate city,
unless they
become free-
men, the Court
will compel the
corporation to
allow the de-
fendant to in-
spect the bye-
law in the cor-
poration books.

DEBT for a penalty under a bye-law, founded on
an ancient custom of the city of *Chester*, whereby
persons are restrained from exercising trades within
the limits of that city, unless they become freemen of
it. The plaintiffs were treasurers of the city, and as
such brought this action against the defendant, who
followed the business of a tanner there. A rule having
been obtained for allowing the defendant the inspection
of the corporation books, so far as respected the bye-
law, stated in the declaration,

D. F. Jones insisted that the defendant was not entitled to an inspection of the corporation books. The
proof of the bye-law in question will be a necessary part
of the plaintiffs' case on the trial, and the defendant has
no more right, beforehand, to the inspection asked for
than he would have if the party suing were a corporation sole, or even a private person suing in his individual
capacity. It is true, that in some cases the court have
granted such inspection, but the more recent authorities
have limited and restrained the right, confining it to
members of the corporation, having, as such, an interest
in the corporation books. The case of the *Brewers'*

Company

Company v. *Benson* (a) appears to have been overturned
in principle by the cases of *Talbot* v. *Villeboys* (b), and
Hodges v. *Atkis.* (c)   In the *Mayor of Southampton* v.
Graves (d) all the authorities were reviewed and inspection was refused.   It may be said that in that case the
action was for tolls, and not upon a bye-law, but the
principle established is, that corporations are not more
bound than private individuals to expose their books to
strangers, though they must to corporators.   If it be
proper that an inspection should be granted, an application should be made to a court of equity, which will
examine into the circumstances, and if leave be granted
will impose proper terms, as was laid down by Lord
Hardwicke, 2 *Vesey*, 620.   Besides, there is here no
affidavit of a demand of inspection, and this court will
not interfere to compel what does not appear to have
been as yet refused.

Chitty, contrà, was stopped by the Court.

ABBOTT C. J.   I cannot say that the defendant is to
be considered as standing altogether in the situation of
a stranger.   The bye-law must be taken to have been
made for the public weal, and for the rule and government of persons resiant, and dwelling within the city.
Now, the defendant falls within that class, though he
be not a member of the corporation.   I think, therefore,
the defendant should be allowed to see the bye-law in
the corporation books, and to have a copy of it; but
the inspection and copy must be confined to the bye-

1824.

HARRISON
against
WILLIAMS.

(a) *Barnes*, 236.   (b) Cited in *Rex* v. *Shelley*, 3 T. R. 142.
(c) 3 *Wils.* 398.   (d) 8 T. R. 590.

M 2   law,

1824.

HABBON
against
WILLIAMS.

law, and the leave must be upon the terms of the defendant paying the town clerk for his attendance to produce the books, and also for the copy furnished.

The other judges concurring,

Rule absolute on these terms.

Wednesday,
July 7th.

Ex parte MIDDLETON.

The driver of a van travelling to and from *London* and *York*, is a carrier within the meaning of the 3 *Car.* 1. *c.* 4., and liable to be convicted in the penalty of 20*s.* for travelling on the Lord's day.

D. F. JONES moved for a certiorari to remove a conviction before the justices of the borough of *Stamford*, in *Lincolnshire*, under the stat. 3 *Car.* 1. *c.* 1. " for the reformation of abuses on the Lord's day, commonly called *Sunday.*" The defendant was the driver of a *van* travelling to and from *London* and *York*, and was stopped in *Stamford* whilst on his journey, and convicted as a carrier travelling with horses on a *Sunday.* D. F. *Jones* contended that this penal statute ought not to be extended beyond its express terms, but should be confined to the mere local pursuit of ordinary occupations, instead of being made to prevent communications between distant places for the public benefit; or at least that it should be confined to such conveyances as were in use at the time of the passing of the act; otherwise, not only every stage-coach, but also every mail-coach, which carried a parcel, or even a passenger, upon a *Sunday,* might be stopped, and the driver subjected to a penalty at every place through which he passed.

Per Curiam. We decline, at present, saying any thing upon the inconvenience suggested as to either

14   stage

stage or mail coaches, but we are clearly of opinion, that a person who has the care of a van is a carrier within the terms of this act of parliament, which ought to receive a liberal construction, being for the better observance of the Lord's day.

Rule refused.

en Philpott. - Jones. 2. Ald & Ell. 41.

WRIGHT and Another, Assignees of GOLDING, against LAING.

THIS was an action brought to recover penalties upon an usurious transaction between the defendant and *Golding* the bankrupt. The declaration consisted of twenty counts, but the principal question turned upon the seventeenth count, which charged that defendant, on the 8th day of *November* 1820, upon a certain corrupt contract made between the defendant and *Golding* on the 25th of *April* 1820, took 22*l*. 10*s*. by way of corrupt bargain and loan for the defendant's forbearance, and giving day of payment to *Golding* of 300*l*. lent to *Golding* on the 25th of *April* 1820, from the time of lending and advancing the same, until the 28th of *October* 1820, when 2*l*. 10*s*. was paid, and for forbearance of 297*l*. 10*s*., residue of the 300*l*., until the 1st of *November*, when 158*l*., other part, was paid; and for forbearing 139*l*. 10*s*., residue of the 300*l*., until the 8th of *November*, when the residue was paid, which 22*l*. 10*s*. exceeds 5*l*. per cent. per annum,

When a person has two demands upon another, one arising out of a lawful contract, the other out of a contract forbidden by law, and the debtor makes a payment which is not specifically appropriated by either party at the time of payment, the law will appropriate it to the debt recognised by law; and therefore, where distinct sums of money were due, one for goods sold, the other for money lent on a usurious contract, and a payment was made which was not specifically appropriated to either debt by debtor or creditor, it was held that the law would afterwards appropriate such payment to the debt for goods sold. Where a bill of exchange was given for the principal money lent and interest to accrue due on an usurious contract, and before the bill became due the lender advanced a further sum of money on the general credit of the borrower, which enabled the latter to pay the bill, it was held that the payment of the usurious interest was complete as soon as the bill was paid.

&c. con-

&c., contrary, &c. At the trial before *Abbott* C. J., at the *London* sittings after last *Michaelmas* term, it appeared from the evidence of *Golding*, that on the 25th of *April*, *Laing* lent *Golding* 300*l.*, upon an agreement that he should have it for six months at 15*l.* per cent.; there was about the same time a purchase of hops by *Golding* of *Laing* amounting to 148*l.* 11*s.* 1*d.*, and to secure the money lent, the interest, and the amount of the hops, *Golding* gave three bills of exchange according to the following account.

Dr. Golding.				Cr.		
Money lent 25th April	£ 300	0	0	By bill due 28th October £ 150	10	1
Interest - -	22	10	0	Ditto due 1st November 158	0	0
Hops sold - -	148	11	1	Ditto due 8th November 162	0	0

Golding also stated, that within a week after the loan he paid to *Laing* 11*s.*, the balance of the above account. The bills were paid when they became due; but *Laing*, on the 30th *October*, lent or advanced to *Golding* another sum of 250*l.*, with which the bills were paid, but it did not appear whether that sum was lent specifically to take up either of the three bills given in respect of the alleged usurious transaction, which were not then due. It was contended on the part of the defendant, that there had not been any payment of the principal or usurious interest, for although the three bills of exchange had been apparently honored when they became due, yet *Golding* had been enabled to honor those which became due on the 1st and 8th of *November*, chiefly by the funds provided by *Laing*. There had therefore been no payment of those bills by *Golding*. The Lord Chief Justice was of opinion, that if the money advanced by *Laing* to *Golding* on the 30th of *October*, was advanced on the

16   general

general account and credit of *Golding*, and not specifically in order to enable him to pay the bills, (although that sum remained unpaid to *Laing*,) yet the bills must be considered as having been paid by *Golding*. If, on the other hand, when the bills had become due, they had been renewed or any distinct loan had been made by *Laing* to enable *Golding* to take them up, and that sum remained unpaid to *Laing*, then the account would not have been closed, and there would not have been any payment of the usurious interest; and he directed the jury to find for the plaintiff, if they were of opinion upon the evidence that the 250*l.* advanced by *Laing* on the 30th of *October*, was advanced upon the general account and credit of *Golding*; and for the defendant, if they thought it was advanced by *Laing*, specifically to enable *Golding* to take up both bills. The jury found for the plaintiffs for 900*l.*, and the verdict was taken on the seventeenth count above set forth. A rule nisi for a new trial having been obtained by *Scarlett* in last *Hilary* term upon the objection taken at the trial, and also upon the ground, that there was not sufficient evidence to support the seventeenth count on which the verdict was taken.

Marryat and *Chitty* now shewed cause. The mode in which the seventeenth count is framed, is according to the appropriation which the law will make of the payments made by the bills of exchange. And it was left to the jury to say, whether the subsequent advances had been made independently of the usurious contract, or specifically to enable *Golding* to take up the bills, and they found the former. The transactions cannot, there-

M 4 fore,

1824.

Wright
against
Laing.

fore, be now blended together so as to protect *Laing* from penalties.

Scarlett and *F. Pollock*, contrà. Although the declaration states various appropriations of the bills as they became due, yet in no one count is the transaction set forth according to its legal or its actual character. The bills were given collectively for the purpose of paying for the hops and for the loan, and as they became due, were no more applicable to the one than the other, and any statement in pleading which gives any appropriation in fact, mistated the transaction. There is no difficulty in setting forth such an agreement as this was in a declaration; the agreement should have been stated as if the bills were given for the whole, and it was not necessary or proper to specify precisely the periods of the separate forbearances, but to aver the giving of the bills and their payment, from which it would have appeared that usurious interest had been taken. All the counts have, however, affected to separate the transaction into parts, and to appropriate the bills in some way or other, which was what the parties had not done or intended to do. As to the other ground, the original debt to *Laing* has never been satisfied, for the bills were chiefly paid by funds supplied by *Laing* himself. He cannot be said to have received payment either of the principal originally advanced, or of usurious interest thereon.

The Court thought clearly, that the finding of the jury, that in fact the subsequent advances were not made specifically to assist in taking up the bills, but generally on account, had disposed of any question as to the payment of usurious interest: and they held, that if

a lender

a lender discounts a second bill to enable the borrower
to take up and pay a former bill, the discount of which
was tainted with usury, that the usury becomes complete
on the payment of the first bill.   On the other point
they took time to consider; and now,

ABBOTT C. J. delivered the judgment of the Court.
This was an action for the penalties of the statute of
usury.   The facts of the case have been very recently
before the court.   It arose on a sale of hops and a loan
of money.   It was not denied, that the loan was made
on a bargain for usurious interest, but it was contended,
that all the bills of exchange had not been in effect paid
by *Golding*, the borrower; and further, that supposing
they had been paid by him, there was not any one count
of the plaintiffs' voluminous declaration properly framed
to meet the case.   We think the evidence shews that
all the bills were paid by the borrower; and we have,
therefore, only to enquire whether any count of the declaration is suited to the case.   By the seventeenth
count, so much of the amount of the first bill of exchange as will cover the price of the hops sold by the
defendant to *Golding*, is appropriated to the payment of
that price; the residue of the amount of this bill, and the
whole of the two bills falling due afterwards are applied
to the payment of the money lent, and of the usurious
interest agreed to be allowed for that loan.   None of the
payments were appropriated by either party at the times
of payment.   If the law ought now to make such an appropriation as the pleader has supposed in this count,
the count will be sustained by the proof, otherwise not.
We think the law ought now to make such an appropriation.   In order to render this matter more simple in
                                                    its

its form, let us suppose a contract made for the sale of
goods at the price of 100*l.* at six months' credit; and as
soon as this contract is made, another and distinct contract to be made for a loan of 93*l.* for the same period of
six months, in consideration of receiving 7*l.* for interest
on the loan; and that on the following day two bills
of exchange are drawn for 100*l.* each, falling due within
three or four days of each other, and also within five or
six days of the day on which the contracts were made,
without any matter to denote the application of either
bill to either of the two contracts. Let us further suppose that the first bill is paid at maturity without any
appropriation of the money by either of the parties, and
that the other bill remains unpaid, and that in this state
of things an action is brought by the seller, who is also
the lender, for goods sold and money lent, without noticing the bills; or that an action is brought by him upon
the last bill, must not the Court say at the trial, for the
furtherance of justice, that the price of the goods has
been paid by the discharge of the first bill, and that the
plaintiff cannot recover on the count for money lent, or
on the second bill, by reason of the illegality of the bargain? We conceive that the Court must say this in the
case I have put. And such an appropriation works no
prejudice to the party, it leaves him only where, by his
own conduct, he placed himself; and in the case I have
put of the payment of one bill and non-payment of the
other, if an action for the penalties of the statute should
be brought, the same principle of law would protect the
defendant, by applying the payment of the first bill to
the legal demand, and not permitting the then plaintiff
to apply it to the illegal demand, that is, to the loan and
interest, although it be precisely of the same amount;
                                                    because

because peradventure the lender might repent the illegal bargain, and refuse to receive the full amount of the second bill, and the law would allow him the opportunity of doing so, that he might not be deemed a receiver of usurious interest, without clear evidence that he had not only bargained to receive, but had actually received, such interest. And if the law will make this appropriation of the payment in the two cases that I have put, in the one instance against the lender, and to prevent him from enforcing an illegal bargain, and in the other instance in favour of the lender, and to protect him from being subject to a penalty for an illegal *bargain only*, it seems very plainly to follow, that a similar appropriation ought to be made by law in the case before the Court; and that the pleader, who is always at liberty to state facts according to their legal operation, is well warranted in the form of this count; and that the count is supported by the evidence. And this, in effect, is only saying, that where a person has two demands, one recognised by law, the other arising on a matter forbidden by law, and an unappropriated payment is made to him, the law will afterwards appropriate it to the demand which it acknowledges, and not to the demand which it prohibits. For these reasons we are of opinion the rule for the new trial must be discharged.

Rule discharged.

The KING *against* The Masters, Keepers, Wardens, and Commoners of the Brewers' Company. (*a*)

The Court will grant a mandamus to admit a copyholder claiming by descent.

THIS was a mandamus to the defendants, as lords of the manor of *Willyatts*, in the county of *Middlesex*, commanding them or their steward to admit *Robert Fossick* to a copyhold tenement, parcel of the manor, which he claimed as heir at law of a person deceased, and also to take a surrender from him to the use of *Martha Winter*, who had advanced 1000*l*. upon mortgage of the premises. The defendants returned, amongst other things, that the prosecutor had claimed to be admitted on the one part, and his sister and her husband on the other part; that the two latter had insisted that the prosecutor was illegitimate; that his father was a quaker; that they produced a register of his birth, which it was contended had been subsequently and surreptitiously inserted; that the homage found that the sister and her husband had made out a primâ facie right to be admitted, and that they had been admitted accordingly.

Chitty being now called upon to support the return, admitted it to be bad, as it only set out what others had stated or found, but contended, that the mandamus ought not to have issued, as the prosecutor claimed by descent; and he cited *Rex* v. *Rennett* (*b*), where the Court held, that as the party claimed by descent, it could answer no purpose to grant the mandamus,

(*a*) This case was heard and determined at the sittings after *Easter* term, but was unavoidably omitted in the preceding volume.
(*b*) 2 *T. R.* 197.

since

since he had as complete a title without admittance as with it, against all the world, but the lord.

1824.

The King
against
The Masters,
&c. of the
Brewers' Co.

Per Curiam. The prosecutor, as heir at law, is entitled to the writ; because, although he has a good title as against every one but the lord, still he has a right to insist upon admittance, to make him a complete copyholder. He may wish to be put upon the homage, or to be put in nomination for various offices, or to surrender to the use of his will; and he has a right to require to be admitted in the present instance, that he may surrender to *Martha Winter*, the mortgagee.

Peremptory mandamus awarded.

The KING *against* The Lord of the Manor of BONSALL and ADAM WOLLEY, Steward of the said Manor.

A rule nisi had been obtained for a mandamus, directed to the defendants, commanding them to admit *Richard Ward*, or the coparceners and heirs of one *Samuel Richardson*, deceased, to a copyhold, close, or parcel of land, consisting of about six acres and a half, situate and lying within the manor of *Bonsall*, which were duly surrendered to the use of *Samuel Richardson* and his heirs, according to the custom of the manor. It appeared, by the affidavits in support of the rule, that *Samuel Richardson*, subsequently to making his will, purchased the copyhold tenement in question, and that it was duly surrendered to the use of him and his heirs for ever; that he died on the 20th of *January* 1823, without having republished his will, leaving *Catherine Richardson* and her three sisters his co-heiresses at law,

who

Semble, that coparceners are entitled to be admitted to copyhold tenements as one heir, and upon the payment of one set of fees.

1824.

The King
against
The Lord of
the Manor of
Bonsall.

who thereby became entitled to the copyhold tenement, subject to a fine of 2s., payable to the lord. They applied at a court baron to be admitted, and the steward demanded for himself fees to the amount of 34l. 13s. 4d. They tendered a sum of 8l. 13s. 4d. It appeared further, that they had agreed to sell the premises to *Richard Ward;* and that they had been prevented from completing such sale, in consequence of the refusal of the steward to admit them. The affidavits in answer stated, that *Samuel Richardson* purchased the premises in 1818, and that previously to that time they had been held as two several and distinct copyhold tenements by two persons, as tenants in common, although *Samuel Richardson* had been admitted to them as one tenement. The steward insisted, that the four coheiresses should be admitted separately as tenants in common for their respective shares to two tenements, upon the payment by each of two sets of fees. They on the other hand insisted, that as coparceners they were entitled to be admitted as one heir, and they tendered two sets of fees for the whole.

The *Attorney General* and *N. R. Clarke* now shewed cause. *Attree* v. *Scutt* (a) is an authority to shew that the premises must be considered as consisting of two tenements, and that the steward is entitled to two sets of fees at least; and although for some purposes several coparceners constitute but one heir, yet, for the purpose of admittance to copyholds, they are rather in the situation of tenants in common than joint tenants. They have not an entirety of interest; but between themselves, to many purposes, they have, in judgment of law,

(a) 6 East, 476.

1824.

The King
against
The Lord of
the Manor of
BONSALL.

several freeholds, and there is no survivorship between them; they can therefore only be entitled to surrender payment of several sets of fees in respect of their separate interests. The reason given for considering the copyhold interest of tenants in common as distinct tenements, viz. that otherwise there might always be a tenant living, and that the lord might never have a fine, applies with equal force to the case of coparceners, inasmuch as the heir of a coparcener becomes a coparcener with the survivors, and there might, therefore, always be a coparcener living. Besides, the case of *Rex* v. *Rennet* (a) is an authority to shew that the court will not grant a mandamus to admit a party claiming by descent.

Campbell, contrà, contended, that a sum double that which the steward could lawfully claim had been tendered to him; for as *Samuel Richardson* had been admitted to the whole of the premises as one tenement the steward had no right now to consider them as two: *Garland* v. *Jekyll* (b); and as all the coparceners make but one heir and one tenant, they were entitled to be admitted, on payment of one fine to the lord and one fee to the steward. *Watkins on Copyholds*, 277. (He was then stopped by the Court.)

ABBOTT C. J. I am of opinion that this rule ought to be made absolute. The case of *Rex* v. *Rennett* was overruled in this court in the late case of *Rex* v. *The Brewers' Company*, where the Court held that a mandamus would lie to compel the admittance of an heir. As to the other question, whether coparceners are entitled to be admitted as one heir, as at present advised, I think that the Lord is bound to admit them as

(a) 2 T. R. 197.   (b) 2 Bing. 275.

1824.

The KING
against
The Lord of
the Manor of
BONSALL.

one heir, and on the payment of such fees as ought to be paid by a single heir. And I entertain considerable doubts whether the steward, after admitting them as one heir, can insist upon taking their surrenders separately; but on that I pronounce no decided opinion. This rule must be made absolute for a mandamus to the defendant, to admit the coparceners on payment of the lawful fees. If the defendants wish to raise the question as to what are the lawful fees upon the admittance of coparceners, or on the surrenders afterwards made by them, they may do so by setting out the facts in a return to the mandamus.

BAYLEY and HOLROYD J. concurred, and intimated a strong opinion that coparceners were entitled to be admitted as one heir, and upon the payment of one set of fees.

Rule absolute.

RULES OF COURT.

Trinity Term, 5 Geo. 4. 1824.

IT IS ORDERED, that no affidavit shall hereafter be used in support of a motion for a new trial in any case, whether criminal or civil, unless such affidavit shall have been made before the expiration of the first four days of the term following the trial, if the cause be tried in vacation: and before the expiration of the first four days after the return of distringas, if the cause be tried in term, without the special permission of the Court for that purpose.

Iṛ

IT IS ORDERED, that in all cases where a rule for a special jury shall have been obtained for the trial of any cause in the county of *Middlesex*, and notice for summoning the same shall be given; such notice, together with the distringas, shall be left at the office of the sheriff of the said county before seven o'clock in the evening next but one before the day on which such jury shall be required to attend, unless such jury shall be required to attend on a *Monday*, and then before seven in the evening of the preceding *Friday*; and that all notices of countermand for summoning special juries shall be left at the said office before twelve o'clock at noon of the day immediately preceding the day for which the jury was to have been summoned.

By the Court.

MEMORANDA.

IN this term *Stephen Gaselee* and *Robert Spankie* of the *Inner Temple*, and *John Adams* of the *Middle Temple*, Esquires, Barristers at Law, were called to the degree of Serjeant, and gave rings with the motto, " Bonis legibus, judiciis gravibus."

Mr. Justice *Richardson* having in the vacation preceding this term resigned in consequence of ill health, Mr. *Gaselee* was appointed a Puisne Judge of the Court of Common Pleas in his stead, and took his seat accordingly on the 5th day of *July*.

END OF TRINITY TERM.

GUTHRIE and BUNYON, Assignees of the Estate
and Effects of SAVERY, a Bankrupt, *against*
FISK and PATTESON, two of the Directors of
the NORWICH Union Society for the Insurance
of Lives and Survivorhips. (*a*)

Where a private act of parliament, entitled " an act to enable a certain insurance society *to sue* and be sued in the name of their secretary," enacted that they might commence all *actions and suits* in his name as nominal plaintiff: Held, that this did not enable the secretary to petition on behalf of the society for a commission of bankruptcy against their debtor.

ASSUMPSIT for money had and received by the
defendants, to and for the use and on the account of
Savery, and for money due on an account stated with him
before he became a bankrupt. There were also counts for
money paid by the plaintiffs, as assignees, for the use of
the defendants, for money had and received by the defendants, to and for the use and on account of the
plaintiffs, as assignees and for money due on an account
stated with the plaintiffs, as assignees, since the bankruptcy. Plea, the general issue, and notice of set-off.
At the trial before *Abbott* C. J., at the *London* sittings
before *Michaelmas* term, 1822, the plaintiffs were nonsuited. A rule nisi was obtained to set aside the nonsuit and for a new trial; and on cause being shewn, a
question arose on the validity of the commission, and
the court directed the facts to be stated for their con-

(*a*) In pursuance of the king's warrant issued ten days before the end
of *Trinity* term, three of the Judges of this court sat, as on former occasions, on the 8th of *July* and the following days until *Saturday* the 17th
of *July* inclusive; and all the Judges sat on *Monday* the 25th of *October*
and the following days, until the first day of *Michaelmas* term. During
that period this and the following cases were argued and decided.

sideration

sideration in the form of a special case, which was as follows: By the act of the 53 *G*. 3. *c*. 216., entitled " An act to enable the *Norwich* Union Society for insurance against loss by fire, to sue in the name of their secretary, and to be sued in the names of their directors, treasurers, and secretary," after reciting, among other things, that several persons had formed themselves into a society, under the name of the *Norwich* Union Society, for insurance against loss by fire, and that difficulties had arisen, and might, from time to time, arise in recovering debts due to the society, and in recovering debts owing by the said society to the individuals members thereof, and other persons dealing therewith, and that it was therefore expedient that such individuals, members, and other persons, should be thereby enabled to commence and prosecute suits and actions at law, and to sue out execution upon judgments obtained by them against such directors and officers of the said society as were thereinafter mentioned,—It was enacted that all actions and suits to be commenced or instituted by or on behalf of the said society, against any person or persons, or body politic or corporate, should and lawfully might be commenced or instituted, and prosecuted in the name or names of the secretary, or secretaries for the time being, of the society, as a nominal plaintiff or plaintiffs, for and on behalf of the society, and that all actions and suits to be commenced or instituted against the society, should be commenced, instituted, or prosecuted against any one or more of the directors, or against the treasurer or treasurers, or against the secretary or secretaries for the time being, of the society, as the nominal de-

N 2

fendant

fendant or defendants for and on behalf of the society. And by the 53 G. 3. c. 215., entitled " An act to enable the *Norwich* Union Society, for the insurance of lives and survivorships, to sue in the name of their secretary, and to be sued in the names of their directors, treasurers, and secretary," the same enactments and provisions were made for and on behalf of the *Norwich* Union Society, for the insurance of lives and survivorships, as were made in the act hereinbefore set forth for and on behalf of the *Norwich* Union Society for insurance against loss by fire. The defendants are, and at the time of making out the deposition of bankruptcy hereinafter mentioned, were two of the directors of the *Norwich* Union Society for the insurance of lives and survivorships; and the same persons are likewise directors of the *Norwich* Union Society for insurance against loss by fire. *Savery*, before his bankruptcy, was a marine insurance broker at *Bristol*, and agent at that place for both the said *Norwich* Union Societies, and as such agent was in the habit of corresponding with, and rendered his accounts to one *Samuel Bignold*, who held the office of secretary to both the said *Norwich* Union Societies. On the 10th of *June* 1820 a commission of bankrupt was issued against *Savery*, upon the petition of the said *Samuel Bignold*, who was described in the petition as secretary to the *Norwich* Union Society for insurance against loss by fire; which petition stated, that *Savery* was indebted to the said society in 100*l*. and upwards for premiums of insurance against fire, had and received by him, *Savery*, to the use of the said society; and upon this petition a commission of bankrupt issued against *Savery*, under the great seal, bearing date on the same day.

Tindal

Tindal for the plaintiffs. Two questions arise in
this case; first, whether it was competent to the secretary of the *Norwich* Union Society to petition for the
commission of bankruptcy; and, secondly, if it was
not, whether these defendants can make the objection.
Upon the true construction of the act it was competent
for the secretary to sue out the commission. The act
is to be considered in the nature of a remedial act, and
therefore should be construed so as to meet any difficulty, the removal of which the legislature may be supposed to have contemplated. The preamble recites,
that "difficulties have arisen, and may, from time to
time, arise, in recovering debts due to the society,"
and the object of the act was to remove those dif-
culties. Now the only effectual mode of recovering
a debt may be by suing out a commission of bankruptcy. The literal meaning of the enacting clause
certainly does not include that mode, but the secretary may take out execution, and a commission of
bankruptcy has been defined to be an action and
execution in the first instance, *Twiss* v. *Massey* (a), ex
parte *Freeman* (b): and although in ex parte *Brown* (c)
it is said to have greater powers than an execution
at law, yet that does not alter the definition, and in
ex parte *Elton* (d), Lord *Eldon* certainly says it is
not to be considered as an "execution at law;" but
the reason which he assigns is, that the distribution of
the effects under it is equitable. From these cases
it is very reasonable that a statute, meant to remove
difficulties in suing, should extend to petitioning for
a commission. To hold otherwise would be a very

(a) 1 *Atk.* 67.   (b) 1 *V. & B.* 41.
(c) 2 *Ves.* jun. 68. (d) 3 *Ves.* 238.

N 3   narrow

narrow construction of the act. In *Com. Dig. Parl.* (R 10) it is said, " every statute ought to be construed according to the intent of the parliament ;" and in (R 13) " the judges expound a case within the mischief and cause of an act, to be within the statute by equity, though it be not within the words." That principle, applied to this case, is decisive in favor of the plaintiffs. But, secondly, these defendants cannot object to the commission ; they are sued as directors of the life insurance company, but they are also directors of the company for insuring from fire, on behalf of which company the commission issued ; they are therefore estopped from disputing it. *Jacaud* v. *French.* (a) [Bayley J. There is this difficulty in the way of that position ; if the defendants were compelled to pay the money sought to be recovered in this action, and afterwards the commission should be superseded, and a valid one issued, they might be compelled to pay it over again.]

F. Pollock, contrà. With respect to the first and principal question, it is well known that the statutes relating to bankrupts are in the first instance construed strictly as to originating the jurisdiction. But when a good commission is established, then they are construed remedially, and therefore liberally. A fortiori, the act now in question should be construed strictly. It is called a public act, but is in truth private, being for the peculiar benefit of the individuals composing the *Norwich* Union Society. Petitioning for a commission of bankruptcy is a proceeding well known, and had it been intended to include it, no doubt the legislature would

(a) 12 *East,* 317.

have

have named it by proper words. The powers given by the act are in derogation of the common law rights of the parties affected by it, and therefore should be construed strictly, as all other powers are. In practice, a secretary to a society is not even allowed to prove under a commission without the leave of the Lord Chancellor. Besides, such a power as that contended for, would be inconsistent with the provisions of the 5 G. 2. c. 30. The secretary could not give the bond required by the twenty-third section of that act.

Tisdal, in reply. When a petition is sued out on a debt due to several, a bond given by one of them is sufficient to satisfy that enactment, *Ex parte Hodgkinson.* (a) [*Holroyd* J. Non constat, that the secretary is a creditor, for he may not be a member of the society.]

BAYLEY J. I am of opinion, that the commission from which alone the plaintiffs derive their right to sue cannot be supported. Unless we see very clearly that the meaning of the legislature goes beyond the words of the statute, we cannot do so. It is a dangerous rule of construction to introduce words not expressed, because they may be supposed to be within the mischief contemplated. The act is entitled, An act to enable the Society *to sue* in the name of their Secretary, and *to be sued* in that and certain other names. The expression *to sue*, generally speaking, means to bring actions, and the maxim, ad ea quæ frequentius accidunt jura adaptantur, applies to this case. Taking out a commission of bankruptcy is a well known mode of recovering a

(a) 2 *Rose*, 172.

debt,

debt, and if the legislature had intended to include that remedy, I should have expected to find more comprehensive words than *to sue*. A commission of bankruptcy is not ordinarily spoken of in that way. The act recites, indeed, that difficulties have arisen, and may from time to time arise in recovering debts due to the society, and those difficulties might be felt whether the proceeding to recover them was by suit or commission of bankruptcy. But had it been intended to extend the remedy beyond suits, words proper for that purpose would most probably have been introduced into the enacting part of the statute. The words there are, that " all actions and suits to be commenced by the society may be brought in the name of the secretary as nominal plaintiff." It is admitted, that those words are not sufficiently large to include the power in question, unless we can give them a more comprehensive meaning than they primâ facie bear. But both the title and the enacting part of the statute authorise a supposition, that the remedy was not meant to extend beyond the instances mentioned. This view of the case is corroborated by referring to the 5 G. 2. c. 30. s. 23., which could not any longer be complied with were the power contended for given to the society. The bond is to be given by the petitioning creditor, and the remedy is to be against him. The act before the court would not give the bankrupt power to sue the society for maliciously issuing a commission, and if it had been intended to give the power of thus suing out a commission, the other power should have been given also. The individuals composing the society could not be sued, for many of them might have opposed the measure. In this, as in all similar cases, we must look at the language used

used by the parties who bring in the act; they should be
careful to use such language as plainly includes all the
cases to which they mean it to apply. In this case they
have not done so, and I think that the rule for setting
aside the nonsuit must be discharged.

HOLROYD J. This statute is in effect a private act,
and must be construed as such, although it is made
public for the special purpose of being judicially noticed
by Courts of justice It is an act giving to individuals certain powers over others, and therefore must be construed
strictly. There is nothing shewing an intention to give
the power in question. It would be attended with this
difficulty in addition to those already pointed out; as
long as the society consisted of the same persons, a debt
of 100l. would be a sufficient petitioning creditor's debt;
but that would not be so if the debt accrued at different
times, and there were a change of the persons constituting
the society, for they are not a corporation. But if the
secretary could sue out the commission, it would be difficult to say whether the debt would or would not suffice.
The statute does not use words which vest the debts in
the secretary. It does not follow that he would be a
creditor at all, and the names of the members of the
society would not be mentioned in the petition, and
therefore it would not appear whose commission it is.
For these reasons, I think that the legislature had in
view only the ordinary proceedings by actions at law,
and perhaps suits in equity.

LITTLEDALE J. concurred.

Rule discharged.

WELLS *against* IGGULDEN.

DEBT for penalties under the 55 *G.* 3. *c.* 137. *s.* 6.

The first count of the declaration stated, that defendant was overseer of the poor of the parish of *Cranbrook*, in the county of *Kent*, and whilst he was such
overseer, to wit, on, &c., at, &c., did, in his own name,
provide, furnish, and supply, for his own profit, certain
goods and provisions for the support and maintenance
of the poor of the said parish in the workhouse of the
said parish, " whereby, and by force of the statute in
such case made and provided, the said defendant forfeited for his said offence the sum of 100*l.*, and thereby,
and by force of the statute in such case made and provided, an action hath accrued, &c." The second count
stated, that defendant, being overseer, provided and
supplied goods and provisions for the maintenance of
the poor of the said parish, (not stating in the workhouse,) and was in other respects like the first. The
third count varied only by stating that defendant was a
person in whose hands the providing for, ordering,
management, control, and direction of the poor of the
parish of *Cranbrook*, was duly placed. Plea, nil debet.
At the trial before *Alexander* C. B., at the last spring
assizes for *Kent*, the plaintiff recovered one penalty of
100*l.*, and in *Easter* term a rule was obtained for arresting the judgment, on two grounds ; first, that it was not
stated in any count of the declaration that the acts done
by the defendant were " against the form of the statute ;" and, secondly, that the declaration did not nega-

tive the exceptions contained in the sixth section of the
act by which the penalty is given.

Abraham shewed cause. The only question upon the
first point is, whether the language of the declaration is
sufficient to bring the offence within the statute, the act
done not being an offence at common law, but made so
by statute. This declaration does shew that the offence
is one created by statute, and that the act done was
against the statute. It first states the facts, and then
says, " whereby and by force of the statute the defendant forfeited 100*l.* for his said offence." It also shews
that the remedy is given by statute, for it alleges in
conclusion, " and thereby, and by force of the statute,
an action hath accrued, &c." In *Coundell* v. *John* (a)
it is said, " where a statute introduces a new law, by
giving an action where there was none before, or by
giving a new action in an old case, the plaintiff need not
conclude contrà formam statuti." The offence in this
case is created and the remedy given by the same statute, it has no relation to any other, and therefore
the decision in *Lee* v. *Clarke* (b) is not in point; but
what was then said by *Lawrence* J. is very important
for the plaintiff. That was an action for a penalty
on the game laws, and the right to recover depended
upon several statutes. The declaration did not conclude contrà formam statuti, but " whereby and by
force of the statute an action hath accrued, &c."
Lawrence J. says, " If it had said *statutes*, in the
plural number, perhaps that might have done, but
it certainly is not sufficient with reference only to
the statute 2 *G. 3. c.* 19., because that alone would not
support the action." In the *Earl Clanricarde* v. *Stokes* (c)

(a) 2 *Salk.* 505.   (b) 2 *East*, 333.   (c) 7 *East*, 516.

the

the offence was created by one statute, and the action given by another; the declaration stated that the act was done " against the form of the statute, by reason whereof, and by force of the statute in such case made, &c., an action hath accrued, &c.," and this was holden good; and from the dictum before cited from *Lee* v. *Clarke*, it may be inferred that the latter allegation would have sufficed by itself, if the same statute had created the offence and given the penalty. The other objection is disposed of by *Jones* v. *Axen* (a), for here the exception comes by way of proviso, and is not incorporated with that part of the act which creates the offence; the plaintiff, therefore, was not bound to take notice of it in his declaration.

Chitty, contrà. The dictum of *Lawrence* J. in *Lee* v. *Clarke* does not amount to any thing like a decision. He merely says, *perhaps* it might have sufficed, if the declaration had said " by force of the *statutes*," in the plural number. · An indictment for an offence created by statute would clearly be bad for want of the conclusion, " contrà formam statuti," (b). In the present instance the allegation " whereby, and by force of the statute, the defendant forfeited 100*l.*" is a conclusion without the statement of sufficient premises, and on a plea of nil debet the only question would be, whether the act had been done as alleged ? Now, all the facts stated might be true, and yet might have happened before the passing of the act. Secondly, the declaration should have negatived the exceptions, they being contained in the same section that creates the offence. [*Holroyd* J. The exception is totally separate from the enactment, it was not, therefore, necessary for the plaintiff to negative it.

(a) 1 *Ld. Raym.* 119.   (b) *Hawk. P. C.* b. 2. c. 25. s. 116, 117.

Had

1824.

Wells
against
Iggulden.

Had it formed a qualification of that which went before, and been incorporated with it, then it would have been necessary, according to the rule laid down in *Stowel* v. *Lord Zouch (c)*, and *Newis* v. *Lark. (d)* Bayley J. Upon that point I have no doubt; statutes are not divided into sections upon the rolls of parliament, and therefore the mere placing of the proviso in the same section of the printed act, does not make it necessary to notice it in pleading, unless it is also incorporated in the enacting sentence; as to the other point

Cur. adv. vult.

On the following day the judgment of the Court was delivered by

BAYLEY J. This was an action on the 55 G. 3. c. 137. s. 6., and a motion was made in arrest of judgment, on the ground that it was not alleged in any count of the declaration, either in the introductory part, that the defendant not regarding the statute did the act in question; nor at the conclusion, that the act done was done against the form of the statute. But the conclusion did state " whereby, and by force of the statute, the defendant hath forfeited, for his said offence, 100*l.*;" and it was argued that that might be considered as a substantive allegation that the act was against the statute. It is observable, however, that those words are stated as an inference of law, and describe the party as forfeiting for his *said offence.* There are several authorities which decide, that in indictments for offences created by statute, and even in actions on statutes giving a penalty to the party grieved, you must state that the act done is against the form of the statute. Thus, in *Doctr. Plac.* 332.,

" If

" If an action be brought against a man, on a statute, the plaintiff should recite the special matter, and say, that it is against the form of the statute;" and in 2 *Hale*, *P. C.* 189. " if an offence be newly enacted, or made an offence of an higher nature, by act of parliament, the indictment must conclude, contrà formam statuti," and this is repeated in p. 192. *Bennet* v. *Talbois* (a) is to the same effect. In *Andrew* v. *The Hundred of Lewknor* (b), the plaintiff declared on the statute of *Winton*, 13 *Edw.* 1., and shewed that he had performed the limitations and ordinances in the statute 27 *Eliz. c.* 13., and concluded, " contrà formam statuti," and it was objected that it ought to have been " contrà formam statutorum," but it was held sufficient, the action being given by the former statute only; and the same point was decided in *Merrick* v. *The Hundred of Ossulston.* (c) Now, the question there agitated could never have arisen, unless it had been considered that it was necessary to conclude either " contrà formam statuti," or " statutorum;" for otherwise the allegation would have been surplusage. In *Lee* v. *Clarke* the question was distinctly raised, and I consider that case as deciding, that in penal actions it is essential to state that the act complained of is against the form of the statute. Since the determination of that case, that of *Lord Clanricarde* v. *Stokes* has been decided, coinciding with the former in principle; but it was there considered that the declaration did, in effect, contain such an allegation. The case of *Coundell* v. *John*, cited from 2 *Salk.* 505., created some doubt in my mind, and I was therefore desirous of looking into it. From the report in *Salkeld*, it would

---

(a) 1 *Ld. Raym.* 149.   5 *Mod.* 307.   (b) *Yelv.* 116.   *Noy.* 125.
(c) *Cas. temp. Hardw.* 409.   *Andr.* 115.

certainly

certainly seem that the allegation, " contrà formam statuti," was considered unnecessary. But that varies from
the other reports of the same case; and looking at that
which is given by *Fortescue* (a), who argued the case, it
appears that the question could not have arisen as stated
by *Salkeld*, and that the doctrine reported by him was not
called for.   It was an action against a wrong-doer, and
two questions arose ; first, whether an action could be
maintained at common law, and, secondly, whether, on
that declaration, the plaintiff could recover under statute
7 & 8 *W*. 3. *c.* 25.   It was not, therefore, a question whether, in an action upon that statute, the declaration must
conclude " contrà formam statuti," but whether the declaration before the Court could be considered as a declaration upon that statute, and it was held it could not.
Salkeld was therefore clearly mistaken as to the grounds
of the decision.   Inasmuch then as this was a penal
action, not even brought by the party grieved, but by
an informer, it appears to us that the statement of the
offence could not be sufficient, unless the facts were set
out and alleged to be done " contrà formam statuti."
The rule for arresting the judgment must therefore be
made absolute.

Rule absolute.

(a) P. 104., by the names of *Kendall* v. *John*.

MURTHWAITE *v.* JENKINSON.

WHEN this case came before the Lord Chancellor
for judgment, his Lordship agreed with the opinion
given by this Court (a) as to the freehold property ; but
with respect to the personalty, held that the limitation
over was good.

(a) 2 B. & C. 357.

E. Fletcher, and Others, Assignees of the Estate and Effects of R. Simpson, a Bankrupt, *against* T. Pogson and G. Thomas, Bail of H. F. Y. Pogson and Isabella his Wife.

Declaration in sci. fa. stated that " R. S., (the plaintiff in the original action,) became bankrupt, whereupon a commission was duly awarded against him, and E. F., R. B., and J. T. (the plaintiffs in the sci. fa.) were duly chosen assignees of the estate and effects of the said R. S. under the commission, and now on behalf of the said E. F., R. B., and J. T., as assignees as aforesaid, we have been informed, &c.:" Held, that this was good, (defendant not having demurred to it,) without an express averment that

DECLARATION in scire facias, after reciting a recognizance entered into by the defendants, as bail in an action brought by *R. Simpson* against *Pogson* and wife, and a judgment for the plaintiff in that action, which is still unsatisfied, proceeded thus: " and whereas the said *R. Simpson* afterwards became bankrupt, within the true intent and meaning of the several statutes made and then in force concerning bankrupts, some or one of them; whereupon a certain commission of bankrupt, under the great seal of the United Kingdom of *Great Britain* and *Ireland*, was duly awarded and issued against the said *R. Simpson*, and *E. Fletcher*, *R. Berry*, and *J. Tiplady*, were duly chosen assignees of the estate and effects of the said *R. Simpson*, under the said commission; and now on behalf of the said *E. Fletcher*, *R. Berry*, and *J. Tiplady*, as assignees as aforesaid, in our said court before us, we have been informed, &c." The issuing of two writs of scire facias and the returns were then set out, and the declaration concluded; " and thereupon the said

an assignment of the bankrupt's effects was made; for that the expression " assignees as aforesaid" might mean " persons to whom an assignment has been made;" and the 5 G. 2. c. 30. s. 26. having directed the choice of assignees to be followed up by an assignment of the effects to the persons chosen, the Court might presume that such an assignment was made.

Semble, that the objection would have been fatal if made the ground of special demurrer.

E. Fletcher,

E. Fletcher, *R. Berry*, and *J. Tiplady*, assignees as aforesaid, pray that execution may be adjudged to them against the said *T. Pogson* and *G. Thomas*, of the damages aforesaid, according to the form and effect of the said recognizance." Plea, that there was no ca. sa. duly issued out against the said *H. F. Y. Pogson* and wife upon the said judgment, and duly returned. Replication, setting out a ca. sa. and return. Demurrer and joinder.

Abraham, in support of the demurrer. The declaration in this case is bad, inasmuch as it does not state that an assignment of the estate and effects of the bankrupt was made to the plaintiffs. It merely avers, that the plaintiffs were chosen assignees; that alone does not give them a title to sue, an assignment to them by the commissioners should also have been set out.

Curwood, contra, referred to the form in *Tidd's App.* 548., and contended, that as the 5 *G*. 2. *c*. 30. *s*. 26. requires that the choice of assignees shall be followed by an assignment to them, it must be presumed that such assignment was duly made.

BAYLEY J. The form adopted in this case follows that given by Mr. *Tidd*, with this exception, that here the word *as* is introduced before *assignees as aforesaid* ; but that makes no difference. The introduction of this form into the collection that I have mentioned does not, indeed, make it an authority, but in general the forms there given are extremely accurate, and we may take it for granted that this form has been in common use. That being so, and the 5 *G*. 2. *c*. 30. *s*. 26. directing that the commissioners *shall* assign the estate of the bankrupt to the persons chosen assignees, I think we are at liberty, on the whole record, to presume that such assignment was made. It is averred that *Fletcher, Berry,* and *Tiplady* were chosen assignees of the estate and effects of the bankrupt, and they are afterwards described as " assignees as aforesaid." That expression may apply not only to persons *chosen* assignees, but to persons being assignees of the estate and effects; that is, to persons to whom an assignment has been made. It is unnecessary to decide whether this would have sufficed had the defendants demurred, but I think, that having pleaded over, they are not in a situation to avail themselves of the objection, as the words are capable of receiving a construction which will support the proceeding.

HOLROYD J. Unless we could say upon this record that the scire facias was sued out after an assignment made to the persons chosen assignees of the bankrupt's estate, it would be insufficient; but there is a well-known rule of law that where, in pleading, matter is stated capable of receiving two constructions, and it is not demurred to, that construction may be given which supports, instead of defeating, the proceeding. Now, this record states the commission, and the choice of certain persons, assignees of the estate and effects of the bankrupt, and then goes on, " now on behalf of *J. F., &c. as assignees as aforesaid.*" If that can be read assignees of the estate and effects, it will suffice even without the allegation of the choice of assignees; but if it only means chosen assignees, it is insufficient. The expression being equivocal, we may, I think, for the reason before given,

put

put that construction upon it which supports the scire facias.

LITTLEDALE J. It appears to me that this declaration could not have been supported, had it been specially demurred to, for it does not clearly shew any thing more than an incipient title in the plaintiffs, to be perfected by an assignment. If it were apparent that they had not a complete title, pleading over would not cure the defect; but the matter being left in doubt I think that it does, for we may take the words as describing the plaintiffs as assignees of the estate of the bankrupt, and we may presume that an assignment was made to them in conformity to the directions of the 5 G. 2. c. 30. s. 26. For these reasons, I think that the demurrer must be overruled.

Judgment for the plaintiff. (a)

(a) See *Winter and Others v. Kretchman*, 2 *T. R.* 45.

1824.

MORRIS and Another *against* ROBINSON.

The master of a ship, which was injured by the perils of the sea, put into the *Mauritius,* and there abandoned the ship and cargo, which were afterwards sold under an order of the Vice-Admiralty Court there, and the proceeds paid into that court. The cargo was not damaged or perishable, nor was there any pressing necessity for the sale of it. The owners of the cargo brought an action on the case against the owners of the ship for wrongfully selling the cargo instead of carrying it to *London,* according to

ASSUMPSIT for money had and received. Plea, the general issue. At the trial before *Abbott* C. J., at the adjourned *London* sittings after last *Trinity* term, a verdict was found for the plaintiffs for 7,000*l.*, subject to the opinion of the Court upon the following case.

The plaintiffs and the defendant were merchants residing in *London.* On or about the third day of *December* 1820, the house of *Macintyre* and Co., of *Calcutta,* merchants, shipped on board the ship *Lady Banks,* whereof *Isaac Valance* was the master, 140 chests of indigo, the property, and an account and risk of the plaintiffs, under three several bills of lading signed by the captain, of which the following are the particulars : One bill of lading for 72 chests, ditto 45, ditto 23, total 140. By which bills of lading, the indigo was to be delivered in the port of *London* to the plaintiffs or their order. The *Lady Banks* sailed from *Calcutta* the 21st of *December* 1820, with the 140 chests of indigo on board, and a cargo of various other merchandise bound for the port of *London,* and afterwards put into *Trin-*

their contract, with a count in trover, and recovered a general verdict for the value of the ship and freight, which was one-fifth of the value of the cargo. They also sent out a power of attorney to an agent at the *Mauritius* to procure from the Vice-Admiralty Court there the proceeds of the sale which had been paid in. The agent demanded them, but they had been previously remitted to the High Court of Admiralty in this country. In an action for money had and received by the owners against the purchaser of the goods : Held, first, that the captain had not any authority to sell the cargo, although acting bonâ fide and under the order of the Vice-Admiralty Court ; secondly, that the recovery against the owners of the ship was no answer to the present action ; thirdly, that the proceeds of the sale at the *Mauritius* not having been paid when demanded, the plaintiffs were in the same situation as if no such demand had been made, and therefore entitled to recover the value of the goods from the defendant.

comalee

comalee for repairs. She sailed from *Trincomalee* on the 17th of *February* 1821, for *London*, and met with tempestuous weather, which occasioned her to become very leaky; during the bad weather about 600 bags of sugar were necessarily thrown overboard, and with much difficulty the ship was conducted to the island of the *Mauritius*, where she arrived on the 24th of *March* 1821, and assistance being procured, she was run upon a sand bank, with a view to the preservation of the ship and cargo, and it was necessary that the ship should be wholly unladen, and that she should be hove down in order to examine and repair the damages which had been sustained. The captain employed a proctor, and on the 24th of *March* petitioned the Vice Admiralty Court of that island, and under an order made by that court, the cargo was landed and deposited in warehouses. An accidental fire having happened at the warehouse where part of the cargo had been deposited, great part thereof was burnt or materially damaged, and it was sold by auction, and twenty-one chests of indigo were (by the proceedings of the Admiralty Court afterwards referred to) reported to be damaged, and were also sold by public auction, but these formed no part of the demand in the present action. After the sale there only remained of the whole cargo, 119 chests of the indigo comprised in the bills of lading before mentioned, and two sample chests of indigo, thirty casks of tallow, some buffaloes' horns, and a few packages of small value. In pursuance of an order of the said Vice Admiralty Court the ship was surveyed, and an estimate was made by competent persons upon oath, that the necessary repairs and other incidental expences to enable the ship to perform her voyage to *England* would amount to the sum of

25,669 dollars; and the surveyors reported, that if the ship had these repairs done to her, she would then be a good sound ship. Two merchants, however, residing at *Port Louis*, declared upon their oath in the proceedings in the Vice Admiralty Court their belief, that the amount of the repairs would far exceed the value of the ship when repaired. The captain had no funds, and could not procure any to pay for the repairs except by the sale of part of her cargo, but there was an opportunity to tranship the indigo from the *Mauritius* for *England* soon after the arrival of the vessel there, and such opportunity afterwards again occurred. Under these circumstances the captain, bonâ fide believing that the repairs would cost at least as much as the estimate before mentioned, thought it best for the interest of all concerned to abandon her and the residue of the cargo; and he accordingly entered protests to that effect on the 9th of *May* 1821. On the 12th of *May*, the judge of the Vice Admiralty Court made an order for the sale of the hull of the ship; and she was accordingly sold by auction, on the 14th of *May* 1821, for 1946 dollars, and her stores, &c. for 7503 dollars. The ship was afterwards repaired at *Port Louis*, and sailed from the *Mauritius* on a voyage to *China* on account of the purchaser. After three surveys, ordered by the Vice Admiralty Court, upon the 119 chests of indigo which remained; and the reports of the surveyors thereupon that they were sound, the said judge, on the 16th of *May* 1821, made the following order: " Let the within goods, abandoned under the protest of the captain of the *Lady Banks*, be forthwith sold by public auction, and the proceeds immediately lodged in the registry of this court." The 119 chests of indigo were, in pursuance of the said order, sold by public auction by the deputy marshal of that court, after having been advertised in the *Gazette*, and otherwise notified to the inhabitants of the island in the most public manner; and in such advertisements and notifications, it was stated that the indigo had been part of the cargo of the ship *Lady Banks*; and that the same would be sold by the order and under the authority of the Vice Admiralty Court, by the deputy marshal of that court. The agent of the defendant then being at the *Mauritius*, who was no party to the proceedings in the Vice Admiralty Court, attended in consequence of the public notification of the sale, and became the purchaser of 20 chests of the indigo, and paid the price for the same into the Court, and the indigo was delivered to him. The defendant's agent, a few days after this sale, purchased from Messrs. *Blaize* and *Baudet*, merchants at *Port Louis*, 32 chests of the said indigo, which they had previously purchased at the auction, and agreed to give an advance of 5½ per cent. upon the price which *Blaize* and *Baudet* had paid for the same at the public sale. The defendant's agent paid *Blaize* and *Baudet* that sum, and received from them the said 32 chests of indigo. The damaged part of the cargo, which was first sold, as before mentioned, produced 11,879 dollars, and the 119 chests of indigo produced 52,321 dollars, and the amount thereof, and of the proceeds of the ship and stores, as before mentioned, reduced, by means of the incidental expences, to 53,846 dollars, or 8109l. 6s. 11d. sterling, have been remitted by the register of the Vice-Admiralty Court to the High Court of Admiralty in *England*, and now remain in the last mentioned court. The 52 chests of indigo, purchased by the defendant's

agent,

agent, formed part of the indigo mentioned in the three bills of lading, and in the following proportions, viz.

15 chests, part of the 72 chests in the first bill of lading mentioned.
19 - - 45 - second ditto.
18 - - 23 - third ditto.

On the 12th of *June* 1821, 20 of the said 52 chests of indigo were shipped on board the *Woodbridge*, and on 12th of *July* the remaining 32 chests were shipped per the *Asia* for the port of *London*. Both ships arrived at that port in the month of *October* 1821; and the 52 chests have been delivered to the defendant. Soon after the indigo arrived in the port of *London*, the plaintiffs gave notice to the defendant, that they were the original proprietors of the said 52 chests of indigo, and claimed the delivery thereof to them, but the defendant refused to deliver the indigo to the plaintiffs, and afterwards sold and disposed of the same, and received the proceeds thereof. In respect of the 72 chests of indigo, contained in the bill of lading first mentioned, the plaintiffs have commenced an action against the owners of the *Lady Banks*, for not carrying the same indigo to *London*, but selling the same unlawfully, as it was alleged, at the *Mauritius*, and the plaintiffs have obtained a verdict against the said owners in that action, under which they will be entitled to recover from the owners to the extent of the value of the ship and her freight; but it is admitted, that the sum which they will receive therefrom will not exceed 1500*l.*, and the 72 chests mentioned in the first bill of lading, were of the value of 7000*l.* and upwards. In respect of the 45 chests of indigo in the second bill of lading mentioned, the plaintiffs, after they had received information of the sale of the indigo, under the circumstances aforesaid, executed

18   and

and sent out a power of attorney to Messrs. *Saunders* and *Wicke*, of the *Mauritius*, empowering them to claim and receive out of the said Vice-Admiralty Court the sum which was produced by the sale of the said 45 chests, and they did accordingly apply to the registrar of the said Vice-Admiralty Court, and claimed to receive such proceeds, but the same had then been remitted to *England*. In respect of the 23. chests of indigo in the third bill of lading mentioned, the plaintiffs have not taken any measures, nor pursued any remedy, except the proceeding in the present action. The 52 chests, so purchased by the defendant's agent, were sound and in good order, and free from damage, when the same were purchased by them at the *Mauritius* as aforesaid, and when they came into the possession of the defendant in *London*.

F. Pollock for the plaintiffs. There are here two questions; the first, whether the plaintiffs ever had a right to bring this action; the second, whether they have lost that right by any of the steps which they have taken in the transaction. *Freeman* v. *E. I. Company* (a) is decisive as to the first question: it was there decided that the captain of a ship has no authority to sell the cargo, except in cases of absolute necessity. Here no necessity is apparent on the case, but the reverse. The goods were not damaged or perishable, they were not sold to repair the ship, or pay other expences. The only difference between the cases is, that here the Vice-Admiralty Court ordered the sale; but it had no authority to do so. Then the circumstance of there being

(a) 5 B. & A. 617.

two

two purchases, one at the auction and the other of those who bought there, makes no difference, for the second was made with full notice, that the vendor purchased at the auction. But it will be urged that the plaintiffs have lost their right of action as to the first parcel, by bringing an action against the owners of the vessel. To that argument there are two answers; first, no judgment has been obtained in that action, the plaintiffs may abandon it, the defendant could not even have pleaded it in abatement had the two actions been concurrent. Again, the remedy against the owner is limited to the value of the ship and freight, which in this instance amounted to 1500*l.*, and the claim exceeds 7000*l.*, as found by the case. If, therefore, the plaintiffs get the 1500*l.*, they may apply it to that part of the indigo in the first bill of lading which did not get into the defendant's hands. As to the parcel bought out of those in the second bill of lading the plaintiffs cannot be prejudiced by sending out a power of attorney to receive the proceeds, for the agent never did receive them; the plaintiffs are, therefore, in the same situation as if that power had not been sent out.

Campbell, contrà. By the sale which took place under the order of the Vice-Admiralty Court, the property in the indigo passed to the defendant. It must be admitted, that the purchase made after the public sale stands on the same footing as the other, but all parties having acted bonâ fide the property was transferred, although the case was not one of strict necessity. The captain may be liable to the shipper, but still if he acts bonâ fide according to the best of his judgment, the foreign purchaser is safe. The case of *Freeman* v. *E. I.*

Company

Company is certainly, to some extent, an authority on the other side, but there the decree of the Vice-Admiralty Court was wanting. [*Bayley* J. We cannot take notice of that decree.] Such an opinion was thrown out in *Reid* v. *Darby* (*a*), but that case was decided on the ground that the register act had not been complied with. It must be presumed that that court acted within the scope of its authority in making the decree. But if that general question be determined in favour of the plaintiffs, still, as to the seventy-two chests, and the forty-five, the owners must be considered as having ratified the sale. The form of the action brought against the shipowner for the seventy-two is material. It was in tort for not carrying them according to contract. The second count alleged that he had sold them: the third was in trover. The action was brought for the whole seventy-two chests, and, therefore, for those which the defendant bought out of that parcel, as well as for the rest. The plaintiffs recovered a general verdict, as appears by the report of the case under the names of *Cannan and Others* v. *Meaburn* (*b*), but the judgment would be best supported on the count in trover, the obligation to transship being very doubtful. It is said that judgment has not been entered up, if so, that is the fault of the plaintiffs and cannot prejudice this defendant. Now a recovery in trover vests the property in the defendant, otherwise, if he sold the goods after the recovery in that action, the new purchaser would also be liable to such an action, and the same would apply to each person into whose hands the goods might pass. It makes no difference that the responsibility of the ship-owner is

(*a*) 10 *East*, 141.   (*b*) 1 *Bing.* 243.

limited

limited by the 53 G. 3. c. 159.; besides, that does not apply to actions of trover. The plaintiffs in that action sought to recover the difference between the proceeds of the sale at the *Mauritius* and the sum which the indigo would have produced here; by so doing they ratified the sale. So also the demand of the proceeds of the forty-five chests amounted to a ratification of the sale: a personal demand by the plaintiff of the defendant would certainly have had that effect, and the demand by the plaintiffs' agent of the registrar of the Vice-Admiralty Court, who may be considered as the defendant's agent in this transaction, has the same effect.

BAYLEY J. There is no doubt but the master of a ship may hypothecate the cargo for the purposes of the voyage, but beyond that he has no right to act as agent for the owner of the goods, unless in cases of absolute necessity. The decree of the Vice-Admiralty Court constitutes the only difference between this case and *Freeman* v. *E. I. Company*. But without meaning to speak at all disrespectfully of that court, I cannot say that I think it had any jurisdiction. The decree can only be looked upon as the fair opinion of a person residing on the spot, for as it is not found as a fact that the court there had jurisdiction, we cannot make it the foundation of our judgment. There was not any necessity for the sale of the cargo; it was not damaged or perishable. It being my opinion then, upon the general question, that the purchaser obtained no property by the act of the person who professed to sell, two questions arise as to the seventy-two chests, to which the former recovery applies, and the forty-five chests, for the proceeds of

which

which the power of attorney was sent out. The whole argument on these two points proceeds on the ground that the defendant had no property in the goods but what he acquired by the confirmation of the plaintiffs. To take the second parcel first; when the owners heard that a wrongful sale had been effected at the *Mauritius,* and that the proceeds were lodged in the Vice-Admiralty. Court, surely they might endeavour to obtain those proceeds without ratifying the sale; but the agent did not succeed in obtaining them; the plaintiffs, therefore, are left in the same situation as if no application had. been made to that court. Then as to the seventy-two chests, the facts stand thus: the plaintiffs brought an action against the owners for the breach of their duty as carriers, with a count in trover. The jury might, on that count, have given the full value of the goods in damages, but their power on the special counts was restricted to a certain amount, and the verdict was restricted to that amount. No judgment has been entered up, and therefore there has been no actual satisfaction. It is argued that the plaintiffs had merely an election to sue the owners for the misconduct of the captain or the defendant for the value of the goods. But independently of the 53 *G.*3. *c.*159., the jury were not bound to make the full value of the goods the measure of the damages in the former action. They might reasonably give small damages, on the ground that an action would lie against the purchasers. If concurrent actions had been brought, that against the owners could not have barred the other; why then should it have that effect because they have been brought at different times? If indeed the plaintiffs were to recover the full value of the goods in each action, a court of equity would interfere

to

to prevent them from having a double satisfaction, but there is nothing in the former action which can, in a court of law, prevent the recovery in this.

HOLROYD J. I am of opinion that all the questions that have been raised must be decided in favor of the plaintiffs. *Freeman* v. *East India Company*, and *Reid* v. *Darby*, shew that the captain has not any authority to sell the cargo, unless in cases of absolute necessity, even although the sale be sanctioned by a Vice-Admiralty Court. With respect to the action against the owners, the verdict recovered in that is not in law sufficient to bar or diminish the plaintiffs' claim in this proceeding. The very ground of that action was, that the sale was wrongful; it cannot therefore be a ratification. But where in trover the full value of the article has been recovered, it has been held, that the property is changed by judgment and satisfaction of the damages. Unless the full amount is recovered, it would not bar even other actions in trover. Here it is plain that the full value had not been recovered on the count in trover; the value of the goods mentioned in that action was 7000*l.*, the verdict 1500*l.*, to which sum the verdict on the other counts was necessarily limited. The probability of a recovery in an action against this defendant might keep down the damages given on the count in trover. In an action against a sheriff for an escape, small damages are often given, on the ground that the debt is not extinguished; and the whole amount may afterwards be recovered, notwithstanding the recovery against the sheriff. The former action brought by these plaintiffs against the ship-owners is not, then, any legal ground for diminishing the sum to be recovered in this.

The

The power of attorney clearly furnishes no defence;
nothing was done upon it; a demand, indeed, was made,
but the money was not given up.

LITTLEDALE J.   I am of the same opinion.   It is
admitted that the sale was not under the pressure of necessity.   As to the decree of the Vice-Admiralty Court,
if it had authority to make it, that should have been
stated in the case.   It has no such power by the law of
nations, and no such authority is exercised by the Court
of Admiralty here.   Suppose an action had been brought
against an officer of that court, and he pleaded a justification, his authority must have been set out.   Then, as
to the recovery in the former action; in the first place
there has been no judgment in that case; and if one
party attempts to avail himself of the technical effect of
such a recovery, the other may set up a technical answer,
viz. that judgment has not been entered up.   But an
action of trover is clearly no bar; unless the full value
has been recovered; here the verdict amounted to little
more than one-fifth of the value.   The justice of the case
then is, that the plaintiffs should be allowed to recover
the residue.   The power of attorney merely amounted
to this; the plaintiffs were willing to waive the tort, and
take the money lodged in the Vice-Admiralty Court;
but they could not procure it.   Surely that ought not to
bar their claim on those who had the goods.   For these
reasons I think that the plaintiffs were entitled to recover for all the indigo purchased by the defendant.

Postea to the plaintiffs.

Ball. v. Banks 3. Scott's NR 497.
Yates v. Aston 4. 2 B 182.

TWOPENNY and BOYS *against* YOUNG.

ASSUMPSIT on a joint and several promissory note,
bearing date *March* the 10th, 1817, given to the
plaintiffs by the defendant and one *Rummen*, for 290*l.*, and
interest, payable on demand. Plea, non-assumpsit. At
the trial before *Graham* B., at the *Kent* Summer assizes,
1823, it appeared, that *Rummen*, a publican, at the time
when the note was given, was indebted to the plaintiffs,
distillers, in the sum of 290*l.*, and being asked for security, got the defendant to join in the note declared
upon. The partnership was soon after dissolved. *Boys*
took upon himself all the debts and credits of the firm,
and carried on the business alone, and continued to deal
with *Rummen* as before, until the end of 1820, during
which period the latter paid him 676*l.* for goods furnished, and interest on the note. A balance of 380*l.*
for the note and goods sold was then due to *Boys*, who
asked for further security, and on the 6th of *January*
1821 *Rummen* gave him a bill of sale, by which (after
reciting that 380*l.* was due to *Boys*, and that for 290*l.*,
parcel of that sum, *Rummen* and defendant had given
the note in question, and that *Boys* having called for
payment, *Rummen* had requested him to accept such
further security as thereinafter mentioned :) as *a further
security Rummen* assigned to *Boys* all his household
goods, &c. By a stipulation in the bill of sale, *Rummen*
was to be allowed to continue in possession during his
life, subject to have it determined, on three days' notice,
at any time afterwards, whilst the said sum of 380*l.*, or

any

any part remained due. *Rummen* continued in possession, and dealt with *Boys* as before, until *March*, 1823, and between that time and the 6th of *January* 1821, he paid *Boys* 500*l.* for goods furnished by him.   In *February* 1823, a commission of bankruptcy issued against *Rummen*, on an act of bankruptcy committed in *October* 1822; and on the 4th of *March* 1823 payment of the note in question was demanded of the defendant. *Marryat* for the defendant, contended, first, that the note was merged in the bill of sale, that being a security of an higher nature; secondly, that the agreement to give three days'- notice, under the bill of sale, was giving time to the principal, and therefore discharged the surety.   The learned Judge overruled the objections, but gave the defendant leave to move to enter a nonsuit. The plaintiff having obtained a verdict, *Marryat*, in *Michaelmas* term, obtained a rule, according to the leave reserved, against which

Abraham now shewed cause.   If the bill of sale had been given in discharge of the promissory note, undoubtedly this action could not be maintained.   But it was merely a *further* security; that is the very expression used in the instrument itself, and being given as a collateral security, it does not take away the remedy on the note; *Drake* v. *Mitchell.* (a)   Neither does the covenant not to sue *Rummen* until after notice operate as a release of the defendant, or as a restraint upon the right of action before existing on the note.   *Dean* v. *Newhall.* (b)

(a) 3 *East*, 251.   (b) 8 *T. R.* 168.

Marryat, contrà. Taking a new security discharged the principal from the old one, and created a new liability, not to be enforced until after three days' notice: that also discharged the surety. The case of *Drake* v. *Mitchell* is no authority on the other side, for there the original security was a specialty, and the new one a mere simple contract. So, also, in *Davey* v. *Prendergrass* (a) the original debt being on bond, it was held, that giving time by parol to the principal did not discharge the surety; but it may be collected from the case, that the judgment of the court would have been different, had the indulgence been given by specialty. In equity the rule is carried to the whole extent contended for in *Davey* v. *Prendergrass*; *Boultbee* v. *Stubbs*. (b)

BAYLEY J. It is not necessary to decide in this case, whether a creditor, by giving time to his principal debtor, does or does not thereby discharge a surety: because I think that the instrument in question did not give time to the principal. It recites, that 380*l.* was due to *Boys*, and that a note had been given for 290*l.*, parcel of that sum, by the defendant and *Rummen*. It then states that *Boys* had called upon *Rummen* for payment, and that the latter requested him to accept a further security, and then contains an assignment of certain property to a trustee for *Boys*. The deed then being intended as a *further* security, and reciting an *existing* security, given by the defendant as a surety, could not have been intended to operate as an extinguishment of all claims upon him. In general, where

(a) 5 B & A. 187.　　　　(b) 18 Ves. 20.

a simple

a simple contract security for a debt is given, it is extinguished by a specialty security, if the remedy given by the latter is co-extensive with that which the creditor had upon the former. We are not called upon to say whether that would be the case when the remedies are not co-extensive; for where there is that in the instrument which shews that the parties intended the original security to remain in force, the new one has not the effect of extinguishing it, as was recently decided in the case of *Solly* v. *Forbes* and *Ellerman*. (a) There, a release was given to one of two partners, with a proviso that it should not operate to deprive the plaintiff of any remedy which he otherwise would have against the other partner; and that he might, notwithstanding the release, sue them jointly. A joint action having been commenced, the party released pleaded the release, to which plaintiff replied, that he sued him only in order to recover against the other; and, on demurrer, the replication was held good. Here, the language of the bill of sale shews that it was intended merely as a further security; that makes the effect of it the same as if an express proviso had been inserted, and prevents it from operating as an extinguishment of the remedy on the note, either as against *Rummen* or the defendant. This rule must therefore be discharged.

HOLROYD J. I am of opinion that the ground of the action which has been brought against the defendant was not extinguished by the deed in question. It is clear from the recital, that it was intended that the note should continue an existing security, and the deed

(a) 2 B. & D. 38.

is

is not strong enough to operate by law in destruction of that intention. The plaintiffs might at any time, notwithstanding the deed, have sued on the note. The deed is a conveyance of personal property, with a condition, that the covenantee may put an end to the covenantor's possession after three days' notice; nor could he have acted on the covenant until after notice had been given. But he does not stipulate not to sue upon the note until after the expiration of the three days. The deed gives no action of an higher nature against the defendant *Young*. The case of *Dean* v. *Newhall* is in point and stronger than this. Had *Boys* covenanted not to sue at all, either on the note or deed, until after the expiration of three days, it would have been exactly in point. The deed, therefore, cannot operate in discharge of the defendant. It is observable, also, that the deed was a security to *Boys* alone, not to *Twopenny* and *Boys*; but, under the circumstances of this case, I do not rely upon that, but upon the intent appearing on the face of the deed.

LITTLEDALE J. concurred.

Rule discharged.

FACEY *against* HURDOM.

CASE for not carrying away tithes. The declaration stated that defendant, in the year 1823, was farmer of the tithes of corn growing on certain closes in the parish of *E.*, in the county of *Cornwall ;* and that plaintiff was tenant and occupier of those closes which were in that year sown with barley and oats; that on, &c. the plaintiff cut the barley and oats, and then and there *lawfully and in due manner* divided, separated, and set out thereon, the tenth part or tithe respectively of the said barley and oats from the nine parts, residue thereof, on the said closes, and there left the same for the use of defendant; and afterwards, to wit, on, &c. at, &c. gave notice thereof to defendant, who did not, nor would, in a reasonable time afterwards carry the same away, &c. Plea, general issue. At the trial before *Bosanquet* Serjt. at the last Spring assizes for *Cornwall*, it appeared that the plaintiff had for several years been tenant of the premises mentioned in the declaration; and that the defendant also had for several years been the farmer of the corn tithes. On the 19th of *September* 1823, and after the corn in question had been put into shocks, each consisting of twelve sheaves, the plaintiff sent notice to the defendant, who lived about a mile and a half from him, that on the following morning he should tithe the corn. It was accordingly tithed by setting out the 10th shock, and the plaintiff began to lead away the other nine parts at seven o'clock in the morning. The defendant had not been there at that time, but one of the

Where, in case for not carrying away tithe-corn, the plaintiff alleged that it was " lawfully and in due manner" set out : Held, that this allegation was satis- . fied by proof, that the tithe was set out according to an agreement between the parties, although it varied from the mode prescribed by the common law.

Whether the whole crop has been left on the ground for a reasonable time after the tithe has been set out, in order that the tithe owner may compare the tenth part with the other nine, is a question for the jury, and not for the Court.

plaintiff's

plaintiff's witnesses, who had assisted in setting out the tithe, stated that he met the defendant at nine o'clock, who said he was coming to tithe the corn; witness answered that it had been done, and that plaintiff was leading it; defendant asked how many dozens (*i.e.* shocks) there were, and did not then complain that he was deprived of the opportunity of comparing the tenth shock with the other nine. Defendant had for four years taken the tithe of the plaintiff's land in kind, and it had during all that time been set out in shocks, and not in single sheaves. It was objected for the defendant, that the plaintiff had not proved his allegation, that the tithe was " lawfully and in due manner" set out; for that, by the common law, it must be set out in the sheaf and not in the shock. The learned Judge thought, that if it was set out according to an agreement between the parties, that would be sufficient, but gave the defendant leave to move to enter a nonsuit on that point. It was then objected, that there was not any evidence of an agreement, or that, at all events, it must be taken to have been subject to a condition that the whole of the corn should remain a reasonable time on the ground, so that the tithe-owner might compare the tenth shock with the others. The learned Judge held, that the reasonableness of the time was a question for the jury, and he left it to them to say, first, whether the tithe was set out according to an agreement between the parties; and, secondly, whether the whole of the corn had been left on the ground for a reasonable space of time. A verdict with 40*s.* damages having been found for the plaintiff, a rule nisi for a nonsuit or new trial was obtained in *Easter* term; and now the Court called upon

Erskine

Erskine and *Carter* to support it. The plaintiff having declared generally, that he set out the tithe lawfully and in due manner, was bound to prove that it was set out as required by the common law. Now, that requires it to be set out in the first convenient state in which the tithe can be collected after the corn is cut, which is in sheaves, *Shallcross* v. *Jowle*. (a) If the plaintiff intended to rely upon a supposed agreement, he should have made that the foundation of his action, otherwise the defendant, not being apprized of the nature of the plaintiff's case, would be taken by surprise. Secondly, the agreement must at all events have been subject to a condition, that the tithe-owner should have a reasonable time for comparing the tithe-shocks with the residue of the corn, and it was for the judge and not the jury to decide whether sufficient time for that purpose had or had not been allowed.

BAYLEY J. I am of opinion that there is not any ground for entering a nonsuit in this case. Although it has been correctly stated, that by the common law the tithe should be set out in sheaves, yet modus et conventio vincunt legem, and therefore if the tithe was set out according to an agreement between the parties, the plaintiff might properly allege that it was " lawfully and in due manner" set out. As to the other points the only question is, whether the learned Judge misdirected the jury, for the Court will not grant a new trial on the ground of the verdict being against evidence where the damages do not amount to 20*l*. Now, there certainly was sufficient evidence of an agreement to be left to the

(a) 13 *East*, 261.

P 4   decision

decision of a jury. Then it has been argued, that the learned Judge should have decided whether the whole of the corn was or was not left on the ground for a reasonable time after the tithe was set out. There certainly are cases where it is for the Judge to say what is a reasonable time, viz. in giving notice of the dishonor of a bill or note. But in this instance the question depended upon a variety of circumstances, such as the residence of the respective parties, the time when notice was given that the corn would be tithed, the state of the weather and other things most proper for the consideration of a jury, and I think that the question was properly left to them. The rule must therefore be discharged.

HOLROYD J.   I think that the proof in this case satisfied the allegation, that the tithe was lawfully and in due manner set out. Where there is not any agreement, the law prescribes the mode in which it shall be done. But the parties may by agreement dispense with that mode, and the tithe set out according to agreement, is lawfully and in due manner set out. It appeared in evidence that the defendant had taken the tithe of corn in kind for four years, and that it had always been set out in the same way. Perhaps that of itself might not have been sufficient, but there was also evidence of an actual agreement, for when the defendant was told that the corn had been tithed, he asked how many dozens or shocks there were; whence it might be inferred, that he had agreed that the tithe should be set out in shocks. The latter circumstance makes an important distinction between this case and *Shallcross* v. *Jowle*.

LITTLE-

LITTLEDALE J. This is an action arising out of the
relative situation in which the parties stood with respect
to each other. The law imposes upon the landholder
the duty of setting out the tithe, and leaving it, together
with the other nine parts, on the ground for a reasonable
time, and then it becomes the duty of the tithe-owner to
carry it away. The mode of setting out the tithe may
either be that which is pointed out by the common law,
or that which is established by custom, or by the particular agreement of the parties. In a declaration against
the tithe-owner for a breach of duty in neglecting to
carry away the tithe corn, it is not necessary to state
the mode of setting it out. It is sufficient to say, that it
was " lawfully and in due manner set out ;" and these
words are equally applicable to the common law mode,
customary mode, or conventional mode. There certainly was evidence from which an agreement might be
inferred, and that was properly left to the jury. I think
that the question of reasonable time was also in this case
properly left to the jury, although it may sometimes be a
question for the Judge, the facts having first been ascertained by the jury. *Darbishire* v. *Parker.* (a) For
these reasons I agree that this rule must be discharged.

1824.

FACEY
against
HURDOM.

Rule discharged.

Coleridge was to have opposed the rule.

(a) 6 *East*, 3.

WALMSLEY *against* ABBOTT.

Where an apo-
thecary, in an
action to reco-
ver the amount
of his bill,
produced in
evidence a cer-
tificate, pur-
porting to be
granted by the
court of ex-
aminers of the
Apothecaries'
Company, and
bearing twelve
signatures,
purporting to
be the signa-
tures of the
persons consti-
tuting that
court, of which
signatures he
proved one,
and gave other
evidence to
shew that the
document was
genuine, and
that he ob-
tained it from
the court of
examiners :
Held, that this
was sufficient,
and that he
was not bound
to prove the
hand writing of
each member of
the court of
examiners who
had subscribed
the certificate.

ASSUMPSIT for an apothecary's bill. Plea, general issue. At the trial before *Garrow* B., at the
last Spring assizes for *Salop*, the plaintiff, in order to
establish his right to sue as required by the 55 G. 3.
c. 194. produced a certificate bearing twelve signatures,
which purported to be those of the persons constituting the court of examiners of the apothecary's company,
and also a signature purporting to be that of their secretary. A witness proved the hand-writing of one of the
examiners, and also of the secretary ; and that another
person, whose name was subscribed to the certificate,
was an examiner, but he was not acquainted with his
hand-writing. The witness had frequently seen certificates granted by the court of examiners, and believed
that which was produced to be a genuine document.
Another witness proved that the plaintiff was examined
at Apothecaries' Hall, that he (the witness) was examined on the same day and passed, and received a
certificate similar to that which was produced by the
plaintiff. It was objected for the defendant that the
55 G. 3. c. 194. ss. 9. and 21. imposed upon the plaintiff
the necessity of proving the signature of at least a majority
of the court of examiners, and that for want of that
proof the certificate produced could not be received in
evidence. The learned judge overruled the objection,
but gave the defendant leave to move to enter a nonsuit. The plaintiff having obtained a verdict, *W. E. Taun-*

ton

ton in *Easter* term obtained a rule nisi to enter a non-suit; against which

Whately (with whom was *Oldnall Russell*) now shewed cause. This question turns upon the ninth, fourteenth, and twenty-first sections of the 55 G. 3. c. 194. The ninth section enacts " that twelve persons shall be appointed as a court of examiners, and that they or the major part of them shall examine all persons desirous of practising as apothecaries, and grant or withhold certificates as they think fit." The fourteenth section enacts, " that after the 1st of *August* 1815 no person who was not in practice before that time, shall practice as an apothecary, unless he shall have been examined by the said court of examiners, or major part of them, and have received a certificate from the said court of examiners, or the major part of them, as aforesaid." The twenty-first section enacts, " that no apothecary shall be allowed to recover any charges claimed by him in any court of law, unless such apothecary shall prove on the trial that he was in practice as an apothecary prior to or on the 5th day of *August* 1815, or that he has obtained a certificate to practise as an apothecary from the said master, wardens, and society of apothecaries as aforesaid." Now, it is not by any part of the act required that the certificate shall be signed by the court of examiners. It is to be granted by them, and, therefore, it is sufficient if the plaintiff gives reasonable evidence that the document produced is genuine. The certificate would have been valid without the signatures, and it would be extremely hard to cast upon the plaintiff the burthen of proving the hand-writing of several persons whose names were unnecessarily subscribed to the instrument. At all events

events they can only be considered as witnesses of its being genuine, and then by proving the hand-writing of one, and that of the secretary also, the plaintiff clearly did sufficient to make the certificate evidence. If it were not a genuine document the plaintiff and those persons who were proved to have signed it, must all have been implicated in a gross fraud, and perhaps even a forgery. But the Court will not presume that such a crime has been committed. The case of *Moises* v. *Thornton* (a) is very different; there the plaintiff, not being able to prove the seal of the University of St. Andrews could not produce any evidence that the diploma was genuine.

W. E. Taunton contrà. The case certainly depends upon the three sections of the 55 G. 3. c. 194., which have been referred to. The fourteenth and twenty-first sections speak of a certificate to be granted *as aforesaid*. Now that refers to the ninth section, where the mode of granting the certificate is described, viz. by the court of examiners, or the major part of them. It is not, therefore, sufficient to prove that a certificate was granted; it must also be shewn that it was granted by a majority of the court of examiners. The signature of the secretary was a mere nullity, for the act of parliament does not recognise any such officer of the court of examiners. Then, in order to prove the granting of the certificate by a majority of the court, the plaintiff was bound to shew that those persons whose names were subscribed to the document were members of the court, and that their signatures were genuine. In *Moises* v. *Thornton*

(a) 8 T. R. 303.

there

there was a stronger case in favor of the plaintiff, for he produced a witness who actually went to the University of *St. Andrew*, and saw the proper officers sign a certificate that a diploma had been granted; yet it was held insufficient, and the plaintiff was nonsuited. [*Bayley* J. That certificate did not purport to be the plaintiff's diploma, and in that case the diploma itself was not authenticated,] neither is this certificate.

BAYLEY J. The ninth section of the 55 G. 3. *c.* 194. requires, that thereafter, before any persons begin to practise as apothecaries, they shall be examined by certain officers appointed by the apothecaries' company, and that the court of examiners, or the major part of them, shall have power to grant or refuse certificates. The fourteenth section prevents any persons from thereafter commencing practice unless they shall have received such certificate, and the twenty-first section prevents such persons from recovering their charges in a court of law, unless they shall have obtained such certificate. It appears to me that putting a fair and reasonable construction upon those provisions, they did not make it incumbent on the plaintiff to prove the hand-writing of all those whose names were attached to the certificate, but only to shew that it was issued by the court of examiners, and that he obtained and received it from them. Now, of those facts there was abundant evidence. It was proved that two of the persons whose names were subscribed were members of the court of examiners, and the hand-writing of one of them was also proved; then the signature of the secretary was shewn to be genuine. The act does not, indeed, require the court to have a secretary, but in fact they have such an officer, and he

signed

signed the certificate as a genuine document issued by the court. Then one of the witnesses proved that the plaintiff had been examined, that he the witness was examined on the same day, and received a certificate corresponding with that which was produced. Upon such evidence I think we are well warranted in concluding, that that document was issued by those who had power to do it, as and for a genuine certificate, and I think that the plaintiff, having given that evidence, had satisfied all that the statute made necessary, and was not bound to prove the signature of each individual constituting the court of examiners.

HOLROYD and LITTLEDALE Js. concurred.

Rule discharged.

TODD and Others *against* THOMAS MAXFIELD.

This Court will order an ex-oneretur to be entered on the bail-piece in all cases where the defendant is entitled to be discharged out of custody; and therefore where a defendant obtained a certificate under a commission of bankruptcy before trial, and did not plead it puis darrein continuance, the Court relieved the bail on motion.

The defendant had become bankrupt thrice, and had not paid 15s. in the pound to his creditors under the second commission: Held, that the third commission was not therefore void, but voidable only.

COMYN had obtained a rule nisi for entering an exoneretur on the bail-piece, upon the ground that the defendant had obtained his certificate under a commission of bankruptcy. It appeared that the action, which was upon a bill of exchange, came on for trial on the 11th of *January* 1824, that judgment was signed on the 19th of *February* 1824, and that a ca. sa. issued, returnable in fifteen days of *Easter*, to which the sheriff returned non est inventus. A writ of scire facias issued against the bail, returnable in five weeks of *Easter*. It

appeared

appeared that the defendant had been declared bankrupt
under three commissions of bankrupt, the first of which
issued in *January* 1808, the second in *November* 1817,
and the third on the 8th of *April* 1823, and that his
estate had not, nor was likely to pay 15*s.* in the pound
under either of those commissions. His certificate under the last commission was allowed by the Lord Chancellor on the 9th of *December* 1823.

Platt shewed cause. The defendant might have
pleaded his certificate puis darrein continuance, and
that being so, the bail are not entitled to relief. That
was expressly decided by the Court of Common Pleas,
in the case of *Clarke* v. *Hoppe.* (a) There the defendant
had become bankrupt pending the action, and obtained
his certificate, and he afterwards permitted judgment to
be signed against him for want of a plea, and the Court
of Common Pleas refused to relieve the bail on motion,
and intimated an opinion that they could not take advantage of the bankruptcy and certificate, in consequence
of the defendant's having neglected to plead it; besides,
the third commission and the certificate obtained under
it are wholly void, the bankrupt not having paid 15s. in
the pound under the preceding commission. *Martin* v.
O'Hara. (b)

Comyn, contrà. The general rule is, that where a
bankrupt is clearly entitled to his discharge, the Court
will order an exoneretur to be entered on the bail-
piece, without the form of a regular surrender by his
bail; and that, even where the certificate is not ob-

(a) 3 *Taunt.* 46.   (b) *Cowp.* 823.

tained

tained until after the return day of the capias ad satisfaciendum. Now it is quite clear, that if the certificate be good, the bankrupt in this case was entitled to his discharge. *Tidd's Practice*, 280., sixth edition. The decision in the case of *Clarke* v. *Hoppe* is certainly at variance with this rule, but that case has never been acted upon in this court. As to the other point, the third commission is still in existence. The fact of the bankrupt's not having paid 15s. in the pound under the other commissions, may be a ground for an application to the Chancellor to supersede the last; but until it is superseded it continues in force, and cannot be treated as a nullity.

Per Curiam. The general rule is, that where the bankrupt is entitled to his discharge, the Court will relieve the bail. Here, the bankrupt was entitled to his discharge if his certificate was valid; and, therefore, this case falls within the general principle. The case of *Clarke* v. *Hoppe* has never been acted upon in this court. As to the other point, the bankrupt has obtained his certificate under the third commission, and unless that commission be absolutely a nullity, the certificate is valid, as long as the commission continues in force. We think that the fact of the bankrupts not having paid his creditors 15s. in the pound under the second commission does not make the subsequent commission void, but that it is voidable only by application to the great seal. This rule must, therefore, be made absolute.

Rule absolute.

— Goode ... Bristow & E. Sept. 29. 1824.

ESDAILE *against* OXENHAM.

TROVER for deeds and pieces of stamped parchment. Plea, general issue. At the trial before *Best J.*, at the last Spring assizes for *Somerset*, it appeared that the plaintiff had, in the year 1819, contracted to purchase an estate of Messrs. *Brickdale*, bankers, at *Taunton*, for 2200*l.* The deeds were prepared at the expence of the purchaser, who paid 1400*l.* in part of the purchase-money. The deeds were sent by the plaintiff's attorney to one *Kinglake*, as attorney for Messrs. *Brickdale*, in order that they might be executed. Messrs. *Brickdale* executed them, and gave them to a servant, that they might be sent back, and he gave them to the defendant, without any particular direction as to what was to be done with them. In order to perfect the conveyance it was necessary that two other persons should execute the deeds, but they refused to do so, and afterwards, and before this action was commenced, plaintiff gave up the contract, and received back 1000*l.* In *November* 1819 the *Brickdales* became bankrupts. At that time they were and still are considerably indebted to the defendant, for business done by him as their attorney. In *January* 1823 the plaintiff demanded the deeds of the defendant, who refused to deliver them up, claiming to have a lien on them for the balance due to him from the *Brickdales.* The plaintiff never tendered the remainder of the purchase-money,

Plaintiff having contracted to purchase an estate of B., had the deeds of conveyance prepared at his own expence, and sent them to B. for execution. B. executed and gave them to a servant to be sent back. The servant delivered them to defendant, an attorney, who had a demand upon B. for business done in his profession. No directions were given to defendant to retain the deeds until the purchase money should be paid. Some necessary parties refused to execute the deeds, and plaintiff having abandoned the contract, demanded the deeds from defendant, who refused to deliver them up, claiming to have a lien for his demand against B. In trover for deeds and stamped

pieces of parchment : Held, that the plaintiff was entitled to recover the deeds at all events, in a cancelled, if not in an uncancelled state. *Littledale J. dubitante.*

but

but offered to pay the defendant any demand he might have for getting the deeds executed. The jury, under these circumstances, found that the *Brickdales* sent the deeds to *Kinglake*, and did not intend that *Oxenham* should get hold of them, and that he detained them for his own demand against the *Brickdales*, not connected with this transaction, and not to secure the payment of the purchase-money, and returned a verdict for the plaintiff, damages 1*s.*; whereupon the learned Judge gave the defendant leave to move to enter a nonsuit, if the Court should be of opinion that defendant had a lien on the deeds. A rule having been obtained accordingly in *Easter* term,

Bayly now shewed cause. It is quite clear, that the defendant had no right to retain the deeds in question on account of the debt due to him from the *Brickdales*. The deeds never belonged to them, and were merely placed in the defendant's hands, that he might return them to the plaintiff. Now his own lien was the only claim which he made when the deeds were demanded, and, therefore, it was not competent for him afterwards to set up a right to retain them for Messrs. *Brickdale*, until the residue of the purchase-money was paid, *Boardman* v. *Sill* (a), *Ogle* v. *Atkinson*. (b) Besides, the *Brickdales* had not any lien. The deeds were prepared at the expence of the plaintiff, the stamps and parchment were his, and therefore, at all events, when the contract was rescinded, he was entitled to have them back in the same state in which they were before the execution by the *Brickdales* took place.

(a) 1 *Campb.* 410. n., and see *White* v. *Gainer*, 2 *Bing.* 23.
(b) 5 *Taunt.* 759. 1 *Marsh.* 323. S. C.

Adam

1824.

ESDAILE
against
OXENHAM.

Adam (with whom were *Scarlett* and *Jeremy*) contrà. The plaintiff cannot recover in this action, for either the defendant is entitled to retain these deeds on account of his lien, or the plaintiff must fail for want of a sufficient title to the deeds in himself. The defendant having a lien as against the *Brickdales* has the same lien against all those who claim under them. Now the only title which the plaintiff can have to these instruments in the character of deeds is derived from the *Brickdales*. [*Holroyd* J. The declaration has also a claim of stamped parchments.] As soon as they were executed the nature of the instruments was changed. The execution was with the assent of the plaintiff, and then he could not make out any title to the deeds, without paying or tendering the remainder of the purchase-money. The case of *Boardman* v. *Sill* is the only one which can be cited, as preventing the defendant from now setting up this defence; and it seems extraordinary that the plaintiff should have a verdict in his favour, without shewing any title to the deeds, merely because the defendant claimed a lien to which his right may be doubtful.

BAYLEY J. I am of opinion that this action is maintainable, and that the verdict was properly found for the plaintiff. It appears, by the finding of the jury, that *Oxenham* at first insisted upon a right of his own: that he failed to establish. The deeds were prepared on behalf of the plaintiff, and at his expence; he paid for the stamps and parchment; and, therefore, before the execution by the *Brickdales*, the property was in him to all intents and purposes. They were to be executed with a view to being returned to him, and not that they might become the property of the *Brickdales*. That

Q 2

being

1824.

ESDAILE
against
OSWESTALL.

being so, the defendant never had a colour for with-holding them, on the ground that the *Brickdales* were indebted to him. He could have no greater right than the *Brickdales*, and upon payment of the purchase-money to them, they could not have retained the deeds. But now the defence set up is not a title in the defend-ant, but the want of a sufficient title in the plaintiff; and it is argued, that the deeds having been executed, the plaintiff cannot demand the possession of them; that is setting up the jus tertii, the right of the *Brickdales* against the right of the plaintiff. If the question were to be considered with reference to these documents in the character of deeds, there might be considerable weight in the arguments, particularly if *it had been shewn that Messrs.* Brickdale *had opposed the delivering up of the* deeds. But these deeds were prepared at the ex-pence of the plaintiff; when sent to be executed they were his property, and there cannot be any doubt that he might have claimed to have them back, if they had never been executed. They were parted with by the plaintiff, that they might be rendered an effectual con-veyance to him from several persons, and that he should have back that conveyance on payment of the purchase-money. Under these circumstances, it was the duty of Messrs. *Brickdale,* the vendors, to procure the execution by all necessary parties. They had no right to execute the deeds unless the others consented; and if they could not procure that consent, the execution by them was wrongful. Now as to the effect of the execution, Messrs. *Brickdale* and the defendant stand on the same footing. It does not, therefore, give the latter any right to withhold from the plaintiff his parchment and stamps. It is possible that the plaintiff may get back the money

paid

paid for the stamps, if he satisfies the commissioners that the contract has been rescinded. I do not say that the plaintiff can insist upon having the deeds uncancelled; but either cancelled or uncancelled he has a right to the possession of them.

HOLROYD J. I am of opinion that the verdict was rightly found in this case. The declaration claimed not only deeds but certain pieces of stamped parchment, and I think that the plaintiff was entitled, at all events, to have the instruments restored to him in a cancelled state, if he was not entitled to have them uncancelled. That being so, the defendant's unqualified refusal to restore them was a wrongful conversion by him. The instruments were the plaintiff's originally, and never ceased to be so. This appears to have been a transaction between a vendor and an intended vendee. Now the person selling is bound to procure the execution of the conveyance by all necessary parties, and if any of them refuse to execute, the contract may be considered as rescinded. Such was the case in this instance, the execution by the *Brickdales* cannot, therefore, put the plaintiff in a worse situation than he was in before. The instruments then remained the property of the plaintiff. If, indeed, they had been executed by all the necessary parties, he could not have claimed them without tendering the residue of the purchase-money; but that was not done, and on the contrary the bargain was abandoned. *Graham* might perhaps have a right to stand in the same situation as the *Brickdales*, he might have cancelled the deeds, but either cancelled or uncancelled he was bound to give them up. But it does not appear that, when the deeds were demanded, the defendant relied on

the

the *Brickdales'* right, he absolutely refused to deliver them up, claiming a right to withhold them altogether. It may be said, that cancelling the deeds will not protect the *Brickdales*, because the estate vested by the execution and delivery of the deeds. But here, from the nature of the transaction, it would be a question for the jury, whether it was not intended that the deeds should operate as an escrow only. Whether that were so or not, the *Brickdales* would at all events have been bound to give them up on the execution of a reconveyance to them at their own expence, they could not retain them altogether. Neither then could *Ovenham* do so, the rule for setting aside the verdict must therefore be discharged.

LITTLEDALE J. I am not prepared to give any decided opinion on this case. It is clear that the defendant has not any right to the deeds in question, nor have the *Brickdales* any right; but I feel a difficulty in saying that the plaintiff has a right to them *as deeds*. There is another question, whether he may not maintain his action for them as mere pieces of stamped parchment. It seems to me, that when the plaintiff delivered them to *Kinglake* to procure the execution of them, he then lost that legal property which would have enabled him to maintain trover. The contract, as it seems to me, still subsisted when the action was brought, and might perhaps have been enforced in equity. There was not any evidence that the *Brickdales* consented to abandon it. The deeds were partially executed, and it appears to me, that until all parties consented to rescind the contract, they would not revert to the state of mere pieces of parchment, and again become the property of

the

the plaintiff in that character. In *Harrison* v. *Parker* (a),
where a person had built a bridge and dedicated it to
the public, it was held that the materials remained his
property; and that when they were severed and taken
away by a wrong-doer, he might maintain trespass for
the asportation. But this case is different; for here, if
the plaintiff had possession of the deeds, he might perhaps be enabled to bring an ejectment; it does not appear what interest in the premises those parties had
who refused to execute the conveyance. There is
another difficulty, the plaintiff never claimed these instruments as mere pieces of parchment, neither had the
defendant any right to cancel the deeds; he had no
authority from the *Brickdales* for that purpose, and on
that ground also I doubt whether the plaintiff was entitled to the possession of the instruments. If the
Brickdales were still solvent, an action would lie against
them for not completing the purchase, and in that case the
plaintiff might recover the value of the parchment and
stamps. At present it seems to me a matter to be settled
rather by a court of equity than by us. If the deeds were
delivered as an escrow, they ought to remain in the
defendant's hands until the payment of the whole of
the purchase-money. Upon the whole, therefore, I
entertain considerable doubts whether the plaintiff has
made out a title to these instruments, either as deeds or
mere pieces of parchment; but, upon the opinions of
my learned Brothers, the rule must be discharged.

Rule discharged.

(a) 6 *East*, 154.

1824.

Bloxsome *against* Williams.

A. not knowing that B. was a horse-dealer, made a verbal bargain with him on a Sunday for the purchase of a horse. The price (which was above 10l.) was then specified, and B. warranted the horse to be sound. It was not delivered, however, until the following Tuesday, when the money was paid: Held, that there was not any complete contract until the delivery of the horse, and consequently that the contract was not void within the stat. 29 Car. 2. c. 7. s. 2. But assuming it to be void, held, secondly, in an action for breach of the warranty, that the purchaser having no knowledge of the fact that the vendor was exercising his ordinary calling on the Sunday, had not been guilty of any breach of the law, and therefore was entitled to recover back the price of the horse.

ASSUMPSIT for breach of the warranty of a horse, with the money counts. Plea, non-assumpsit. At the trial before *Park* J. at the last Spring assizes for the county of *Berks*, 1823, it appeared that the defendant was the proprietor of a stage-coach, and a horse-dealer. The plaintiff's son was travelling on a *Sunday* in defendant's coach, and while the horses were changing made a verbal bargain with the defendant for the horse in question for the price of thirty-nine guineas; the latter warranted the horse to be sound, and not more than seven years old. The horse was delivered to the plaintiff on the following *Tuesday*, and the price was then paid; there was no evidence to shew that the plaintiff's son knew at the time when he made the bargain that the defendant exercised the trade of a horse-dealer. The horse was unsound and seventeen years old. It was objected on the part of the defendant that the plaintiff could not recover, on the ground that the bargain, having been made on a *Sunday*, was void within the 29 *Car.* 2. c. 7. s. 2.; the learned judge overruled the objection, and the plaintiff obtained a verdict for the price of the horse. A rule nisi having been obtained in the following term for a new trial,

W. E. Taunton and *Talfourd* now shewed cause, and contended, first, that there was not any complete contract on the *Sunday*, the verbal bargain being void by the statute of frauds. The contract, therefore, only became com-

plete

plete on the *Tuesday,* when the horse was delivered to and accepted by the defendant. Assuming it, however, to have been void, it only became so in consequence of the defendant's having exercised his ordinary calling of a horse-dealer on the *Sunday, Drury* v. *Defontaine.* (a)   The fact of that being his ordinary calling was not known to the plaintiff; he therefore did not concur in any breach of the law, and is entitled to recover back his money which has been paid upon a void contract.

Jervis and *G. R. Cross* contrà.   The contract when completed refers back to the day when the bargain was made, and if that be so, then it is clearly void within the words of the 29 *Car.* 2. *c.* 7., because the defendant, when he made the contract, was exercising his ordinary calling.   The policy of the statute was to prevent any person from exercising his usual business on the *Sunday.*   The object of the statute therefore will be best answered by not allowing the plaintiff to recover back his money, which has been paid in pursuance of a contract made in breach of the law.

BAYLEY J.   The statute 29 *Car.* 2. *c.* 7. *s.* 1. enacts, that no tradesman, artificer, workman, colourer, or other person whatsoever, shall do or exercise any worldly labour, business, or work of their ordinary callings upon the Lord's day, and that every person, being of the age of fourteen years or upwards, *offending* in the premises, shall, for every such offence forfeit five shillings.   In *Drury* v. *Defontaine* it was held that the vendor of a horse who made a contract of sale on a *Sunday,* but not in the exercise of his ordinary calling, might

(b) 1 *Taunt.* 131.

recover

recover the price. I entirely concur in that decision, but I entertain some doubts whether the statute applies at all to a bargain of this description. I incline to think that it applies to manual labour and other work visibly laborious, and the keeping of open shops. But I do not mean to pronounce any decision upon that point; my judgment in this case proceeds upon two grounds; first, that there was no complete contract on the *Sunday*, and secondly, assuming that there was, that it is not competent to the defendant, who alone has been guilty of a breach of the law, to set up his own contravention of the law as an answer to this action at the suit of an innocent person. As to the first point the statute of frauds enacts, " that no contract for the sale of goods, &c. shall be good, except the buyer shall accept part of the goods so sold, and actually receive the same, or give something in earnest to bind the bargain, or that some note or memorandum in writing of the bargain be made." Now in this case there was no note in writing of the bargain, and on the *Sunday* all rested in parol, and nothing was done to bind the bargain. The contract, therefore, was not valid until the horse was delivered to and accepted by the defendant. The terms on which the sale was afterwards to take place were only specified on the *Sunday*, and those terms were incorporated in the sale made on the subsequent day. Assuming, however, that the contract was perfect on the *Sunday*, the defendant was the person offending within the meaning of the statute by exercising his ordinary calling on the *Sunday*. He might be thereby deprived of any right to sue upon a contract so illegally made, and upon the same principle any other person knowingly aiding him in the breach of the law, by becoming a party to such a contract, with the

the knowledge that it was illegal, could not sue upon it. But in this case the fact that the defendant was a dealer in horses was not known to the plaintiff or his son, he therefore has not knowingly concurred in aiding the defendant to offend the law, and that being so, it is not competent to the defendant to set up his own breach of the law as an answer to this action. If the contract be void as falling within the statute, then the plaintiff, who is not a particeps criminis, may recover back his money, because it was paid on a consideration which has failed. For these reasons I think this rule must be discharged.

HOLROYD and LITTLEDALE Js. concurred.

Rule discharged.

Lord BAGOT *against* WILLIAMS.

ASSUMPSIT for money had and received. Plea, first, non-assumpsit; secondly, that on the 7th day of *September* 1822, at the court of our lord the king, in and for the lordship or dominion of *Dyffryn Clwyd*, within the town of *Ruthin*, then held at *Ruthin* aforesaid, in the lordship and county aforesaid, and within the jurisdiction of said last mentioned court, before *A. B.* then chief steward of said last mentioned court, plaintiff levied his certain plaint against defendant in a certain plea of debt of 4000*l.*, upon and for the very same identical

had received on account of the plaintiff, and as his steward, different sums of money at different times, and that on the investigation of the accounts, the plaintiff found that there was due to him a much larger sum than that for which he had declared in the inferior court, but that he had proceeded for the smaller sum, under the belief that the defendant had no available property beyond that amount, defendant in that action suffered judgment by default, and plaintiff verified for 3400*l.* : Held, that all the sums which the plaintiff knew the defendant had received at the time when he commenced the action in the inferior court, were to be considered as causes of action, in respect of which he had declared and recovered the judgment.

causes

Assumpsit for money had and received. Plea, a judgment recovered for want of a plea for 4000l. in an inferior court in Wales for the same causes of action. Replication, that the causes of action were not the same, and issue joined thereon. At the trial, it appeared that the defendant

causes of action as those whereof plaintiff hath above in his declaration complained against defendant; and such proceedings were thereupon had, that afterwards, to wit, on the 5th day of *October* 1822, &c. plaintiff by the consideration and judgment of the court, according to the custom of the same court, recovered against defendant his said debt, and 6*l.* 18*s.* for his damages, which he had sustained as well on occasion of the detaining his said debt as for his costs and charges by him about his suit in that behalf expended, whereof defendant was convicted as by the record, &c.

Replication, that the causes of action in the declaration in this action mentioned, were not the same identical causes of action as those in the second plea mentioned, and for and in respect whereof the said supposed judgment in the second plea mentioned was recovered. At the trial before *Garrow* B., at the last Spring assizes for the county of *Salop*, the following facts were proved. The defendant had been the steward of the plaintiff, and in that character, between *November* 1821 and *April* 1822, had received various sums of money arising from the sale of the plaintiff's timber, exceeding considerably 3400*l.* In *June* 1822 he received two other sums on the plaintiff's account. In *September* 1822 he ceased to be the plaintiff's steward. The steward who succeeded the defendant was called as a witness, and he stated, that in *August* 1822, he investigated the defendant's accounts, and found that there was due from him to the plaintiff a sum of 7000*l.*; that in that estimate he took into consideration all the sums claimed in the present action, except a sum of 46*l.* which the defendant had received on account of rent at *Christmas* 1821. The fact of the defendant's having received that sum had only come to his (the witness's) knowledge since the judg-

ment

ment was obtained in the court at *Ruthen*. After he, the witness, had investigated the accounts, he directed the action to be brought in the inferior court for 4000*l.*, and judgment having passed by default, he verified for 3400*l.* only, because the defendant (as he then thought) had not any property in value exceeding that sum. Upon these facts the learned Judge was of opinion, that whatever constituted a subsisting debt at the time when the proceeding in the inferior court was instituted, and was known to be so by the agent who managed the whole transaction, was to be considered as included in and constituting one entire cause of action; and he therefore directed the jury to find a verdict for the plaintiff for 46*l.*, but reserved liberty to the plaintiff to increase the verdict as the court should afterwards direct. A rule nisi having been obtained for that purpose,

Patteson shewed cause. The causes of action in respect of which the plaintiff now seeks to recover, are the same as those for which he has already obtained judgment in the inferior court. It is clear that all the sums now claimed might have been recovered in the former action, and it is not competent to a party to split his demand into parts, and bring separate actions for every distinct item in an account. Here the plaintiff's agent knew at the time when he instituted the first suit that all the sums now claimed (except the sum of 46*l.*) were due to the plaintiff. If the defendant had pleaded, and issue had been taken on the plea, evidence might have been given in respect of all the sums which the plaintiff knew to be due; and if such evidence had been given, and the plaintiff had consented to take a verdict for a less sum than that actually proved to be due, he would have been

causes of action as those whereof plaintiff hath above in his declaration complained against defendant; and such proceedings were thereupon had, that afterwards, to wit, on the 5th day of *October* 1822, &c. plaintiff by the consideration and judgment of the court, according to the custom of the same court, recovered against defendant his said debt, and 6l. 18s. for his damages, which he had sustained as well on occasion of the detaining his said debt as for his costs and charges by him about his suit in that behalf expended, whereof defendant was convicted as by the record, &c.

Replication, that the causes of action in the declaration in this action mentioned, were not the same identical causes of action as those in the second plea mentioned, and for and in respect whereof the said supposed judgment in the second plea mentioned was recovered. At the trial before *Garrow* B., at the last Spring assizes for the county of *Salop*, the following facts were proved. The defendant had been the steward of the plaintiff, and in that character, between *November* 1821 and *April* 1822, had received various sums of money arising from the sale of the plaintiff's timber, exceeding considerably 3400l. In *June* 1822 he received two other sums on the plaintiff's account. In *September* 1822 he ceased to be the plaintiff's steward. The steward who succeeded the defendant was called as a witness, and he stated, that in *August* 1822, he investigated the defendant's accounts, and found that there was due from him to the plaintiff a sum of 7000l.; that in that estimate he took into consideration all the sums claimed in the present action, except a sum of 46l. which the defendant had received on account of rent at *Christmas* 1821. The fact of the defendant's having received the rent had only come to his (the witness's) knowledge since the judg-

ment

ment was obtained in the court at *Ruthen.* After he, the witness, had investigated the accounts, he directed the action to be brought in the inferior court for 4000*l.*, and judgment having passed by default, he verified for 3400*l.* only, because the defendant (as he then thought) had not any property in value exceeding that sum. Upon these facts the learned Judge was of opinion, that whatever constituted a subsisting debt at the time when the proceeding in the inferior court was instituted, and was known to be so by the agent who managed the whole transaction, was to be considered as included in and constituting one entire cause of action; and he therefore directed the jury to find a verdict for the plaintiff for 46*l.*, but reserved liberty to the plaintiff to increase the verdict as the court should afterwards direct. A rule nisi having been obtained for that purpose,

Patteson shewed cause. The causes of action in respect of which the plaintiff now seeks to recover, are the same as those for which he has already obtained judgment in the inferior court. It is clear that all the sums now claimed might have been recovered in the former action, and it is not competent to a party to split his demand into parts, and bring separate actions for every distinct item in an account. Here the plaintiff's agent knew at the time when he instituted the first suit that all the sums now claimed (except the sum of 46*l.*) were due to the plaintiff. If the defendant had pleaded, and issue had been taken on the plea, evidence might have been given in respect of all the sums which the plaintiff knew to be due; and if such evidence had been given, and the plaintiff had consented to take a verdict for a less sum than that actually proved to be due, he would have been

and in that case it may have included the same causes of action which are the subject of this action, for money had and received. It appears that the parties did not go before a jury upon a writ of enquiry; but that judgment having passed by default, the agent of the plaintiff, by his affidavit of verification, proved the debt and, fixed the amount; he thereby put himself in the place of a jury. Whatever facts were known to him, therefore, may be considered in the same light as if they had been laid in evidence before a jury, and they had drawn a conclusion from them; and if a jury, after having in evidence before them all the facts which were known to the plaintiff's agent, had found that 3400*l.* was the sum due, it is quite clear that the plaintiff could not maintain a second action in respect of any of the sums of money which had been brought under the consideration of the jury. In this case the agent of the plaintiff proved that he was aware at the time when the action was commenced in the inferior court, that all the sums now claimed in the present action were due to the plaintiff except the sum of 46*l.*; and that being so, I am of opinion that all the other items must be considered as constituting the causes of action, in respect of which judgment was recovered. The rule for a new trial must be discharged.

BAYLEY J. The case of *Seddon* v. *Tutop* is distinguishable from the present: the ground of the decision in that case was, that no evidence had been given in the first action, on the count for goods sold and delivered, but that the plaintiff recovered a verdict merely on the count for the promissory note; and it was held that the judgment in that action was no bar to his re-

covering

covering in a subsequent action for goods sold. In this case Lord *Bagot*, at the time when the first action was commenced, had a demand on the defendant, not for one specific sum of money, but for different sums of money received by the defendant on his account, from different persons and at different times. His agent knew that he had claims in respect of all the sums now claimed; except 40l., and having that knowledge he formed an opinion that 3400l. was the whole sum which Lord *Bagot* ought to claim; and if he acted upon that opinion, it is much the same thing as if a plaintiff in a cause at nisi prius having a demand of 60l., consisting of three sums of 20l., which became due to him at different times, consented to take a verdict for 40l. If the jury in such a case, at the suggestion of the plaintiff, reduced the verdict to 40l. he would be bound by it; and could not afterward bring a second action for the other 20l. It seems to me that he is equally bound by his own act in this case, as he would have been by the verdict of a jury in the other, and that having chosen to abandon his claim once, he has done it for ever.

HOLROYD J. concurred.

Rule discharged.

1824.

Holmes against Love and Tucker

A tenant conveyed his interest in leasehold premises to trustees for the benefit of his creditors, by deed containing a proviso, that if all and every of the creditors should refuse to execute or consent to the deed within six months from the date thereof it should be void: Held, that the non-execution of the deed by a particular creditor was not evidence of a refusal by him to execute or assent, but that it was incumbent on a party seeking to avoid the deed to shew a positive refusal to execute or assent to the deed.

ACTION for use and occupation. Plea, general. Issue. At the trial before *Burrough* J. at the last Spring assizes for the county of *Kent*, it appeared that in *June* 1821 the plaintiff had agreed to let one *Edwards* a farm called *Aston Farm*, at a rent of 250l. for fourteen years from *Michaelmas* 1821, determinable at seven or ten years, by the landlord or tenant, upon giving twelve months' notice. *Edwards* took possession in *October*, 1821, and becoming embarrassed in his circumstances, on the 8th of *November* 1822, by deed made between him of the first part; the several persons whose names were subscribed as creditors of the second part; *Thomas Woodman* and the two defendants (being also creditors) of the third part; reciting that *Edwards* was seised of freehold and leasehold hereditaments, and possessed of goods and chattels and personal estate; and that he was indebted to his creditors in several sums of money, which he was unable to pay; assigned to *Woodman*, *Love*, and *Tucker*, all his freehold and leasehold property, and all other his personal estate whatsoever in trust, to sell by auction or private contract all his real and personal property, and get in all monies, debts, &c., and after paying the costs of carrying the trusts into execution, then to divide the residue rateably and proportionably among the creditors who should execute the deed. That the deed contained the following proviso: That if all and every the creditors of *Edwards* whose debts respectively had vested in them by the assignment, and

amounted to more than 5l., should *refuse to execute or otherwise consent to the deed* within six months from the date thereof, that then and in such case the same deed, and every article, matter, and thing therein contained, should cease and become void to all intents and purposes. This deed was executed by *Edwards* and the two defendants, *Love* and *Tucker*, but not by all the creditors, nor by *Woodbury* the other trustee; but there was no evidence to shew that he, or any of the creditors had positively refused to execute or consent to the deed. *Griffiths*, the attorney who prepared it, was a creditor for 15l., and he told one of the defendants, at the time when it was executed, that it was void in consequence of the proviso. Immediately after the execution of the deed the defendants proceeded to the premises to take possession, but they found a sheriff's officer in possession under a fi. fa., at the suit of a creditor, and also under a distress for rent, at the instance of the plaintiff. They paid the execution creditor his debt, and afterwards paid the plaintiff the rent to *Michaelmas* 1822. On the 27th of *November* they sold all the live and dead stock upon the premises by auction, and kept a person in possession till *February* 1823. *Edwards* afterwards continued in possession and management of the farm, and the defendants paid the rent up to *Lady-day* 1823. The plaintiff, at the trial, attempted to shew, that *Edwards* continued in possession, in the character of agent to the defendants, from *February* until *Michaelmas* 1823, but, upon that point, there was contradictory evidence. It was contended, That the plaintiff was entitled to recover the rent from the defendants, whether they continued in the actual occupation or not, because the legal interest in the premises had vested in them by the assignment, and

R 2 continued

continued in them during the whole period for which the
rent was claimed. For the defendants, however, it was
contended, that as the deed was not executed by all the
creditors, the non-execution amounted to a refusal to
execute or consent to it, and that it became void on the
9th of *May* 1823, and, therefore, that the defendants
had not the legal interest in them at the time when the
rent claimed became due. The learned Judge was of
opinion that the deed did become void at that time,
and that the defendants were not liable for the rent
claimed unless they continued in possession after that
period : and he told the jury to find for the plaintiffs,
if they thought that, after *February* 1823, *Edwards*
held the premises as the agent of the defendants ; but
if they thought that he then continued in possession on
his own account, to find for the defendants. A verdict
having been found for the defendants, a rule nisi was
obtained for a new trial in last *Easter* term, on the
ground that the deed was not defeated by the mere
omission of the creditors to execute, but that it was
necessary to shew an actual refusal.

E. Lawes now shewed cause. The non-execution of
the deed by the creditors was primâ facie evidence of a
refusal on their part to execute or assent to it. In assumpsit for money due upon simple contract, the declaration always contains an averment, that the defendant refused to pay, yet in such cases, when the legal
liability is once established, the non-payment is always
considered sufficient evidence of a refusal to pay. Besides here, *Griffiths*, a creditor, stated, when the deed
was executed by the defendants, that it was void in con-

sequence

sentence of the proviso. It must be taken, therefore, that he refused to execute it.

Selwyn and *Carter*, contrà. The tenant's interest in these premises vested by the deed in the defendants, liable to be divested upon a condition subsequent. That being a condition, the effect of which is to defeat an estate already vested, must be construed strictly; and so construing the proviso, it is quite clear, that it was necessary to prove an actual refusal to execute or assent to the deed, in order to make it void.

BAYLEY J. In order to entitle the plaintiff to maintain this action for use and occupation, the defendants must, during the period for which the rent is claimed, either have been in the actual occupation of the premises, or must have had the legal interest vested in them. The jury have found, that the defendants were not in the actual occupation of the premises. In *November* 1822 the tenant assigned his interest to the defendants, and they took possession under the deed. There is a proviso in it, that the deed shall be void, if all and every the creditors of *Edwards*, whose debts amounted to more than 5l., shall refuse to execute or consent to the deed within six months from the date thereof. It is said that the deed is void, because all the other creditors did not execute, or otherwise consent to the deed. But the proviso makes the deed void only in case any of the creditors refuse to execute or consent. The question is, therefore, did they or any of them refuse to execute or consent to the deed? There is no evidence of that, and if any had refused it was a matter capable of easy proof; for whoever went round

R 3   with

with the deed to ask the creditors to execute it, might here proved the refusal. It has been said, that what passed with *Griffiths* shews, that the deed was void, but his saying that it would be void does not prove it to be so. I think that the deed clearly vested the whole interest in the assignees, and then, unless it was divested out of them by the absolute refusal of some one of the creditors, to execute or otherwise consent to the deed, that interest which had once vested continued in them; that being so, they are clearly liable for this rent. The rule for a new trial must, therefore, be made absolute.

HOLROYD J. By the deed of assignment the interest in the premises became legally vested in the defendants, and there is nothing to shew that it was ever divested out of them; for there is no evidence of a refusal by any one of the creditors, to execute or consent to the deed; and until there was such refusal, the estate which had once vested in the assignees, would continue in them by virtue of the original assignment.

LITTLEDALE J. I am clearly of opinion, that all the interest which the tenant had in these premises vested in the defendants by the assignment. By the proviso the estate conveyed by the deed might become void upon the refusal of any of the creditors to execute or assent to the deed. Now that being a condition, the effect of which is to destroy an estate, must be construed strictly. In 1 *Inst.* 219 b, it is laid down, that a condition that is to create an estate is to be performed by construction of law, as near the condition as may be, and according to the intent and meaning of the condition; albeit, the letter and words of the condition cannot be performed.

But

But other statutes or another condition that destroys an estate, is that is to be taken strictly, unless to be had under special cases." Applying that rule to the present case, I am of opinion, that the mere non-execution of the deed does not amount to a refusal to execute or consent, within the meaning of this proviso. It has been said, that in the common case of a debt the neglect to pay is considered equivalent to a refusal; but in that case the debt becomes absolute, by the non-payment of the money at the time when it ought to be paid. Thus, where a bond is conditioned to be void, upon the payment of a sum of money upon a given day, the non-payment of the money on that day enables the party to put the bond in suit. (a) But if the bond be for the payment of a given sum of money, with a condition that it shall be void if a person shall refuse to do a particular thing, in that case, in order to defeat the bond, it would be necessary to shew an actual refusal. The mere omission to do the particular thing required, would not be sufficient. So in this case, in order to defeat the estate which was actually vested in the defendants, I think it was necessary to shew an actual refusal to execute or consent to the deed.

Rule absolute.

This case was again tried before Abbott C. J. at the Kent Summer assizes 1824, when the point decided by the above Judges was fully discussed, and the Lord Chief Justice concurring in the judgment delivered by them, ruled the case for the city, and a verdict was found for the plaintiff.

(a) See Winter v. Moseley, 2 B. & A. 802.

R 4

1824.

CURTIS, Baronet, and Another *against* The Hundred of GODLEY.

By the black act 9 G. 1. c. 22., any person who shall unlawfully and maliciously kill, maim, or wound any cattle, or cut down or otherwise destroy any trees planted in any avenue or growing in any garden, orchard, or plantation for ornament, shelter, or profit, shall be adjudged guilty of felony, and the inhabitants of the hundred are to make satisfaction to the persons damnified by the cutting down or destroying any trees which shall be committed by any offenders against the act: Held, that in order to make the malicious destruction of trees a felony within this statute, the act done must pro-

THIS was an action against the hundred, brought to recover satisfaction for damages sustained by the plaintiffs, by reason of some person unknown having wilfully, maliciously, and feloniously, destroyed 160,000 fir trees of the plaintiffs, standing and growing for profit in their plantations, situate, &c. Plea, general issue. At the trial before *Alexander* C. B., at the last Spring assizes for the county of *Surrey*, it appeared that, on the 6th day of *May* 1823, the plantation of the plaintiffs, which was at a distance of a mile from any dwelling-house, had been destroyed by fire; but that the fire had commenced in an adjoining plantation belonging to one Mr. *Laurel;* and that it burnt through his plantation for about a mile in length before it reached that of the plaintiffs. The spot where the fire commenced was half a mile distant from any regular road, or from any house. Some remains of dry fir were found near the place where the fire had been kindled, and seemed to have been placed there for the purpose of making a fire. It was objected by the defendants' counsel, that the action could not be supported against the hundred, because, if the fire were even kindled maliciously, still no offence was committed against the 9 G. 1. c. 22., which statute

ceed from a malicious motive towards the owner of the trees, and therefore where an action was brought against the hundred by a party damnified, in consequence of his plantation having been destroyed by fire, and it appeared that the fire had commenced at the distance of a mile from his plantation, and in adjoining grounds belonging to a different proprietor, it was held that there was not any evidence that the act was done from motives of malice towards the plaintiff, and therefore that no offence had been committed against the statute, and that the action consequently was not maintainable against the hundred.

alone

alone gave the party damnified a remedy against the
hundred, the 1 *G.* 1. *c.* 2., and the 6 *G.* 1. *c.* 16., giving
the action against the inhabitants of the *parish town* and
vill; and the 22 *G.* 2. *c.* 36. *s.* 8. against the inhabitants
of the hundred or of the parish town, &c. at the option
of the party damnified in those cases only where the act
done constituted an offence against the 9 *G.* 1. *c.* 22.
The words of that statute are, " that if any person or
persons shall unlawfully and maliciously kill, maim, or
wound any cattle, or cut down or otherwise destroy any
trees planted in any avenue, or growing in any garden,
orchard, or plantation, for ornament, shelter, or profit."
And it was contended, that the words *otherwise destroy*
did not mean to destroy by fire, but that it imported
destruction ejusdem generis, as cutting down, the very
next sentence of the act making it an offence to set fire
to any house, &c. not including trees. Secondly, that
the word *plantation* following the words " garden or
orchard," meant a plantation contiguous to a dwelling-
house. The Lord Chief Baron reserved to the defendants liberty to move to enter a nonsuit in case the verdict should be against them, and directed the jury to
find for the plaintiffs if they thought upon the evidence
that the fire was kindled wilfully, but otherwise, for the
defendants. A verdict having been found for the defendants, a rule nisi was obtained in the following term for
a new trial, upon the ground that the verdict was against
evidence ; and now *Bolland* was heard against the rule,
and *Marryat* and *Chitty* in support of it. The questions
discussed were, first, whether the verdict was proper upon
the evidence; and, secondly, whether the action was
maintainable against the *hundred.* It was contended
upon the grounds taken at the trial that it was not.
It is unnecessary to state the argument here, because the

1824.

Cases
against
The Hundred
of Godley.

Court

Court ultimately pronounced their judgment upon a
point not noticed at the bar.

Cur. adv. vult.

BAYLEY J. The question submitted to the jury in
this case was, whether the plantation were wilfully set on
fire; they found that it was not. But if we were satisfied that this action was properly brought against the
hundred, we think that upon the terms of the plaintiffs paying the costs of the first trial, it might be fitly
submitted to the consideration of another jury. But
we are of opinion, that even if the plantation had been
wilfully set on fire, still that there would not have been
any offence committed against the statute 9 *G.* 1. *c.* 22.,
and therefore that the action was not properly brought
against the *hundred.* The other statutes cited give to the
party dammified an action against the inhabitants of the
parish or *town,* &c. The statute 1 *G.* 1. *st.* 2. *c.* 48.,
entitled " An act for the encouragement of the growth
of timber," enacts, that if any person shall maliciously
break down, cut up, pluck up, throw down, bark, or
otherwise destroy, &c. any timber trees, fruit trees, or
any other trees, the party dammified shall recover satisfaction from the inhabitants of the *parish,* town, or vill.
The statute 6 *G.* 1. *c.* 16. recites, that doubts had arisen
whether the former act extended to offences committed
in the day time, and gives the remedy against the inhabitants of the *parish,* &c. adjoining the wood, whether
the act be done by day or night." The 29 *G.* 2. *c.* 36.
s. 9. reciting that by the 9 *G.* 1. *c.* 22. it was enacted, that
the inhabitants of the hundred should make satisfaction
to every person for damage sustained by the cutting
down or destroying any trees which should be done or
committed by any offender against that act, to be recovered

1824.

Crew
v.
The Hundred

veral as therein directed; and reciting also, that doubts
had arisen whether the provisions made by that act had
not repealed and annulled the remedy given by the statutes
1 G. 1. c. 2., and the 6 G. 1. c. 16., and for obviating the
doubts, enacts, that it should be lawful for any person to
take remedy either against the parish, town, hamlet, vill,
or place where any of the *said* offences shall be committed according to the powers given by the former acts, or
against the hundred, wherein any of the *said* offences shall
be committed, as to such persons shall seem most meet.
The words "said offences" refer to the offences created
by 9 G. 1. c. 22. The statute 13 G. 3. and subsequent
statutes do not give any remedy against the hundred.
All these acts therefore give the remedy against the inhabitants of the parish, town, or vill. The 9 G. 1. c. 22.
being the only statute which gives any remedy against
the hundred, and the 29 G. 2. c. 36. giving an option to the party damnified, to bring his action either
against the hundred or against the parish, town, or vill,
&c. in cases where the person committing the act is an
offender against the statute 9 G. 1. c. 22. The question
therefore in this case is, whether the person or persons
who did the act whereby the plaintiff has been damnified,
were offenders against that statute. The words are,
"that if any person shall unlawfully and maliciously
kill, maim, or wound any cattle, or cut down, or otherwise destroy any trees planted in any avenue, or growing
in any garden, orchard, or plantation for ornament
shelter or profit." To constitute an offence within this
clause, it is essential that the act should be done unlawfully and maliciously. The term maliciously in this
part of the act of parliament, means malice against the
owner of the property damaged. This has been the
uniform current of authorities upon both branches of
this

this part of the clause. It was ruled, upon the branch for maiming cattle by *Heath* J., in *Rex* v. *Pearce*, tried at *Gloucester* 1789, and in *Rex* v. *Kean* (a), *Old Bailey* 1789, that in order to bring the offender within the statute, it was necessary to shew that the maiming of the animal was done from malice against the owner of it, and not from any angry or passionate disposition against the beast itself. The same point was ruled by *Hotham* B. and *Heath* J. in *Shepherd's* case. (b) In all these cases the prisoners were acquitted. But in *Michaelmas* term 1822, the same point was decided by all the judges in a case where the prisoner had been convicted. That was the case of the *King* v. *Austis*. There the indictment was for killing, maiming, and wounding a sheep of *Mary Clare*. It appeared that the prisoner acted from malice, not against *Mary Clare*, but against *Joseph* her son and manager. The judges held, that as *Joseph* could in no respect be deemed owner, the conviction was wrong. All these cases were decided on the first branch of the clause respecting the maiming of cattle, but the words *unlawfully and maliciously* apply to and must receive the same construction in both branches. In commenting on this statute, and the statutes 6 *G*. 3. *c*. 36. & *c*. 48., Mr. *East*, after noticing several points in which they differ, observes; " The most important distinction of all, is the view and intent of the Black Act contrasted with the other statutes. Supposing that the words ' wilfully and maliciously,' which occur in the preamble of the statute 6 *G*. 3. *c*. 36., of which the first only is used in the enacting part of the 6 *G*. 3. *c*. 48., are a descriptive part of the offence under those statutes, yet the whole scope of those statutes, which were

(a) 2 *Leach*, 594.   (b) 2 *Leach*, 609.   (c) 2 *East's* P. C. 1062.

intended

intended for the protection of the property itself from depredation, shews that the word ' maliciously' is only to be taken in its most general signification, as denoting an unlawful and bad act, an act done malo animo, from an unjust desire of gain, or a careless indifference of mischief. Whereas in order to bring an offender within the penalty of death under the Black Act, the malice must be personal against the owner of the property. This has been expressly holden with respect to the offence of killing, maiming, or wounding cattle: and the two offences are described in the same paragraph of the clause, and must therefore have the same construction." Since the publication of that work, the question upon the latter branch of the clause has come under the consideration of the judges in the case of *The King v. Taylor* in *Hilary* term 1819. In that case one *Knevett* had many young apple and pear trees in his garden from four to six feet high. The prisoner, from malice to *Knevett*, cut down about 100 and left them. Many were cut below the grass, and might shoot again and be regrafted, and would bear again in five or six years. The jury found that the trees, though cut down, were not totally destroyed, and upon this finding the judges were unanimous that these were trees within the act, because they were growing for profit, and that cutting them down without total destruction was sufficient to bring the case within the act; and that the 9 G. 1. *c.* 22. was not repealed by the statutes of the 6 G. 3. *c.* 36. & *c.* 48., because they applied to cases where there was no malice against the owner, and the conviction was held to be right. One of the questions in that case was, whether the destruction of trees in gardens, orchards, and plantations, continued an offence under the 9 G. 1. *c.* 22., notwithstanding the subsequent pro-

visions

is, that wherever the interest of the covenantees is joint, although the covenant be in terms joint and several, the action follows the nature of the interest, and must be brought in the name of all the covenantees; but where the interest of the covenantees is several they may maintain separate actions, although the language of the covenant be joint. Looking only to the language of the covenant in this case, it would appear to be a joint covenant; but the interest of the covenantees is several, each of them having a distinct interest in the annuity payable to him. The interest, therefore, being several, the covenant must also be several, and, consequently, this action is properly brought by the executor of that covenantee whose annuity was in arrear. The cases cited on the part of the defendant are distinguishable from the present, because in each of those cases one of the covenantees had no interest whatever; and the covenant was not only joint in its language, but it was for the performance of one entire thing. Here, the covenant is for the payment of two distinct annuities. In *Rolls* v. *Yate* the covenant was for the payment of one entire sum to one of two covenantees. It was not only, therefore, joint in its language, but the two covenantees had a joint legal interest, although one of them only was to derive a benefit from it. The same observation applies to the case of *Anderson* v. *Martindale*; the covenant there was to pay one annuity to one of the two covenantees. Here, the covenant is for the payment of a distinct annuity to each of the covenantees, and, therefore, the interest is clearly several.

Judgment for the plaintiff.

PARKER *against* RAMSBOTTOM and Others.

THIS was a feigned issue, directed by the Court of
Chancery, to try the two following questions, viz.
first, whether the plaintiff was legally entitled to prove
any, and what debt, under a commission of bankrupt
issued against *Edward Penfold, John Springett,* and
William Margesson Penfold, bearing date the 29th of
March 1816; and, secondly, whether, in respect of
such debt as was proveable under the commission, the
plaintiff had any legal lien upon any, and which of
the securities mentioned in the schedule annexed to
a certain indenture, bearing date on or about the
13th *July* 1814, and made between the plaintiff of the
first part, *John Springett* of the second part, and *Edward*

A. B. and *C.*
carried on the
business of
bankers in co-
partnership.
A. advanced
large sums of
money to the
concern, which
he raised by
selling out
stock, and he
took separate
bonds for
18,000*l.* from
B. and *C.*, con-
ditioned for
the replacing of
9000*l.* 3 per
cent. consols
by each, being
their respective
proportions of
the stock sold
by *A.* The stock

not being replaced, *A.* brought actions, and recovered judgments on the bonds. *A.* afterwards
retired from the concern, and at that time 20,000*l.* 3 per cent. consols was due to him;
by the deed of dissolution *B.* and *C.* covenanted to replace it by four instalments, and that
if they failed to do so *A.* might resort to the judgments recovered on the bonds; and
further, that he should have a lien on certain specified securities for that debt, and also, as
an indemnity against partnership debts, which they covenanted to pay. One instalment
was replaced when due, but *B.* and *C.* having failed to replace the second, a new arrangement (not under seal) was entered into, whereby it was agreed that the transaction should
be considered as a loan of money from the first, and that the sum produced by the sale of
the 15,000*l.* 3 per cents. which remained due, which was 10,083*l.*, should be the debt, and
be repaid at a future day with 5 per cent. interest. The value of 15,000*l.* 3 per cent.
consols at the date of this last agreement was 8437*l.* Before any part of the 10,085*l.* was
paid, *B.* and *C.* became bankrupts, and at the issuing of the commission, two out of the
three remaining days fixed by the deed of dissolution for the re-transfer of stock had
passed: Held, that the second agreement was void for usury, but that the deed of dissolution remained binding, and that *A.* might prove under the commission against *B.* and *C.*
for the 15,000*l.* 3 per cent. consols, the value of the two instalments due before the bankruptcy to be ascertained by the price of consols on the days when those sums respectively
became due; the value of the third to be taken at the price of consols on the day when the
commission issued, with a rebate for the interval between that day and the day fixed for the
re-transfer of that instalment; and further, that *A.* still had the lien given by the deed.
A. having paid certain old partnership debts after he left the concern: Held, secondly, that
he might prove for those also. Whilst *A.* remained in the bank he received interest upon
his advances without any deduction for property tax: Held, thirdly, that no deduction was
to be made in respect of that from the sum to be proved by him, inasmuch as it did not
appear that the bankrupts had accounted to government for the property tax on the monies
so paid.

Penfold of the third part, and which securities were as follows. A mortgage from *William Elgar* of *Maidstone*, in the county of *Kent*, to *R. Parker, J. Springett,* and *E. Penfold,* for securing 10,000*l.* and interest. A bond from the Earl of *Romney* to *R. Parker, J. Springett,* and *E. Penfold,* and a promissory note of Mr. *W. Archer,* of *Maidstone,* to the said last mentioned persons, for 1000*l.* and interest. The plaintiff in his declaration as to the first question averred, that he was entitled to prove a debt, to wit, 30,000*l.* under the said commission; and as to the second question, that in respect to the said debt he had a legal lien upon all the said securities. These several averments were denied by the defendants in their pleas, and issues were joined thereon. At the trial before *Abbott* C. J., at the *Middlesex* sittings after *Easter* term 1823, a verdict was found for the plaintiff upon both issues, subject to the opinion of the Court upon the following case. The plaintiff, in *December* 1787, entered into partnership with *E. Penfold* and *J. Springett* as bankers at *Maidstone,* in the county of *Kent,* for a term of twenty-one years, which expired on the 31st of *December* 1808. In *January* 1809, an agreement was entered into between the partners to continue the partnership for a further term of seven years upon the same terms as before, except that the plaintiff should, instead of an equal division of the profits, receive one-tenth of the profits beyond the other partners; by this agreement it was settled, that the plaintiff should receive four-tenths of the profits of the concern, *E. Penfold* three-tenths, and *J. Springett* the remaining three-tenths. In the course of the year 1810, it became necessary that advances should be made to the bank, and on the 17th of

July in that year, the plaintiff advanced to the bank for
the use of the partnership the proceeds of a sum of
30,000*l.* 3 per cent consols, and subsequently a further
sum of 18,200*l.* of the same stock. Before the 1st of
January 1813, by various repayments to the plaintiff,
the advances were reduced to 30,000*l.* 3 per cent. consols, and on that day *E. Penfold* and *J. Springett* made
and executed two several bonds to the plaintiff in the
penal sum of 18,000*l.* each. The condition subjoined
to each was the same, with the change only in the
names of the obligors, and was for the replacing of
9000*l.* 3 per cent. consols on or before the 1st *January*
1814, and payment of the dividends by way of interest in the mean time. In *October* 1813, the sum of
10,000*l.* 3 per cent. consols was reinvested in the plaintiff's name out of the funds of the bank. After the sum of
30,000*l.* consols was advanced as aforesaid, *Parker* insisted upon receiving payments equal to the dividends
without any deduction of the property tax, and he always afterwards had credit in his private account for
an amount equal to the dividends without any deduction
of the property tax upon all the stock remaining due
down to the period of the dissolution of partnership
hereinafter mentioned. He had also credit in his said
account, with his privity, for interest upon the said
payments from the time when such dividends became
due until the same were paid. Interest was not allowed to the customers of the bank unless they left
it for a given period, and then only on a special agreement. The stock mentioned in the conditions of the
bonds was not replaced according to the terms of the
condition, viz. on the 1st day of *January* 1814, on
which day the market price of the stock was 61$\frac{5}{8}$,

S 2   whereby

whereby the bonds became forfeited; and in *Easter* term 1814, the plaintiff signed judgment in two several actions which had been brought by him in *Hilary* vacation in the Court of King's Bench upon the two bonds. On the 5th of *July* 1814, the partnership between the plaintiff and *E. Penfold* and *J. Springett* was dissolved by the plaintiff withdrawing himself from the concern; and on the 13th of the same month of *July* a deed of dissolution of copartnership between the said parties was executed by them. This deed began by reciting, that the parties had carried on the business of a banker under articles of partnership, by which *Parker* was entitled to four-tenths, and each of the others to three-tenths, of the concern; that *Parker* had advanced large sums for the use of the concern; and that *J. Springett* and *E. Penfold* had, by their respective bonds, secured the retransfer to *Parker* of 9000*l.* and 9000*l.* 3 per cent. consols on the 1st of *January* 1814, with the dividends; and that those sums not being retransferred at the day fixed, *Parker* had commenced actions and recovered judgments on those bonds; that the several sums of 9000*l.* and 9000*l.* 3 per cent. consols had not been replaced; and that the further sum of 2000*l.*, like annuities, was also due to *Parker*; that 1139*l.* was standing to *Parker's* credit in the partnership books under the head of profit and loss; and that he had agreed to assign to *E. Penfold* his share in the concern, and the said sum of 1139*l.*, upon having such indemnity against the partnership debts, and such security for the retransfer of the several sums of 9000*l.*, 9000*l.*, and 2000*l.* stock as thereinafter mentioned. The deed contained an assignment by *Parker* to *E. Penfold* of the sum of 1139*l.* and his share in the concern, and covenants by *Springett* and *E. Penfold* to pay the part-

nership

nership debts and indemnify *Parker* against them; and they further covenanted, that the several sums of 9000*l.*, and 9000*l.*, and 2000*l.* 3 per cent. consols, and the interest and dividends, should be transferred and paid to *Parker* by four equal instalments, on the 5th of *January* and the 5th of *July* in the years 1815 and 1816; and that, if default should be made in payment of the said sums or any part thereof, it should be lawful for *Parker* to proceed in the actions before mentioned without reviving the judgments.   They also covenanted, that certain securities specified in a schedule thereunder written, (being the same that were mentioned in the issue,) should, together with the monies payable in respect of them, be retained by *Parker* for two years as an indemnity against partnership debts, and should also be retained until the whole of the said sums of 9000*l.*, 9000*l.*, and 2000*l.* 3 per cent. consols and dividends should be paid.

The dissolution of partnership was proposed by the plaintiff. At that time the bank had sustained considerable losses, for two or three years before no profits had been divided, but the whole of such profits had, at the suggestion of the plaintiff, been carried to a fund, called the reserve fund, to pay off the losses; and at the time of the proposal for and of the dissolution, the concern was known by both parties to be insolvent as a separate establishment, and was believed by both to be deficient to the amount of 7000*l.*, although as to the public it was solvent, because the plaintiff and the defendant *E. Penfold* had both considerable private property.   After the plaintiff had thus retired from the partnership, *E. Penfold* and *Springett* admitted *William Margesson Penfold*, a son of the former, as partner in the concern, and they together continued the banking business until their failure and bankruptcy, as hereinafter mentioned. The first instalment of 5000*l.* 3 per cent. consols was paid under the deed of dissolution; but the second instalment not having been paid according to the terms of that deed, a negociation took place between *E. Penfold* and *Springett* and the plaintiff upon the subject of such default; and on the 6th of *September* 1815, the following agreement was entered into between the plaintiff and the said *E. Penfold* and *Springett*, viz.: " Memorandum, this 6th day of *September* 1815, that it is agreed between *R. Parker* and *E. Penfold*, on behalf of themselves and co-partners in the *Kentish* bank, with reference to their articles of separation in regard to the replacing of stock therein mentioned belonging to Mr. *Parker*, that the second instalment, which should have been replaced in *July* last, of 5000*l.*, and the two future instalments of 5000*l.* each, shall be accounted for in money at the price originally sold out, and the said *E. Penfold* and Co. released from the replacing thereof, and that they shall pay to *R. Parker* interest at 5 per cent. half yearly, on the 5th of *January* and 5th of *July* every year, until the principal and all interest shall have been repaid. *Parker* is to retain all the securities now held by him, except *Archer's* note of 1000*l.*, and a tan yard and premises adjoining, contained in lot second of particulars of sale of *Elgar's* premises, of 28th of *July* 1814, in lieu of which a bond is to be forthwith made and executed by *E. Penfold* to *R. Parker*, to make good any deficiency at the final payment and closing of this account between them. In consideration of the circumstances, and for accommodation of the *Kentish* bank,

R. Parker

R. Parker agrees to postpone the payment of the debt, viz. 5041*l.* 17*s.* 6*d.*, one half part thereof until the 5th day of *July* 1818, and the second half part with all interest due thereon till the 5th of *July* 1820. The amount of the 15,000*l.* consols, at the price sold out, is agreed to be in money 10,083*l.* 15*s.* In case any part of these securities should be sold, the produce is to be paid to Mr. *Parker* on account and in reduction of the within instalments." On the 17th of *July* 1810, at which time the stock was sold out, the market price was 67¼, making the proceeds 10,083*l.* 15*s.* On the 6th of *September* 1815, the market price was 56¼, making the proceeds or value of the stock at that date 8437*l.* 10*s.* Under and in pursuance of this agreement the plaintiff gave up to *E. Penfold* and *Springett* the promissory note of *Archer* for 1000*l.*, mentioned in the schedule to the deed of dissolution, and also his security upon the tan-yard and premises adjoining, mentioned in the memorandum of agreement; and in like performance of the said agreement, on the 10th *October* 1815, *E. Penfold* and *Springett* executed a joint and several bond to the plaintiff, in the penal sum of 10,000*l.*, conditioned for the payment by them, or either of them, to the plaintiff, on the 6th of *July* 1820, of all such part and so much of the said debt or sum of 10,083*l.* 15*s.*, and interest, at the rate of 5 per cent. per annum, on the 6th day of *July* 1820, as should then remain due and owing to the plaintiff, the money to be ultimately recoverable thereon, being limited not to exceed the sum of 5000*l.* On the 10th of *October* 1815, the market price of stock was 58¼. On the 29th of *March* 1816 a commission of bankrupt was issued against *E. Penfold*, *J. Springett*, and *William Margesson Penfold*, under which they were found and

S 4   declared

declared bankrupts; and the defendants in this case were chosen assignees under the commission. At the time of the bankruptcy, several of the debts which were due from the partnership of the [plaintiff and *E. Penfold* and *Springett*, and which *E. Penfold* and *Springett* had covenanted by the deed of dissolution to pay, remained unpaid, and the plaintiff, since the bankruptcy, has paid some of them. The amount of the property tax upon the dividends of the stock remaining due, for which dividends the plaintiff had credit, without allowing a deduction of property tax, was 261*l.* 18*s.* on the 1st *January* 1813, 411*l.* 18*s.* on the 5th *July* 1814, and on the 6th *September* 1815, and at the time of the bankruptcy was 464*l.* 8*s.*

Tindal, for the plaintiff. The plaintiff is entitled to prove under the commission against the two persons who were partners at the time when he left the concern, a debt to be calculated on the basis of the agreement bearing date *September* 6th, 1815. If, however, the Court shall be of opinion that there is any valid objection to that agreement, then the plaintiff may resort to the deed of dissolution, and prove a debt to the amount appearing to be due according to that deed. It is objected to the agreement of *September* 6th, 1815, that it was void for usury. But the situation of the parties shews the contrary. By the deed of dissolution four days were fixed, on each of which a certain amount of stock was to be replaced. One portion of stock was replaced on the first day specified. Another day, before which stock had fallen, arrived, and the lender was then willing to take back the stock, and abide by the loss already incurred, or to accept at a future day the ori-

ginal

ginal value of the stock, giving to the borrower the chance of benefit by a future rise in the value. By that agreement the lender might forego a considerable advantage; and it is a well established rule in this branch of the law, that where the amount of the principal is put in hazard, the contract is not usurious, although more than 5l. per cent. interest be reserved; *Button* v. *Downham* (a): and that principle governs all cases of life annuities. So here it is clear, that the plaintiff might not receive so much under the last agreement as under the deed of dissolution, part of the sum to which he was originally entitled was therefore put in hazard; *Maddock* v. *Rumball* (b); which case also shews that the present is not, as will perhaps be contended, a transaction within the 7 G. 2. c. 8., commonly called the Stock-jobbing act. *Boldero* v. *Jackson* (c) may be cited to shew that the contract here was usurious, but the two cases are very different; there the illegal contract was complete at the moment; here the debtors had the chance of the benefit to be derived from a fluctuation of the stocks during a period of eighteen months. But, secondly, if the second contract be considered usurious, still the former arrangement for payment of the debt due to the plaintiff, contained in the deed of dissolution, remains legal and binding, *Com. Dig. Usury* (B); *Pollard* v. *Scholey* (d), *Ferrall* v. *Shaen*. (e) If that be so then clearly the plaintiff may prove under the commission for the value of those instalments of stock which ought to have been replaced before the commission; for this case differs from *Utterson* v. *Vernon* (f), inasmuch as there no

(a) *Cro. Eliz.* 645. (b) 8 *East*, 304.
(c) 11 *East*, 612. (d) *Cro. Eliz.* 20.
(e) 1 *Saund.* 294. (f) 3 *T. R.* 539. 4 *T. R.* 570.

day

day was fixed for the re-transfer of the stock, and the decision proceeded on that ground. With respect to the last instalment, for the re-transfer of which the day had not arrived before the bankruptcy, *Ex parte King* (a) is an authority for saying that the proof may extend to that also; for bonds were originally given, conditioned for replacing the stock, and judgments were obtained upon them; and the deed of dissolution provides, that in case of any future default, the plaintiff shall be at liberty to resort to those judgments. Thirdly, the plaintiff is clearly entitled to prove for those old partnership debts which he has paid since the bankruptcy. Some argument will be raised as to the deduction of the property tax, but it does not appear that the bankrupts ever accounted for it to government. The question of lien is involved in the first two questions, for if the second agreement is void, and the original one remains valid, then the plaintiff is entitled to a lien on the securities specified in the schedule to the deed of dissolution.

Parke, contrà. The plaintiff, in this case, has no right to prove under the commission for any thing more than the old debts which he has paid since the bankruptcy, nor has he any lien beyond the amount of those debts. The agreement made in *September* 1815 was clearly usurious, and if so, the plaintiff has no right to prove, for he cannot recur to the former securities; the deed of dissolution made in 1814 being satisfied by the subsequent arrangement. Even if that were not so, the proof contended for could not be admitted, as the

(a) 8 *Ves.* 334.

plaintiff

plaintiff has only a claim to unliquidated damages for not replacing stock. The agreement of *September* 1815 was clearly a shift and contrivance to cover usury. At that time one portion of stock had been replaced; as to another, default had been made, and the remaining instalments were to be transferred at future days. The real debt due to the plaintiff in *Sept.* 1815 was the then market price of the 15,000l. stock, viz. 8437l. 10s.; but the sum which the plaintiff stipulated to receive was 10,083l. 15s. and interest thereon. The bargain then was the same as if the value of the stock had at that time been lent, to receive more afterwards than the principal and interest. The agreement may be considered the same as if the stock had been replaced, and immediately sold out again, in order to lend the proceeds; in which case it would manifestly have been a corrupt bargain for the forbearance of money, in consideration of a return of more than the principal and legal interest. In substance and effect it was an agreement to indemnify the plaintiff for a past loss by a fall in the price of stock, in consideration of future forbearance. Or it may be likened to lending stock on an agreement to take it at more than the market price. Such a contract is clearly usurious, *Moore* v. *Battie* (a), *Doe* v. *Barnard* (b), *Boldero* v. *Jackson.* (c) As to the second question which arises, if the agreement of *September* 1815 is void, it must be admitted, that where a bonâ fide debt is due, that is not invalidated by a subsequent agreement for usurious interest, according to *Pollard* v. *Scholy* and *Gray* v. *Fowler* (d): but in those cases the nature of the

(a) 1 *Eden*, 273.　　　(b) 1 *Esp.* 11.
(c) 11 *East*, 612.　　　(d) 1 *H. Bl.* 462.

original

original debt was not altered. [*Abbott* C. J. Could you plead the second agreement in bar of an action of covenant on the deed of dissolution; would it not be pleading simple accord without satisfaction to an action on a specialty?] The new agreement operated as a satisfaction, it is to be considered altogether a new transaction; *Israel* v. *Douglas* (a), *Wade* v. *Wilson* (b), *Hollingworth* v. *Parkhurst* (c), *Dobson* v. *Lockhart.* (d) But if the Court should think that there is a technical difficulty in calling the second agreement a satisfaction of the first, still in equity it is so; and that is a sufficient ground for rejecting the proof sought for. At all events, the plaintiff cannot prove for that instalment of stock which was not due at the time of the bankruptcy; and no case has been cited to shew that he may prove for the others. The sum payable for property tax must also be deducted from the amount to be proved, for the plaintiff had no right to that. [*Littledale* J. You do not shew that the bankrupts accounted to government for the property tax.] Lastly, the deed of dissolution was void, as against the creditors of the firm. The parties knew the concern to be at that time insolvent, that deed, therefore, gave a fraudulent preference to the plaintiff, and the assignees may take the same objection to it that the creditors might, *Anderson* v. *Maltby.* (e)

ABBOTT C. J. I am of opinion that the plaintiff is entitled to prove under the commission issued against *E. Penfold, Springett,* and *W. M. Penfold,* and, consequently, that he has a lien upon the securities mentioned

(a) 1 *H. Bl.* 239.   (b) 1 *East,* 195.
(c) *Noy.* 2.   (d) 5 *T. R.* 133.
(e) 4 *Br. C. C.* 423   2 *Ves. jun.* 244. *S. C.*

in

in the case. The agreement bearing date *September* 1815, is, in my judgment, usurious and void; for it secures to the plaintiff 10,083*l.* for the stock remaining unpaid, which was at that time of considerably less value. It is manifest that the difference was taken for the forbearance. But the effect of holding that agreement void is to set up the original agreement, which was lawful, and make that binding on the parties. It has been so held in transactions of money lent, and I can see no difference in this respect between a loan of money and of stock. If the case had rested on the deed alone, *Parker* could only have proved for those sums which were to have been transferred on days passed before the bankruptcy, and could not have proved for that which remained to be transferred at a future day. But before the execution of the deed of dissolution two bonds had been given for 9000*l.* each to secure the monies advanced by *Parker*, and judgments had been obtained upon them. The deed of dissolution contains a provision, that unless the terms of it were performed *Parker* might resort to the judgments; and that brings in the sum of 2000*l.* mentioned in the deed, which was not otherwise provided for. Those judgments then stand as a security for 15,000*l.* stock, for which *Parker* may consequently prove, the value of the two instalments of 5000*l.* each which ought to have been transferred on days passed before the bankruptcy, to be calculated at the market price of the stock on those days respectively, and of the remaining 5000*l.* at the price on the day of the issuing the commission, with a rebate for the interval between that day and the day appointed for the transfer of that instalment. In addition to those sums, *Parker* is also entitled to prove for the old partnership debts that he has paid. The only remaining point is respecting

the

the property tax; there is so much obscurity in the clause of the act respecting the deduction of it, that I cannot say that the bankrupts are at this distance of time entitled to reclaim that which they appear to have paid voluntarily, especially as it does not appear that they ever paid the money to government. If the agreement of 1815 has not the effect of avoiding the deed of dissolution, it follows that it cannot deprive *Parker* of his lien on the securities mentioned in that deed. The observation as to the deed being a fraud upon the other creditors, is answered by the case which states that the concern was solvent as to the public, although insolvent as a separate establishment.

BAYLEY J. I have not any doubt that the agreement of *September* 1815, was usurious. The statute 8 *Ann.* st. 2. c. 16. applies to loans of money's worth, as well as money itself. The original contract was for a return of the stock lent, that was a legal bargain. The stock when originally sold produced 10,083*l.*, but in *September* 1815, it was worth only 8437*l.*, and therefore, when the new bargain was made, *Parker* lent a thing of the value of 8437*l.* only, and stipulated for a return of 10,083*l.*, with 5 per cent. interest on the latter sum. That was clearly usurious. Then the question arises whether that destroys the former bargain? I am of opinion that it does not. There are many authorities for saying that a bargain for usurious interest upon a pre-existing debt does not bar a claim for that debt. It has been argued that the second bargain changed the nature of the transaction, and that it must be considered as if the stock had been replaced, and then resold. But that is contrary to the real facts of the case, and

Gray

Gray v. Fowler, which was cited at the bar, is an express authority for the plaintiff on this point. Putting the statutes of usury out of the question, if an action had been brought by *Parker* on the deed the bankrupts could not have pleaded the second bargain as an answer; that would have been accord only, but that without satisfaction also is a bad plea to an action founded on a specialty. Then what was the debt secured by the deed of dissolution? It was 20,000*l.* 3 per cent. consols, to be transferred on several days. The first instalment only was duly transferred; for the others *Parker* may, I think, prove in the manner stated by my Lord Chief Justice. He may also prove for the partnership debts which he has paid. As to the property tax, if I could see clearly by the case that the money paid to *Parker* had before paid property tax, and that he knew it, I should hesitate to say that no deduction is to be made in respect of it, inasmuch as he and the bankrupts did not stand upon an equal footing, and it can hardly be taken as a voluntary payment by them.

HOLROYD J. I take the same view of this case both as to the power of proving and the claim of a deduction in respect of the property tax. The agreement made in *September* 1815, was usurious on the grounds already stated; but whether that agreement be or be not void, and laying the statutes against usury out of the question, still it did not put an end to the deed. It has been urged that the new contract amounted to a performance of the former covenants; but I think it did not, and if so, then, even if the second agreement continued in force, an action might nevertheless have been brought

on

on the covenant in the deed; the second agreement being only by parol, could not operate to discharge the deed unless the covenants were satisfied. I think that it was not a performance, but a substitution for the former transaction, and therefore differs from *Wade* v. *Wilson*, and all that class of cases. Then the question is, whether under the former deed and securities there was a proveable debt. I am of opinion that there was, and that under the judgments the sum of 2000*l.*, which was not otherwise provided for, may be proved, as well as the remainder of the debt.

LITTLEDALE J. I think that the agreement of 1815 was usurious. It appears that when the stock was lent in 1810, the market price was 67½*l.*; it may, therefore, be considered as if *Parker* had originally lent his money at less than 5 per cent. interest. But then from 1810 to 1815 he had the chance of a rise in the funds, and therefore had not after that time a right to have the transaction considered as a loan of money from the beginning. In the next place, I think that the second agreement being by parol, cannot be considered a performance of the first, which was by deed. Accord and satisfaction may be pleaded to a deed, but here there was accord only, without satisfaction. As to the other points respecting the property tax and the plaintiff's right of lien, I quite agree with what has fallen from my Lord Chief Justice and my learned brothers.

Judgment for the plaintiff.

WHITE and Another, Executors of W. WHITE, deceased, *against* ANN WRIGHT.

ASSUMPSIT on a special agreement, bearing date the 31st of *August* 1815, breach not re-transferring stock, viz. 400*l.* 3 per cent. consols, either on the transfer day next after the expiration of one year from the date of the agreement, or at any other time before or afterwards, and for not paying the interest and dividends thereon. The declaration contained several special counts, some for not transferring the stock on the next transfer day next after the expiration of one year from the date of the agreement, others for not transferring within seven days after notice given to the defendant, viz. within seven days after the 3rd of *December* 1822, and other counts for the non-payment of the interest and dividends: to which the defendant pleaded several pleas; first, non-assumpsit, and three special pleas of usury, upon which the replication took issue. At the trial before *Alexander* C. B., at the last Spring assizes for *Surrey*, a verdict was found for the plaintiffs, damages 400*l.*, subject to the opinion of the Court upon the following case. By memorandum of an agreement made the 31st of *August* 1815, between the defendant, *Ann Wright*, and the testator *W. White*, (reciting, that the said *W. White* did, on the 29th day of *August* instant, at the request of the said *Ann Wright*, sell out for her accommodation 400*l.* stock in the 3*l.* per cent. consolidated bank annuities, at the price or sum of 55*l.* 15*s.* per cent., and which 400*l.* stock pro-

Where the lender of stock reserved to himself the dividends by way of interest, and the option of deciding at a future day whether he would have the stock replaced, or the sum produced by the sale of it repaid to him in money with 5 per cent. interest: Held, that this bargain was usurious, and that it made no difference whether the whole of the agreement was contained in one instrument, or whether the lender procured the execution of two instruments, by one of which he might compel the replacing of the stock, by the other the payment of the money and interest.

T   duced

duced the sum of 223*l.*, which *W. White* hath lent and advanced to *Ann Wright*, on her bond bearing even date herewith, and also on security of a conditional surrender, of the same date, of certain copyhold premises in the manor of *Epsom*, which she, *Ann Wright*, doth hereby admit and acknowledge. And whereas, previous to the said *W. White's* selling and transferring the said 400*l.* three per cent. consolidated annuities for the accommodation of *Ann Wright*, she did agree with *W. White*, within the time or space of one year from the date hereof, if thereto required by *W. White*, his executors, administrators, or assigns, to transfer, or cause or procure to be transferred unto and to the account of him, *W. White*, his executors, &c. the like sum of 400*l.* stock as aforesaid in the said 3*l.* per cent. consols, and likewise to pay, answer, and make good unto him, *W. White*, his executors, &c. all dividends, interest, and produce which in the mean time he, *W. White*, his executors, &c. could have received or would have been entitled to in case the said 400*l.* stock had remained standing in the books of the Governor and Company of the Bank of *England*, in the name and as the property of him, *W. White*, his executors, &c.) *Ann Wright*, for herself, her heirs, executors, or administrators, agreed with *W. White*, his executors, administrators, or assigns, that she, her heirs, executors, &c. should and would, at her and their own proper costs and charges, on the request of *W. White*, his executors, &c., on the next transfer day next after the expiration of one year from the day of the date of that agreement, or at any subsequent transfer day when thereto requested as aforesaid, transfer unto and to the account of him, *W. White*, his executors, &c. in

the

the books of the said Governor and Company, 400*l*. like stock as aforesaid in the said fund of the said Governor and Company, and likewise should and would in the mean time pay unto him, *W. White*, his executors, &c. all dividends, interest, and produce which he, his executors, &c. could have received or would have been entitled unto in case the said 400*l*. stock had remained and continued standing in the books of the said Governor and Company in the name and as the property of him, *W. White*, his executors, &c. At the same time the defendant executed and delivered to the testator a bond, dated the 31st of *August* 1815, in the penal sum of 440*l*., conditioned for the payment of 223*l*. and interest to *W. White* on the 31st of *August* 1816. Defendant also made the conditional surrender of her property in the manor of *Epsom*, alluded to in the agreement. After *W. White's* death, viz. on the 3rd of *December* 1822, the defendant was requested to re-transfer the stock within seven days from that time. The price of 3 per cent. consols on the 31st of *August* 1815, was 55¾ per cent., and on the 3rd of *September* 1816, 61¼ per cent., and on the 25th of *March* 1824, being two days before the trial, the price was 94½.

Chitty, for the plaintiff. It will be contended for the defendant in this case, that the contract sued upon was usurious, and *Barnard* v. *Young* (a) will probably be relied on as an authority in point. It is, however, very distinguishable. There it was expressly stated, that the lender was at all events to have the option of receiving

(a) 17 *Ves.* 44.

T 2   the

the amount produced by the sale of the stock, or of having the stock replaced. Here the borrower was at liberty to replace the stock at any time within a year after the loan, and according to *Roberts* v. *Trenayne* (a), that power prevented the contract from being usurious. (*Bayley* J. In the case there put, the lender was to receive no interest in the mean time.) But a mere *loan* of stock is not usurious, and this was in effect a loan of stock for the first year, for the borrower might at any time have discharged the debt by replacing the stock. (*Holroyd* J. The defendant was to replace the stock *if requested*.) If a man is bound to do a thing on request, he may do it before. 1 *Roll. Abr.* (R) *pl.* 4, 5.

Comyn, contrà, was stopped by the Court.

ABBOTT C. J. I am of opinion that the case of *Barnard* v. *Young* was rightly decided, and that this is not to be distinguished from it; unless, indeed, it makes a difference that the contract was to be executed by means of two separate instruments instead of being comprised in one. But it was long ago decided in *Roberts* v. *Trenayne*, that such a circumstance makes no difference. It is true, that in *Barnard* v. *Young* the agreement gave *in words* an option to the lender, either to have the stock replaced or the produce paid to him in money. But the two instruments given to the lender in this case produce the same effect, for he might, were it not for the statutes of usury, enforce either the bond for payment of the money, or the agreement to replace the stock. In *Barnard* v. *Young*, the defendant had

(a) *Cro. Jac.* 507.

lent

lent a sum of 10,000*l.*, and that not being repaid at the time specified, a new agreement was entered into, securing to him at a future day either so much stock as the 10,000*l.* would have purchased at the time when it ought to have been paid, or the sum of 10,000*l.* in money at his own option; and there was an undertaking at all events to pay 5*l.* per cent. interest on the principal sum. The Master of the Rolls in giving judgment says, " The lender is at his election to have his principal and interest, or to have a given quantity of stock transferred to him. His principal never was in any hazard, as he was at all events sure of having that with legal interest, and had the chance of an advantage if stock rose. It was usurious to stipulate for that chance. In fact, the stock did rise, and if the contract had been performed, he would have had principal and interest and a very large premium." I cannot distinguish that case in substance and effect from this. Here, if the lender, after receiving 5 per cent. interest on his money, had afterwards, on a rise in the stocks, compelled the defendant to replace the stock sold, he would, as in that case, have had principal, interest, and a premium besides. That is an advantage which by law he was not entitled to contract for. The contract was therefore usurious, and a nonsuit must be entered.

BAYLEY J. Looking at the facts of this case, I am clearly of opinion that it falls within the statute of usury, 12 *Ann.*ᵗ *st.* 2. *c.* 16., which enacts, " that all bonds, contracts, and assurances whatsoever for payment of any principal whereupon or whereby there shall be reserved or taken above the rate of 5*l.* in the 100*l.* for a year, shall be utterly void." If then more than

T 3   5*l.* per

5*l.* per cent. per annum be reserved by means of a collateral advantage either by way of option or otherwise, it is within the statute. A party may lawfully lend stock as stock to be replaced, or he may lend the produce of it as money, or he may give the borrower the option to repay it either in the one way or the other. But he cannot legally reserve to himself a right to determine in future which it shall be. It is not illegal to reserve the dividends by way of interest for stock lent, although they may amount to more than 5*l.* per cent. on the produce of it, for the price of stock may fall, and then the borrower would be a gainer; but the option must be made at the time of the loan. The instruments set out in this case, shew that an option to be exercised in future was reserved. It has been argued that the agreement enabled the defendant at all events, if she chose, to replace the stock; but the agreement is to replace it *if required,* and the bond gave the lender power to enforce the repayment of the principal, which was never put in hazard. Upon principle, therefore, as well as on the authority of the case of *Barnard* v. *Young,* I think that the plaintiffs are not entitled to recover in this action.

H<small>OLROYD</small> J. I am of opinion that this contract is usurious, and cannot be distinguished from that which was decided to be so in *Barnard* v. *Young.* The case of *Roberts* v. *Trenayne,* shews that the effect is the same whether the contract be contained in one instrument or in several. If the produce of stock is lent with an agreement that it shall be returned in money, and the dividends are in the mean time reserved by way of interest, that is usurious if the dividends amount to more

than

than 5*l.* per cent. on the produce of the stock. This case is still stronger, for the dividends did amount to more than 5 per cent. on the sum produced by the stock, and in addition to that the lender had the further benefit of choosing at a future time whether the repayment should be made in stock or money. He was, therefore, entitled at all events to the principal, and more than 5 per cent. interest, and the chance of a still greater profit if the price of stocks happened to rise.

LITTLEDALE J. I am of the same opinion. The dividends reserved in this case amounted to more than 5 per cent. on the produce of the stock. But the law allows that, if it be bonâ fide a mere loan of stock to be replaced, for then, if the stocks fall, part of the principal is lost. Here no part of the principal was put in hazard. The bond was given absolutely for repayment of the money at a certain day, and no option was given to the borrower as to repaying the money or replacing the stock. Such a contract is usurious, and no action can be founded on it.

Judgment of nonsuit.

1824.

The East India Company *against* Tritton and Others.

Certain bills of exchange, drawn upon and accepted by the *E. I.* Company in favor of *W. H.* in *India*, were afterwards indorsed to *D.* and *C.* by an agent for *W. H* , under a supposed authority given by a power of attorney, which was seen and inspected by the acceptors; *D.* and *C.* indorsed the bills to *B.* and Co., their bankers, in order that the latter might, as their agents, present them for payment when due; *B.* and Co. put their names on the back of the bills, presented them for payment, and received the amount, which they soon after paid over to

ASSUMPSIT. The first count of the declaration stated, that before the time of making the promise by the defendants thereinafter next mentioned, in parts beyond the seas, to wit, at *Fort St. George*, in the *East Indies*, that is to say, in *London*, one *G. G. Keble*, by order of the Honorable the Governor in Council there, and according to the usage and custom of merchants, had made three certain bills of exchange in writing, and then and there directed the same to the Honorable the Court of Directors of the *East India* Company in *London;* by one of which said bills of exchange, bearing date on the 20th of *January* 1809, the said *G. G. Keble* requested the drawees thereof, at three months' sight of that second of exchange (first or third not being paid) to pay or cause to be paid unto one *W. Hope*, Esquire, or his order, in *London*, the sum of 8940*l.* sterling, (the declaration then set out two other bills in the same form, one for 13,200*l.*, the other for 1140*l.*,) which said bills of exchange the said plaintiffs afterwards, to wit, on &c., at &c., upon sight thereof by one *W. Ramsay*, their agent in that behalf, duly ac-

their principals. It was afterwards discovered that the power of attorney given by *W. H.* did not authorise his agent to indorse the bills, and the administrator of *W. H.*, in an action against the acceptors, recovered the amount of them. The acceptors then brought an action against *B.* and Co., and declared on a supposed undertaking by them, that they, as holders, were entitled to receive the amount of the bills. The jury found that the plaintiffs paid the bills on the faith of the power of attorney, and not of the indorsement by the defendants, and that the latter paid over the money before they had notice of the invalidity of the first indorsement. Held, that, under these circumstances, the plaintiffs could not recover against the defendants.

Semble, that an indorser does not impliedly warrant the validity of prior indorsements.

cepted,

cepted, according to the said usage, &c., and according
to the form of the statutes in that case made and provided; the declaration then stated, that when the bills
became due they were presented by the defendants, then
being the holders thereof, to the plaintiffs for payment,
and that at the time of the presentment of the said
several bills of exchange to the plaintiffs for payment as
aforesaid, each and every of the said bills of exchange
purported to be indorsed by the said *W. Hope*, by one
J. Card, as the agent for, and by procuration of the said
W. Hope, to Messrs. *Davies* and *Card*, who indorsed
them to the defendants.   The declaration then alleged,
that, at the time of the presentment of the bills for payment, the defendants, according to the said usage, &c.,
had made their indorsement in writing upon each of the
bills, their names, style, and firm of dealing, of *Barclay*,
Tritton, and Co. being thereon respectively written and
then remaining thereon, and had thereby appointed the
said sums of money in the said bills respectively mentioned to be paid to the bearer thereof respectively;
and the defendants then and there asserted and affirmed,
that they the defendants were then and there entitled, as
such holders of the said bills of exchange as aforesaid,
to receive the several sums of money therein mentioned
respectively; and the plaintiffs in fact say, that they, relying upon the indorsement by the defendants so being
upon the said bills as last aforesaid, and upon the said
assertion and affirmation of the defendants, did then and
there pay to the defendants, so being the holders of the
said several bills of exchange, the several sums of
money mentioned in the same, then and there amounting to the sum of 23,282l. 6s. 6d. Averment, that the
indorsement by *Card* was made without any authority
from

from *W. Hope*, and that before the indorsements were made by *Card*, to wit, on the 14th of *March* 1809, the said *W. Hope* had departed this life in parts beyond the seas, to wit, at &c. The declaration then set out a grant of administration to *James Murray* afterwards and after such payment as aforesaid, to wit, on the 13th of *February* 1812, and of administration de bonis non to *John Murray*, on the 31st of *October* 1814; and that *John Murray*, within six years after the grant of administration to *James Murray*, commenced an action against the present plaintiffs, to recover the amount of the said bills and interest, and in *Michaelmas* term, 2 *G.* 4., recovered 35,827*l.*, which plaintiffs afterwards paid: of all which premises the defendants afterwards, to wit, on &c., at &c. had notice; by reason of which said several premises last mentioned, the defendants then and there became liable to pay to the plaintiffs the said sum of money last mentioned, whenever they the defendants should be thereunto afterwards requested, and being so liable, promised to pay it.

The second count alleged, that the bills were indorsed by defendants, and that plaintiffs paid them, relying on the indorsement, and omitted the statement of any such assertion or affirmation by the defendants, as that set out in the first count.

The third count alleged, that defendants indorsed the bills to the plaintiffs, and that they relying on the indorsement, paid.

The fourth count stated, that in consideration that the plaintiffs would pay the defendants being the holders of the bills, defendants promised that they would save harmless and indemnify the plaintiffs from any loss or damage by reason of the payment of the bills; and

after

after setting out the proceedings by *John Murray*, as in
the first count, assigned as a breach, that the defendants
had not saved them harmless.

The fifth count stated, that defendants undertook
and promised, that they were entitled, as holders of the
bills, to receive the several sums of money therein mentioned, and that they would indemnify the plaintiffs.
Averment, that they were not, as holders, entitled to
receive the money, and breach, that they did not indemnify the plaintiffs.

The sixth count was on a promise to indemnify the
plaintiffs if they, the defendants, were not entitled to
receive the money on the bills. To these the common
money counts were added. Pleas, 1st, non assumpsit;
2dly, to the first six counts, actio non accrevit infra sex
annos; to the others, non assumpsit infra sex annos.
Issue thereon. At the trial before *Abbott* C. J. at the
London sittings after *Trinity* term 1823, a special verdict
was found, which stated in substance as follows. The
several bills mentioned in the declaration were drawn
and accepted as therein alleged. Afterwards, and when
the said bills became due and payable, to wit, on, &c.,
the same were presented for payment to the plaintiffs by
the defendants and one *R. Barclay* since deceased, then
being bankers in *London*, and holders as the bankers and
agents of and for Messrs. *Davies* and *Card*, as hereinafter
mentioned, by the hands of one *W. Bell*, then being the
clerk and servant of the defendants and *R. Barclay* since
deceased, in that behalf. At the time of the presentment
of the said several bills of exchange to the plaintiffs for
payment, each and every of the said bills of exchange had
indorsements upon them in the words following; that is
to say, " Pay Messrs. *Davies* and *Card*, or their order,
per

per procuration of *William Hope. J. Card.*" " Pay
Messrs. *Barclay, Tritton,* and company, or order.
Davies and *Card.*" " *Barclay, Tritton,* and Co.*" On
the 7th of *October* 1800, *W. Hope* executed a power of
attorney to *Card.* (The power was then set out, being the
same mentioned in *Murray* v. *East India Company.*(a))
The first indorsement was in the proper hand-writing
of *J. Card,* and before the time of the presentment of
the said three bills of exchange for payment, and previously to the payment thereof, the said power of
attorney was produced to the plaintiffs for their inspection, and the same was inspected by them accordingly; when the said power of attorney was so produced, an entry thereof was made by the plaintiffs
in a register kept by them in their treasurer's office,
for the entry of powers of attorney to be acted upon
in. paying monies for the plaintiffs at such office,
where all payments by the plaintiffs were and are
made. . *W. Hope* died on the 14th of *March* 1809, but
neither the plaintiffs nor the defendants and *R. Barclay,*
since deceased, nor *J. Card,* at the time of the payment of the said bills of exchange hereinafter mentioned, had any knowledge of the death of the said
W. Hope. The bills were indorsed by *Davies* and
Card, and the defendants, as alleged. Upon the presentment of the said bills of exchange to the plaintiffs
by the said *W. Bell,* then being a clerk and servant
of the defendants and *R. Barclay,* since deceased,
the plaintiffs did pay to the said *William Bell,* as
such clerk and servant of the defendants, and *R.
Barclay,* since deceased, the several sums of money re-

(a) 5 *B. & A.* 204.

spectively

spectively mentioned in the same bills of exchange, amounting together to the sum of 23,282*l.* 6*s.* 6*d.*, which were received by the defendants and *R. Barclay* accordingly. The said payment of the said bills of exchange was so made by the plaintiffs to the defendants and *R. Barclay*, since deceased, on the faith of *John Card*'s indorsement on the said bills of exchange, and of the said power of attorney from the said *W. Hope* to *J. Card*, and not on the faith of the indorsement of the defendants and *R. Barclay* on the said bills of exchange. Long before, and at the time of the payment of the said bills of exchange as aforesaid, *Davies* and *Card* kept a banking account with the defendants and *R. Barclay*, since deceased, who then carried on the trade or business of bankers in the city of *London* in copartnership together, and which said last-mentioned *R. Barclay* died before the commencement of this action. *Davies* and *Card*, on the 17th of *October* 1809, specially indorsed the said bills of exchange as aforesaid to the defendants and *R. Barclay*, since deceased, and delivered the same to the defendants and *R. Barclay*, that they, as the bankers of the said *Davies* and *Card* might, in the usual course of banking business, receive payment of the said bills of exchange when the same should be due, for and on account of the said *Davies* and *Card*, the defendants and *R. Barclay* not having had at any time any interest in the said bills of exchange or the proceeds thereof. The defendants and *R. Barclay*, since deceased, received the money as agents for *Davies* and *Card*, who drew out the whole of it on the 11th of *December* 1809. The grant of administration to *James Murray*, and afterwards of administration

ministration de bonis non to *John Murray*; the action
by him against the *East India* Company; the notice of
such action to the defendants; the recovery by the
plaintiff in that action, and payment of the money recovered to him by the *East India* Company; and the
notice of that fact to the defendants, were then found,
as alleged in the declaration.

The case was now argued by

Tindal, for the plaintiffs. Upon the whole of the
record in this case it appears that the plaintiffs have
paid the bills in question twice over; and the point now
to be determined is, whether they have brought their
action against the right persons to recover the money so
paid. Each of the special counts contains an allegation
that the indorsement of the defendants was on the bills
when they were presented for payment. That, in law,
imports a warranty that they were the true and lawful
holders of the bills. When the name of the drawer of
a bill has been forged, the acceptor having paid it to an
indorsee, cannot recover back the money, *Smith* v.
Chester, (a) but that is on the ground that the acceptor
is bound to know the drawer's hand-writing. Here it
appears that the name of the first indorser was written
without his authority; but the defendants, by demanding
the money, and putting their names on the bills, impliedly warranted that they could, if necessary, produce
evidence of the first indorsement. This follows from
what was said by *Chambre* J. in *Smith* v. *Mercer*. (b)
The plaintiffs in that case had, as bankers of the supposed acceptor of a bill, paid the amount to the defend-

(a) 1 *T. R.* 654.   (b) 6 *Taunt.* 83.

ants,

ments, the holders, who indorsed it before it was presented for payment. The acceptance was afterwards discovered to be a forgery, and an action was brought to recover back the money so paid. That learned Judge says: " The defendants have paid their money for that which is of no value; they have thereby sustained a loss, and they ought not to be permitted to throw that loss upon another innocent man, who has done no act to mislead them; and still less ought they to be so permitted where, instead of being misled by any act of the plaintiffs, they themselves have given the appearance of authenticity to the instrument by their own indorsement, which was a sort of warranty of its genuineness at a time when the forged acceptance made a part of the instrument." So here the names of *Barclay* and Co. on the back of the bills amounted to a sort of warranty that the prior indorsements were made by persons having proper authority for that purpose. On the other side, three objections will probably be made. 1st, That the action is barred by the statute of limitations; 2dly, that the bills were paid by the plaintiffs on the faith of the power of attorney, and not of the indorsement by *Barclay* and Co.; 3dly, that the defendants received the money as mere agents, and paid it over to their principal before they had any notice that *Card* had not authority to indorse the bills. [*Abbott* C.J. You had better begin with the second objection, for unless that can be obviated, it will not be necessary to discuss the others.] If the indorsement by *Barclay* and Co. amounts to a warranty, it is no answer to say that the money was not paid on the faith of that warranty. If goods are furnished to *A.* and a warranty of the payment is given by *B.*, it would be no defence to an action on that warranty

ranty against·*B.* to show that at the time of the sale his credit was not so good as *A.*'s, and that the goods were furnished on *A.*'s credit, and not on-the credit of the warranty. So here, although the bills were paid on the faith of the indorsement by *Card* under the power of attorney given to him, that is no answer to this action if the indorsement by *Barclay* and Co. is to be considered as a warranty. To support the next objection, viz. that the defendants received the money as agents, *Sadler* v. *Evans* (a) will probably be relied on; but there all parties knew that the defendant received the money as agent. Here there is nothing to show that the *East India* Company knew the defendants to be agents. Under such circumstances an action will lie against the agent to recover back the money wrongfully paid to him. *Snowdon* v. *Davis.* (b) [*Bayley* J. There the defendant wrongfully took the money in the first instance.]

Campbell, contrà, was stopped by the Court.

Abbott C. J. I am clearly of opinion that the plaintiffs cannot maintain this action. It is found as a fact by the special verdict that before the bills were paid the plaintiffs took all such steps as they judged fit to satisfy themselves that the first indorsement by *J. Card* was made by virtue of a sufficient authority. The power of attorney was not produced by the defendants; nor does it appear that they ever saw it, or had any means whatever of forming a judgment as to its sufficiency. But laying that part of the case aside, it further appears that after the *East India* Company, who had full means

(a) 4 *Burr.* 1984.   (b) 1 *Taunt.* 359.

of

of knowledge, had made all such inquiries as they thought fit, the defendants, who are perfectly innocent parties, received the money as agents and paid it over to their principals. As soon as the defendants received the money *Davies* and *Card* might have maintained an action against them for it; they were, therefore, bound to pay it over. Perhaps, indeed, they might have refused to do so had the money remained in their hands until the insufficiency of *J. Card's* authority to indorse the bills was discovered; but in fact the whole had been paid over before any such discovery was made. The plaintiffs, therefore, cannot now call upon them to restore money which is not in their hands, and which they had no right to withhold from their principals. For these reasons our judgment must be for the defendants.

BAYLEY J. The most favourable view of this case for the plaintiffs, is to say that both parties are innocent and free from blame; but even then the maxim "potior est conditio possidentis" applies. And it is to be observed, that all the means of ascertaining the extent of *Card's* authority were within the reach of the plaintiffs, and notwithstanding that, they thought fit to pay the money. Great injustice would be worked if they were now allowed to recover it back. The defendants did not take the bills immediately from *Card*, but mediately through *Davies* and *Card*; they had not, therefore, any right to see the power in the hands of *Card*, nor am I prepared to admit that every indorser warrants the genuineness of the prior indorsements. But it is not necessary to decide or discuss that question. The power was shewn to the plaintiffs, it was for them to judge of the extent of the authority given by it. The imputation of negligence does therefore attach upon the plaintiffs, but not upon the defendants. The latter received the money as agents and have paid it over, it would be extremely unjust to make them refund the money. I am therefore of opinion, that the plaintiffs cannot recover in this action.

Holroyd J.   I agree entirely both in the principles of law which have been stated by my Lord Chief Justice and my Brother *Bayley*, and in the application of them to this case.   The money was paid by the plaintiffs, not on a mistake of fact but of law, the case of *Bilbie* v. *Lumley* (a) is therefore sufficient to dispose of this question. The plaintiffs had the means of knowledge in their power, and acted upon the information which they obtained.   It turned out that *Card* had not any authority to indorse the bills, but I think the defendants were entitled to presume that the indorsement was properly made, and were justified in receiving the money, and when they had received it, they could not have resisted an action brought for it by their principals.   Here was no express promise to repay the money to the plaintiffs if the indorsement proved insufficient, nor can any such promise be implied from the facts of the case.   The defendants have paid over the money to persons who could by law have compelled them to do so, the plaintiffs then cannot be entitled to recover in this action.

Littledale J.   The whole of the argument for the plaintiffs was founded on the supposition, that a person presenting a bill for payment gives a warranty that the

(a) 2 *East*, 469.

indorse-

indorsements are genuine and made under a proper authority. Here, certainly, there was not any express warranty, and I am not aware of any case which says that such a warranty is to be implied. The dictum of *Chambre J.*, which has been cited, is only that it is a *sort* of warranty. In the present instance, upon the facts found by the special verdict, there was nothing like an implied warranty or even a representation. The plaintiffs paid on the faith of the power of attorney, which was shewn to and examined by them. Clearly, the law will not imply a warranty by the defendants, that *Card* had power to indorse the bills when the plaintiffs had the means of ascertaining the extent of his authority, and the defendants had not. If, therefore, in general, there were an implied warranty, of which however I am not aware, it would in this case be negatived by the finding of the jury. Upon the whole then it appears, that there is not any ground for the claim made in this action.

1824.

The EAST INDIA Co.
against
TRITTON.

Judgment for the defendants.

LEWIS *against* CATHERINE LEE.

ASSUMPSIT for goods sold, money lent, &c. Plea, praying judgment of the writ, because, before and at the time of suing out the writ of the plaintiff, she, the said *Catherine*, was and now is married to one *Francis Lee*, who is still living, to wit, at, &c. And this, &c. wherefore because he is not named in the said writ, she prays judgment thereof, and that the same be quashed.

A woman divorced a mensa et thoro for adultery, and living separate and apart from her husband, cannot be sued as a feme sole,

U 2

Repli-

Replication, that the said writ, by reason of any thing by the said *Catherine* in her said plea alleged, ought not to be quashed, because, before the time of making the said several promises and undertakings in the declaration mentioned, the said *Francis Lee* exhibited a libel in the Arches Court of *Canterbury* against the said *Catherine*; and that the said *Francis*, on the 4th day of *December* 1814, obtained against the said *Catherine* in the said court, a definitive sentence of divorce from the bed and board of, and mutual cohabitation with, the said *Francis*, for adultery committed by the said *Catherine* with one *A. B.*; and that, before and at the time of the making of the said promises and undertakings in the declaration mentioned, and from thence, until and at the time of issuing out the said writ of the plaintiff against the said *Catherine*, and still, she, the said *Catherine*, lived divorced, separate, and apart from the said *Francis Lee*, her husband; and that she, the said *Catherine*, during all the time aforesaid, and still, had a large, ample, and sufficient allowance, as and for her separate maintenance, and which allowance had been during all that time paid to her, to wit, at, &c. And that the said *Catherine*, so being divorced, separate, and apart from her said husband, and having such allowance, the said several promises in the declaration mentioned, were made by the said *Catherine* as a feme sole upon her own separate credit and account, and not upon the credit or account of her said husband, to wit, at, &c. And this, &c. wherefore he prayed judgment, and that the said writ might be adjudged good, and that the said *Catherine* might answer over thereto, &c. Demurrer.

Dover in support of the demurrer. The replication is bad in point of form, because it refers to the promises

in

in the declaration and not to the writ, of which the plea prays judgment. It therefore goes beyond the plea, to which it ought to be an answer, and is bad as a departure from it. Secondly, it contains double matter. The plaintiff relies upon two points : first, the divorce; and, secondly, that credit was given to the defendant as a feme sole. These two facts have no connection, and do not constitute one proposition. Thirdly, the divorce is informally pleaded, for it ought to have been shewn before whom, and for what cause, it took place, *Comyn's Dig. Abatement*, (H) 43., 1 *Co. Lit.* 303. a. But, fourthly, the replication is no answer to the plea, because it does not shew that the defendant had ceased to be a feme covert; and it is quite clear, that if she continued a feme covert, she was not liable to be sued alone. *Gilchrist* v. *Brown* (a) shews that a feme covert living apart from her husband and in adultery, cannot be sued as a feme sole; and the law is the same even if she lives separate, and has alimony pending the suit in the Ecclesiastical Court, and obtains credit in her own name, *Ellagh* v. *Leigh.* (b) In *Marshall* v. *Rutton* (c), all the former cases were reviewed, and it was fully established, that a feme covert cannot bring an action while *the relation of marriage subsists,* and she and her husband are living in this kingdom, notwithstanding she lives separate from her husband, and has a separate maintenance secured to her by deed. If the defendant, therefore, be still a feme covert, this falls within the rule laid down in these cases. Whether she be a feme covert or not depends upon the effect which the common law courts will give to a sentence of divorce a mensa et thoro. Now, at com-

(a) 4 T. R. 766.   (b) 5 T. R. 679.   (c) 8 T. R. 545.

mon

mon law a wife could not sue without her husband, except in cases where he was supposed to be civiliter
mortuus. In *Co. Lit.* 132 *b.* Lord *Coke* says, "that a
wife is disabled to sue without her husband, as much as
a monk is without his sovereign, and he mentions Sir
Robert Belknap's case as an exception. He was exiled
or banished for *life* beyond sea, and his wife was allowed
to sue out a writ in her own name, he being alive."
And Lord *Coke* afterwards observes, "that a deportation
for ever into a foreign land, like to profession, is a civil
death, and that is the reason that the wife may bring an
action or may be impleaded during the natural life of
her husband; and so, if by an act of parliament the
husband be attainted of treason or felony, and saving
his life, is banished for *ever* as *Belknap* was, this is a
civil death, and the wife may sue as a feme sole; but if
the husband have judgment to be exiled but *for a time,*
which some call a relegation, that is no civil death."
Unless, therefore, the sentence of divorce a mensa et
thoro, operates as a civil death of the husband, it is clear
that the wife cannot be sued as a feme sole. Now, here
the divorce is for adultery, and though at one time it
was held that that was a ground of divorce, a vinculo
matrimonii; it was afterwards solemnly settled in *Foljambe's* case in 44 *Elizabeth* (a), that it was only ground
of divorce a mensa et thoro, and this alteration of the
law may account for some of the dicta to be found in
the older cases. The sentence of divorce a mensa et
thoro does not extinguish the obligations attending the
relation of husband and wife, but merely suspends them
and operates only as a temporary separation. The

(a) *Moore*, 683. *Noy.* 100.

sentence,

sentence, so far from dissolving the matrimonial tie, by its very tenor contemplates the possibility of reconciliation and renewed cohabitation, and it is in conformity to this notion that the injured party, before becoming entitled to the benefit of the sentence, is obliged to enter into a bond to lead a chaste and continent life without contracting marriage during the life of the defendant. The words of the sentence are, "We do declare that the said *A. B.* ought by law to be divorced and separated from bed, board, and mutual cohabitation with the said *C. D.,* her husband, *until they shall be reconciled to each other,* and we do divorce, &c. bond being given." (a)   It is evident, therefore, that the sentence contemplates only a temporary separation, and resembles the case put by Lord *Coke,* where the husband is exiled but for a time.   It does not operate, therefore, as a civil death of the husband does.   In that case the woman is considered as a widow.   Such a sentence does not bar dower, *Co. Lit.* 32., *Stowel's* case (b), nor bastardize the issue (c), nor determine an estate to the husband for the life of his wife.   At common law, therefore, the effect of such a sentence was not to destroy the relation of husband and wife, and to make the woman a feme sole. By the 13 *Ed.*1. *s.*1. *c.*33., a woman who elopes with, and continues with, an adulterer, loses her dower; but that is by the positive enactment of the legislature.   If parties separated by divorce a mensa et thoro marry again, they may be proceeded against in the Ecclesiastical Courts, although they are not indictable for felony under the 1 *Jac.*1. *c.*11., because they are within the exception in

(a) *Poynter on Marriage and Divorce,* 182.
(b) *Godbold,* 145. *Noy.* 108. But see, contrà, *Roll's Abr. Dower,* p. 13.
(c) *Burn's Eccl. Law,* tit. *Marriage,* 502.

the

the third section; but it is quite clear from *Porter's* case (*a*), that if they had not been expressly excepted, they would have been within the enacting clause. It is clear, then, that the sentence of divorce a mensa et thoro has not the effect of putting an end to the coverture of the woman; and that being so, *Hatchett* v. *Baddeley* (*b*), and *Marshall* v. *Rutton* (*c*), shew that she cannot be sued as a feme sole.

Abraham, contrà. The authorities cited on the other side establish this principle, that it is not in the power of parties, by their private agreement, to alter the character and condition, which by law results from the state of marriage. But here, that character and condition is altered, not by the agreement of the parties, but by the sentence of a court of competent jurisdiction. In *Ellagh* v. *Leigh* (*d*) proceedings had been instituted in the Ecclesiastical Court, and alimony had been allowed; but no adjudication had taken place upon the matter before the court. In this case the replication states, that the Ecclesiastical Court pronounced a definitive sentence of divorce from bed and board, and that the parties did live separate at the time when the action was brought. It does not appear that the separation was to be temporary; it might continue during their lives. In 3 *Salkeld*, 138. it is said, that a divorce for adultery was anciently a vinculo matrimonii, and, therefore, in the beginning of the reign of Queen *Elizabeth*, the opinion was, that after divorce, the parties might marry again; but in *Foljambe's* case (*e*), that opinion was changed, and it was held to be only ground of divorce a mensa et thoro;

(*a*) Cro. Car. 461.   (*b*) 2 Blac. 1079.
(*c*) 8 T. R. 545.   (*d*) 5 T. R. 679.
(*e*) Moore, 683. Noy. 100.

and

and according to *Stephens* v. *Totty* (a), after a divorce causa adulterii, a release by the husband of an obligation made to his wife before marriage was adjudged good. Admitting, therefore, that a sentence of divorce a mensa et thoro does not wholly destroy the relation of husband and wife, still it operates as a suspension of that relation so long as the parties continue to live separate in pursuance of the sentence; and upon that ground, children born during such separation, are primâ facie bastards, *The Parish of St. George* v. *St. Margaret, Westminster*. (b) Here it is stated, that the wife did, at the commencement of the action, live separate and apart from her husband: she, therefore, was not at that time a feme covert.

ABBOTT C. J. There is no authority to shew that a sentence of divorce a mensa et thoro for adultery so far destroys the relation of husband and wife as to make the latter a feme sole. In *Hatchett* v. *Baddeley* (c), *Blackstone* J. says, that a feme covert cannot be sued alone unless in the known excepted cases of abjuration, exile, and the like, where the husband is considered as dead, and the woman as a widow, or else as divorced a vinculo. In *Hyde* v. *Price* (d), the then Master of the Rolls, Lord *Alvanley*, after citing this dictum, says, that he had taken the pains to look at all the cases on this subject which were collected in *Lean* v. *Schutz* (e), and that they all shewed that, subject to the exceptions mentioned by Mr. Justice *Blackstone*, no action could be maintained against a married woman; and in

(a) *Cro. Eliz.* 908.   (b) 1 *Salk.* 123.
(c) 2 *Black.* 1082.   (d) 3 *Ves.* 443.
(e) 2 *Bl.* 1195.

Marshall

1824.

Lewis
against
Lee.

Marshall v. *Rutton*, which was argued before the twelve Judges, Lord *Kenyon*, in delivering the judgment of the court says, "We find no authority in the books to shew that a man and his wife can, by agreement between themselves, change their legal capacities and characters, or that a woman may be sued as a feme sole, while the relation of marriage subsists, and she and her husband are living in this kingdom." *Now* in this case it is clear, from the authorities cited, and from the terms of the sentence which have been referred to, that a divorce for adultery does not destroy the relation of marriage, but that it merely suspends for a time some of the obligations arising out of that relation. The relation of marriage, therefore, still subsisting, and the defendant still continuing a feme covert, according to all these authorities, she cannot be sued without her husband. The judgment of the Court must, therefore, be for the defendant.

Judgment for the defendant.

BUSHBY and Another, Executors of J. BUSHBY, *against* JOHN MILBOURN DIXON, Heir of JOHN MILBOURN DIXON, deceased.

A. B., seised of lands in fee simple, at the time of her death in the possession of a tenant from year to year, died, leaving *C. D.* her heir at law. No rent was ever paid to him, it being supposed that the lands passed to a devisee under the will of *A. B.* After the death of *C. D.*, his son and heir at law brought ejectment, and recovered the lands. In debt against the son, as heir of *C. D.*, on a bond given by the latter, to which the son pleaded no assets by descent from his father, it was held, that the father was *seised, in fact,* of the lands in question, that they descended from him to his son, and were, *therefore,* assets in the hands of the latter, liable to the bond debt.

DEBT on a bond, dated the 12th of *November* 1795, executed by *John Milbourn Dixon*, deceased, and *Lucy Dixon*, deceased, to *John Bushby*, deceased, in the

penal

penal sum of 360*l.*, conditioned for the payment of
180*l.*, with interest, at 4¾ per cent. on the 12th of *November* 1796. The first plea was non est factum. The
second solvit ad diem. The third solvit post diem. On
which pleas respectively issues were joined, and found
for the plaintiff. The last plea and issue thereon were
as follows: that defendant ought not to be charged with
the said debt, by virtue of the said supposed writing
obligatory, because he, the said defendant, hath not, nor
at the time of the exhibiting the bill of the said plaintiffs
in this behalf, nor at any time before or since, had he
any lands, tenements, or hereditaments by descent from
the said *John Milbourn Dixon,* in fee simple; and this,
&c., wherefore he prays judgment if he, the said defendant, as heir of the said *John Milbourn Dixon* deceased, ought to be charged with the said debt by virtue
of the said writing obligatory. Replication, that the
defendant hath, and at the time of the exhibiting of the
bill of the plaintiffs in this behalf, had sufficient lands,
tenements, and hereditaments by descent from the said
John Milbourn Dixon in fee simple, wherewith the said
defendant could, and might, and ought to have satisfied
the said debt above demanded. At the trial before
Holroyd J., at the Summer assizes for *Cumberland,* 1823,
a verdict was found for the plaintiffs on this last issue,
subject to the opinion of the Court on the following
case. The obligor, *Lucy Dixon,* at the time of making
her will, and also of her death as hereinafter mentioned,
was seized in fee of the adjoining tenements of *Catlowdy*
and *Simeons Onset,* being both of freehold tenure, and
situate in the parish of *Kirk Andrews upon Esk,* in the
county of *Cumberland;* and by her will duly executed,
devised her messuage or tenement, called *Catlowdy,* to

her

her daughter *Ann*, the wife of *John Milbourn*, for her life with power to dispose thereof by will. *Lucy Dixon* died so seised, on the 15th of *June* 1797. At the time of making her will, and also of her death, both *Catlowdy* and *Simeons Onset* were occupied as one farm, being in the possession of the same person as tenant from year to year of the whole, under one rent; which person continued in possession as tenant until the year 1807. From the time of the death of *Lucy Dixon*, *Ann Milbourn*, and *John Milbourn* her husband, contending that *Simeons Onset* passed by this devise, received the rents of both estates during her life. *Ann Milbourn* died in 1801, and after her death, her husband *John Milbourn* received the rents and profits both of *Catlowdy* and *Simeons Onset*, as tenant by the curtesy until his death, which took place in *June* 1815. In 1807, the said *John Milbourn* granted a lease of the two tenements to *John Forster* and *Adam Forster* for nine years, under which the lessees held the possession, and paid the rent to *John Milbourn* during his life; the last rent which was paid by them to *John Milbourn* was at *Whitsuntide* 1815, and then due, which was subsequently to the death of *John Milbourn Dixon*, the other obligor, which took place on the 27th of *April* 1815. The obligor *John Milbourn Dixon* was the heir at law of *Lucy Dixon*, and he, in *Hilary* vacation 1815, served a declaration in ejectment upon the tenant in possession of *Simeons Onset*, claiming it as heir at law of *Lucy Dixon*, but he died as before stated, on the 27th of *April* 1815, and no further proceedings took place therein. The defendant, after the death of his father, brought another ejectment, and after obtaining a judgment by default, recovered the possession of *Simeons Onset* in *Trinity* vacation 1815.

After-

Afterwards one *Isaac Milbourn*, the son of the said *Ann Milbourn*, brought an ejectment for the same premises, which was defended by *J. M. Dixon* the present defendant, upon the trial of which a verdict was found for the defendant, and a rule nisi having been obtained to set aside that verdict, the Court of King's Bench upon argument discharged the rule, being of opinion that *Simeons Onset* did not pass either by the will of *Lucy Dixon* or of *Ann Milbourn*. The question for the opinion of the Court is, whether the present defendant took *Simeons Onset* by descent from his father.

Patteson for the plaintiff. The simple question to be decided is, whether the defendant's father was ever actually seised of *Simeons Onset*, for it must be admitted, that a seisin in law in the father is not sufficient to make the estate assets in the hands of his son, *Co. Lit.* 11 *b.* n. 3. The case states, that the estate in question at the time of *Lucy Dixon's* death was in the possession of a tenant from year to year. At that time *J. M. Dixon*, the father, could not enter by reason of the outstanding term, but the possession of a tenant for years is the possession of the person entitled to the freehold; the father was therefore seised in fact immediately on the death of *L. Dixon*. In *Co. Litt.* 15 *a.* this very case is put, and the same was held respecting a copyhold in fee in *Brown's* case. (a) In note 82. to *Co. Litt.* 15 *a.* Mr. *Hargrave* cites *Jenk.* 242. as shewing that the entry of a devisee for years will make a possessio fratris, *Vin. Abr. Descent* (K), *pl.* 34. *S. C.* So in *Goodtitle* v. *Newman* (b), the possession of guardian in socage was held to

(a) 4 *Co.* 21. *Moore*, 125.   (b) 3 *Wils.* 516.

ne

be the possession of the heir. The possession of tenant for years has also been holden sufficient to give *actual* seisin to a feme covert so as to make her husband tenant by the curtesey, *De Grey* v. *Richardson.* (a)   If then the possession of the tenant was the possession of *J. M. Dixon*, he was actually seised on the death of *L. Dixon.* The subsequent payment of rent to the supposed devisee of *Simeon's Onset* might be a disseisin of *J. M. Dixon*, but could not be an abatement. The possession of the tenant for years protected the heir from abatement, *Co. Lit.* 243 a. [*Bayley* J. If the present defendant had claimed the lands in question in a real action as heir of the father, could he say that his father was seised by taking the esplees?] He might, for although rent was paid to another, yet the tenant must be considered as taking the esplees or profits of the lands for the use of the person entitled to the freehold, the possession of the tenant being in law his possession. It is even doubtful, whether the payment of rent to a third person amounted in this case to a disseisin of *J. M. Dixon*, as it was paid to the devisee under a mistake, and not with intent to work a disseisin, *Litt. s.* 396. *Williams* v. *Thomas* (b), *Doe* v. *Perkins* (c), *Jarrett* v. *Weare* (d), *Hall* v. *Doe.* (e)

Tindal contrà. Looking at the whole of this case, it appears that the obligor had not any such seisin of the estate in question as to make it descendible from him to the defendant. *L. Dixon* died seised on the 15th of *June* 1797. *Ann Milbourn*, and *John* her husband, re-

---

(a) 3 *Atk.* 469.   (b) 12 *East*, 141.
(c) 3 *M. & S.* 271.   (d) 3 *Price*, 575.
(e) 5 *B. & A.* 687.

ceived the rents from that time till 1801, when *Ann* died, the rents were then received by *J. Milbourn*, claiming to be tenant by the curtesy up to *Whitsuntide* 1815; before which time, viz. on *April* the 27th in that year, *J. M. Dixon* died. It is plain, therefore, that the obligor never enjoyed the profits of the estate, and the authorities which have been cited do not shew that under the circumstances of this case he was seised in fact. In *Co. Litt.* 15 a. which has been referred to, he speaks of the son dying " before entry or receipt of rent." Those words manifestly imply that he speaks of a case where the rent would have been paid to the son if he had lived till it became due, and not of a case where there has been a denial of his title as in this case. Here the rent was received by another person under a claim of right as devisee under the will of *L. Dixon.* So in the case cited from *Jenk.* 242. where the entry of the devisee was held to be an entry for the heir at law, there was no adverse claim; again, in *Good-title* v. *Newman,* there was an actual entry by the guardian in socage. Here the plaintiff cannot recover, unless he succeeds in shewing that a person who was kept out of the enjoyment of the freehold during his whole life by an adverse agreement between the tenant and a third person, was nevertheless actually seised of the freehold. This would have been a disseisin if the obligor had entered or received rent, *Roll. Abr. Disseisin* (C), *pl.* 8. *Bro. Abr. Disseisin, pl.* 96. But as he had not entered or received rent it was an abatement, for if the obligor having received rent would have been disseised by a subsequent payment of it to another, why should not the payment of it to another ab initio, prevent him from ever becoming seised. In *Com. Dig.*
Abatement

Abatement (A 1.), it is defined to be " when on a dying seised, one without right enters before the heir." And in *Co. Litt.* 277 *a.* it is said, than an abator takes away the freehold in law descended to the heir. The question put as to the bringing a real action is also important, for how can it be said that the obligor took the esplees, when *John Milbourn* and his wife received all the rent which was paid for the land.

ABBOTT C. J. I am of opinion that the verdict on the last issue must be entered for the plaintiffs. It is clear that if the obligor was ever actually seised of the estate in question, for however short a time, the defendant takes it by descent from him. But the seisin of the obligor must be shewn to have been a seisin in fact. That is also necessary to make a possessio fratris, so as to cause the descent of an estate to a sister of the whole blood, in preference to a brother of the half blood; and therefore whatever seisin suffices in the latter case will suffice to charge the defendant in this action. Adverting to the doctrine on this point in *Co. Litt.* 15 *a.* we find it laid down thus: " If the father maketh a lease for years, and the lessee entreth, and dieth (*a*), the eldest son dieth during the term, before entry or receipt of rent, the youngest son of the half blood shall not inherit, but the sister; because the possession of the lessee for years (and a tenant from year to year is to be considered a lessee for years for this purpose,) is the possession of the eldest son so as he is actually seised of the fee simple, and consequently the sister of the whole blood is to be heir." This establishes that the posses-

(*a*) i. e. the father dieth.

sion

sion of a tenant for years, being a rightful possession, is considered in law as the possession of the heir, and therefore gives him a seisin in fact. On the authority of this doctrine, which has been very often recognized in other cases, I think that we are bound to say that the obligor, *J. M. Dixon*, was for a time seised in fact of *Simeon's Onset*, and consequently that the defendant had the land by descent from him, and is thereby rendered chargeable in this action.

BAYLEY J. It is clear on which side the justice of this case lies, for as heir either of *Lucy Dixon* or of his father, the defendant is certainly liable to discharge this bond. But still we must see that he is properly charged as heir of his father, in order to give judgment for the plaintiffs in this action. It seems to me that the taking of the esplees by the tenant is a taking for the person seised of the freehold. In *Ratcliffe's* case (a) there is this passage relating to the doctrine of possessio fratris, " If the elder son enters, and by his own act hath gained the actual possession, or if the lands were leased for years, or in the hands of a guardian, and the lessee or guardian possess the land, there the possession of the lessee or guardian doth vest the actual fee and freehold in the elder brother." Where there is no one in possession at the death of the ancestor, there must be an actual entry by the heir to give him the seisin in fact. But when there is a tenant, his possession becomes that of the heir immediately on the death of the ancestor. The subsequent misconduct of the tenant in paying rent to another person, or the mistake of the heir as

(a) 3 Co. 42.

to his rights, cannot by relation alter the nature of the seisin which he before had. In this case, therefore, I am of opinion that the defendant took the land in question by descent from his father, and that the verdict on the last issue must be entered for the plaintiffs.

HOLROYD J. I think that the defendant is liable to this action as heir of his father, having received lands by descent from him, his father having been seised of them in fact. Lord *Coke* puts the two cases of a man dying seised of lands in his own possession, and of lands in the possession of a tenant for years. If he is in possession himself the freehold descends on the heir, and he is immediately seised in law, but not in fact. In *Co. Litt.* 277. *a.* speaking of an abator, he says : " Abate is both an *English* and *French* word, and signifieth, in its proper sense, to diminish or take away; as here by his entry he diminisheth and taketh away the freehold *in law* descended to the heir." And again : " A disseisin is a wrongful putting out of him that is *actually* seised of a freehold. An abatement is when a man died seised of an estate of inheritance, and between the death and the entry of the heir an estranger doth interpose himself, and abate." So that if a man die seised of land in his own possession, and the heir does not enter, and a third person does, that which would have been a disseisin if the heir had entered, is an abatement. Again, in *Co. Litt.* 243 *a.*, it is said, that if the ancestor leases for years, and dies, the possession of the lessee for years maketh an *actual* freehold in the eldest son. Thus, the case of an ancestor dying seised of lands in the possession of a tenant for years, is, in this respect, put on a different footing from his dying seised where there is no tenant; and in the former case the heir has such a seisin as renders the land descendible from him. And if there be an actual seisin in the heir, that will not be defeated ab initio by a subsequent neglect on his part to claim rent, or on the part of the tenant to pay it. The lessee was bound to pay rent to the lessor and his heirs, and therefore cannot be permitted to say that he took the esplees for any one else. The defendant in this case then must claim the land by descent from his father, the obligor, and is liable to be charged with the bond debt.

LITTLEDALE J. I also am of opinion that the plaintiffs are entitled to recover on the third issue. If the obligor was ever actually seised, the defendant takes by descent from him. At the moment of *Lucy Dixon's* death, the obligor did become actually seised, for the possession of the tenant for years is the possession of the owner of the freehold. In the old entries of pleadings in real actions leases for years are never noticed; it is never said that the land descended from *A.* to *B.* subject to a term. In those days it was considered that the tenant was in the nature of a bailiff or servant, and therefore that he took the esplees for the benefit of the owner of the freehold. (a) But stress has been laid on the fact of rent being paid to a third person. That, however, makes no difference. Although no rent was paid to the obligor, still at the moment of *Lucy Dixon's* death the possession of the tenant was the possession of her heir. He then became immediately seised in fact. It is immaterial to this question whether he was after-

(a) See *Gilb. Ten.* 34. *Co. Litt.* 239 b. n. 2. *Watk. on Descents,* 108.

X 2   wards

wards disseised or not, the land descended from him to
the defendant, who is therefore liable to discharge the
bond of his ancestor.

Judgment for the plaintiffs.

BARFORD, Administrator of N. PITTS, *against*
VINCENT STUCKEY.

*A. and B. by
deed, (reciting
that C. had left
them estates in
strict settle-
ment, with re-
mainder over
on failure of
issue male, to
D.,) out of their
regard to D.,
and considering
that C. had
made no oth-
provision for
him, agreed
with D., his
executors and
administrators,
to pay him an
annuity for
twenty-one
years, if A. and
B., or the sur-
vivor of them
should so long
live ; and in
case of the
death of D.
within the term,
to his child or
children, if any,*

DEBT upon an annuity deed, bearing date the 11th of
May 1810, between *B. J. Bartlett* and *Vincent
Stuckey* of the one part, and one *Nathaniel Pitts* of the
other part. The deed, which was set out on oyer, recited that *John Stuckey*, deceased, by his last will gave
and devised to two trustees therein named, and their
heirs, certain lands and hereditaments in his will mentioned, habendum, to the trustees, and their heirs, to
the use of *B. J. Bartlett* and his assigns, for life, with
remainder to his first and other sons, &c. ; and in default of issue male of *B. J. Bartlett*, remainder to the
use of *Vincent Stuckey* and his assigns, for life ; remainder to his first and other sons ; and in default of
issue male of *Vincent Stuckey*, remainder to the use of
Nathaniel Pitts and his assigns, for life, with divers remainders over ; and reciting also that *J. Stuckey*, the
testator, by his will devised to the trustees certain other

in such proportions as *D.* should appoint, or in default of appointment, to all of them
equally ; and if there should be no child, to his then wife, so long as she should remain a
widow. *D.* covenanted with *A.* and *B*, their executors, &c., that in case he or his heirs
should come into possession of the said estates under the will of *C.*, then that he, *D.*, his
heirs, executors, or administrators, should pay to the executors or administrators of *A.* and
B., or the survivors of them, all sums of money received by him, his children, or wife, for
and on account of the annuity. *D.*, his wife and child, died within the term, and it was
held that the deed did not operate as the grant of an annuity for the term of twenty-one
years absolutely, but that it was determinable by the death of the grantee, his children and
wife, and therefore that *D.*'s administrator was not entitled to claim payment of the annuity.

lands

lands and hereditaments in the will also mentioned, to
hold to them and their heirs, to the use of *V. Stuckey*
and his assigns for life; remainder to the use of his first
and other sons; and in default of issue male of *V.
Stuckey*, remainder to the use of *B. J. Bartlett* and his
assigns for life; remainder to the use of his first and
other sons; and in default of issue male of the said
B. J. Bartlett, remainder to the said *Nathaniel Pitts* and
his assigns, with divers remainders over. The deed
then recited, that *Bartlett* and *Vincent Stuckey*, in consideration of the great regard and esteem which they
had for *Pitts*, and considering that the testator had not
by his will made any further provision for *Pitts*, agreed
to grant him an annuity of 500*l.* per annum for the
term of 21 years, in case they should so long live; and
in the event of either of their deaths within the said
term, then if the survivor should so long live, and be in
actual possession of all the said settled hereditaments,
• to commence from the 25th *March* then last past, to be
paid half-yearly; *and in case of the death of* Nathaniel
Pitts before the expiration of the said term of 21 *years*, they,
the grantors, agreed that they, or the survivor of them,
would pay the said annuity for the term aforesaid, subject as aforesaid to and for the use and benefit of the
child and children of *N. Pitts* (if any) in such proportion as he, *N. Pitts*, should by deed or will appoint;
and in default of appointment, for the benefit of all his
children equally; but in case there should be no child
of *N. Pitts* living at the time of his decease, happening
within the said term, then the said annuity was to be
paid in like manner for the then remainder of the said
term of 21 years, in case the said grantors, or the survivor of them, should be then living, unto his then

X 3   wife,

wife, for and during such period only of the said term as
she should continue his widow; which said annuity it
was agreed should be paid by the grantors in certain
specified proportions; and it was also agreed that if on
the death of either of the grantors within the said term,
the survivor of them should be in the possession of the
said hereditaments and premises, then the annuity should
be paid, as before stipulated, by such survivor for the
then remainder of the said term of 21 years, in case
such survivor should so long live; but in case N. Pitts
or his heirs should at any time during the said term
come into possession of the said manors, messuages,
farms, lands, and hereditaments, under the limitations
in the will of *John Stuckey* expressed, or should otherwise by operation of law obtain or get into possession of
the hereditaments and premises by the will of *J. Stuckey*
devised, then the said annuity was to cease and be
utterly void; and then, in either case, N. Pitts, his
heirs, executors, &c. were to repay to the grantors respectively, and to the survivor of them, their, and his
executors and administrators, in the proportions aforesaid, all sums of money by him, N. Pitts, *his children,
or wife, received* for or on account of the said annuity.
It was therefore witnessed, that for the considerations
aforesaid, they, *B. J. Bartlett* and *V. Stuckey*, did by the
said agreement for themselves severally and respectively
promise and agree to and with N. Pitts, his executors,
and administrators, that they, the grantors, should and
would, during the said term of 21 years, to commence
as aforesaid, in case they should so long live, well and
truly pay or cause to be paid unto N. Pitts, or in case
of his death within the said term, then unto or for the
use of his child or children, if any, but if not, then unto
his then present wife, in case she should remain his

                                                    widow,

widow, an annuity or clear yearly rent or sum of 500*l.* of lawful money, &c. in the proportions and shares thereinbefore mentioned, by two equal half-yearly payments, on the 29th *September* and the 25th day of *March* in every year, together with a proportionable part of the said annuity up to the time of the decease of the survivor of them, the grantors, in case they should both die before the expiration of the said term of 21 years, and such survivor should happen to die between any of the said half-yearly days of payment, and before a full half-yearly payment should become due and payable, without any deduction, defalcation, or abatement of any sort or kind, parliamentary or otherwise howsoever, the first payment to be made and begin on the 29th day of *September* then next ensuing the date thereof. There then followed a covenant by *Pitts*, that in case he or his heirs should at any time during the term come into the possession of the land, &c. under the limitation in the will of *V. Stuckey*, that he, *Pitts*, his heirs, executors, and administrators, should pay to the executors and administrators of the grantors, or the survivor, all sums of money received by him, his said children or wife, for and on account of the same annuity. There were averments that *Pitts*, his wife, and child, died within the term of 21 years; and that plaintiff took out administration of the effects of him and his child. Breach, annuity in arrear. Demurrer and joinder; and judgment for defendants in C. P. (*a*), whereupon a writ of error was brought.

Tindal, for the plaintiff in error. By this deed *Pitts* was entitled to an annuity for twenty-one years absolute. The Court of Common Pleas held, that the

(*a*) 1 *Bing.* 225.

X 4   annuity

annuity was to continue only for the life of *Pitts*, his
children, and his wife; but the deed must be construed
according to the fair import of the language used. The
words of the grant are, that the grantors had agreed to
grant him an annuity of 500*l.* per annum for the term
of 21 years, *in case they should so long live;* and in the
event of their deaths within the term, then if the survivor
should so long live. That is a grant of an annuity
for the term of 21 years absolutely, and the covenant
for the payment of the annuity is consistent with the
words of the grant, for that covenant is with *Pitts*, his
executors, and administrators, to pay the annuity during
the said term of 21 years, to him, or his children or his
widow. There is nothing in the granting part to limit
the term of the grant, except the death of the grantors
themselves. The subsequent clause, by which they
agree, in case of the grantee's death, to pay the annuity
to his children, as he shall appoint, or to his then wife,
does not limit the duration of the annuity; it only regulates the mode of payment, and gives the grantee a
special power of appointment of the persons to whom
the payment shall be made; and there being no such
persons in existence, the special appointment fails. The
payment must, therefore, be made to the personal representative of the grantee. If the grantors had intended
that the annuity should cease upon the death of the
children and the wife during the term, they would, in
that part of the deed where it is stipulated to pay the
annuity, in case of the death of *Pitts*, to the children
and wife, have introduced the words of condition, in
case they should so long live. It is evident, from the
introduction of those words in the previous clause, that
they knew how to introduce words of condition when

20   they

they thought proper. The agreement to pay the annuity to the wife and children does not necessarily limit the duration of the annuity. The recital may be relied on to shew, that it was the intention of the grantors that the deed should not be construed strictly according to the words of the granting part, but that it was a voluntary grant on their part, and should be construed with reference to the intention disclosed in the recital, from which it appears to have been their intention to make a provision for the grantee, his children and wife; but this being a grant by deed must be construed more strictly than if it was contained in a will, and the words of the grant being those of the grantors must be taken most strongly against themselves, *Sheppard's Touchstone*, 88., 2 *Black. Com.* 380. In *Germain and Wife* v. *Orchard* (a), a termor granted a term of 1000 years to the grantee, his executors, administrators, and assigns, habendum after the death of the grantor and his wife for the residue of the term of 1000 years: the habendum being repugnant to the premises, it was held to be void, and that the grantee took the term presently. Secondly, the recital of the agreement does not make out that it was the intention to confine the annuity to the life of *Pitts*, his wife, and children. Suppose the wife and children had died in the lifetime of *Pitts*, what words are there to limit the annuity to the term of 21 years. Or suppose his child had died in his lifetime, leaving a son, surely the grantors must have intended that the grandson should have the annuity for the residue of the term of 21 years, yet if the construction contended for on the other side be right, he would have nothing.

1824.
———
BARFORD
against
STUCKEY.

(a) 1 *Salk*, 346.

Peake

Peake Serjt., contrà. , It is true, that where the language of an instrument is ambiguous, the words are to be taken most strongly against the person using them. Here there is no ambiguity. The intention is to be collected from the whole deed; that intention was to do a generous and voluntary act towards the grantees. It is more consistent with that intention that they should make a provision for *Pitts* and his family, and not give the annuity absolutely, so that he might sell or dispose of it. The concluding covenant removes all doubt as to the true construction of the deed. By that *Pitts* covenants, not merely to repay the money which he had received, but also the money received by his wife and children; but he does not covenant to pay any money the assignees of the annuity might receive, or that his executors should pay any money they might receive. (He was then stopped by the Court.)

ABBOTT C. J. We have no doubt that, upon the true construction of this deed, *Pitts* the grantee was entitled to an annuity for the term of 21 years, determinable however by his death. This was a voluntary grant. It appears by the recital in the deed, that the testator having devised his estates to the two grantors for life, and to their issue in tail male, with an ultimate remainder to *Pitts*, they out of regard to him, and considering that the testator had made no other provision for him, had agreed to grant him an annuity of 500*l.* for the term of 21 years, in case they the grantors or the survivor of them should so long live. Now it has been said, that this is an absolute grant for 21 years, and that would be so if the deed had stopped here; but the words which immediately follow shew clearly, that the

16   grantors

1824.

BARFORD
against
STUCKEY.

grantors did not intend that the annuity should continue absolutely for the term of 21 years. Those words are, " In case of the death of *Pitts* before the expiration of 21 years, they agree to pay the annuity for the use of his child or children, if any, in such proportions as he should appoint; or in case he should leave no child surviving him, then to his then present wife, so long as she should continue his widow." Now I think the words " in case of the death of *Pitts* before the expiration of 21 years," are to receive the same construction as if the grant had been " to *Pitts* for 21 years in case he shall so long live." This clause provides for a mode of payment in the event of his death different from that which would have taken place if the annuity had been granted to him absolutely for the term of 21 years. In that case it would have been payable to his personal representatives; but by this clause it is to be applied for the benefit of such of his children as he should by deed or will appoint; and in default of appointment, among his children equally; and if he should leave no child surviving him, then to the use of his then present wife, so long only as she should continue his widow. These provisions are inconsistent with the fact of the grantee's having an absolute interest in the annuity for the term of 21 years; his interest was to cease on his death, and the future payments were not to constitute part of his personal estate. Without relying, therefore, upon the concluding covenant, (the language of which, however, is strong to shew that it was the intention of the grantors to provide only for the grantee and his immediate family,) I am of opinion, that, giving a reasonable construction to the words of the grant itself, they are sufficient to give an annuity to *Pitts* for the term of 21 years, determinable by his death within

that

that period, then to his children as he shall appoint, determinable by their death, then to his wife, determinable by her death, or by her ceasing to continue his widow.

BAYLEY J. Considering the purpose and the language of the deed, I think that this annuity was to cease, in case the first grantee, his children and wife, died during the term. The object clearly was, to provide for the grantee and his immediate family, and that object would be fully answered by making the annuity payable first to him, then to his children, then to his wife, without giving him an absolute power of disposing of it by sale or otherwise; but if the words of the granting part, construed together with the recital, left any doubt as to the intention of the grantors, that doubt is wholly removed by the manner in which the covenant for the payment of the annuity is framed, and by the introduction of the words executors and administrators in some places, and the omission of them in others. The covenant to pay is with Pitts, his executors, &c.: the latter words are properly introduced into this part of the covenant, in order to enable the personal representatives of Pitts to recover the arrears of the annuity which might be due at the time of his death, but the covenant is, to pay the annuity to Pitts, omitting the word executors, and in the event of his death, to his children or his widow. Again, in the clause for repayment of the annuity, Pitts covenants that he, his executors, &c., shall pay to the executors of the grantors all such sums of money received by him, Pitts, his children or wife, on account of the annuity, but he does not covenant to pay any money which his assignees or

executors

executors might receive. Considering, therefore, the
recital, and the language of the grant and of the covenants, I think that there is no reasonable ground for
doubting that the object of the grantors was to make a
personal provision for the grantee, his children and wife,
and no further; and that being so, the judgment of the
Court of Common Pleas must be affirmed.

HOLROYD and LITTLEDALE Js. concurred.

Judgment affirmed.

1824.

BARFORD
against
STOCKEY.

LITTLETON and Another *against* CROSS and MOODY, Executors of HUGH LUSH, deceased.

DECLARATION of *Hilary* term. 3 G.4., upon an
indenture made between Sir *R. C. Hoare*, Bart.,
and the plaintiffs of the one part, and *Hugh Lush*, deceased, of the other part, by which, in pursuance of
an agreement for an exchange of lands, *Lush* granted,
bargained, sold, and exchanged to the plaintiffs, their
heirs and assigns, a cottage or dwelling-house, lands,
hereditaments, and premises, habendum to the plaintiffs,
their heirs and assigns, for ever. Covenant by *Lush* for
good title and for quiet enjoyment. Breach, that *Lush*
had not good title, and that plaintiffs were evicted by
two persons having lawful title. Plea, that the defend-

By fiction of
law, all judg-
ments are sup-
posed to be re-
covered in
term, and to
relate to the
first day of the
term; but in
practice judg-
ments are fre-
quently signed
in vacation,
and where the
purposes of
justice require
that the true
time when the
judgment was
obtained should
be made appear,
a party may
shew it by

averment in pleading; therefore, in an action against an executor for breaches of covenants
in an indenture made by his testator, the defendant having pleaded in chief plené administravit and a retainer for a simple contract debt, upon which issues were taken and
joined, and then puis darrein continuance, a judgment recovered upon a bond of the testator's after the last continuance, (being the last day of *Trinity* term,) to wit, on the second
day of *August*, as of *Trinity* term preceding; to which the plaintiff replied, that the
defendants had notice of the bond before the commencement of the action: Held, upon
demurrer to the replication, that the plea was well pleaded, and was an answer to the
action.

ants

ants had fully administered all and singular the goods
and chattels of the testator. Secondly, a retainer by
Cross, one of the executors, with the assent of the other,
on account of a promissory note given by the testator to
Cross the executor for 100*l.*; and that, at the time of
his death, the same was due; and that the defendants
had fully administered all the goods and chattels of the
deceased, except goods and chattels of the value of 56*l.*
which were not sufficient to satisfy the debt due to *Cross*
the executor. Replication, of *Trinity* term, that the
defendants had assets of the value of the damages sustained by the plaintiffs by reason of the breaches of covenant. Rejoinder, which was of *Hilary* term 4 *G.4.*,
joining issue upon the replication. At the assizes at
Bridgwater, on the 2d *August* 1823, the defendants
pleaded puis darrein continuance, that one *Thomas Cross*,
after the death of *Lush*, to wit, in *Trinity* term in the
4th year of *G.4.*, by bill without the king's writ, had
impleaded the defendants, as executors in a certain plea
of debt, for the sum of 800*l.* upon a writing obligatory
entered into by *Lush* in his lifetime to *Thomas Cross;*
and such proceedings were thereupon had in the said
plea of debt, that the said *Thomas Cross* afterwards, *and
after the last continuance of this said* cause, that is to say,
after the 18th day of *June* in the year last aforesaid,
from which day, until the 6th day of *November* in *Michaelmas* term next, unless the justices assigned to hold
the assizes for the county of *Somerset* should first come
on the 2d day of *August* in the year last aforesaid, this
said cause continued, to wit, on the said 2d day of
August as of last *Trinity* term, in the 4th year of the
reign of *G.4.* as aforesaid, recovered a certain judgment
of the Court of King's Bench against the said defend-
                                                        ants

-ants as executors as aforesaid, whereby it was considered that the said *Thomas Cross* should recover against the said defendants the sum of 800*l.* and 84*s.* for his damages and costs. After averring that the judgment was still in force, the defendants pleaded that they had fully administered all the goods and chattels, except goods and chattels of the value of 56*l.* which were not sufficient to satisfy the debt and damages recovered by the judgment. Replication, that the defendants before the exhibiting of the bill of the plaintiffs, to wit, on the 1st of *January* 1823, at, &c., had notice of the said writing obligatory and debt in the same plea mentioned. Demurrer and joinder.

Campbell in support of the demurrer. *Prince* v. *Nicholson* (a) is an authority to shew that an executor may plead puis darrein continuance, a judgment recovered in a suit subsequently commenced, and that the plea is not invalidated by the executor's having suffered judgment to pass against him voluntarily. That case is not distinguishable from the present. (He was then stopped by the Court.)

E. Lawes, contrà. This case is materially distinguishable from that of *Prince* v. *Nicholson*. The judgment in this case having been signed in vacation, must have been obtained under a warrant of attorney given by the defendants, they therefore became actors. Besides, here it is *admitted* upon the pleadings that the defendants, before the commencement of this action, had notice of the bond upon which the judgment was recovered. That

(a) 1 *Marsh.* 280. S. C. 5 *Taunt.* 333.

fact

fact distinguishes this from any other case. The defendants endeavoured to defeat the plaintiffs, as well as the present judgment creditor, by pleading two false and frivolous pleas; and then after allowing the plaintiffs to continue their suit to the very day of trial, they set up a collusive judgment given to that creditor, which is another fraud upon the plaintiffs. If they had intended to prefer this creditor, of whose claim they had notice, they ought to have done it in the first instance. The plea is bad in point of law. It describes the judgment as recovered in vacation as of the preceding term. Now, a judgment can only be recovered during the term while the Court is sitting in banc. Judgments by the practice of the Court may be signed during the vacation, but then, in contemplation of law, they are judgments of the preceding term. It ought to have been stated in pleading according to its legal effect. [*Holroyd* J. In *Bodsworth* v. *Bowen* (a), where a bill was filed against an attorney in vacation, it was held that the day of filing might be inserted in the memorandum, and the form given is, " that on, &c. a day after the cause of action accrued, the plaintiff brought into the office of the clerk of the declarations, according to the course and practice of the Court, his certain bill against the defendant and filed the same as of *Michaelmas* term."] That form ought to have been pursued in this case, but the defendants have alleged that the judgment was recovered in the vacation, which is impossible. They ought to have pleaded, that the judgment was signed in the vacation according to the practice of the Court, whereby it became a judgment as of the preceding term. In that case the judgment would relate back to the first day of that term, and would be no answer to the action by way

(a) *5 T. R. 325.*

of

of plea puis darrein continuance, because it was a judgment recovered before the last continuance.   Besides,
the plea is inconsistent with the other pleas pleaded.
In *Vaughan* v. *Brown* (a), it was held that a matter which
was in esse at the time of the first plea, could not be taken
advantage of by way of plea puis darrein continuance; and
Lee C. J. was of opinion, that the same rule applied
where the non-existence thereof was owing to the laches
of the party.

Campbell in reply.   The plaintiffs might have applied
to the court to have the judgment set aside if it was
obtained fraudulently, or they might have replied per
fraudem; but they have pleaded over, and have thereby
admitted the judgment to be valid.   Besides, *Prince*
v. *Nicholson* is an authority to shew that an irregular
judgment may be taken advantage of by executors until
it be set aside.   Now it is a general rule, that any matter
constituting a good ground of defence which has arisen
after the last continuance, may be pleaded.   Here,
there was no judgment in existence before the 2d of
August; and, therefore, according to the general rule,
it is a matter which may be pleaded by the defendants,
puis darrein continuance.   Secondly, it does sufficiently
appear upon the pleadings that the judgment was obtained after the last continuance.   There is a positive
averment, that it was recovered after the last continuance, to wit, on the 2d of *August*.   A judgment recovered
at that time could not have been pleaded before the last
continuance.   If the defendants, therefore, cannot avail
themselves of this matter of defence by plea puis darrein continuance, they will be deprived of it altogether.

1824.

LITTLETON
against
CASS.

(a) *Andrews*, 332.

If there is any possible case in which a judgment could legally be pronounced after the last continuance and before the trial, it ought to be presumed to have been so done. Now, it may have been pronounced at the sittings in banc after term.

ABBOTT C. J. I am of opinion that this plea is properly pleaded, and that the defendants are entitled to the judgment of the Court. The situation of an executor is frequently one of great difficulty. The law imposes on him the burthen of paying the debts of the testator in a particular order; and, on the other hand, it confers on him certain privileges. One of those privileges is, that he has a right to retain for his own debt in preference to all other creditors of equal degree; and that, among creditors of equal degree, he may pay one in preference to another. He may even, after actions are commenced against him by a creditor on simple contract, confess a judgment in favor of another creditor of equal degree, and thus give the latter a preference. That was expressly decided in *Prince* v. *Nicholson.* The action was for goods sold to the testator, the executor pleaded in chief non assumpsit, and at nisi prius pleaded puis darrein continuance, a plea of three judgments recovered against him, as executor, in the same term in actions of debt, which were commenced also in that term for money borrowed by the testator, and plenè administravit præter 300*l.* the amount of those judgments. That case was argued with great learning and ability. One of the objections was, that the executor having pleaded in chief, could not plead another judgment recovered against him as executor since the last continuance, because such judgment must have been suffered voluntarily. The judgment of the Court was

delivered.

delivered by Lord Chief Justice *Gibbs*, who was a
lawyer of great eminence in every department of his
profession, and peculiarly skilled in the science and
practice of pleading. The Court of Common Pleas
decided that the plea was not invalidated by the defendant's having suffered judgment to pass against him
voluntarily. Now, the present case is not distinguishable from that, and must be governed by it. It is said,
however, that in this case the judgment was entered up
on a warrant of attorney. I doubt whether there be
sufficient facts to enable us to draw that inference; but
if there be, the same inference might have been drawn
from the facts in *Prince* v. *Nicholson*, for the judgments
were obtained in the same term in which the actions
were commenced. I am, therefore, of opinion that the
defendants were authorized by law to confess a judgment in favor of another creditor even after the commencement of the present action, and that the judgment
so recovered is an answer to the present action. The
remaining objection, which is one of some difficulty, is,
that the plea describes the judgment to have been recovered after the last continuance of the said cause, to
wit, on the 2d day of *August* as of *Trinity* term preceding. The plaintiff by his replication has admitted
the fact, and the question is, whether we can give effect
to it as a judgment recovered on that day, or whether
we are bound to treat it as a judgment recovered in the
preceding term. If it is to be considered as a judgment
recovered in the term, then by fiction of law it relates
back to the first day of that term, and, of course, must
be considered as having been recovered before the last
continuance. If that be the legal effect of the judgment described in this plea, and the executor is pre-

Y 2   cluded

cluded from shewing the fact to be contrary to that which the fiction of law supposes, he will be deprived of the privilege allowed him by law of pleading a judgment actually recovered against him after the last continuance. It is a general rule, that where it is for the interest of the party pleading to shew that a proceeding did not take place at the precise time when by fiction of law it is supposed to have happened, it is competent for him to do so. Where a bill is filed against an attorney in vacation, which by fiction of law is supposed to take place in term, it is competent to the party filing the bill to shew the very day when the bill was filed. And so in the case of writs which are supposed to issue in term, it is competent to a party to shew the time when they actually issued, if that be necessary in order to avail himself of the statute of limitations. Now in this case it is the interest of the defendants, who plead the judgment, to shew that the judgment was not recovered until after the last continuance; and I think that they may be permitted, by averment, to shew that in point of fact the judgment was recovered after that continuance; and that being so, the judgment described in this plea may be considered to have been obtained in the vacation, and after the last continuance. The judgment of the Court must therefore be for the defendants.

Bayley J. An executor has a right to pay one creditor in preference to another of the same degree, and he has it in his election to give a preference by confessing a judgment to one of several creditors of equal degree, who have brought actions against him. In some instances executors may possibly act capriciously, but there are many where, in the exercise of a sound discretion,

discretion, they may with great propriety prefer one creditor to another; and I think it highly probable in this case that the defendants were well warranted in confessing a judgment to the bond creditor, though that might ultimately prejudice the plaintiffs, who had only a claim to unliquidated damages for breach of covenant. It is quite clear, however, that the defendants had a right to prefer the one to the other; and that if this judgment, instead of being pleaded as a plea puis darrein continuance, could have been originally pleaded in bar, it would have been a good answer to the action. Unless, therefore, the defendants are precluded from availing themselves of this defence by the form of pleading it, they ought to be allowed their privilege of giving the bond creditor a preference in this case. The difficulty propounded is this: that the defendants have described this as a judgment recovered in the vacation as of the preceding term; and if it be considered a judgment of that term, it relates back to the first day of that term; and then it must be taken to be a judgment recovered before the last continuance. As, however, the fact of this judgment having been recovered against them after the last continuance is a good defence to the action if it can be pleaded, it will operate as a great injustice upon the defendants if, by a fiction of law, they are to be precluded from pleading it. The rule is, in fictione juris subsistit æquitas. Wherever, therefore, a fiction of law works injustice, and the facts which by fiction are supposed to exist are inconsistent with the real facts, a court of law ought to look to the real facts. Where a latitat is sued out after the expiration of six years from the time when the cause of action arose, but bearing teste before, a party relying

Y 3   upon

upon the statute of limitations is permitted to shew the true day when it was sued out. In that case, by fiction of law, the latitat, though sued out after the term, is supposed to have issued in the preceding term; but a party seeking to avail himself of that which is a legal defence to the action, and the validity of which depends upon the actual time when the writ was sued out, is permitted to shew it. So in this case the fiction of law is that the judgment is recovered in the term, and the term being considered but one day, it relates to the first day of the term; but, in point of fact, judgments are constantly obtained in the vacation. If, therefore, the purposes of justice require that in order to enable the defendants to plead the judgment recovered against them, they should be permitted to shew that it was recovered not, as the fiction of law supposes, in the preceding term, but after the last continuance and in the vacation, they ought to be permitted to do so. Now, it is quite clear that unless the judgment was recovered after the last continuance, it could not be pleaded at Nisi Prius puis darrein continuance, but ought to have been pleaded in banc. If, however, it was obtained after the last continuance it could not have been pleaded in banc. If it was in fact obtained at the time stated in the plea, and the defendants are not allowed to shew that by averment, they will be wholly precluded from setting up this judgment as an answer to the action. The purposes of justice, therefore, require that the defendant should be permitted to shew by averment that this judgment was obtained in vacation. It is averred in the plea that the judgment was recovered in vacation as of the preceding term. The fair meaning of that allegation is, that the judgment

ment was given in vacation so as to take effect as of that term. If that be the fact, it could not have been pleaded as a judgment recovered before the 18th day of *June* the next preceding continuance; and as the judgment recovered against the defendants in the vacation is, in point of law, a defence to the action, the fiction of law by which the judgment is supposed to have been recovered in the preceding term ought not to prevail so as to prevent their pleading the judgment as a defence to the action. Besides, by the 3 G. 4. c. 102. the Court does sit in banc, and pronounce judgments in vacation, although those judgments are entered up as of the preceding term. The averment that the judgment was recovered on the 2d of *August* being under a videlicet might be rejected; and then it might be taken to have been recovered on some day when the Court, sitting in banc out of term, might legally pronounce judgment. The plaintiff, too, has not replied nul tiel record, but has pleaded over, and relied upon the notice. This, therefore, ought to be presumed to be a regular judgment, upon the principle omnia præsumuntur rite esse acta. For these reasons I think that this plea is properly pleaded, and that the judgment of the Court must be for the defendants.

HOLROYD J. I think that the plea puis darrein continuance, is an answer to this action, notwithstanding the fact alleged in the replication, that the defendants before the commencement of the action had notice of the bond, and that the plea is to be taken to have been pleaded since the last continuance. According to the case of *Prince* v. *Nicholson*, it makes no difference that the defendants had knowledge of the debt upon which

the

the judgment was recovered. That case is in no respect different from the present, and it shews that a judgment recovered against the defendant since the commencement of the action may be pleaded puis darrein continuance. I think that decision was founded upon just and proper reasons. There being no doubt, therefore, that the executors had power to prefer one creditor to another, the only question is, whether the defendants have pleaded this plea puis darrein continuance within due time. Now, in contemplation of law, independently of the late act, a judgment is considered as given during the term when the court sits in banc. The court, however, is not thereby estopped from taking notice of the practice which has long prevailed of entering up judgments in vacation, or from enquiring as to the precise time when the judgments are given. The fiction of law is, that all writs are supposed to issue in term, and generally speaking, a party is estopped by the teste of the writ from disputing the time when it issued. But where it is necessary for the purposes of justice that a party shall be permitted to shew that it in fact issued in vacation, he is permitted to do so, and therefore it has been decided, that a defendant, in order to avail himself of the statute of limitations, may shew the very time when the writ issued. That was decided in *Johnson* v. *Smith.* (a) Lord *Mansfield* there lays down the true principle applicable to this case. He says, " The Court would not endure that a mere form or fiction of law introduced for the sake of justice, should work a wrong, contrary to the real truth and substance of the thing." But, if the fiction of

(a) 2 *Burr.* 950.

law

law that judgments are pronounced only in term were
to prevail in this case, when in point of fact the judgment was obtained in vacation after the last continuance, it would work a wrong by depriving the defendants of a legal defence to the present action. Lord
Mansfield afterwards says, " The reason why nobody
shall be permitted to aver that a judgment was signed
after the first day of the term is, because the fact is not
relevant. The legal consequences do not depend upon
the truth of the fact on what day the judgment was completed, but upon the rule of law that it shall be deemed
complete, and bind to all intents and purposes by relation." In this case the fact is relevant, the legal consequences of the judgment do depend upon the truth of
the fact whether it was completed before or after the
last continuance. If there was not any complete judgment before the 2nd of *August*, the defendants may
avail themselves of it by plea; if, on the other hand, the
judgment by relation was complete on the first day of
the preceding term, then the defendants cannot plead it
puis darrein continuance. Lord *Mansfield* afterwards
says, " the moment the law said that judgments should
bind purchasers *only from the signing*, it followed that
in the case of purchasers the *time* of signing might be
shewn." This reasoning applies strictly to this case.
The law says, that an executor may plead in answer to
an action, a judgment obtained against him since the
last continuance. In order, therefore, to avail himself
of that defence, he must be permitted to shew the time
when the judgment was actually obtained. The principle is, that in all cases where for the purposes of justice it becomes necessary that the true time when any
legal proceedings took place should be ascertained, the
fiction

LYTTLETON
against
CROSS.

fiction of law is not to prevail against the fact. Now, by law, a judgment recovered against an executor since the last continuance is a good matter to plead in bar, such a judgment has been obtained, and the defendants have pleaded it: the plaintiff objects that by fiction of law, this judgment, although actually obtained after the term, must be supposed to have been given in term, and cannot be pleaded in answer to the action. The fiction of law is in this case inconsistent with the fact, and if it prevailed, would work great injustice, and, therefore, according to the principle laid down by Lord *Mansfield*, it is competent to the party to shew the actual time when the judgment was obtained. If that be so, then this judgment, which was in fact obtained after the last continuance, is properly pleaded.

LITTLEDALE J. This action being founded upon a specialty, and the judgment pleaded being also founded upon a specialty, I have no doubt that the executors had the right to prefer one creditor to another by confessing judgment, and that if the judgment were recovered before the plea pleaded it might be pleaded in bar; or if recovered before the trial, after issue joined, it might be pleaded puis darrein continuance. I accede entirely to the doctrine laid down in *Prince* v. *Nicholson*, but in that case the plea was pleaded in term, with a special memorandum, so that it appeared upon the record that the judgment mentioned in the plea had been obtained before the trial. The difficulty which I have felt during the course of the argument is, that it does not primâ facie appear upon this record that the judgment was obtained since the last continuance. It seems to me that the defendants are obliged to resort to a fiction

of

of law against the real fact. They allege that judgment was recovered on the 2d of *August*. Now I doubt whether the signing of the judgment on the 2d of *August* was any thing more than the execution by the officer of the court of an authority to enter up judgment as of the preceding term. When the judgment is signed, it is by relation a judgment of the first day of that term, and it is the judgment which gives the debt the precedence, and enables the defendants to plead it as an answer to this action. The obtaining of that judgment is the gist of the defence. Although, however, I have entertained doubts whether the judgment can be considered to have been obtained on the 2d of *August*, yet upon the whole those doubts are not of such a nature as to induce me not to concur in the judgment given by the rest of the Court. The reasoning of Lord *Mansfield* in *Johnson* v. *Smith* applies strongly to the present case, and, upon the whole, I think that the judgment ought to be for the defendants.

Judgment for the defendants.

MOORE *against* RAWSON.

The right to light is acquired by enjoyment, and may be lost by a discontinuance of the enjoyment, unless the party who ceases to enjoy at the same time does some act to shew an intention of resuming the enjoyment within a reasonable time. And, therefore, where in case by a reversioner for obstructing lights, it appeared that the plaintiff's messuage was an ancient house, and that adjoining to it there had formerly been a building, in which there was an ancient window, next the lands of the defendant, and that the former owner of the plaintiff's premises, about seventeen years before, had pulled down this building, and erected on its site another with a blank wall, next adjoining the premises of the defendant; and this latter, about three years before the commencement of the action, erected a building next the blank wall of the plaintiff, who then opened a window in that wall in the same place where the ancient window had been in the old building: it was held, that he could not maintain any action against the defendant for obstructing the new window; because, by erecting the blank wall, he not only ceased to enjoy the light, but had evinced an intention never to resume the enjoyment.

CASE for obstructing *lights*. Plea, not guilty. At the trial before *Hullock* B., at the last Spring assizes for the county of *Derby*, it appeared, that the plaintiff was seised in fee of a messuage and building, with a yard, garden, and appurtenances, situate at *Ripley*, in that county, in the occupation of a tenant from year to year. The defendant was the owner of other messuages and premises next adjoining the plaintiff's, on the northern side thereof. The plaintiff's messuage was an ancient house, and adjoining to it there had been a building formerly used as a weaver's shop. The old shop had *ancient windows*, for the convenience of light to the weavers who worked looms there. About seventeen years ago the then owner and occupier of the premises took down the old shop, and erected on the same site a stable, having a blank wall next adjoining to the premises of the present defendant. This building had latterly been used as a wheelright's shop. About three years ago, and while the plaintiff's premises continued in this state, the defendant erected a building next to the blank wall, and the plaintiff then opened a window in that wall, in the same place where there had formerly been a window in the old wall, and the action was brought for the obstruction of this new window by the building so erected by the defendant. The learned Judge directed the jury to find

a verdict

a verdict for the plaintiff, but reserved liberty to the
defendant to move to enter a nonsuit. A rule nisi having
been obtained accordingly,

Vaughan Serjt. and *N. R. Clarke* shewed cause. Every
man, primâ facie, is entitled to enjoy all the light and air
which come to his own land. The enjoyment of lights
for twenty years, in a particular mode, is presumptive
evidence of a grant by the owner of the adjoining land
of the privilege so to enjoy the light. Here, the
former owners of the plaintiff's premises enjoyed the
light for that period, they must therefore be taken to
have had a grant from some person capable of making
it; and that being so, the right which was once vested
in the owners of the plaintiff's premises, could not be
divested out of them, except by a release of the right so
granted to them, or by a non user of the right for
such a length of time as would warrant the presumption of a release. If, therefore, there had been a non-
user for twenty years, a release might be presumed, but a
non-user for a less period does not warrant such a presumption. In *Lethbridge* v. *Winter* (a) a gate had been
erected in a place where a similar gate had formerly
stood, but where, for the twelve years preceding, there
had been none. It was contended for the defendant,
that from suffering the gate to be down so long, and
permitting the public to use the way without obstruction
for so many years, the plaintiff, and those under whom
he claimed, must be considered as having completely
dedicated the way to the public, and that the gate could
not be replaced. The plaintiff recovered a verdict, and
the Court of King's Bench refused to grant a rule *nisi*
to set it aside. This is an authority to shew, that a party

(a) 1 *Campb.* 263.

does

does not lose his rights by a mere non user for twelve years.

Denman and *Reader*, contrà. Light, air, and water are primâ facie publici juris, but individuals may acquire a right to them by occupancy or enjoyment, and if the right is acquired by enjoyment, it may also be lost by a discontinuance of it. The period of enjoyment necessary to give an individual an exclusive right to enjoy light, air, and water, is fixed by the municipal law of the country, and, by the law of *England*, that period is twenty years, but as the right is acquired by enjoyment, it may be lost by non user, unless the party who has appropriated to himself the light, air, or water, at the time when he discontinues the use, does some act to indicate to others his intention to resume it within a reasonable time. Here, the plaintiff or the former owner of his premises did no act of that kind. On the contrary, the erecting of the blank wall on the site of that which formerly had the windows, indicated an intention not to resume the enjoyment of the light in the mode in which they formerly had it. It is true, that twenty years being the fixed period necessary to give an exclusive right to enjoy the light in a particular mode derogatory to the rights of others, it has been usual to direct juries in such cases to presume that such right has been transferred to the owner of the property who has so enjoyed it, by the owner of the adjoining land, by an instrument adapted to convey such right. Now the right to the light being incident to the land itself, the right to enjoy in a particular mode a portion of the light which primâ facie belongs to the owner of the adjoining land, and which he may appropriate to his own use, is an easement annexed to the land, and must

be

be transferred by deed. In ordinary cases, where the enjoyment of the light in the particular mode has continued down to the very time of the obstruction complained of, it has been usual to presume a deed of grant from the person who had the fee simple of the adjoining land, such a deed alone being consistent with the facts of the case. But the facts of this case do not make it necessary to presume that there was any such grant. It is consistent with those facts that the owner of the land adjoining the plaintiff's may have entered into a covenant with the former owners, to allow them, or those deriving title under them, the enjoyment of the light in the mode in which it had been formerly enjoyed for a term of years, determining at the time when the former owner of the plaintiff's premises built the blank wall. Such a deed is consistent with the enjoyment proved, and the jury ought not to be directed to presume any other deed than that which is necessary to account for the enjoyment. In *Barker* v. *Richardson* (a), where lights had been enjoyed for more than twenty years, contiguous to land which within that period had been glebe land, but was conveyed to a purchaser under 55 G. 3. c. 147., it was held, that no valid grant could be presumed, inasmuch as the rector, who was mere tenant for life, could not grant the easement.

ABBOTT C. J. I am of opinion that the plaintiff is not entitled to maintain this action. It appears that many years ago the former owner of his premises had the enjoyment of light and air by means of certain windows in a wall of his house. Upon the site of this

(a) 4 *B. & A.* 579.

wall

wall he built a blank wall without any windows.   Things continued in this state for seventeen years.   The defendant, in the interim, erected a building opposite the plaintiff's blank wall, and then the plaintiff opened a window in that which had continued for so long a period a blank wall without windows, and he now complains that that window is darkened by the buildings which the defendant so erected.   It seems to me that, if a person entitled to ancient lights pulls down his house and erects a blank wall in the place of a wall in which there had been windows, and suffers that blank wall to remain for a considerable period of time, it lies upon him at least to shew, that at the time when he so erected the blank wall, and thus apparently abandoned the windows which gave light and air to the house, that was not a perpetual, but a temporary abandonment of the enjoyment; and that he intended to resume the enjoyment of those advantages within a reasonable period of time. I think that the burthen of shewing that lies on the party who has discontinued the use of the light.   By building the blank wall, he may have induced another person to become the purchaser of the adjoining ground for building purposes, and it would be most unjust that he should afterwards prevent such a person from carrying those purposes into effect.   For these reasons I am of opinion, that the rule for a nonsuit must be made absolute.

BAYLEY J. The right to light, air, or water, is acquired by enjoyment, and will, as it seems to me, continue so long as the party either continues that enjoyment or shews an intention to continue it.   In this case the former owner of the plaintiff's premises had acquired a right to the enjoyment of the light; but he chose to relinquish that enjoyment, and to erect a blank

wall

wall instead of one in which there were formerly windows. At that time he ceased to enjoy the light in the mode in which he had used to do, and his right ceased with it. Suppose that, instead of doing that, he had pulled down the house and buildings, and converted the land into a garden, and continued so to use it for a period of seventeen years; and another person had been induced by such conduct to buy the adjoining ground for the purposes of building. It would be most unjust to allow the person who had so converted his land into garden ground, to prevent the other from building upon the adjoining land which he had, under such circumstances, been induced to purchase for that purpose. I think that, according to the doctrine of modern times, we must consider the enjoyment as giving the right; and that it is a wholesome and wise qualification of that rule to say, that the ceasing to enjoy destroys the right, unless at the time when the party discontinues the enjoyment he does some act to shew that he means to resume it within a reasonable time.

HOLROYD J. I am of the same opinion. It appears that the former owner of the plaintiff's premises at one time was entitled to the house with the windows, so that the light coming to those windows over the adjoining land could not be obstructed by the owner of that land. I think, however, that the right acquired by the enjoyment of the light, continued no longer than the existence of the thing itself in respect of which the party had the right of enjoyment; I mean the house with the windows; when the house and the windows were destroyed by his own act, the right which he had in respect of them was also extinguished. If, indeed, at the time when he

VOL. III.   Z   pulled

pulled the house down, he had intimated his intention of rebuilding it, the right would not then have been destroyed with the house. If he had done some act to shew that he intended to build another in its place, then the new house, when built, would in effect have been a continuation of the old house, and the rights attached to the old house would have continued. If a man has a right of common attached to his mill, or a right of turbary attached to his house, if he pulls down the mill or the house, the right of common or of turbary will primâ facie cease. If he shew an intention to build another mill or another house, his right continues. But if he pulls down the house or the mill without shewing any intention to make a similar use of the land, and after a long period of time has elapsed, builds a house or mill corresponding to that which he pulls down, that is not the renovation of the old house or mill, but the creation of a new thing, and the rights which he had in respect of the old house or mill, do not in my opinion attach to the new one. In this case, I think, the building of a blank wall is a stronger circumstance to shew that he had no intention to continue the enjoyment of his light than if he had merely pulled down the house. In that case he might have intended to substitute something in its place. Here, he does in fact substitute quite a different thing, a wall without windows. There is not only nothing to shew that he meant to renovate the house so as to make it a continuance of the old house, but he actually builds a new house different from the old one, thereby shewing that he did not mean to renovate the old house. It seems to me, therefore, that the right is not renewed as it would have been, if, when he had pulled down the old house, he had shewn an intention

to

to rebuild it within a reasonable time, although he did not do so eo instanti.

LITTLEDALE J. According to the present rule of law a man may acquire a right of way, or a right of common, (except, indeed, common appendant) upon the land of another, by enjoyment. After twenty years' adverse enjoyment the law presumes a grant made before the user commenced, by some person who had power to grant. But if the party who has acquired the right by grant ceases for a long period of time to make use of the privilege so granted to him, it may then be presumed that he has released the right. It is said, however, that as he can only acquire the right by twenty years' enjoyment, it ought not to be lost without disuse for the same period; and that as enjoyment for such a length of time is necessary to found a presumption of a grant, there must be a similar non-user, to raise a presumption of a release. And this reasoning, perhaps, may apply to a right of common or of way. But there is a material difference between the mode of acquiring such rights and a right to light and air. The latter is acquired by mere occupancy; the former can only be acquired by user, accompanied with the consent of the owner of the land; for a way over the lands of another can only be lawfully used, in the first instance, with the consent, express or implied, of the owner. A party using the way without such consent would be a wrong doer; but when such a user, without interruption, has continued for twenty years, the consent of the owner is not only implied during that period, but a grant of the easement is presumed to have taken place before the user commenced. The consent of the owner of the land was necessary, however, to make the user of the way (from

Z 2

which

which the presumption of the grant is to arise) lawful in the first instance. But it is otherwise as to light and air. Every man on his own land has a right to all the light and air which will come to him, and he may erect, even on the extremity of his land, buildings with as many windows as he pleases. In order to make it lawful for him to appropriate to himself the use of the light, he does not require any consent from the owner of the adjoining land. He therefore begins to acquire the right to the enjoyment of the light by mere occupancy. After he has erected his building the owner of the adjoining land may, afterwards, within twenty years, build upon his own land, and so obstruct the light which would otherwise pass to the building of his neighbour. But if the light be suffered to pass without interruption during that period to the building so erected, the law implies, from the non-obstruction of the light for that length of time, that the owner of the adjoining land has consented that the person who has erected the building upon his land shall continue to enjoy the light without obstruction, so long as he shall continue the specific mode of enjoyment which he had been used to have during that period. It does not, indeed, imply that the consent is given by way of grant; for although a right of common (except as to common appendant) or a right of way being a privilege of something positive to be done or used in the soil of another man's land, may be the subject of legal grant, yet light and air, not being to be used in the soil of the land of another, are not the subject of actual grant; but the right to insist upon the non-obstruction and non-interruption of them more properly arises by a covenant which the law would imply not to interrupt the free use of the light and air. The right, therefore, is acquired by mere

occupancy,

occupancy, and ought to cease when the person who so acquired it discontinues the occupancy. If, therefore, as in this case, the party who has acquired the right once ceases to make use of the light and air which he had appropriated to his own use, without shewing any intention to resume the enjoyment, he must be taken to have abandoned the right. I am of opinion, that as the right is acquired by mere user, it may be lost by non-user. It would be most inconvenient to hold, that the property in light and air, which is acquired by occupancy, can only be lost where there has been an abandonment of the right for twenty years. I think, that if a party does any act to shew that he abandons his right to the benefit of that light and air which he once had, he may lose his right in a much less period than twenty years. If a man pulls down a house and does not make any use of the land for two or three years, or converts it into tillage, I think he may be taken to have abandoned all intention of rebuilding the house; and, consequently, that his right to the light has ceased. But if he builds upon the same site, and places windows in the same spot, or does any thing to shew that he did not mean to convert the land to a different purpose, then his right would not cease. In this case, I think that the owner of the plaintiff's premises abandoned his right to the ancient lights, by erecting the blank wall instead of that in which the ancient windows were; for he then indicated an intention never to resume that enjoyment of the light which he once had. Under those circumstances, I think that the temporary disuse was a complete abandonment of the right.

. Rule absolute.

QUEIROZ and Others *against* TRUEMAN and Another.

*A. and Co.,
merchants at
Rio Janeiro,
consigned cot-
tons to B. in
this country for
sale, and sent
bills of lading,
which shewed
that the cottons
were sent on
account and
risk of the con-
signors. B.
employed C.
and D., brokers
at Liverpool, to
effect the sales,
which they did;
some at a credit
of ten days, and
bills at three
months; others
for cash in one
month. C. and
D. made large
advances to B.,
and received
the proceeds of
the cottons
when due.
Before that
time B. had
become bank-
rupt. In an
action by A.
and Co. against
C. and D. for
money had and
received: Held,
that the latter
were not en-
titled to retain
for the advances
made by them*

ASSUMPSIT for money had and received. Plea, general issue. At the trial before *Abbott* C. J. at the *London* sittings after *Trinity* term 1820, a verdict was found for the plaintiffs for 3796*l.* 5*s.* 8*d.*, subject to the opinion of the Court, on a case in substance as follows: The plaintiffs carry on business as merchants at *Rio de Janeiro*, under the firm of *Queiroz* and Co. Defendants are cotton brokers in *London*. One *Caumont* of the city of *London*, commission merchant, for some years before the transaction in question arose, had been in the habit of receiving cotton on consignment from the plaintiffs, and other foreign correspondents, to be sold by him on their account; but had not imported any cotton on his own account. He had been in the habit of employing sundry brokers, and, amongst others, the defendants, as brokers to sell the cotton so consigned to him. *Needham* and Co. were cotton brokers at *Liverpool*, employed by the defendants, with whom the defendants divided the commission upon the sales effected by them, and for whom they were responsible. In the beginning of *July* 1818, *Caumont* received a bill of lading of 165 serons of cotton, shipped by the plaintiffs in the *Aurora*, from *Rio de Janeiro* to *Liverpool*, and agreed with the defendants that they

to B., for that he was a factor for sale only, and had no authority to pledge the goods, and that the plaintiffs were entitled to recover the net proceeds, deducting such sums only as B. could have retained   A. and Co., when they consigned the cottons to B., requested him to make remittances in anticipation of sales: Held, secondly, that this request did not give B. any special authority to pledge the goods.

should

should sell these cottons through the medium of Needham and Co., together with certain other cottons, but which were not the property of the plaintiffs, consigned to him by the same vessel. On the 15th of July 1818, Caumont wrote to the defendants, inclosing four bills of lading of the before mentioned cottons, and desiring that they would send them to Needham and Co. and request them to do the needful as to the sale of the cottons. The bill of lading of the 165 serons of the plaintiffs, inclosed in the foregoing letter, was dated at Rio de Janeiro, the 25th of April 1818, and expressed that the cotton, viz. two serons marked Q. and L., and 163 serons marked Q. and C., were shipped by Queiros and Co., and were to be delivered in their name, and on their account and risk, to Caumont, or to his order, paying the freight, &c. therein mentioned. This bill of lading was indorsed by Caumont specially to the defendants, and by them to Needham and Co. On the 15th of July defendants wrote to Needham and Co. inclosing the said four bills of lading, in which letter was the following passage: " When these cottons are sold, the proceeds must go to our credit. Indeed you are to know no other persons than us in the business, as we shall have to advance on them." On the 10th of September, Caumont wrote to the defendants as follows: " According-ing with what we mutually agreed together respecting the advances which I requested you to make me on the undermentioned cotton consigned for my account, and under your care to Needham and Co. of Liverpool, I have drawn upon you 1500l. under yesterday's date, at two months, and 1500l. same date, at three months, to which I request your acceptance, placing the same to your credit, when due, and against the net proceeds of

the

the cotton." He then mentioned the several parcels of cotton included in the four bills of lading as before stated, and a small parcel from *Maranham* as consigned on his account to *Needham* and Co. The two bills for 1500*l.* each were accepted by the defendants, and duly paid. *Caumont* got them discounted shortly after they were accepted. The *Aurora* arrived at *Liverpool* on the 28th of *August* 1818, with the said 165 serons of cotton on board, and *Needham* and Co. obtained possession of and sold the cotton at *Liverpool* at ten days, and bills at three months, being the usual credit in that trade at *Liverpool*, according to which at the end of ten days bankers' bills are to be given not exceeding three months; if the bills have less than three months to run, interest is allowed for the difference of time. Such bankers' bills pass current at *Liverpool* as cash. On the 26th of *July* 1818, *Caumont* received bills of lading of sixty bags of cotton, the property of the plaintiffs, shipped by their agents in the *Riga* packet from *Pernambuco* for *London*. In these bills of lading, which were dated *June* the 2d, 1818, it was expressed that the cottons marked Q. V. and C. were shipped by *Antonio Soares* for account and risk of *Queiroz* and Co. of *Rio de Janeiro*, and were to be delivered in their name to *Caumont*. The *Riga* packet arrived at *London* with the said sixty bags of cotton on the 26th of *July* 1818. *Caumont* employed the defendants to sell them, and on the 23d of *September* sent them a delivery order for the cotton inclosed in the following letter, dated *London*, *September* 23d, 1818. " Referring to my letter of the 10th instant, advising two drafts, together 3000*l.*, in anticipation of net proceeds of some cottons consigned on my account, and under your care, to *Needham* and

Co.

Co. of *Liverpool*, I have now to advise, for the same objects, my new drafts upon you for 1200*l.* at three months' date, and herewith hand you a delivery order for sixty bags *Pernambuco* cotton of mine in the *London* Docks, ex *Riga* packet, on account of which I likewise draw on you 800*l.* at two months' date." The bills mentioned in the foregoing letter were accepted, and duly paid by the defendants. *Caumont* got them discounted shortly after they were accepted. Defendants got possession of the sixty bags of cotton under the said delivery order, and sold them on the 16th of *December* 1818. On the 11th of *November* 1818, *Caumont* received bills of lading of 110 bags of cotton, the property of the plaintiffs, shipped by their agents in the *Isabel* from *Pernambuco* for *London*. These bills of lading were exactly in the same form as those for the cotton by the *Riga* packet. If goods imported come from abroad on account of the shippers, the usage is to put the initials of the shippers in the bill of lading in the manner pursued in the bills of lading above set out. If they come on account of the consignee, they are marked differently with such marks as the consignee directs. The *Isabel* arrived in the port of *London*, with the 110 bags of cotton on board, on the 16th of *November* 1818; *Caumont* landed them, and entered them in his own name in the *London* Docks, and employed defendants to sell them. Defendants sold sixty bags on the 10th of *December*, and the remainder on the 16th. On the 1st of *January*, *Caumont* wrote the following letter to the defendants: " According to our verbal agreement, I request your giving to the bearer of this a cheque for 1000*l.*, on account of cotton which you have sold for me, and of which you have received

the

the delivery orders." A cheque for 1000l. upon the defendants' bankers was given by them the same day to Caumont, and duly paid. On the 9th of January 1819, Caumont stopped payment, and on the 4th of February a commission of bankrupt was sued out against him, under which he has been duly declared a bankrupt. The cotton by the Aurora was sold in four parcels on the 21st of September, the 27th of November, 28th of November, and the 4th of December, which were paid for respectively by bills becoming due on the 4th of February, the 7th of March, 8th of March, and 17th of March. The net proceeds amounted to 1506l. 16s. 5d., from which Caumont, as between him and the plaintiffs, was entitled to certain charges whereby it would be reduced to 1458l. 19s. 8d. The cottons by the Riga packet were sold on the 16th of December 1818, on the terms of cash in one month, discount 1½ per cent. The net proceeds amounted to 790l. 11s. 11d., from which Caumont, as between him and the plaintiffs, was entitled to certain charges whereby it would be reduced to 696l. 13s. 2d. The cottons by the Isabel were sold at the same time, and on the same terms. The net proceeds amounted to 1498l. 16s. 4d., from which sum Caumont, as between him and the plaintiffs, was entitled to charges by which it would be reduced to 1430l. 4s. 8d. On the 18th of September 1819, the defendants were, for the first time, called upon by the plaintiffs to account to them for the proceeds of the cotton so sold as aforesaid. On the 9th of May 1818, the plaintiffs wrote to Caumont, enclosing a bill of lading and invoice of the 165 serons of cotton by the Aurora, and saying, " We expect that you will send us some remittances on account of the proceeds consigned to you, though they be not yet sold,

as is customary, in order to encourage us thereby to
send you more frequent consignments." On the 9th
of *December* 1818, *Caumont* wrote to the plaintiffs,
enclosing a remittance of 1850*l.*; but of that only
883*l.* 14*s.* 7*d.* was ascribable to the above consignments. The account sales were rendered by the defendants to *Caumont* of the 165 serons by the *Aurora*
on the 8th of *January*, and of the sixty bags by the
Riga packet, and the 110 bags by the *Isabella* on the
18th of *January* 1819. The balance of accounts between *Caumont* and the defendants was settled between
defendants and *Caumont's* assignees on the 5th of *March*
1819, and the sum of 185*l.* 11*s.* 5*d.*, the amount thereof,
was then paid to the latter. The balance arose from
the sale of other goods besides those belonging to the
plaintiffs. The sum of 3796*l.* 3*s.* 8*d.*, for which the
verdict was taken, is the amount of the net proceeds of
the three consignments; but as between *Caumont* and
the plaintiffs they would only be entitled to a balance of
2611*l.* 15*s.* 5*d.*, in estimating which credit is given for
the 883*l.* 14*s.* 7*d.* remitted by *Caumont* to the plaintiffs.
The case was now argued by

Campbell, for the plaintiffs. *Queiros* and Co. are entitled to recover the sum of 2611*l.* 16*s.* 5*d.*, in this
action. It is difficult to conjecture any defence that
can be set up. The cottons were the property of the
plaintiffs, and were consigned by them to *Caumont* to be
sold on their account. The defendants were employed
by *Caumont* to effect the sales, which they did, and got
all the proceeds into their hands. The only question
then is, whether they have paid over those proceeds to
Caumont, or have a right to set off against the present
demand

demand a debt due to them from him. . It appears by the case that they never paid over to *Caumont* the proceeds which they received. Then have they a right to set off the debt which he owed them for their advances? They cannot have any such right unless *Caumont* had authority to pledge the goods. It must be admitted that under such circumstances, the defendants, as pawnees, would have a lien for their advances; the question, therefore, is, whether *Caumont* had such authority. By the law of *England* a factor for sale cannot pledge, *Patterson* v. *Tash*(a), *Martini* v. *Coles*(b); nor did the correspondence in this case give him any special authority to do so. The plaintiffs merely say they hope that *Caumont* will make remittances in anticipation of sales. Surely that is not so strong as if they had drawn bills upon *Caumont,* and he had accepted them; but it has been held that such a course of dealing does not give a factor authority to pledge the goods of his principal, *Graham* v. *Dyster* (c), *Kuckein* v. *Wilson* (d), *Fielding* v. *Kymer* (e), reported as *Gill* v. *Kymer,* 5 *B. Moore. Duclos* v. *Ryland,* in a note to that report, is also in point. There does not then appear to be any answer to this demand, and the plaintiffs are entitled to retain the verdict to the extent of the balance due to them.

Jones, contrà. It is certainly too late to contend that a factor for sale has a general authority to pledge the goods of his principal, for although many learned judges have expressed doubts as to the expediency of the rule of

(a) 2 *Str.* 1178.   (b) 1 *M. & S.* 140.
(c) 2 *Stark.* 21.   (d) 4 *B. & A.* 443.
(e) 2 *B. & B.* 639.

law

law on this point, yet they have felt themselves bound by decided cases. But where a special authority is given, or where no injury is done to the principals, advances to the factor may be available against them. Here, authority to pledge was given by the letter of the plaintiffs, they ask for advances of money before the sales took place. This is distinguishable from *Fielding* v. *Kymer*, for there the bills accepted by anticipation were to be paid out of the proceeds of the goods. If *Caumont* had made advances he would have had a lien on the goods, why then should not the defendants have the same, as they advanced the money? But, secondly, the plaintiffs have not been injured by the advances made to *Caumont*. All the cottons sent by the *Aurora* were sold on or before the 4th of *December ;* in ten days from that time bills, which at *Liverpool* are current as cash, were to be given; had *Caumont* sold the goods without the intervention of the defendants, he might, at the expiration of the ten days, have demanded the bills, and by that means have obtained the whole of the proceeds. If then, but for the employment of the defendants, he would have been in a situation to claim the whole proceeds before he became bankrupt, the defendants cannot have injured the plaintiffs by advancing to him a part. The consignments by the *Riga* packet and *Isabel* stand on a different footing, for it does not appear that the defendants ever saw the bills of lading of those goods; they might therefore suppose them to be *Caumont*'s property.

ABBOTT C. J. The principle of law on which this case must be decided is not of modern introduction, but has been recognised in a variety of modern cases. Some doubts having been lately thrown on the expediency of
that

that law, I think it right to express my opinion, that it is one of the greatest safeguards which the foreign merchant has in making consignments of goods to be sold in this country. And I should be extremely sorry (if I may be allowed to use such an expression when sitting in this place,) if that law were to be abolished. In the present case it must be taken, that the defendants might have known that all the cottons were consigned to Caumont as a factor, they might have asked to see the bills of lading, the means of knowledge were therefore within their reach, and the voluntary blindness of one party ought not to be allowed to prejudice another. It has been argued, that if the sales had been effected by Caumont immediately without the intervention of the defendants, he would have received the whole proceeds, and then the plaintiffs would have been in as bad a situation as if the lien now claimed by the defendants is allowed. But I think it very unlikely that Caumont would, under such circumstances, have received the proceeds. Upon the facts appearing in this case, it is extremely probable that he would have stopped payment in September but for the advances made by the defendant, which enabled him to hold up his head for a time. It is much better for all parties, when persons are insolvent, that they should stop at once and allow their property to be fairly divided amongst their creditors, rather than struggle on a little longer perhaps to relieve some creditors by drawing in a new set of sufferers. The money advanced in this case was for Caumont's use, and not for the plaintiffs; the defendants then have received the proceeds of the goods, and have not paid them over to the principals. Caumont in the first instance had no authority to pledge, nor did he derive any from

the

1824.

Garratt
against
Gummett

the correspondence. The plaintiffs are therefore entitled to a verdict for the net proceeds of the goods, deducting such charges as Caumont was entitled to make; and also the sum which he remitted on account of these goods; that leaves a balance of 261l. 15s. 9d. due to the plaintiffs.

BAYLEY J. It has been frequently decided in favor of foreign merchants, that a factor cannot pledge the goods consigned to him for sale. I cannot help thinking that this rule of law has operated much to increase the foreign commerce of this kingdom by holding out to consignors, that if the factor goes beyond the authority vested in him it shall not work a prejudice to his principal. I entirely concur in saying, that in my judgment this, as a measure of policy, ought not to be altered. The rule is founded upon a very plain reason, viz., that he who gives the credit should be vigilant in ascertaining whether the party pledging has or has not authority so to deal with the goods. That knowledge may always be obtained from the bill of lading and letters of advice. Here, the advances were made by the defendants, who either had knowledge or the means of obtaining it. The facts of this case, therefore, go beyond what was proved in some of those in which it has been held, that a factor for sale cannot pledge. The letter which has been relied on did not confer any special authority to pledge, but merely asked for advances out of Caumont's funds. But even admitting that it gave authority to pledge for the purpose of making remittances, the defendants should have seen to the application of the money advanced. It is said that the principals have not been damnified, for that if the defendants had not made advances,

Caumont

Caumont might have demanded the bills: but had they been given to him it would have been his duty to keep them for his principals, and we ought not to presume that he would have acted so dishonestly as to indorse them away. With respect to those goods which were to be paid for in cash on the 16th of *January, Caumont* had before then become bankrupt, and a purchaser acting bonâ fide, or a disinterested agent would not then have paid the money to him, knowing him to be a factor, but the payments by anticipation deprived his principals of that advantage. Upon the whole then, I think that the plaintiffs are entitled to recover the net proceeds of the goods, deducting those sums only which *Caumont* would have a right to deduct.

HOLROYD J. I entirely agree with what has been said respecting the rule of law, its policy and application to the present case. The goods were the property of the plaintiffs, and must be taken to have been sold for them, but the money has not been paid to them; the defendants therefore having received it, are responsible. It is said, that the letter written by the plaintiffs gave *Caumont* power to pledge, but it had no such effect. It would merely have given to him a lien for his advances, if he had not otherwise been entitled to it, and by no means takes this case out of the general rule of law.

LITTLEDALE J. expressed no opinion, having been concerned in the case when at the bar.

Postea to the plaintiffs, verdict to be entered for 2611*l.* 15*s.* 5*d.*

~ uchunch. .. Lugta 1. 2 Sept 24 __1824.__

M. PETRIE *against* JOHN BURY and Another, Executors of JAMES BURY.

COVENANT. The declaration stated, that, by a certain indenture, purporting to be made between *James Bury* of the first part, *Patience Petrie* of the second part, and the plaintiff, one *Beddome*, and the said *John Bury*, of the third part (which indenture, sealed with the seal of *James Bury*, plaintiff, brought into court and averred, that *Beddome* and *John Bury* did not at any time seal or deliver the said indenture) reciting, that a marriage was intended to be solemnized between *James Bury* and *Patience Petrie* ; in consideration thereof *James Bury* covenanted with the plaintiff, *Beddome*, and *John Bury*, that in case the marriage took effect and the said *Patience* should survive him, his heirs, executors, or administrators should pay to them the said plaintiff, *Beddome*, and *John Bury*, an annuity of 200*l.*; for the use of the said *Patience*. Averment that the marriage did take effect, that *Patience* survived her husband, and was then still living, and that 250*l.* of the annuity was in arrear. Defendants set out the deed on oyer and demurred. Joinder in demurrer.

Where, in covenant against the executors of A. B., plaintiff declared that A. B. covenanted with him and two others, that his executors, &c. should pay to them an annuity for the use of a third person, and averred that the other two never sealed the deed : Held, on demurrer, that all joint covenantees who may sue must sue, and that the declaration was bad, inasmuch as it did not appear that any of the covenantees had not assented to the deed although they did not seal it.

Quære, whether the declaration would have been sufficient if it had averred that the two covenantees not joined, had refused to assent to the deed?

Wightman, in support of the demurrer. The question upon this demurrer is, whether an action can be maintained by one of three joint covenantees, because the other two did not execute the deed. It is clear that the others might have joined in the action, *Clement* v. *Hen-*

ley (a); and if so, they must join. This is like the case of executors who must join, even if they have renounced before the ordinary. *(b)* In this case there is no averment of dissent, no disclaimer of the covenant; for any thing that appears, the persons not joined may hereafter execute the deed; *Vernon v. Jefferys. (c)* In that case, certainly, there does not appear to have been any averment that the parties not joined did not execute the deed; but in other respects this is a much stronger case for the defendants, for here there are no mutual covenants; the covenant is all on one side, to pay an annuity to three persons for the use of a fourth.

F. Pollock, contrà. The case of *Clement v. Henley* is in favor of the present plaintiff, for if it was then necessary to have a decision, that parties not having executed might join in suing, it can hardly be supposed that they might not have abstained from joining in the suit. The other case of *Vernon v. Jefferys* proves, that where it is shewn by averment that some of the covenantees have not executed, an action may be maintained by those who have. The plaintiff having averred that the persons not joined did not execute this deed, it was at all events incumbent on the defendant to shew their assent, or some other act of theirs to make them parties to the covenant.

Wightman, in reply. If the argument on the other side be good the covenant in question might be with one person now, with two a week hence, and afterwards with three; and several actions might be maintained for the same breach.

(a) 2 Roll. Abr. Fait (F), pl. 2.   (b) See Henslow's case, 9 Co. 37.
(c) 2 Str. 1146.   7 Mod. 358. S.C.

ABBOTT

ABBOTT C. J. I am of opinion that this action is not maintainable. It is founded on a deed made in contemplation of marriage, whereby *James Bury* covenanted with three persons, that, in case his intended wife should survive him, his heirs, executors, or administrators should pay to them an annuity for her use. The action is brought by one of those covenantees alone, and the declaration alleges that the others did not seal the deed. It is clear, upon decided cases, that such parties may sue together with those who have sealed. The question is, whether if they *may* they *must* join in the suit. We are not called upon to consider the effect of an express disclaimer, renunciation, or refusal by the other covenantees, for nothing of that kind is alleged. Trustees very often assent to a trust without executing the deed which creates it, and they may assent at any time, and without an express allegation of dissent that will not appear. Assent is therefore to be presumed, and on that ground my judgment is founded. The case is analogous to that of executors who, when they may, must join in suing. The recital in the 21 *H.* 8. *c.* 4. shews that an opinion then prevailed, that where one of several devisees in trust to sell *refused* to act, no sale could take place. It does not speak of the mere absence of assent, but of an actual refusal. In this case, therefore, I think that it was not sufficient to say that the other covenantees did not seal; they might sue notwithstanding; and as they might, I think that the action cannot be maintained without them.

BAYLEY J. By the deed in question, *James Bury* covenanted that his heirs or executors should pay the

A a 2 annuity

annuity to three persons. It appears on the face of the deed to have been his intention that the money should go into the hands of the three, and that there should be the security of them all for the due application of the money. It is a general rule, confirmed by the late case of *Scott* v. *Goodwin* (a), that all joint covenantees or obligees must sue. In this case, therefore, the plaintiff was wrong in suing alone, without shewing some special title so to do. The defendants have a right to say, the contract was never made with you alone, but with you together with two others. It may be beneficial to the defendants to have the action brought by the three, for they may possibly have a defence against them all, which is not available against one of them. Here the plaintiff has done nothing more than shew, that two of the covenantees did not seal, but they may still be covenantees; they may have assented to the deed, and unless the declaration shews that they have no right to be considered covenantees it is insufficient.

HOLROYD J. The plaintiff is not entitled to sue alone on this covenant; it was made with three persons, and although two of them did not seal the deed, yet it is not in law converted into a covenant with one. No intention that it should be so is shewn, and by law the covenant does not import that. Supposing the others had executed, the present plaintiff would not by himself be entitled to receive the whole or any part of the money; and there is nothing to shew an intention that he should have any such right, in the event of the neglect of the others to execute the deed. There are many

(a) 1 B. & P. 67.

cases which shew that all joint covenantees may sue, although they have not sealed, and if so, I think that they
must sue, and, consequently, this plaintiff cannot recover
alone.

LITTLEDALE J. concurred.

Judgment for the defendants.

MAYFIELD *against* WADSLEY.

INDEBITATUS assumpsit for crops of wheat, hay,
and corn, and for goods bargained and sold to the
defendant, and goods sold and delivered. Plea, non-
assumpsit. At the trial before *Hullock* B. at the last
Spring assizes for the county of *Lincoln*, it appeared,
that the plaintiff being the occupier of a farm, quitted
the same on the 25th of *March* 1821, and was succeeded
by the defendant's son-in-law, *George Mayfield*. The
plaintiff had sown forty acres with wheat; and it appeared by the testimony of a witness who valued the crops,
that in *February* 1821 a verbal agreement was made
between the plaintiff and the defendant, and that

A. being the occupier of a farm, quitted the same on the 25th of March 1821, and was succeeded in the possession by B. A. had sown forty acres with wheat, and it appeared that at a meeting between A. and B. in February 1821, A. asked B. if he would take the forty acres of wheat at 200l. telling him, that if he

did not, he should not have the farm. *B.* said that he would take it. A person present
then valued the dead stock, and having so done, asked to whom he was to value it; *B.*
said that it was to be valued to him, and then promised to pay *A.* for the wheat and the
dead stock on a given day, and he did pay a sum of money on account. *B.* afterwards
had possession of the farm, the growing wheat, and the dead stock : Held, that, in indebitatus assumpsit for crops bargained and sold, and goods sold and delivered, the contract for
the dead stock was distinct from any contract for the sale of the growing wheat, and that
possession of the farm, and therefore that *A.* was entitled to recover to that amount : Held,
also, by *Bayley* and *Holroyd* Js., *Littledale* J. dissentiente, that as *B.* had had the growing
wheat, and had made a part payment on account, *A.* was entitled in this action to recover
the remainder of the price agreed to be paid for it.
 Where a plaintiff has recovered a verdict for a sum of money, composed of several items,
some of which he was not in strict law entitled to recover under the declaration in that
action, but which he would be clearly entitled to recover by declaring in a different form,
the court will not reduce the damages. Per *Abbott* C. J.

A a 3   on

on that occasion the plaintiff asked the defendant if he
would take the forty acres of wheat at 200l., telling him,
that if he did not he should not have the farm; the defendant then said that he would have the wheat. The
witness then proceeded to value the dead stock, and
after having ascertained its value to be 40l. 8s. 6d.,
asked to whom it was to be valued, the defendant said
to him. There was a machine on the farm, which was
also valued at 4l. 10s. *Wadsley* afterwards said to *Mayfield,* " Have you any objection to give *me* possession of
the farm;" and upon *Mayfield's* asking when he would
pay him, *Wadsley* said, that if he would meet him on
the 8th of *March* he would pay him the money for the
wheat and the dead stock, and the machine. It appeared
further, that about a fortnight before the trial, the defendant acknowledged that he had paid 75l. on account
of this money, but said that he would pay no more.
Upon this evidence the learned Judge told the jury that
the plaintiff was entitled to a verdict for the whole sum
sought to be recovered, if they were of opinion that the
defendant had agreed to pay for the wheat to be taken
by *George Mayfield,* because in that case there was a
part performance of the contract, *George Mayfield* having
had the wheat, and the defendant having paid 75l. on
account. The jury found a verdict for the plaintiff for
169l. 18s. 6d., the balance due after deducting the 75l.
A rule nisi was obtained in *Easter* term last for entering
a nonsuit, on the ground that there was no evidence to
shew that there had been any part performance of the
contract by the defendant, because it did not appear that
the possession of *George Mayfield* was the possession of
the defendant, or that the 75l. had been paid by him on
account of the wheat, and, secondly, that even if there

was

was a part performance, still this action was not maintainable within the fourth section of the statute of frauds, the bargain for the dead stock, &c. being subsidiary to a contract relating to the sale of an interest in land.

Denman C. S. and *Pennington* now shewed cause. *George Mayfield* having had possession of the farm, and his possession being that of the defendant, the latter having paid 75*l.* on account of the wheat and dead stock, cannot now rescind the contract. It is a contract executed and cannot be treated as a nullity, *Crosby* v. *Wadsworth.*(a) In *Parker* v. *Staniland*(b) it was held, that indebitatus assumpsit would lie for crops of potatoes bargained and sold, although they were in the ground at the time of the contract, because no interest in the land passed, but a mere right to go upon the land to gather the potatoes. So in *Poulter* v. *Killingbeck* (c), it was held, that indebitatus assumpsit would lie for moieties of crops of wheat sold by the plaintiff to the defendant, and reaped for his use. There the plaintiff had let land to the defendant, from which he was to take two successive crops, and to render the plaintiff a moiety of the crops, in lieu of rent. While the crops of the second year were on the ground an appraisement was taken by both parties, and the value ascertained, and it was held, that the special agreement was executed by the appraisement. But here, at all events, the plaintiff is entitled to recover the value of the dead stock, under the count for goods sold and delivered. It was a separate contract, and *Mayfield* accepted the goods, and acceptance by him is an acceptance by the defendant, and, consequently,

(a) 6 *East*, 602.   (b) 11 *East*, 362.   (c) 1 *Bos. & Pul.* 397.

A a 4

25

as to the dead stock, it is a case within the exception of the statute of frauds.

Clarke and *Reader*, contrà. There was no evidence to shew that the contract had been executed by the defendant, or that he contracted on his own account. It appeared that *G. Mayfield* obtained possession of the farm, but there was nothing to identify him with the defendant, so as to make the possession of the one the possession of the other. It does not even appear that the 75l. was paid by the defendant on account of the wheat. Then, if there was no part execution of the contract, the plaintiff clearly could not maintain an action upon it. But even admitting a part execution, the case is not altered, for the fourth section of the statute of frauds says, that no action shall be maintained upon a contract relating to the sale of an interest in or concerning lands, unless it be in writing. This was a sale of growing wheat, and of the interest which the plaintiff then had in the farm: the contract for the dead stock was merely subsidiary to that. There is not a syllable in the fourth section of the statute of frauds making such a contract binding when partly performed. The provision to that effect relates entirely to sales of goods and chattels which would otherwise be void by the operation of the 17th section. If in this case there had been a mere sale of goods and chattels, part performance might have taken the case out of that section: but being a sale of an interest in land, it would be directly in contravention of the fourth section to allow the plaintiff to maintain this action.

ABBOTT C. J. It appears to me, plainly, from the evidence

evidence in this case, that the defendant contracted to
have possession of the farm, and to pay 200*l.* for the
forty acres of wheat, and specific sums of money for the
dead stock and for the machine. The bargain was
clearly made by the defendant, and apparently for himself. He desires the dead stock to be valued to him,
and he says to *Mayfield,* " Have you any objection to
give *me* possession of the farm?" It is said, that whatever may have been the treaty originally, there is no
evidence to shew that it was carried into execution by
Wadsley; and if there were no other evidence in the
case than that which I have stated, I am not prepared
to say we could have inferred that the possession of
George Mayfield was the possession of the defendant.
But it appears further, that the defendant, a fortnight
before the trial, acknowledged that he had paid 75*l.* on
account of the money due for the wheat and the dead
stock. It is clear, therefore, that he either took possession himself and gave possession to *Mayfield,* or that
Mayfield was originally put in by him; and, therefore,
that the possession of the one was the possession of the
other. But it is contended, that as this was a verbal
contract, partly for the sale of an interest in land, and
partly for goods, being void in part, it must be void in
toto. Perhaps that might be so, if it had been one entire contract made at one time and for one price, but here,
there were distinct contracts, and separate prices were
fixed. In the first instance a bargain was made for the
wheat at 200*l.* It may be inferred from the conversation,
that some previous agreement had been made with respect
to the giving up of the farm, but it does not appear what
that contract was, or whether it included any stipulation
about the wheat or dead stock; the only thing proved
was, that a contract having first been made for the wheat

at

at 200l., the witness proceeded to value the dead stock, and
after an interval of time, during which he had ascertained
the value, he asked to whom it was to be valued, and the
defendant said " to him." That is the only evidence
of any contract for the dead stock. I have no doubt,
therefore, that the plaintiff is, at all events, entitled to
recover for the price of the dead stock which *Mayfield*
afterwards had. The defendant having paid 75l. on account generally, and not having made any specific appropriation of that sum at the time of payment, the
party receiving it was entitled to apply it to any just
demand that he had upon him. He might, therefore,
apply it to the demand which he had in respect of the
crops, and may fairly insist that the debt for the dead
stock and the machine still remains; and that being so,
the defendant can at most be entitled only to have the
damages reduced. But if the Court cannot order a
nonsuit, then it becomes a question, whether we ought
in this case to make a rule for reducing the damages.
Supposing that the plaintiff cannot recover the residue
on a declaration for crops bargained and sold, founded
on the original contract, on the ground that it is void by
the statute of frauds, yet I think he may recover on a
declaration, stating that the defendant was indebted for
the value of crops sown by the plaintiff on land in his
possession, and which the defendant was allowed to take,
and for which he promised to pay. If the plaintiff is in
strict law entitled to recover part of his demand in this
action, and in another form of action would be entitled
to recover the residue, we ought not to reduce the damages in this case, for this would only have the effect
of putting both parties to further expence, when the
final result must be the same.

BAYLEY

BAYLEY J. The defendant, in this case, bargained for the possession of the farm for *George Mayfield*; he was identified with the defendant, and then his possession was the possession of the defendant, and the performance of the contract by him would be performance by the defendant. The jury have found, that the defendant did agree to pay for the wheat to be taken by *George Mayfield*. It is said that there was no evidence to justify the learned Judge in leaving that question to the jury, but I think there was very strong evidence of such an agreement by the defendant. The plaintiff asked the defendant if he would have the wheat at 200*l.* or not, and told him if *he* would not have it at that price, he should not have the farm; and then, when the witness asked to whom he was to value the dead stock, the defendant said "to me;" and afterwards, *Wadsley* says to *Mayfield*, "Have you any objection to give *me* possession of the farm," and then he promises that he will pay for the wheat and the dead stock on the 7th of *March*. He afterwards does pay 75*l.*, on account of the wheat and the dead stock, and within a fortnight before the trial he acknowledges that he had so paid it. That circumstance shews that he contracted for the benefit of *George Mayfield*; for unless possession of the farm and goods had been delivered according to the contract, the defendant would no doubt have demanded to have the money back. If there was a delivery according to the contract there ought not to be a nonsuit; for then, as to the 44*l.*, the price of the dead stock, the statute of frauds is out of the question. The 75*l.* paid on account cannot now be appropriated to that demand, inasmuch as the defendant did not so appropriate it at the time of payment. As to the residue of the demand for the crops, the

the defendant contracted for them as crops, and he, or *Mayfield* by his authority, received them as crops. Under these circumstances, I am inclined to think that the statute of frauds does not apply, and that the plaintiff may recover in this action.

HOLROYD J. I incline to think that the plaintiff is entitled to retain his verdict for the whole amount. There is abundant evidence to shew that the contract has been executed, and that possession of the farm has been delivered to the defendant, or to *George Mayfield*, by his authority. The defendant, a fortnight before the trial, acknowledged that he had paid 75*l.* and no more. Now if he had not had possession he would have said that he was entitled to have that money back again, and if he had possession of the wheat, then, unless the case be within the statute of frauds, the plaintiff is entitled to recover his whole demand. In 1 *Ld. Raymond*, 182, *Treby* C. J. said, that a sale of timber growing upon the land need not be in writing, because it was but a bare chattel, and to that opinion *Powel* J. agreed. In some cases, therefore, crops growing upon the land may be considered as goods and chattels, and crops agreed to be taken by an incoming of an outgoing tenant may be recovered under a count for goods bargained and sold. But it is said, that from what passed at the time of the appraisement, it appears that the parties bargained for an interest in the land. It seems to me that there was nothing more than a conditional agreement for the crops in the event of the defendant having the land. The taking of the land might have been by an agreement with the

lessor,

lessor, and if in that case a separate action had been brought against the defendant for not taking the farm, the conditional agreement for the goods would not have been avoided by the statute of frauds. But there was no evidence of any engagement that the offgoing tenant should assign his interest in the land to the defendant, and that might cease at *Lady-day* when the possession was to be given up. He, therefore, had no interest in the land to part with; and that being so, the contract was not for the sale of any interest in the land, and the rule for a nonsuit must be discharged. I think also, that under the circumstances of this case, the defendant is not entitled to have the damages reduced.

LITTLEDALE J. I think that *George Mayfield* and defendant are sufficiently identified, and that the case is to be considered as if the defendant had had the same benefit from the contract as *George Mayfield*; the verdict is therefore right for the price of the dead stock and for the machine, because even if there were a contract for the sale of an interest in land upon which no action would lie, still as a distinct price was to be paid for the value of the dead stock, the action would lie for the value of that, there being nothing to affect that part of the agreement. In equity and conscience it is clear that the defendant is liable to pay the full amount, but I have considerable doubt whether this or any other action can be maintained for the value of the growing crops. I think that in effect this was a contract relating to the sale of an interest in land. If the giving up of the land was any part of the consideration for the defendant's agreeing to take the wheat which was then sown in the land, the wheat must be considered as part of the land itself.

itself. It is true, that in some cases there may be a contract for the growing crops, independently of the land itself; but where the land is agreed to be sold, and the vendee takes from the vendor the growing crops, the latter are considered part of the land. It by no means follows, therefore, that because the crops formed the subject of a distinct valuation, they were the subject of a distinct contract of sale. Most of the cases where this question has arisen, were upon contracts for growing wheat, potatoes, and things of that nature, distinct from any assignment or letting of the land, and they have been held not to be within the statute. Here the agreement did not relate to the mere sale of the produce of the land. It does not distinctly appear what interest the plaintiff had, whether he was owner or tenant of the land, but I collect that he had some interest in him which would continue after *Lady-day*. The expressions used shew that the plaintiff had a power to let the defendant have the land or not; then as the land was to be given up, I cannot help thinking that the crops were part of the land. Crops of corn may be sold under a fi. fa., but although crops are separately valued, yet, if they are transferred with the land, the party takes them as part of the land. In this case they were not made the subject of a distinct sale, but only of a distinct valuation. The consideration for paying the 200l. was not merely for the benefit of the crops, but the possession of the land for which the defendant had contracted: if the plaintiff had been the owner of the land, and this had been a parol letting, then, perhaps, he might have maintained this action. The contract for crops in that case would have been subsidiary to another parol contract, legal and binding, and

not

not within the statute. So, if there had been an under-lease; but if there is an assignment it is otherwise; then the statute requires it to be in writing, and the contract for crops growing on the land would be subsidiary to the contract for the land; and I rather collect that in this case it was an assignment. A parol agreement for the sale of crops may be good also between the out-going and the incoming tenant; but then there would be no sale of any interest in the land, for that would come from the landlord. Since then it seems that the plaintiff had some interest in the land, it appears to me, that the crops were part of the land; but I express this opinion with diffidence after the opinion delivered by my lord and my brothers. I am, however, satisfied that the verdict was right for the 44*l*. 8*s*. 6*d*. for the dead stock and machine, and that the defendant ought in justice to pay the residue.

Rule discharged.

[handwritten marginalia]

Storer and Others, Assignees of Fletcher, a Bankrupt, *against* Hunter.

By lease, the lessor demised to the lessee a colliery, and all the engines, machinery, and other implements, effects, and things then lying on or about the colliery, or used or employed therewith, and mentioned in a certain inventory and valuation then made, habendum for twenty-one years, at a certain rent therein mentioned. The lease contained a proviso for re-entry in case the rent should be in arrear for the space of thirty days; and also a proviso, that on the expiration, or other sooner determination of the demise, the lessee should leave and yield up to the lessor all engines, machines, effects, and things belonging to and used in the said colliery, and that an inventory and valuation should, three months previous thereto, be made and taken by two indifferent persons, to be appointed by the parties respectively, or by an umpire, and such inventory should be compared with the then present inventory and valuation, and that the difference in the value of the engines, &c. should be paid by the landlord or tenant to the other, according as it was greater or less than the value at the time of the letting. The tenant entered and occupied the colliery, machinery, &c., and failing in the payment of the rent, the lease became forfeited, and the landlord recovered a judgment in ejectment in *Trinity* term 1818, but did not execute his writ of possession until the 9th of *November* 1819. On the following day the tenant committed an act of bankruptcy. The lease having become forfeited by the act of the tenant, no inventory or valuation of the machines, and other effects and things belonging to the collieries, was made three months before the determination of the demise: Held, however, as the tenant by his own act had determined the lease, and had thereby rendered it impracticable for the landlord to have a valuation made three months before the determination of the demise, that the latter was entitled, without any such valuation having been made, to resume the possession of the fixtures, machinery, and other effects used in the colliery upon the determination of the demise by such forfeiture; and that he was entitled to resume such possession even of new machinery erected by the tenant during the term.

Held, secondly, that the tenant never had, under this demise, the possession, order, or disposition of the fixtures or moveable articles within the meaning of the 21 *Jac.* 1. c. 19., but a mere qualified right to use them during the term; and if they had been in his possession, &c. within the meaning of the statute, that would have ceased when the landlord resumed possession on the 9th of *November*.

During the intermediate time between the recovery of the judgment in *Trinity* term 1818, and the execution of the writ of hab. fac. poss. on the 9th *November* 1819, the bankrupt continued to work the colliery, and to have the use of the machinery and implements: Held, that during this period the bankrupt had not the order or disposition of the machinery and implements within the meaning of the statute of *James*.

TROVER for engines, cylinders, pumps, whimsies, gins, rail roads, and other implements belonging to two collieries, Plea, not guilty. At the trial before *Hullock* B., at the Spring assizes for *Derby*, 1824, the following facts were proved. The plaintiffs were

assignees

assignees under a commission of bankrupt which issued against *Fletcher* on the 16th of *November* 1819, upon an act of bankruptcy committed on the 10th of *November*. The bankrupt held two collieries as tenant to the defendant under a lease, whereby defendant demised the said collieries to the bankrupt; and also all the engines, gins, machinery, rail roads, and other · implements, effects, and things, then being in and upon or about the said collieries or coal works, or used or employed therewith; and also all the boats and waggons used· for the purpose of the said collieries, and other effects incident or belonging thereto, and particularly mentioned and described in an inventory and valuation ¬thereof taken by Mr. *J. Woodhouse*, in or about the month of *January* 1810, with the usual powers to work and carry on the collieries from the 1st *January* 1810, for twenty-one years, at the rent of 10*l.* for every 100*l.*, for· which coals, slack, and cokes should be sold from the said collieries during the said term, and so in proportion, &c. to be paid quarterly.   Then followed a covenant by *Fletcher* for payment of rent, and a proviso for re-entry in case the rent should during the said· term be in arrear and unpaid by the space of thirty days after the same should respectively become ·due.   And it was provided that, on the expiration or other *sooner determination* of the demise, the said *James Fletcher* should and would leave and yield up unto the said *W. H. Hunter*, his heirs, &c. all and singular the engines, gins, machines, rail roads, machinery, effects, and things belonging to and used in the said collieries or coal works; and that an inventory and valuation should, three months· previous thereto, be made and taken by two indifferent persons to be for that purpose appointed

VOL. III.   B b   by

by the said *W. H. Hunter* and *James Fletcher*, or their
representatives, or by an umpire to be appointed by the
two referees, in case they should differ about the same;
and such inventory and valuation should thereupon be
compared with the then present inventory and valuation;
and in case the amount thereof should fall short of the
amount of the then present valuation, which had been
made and signed by the said *J. Woodhouse*, the difference
should be paid by the said *J. Fletcher* unto the said
W. H. Hunter, his heirs, &c. on demand; but in case
the amount of the inventory and valuation to be taken
as aforesaid on the expiration or other sooner determination of the demise, should exceed the amount of the
then present inventory or valuation, then *W. H. Hunter*,
his heirs, &c. should pay unto *J. Fletcher*, his executors,
&c. the difference in value thereof, within three months
from the time of such valuation being made. The inventory mentioned in this lease was produced in evidence,
and it appeared to contain a valuation of all the machinery, fixtures, and moveable articles used in the
colliery. By virtue of this demise *Fletcher* took possession of the collieries, engines, &c., and continued in
possession until the 9th of *November* 1819, when *Hunter*
was put into possession under a writ of hab. fac. poss.
issued on a judgment obtained by him in *Trinity* term
1818, in an action of ejectment, commenced for a forfeiture by non-payment of rent. Whilst the bankrupt
was in possession, he expended considerable sums on
the machinery used in working the collieries; he put up
a new engine at an expense of 2,000*l*., and after the
judgment in the ejectment was obtained, he put in a new
boiler which cost 60*l*. It appeared by the evidence of
various witnesses, that in some instances the machinery
                        and

and implements used in working collieries were bought
by the tenant, and then it was usual for him to take
them away at the determination of the term, and that in
others the landlord demised the machinery, &c. together with the colliery, and took them back with the
colliery when the tenancy expired. Upon this evidence it was contended by the counsel for the plaintiffs, that they were entitled to recover the value of all
the machinery and implements, fixtures as well as
moveables, on the ground that they were in the possession of the bankrupt as apparent owner, during the
whole of his tenancy, or if not, still that the landlord had
suffered the bankrupt to continue the apparent owner
of the whole property, from the time when the judgment in ejectment was obtained. Secondly, that at all
events they were entitled to recover the value of the
moveables. On the part of the defendant it was contended that the property in all the machinery and
implements, moveables as well as fixtures, vested in
the landlord as soon as the lease became determined
by the forfeiture. The learned judge left it to the
jury to find upon the evidence whether the bankrupt's
possession constituted a reputed ownership in him at
the time of the act of bankruptcy, and if they were of
that opinion, then he directed them to find for the
plaintiffs, for the value of the moveables, but he reserved
liberty to the defendant to move to enter a verdict for
him, or a nonsuit in case this court should be of opinion
that the whole property in the fixtures and moveables
vested in the landlord when the lease became forfeited ;
and he further reserved liberty to the plaintiffs to move
to increase the damages if they thought fit. The jury
found a verdict for the plaintiffs for the value of the
moveable articles on the collieries, at the time when the

act of bankruptcy was committed. A rule nisi for entering a verdict for the defendant or a nonsuit having been obtained in last *Easter* term.

Denman, Reader, and *N. R. Clarke,* shewed cause. The fixtures, machinery, and other implements belonging to and used in this colliery, were at the time of the act of bankruptcy in the possession, order, and disposition of the bankrupt, with the consent of the true owner within the meaning of the 21 *Jac.* 1. *c.* 19. During the continuance of the term the bankrupt had not merely the use of the machinery and implements, but he had the power of changing, removing, or adding to them, and he actually erected a new engine at a great expence. His possession, therefore, differed materially from that of the occupier of a ready furnished house. The defendant put an end to the tenancy, and treated the bankrupt as a trespasser by bringing an ejectment for a forfeiture in *Hilary* term 1818, and obtained a judgment against him in *Trinity* term 1818. At that time, therefore, he might have obtained possession of the collieries and the fixtures, and have notified to the world that the fixtures and other things were his and not his tenant's. But he allowed the bankrupt to continue in possession of the machinery, and to appear to the world as the owner till the 9th of *November* 1819. During the whole of that period the property was in the possession, order, and disposition of the bankrupt, with the permission of the true owner. *Horn* v. *Baker* (a) was a much stronger case than the present; there the bankrupt had the vats demised to him, with a power of purchasing; here the bankrupt not only had the use of the things demised, but he had the power of changing

(a) 9 *East,* 215.

them.

them. It is one of the very cases contemplated by the statute; and if he was once the reputed owner, then according to *Lingard* v. *Messiter* (a) he continued the reputed owner until it was notified to the world that the ownership had ceased. Here the defendant did nothing to inform the world that the bankrupt had ceased to be the reputed owner. But, secondly, the bankrupt was not only the reputed owner, but he was the actual owner of a considerable part of this property; for he had erected a new engine at a considerable expense, and there was no evidence to shew that that was substituted for any other which had been on the premises at the commencement of the term. The plaintiffs, therefore, are at all events entitled to recover for the value of that engine. [*Bayley* J. Did not the property in all the fixtures and moveables on the colliery vest in the landlord upon the determination of the lease?] That would have been the case if the lease had expired by effluxion of time, and an inventory and valuation had been made three months before the expiration of the term. But the terms of the proviso are, that the tenant should, on the determination of the demise, deliver up the machinery and other things upon the premises, and that an inventory and valuation should be made three months previously thereto, and that the difference between that valuation and the one made at the commencement of the lease should be paid by the landlord to the tenant, or vice versa according to circumstances. No such valuation having been made, the tenant was not, at the expiration of the term, bound to deliver up the things to the landlord; they, therefore continued the property

(a) 1 *B. & C.* 308.

of

of the tenant. The terms of the lease are not sufficient to shew that the things became absolutely the property of the landlord in the event of the lease having been determined by forfeiture, they were only to become so in the event of its determining by effluxion of time, and in case a valuation were made three months before the term expired. That event has not happened, and, therefore, the property did not vest in the landlord when the lease became forfeited.

ABBOTT C. J. I am of opinion that the rule for a nonsuit ought to be made absolute. Judging from the facts adduced in evidence, I am bound to state, that in my opinion there is no evidence to prove that *Fletcher* ever had the absolute ownership of the machinery and other things belonging to these collieries. I think that he had merely a qualified property in them subject to the terms of the lease under which he held them; and if that be so, then this case is very distinguishable from *Lingard* v. *Messiter*, and *Kirkley* v. *Hodgson* (a), because in those cases the bankrupt had once been the absolute owner of the property. The terms of the lease manifestly shew that the lessee never had the absolute ownership of the fixtures or the moveables in the collieries. It contains a proviso for re-entry of the landlord in case the rent should be in arrear above thirty days; and then, that on the expiration or other sooner determination of the demise, the bankrupt should yield up to *Hunter*, all the machinery, effects, and things, belonging to and used in the collieries; and that an inventory and valuation should, three months previous thereto, be made in the

(a) 1 B. & C. 588.

manner

1824.

Stourbridge
against
Hussell.

manner therein mentioned. It is clear, therefore, from these provisions, that the nonpayment of the rent might lead to a determination of the lease by forfeiture, but if it was not so determined, then it would expire by effluxion of time at a given period. If it did so expire, a valuation of the fixtures was to take place, three months previously to such expiration: but if it expired otherwise than by lapse of time, as, for instance, by some act of the tenant amounting to a forfeiture, it is clear that it could not be intended that three months' notice should be given by the landlord of his intention to take the machinery and other things, because it would be impossible. The effect of the proviso, therefore, is, that whenever the lease expired, the landlord was to be entitled to resume, at a certain valuation, the possession of the collieries, and the machinery, effects, and things, whether moveable or immoveable, belonging to and used in the same. If the things on the collieries at the determination of the lease exceeded the value of those mentioned in the inventory made on the tenant's entering into possession, then the landlord was to pay the tenant the difference. If, on the other hand, they were found to be of less value, the tenant was to make up the deficiency to the landlord. Now such a mode of valuation having been stipulated for, it is manifest that new articles brought on by the tenant during the term were intended to be included in this valuation. It never can be supposed that those things only which were on the collieries when the tenant entered were to be valued. During such a term there must necessarily be considerable wear and tear, and new articles would be required; and whenever the lease expired, the landlord was entitled to have the possession of all the articles which might then

be

be found on the collieries, paying for the same according to the valuation prescribed by the terms of the lease. The very terms of the proviso contemplate the purchase of new or additional articles by the tenant, and manifestly shew that such articles were intended to be included; and the schedule annexed to the lease contains an account of moveable as well as fixed articles. If, then, the bankrupt never had an absolute ownership, but only a qualified right to the use of the articles during the term, what is there to shew that he ever had any reputed ownership? In *Horn* v. *Baker*, it did not appear to have been the usage to demise the vats and other utensils which necessarily belong to a distillery; but here it appears by the evidence, that in some instances the articles used in collieries belong to the tenants, in others they do not; that though in some cases the landlord in demising collieries permits the lessee on certain conditions to have the use of the fixtures and other things during the demise, yet in other instances they belong absolutely to the lessee. Then, if the possession of such things is consistent with the fact of a person being absolute owner, and also of his not being absolute owner, the mere possession of such things ought not to raise an inference in the mind of any cautious person acquainted with the usage that the person in possession is the owner. If it had not been the usage for the owners of collieries ever to demise the machinery and other things used in the colliery; then possession by the lessee would be evidence of reputed ownership; but there being such an usage, the mere possession of such things is not evidence of reputed ownership; and no evidence having been adduced to shew that the bankrupt ever had the absolute ownership

ownership in the articles used in these collieries, I am of opinion that the jury ought upon these facts to have given a verdict for the defendant; but I think it better that the rule for entering a nonsuit should be made absolute, because in that case the plaintiff will not be precluded from bringing another action.

BAYLEY J. It appears to me, that in this case the property in the collieries, and in the fixtures and moveables belonging to and used in the collieries, became vested in the landlord whenever the lease expired, either by effluxion of time or by forfeiture, and that the bankrupt had not, at the time of his bankruptcy, or at any other time, any reputed ownership in such property, so as to bring it within the operation of the statute of the 21 *Jac.* 1. *c.* 19. I am also of opinion, that whatever fixtures and other things were brought to the collieries by the tenant, either to supply the deficiency made by wear and tear, or otherwise to promote the works of the collieries, cannot be considered as belonging to the tenant at the time when the lease became determined, whether that was by forfeiture or by the completion of the term. All the property in the fixtures and other things used in the colliery then became the landlord's, subject to the terms of the proviso by which he was to allow the tenant for any increase in the value of the things left on the collieries. The tenant, therefore, never had the possession, order, or disposition of such property, within the meaning of the statute 21 *Jac.* 1. *c.* 19. He had merely a right to use them during the term, and when that right ceased by the expiration of the term, the absolute property in them vested in the landlord. But then it is said that he had the apparent owner-

ownership. In order to try whether that was so, we must consider the character of this possession in the place where the possession occurred, and where he is supposed to have had the reputed ownership. The mere possession of a furnished house does not of itself induce a prudent and cautious man to believe that the occupier is the real owner of the furniture, because in such cases he knows that the property in the furniture frequently belongs to the landlord. In order to ascertain, therefore, whether the party in possession is entitled to the character of owner, further enquiry becomes necessary; for the possession being such that he either may or may not be the owner, the party about to trust him is not entitled to conclude, from the mere possession, that he is owner. In such a case he is bound to enquire upon what terms the property has been taken, and he ought also to enquire what the nature of the usage is, in the place where the property is situate. Now this is the case of a ready-furnished colliery, if I may be allowed the expression; and as it appears that the machinery and other things on collieries sometimes belong to the landlord and sometimes to the tenant; it must depend upon the bargain between the landlord and tenant, to what character the latter is entitled. If a house or colliery be ready furnished and taken on lease; in order to ascertain the ownership of the furniture, the enquiry should be, did the tenant take the naked house or colliery, or did he take it furnished? and if the result of the enquiry be that he did not take the naked colliery, but also took all the engines, machinery, effects, and things used in the collieries mentioned in an inventory and valuation, made at the time when the tenant entered; then the fact of his taking all these things mentioned

mentioned in the inventory, may be considered as notice
to the neighbourhood of the character of the transaction;
for as there was a valuation there could be no difficulty
in finding out the valuer, and he could have stated whether the valuation was made to a purchaser or to a tenant.
I cannot conceive, that, in this case, where the property
in the collieries previously belonged to *Hunter*, the mere
fact of *Fletcher's* taking the collieries could have raised
in the minds of the neighbours the belief that he had become the actual owner of the property in and about the
collieries; and if that belief were not justified in the
first instance, there is no proof of any thing which afterwards occurred to justify the supposition of such ownership. There is nothing to shew that any distinction was
made between fixtures and articles of a moveable nature;
and the provisions of the lease and the inventory lead to
a contrary conclusion. And if the articles originally
belonged to the landlord, the presumption is (bearing in
mind the provisions of the lease) that when the tenant
introduced new articles, they were for the purpose of replacing others, and then the substituted articles must be
considered on the same footing as those originally leased
by the landlord. If that were not so, there might be
some weight in the distinction made between moveables
and fixtures; but all the things used in the working of
the collieries, whether they were there when the tenant
entered into possession, or were supplied during his occupation, are treated as fixtures. In *Horn* v. *Baker* it
was held, that the leasing party was entitled to recover
all the fixtures, except such as the tenant was justified
in removing, because they did not come within the
meaning of fixtures in such trade; but when usage does
not establish a right to remove, then it depends upon

the

the bargain between the parties; and this is an answer to the argument urged, that if the tenant had not a right to remove such articles as were enumerated in the lease, yet he might remove those which were subsequently introduced. Again, the statute of the 21 *Jac.* 1. *c.* 19. speaks of property in the possession, order, and disposition of the bankrupt at the time of his bankruptcy. Now, assuming that these things were once in the possession, order, and disposition of the bankrupt, I think that they did not so continue down to the time of the act of bankruptcy; for the defendant took possession of the coal mine the day preceding the act of bankruptcy; and when a landlord takes possession of a coal mine, he takes possession of every thing connected with it, which the tenant has not a right to carry away. If he takes possession of any thing which the tenant has a right to take away, the property, as to that, still continues in the tenant; but if by the bargain between the landlord and tenant, the latter has no right to remove any thing from the land, then, when the landlord takes possession of the land, he takes possession of all the moveables on it. In this case the tenant had not any right to remove either the fixtures or moveables; and, therefore, when he was turned out of possession, he ceased to have any right whatever over them. That being so, this case is decided by the facts. The landlord took possession on the 9th of *November*, and the act of bankruptcy was not committed till the following day; and when he took possession of the land he took possession of all the articles then on the collieries, subject to the stipulation to pay for them, if the value exceeded that of the articles mentioned in the inventory. If there had been no such stipulation for payment, those things could not have

been

been taken from *Hunter*, for *Fletcher* had no right to
remove them; the possession shifted to him who had a
right to possess the land; the machinery and other
things belonging to the colliery, according to the lease,
going back to the landlord whenever such lease should
expire.   Had the lease expired by effluxion of time,
a valuation was to take place three months previous to
such expiration.   Here there had not been any valuation, nor had the three months' notice been given; but
that notice became impossible, from the manner in which
the determination of the lease took place.   But in whatever
way the lease was determined, it was expressly provided,
that the things belonging to or used in the collieries
should be left.   The effect of the lease was, that if the
three months' notice could be given it was to be given;
but if it could not, still the things were to be left on the
colliery, and a valuation was to take place, with reference to the things on the collieries at that time, and as
compared with the property when the tenant entered
into the occupation.   The balance, either way, was to
be received or paid by the landlord or tenant, as the
case might be.   An increase of value could not be contemplated by the parties, so as to require any thing to
be paid by the landlord to the tenant, unless it were
intended to include new things brought to the collieries
for the purpose of working them by the tenant during his
occupation.   The lease included every thing, and it was
reasonable that it should do so, for the value of the articles
would have been greatly prejudiced by a removal of them;
but no injustice could be done to either party if the difference on valuation was to be paid by one to the other.
These reasons satisfy me, that though the bulk of what
the tenant put up might be great, it was not to be
thence

thence inferred, that he had a visible ownership; and if he ever had the visible possession or ownership, so as to bring the case within the statute of *James*, I think that it had been determined, by the act of the landlord in taking possession of the collieries. In *Horn* v. *Baker* the enquiry was, whether the lessee, from the usage among distillers, had a right to the vats and utensils; and the jury found that it was not usual to leave them on the premises. The conclusion from that was, that vats and utensils were not included in what are termed fixtures. But in this case, according to the evidence, the usage is both ways, and if so, then it becomes the duty of a party about to trust the tenant, to enquire what was the particular agreement respecting these collieries. It has been urged, that the landlord had his judgment in the action of ejectment long before the writ of possession was executed, but the judgment in ejectment did not vary the right of the landlord; and before that judgment was obtained the bankrupt had not the visible possession in the eye of the law. For these reasons I think the rule for entering a nonsuit must be made absolute.

Holroyd J. I am of opinion that this action of trover cannot be maintained by the assignees, because the bankrupt, at the time of his bankruptcy, had not any right of possession in the fixtures and other things used in the collieries. I am also of opinion, that he had not the possession, order, or disposition of these things, within the meaning of the statute of the 21 *Jac.* 1. *c.* 19. By the lease, the landlord demised not the colliery only, but the fixtures and moveable articles used in the colliery; and it is one of the stipulations of the lease, that

the

the tenant shall, at the expiration, or other sooner determination of the demise, deliver up to the landlord the machinery and other things belonging to and used in the colliery, and a compensation is secured to the landlord or tenant, in the event of such things being improved or deteriorated in value when the lease is determined. But, at all events, the lessor was to have delivered up to him not merely the things demised, but all those found on the collieries at the determination of the demise. It is immaterial whether the term were fully completed or not, for these provisions were to be complied with on the expiration or other sooner determination of the term. So that provision was made for an earlier determination than the full period mentioned in the lease. The lease provides also that the valuation made at the determination of the demise should be compared with the valuation mentioned in the lease, and that the difference between the two valuations should be paid by the landlord, if the value at the end of the term exceeded that mentioned in the inventory; by the tenant, if it was less. The language of this proviso evidently applies to all the things brought to the colliery during the term, and remaining there at the determination of it, whether the tenant continued to the end of the term granted or not. The colliery and other things were at all events to be given up. If the demise were determined by the act of the tenant, still there must have been an inventory to ascertain whether any compensation was to be made by the landlord to the tenant, or by the tenant to the landlord, for any increase or deficiency in the value of the articles belonging to or used in the collieries. And if that provision applied to the things demised, it must also extend to the things substituted in lieu of them; for

it

it was provided that all the machinery, effects, and other things used in the collieries should be given up to the landlord, subject to the valuation and payment. The things demised, therefore, never became the property of the tenant so as to empower him to take them away. They remained the general property of the landlord, subject to the terms and provisions of the lease, the tenant having the right to use them so long as he complied with the conditions of the lease, and being bound to deliver them up at the determination of the tenancy. The tenant failed to comply with the conditions of the lease, and committed a forfeiture; his right to the use and possession of these things was then at an end, and they became the absolute property of the landlord. The bankrupt, therefore, or his assignees, have not any right to the possession of these things. I am also of opinion that this case does not come within the statute of *James.* This was a demise to the bankrupt of the machinery and the other things used in the colliery; and the mere possession of the things demised does not shew that they were in fact or law put into the possession, order, or disposition of the tenant within the meaning of the 21 *Jac.* 1. *c.* 19. He had a mere qualified right to use them, but not the power of disposition. But if they were in his possession, order, and disposition, they did not continue so at the time of the act of bankruptcy; for the landlord took possession of the colliery on the preceding day under the writ of *hab. fac. poss.*, and having a right also to resume possession of the machinery and other things used in the colliery, I think, that by taking possession of the colliery, he had virtual possession of the machinery and other things belonging to and used in the colliery. For these reasons
I think

I think that the rule for entering a nonsuit should be made absolute.

LITTLEDALE J. I also think that where the usage does not decide whether fixtures and other things used in a colliery are the property of the landlord or the tenant, that must depend on the agreement between the parties. It was decided in the cases of *Ryall* v. *Rolle* (a), and *Horn* v. *Baker*, that fixtures were not goods and chattels within the meaning of the statute of *James*. In this case the chattels used in the colliery were as much the subject of demise as the collieries themselves. In the inventory mentioned in the lease all the moveables and immoveables are enumerated, and that shews the nature of the bargain between the parties. The possession of the tenant under the lease was not such a possession as the statute of the 21 *Jac.* 1. c. 19. contemplated; his possession is recognized by the law in the same way as the possession by the tenant of the furniture in a ready-furnished house, derived from a lessor under a contract. The possession of a factor might be said to be evidence of a reputed ownership, but it has been decided that he has not such an ownership within the statute of *James*. Here it is stipulated in the lease, that at the end or other sooner determination of the demise, all the things upon the colliery should be given up to the landlord. But as many things might be required to be replaced and new machinery might have been introduced so as to make the value of the property greater at the end

(a) 1 *Atk.* 165.

than it was at the beginning of the term, the lease contains a stipulation for compensation for the value as compared with that mentioned in the inventory at the beginning of the term, and accordingly it is provided, that at the determination of the demise the landlord should make compensation to the tenant if the value exceeded that mentioned in the original inventory. There is no pretence for saying that if there had been no bankruptcy during the term, those things would at the end of the term have been the property of the tenant: in the event of a subsequent bankruptcy they certainly could not have belonged to the assignees. But it is said that, as the lease provided that a valuation of the things on the colliery should be made three months previous to the expiration or other sooner determination of the demise, the landlord was only entitled to the possession of those things, provided such valuation was made and he paid the difference, if any there was, between the then and the former value. But I think this stipulation respecting the valuation applies only to cases where it was possible for the landlord to give notice to the tenant to appoint a valuer, so that the valuation might be made. Here notice was not practicable, because the lease was determined by forfeiture, and that forfeiture originated with the tenant, and he alone therefore could have given any notice of his intention to determine the lease. The landlord had a right to re-enter whenever the rent should be in arrear thirty days. He was entitled to serve an ejectment the very day after the thirty days had expired. It was impossible for him to give the tenant notice to appoint a valuer three months before the demise was determined

by

1824.

Brooke
against
Harris.

by the nonpayment of rent; and as the landlord had expressly reserved to himself a right to resume possession of the machinery and implements, on the expiration or *other sooner determination of the demise*, he would be wholly deprived of the benefit of that stipulation if the construction now contended for on the part of the plaintiffs were to prevail. It never could, therefore, be the intention of the parties to make it a condition precedent to the landlord's right to resume the possession of the machinery, that there should be a valuation made three months before the lease was determined, when it was determined by the act of the tenant, and the intention to determine it must have been unknown to the landlord. It has been urged that the fact of the landlord's having allowed the bankrupt to continue in possession from the time when he recovered the judgment in ejectment until the time when the writ of possession was executed, changed the situation of the parties, and that from that time the bankrupt no longer held possession under the lease, but was allowed to have the apparent ownership by the permission of the landlord. This argument pressed upon my mind for some time, but I think upon the whole it is not entitled to any great weight, because, before any ejectment was brought, the tenant had not the possession, order, or disposition of the property, and therefore, after the judgment was obtained, the parties were in the same relative situation as before. The circumstance of the landlord's not putting the judgment in execution did not give the tenant any right over the property which he had not before. It did not give him the power of selling or disposing of it. The tenant having put an end to the lease, the landlord had a right to resume possession

C c 2   of

of the collieries, and of the property used in working
the same, and his not making use of the judgment in
ejectment did not in any way affect his right, or make
any apparent alteration in the character of the tenant's
possession. Upon the whole, I think that the rule for
entering a nonsuit ought to be made absolute.

Rule absolute. (a)

Vaughan Serjt., *Clarke*, and *Marryat* were to have
supported the rule.

(a) The landlord took possession of the colliery under the hab. fac.
poss. on the 8th of *November.*

Doe, on the several Demises of Benjamin Maddock and Jane Garratt his Wife, and Thomas Moore and Ann his Wife, *against* John Lynes and Thomas Walker.

*T. C., possessed
of lands for the
residue of a
long term of
years, by in-
denture of
three parts,
dated Novem-*

EJECTMENT on the joint and several demises of
Benjamin Maddock and *Jane Garratt*, otherwise
Jane his wife, and *Thomas Moore* and *Ann* his wife,
against *John Lynes* and *Thomas Walker*, to recover a

ber 1st, 1771, between *T. C.* of first part, *J. W.* and *T. L.* of second part, and *E. K.* of
third part, in consideration of an intended marriage between *T. C.* and *E. K.*, " and for
the considerations mentioned and expressed in a certain indenture of three parts, intended
to bear date after the date thereof, and made between *T. C.*, *S. H.*, and *J. H.* of the first
part, *W. C.* and *J. K.* of the second part, and *E. K.* of the third part, and for other good
considerations," assigned the said lands to *J. W.* and *T. L.* for the residue of the said term
upon trust to permit and suffer *T. C.*, his executors, &c. to receive the rents for his own
use until the solemnization of the intended marriage, and afterwards to permit *T. C.* to
receive the rents for his life, and afterwards to permit the wife to receive the rents for her
life, and upon other subsequent trusts. By indenture of three parts, dated *November* 2d,
1771, between *T. C.*, *S. H.*, and *J. H.* of the first part, *W. C.* and *J. K.*, of the second part,
and *E. K.* of the third part, *T. C.* enfeoffed *W. C.* and *J. K.* of the lands mentioned in the
deed of *November* 1st, 1771, upon certain trusts. The deed contained a power of attorney
to deliver seisin, and a memorandum of livery of seisin was indorsed upon it. *T. C.* continued in possession of the lands from the 1st of *November* 1771 till the time of his death
in 1809. In ejectment against the executor of *T. L.*, who survived *J. W.*: Held, that
the term " assigned to *J. W.* and *T. L.*" was not destroyed by the feoffment, because it
did not appear that they ever assented to it.

messuage

messuage and certain closes called the *Brockeys*, situate in the parish of *Barwell*, in the county of *Leicester*. The defendant, *J. Lynes*, defended as landlord, and *T. Walker*, the other defendant, defended as tenant in possession of the premises. At the trial before *Holroyd J.*, at the *Leicester* Summer assizes 1822, the jury found a verdict for the plaintiff, subject to the opinion of this Court on the following case.

Jane Maddock the wife of *Benjamin Maddock*, and *Ann Moore* the wife of *Thomas Moore*, were the co-heiresses of *T. Cooper*, who died on or about the 23d of *February* 1809, without issue and intestate, and was at the time of his death in possession, and the actual occupation, of the said messuage and closes. The said *T. Cooper* was possessed of the whole of the premises for the remainder of long terms of years, created by leases granted by the Honorable *John Grey*, lord of the manor of *Barwell*, in the time of Queen *Elizabeth*. By indenture of assignment duly executed by the parties thereto, bearing date 1st of *November* 1771, and made between the said *T. Cooper* of the first part, *J. Wileman* and *J. Lynes* of the second part, and *E. Kiss* of the third part, reciting *T. Cooper's* title to the lands therein mentioned, for the remainder of three several terms of years, viz., two of 10,000 years, and the other of 1000 years; it was witnessed, that in consideration of a marriage intended to be had between *T. Cooper* and *E. Kiss*, and for the considerations mentioned in a certain indenture of three parts, intended to bear date after the day of the date thereof, (meaning a certain indenture of feoffment, hereinafter set forth,) and made between *T. Cooper* and *S. Heyrick*, and *J. Heyrick*, of the first part, *W. Cooper* and *J. Kiss*

C c 3

of

1824.

Doe dem.
M'Iddock
against
Lyne.

of the second part, and the said *Elizabeth Kiss* of the third part; and in consideration of 5*s.* to the said *T. Cooper*, paid by the said *John Wileman* and *T. Lynes*, and for divers other good causes and considerations, *T. Cooper* did bargain, sell, assign, transfer, and set over unto *J. Wileman* and *T. Lynes*, their executors, administrators, and assigns, all the said recited messuage, closes, hereditaments, and premises with their appurtenances, and all other leasehold closes, lands, and hereditaments whatsoever of the said *T. Cooper*, lying and being in the lordship of *Barwell* aforesaid: and all the estate, &c.; to hold unto *J. Wileman* and *T. Lynes*, their executors, administrators, and assigns, for the residue of the said terms of 10,000 years, 10,000 years, and 1000 years; subject, nevertheless, to the trusts and proviso thereinafter declared, viz., upon trust to permit and suffer *T. Cooper*, his executors, administrators, and assigns, to receive the rents for his and their own use; and that the said terms might be disposed of as he, *T. Cooper*, should direct, until the said intended marriage should be solemnized; and after the solemnization thereof, in trust to permit and suffer *T. Cooper* and his assigns to enjoy and receive and take the rents and profits of the premises for so long time of the said term and terms as should incur during the life of *T. Cooper*; and after his decease, upon trust to permit and suffer the wife to receive the rents during her life; and after her death, to permit the first son of the marriage to receive the rents during such time of the term as he should happen to live; and in case he should die before twenty-one, then the second and other sons successively; and in case there should be no issue male of the marriage, then to permit all and every the daughters

tors to receive the rents so long as they should live ; and
if any such daughter or daughters should attain the age
of twenty-one years, in trust for such daughter or daughters, and her executors, administrators, and assigns ;
and in case there should be no issue of the marriage, or
in case all such issue should die before the age of twenty-
one years, in trust for the executors and administrators of *T. Cooper.* There was a proviso enabling the
husband and wife, with the consent of the trustees, to
revoke those uses or trusts, and to appoint fresh ones ;
and a covenant by *T. Cooper*, that the premises should
remain during the remainder of the term in the trustees,
without any disturbance by him or any person claiming
under him, and also a covenant for further assurance.

By indenture of feoffment, duly executed by the parties thereto, bearing date the 2d of *November* 1771, and
made between the said *T. Cooper* and *S. Heyrick*, and
J. Heyrick, therein described of the first part, *W. Cooper*
and *Joshua Kiss*, therein described of the second part, and
Elizabeth Kiss of the third part; it was witnessed, that in
consideration of a marriage then intended to be solemnized between *T. Cooper* and *E. Kiss*, and of a considerable marriage portion which *T. Cooper* would receive
with *E. Kiss* on the solemnization of the marriage, and
for the making a jointure and provision of maintenance
for *E. Kiss* in lieu of dower in case the marriage should
take effect, and she should happen to survive *T. Cooper*,
and for the settling and assuring the messuage, closes,
lands, and hereditaments therein described, to the several
uses, and under and subject to the proviso, condition,
or agreement therein expressed; and also in consideration of 10s. a piece to *T. Cooper*, *S. Heyrick*, and *J.
Heyrick*, paid by *W. Cooper* and *Joshua Kiss*, and for

C c 4

divers

divers other good and valuable causes, *T. Cooper* did grant, bargain, sell, alien, enfeoff, and confirm, and *S. Heyrick* and *J. Heyrick*, by the direction and appointment of the said *T. Cooper*, did, according to their several respective estates therein, bargain, sell, alien, enfeoff, and confirm, unto *W. Cooper* and *Joshua Kiss*, their heirs and assigns, the said messuage and closes called the *Brockeys*, and their appurtenances to hold unto *W. Cooper* and *J. Kiss*, their heirs and assigns, to such uses as the same premises respectively stood limited to before the execution of the said indenture until the solemnization of the said marriage; and after the solemnization thereof, to the use of said *T. Cooper* and his assigns for the term of his natural life, without impeachment of waste; and after his decease, to the use of the said *E. Kiss*, and of her assigns for her natural life for her jointure, and in lieu of all dower and thirds; and after the decease of the survivor of them, the said *T. Cooper* and *E. Kiss*, to the use of the heirs of the body of the said *T. Cooper*, on the body of the said *E. Kiss* lawfully to be begotten; and in default of such issue, to the use of the heirs and assigns of the said *T. Cooper* for ever. Then followed a proviso enabling *T. Cooper* and *E. Kiss*, during their joint lives by deed, with the consent of *W. Cooper* and *J. Kiss*, or the survivor, or his executors or administrators, to revoke the aforesaid uses or trusts, and limit fresh uses or trusts. *T. Cooper* by that deed covenanted, granted, and agreed for himself, his heirs, executors, and administrators, to and with *W. Cooper* and *J. Kiss*, and their heirs, that the premises should remain to the uses and subject to the proviso aforesaid, and be quietly enjoyed accordingly without any interruption by *T. Cooper*, his heirs or

assigns,

assigns, or *S. Heyrick* and *J. Heyrick*, or either of them, their, or either of their heirs or assigns, or any persons whomsoever claiming or to claim under them, or any of them. The indenture also contained a power of attorney from *T. Cooper, S. Heyrick*, and *J. Heyrick*, to *William Ward*, to deliver seisin of the messuage and premises by the said deed granted and enfeoffed, unto *W. Cooper* and *J. Kiss*, to hold to them, their heirs and assigns, according to the purport, true intent, and meaning of the said indenture. The following memorandum of livery of seisin was endorsed on the said deed: " Be it remembered, that on the 5th day of *November*, in the year of our Lord 1771, the within named *William Ward*, by virtue and in execution of the power and authority to him given and granted by the within written indenture, did enter into, and upon the messuage or tenement, and one of the closes within granted, in the name of the whole of the within granted hereditaments and premises, and take full and peaceable possession and seisin thereof, in the name of the whole of the within granted hereditaments and premises; and immediately after deliver over the same unto the within named *William Cooper* and *Joshua Kiss*, to hold to them, their heirs and assigns, according to the tenor, purport, true intent, and meaning of the within written indenture."

T. Cooper continued in possession and the actual occupation of the premises, in the indentures of the 1st and 2d *November* 1771, mentioned from the time of executing the indentures until his death in 1809, and paid an annual chief rent of sixpence for part of the premises to the lord of the manor of *Barwell. Wileman*, one of the trustees, under the indenture of the 1st *November* 1771,

1771, died in *June* 1785, and *T. Lynes*, the other trustee under the said indenture, died in *April* 1787, and made by his will the defendant, *John Lynes*, his executor. Upon the death of *T. Cooper*, *J. Lynes* the defendant as agent for the widow, *Elizabeth Cooper*, who was entitled to a life interest under the trusts or limitations of each of the said indentures of the 1st and 2d of *November* 1771, let the premises to the defendant *Thomas Walker*, and received the rent of the same for her life. The chief rent above mentioned was paid to the lord of the manor during the lifetime of Mrs. *Cooper*, and since her decease, by the said *John Lynes* down to the year 1816.

The premises sought to be recovered by the action, are the whole of the premises granted by the indenture of feoffment of the 2d *November* 1771, and are the same as are comprised in the terms of 10,000 years, 10,000 years, and 1000 years, in the deed of assignment of the 1st *November* 1771 mentioned. The marriage of *Elizabeth Kiss* and *Thomas Cooper* was solemnized. They had no issue of the marriage, and *T. Cooper* died in possession of the said premises. His wife *Elizabeth* survived him, and died on or about the 9th day of *April* 1810.

Preston, for the plaintiff, made two points, first, by the feoffment, *Cooper* acquired the fee absolutely, and an estate in fee rightful, as against all persons except the reversioner. Secondly, by means of the feoffment the term was forfeited and extinguished, and the right under the term barred. As to the first point, the authorities are uniform from the time when *Bracton* wrote down to the time

time when the case of *Taylor* v. *Horde* (a) was decided. In *Littleton*, s. 611. it is laid down, that "when a tenant for life maketh a feoffment in fee, by such a feoffment the fee simple passeth.   So a tenant for years may make a feoffment, and by his feoffment the fee simple shall pass ; and yet he had at the time of the feoffment made but an estate for term of years."   Lord *Coke*, in commenting upon this passage, says, that by the feoffment, the fee simple passes by force of the livery, and that it is a disseisin to the lessor.   [*Holroyd* J.   In *Taylor* v. *Horde*, Lord *Mansfield* considers it as a disseisin only at the election of the lessor.   In 1 *Burr.* 112. he says, " if the lessee for life or years makes a feoffment, the lessor may still distrain for the rent, or charge the person to whom it is paid as a receiver ; or bring an ejectment, and choose whether he will be considered as disseised ;" and he cites in support of that position *Metcalf and Kynaston* v. *Parry*, a manuscript case, decided by the Court of Exchequer in 1748.   " Tenant in tail of lands leased by his father to a second son for lives, (under a power) upon his father's death, received the rent from the occupier as owner, and as if no such lease had been made, during his whole life.   He suffered a common recovery.   It was holden that this was only a disseisin of the freehold *at election,* and that, therefore, he could not make a good tenant to the præcipe, and the recovery was adjudged bad."]   In that case there was a mere receipt of the rent.   No actual disseisin by the eldest son.   The freehold was in the second son by force of the lease.   The opinion of Lord *Mansfield* is the only authority in support of the position cited from *Tay-*

(a) 1 *Burr.* 60.

lor

lor v. *Horde,* and it is at variance with the doctrine laid down by *Littleton* and Lord *Coke.* The feoffee is not tenant to the lessor. A feoffment is necessarily a disseisin in fact, except as between the lord of the seignory and his tenant. *Bracton, lib. 2. c.* 14. adverts to the very case of a stranger entering upon a vacant possession and making a feoffment, and states the law to be, that it gives a fee as between the feoffor, the feoffee, and all others who have not the right, and that even in process of time it may become good against the person who has the right. (*a*) The feoffment may perhaps be void against other persons on the ground of fraud, or it may be void against the reversioner where the tenant continues in possession and pays the rent. In 1 *Inst.* 330 *b.* it is said, that the feoffor may annex a warranty, whereupon the feoffee may vouch him; and in 367 *a.,* that if a lessee for years, or tenant by elegit, &c., or a disseisor incontinent make a feoffment in fee with warranty, if the feoffee be impleaded he shall vouch the feoffor, and after him his heir also; because this is a covenant real, which binds him and his heirs to recompence in value if they have assets by descent to recompence; for there is a feoffment de facto and a feoffment de jure: and a feoffment de facto made by them that have such interest or possession as is aforesaid, is good between the parties, and against all men but only against him that hath right." In *Focus* v. *Salisbury* (*b*), Lord *Hale* takes the distinction between a tenant for life and for years; and says, if lessee for years be, the remainder over for life, and the lessee levy a fine and five years pass, the lessor is not barred by any non-claim, because the fine operates

(*a*) See *Butler's* note to *Co. Litt.,* 330. *b.*   (*b*) *Hardr.* 400.

nothing,

nothing, and " partes ad finem nihil habuerunt". may
be pleaded to it; otherwise it is where a tenant for life
levies a fine, for he has a freehold, and his fine displaces
the remainders, and therefore an entry is requisite within
five years after the death of the tenant for life; and,
therefore, when a lessee for years or at will is to levy a
fine, it is usual for the lessee to make a feoffment first,
to displace the other estates. " In *Whaley* v. *Tankred* (a),
C. Meynell, tenant for ninety-nine years, if he should
live so long, remainder to *E. Meynel* in tail, on the 14th
of *October* 1656, enfeoffed the defendant and his heirs,
and in *Hilary* 1656 levied a fine, sur conusans de droit
come ceo, &c., with proclamations to the same *C. Tankred*,
to the use of him and his heirs, who entered accordingly. On the 28th of *August* 1661 *E. Meynel* died.
C. Meynel, on the 18th *March* 1664, died; on the 10th
April, 23 *Car.* 2., 1672, the lessor of the plaintiff being
eldest son and heir of *E. Meynel*, entered, and the question
was, whether his entry was lawful, or whether *E. Meynel*
ought to have entered within five years after the fine
levied, or should have other five years after the death of
C. Meynel. (b) And it was resolved that he should have
five years after the expiration of *C. Meynel's* estate by
his death, and that there was no difference between the
lessee for life and the lessee for years as to this point."
[*Bayley* J. Does a feoffment destroy a term created to attend an inheritance?] It does if the trustee of the term
is acting in privity and concert with the feoffor. All
these authorities shew that a feoffment by tenant for
years will give a fee against all persons except the rightful owner. The case of *Taylor* v. *Horde* was rightly de-

(a) *Sir T. Raym.* 219.

(b) By the report of this case in 2 *Lev.* 51. it appears that the heir
was an infant at the time of *C. Meynel's* death.

cided

feoffment. If a tenant in tail make a feoffment his feoffment creates a discontinuance. The statute of *Westminster* gave as a remedy for disseisin, the assize of novel disseisin. That remedy formerly stood in the place of the modern action of ejectment. It was frequently a proceeding founded on fiction, and parties were in many cases allowed to consider themselves disseised, in order to try the right by this speedy remedy; and many of the disseisins which were redressed by this proceeding were disseisins at election only. There were formerly only two cases of actual disseisin, entry into the possession by force or entry on a vacant possession; or a feudal act by a person who obtained the possession rightfully, as lessee for life or years, or person having a mere naked possession. If tenant for years or for life makes a feoffment, his wife will be entitled to dower, because he gains a fee by the feoffment, and the feoffee who derives title from the feoffor is estopped from saying that the latter had not a fee while the wife of a tenant for life who makes a lease to another, for the life of that other, will not be dowable. (a) The party disseised has not any right to treat this as a disseisin at election. If there be tenant for years, and a stranger wishes to make a feoffment, so as to work a disseisin, there must either be an ouster of the tenant for years, or his consent must be obtained to the livery. To make a feoffment good and valid nothing except possession is necessary; but if the tenant for years does consent to the feoffment which is a wrongful act, and a feudal alienation against the reversioner, that assent to livery of seisin made by a stranger is a forfeiture; it is an attornment to a stranger; a recognition of a title in him to the

(a) *Preston* on Estates, tit. *Dower*, 555. 1st edition.

prejudice

prejudice of the rightful owner. In this case, if the assignee of the term had entered immediately after the feoffment, claiming the term, he would have restored the seisin to the reversioner. In *Littleton, s. 472.* it is said, if a man be disseised by two, if he release to one of them he shall hold his companion out of the land, and by such release, he shall have the sole possession and estate in the land. But if a disseisor enfeoff two in fee, and the disseisee release to one of the feoffees, this shall enure to both the feoffees. The cause of the diversity between these two cases is sufficiently obvious; in the latter case the feoffees come in by title, i. e., by feoffment or feudal contract, while in the former case the disseisors come in by wrong. Lord *Coke*, in commenting on this passage, observes, " This is to be understood where tenant in fee simple is disseised and releases; for if tenant for life be disseised by two, and he releaseth to one of them, this shall enure to them both, for he to whom the release is made hath a larger estate than he that releaseth, and therefore cannot enure to him alone, to hold out his companion; for then, should the release enure by way of entry and grant of his estate, and, consequently, the disseisor to whom the release is made, should become tenant for life, and the reversion revested in the lessor; which strange transmutation and change of estates in this case the law will not suffer. But if lessee for years be ousted, and he in the reversion disseised, and the lessee release to the disseisor, the disseisee may enter, *for the term for years is extinct and determined.* But otherwise it is in the case of a lessee for life, for the disseisor hath a freehold, whereupon the release of tenant for life may enure; but the disseisor hath no term for years whereupon the release of the

lessee for years may enure." This passage is an authority to shew that the term for years was extinguished by
the feoffment, and that the lord had a right to enter as
soon as that feoffment was made. [*Littledale* J. It is
quite clear that the feoffment is of no avail unless it was
made with the consent of the termor. Now it appears, that
at the time when it was made the term had been assigned,
and there is nothing to shew that the assignees knew or
assented to the feoffment that was afterwards made.]
The assent of the trustees appears by the terms of the
assignment, for it refers to an indenture of three parts,
to be made on the following day, and that was the feoffment. At all events the assignor, as soon as he made
the feoffment, may be considered as claiming adversely
to the trustees, and the feoffment and assignment were
parts of the same transaction, and that species of injury
to the reversioner, which gave him a right to enter
for a forfeiture, by reason of the attempt to gain the fee,
and change the tenancy to his prejudice.

Tindal contrà was stopped by the court.

ABBOTT C. J. I am of opinion that the plaintiff is
not entitled to recover in this case. My judgment is
founded upon the ground that the feoffment did not
operate to destroy the term of years, because it does not
appear to have been made with the consent of those who
had the term. At the same time, however, I beg that
I may not be considered as giving my assent to the doctrine which has been advanced upon the first branch of
the case. There is so much good sense in the doctrine
laid down by Lord *Mansfield*, that I should be sorry to
find any ground for saying that it could not be supported.

ported. It is admitted in this case, that if there be a
lessee for term of years in possession, and a feoffment
be made by a stranger, that that feoffment would not be
good unless the lessee assented to it. Now at the time
when the feoffment in this case was made, *Cooper* had
ceased to be the lessee for the term of years, for the
very day before the feoffment was executed he had conveyed his interest in the term to two trustees. On the
2d of *November*, therefore, the day when the feoffment
was executed, the term was in them. Is there any thing
on the face of this case to shew that they assented to the
feoffment? If that assent was given, it ought either to
have been expressly found, or facts should have been
stated, necessarily leading to the conclusion that such
consent was given ; but no such facts are stated in this
case. It appears, indeed, by the recital in the indenture
of assignment, that it was made in consideration of a
marriage intended to be had between the assignor and
Elizabeth Kiss, and for the considerations mentioned and
expressed in a certain indenture of three parts, intended
to bear date the day after the date of the assignment,
and made between *T. Cooper*, *S.* and *J. Heyrick*,
W. Cooper, and *J. Kiss* and *Elizabeth Kiss*. Now I
cannot, from this recital, collect that the assignees accepted the term upon certain trusts, for the purpose of
enabling *Cooper* to make a feoffment, and so destroy the
term, and defeat the trusts. The intended deed is not
called an indenture of feoffment in the deed of assignment, and I cannot, therefore, say that these trustees
were informed that an indenture of feoffment was intended; and one reason why we should not presume
that they assented to such a deed is, that the objects of
the assignment would thereby be defeated. Then it is

D d 2   argued,

argued, that *Cooper's* possession was adverse to the trustees of the term; but I cannot accede to that, because, by the assignment, he was to have the beneficial enjoyment, so that his possession was consistent with the terms of the trust. The foundation of the argument urged in this case therefore fails, because there is nothing to shew that the trustees assented to the destruction of that term, or to the feoffment which was afterwards executed. Whether this feoffment worked a forfeiture or not may be a question between the reversioner and the lessee; but not appearing to have been made with the assent of the assignees of the term, it is of no avail against them. For these reasons, I think the judgment of the Court must be for the defendant.

BAYLEY J. It is conceded that the rightful fee is, or ought to be, in the original lessor, or in his representatives. Here, an attempt has been made to turn the term into a wrongful fee, and so to vary the relative situation of the lord and third persons. One of the consequences that would result from the doctrine contended for in argument would be, that this property, which before would have been liable as a chattel interest to the payment of debts, would be transmitted to *the heir at law* free from those burthens to which it would be liable in the hands of the personal representative. It is said that, since the introduction of common recoveries, it has been the common practice with conveyancers to make a feoffment with livery of seisin of the land to the person against whom the writ of entry was intended to be brought: the opinion being, that the feoffment was the most secure conveyance by which a tenant to the præcipe could be made; because, if the feoffor is in possession at the

1824.

Doe dem.
Maddock
against
Lynes.

the time when the livery of seisin is made, the feoffment is supposed to pass a good estate of freehold either by right or by wrong. But a court of law ought to set its face against deeds which are intended to work fraud or wrong; and I am glad, that in this case there is sufficient ground for saying, that the feoffment is not to take effect. It is a general rule, that unless the persons entitled to the actual possession concur in the feoffment, it will not defeat their interest. That being so, the term in this case continued against all persons but the lord. It is unnecessary to say whether it continued as against him; for in this case, the day before the feoffment was executed, the interest which *Cooper* had had in the term was assigned to two trustees. They then took the legal interest in the term upon trusts which would probably continue for a long time, and it was their duty not to lend themselves to any act tending to defeat that interest. We must presume that they did their duty, and, therefore, that they did not concur in any act to defeat the term. It is not found as a fact in the case, that the feoffment was executed with their consent; and if it was not, then it is conceded that the term was not destroyed, because the trustees were entitled to the actual possession, and we must therefore presume that they had it. As it does not appear, therefore, that the feoffment was made with their concurrence, the term is not defeated. The lord may, if he pleases, insist upon the forfeiture, and that will raise a different question which it is not necessary now to decide.

HOLROYD J. I think, even supposing that it had appeared by the facts of this case, that the trustees of the term had assented to the feoffment, the term would

not

not thereby have been destroyed, except at the election of the lord, who might have taken advantage of it. But consent is not to be presumed, and it is not found as a fact, nor are any facts stated which would necessarily lead to the conclusion that there was such a consent. It is admitted, that a feoffment by a stranger would not operate as a destruction of the term. The passages cited from *Littleton* and Lord *Coke* upon the general nature of disseisin, are considered by Lord *Mansfield* to apply to disseisin by election. In this case the actual possession continued the same as if the term had continued, and the parties had enjoyed the possession under the term; and if so, then the possession is to be considered as founded upon the right, and not upon the wrong, by analogy to the principle of remitter. The greatest mischief might arise in cases of this kind, if secret conveyances like these were to operate against parties really interested. The nature of a feoffment and disseisin are materially altered since the time when *Littleton* wrote. Such a case as this differs materially from that where an actual ouster of the freeholder formerly took place. The latter then no longer performed the services. There was not only a change of possession, but the person taking possession was adopted by the lord, and allowed by him to perform all the functions of tenant. It has been admitted, that in order to make the feoffment effectual in this case the tenant ought to have been ousted, or that his consent ought to have been gained. For these reasons I think that the lessor is not entitled to recover.

LITTLEDALE J. concurred.

Judgment for defendant.

CASES

Court of KING's BENCH,

Michaelmas Term,

In the Fifth Year of the Reign of GEORGE IV.

YOUNG *against* MILLER.

Saturday,
November 6th.

THIS cause was referred to two arbitrators, one named by each party, and such third person as should be chosen by the other two; the award of any two to be binding. The arbitrators not coinciding in the appointment of a third, agreed that each should name one person, and that they should then toss up for choice. The plaintiff's arbitrator won, and appointed the person whom he had before named. An award in favor of the plaintiff having been made by these two, a rule was obtained to set it aside, on the ground that the third arbitrator had been improperly appointed.

Where a cause was referred to two arbitrators specially named, together with a third, to be chosen by them, and the award of any two was to be binding; and they agreed that each should name one person, and that the right of selecting one of those so named should be determined by lot: Held, that this mode of appointing the third arbitrator was bad, and a sufficient ground for setting aside the award.

Tindal

Tindal shewed cause, and contended, that as two persons were named before the arbitrators tossed up, one of whom the winner was bound to appoint, this case was to be governed by *Neale* v. *Ledger*.(a), where Lord *Ellenborough* held, that, under such circumstances, this mode of appointing a third arbitrator was not objectionable.

Parke, contrà. This case is distinguishable from *Neale* v. *Ledger*, for there, the parties out of whom the choice was to be made, were named before any thing was said about tossing up, and that mode of selection was resorted to because the two persons proposed were considered to be equally eligible. Here, the agreement to appoint by lot was made before the nomination of the two persons, of whom one was to be appointed. This is much more like *Wells* v. *Cooke* (b), where such a proceeding was considered sufficient cause for setting aside the award.

Per Curiam. This rule must be made absolute. The present case bears a much greater resemblance to *Wells* v. *Cooke* than to *Neale* v. *Ledger*. The agreement to toss up preceded the nomination of the two persons out of whom the choice was to be made. Each of the arbitrators had then precluded himself from the opportunity of objecting to the person nominated by the other, however unfit he might be for the office which he was to discharge.

Rule absolute.

(a) 16 *East*, 51.　　　　　(b) 2 *B. & A.* 218.

1824.

ROGERS *against* JONES.

Monday,
November 8th.

THIS was an action of trespass for false imprisonment, brought against the defendant, a justice of
peace. At the trial before *Park* J., at the last Summer assizes for the county of *Hereford*, the plaintiff
proved a commitment by the defendant, reciting, that a
certain quantity of wood, the property of *T. D.*, had
been cut and spoiled, and taken and carried away, and
that he had just cause to suspect that the plaintiff did
cut, &c., and carry away the same, and that two ashen
trees stolen were found on the plaintiff's premises, and
that he could not give any satisfactory account how he
came by the same; and, therefore, that he, defendant,
convicted plaintiff of cutting, spoiling, taking, and carrying away wood, the property of *T. D.*; and the defendant
ordered the plaintiff, within the space of twenty-five days
then next ensuing, to pay to *T. D.* 11s., in satisfaction
of the damage done, and also ordered the plaintiff, within
the same space of twenty-five days, to pay to the overseers
of the parish, for the use of the poor, 20l. for the said offence, and plaintiff was committed for disobeying this
order. On the part of the defendant a conviction
was produced, by which it appeared that the plaintiff was convicted, under the 6 *G. 3. c.* 48., for that
he, on, &c., did go into the wood grounds belonging
to *T. D.*, of, &c., and did cut, spoil, take, and
admissible for that purpose. Quære, whether it was admissible in mitigation of damages.

In an action against a magistrate, for false imprisonment the plaintiff proved a commitment for a certain alleged offence. The defendant proved a conviction of the plaintiff for an offence differing from that recited in the commitment: Held, that this conviction was no justification of the imprisonment.

The defendant, in order to deprive the plaintiff of his costs under the 43 G. 3. c. 141., tendered evidence to shew that the offence mentioned in the conviction had actually been committed by the plaintiff: it was held, however, that that statute applied only to cases where convictions had been quashed, and, therefore, that the evidence was not

felo-

feloniously carry away two ash trees of the said *T. D.*, not having the consent of the said *T. D.*, the owner of the said woods, nor of any other person entrusted with the care thereof, for which offence the plaintiff was ordered to pay the sum of 20*l.*, together with the sum of 3*l.* 0*s.* 6*d.*, for the charges and expences attending the said conviction, this being his first offence; and it was contended, that as this conviction was good upon the face of it, it was evidence of all the facts stated in it, and a justification of the imprisonment; but the learned Judge was of opinion that the commitment not being founded on the same statute was not justified by the conviction. Evidence was then tendered to shew that the plaintiff had been guilty of the offence imputed to him; but the learned Judge thought it inadmissible, and the plaintiff obtained a verdict for 23*l.*

Sir *W. Owen* now moved for a new trial. It is a general rule, that in trespass against a magistrate, a subsisting conviction, good upon the face of it, for an offence within his jurisdiction, being produced on the trial, is sufficient evidence of the facts stated in it, and a bar to the action; *Strickland* v. *Ward* (a), *Massey* v. *Johnson* (b), *Brittain* v. *Kinnaird* (c), and *Gray* v. *Cookson.* (d) Now here, the conviction produced is of an offence on the 6 *G.* 3. *c.* 48. It is, therefore, evidence that the defendant was guilty of the offence charged in it, and that it was a matter within the jurisdiction of the convicting magistrate. It is true, that the plaintiff shewed a commitment by the defendant under an old statute, stating an offence not founded on the 6 *G.* 3.,

(a) 7 *T. R.* 633.   (b) 12 *East,* 67.
(c) 1 *Brod. & B.* 432.   (d) 16 *East,* 13.

but

but a magistrate may draw up his conviction after the
party has been committed; *Gray* v. *Cookson*. (a) Secondly,
the learned Judge ought to have received evidence to
shew that the defendant actually committed the offence
charged in the conviction, because, by the 43 *G.* 3. *c.* 141.
it is enacted, that in all actions brought against any justice, for or on account of any conviction made by him,
under any act of parliament, or for any act done or commanded by him for the levying any penalty, apprehending any party, or about carrying such conviction into
effect, in case such conviction shall have been quashed,
the plaintiff, besides the value of the penalty which may
have been levied, shall not recover any more damages
than 2*d.*, nor any costs of suit, unless it shall be expressly alleged in the declaration in such action, which
shall be an action on the case only, that such acts were
done maliciously and without any reasonable or probable
cause; and by *s.* 2. of the same statute the plaintiff
shall not recover back the penalty levied, nor any damages or costs, if the justice proves at the trial that the
plaintiff was guilty of the offence. The learned judge
was of opinion that the statute applied to those cases
only where the conviction had been quashed; but that
construction is liable to this inconsistency, that it would
put a magistrate in a better situation when his conviction
has been quashed than when a valid conviction exists,
which would be absurd and unjust. The statute is in
the alternative. The words " in case such conviction
shall be quashed," apply only to the latter part of the
sentence, to acts done for or about the carrying of the
conviction into effect, and not to the former words,
" for any act done or commanded by the justice for the

(a) 16 *East*, 13.

levying

levying any penalty, apprehending any party," &c. Besides, at all events, the evidence ought to have been received in mitigation of damages.

Per Curiam. The commitment and conviction do not connect themselves together. A magistrate cannot justify a commitment for one offence by a conviction for another and different offence. Here, the plaintiff has been imprisoned under a commitment for disobedience to an order of a magistrate, by which he was directed to pay 11s., as a recompence to the owner of the wood taken, and 20l. to the overseers of the poor of the parish. It is difficult to say that that order and commitment are founded on any statute. It would appear that the magistrate intended to proceed on the 15 *Car.* 2. *c.* 2., but the punishment is not warranted. The conviction upon which the magistrate relies, as a justification for this imprisonment, is founded on the 6 *G.* 3. *c.* 48., by which it is made an offence, wrongfully and maliciously to cut down trees without the consent of the owner. That conviction would have been an answer to an action for a commitment, in respect of the offence mentioned in it; but it is no justification of imprisonment for any other offence. As to the other point, it was held by this Court, in *Gray* v. *Cookson*, that the 43 *G.* 3. *c.* 141. applied only to cases where the conviction had been quashed. If the argument urged to-day were to prevail, a magistrate might convict on insufficient evidence, and afterwards be permitted to shew that sufficient evidence might have been adduced to justify the conviction. The only other point is, whether this evidence ought to have been admitted in mitigation of damages. Now even supposing it to have been admissible, as the commitment was illegal, and the

jury

jury have only given the plaintiff a verdict for 23*l*., which was the sum that he must have paid, in order to relieve himself from that illegal imprisonment, we cannot say that under such circumstances, a less sum ought to have been given.

Rule refused.

Doe Dem. Jackson *against* Wilkinson.

EJECTMENT. At the trial at the last assizes for *Chester*, it appeared that the action was brought to recover possession of a small piece of land by the side of a turnpike road. About thirty-three years ago the defendant enclosed the land in question, which was then waste. One *Trafford* was then owner of the freehold of the land on each side of the road. In 1808 the lessor of the plaintiff purchased the estate of *Trafford*. In 1816 he demanded 6*d*. rent of the defendant, who paid it on three several occasions. Nothing was said to him about the right in which the rent was claimed. In 1822 notice to quit was given, which he refused to comply with, contending that he had a right to the close. The learned Chief Justice of *Chester* told the jury that, if they believed the evidence as to payment of rent, they must find for the plaintiff. A verdict having been found accordingly,

D. F. Jones moved for a rule nisi for a new trial. The learned Chief Justice was wrong in treating payment of rent as conclusive in this case. It did not appear that the defendant had any intimation of the right in which the payment was demanded. It was very probably paid through fear or mistake. It should at all events have

been

Defendant enclosed a small piece of waste land by the side of a public highway, and occupied it for thirty years without paying any rent; at the expiration of that time, the owner of the adjoining land demanded 6*d*. rent, which defendant paid on three several occasions. In ejectment: Held, that this, in the absence of other evidence, was conclusive to shew that the occupation of defendant began by permission, and entitled the plaintiff to a verdict.

been left to the jury to say whether the defendant paid the money as tenant. *Fenner* v. *Duplock*. (a)

ABBOTT C. J.   I think that the learned Chief Justice was warranted in treating the payment of rent as conclusive evidence that the former occupation by the defendant was a permissive occupation; which view of the case was strongly corroborated by the situation of the piece of land in dispute.   Then, the only question was, whether the evidence given was true, and it is not pretended that any doubt existed on that point.

HOLROYD J. (b)   In *Bull. N. P.* 104. it is said, " A distinction has been taken, and allowed by all the Judges, on a case reserved by *Pengelly* C. B., that if a cottage is built in defiance of a lord, and quiet possession has been had of it for twenty years, it is within the statute; but if it were built at first by the lord's permission, or any acknowledgment have been since made, (though it were one hundred years since,) the statute will not run against the lord."   Here the payment of rent was an acknowledgment that the occupation was by permission.   Had the defendant known that the lessor of the plaintiff could not otherwise prove a tenancy, it is probable that he would not have paid the rent; but having paid it, the tenancy is acknowledged.

LITTLEDALE J. concurred.

Rule refused.

(a) 2 *Bing.* 10.   (b) *Bayley* J. had gone to Chambers.

BISHOP and Others, Assignees of HORNBLOWER, a Bankrupt, *against* CRAWSHAY and Others.

TROVER for iron hoops, bars of iron, &c. Plea not guilty. At the trial before *Park* J. at the Summer assizes for the county of *Stafford*, 1824, the following appeared to be the facts of the case: *Hornblower*, the bankrupt, carried on business at *Briarly Hall, Staffordshire.* The defendants were iron merchants, resident in *London.* On the 26th of *January* 1822, the defendants sent orders to the bankrupt to make the articles which were the subject of the present action, and they were made pursuant to that order, and were loaded on board barges on the 8th *February* to be forwarded to the defendants, and were landed at their wharfs in *London* on the 25th of *February* 1822. The value of the goods was 167*l.* On the 5th *February Hornblower* committed an act of bankruptcy, and on the 6th he drew a bill on the defendant for 400*l.*, which the latter accepted on the faith that the orders would be executed. On the 15th a commission issued against *Hornblower.* The defendants were in the habit of accepting bills for the bankrupt before the arrival of the goods ordered by them. Upon these facts it was contended that this was a case provided for by the 1 *Jac.* 1. *c.* 15. *s.* 14., which enacts " that no debtor of the bankrupt shall be thereby endangered for the payment of his debt truly and bona fide to any such bankrupt before the act of bankruptcy was committed, and when the bill was accepted by *A.*, and therefore this was not a payment protected by the 1 *Jac.* 1. *c.* 15. *s.* 14., because *A.* was not a debtor of *B.* at the time when the acceptance was given.

A., a merchant in *London*, ordered goods to be made by *B.*, a manufacturer in the country. The goods were made to order, but before they were forwarded to *A.*, *B.* committed an act of bankruptcy, and afterwards shipped the goods, having previously, but after the act of bankruptcy, drawn upon *A.* a bill of exchange for a larger sum than the price of the goods ordered, which bill *A.* accepted, not then knowing that *B.* had committed an act of bankruptcy. The goods having afterwards come to the possession of *A.*, it was held, that the assignees were entitled to recover them, because the property in them remained in the bankrupt, both at the time when

such

·such time as he should understand or know that he was become bankrupt." But the learned Judge was of opinion that it was not a case within that clause of the statute, and the jury, under his direction, found a verdict for the plaintiff for the value of the goods.

W. E. Taunton now moved for a new trial, and contended that this case was to be governed by that of *Cash* v. *Young*.(a) There *A.* bought goods of a trader who had committed a secret act of bankruptcy, and paid for them bonâ fide without knowledge of the bankruptcy, and it was held that the assignees of the seller could not maintain trover for the goods, the payment being protected by the 1 *Jac.* 1. *c.* 15. *s.* 14. Now that case is expressly in point; for here the defendants accepted the bill for 400*l.* on the faith that their order for the goods would be executed, and without knowledge of the bankruptcy. That acceptance was equivalent to payment. [*Bayley* J. A payment made before the goods are delivered is not a payment made in the usual course of trade.] The learned Judge ought, at all events, to have left it to the jury upon the evidence to find whether the goods were bought and paid for bonâ fide, and in the usual course of trade.

Abbott C.J. I think that the direction of the learned Judge was right, and that there was no question of fact in this case which could properly be left to the jury. It appears that the defendants had from time to time been in the habit of accepting bills for the bankrupt before the delivery of goods which they had

(a) 2 *B. & C.* 415.

ordered,

1824.

Baxter
against
CRAWSHAY.

ordered, and that in this instance they had given an
order to the bankrupt for goods to the amount of 160*l.*,
and that he drew on the defendants not for the price of
those goods, but for a larger sum; and that the bill was
accepted a few days after the goods were put on board
the lighter, and before they were delivered to the defendants. Now the only question is, whether the acceptance of that bill was a payment of a debt by a *debtor*
within the meaning of the 1 *Jac.*1. *c.*15. *s.*14. In order
to bring a case within this provision the person paying
the money must at the time of the payment be a debtor
of the bankrupt. In this case the defendants were not
debtors to the bankrupt at the time when they accepted
the bill. For until the goods ordered were actually
delivered no debt was contracted by them; and, therefore, it is not a case within the statute. In *Cash* v.
Young there was a doubt whether the payment was
made bona fide or for a special purpose, and the
question was left to the jury whether the goods were
bought and paid for in the ordinary course of trade,
and they found that fact for the defendant; and then
the question raised upon the statute was, whether,
supposing the payment to have been made bona fide,
the words " debtor of the bankrupt" included a person
who after the act of bankruptcy had become a debtor;
and the mischief and inconvenience of holding the contrary was pointed out in the argument. If the assignees
had been entitled to recover, no person could with safety
buy and pay for goods any where out of the city of
London. The defendant would not have been able to recover back the money paid to the bankrupt, and would
thereby have been endangered by such payment although
made bona fide, and. the assignees would have had

VOL. III.   E e   the

the benefit both of the money and of the goods. But in the present case the defendants were not debtors to the bankrupt at the time when they accepted the bill; he had no claim on them at that time, and if he had not become bankrupt, he could not in respect of any demand then existing have maintained any action upon the bill. The defendants, therefore, not being debtors of the bankrupt at the time when they accepted the bill, and there being no evidence to shew that the bill was specifically appropriated to the payment of the price of these goods, I am of opinion that it is not a case within the statute, and that there is no ground for a new trial.

BAYLEY J. If there was any evidence in this case to shew that either by the usage of the trade or by an express bargain between the parties, the defendants were to make advances for the specific articles while they were making, then they might be considered thereby to have acquired a property in those articles. In *Woods* v. *Russell* (a), *Paton*, a ship-builder, agreed to build a ship for *Russell*, and the latter was to pay for the same by four instalments at stated times during the progress of the work. Three instalments were paid, but before the fourth became due, or the ship was finished, *Paton* became bankrupt, and in an action brought by the assignees to recover the value of the ship, the Court intimated a strong opinion that the payment of those instalments appropriated specifically to *Russell* the very ship in progress, and vested in him a property in the ship. In this case, however, it does not appear that there was any such usage of trade, or any

(a) 5 B. & A. 942.

specifi

specific bargain between the parties.   Then if that be
so, the property in the goods remained in the bankrupt,
and passed to his assignees under the commission.
And there can be no doubt that this is not a case within
the 1 *Jac.* 1. *c.* 15. *s.* 14., because, assuming the giving
of the acceptance to be equivalent to payment, the defendants were not the *debtors* of the bankrupt at the
time when that acceptance was given.

HOLROYD J. I think that the property in these goods
remained in the assignees, and that they are not to be
considered as having been paid for them by reason of
the acceptance.   The bill was not drawn specifically for
the price of these goods, and although it was accepted
in the confidence that the order given for the goods
would be executed, yet so long as that order was not
executed but only in a course of execution, no property
in the goods passed to the defendants.   In *Woods* v.
Russell, the stipulation was that payment should be
made from time to time while the vessel was building,
and those payments were expressly appropriated to that
particular subject matter.   In this case the goods were
made, but until the money paid was appropriated to
these particular goods, the defendants could not have
maintained trover for them if they had been even sold
to another person.   It is clear, therefore, that the assignees had a sufficient property in these goods to enable
them to maintain this action, unless indeed there was
a payment within the statute of 1 *Jac.* 1. *c.* 15. *s.* 14.
Now there was no existing debt due from the defendants
to the bankrupt at the time when they accepted the bill,
and it was not certain that there ever would be such a
debt: and as there was no appropriation of the ac-

ceptance

1824.

BISHOP
against
CRAWSHAY.

ceptance as a payment for these particular goods, the money paid in consequence of that acceptance cannot be considered a payment made by a debtor of the bankrupt within the meaning of the 1 *Jac.* 1. *c.* 15. *s.* 14.

LITTLEDALE J. concurred.

Rule refused.

Monday,
November 8th.

SHELDON *against* COX.

A. agreed to give a horse, warranted sound, in exchange for a horse of B. and a sum of money. The horses were exchanged, but B. refused to pay the money, pretending that A.'s horse was unsound: Held, that it might be recovered on an indebitatus count for horses sold and delivered.

ASSUMPSIT. The declaration contained special counts for money agreed to be paid on an exchange of horses, indebitatus counts for horses sold and delivered, and the money counts. At the trial before *Bayley* J. at the last *York* assizes, it appeared that the plaintiff had agreed to exchange with defendant a black horse, warranted sound, for a bay mare, and forty guineas, and five guineas more if the black horse suited. The horses were exchanged, but the defendant afterwards contending that the black horse was unsound, refused to pay the money. The evidence did not support any of the special counts, and it was objected for the defendant that the plaintiff could not recover on the common counts. The learned judge held, that as nothing but the payment of money remained to be done between the parties, the plaintiff might recover on the common counts, and he had a verdict accordingly for 47*l.* 5*s.*

Scarlett moved for a rule nisi to enter a nonsuit, or for a new trial on the ground taken at the trial.

There

There is not any authority deciding that in such a case as the present, indebitatus assumpsit will lie. *Leeds* v. *Burrows* (a), was a mere case of the sale of certain goods, to be valued between an outgoing and an incoming tenant. When the valuation was made and possession was delivered to the incoming tenant, no doubt assumpsit for goods sold and delivered might be maintained. But here the nature of the contract was not altered by the part performance, it was therefore incumbent on the plaintiff to declare specially.

1824.

SHELDON
against
COX.

Per Curiam. The plaintiff delivered a horse to the defendant to be paid for partly by a horse of the defendant, and partly by money. The defendant delivered his horse but refused to pay the money. It is difficult to suggest any reason why that sum may not be recovered in a common count as part of the price of a horse, sold and delivered by the plaintiff to the defendant.

Rule refused.

(a) 12 *East*, 1.

SKAIFE and CARIS *against* JACKSON.

Tuesday,
November 9th.

ASSUMPSIT for money had and received. Plea, the general issue. At the trial before *Bayley* J., at the last *York* assizes, it appeared, that defendant had

In assumpsit by two co-trustees for money had and received to their use, the defendant produced a receipt for the money given by one of the plaintiffs: Held, that this was not conclusive, and that evidence was properly admitted to shew that the giving of the receipt was a fraudulent transaction, and that the money had not been paid.

received

received a sum of money belonging to the plaintiffs, as co-trustees. In answer, the defendant produced a receipt for the money, signed by *Caris*, and it was contended, that this estopped the plaintiffs from shewing that the money had not been paid over to them. The learned Judge held that the plaintiffs were not estopped, but gave the defendant leave to move to enter a nonsuit. Evidence being produced to shew that the giving the receipt was a fraudulent transaction, the plaintiffs obtained a verdict; and now

Brougham moved for a rule nisi to enter a nonsuit. If the receipt was obtained by fraud that might have been ground for an application to the equitable jurisdiction of the Court, to prevent its being set up as a defence; but as that was not done, evidence of fraud was not admissible at the trial as an answer to the receipt. If *Caris* had been the sole plaintiff the receipt would clearly have been an answer to the action; *Abner* v. *George* (a); he could not set up his own fraud; and the same appears to be the case, where the party giving the receipt is interested jointly with another; *Henderson* v. *Wild*. (b)

ABBOTT C. J. I am of opinion that we ought not to grant a rule in this case. The receipt was not a discharge of the action, nor was it pleadable in bar; but a release is, and although fraudulent, a court of law can only avoid it by equitable interference. A receipt is very different, and is nothing more than a primâ facie acknowledgment that the money has been paid. It

(a) 1 *Campb.* 392.   (b) 2 *Campb.* 561.

is

is said, that a party cannot set up his own fraud; but
the maxim " nemo allegans turpitudinem suam est au-
diendus," more properly applies to the defendant than
to the plaintiffs. It is admitted that the money was not
paid; we ought not, then, to allow the receipt to operate as a defence to the action.

LITTLEDALE J.(a) I am of the same opinion. The receipt
was not an estoppel, and the circumstances under which
it was obtained might be shewn. It amounted to nothing
more than a parol acknowledgment of payment. But this
case is not put on the footing of estoppel only; it is said
that the receipt was given to defraud the cestui que
trust, and that in pari delicto potior est conditio possidentis. But that maxim is inapplicable, for one of the
plaintiffs is not in delicto, and the defendant ought not,
against him, to be allowed to set up his own fraud. If
there had been but one plaintiff, and he had been party
to the fraud, the question might have been very different.

Rule refused.

(a) *Holroyd* J. was in the Bail Court.

BENTALL and Others, Assignees of BAKER and
FARNLEY, Bankrupts, and DYER *against* BURN.

ASSUMPSIT for goods bargained and sold, and goods
sold and delivered by *Dyer* and the bankrupts,
before their bankruptcy. This was an action brought to

A hogshead of
wine in the
warehouse of
the *London*
Dock Company
was sold for
18l., and a delivery order given to the vendee. There was no contract in writing: Held,
that the acceptance of the delivery order by the vendee was not an actual acceptance of the
wine within the statute of frauds.

recover 13l. 14s., the price of a hogshead of Sicilian wine sold to the defendant by the bankrupts, they being copartners with the other plaintiff, *Dyer*, who resided in *Sicily*. At the trial before *Abbott* C. J., at the *London* sittings after last *Trinity* term, it appeared that the bankrupts had, on the 15th of *February* 1822, sold, in the name of and on account of the firm, to the defendant a hogshead of *Sicilian* wine, then lying in the *London* docks, at the price of 13l. 14s., and at the same time a delivery order and invoice were made out and sent to the defendant, signed by the firm. But there was no contract in writing. On the 5th of *June* the defendant, on being applied to for payment, said, that the former order had been lost, and that the wine had not been transferred to him in proper time, and he had, consequently, lost the sale of it; that he had not been allowed to taste it. It was proved that a delivery order is given where the wine is intended to be speedily removed, and that the party receiving it may get the goods mentioned in the order, upon producing it at the *London* docks, and paying the charges, which are always deducted from the price. Upon this evidence the Lord Chief Justice was of opinion, that the acceptance of the delivery order by the vendee was not equivalent to an actual acceptance of the goods, within the meaning of the statute of frauds; and he directed a nonsuit to be entered, with liberty to the plaintiffs to move to enter a verdict for them, for the price of the wine.

Barnewall now moved accordingly. The acceptance of the delivery order by the vendee was equivalent to an actual acceptance of the wine itself, for it was proved, that, upon production of the order at the *London* docks,

he

he might have obtained immediate possession of the
wine. In Chaplin v. Rogers (a), Lord Kenyon says,
" Where goods are ponderous and incapable of being
handed over from one to another, there need not be an
actual delivery; but it may be done by that which is
tantamount, such as the delivery of the key of the warehouse in which the goods are lodged, or by delivery of
other indicia of property." Now here, the wine was not in
the warehouse of the vendor, and he, therefore, could
not give the vendee the key, but he gave him that which
enabled him to acquire the same dominion over it as if
he had the key. In Searle v. Keeves (a), which was assumpsit, for not delivering rice pursuant to contract,
there was no proof of any contract in writing, but the
plaintiffs produced an order on Bennett and Co., to deliver to them 20 barrels of rice, signed by Keeves, and a
witness, proved that Keeves told him that he had sold
that quantity of rice to Searle. The plaintiff then proved
the delivery of the order for the rice to the warehouseman of Bennett; Keeves afterwards countermanded that
order, and Bennett refused to deliver. And Eyre C. J.
held, that the statute of frauds did not attach, because
there had been a delivery of the whole. Keeves, the
defendant, gave an order for the delivery on Bennett and
Co., in whose possession the rice then was; that satisfied the statute. Now that case is expressly in point.
It may perhaps be said, as the London Dock Company held the wine as the agents of the vendors, that
it must continue the property of the latter until the
London Dock Company consented to hold it as the
agents of the vendee; that they might refuse to become

(a) 1 East, 194.   (b) 2 Esp. 598.

the

the agents of the latter. That argument might apply to the case of a common warehouseman, but the dock company having accepted a certificate from the treasury, under the warehousing act of the 43 G. 3. c. 132, have the exclusive privilege of warehousing wines before the duties are paid, and they are, therefore, bound to receive the goods into their warehouses, and to transfer them from buyer to seller, when required so to do, *Allnutt v. Inglis.* (a)

Per Curiam. There could not have been any actual acceptance of the wine by the vendee until the dock company accepted the order for delivery, and thereby assented to hold the wine as the agents of the vendee. They held it, originally, as the agents of the vendors; and as long as they continued so to hold it the property was unchanged. It has been said, that the *London* Dock Company were bound by law, when required, to hold the goods on account of the vendee. That may be true, and they might render themselves liable to an action for refusing so to do; but if they did wrongfully refuse to transfer the goods to the vendee, it is clear that there could not then be any actual acceptance of them by him until he actually took possession of them.

Rule refused.

(a) 12 *East*, 527.

1824.

Tuesday,
November 9th.

TRIPP *against* THOMAS.

CASE for words imputing subornation of perjury. Judgment by default. At the execution of the writ of enquiry the plaintiff offered no evidence, but his counsel addressed the jury, and they assessed the damages at 40*l.*

Ludlow now moved to set aside the inquisition, and contended that the jury were not justified in giving damages without some evidence by which they might be guided in fixing the amount; or that the damages should, at all events, have been nominal.

ABBOTT C. J. I think that we cannot disturb the finding of the jury. The defendant by suffering judgment by default admitted the speaking of the words as alleged in the declaration. It was, therefore, unnecessary to give evidence to that effect. The plaintiff did not produce any evidence in aggravation, it cannot therefore be presumed that the jury were misled, or that they estimated the damages on erroneous grounds.

Rule refused.

In case for words, defendant suffered judgment by default. At the execution of the writ of inquiry, the plaintiff offered no evidence, and the jury assessed the damages at 40*l.*: Held, that it was not incumbent on the plaintiff to give any evidence, and that the jury were not, under such circumstances, bound to give nominal damages only.

1824.

WILKINSON and Others *against* JOHNSON and Others.

Certain bills of exchange purporting to have, amongst others, the indorsement of *H.* and Co., bankers of *Manchester*, were presented for payment in *London*, at a house where the acceptance appointed them to be paid. Payment being refused, the notary who presented them, took them to the plaintiff, the *London* correspondent of *H.* and Co., and asked him to take up the bills for their honor. He did so, and struck out the indorsements subsequent to that of *H.* and Co., and the money was paid over to the defendants, the holders of the bills. The same morning, it was discovered that the bills were not genuine, and that the names of the drawer, acceptor, and *H.* and Co. were forgeries. Plaintiff immediately sent notice to the defendant, and demanded to have the money repaid. This notice was given in time for the post, so that notice of the dishonor could be sent the same day to the indorsers: Held, that the plaintiff having paid the money through a mistake was entitled to recover it back, the mistake having been discovered before the defendant had lost his remedy against the prior indorsers : Held, secondly, that the rights of the parties were not altered by the erasure of the indorsements, that having been done by mistake, and being capable of explanation by evidence.

ASSUMPSIT brought by the plaintiffs to recover back the sum of 589*l*.6*s*.8*d*., paid by them as they alleged in mistake on three bills of exchange. At the trial before *Abbott* C. J., at the *London* sittings before *Michaelmas* term 4 G. 4., a verdict was found for the plaintiffs, subject to the opinion of the Court upon the following case. About eleven o'clock on the morning of *Monday*, the 3d of *February* 1823, a notary public, who had been employed by Messrs. *Smith*, *Payne* and *Smith*, to note three bills of exchange which became due on the *Saturday* preceding, and which he had on that day presented for payment at the house of Messrs. *Masterman* and Co., where they were made payable, and refused payment, called, in consequence of the dishonor of the said bills, but without any order from *Smith*, *Payne* and *Smith*, with the said bills at the banking house of the plaintiffs, who carry on trade and business in partnership together as bankers in *London*, for the purpose of the same being taken up by the said plaintiffs, for the honor and on account of Messrs. *A. Heywood*, Sons and Co., who appeared to be indorsers upon the said bills, and whose *London* bankers the said plaintiffs then were, and still are. The follow-

ing

ing is a copy of one of the said bills of exchange, and of the several indorsements thereon.

No. 214*l.* 10*s.*

" *Liverpool, October* 30th 1822.

" Three months after date, pay to the order of *Charles Thompson,* Esq., two hundred and fourteen pounds ten shillings sterling, value received as advised.

" *Cropper, Benson,* and Co.

" To Messrs. *Birly* and
Hornby, Manchester.

" To be paid at *Masterman's, London.*"

The names *Birly* and *Hornby* were written across the bill, and it was indorsed, "*Charles Thompson, A. Heywood,* Sons and Co.; pay to the order of Mr. *Henry G. Harvey, Geo. Green, Henry G. Harvey,* pay Messrs. *H.* and *T. Johnson* and Co., or order *Gordon, Batt* and Co., *H.* and *T. Johnson* and Co.*"* The other bills were the same in form and had the same indorsements, they were drawn for 187*l.* 8*s.* 4*d.* each. The notary, who presented the bills at the house of the plaintiffs, was employed to present and note them as aforesaid, by *Smith, Payne* and *Smith,* bankers in *London,* who held the same as the bankers and agents of the defendants who are in partnership together. The plaintiffs believing that the bills were genuine bills, and that the indorsements in the names of *A. Heywood,* Sons and Co., were their genuine indorsements, took up the same for the honor, and on the account of the said *A. Heywood,* Sons and Co., and forthwith paid to the notary who presented the bills, the sum of 589*l.* 6*s.* 8*d.,* being the amount of the several bills, which was carried by the notary and paid to *Smith, Payne* and *Smith,* as the bankers

of

of the defendants, and the clerk of *Smith, Payne* and Co., immediately entered the same in their counter book. The clerk of the plaintiffs, upon paying the said sum to the notary, struck out all the indorsements on the bills, subsequent to that of Messrs. *A. Heywood,* Sons and Co. Immediately after the bills were so paid, by the plaintiffs, it was discovered that the same were not genuine bills, but that the names of the drawers and acceptors, and the names of *A. Heywood,* Sons and Co., on whose account the payment had been made, were forgeries. Upon the same day and before the hour of one o'clock, the plaintiffs gave notice to the defendants, and also to *Smith, Payne* and *Smith,* that the bills were discovered not to be genuine bills, but that the same were forged in the particulars before mentioned; and as well *Smith, Payne* and Co., as also the defendants, were at the same time informed that the names of the indorsers, subsequent to the indorsement purporting to be the indorsement of *A. Heywood,* Sons and Co., had been struck out by mistake, and under the belief, that the indorsement purporting to be the indorsement of *A. Heywood,* Sons and Co. was genuine, and the plaintiffs then demanded of *Smith, Payne* and *Smith,* and of the defendants, the money which been. paid by the plaintiffs as aforesaid, which *Smith, Payne* and *Smith,* and the defendants, refused to return. It was afterwards agreed, without prejudice, by the plaintiffs and defendants, that the defendants should return the bills to the indorsers from whom they received them, which was done accordingly, and such indorsers had due notice as well of the presentment of the bills of exchange, at the place where payable, and of their being dishonoured, as also of the circumstances above detailed; but the indorsers refused

to

to take them up, on the ground that the bills had been paid by the plaintiffs; and also on the ground, that the indorsements before mentioned had been struck out, and that the indorsers had thereby lost their remedy over.

The case was argued at the sittings in banc after last term, by *Tindal* for the plaintiffs, and *R. V. Richards* for the defendants; and again, before this term, by *Tindal* for the plaintiffs, and *Parke* for the defendants.

Arguments for the plaintiffs. There are several circumstances in this case which distinguish it from all those which at first sight seem adverse to the claim of the plaintiffs. In the first place, the plaintiffs were not parties to the bills, there was not therefore any duty on their part to know the handwriting on the bills and to pay them. The bills were presented to the plaintiffs by the agent of the defendants, who, by so doing, must be considered as having represented them to be good and genuine bills. The mistake was discovered, and notice of it given so early, that there was ample time to send by that day's post to the prior indorsers, information of the non-payment of the bills, so that the mistake did not deprive the defendants of their right to recover against any of those parties. In *Smith* v. *Mercer* (a), the plaintiffs were the bankers of *Evans* the drawee, whose acceptance was forged. There was a supposed direction by him to them, to pay the bill. It was their duty to obey the direction if given by their customer, and they were also bound to make themselves acquainted with his hand-writing. Again, the mistake there was not

(a) 6 *Taunt.* 76.

dis-

1824.

WILKINSON
against
JOHNSON.

discovered until a week afterwards, when the party presenting the bill had lost his remedy over. The opinion of *Gibbs* C. J. was founded on the latter circumstance. It is true, that *Dallas* C. J. and *Heath* J. took the larger ground of want of caution in the plaintiffs, but *Chambre* J. differed altogether, and thought they were entitled to recover, as having paid their money upon a consideration that failed. The point decided in *Smith* v. *Chester* (a) was, that the acceptor cannot dispute the hand-writing of the drawer, and that, although it be a forgery, he must pay the bill. But these plaintiffs were not acceptors, no duty was incumbent on them; they merely took up the bills for the honor of a supposed indorser; and the last observation is also applicable, as distinguishing this case from *Price* v. *Neale.* (b) The case most resembling it is *Jones* v. *Ryde* (c), there the defendant having got the plaintiff to discount a navy bill, which turned out to be forged, was held liable to refund the money, although both parties were at the time equally ignorant of the forgery. *Bruce* v. *Bruce* (d) was a similar case, and was governed by the decision in *Jones* v. *Ryde.* It may be said that the plaintiffs, by striking out the indorsements subsequent to that of *Heywood* and Co., have deprived the defendants of their right of action against the parties. But that is not so, the names were struck out under a mistake, and that may be explained by evidence, as might be done if a name had been blotted out by accident, or one name had by mistake been erased instead of another.

(a) 1 *T. R.* 654.   (b) 3 *Burr.* 1354.
(c) 5 *Taunt.* 488.   (d) 5 *Taunt.* 495.

Argu-

Arguments for the defendants. The plaintiffs are not
entitled to recover in this action. The rule that money
paid under a mistake of facts may be recovered must be
admitted. But there are two exceptions; first, where the
party paying is more in fault than the receiver; secondly,
where restitution cannot be made without injury to the
party repaying the money. Both these exceptions are
applicable to this case. As to the first, *Smith* v. *Mercer*
is directly in point. The payment by the plaintiffs was
the same as if it had been made by *Heywood* and Co.,
who would undoubtedly have been bound by it. The
plaintiffs were in the situation of acceptors for honor.
If an express acceptance had been given, they would have
been estopped by it, but it makes no real difference that the
acceptance and payment were concurrent acts. In *Price*
v. *Neale*, one of the bills was paid without actual acceptance, but that payment was held to be binding. Secondly,
restitution cannot be made without injury to the defendants, for their situation has been altered by the erasure
of the indorsements; they cannot be placed in statu quo.
It may be questionable whether the indorsers are not
altogether discharged, the erasure having been made
intentionally and with a view to discharge them. But,
supposing that not to be the case, still the explanation
of the mistake would impose great expence and difficulty
on the defendants in suing those indorsers, and it is
very doubtful whether they could recover those expences
in an action against the present plaintiffs for defacing
the bills, for that was done with the consent of their
own agent.

Cur. adv. vult.

The judgment of the Court was now delivered by

ABBOTT C. J. This case was argued before three of the Judges at the sittings in the adjoining room, and again before the whole Court at the sittings before the present term. In the argument two points were made. First, whether the plaintiffs could have recovered back the money which they paid on the bills in question, supposing they had not struck out the indorsements subsequent to the name of *Heywood* and Co., for whose honor they paid the bills. Secondly, whether their right to recover was defeated by that act.

Upon the first question, the cases of *Jones* v. *Ryde* (a) and *Bruce* v. *Bruce* (b) were cited for the plaintiffs; and *Price* v. *Neale* (c) and *Smith* v. *Mercer* (d) for the defendants. The general rule of law is clear and not disputed; viz. that money paid under a mistake of facts may be recovered back, as being paid without consideration. To this rule, the two cases cited for the defendant are an exception. The question is, whether the present case be properly within the rule, or within the exception. The case of *Price* v. *Neale*, was that of a man upon whom two bills of exchange falling due at different times were drawn: he paid the first when presented at maturity, not having accepted it, and accepted and paid the second. This was all done under a mistaken opinion that the signature of the supposed drawer was genuine. Some time afterwards, it was discovered that the signature of the drawer was forged. The decision of Lord *Mansfield* against the plaintiff appears not to have been grounded on the delay, but rather upon the general principle, that an acceptor is bound to know the hand-writing of the drawer, and that it is rather by his

(a) 5 *Taunt.* 488.   (b) 5 *Taunt.* 495.
(c) 3 *Burr.* 1354.   (d) 6 *Taunt.* 76.

fault

1824.

WILKINSON
against
JOHNSON.

fault or negligence than by mistake, if he pays on a forged signature. The case of *Smith* v. *Mercer* was that of a banker at whose house a bill purporting to be accepted by one of his customers was made payable. The forgery of the acceptor's name was not discovered until the end of a week. In this case Mr. Justice *Chambre* thought the plaintiffs entitled to recover. The other Judges were of a different opinion. Mr. Justice *Dallas* appears to have founded his judgment principally on the supposed fault or neglect of the plaintiffs, who ought to have known the signature of their customer; though he also notices the delay, and the inconvenience that might thereby result to the holders of the bill. Mr. Justice *Heath* appears to have given his judgment entirely on the ground of the fault or neglect of the plaintiffs, who could not, in his opinion, be in a different situation from that in which their customer would have stood if he had paid the bill himself. The Lord Chief Justice *Gibbs* grounds his judgment on the delay as sufficient for the decision of the cause; at the same time, however, declaring that he does not mean thereby to express his dissent from the larger ground on which the case had been put by the other two Judges.

Now, if we compare the facts of the present case with those of the two cases before mentioned, we shall find some important difference. The plaintiffs were not the drawees or acceptors of the bills, nor the agents of any supposed acceptor. They discovered the mistake in the morning of the day they made the payment, and gave notice thereof to the defendants in time to enable them to give notice of the dishonor to the prior parties, which was accordingly given. The plaintiffs were called upon to pay for the honor of *Heywood* and Co., whose

names

names appeared on the bills among other indorsers. The very act of calling upon them in this character was calculated in some degree to lessen their attention. A bill is carried for payment to the person whose name appears as acceptor, or as agent of an acceptor, entirely as a matter of course. The person presenting very often knows nothing of the acceptor, and merely carries or sends the bill according to the direction that he finds upon it; so that the act of presentment informs the acceptor or his agent of nothing more than that his name appears to be on the bill as the person to pay it; and it behoves him to see that his name is properly on the bill. But it is by no means a matter of course to call upon a person to pay a bill for the honor of an indorser; and such a call, therefore, imports on the part of the person making it, that the name of a correspondent, for whose honor the payment is asked, is actually on the bill. The person thus called upon ought certainly to satisfy himself that the name of his correspondent is really on the bill; but still his attention may reasonably be lessened by the assertion, that the call itself makes to him *in fact*, though no assertion may be made *in words*. And the fault, if he pays on a forged signature, is not wholly and entirely his own, but begins at least with the person who thus calls upon him. And though, where all the negligence is on one side, it may perhaps be unfit to inquire into the quantum, yet where there is any fault in the other party, and that other party cannot be said to be wholly innocent, he ought not, in our opinion, to profit by the mistake, into which he may by his own prior mistake have led the other; at least, if the mistake is discovered before any alteration in the situation of any of the other parties, that is, whilst the remedies of all the parties entitled to

remedy

remedy are left entire, and no one is discharged by laches. Further, it is not easy to reconcile the opinion of some of the judges in *Smith* v. *Mercer*, with the prior judgment of the same court in *Bruce* v. *Bruce*. That was the case of a victualling bill, of which the sum was altered and enlarged, and in this alteration the forgery consisted. The whole sum was paid at the victualling office when the bill was presented by the bank of England, but the forgery being discovered, the bank paid back the difference, and then called upon their customer, the plaintiff, who repaid the bank, and brought his action against the defendant, from whom he had received the bill in its altered state. Now, if the payment of the whole sum at the victualling office could not by law be rescinded on the ground of mistake, the refunding of part by the bank, and afterwards by the plaintiff, was an act done in their own wrong, and consequently not binding upon the defendant, nor giving a right of action against him. We think the present case approaches in principle nearer to that of *Bruce* v. *Bruce*, than to either of the other two. We think the payment in this case was a payment by mistake and without consideration to a person not wholly free from blame, and who ought not, therefore, in our opinion, to retain the money, unless the act of drawing the pen through the names of the other indorsers will have the effect of discharging them, and thereby deprive the defendants of their rights to resort to them; which brings me to the second question in this cause. And upon this second question we are clearly of opinion, that the defendants have not been deprived of their right to resort to the prior indorsers. The striking out an indorsement by mistake cannot, in our opinion, discharge the indorser; it would be most

mis-

mischievous to commerce to hold that it should." In the case of *Fernandez* v. *Glynn and Others*, which was tried before Lord *Ellenborough* at *Guildhall*, at the sittings after *Michaelmas* term 1806, it appeared that a check drawn upon the defendants, who were bankers in the city, by one of their customers, was passed through the clearing house, and taken from thence to the defendant's shop by one of their clerks, and there another clerk drew his pen through the name of the drawer as usual when a check is intended to be paid ; but it being soon afterwards known that a check to a very large amount, drawn by a third person, and paid into the defendant's house by the drawee of this check, was dishonored, the same clerk wrote under the name, the words "cancelled by mistake," and signed his initials, and in that state the check was before five o'clock returned to the bankers to whom the plaintiff had delivered it, and was received back by them. It was contended for the plaintiff, that this cancellation amounted to an acceptance of the check, or an acknowledgement that the defendants had money in their hands to pay it, and was irrevocable. It was proved, however, to be usual to return and take back before five o'clock, checks passing through the clearing house, and thus cancelled, if the words "cancelled by mistake" were written on them as in the present case, and the plaintiff was non-suited. (*a*) Now this case shews, that the act of drawing a pen through a name on such instruments is not considered among mercantile men to be an act so absolute in itself as not to be recalled and annulled, if done by mistake. We think that, in the present case, the mistake may be

---

(*a*) See a note of this case 1 *Campb.* 426.

shewn,

shewn, and that the indorsers are not discharged. If, indeed, it shall hereafter appear that the defendants are put to any additional expence, by extra proof or otherwise, on account of this improvident act of the plaintiffs, which is very unlikely, they may possibly maintain a special action upon the case to recover a compensation to the extent of the injury they sustain, but this does not necessarily extend to the whole consideration, and if not, it furnishes no defence to the present action. The verdict, therefore, is to be entered for the plaintiffs.

Postea to the plaintiffs.

VAN WART *against* WOOLLEY, LEWIS, MOILLIET, and GORDON.

ASSUMPSIT against the defendants, as the bankers and agents of the plaintiff, for neglecting to give due notice of the non-acceptance of a bill of exchange which the plaintiff had delivered to them to get accepted; in consequence of which laches the plaintiff alleged that, as the payee, he was prevented from giving due notice of the dishonor to the drawers *Alexander Cranston* and Co., and also to Messrs. *Irving, Smith,* and *Holly,* from whom he had received the bill, and

A. and Co., resident in *America,* employed *B.,* resident at *Birmingham* in this country, to purchase and ship goods for them. On account of such purchases, they sent to *B.* a bill, drawn by *C.* in *America* on *D.* in *London,* but did not indorse it.

B. employed his bankers to present the bill for acceptance. *D.* refused to accept, but of this the bankers did not give notice until the day of payment, when it was again presented, and dishonored. Before the bill arrived in this country *C.* became bankrupt, and he had not, either when the bill was drawn, or at any time before it became due, any funds in the hands of *D.*, the drawee. In an action by *B.* against the bankers for neglecting to give him notice of the non-acceptance of the bill: Held, that inasmuch as *A.* and Co., not having indorsed the bill, were not entitled to notice of the dishonor, and still remained liable to *B.* for the price of the goods sent to them, and the drawer was not entitled to notice, as he had no funds in the hands of the drawee, *B.* could not recover the whole amount of the bill, but such damages only as he had sustained in consequence of having been delayed in the pursuit of his remedy against the drawer.

F f 4

who

who would have been liable to pay him the sum therein
mentioned, if they had received due notice of its dishonor; but now by the defendants' neglect are discharged from that obligation, and have refused to pay;
and whereby the plaintiff also alleged, that he had lost
his remedy against the drawers and the said Messrs.
Irving, Smith, and Holly. Plea, general issue. At the
trial before Abbott C.J. at the London sittings after
Michaelmas term 1828, a verdict was found for the
plaintiff, subject to the following case:—

The plaintiff residing at Birmingham, received from
his correspondents, Irving, Smith, and Holly, of New
York, in the United States of America, a bill of exchange for 500l., dated New York, 6th June 1818, and
drawn by A. Cranston and Co. upon Greg and Lindsay
in London, and payable sixty days after sight to the
order of the plaintiff. The letter inclosing the bill
stated it to be a further remittance on account of an
order for hardware. On Tuesday the 2d of July 1818,
the plaintiff delivered the bill to the defendants, who
are bankers at Birmingham, to get it duly accepted by
the drawees, who were resident in London, and the defendants received the bill for that purpose, and forwarded
the same on the following day to their town correspondents and agents, Sir John Lubbock and Co., bankers in
London, who, on the 8th of July, presented the bill to
the drawees for acceptance. The drawees having, on
the 1st of July 1818, received advice of the bill being
drawn from Cranston and Co., had written for directions
as to accepting the same to James Alexander and Co. of
Belfast, in Ireland, and not having received any reply
from those parties, gave the following answer to Lubbock and Co.: " Greg and Co. have written for advice,

will

will desire Lubbock and Co. to have it only noted for the present." In consequence of such request, Lubbock and Co. did not protest the bill for non-acceptance, or give notice to the defendants or to the plaintiff of the refusal to accept until the 10th of September 1818. On that day they sent a letter containing such notice by the post, which was received by the defendants on the 11th, the bill having been presented for payment on the 9th of September, and protested on that day for non-payment. The defendants did not give any notice to the plaintiff of the refusal of the said drawees to accept the bill until the 11th of September 1818, being the day the defendants received the bill from Lubbock and Co. This was the first notice to the plaintiff of such dishonor, which notice being accompanied with a protest. The defendants were for some time before, and at the time when the bill of exchange was delivered to them, the general bankers of the plaintiff, and invariably charged the plaintiff commission on all the transactions which passed between him and the defendants as his bankers, and did actually charge him, in their banking account with him, commission on this bill of exchange at the rate of six shillings per cent.; and the defendants further charged the plaintiff with the sum of 1l. 16s., the amount paid for noting for non-acceptance, and for protesting the same for non-payment, and charges. On the 9th of September 1818, the bill was presented to the drawees for payment, and dishonored. The drawees had no funds or effects of the drawers in their hands at the time when the bill was originally drawn, nor at any time prior to its coming to maturity; nor had they any expectation of assets of the drawers to meet the bill; but the drawees had been accustomed to accept for the

drawers

drawers under the guarantee of *J. Alexander* and Co. of *Belfast*, for 10,000*l.*, which amount had been overdrawn. The drawers before the bill was drawn, had been accustomed to draw on the drawees to a larger amount than the said sum of 10,000*l.*; but the drawees had never accepted any bills beyond the guarantee of 10,000*l.*, unless they were covered by other resources. The drawees had by letter of the 3d of *July* 1818, addressed to the drawers, declined accepting the said bill, unless they should receive further advice from *Alexander* and Co. *Cranston* and Co., the drawers, became bankrupts, in *New York*, on the 6th of *July* 1818, and the produce of their estate will be about 2*s.* in the pound.

It appeared that *Irving* and Co. employed the plaintiff to purchase goods for them in *England* by commission, and had ordered goods to a much greater amount than 500*l.*; which goods were sent out by the plaintiff to *America*, the bill of exchange having been remitted and sent by *Irving* and Co. to the plaintiff, for and on account and in part payment of the price of the said goods. *Irving* and Co. did not indorse their names on the bill of exchange, and were wholly unknown to the defendants. The plaintiff sent the bill of exchange, on the 12th of *September* 1818, to *Irving* and Co., requesting them to pay the amount of the bill of exchange; but on the 9th of *March* 1819, they wrote to plaintiff and refused so to do, returning the bill of exchange, and insisting that they were discharged from liability to make such payment, in consequence of their not having had due notice of the non-acceptance of the bill of exchange; whereupon the plaintiff, on the 1st of *April* 1819, returned the bill to the defendants, who

refused

refused to pay the same. The usual time of passage from *England* to *New York*; and back, was generally about ten weeks. This case was argued at the sittings before this term by *Chitty* for the plaintiff, and *Abraham* for the defendant.

For the former it was contended, that the defendant being an agent receiving compensation for his trouble, was liable for any damage arising by reason of his negligence; and that in consequence of his neglect a difficulty had arisen respecting the bill, and that the plaintiff had a right either to have the bill paid, or to have a clear remedy over against the drawer, or the person from whom he received the bill. It is not clear that the drawers would not be discharged. At all events, a difficulty was imposed on the plaintiff by the act of the defendants. In *Owenson* v. *Morse* (a), it was held, that if the seller of goods takes notes or bills for the price without agreeing to run the risk of their being paid, that is not to be considered as payment. The plaintiff, therefore, originally had a remedy against *Irving, Smith,* and Co., but he has now lost it. He has made the bill his own as against them, for they were entitled to notice of the non-acceptance from him. They were in the situation of sureties, and a surety, though not a party to the bill, may be discharged by want of notice, *Phillips* v. *Astling*. (b) For the defendant it was contended, that the plaintiff had sustained no damage in consequence of not having received notice of the non-acceptance. Prima facie notice to the drawer is necessary; but if it appear from special circumstances that he sustains no loss from want of notice, then it

(a) 7 T. R. 64.   (b) 2 Taunt. 206.

becomes

becomes unnecessary. Now, here the drawer had no funds in the hands of the drawee, and therefore notice was not necessary. As to *Irving, Smith*, and Co. their names were not upon the bill, and they therefore were clearly not entitled to notice, *Swinyard* v. *Bower* (a), *Holbrow* v. *Wilkins* (b); and, for the same reason, they are still liable to the plaintiff for his demand against them, *Ex parte Blackburne.* (c)

Cur. adv. vult.

ABBOTT C. J. now delivered the judgment of the Court, and after stating the facts of the case, proceeded as follows:

Upon this state of facts it is evident that the defendants (who cannot be distinguished from, but are answerable for their *London* correspondents, Sir *John Lubbock* and Co.) have been guilty of a neglect of the duty which they owed to the plaintiff, their employer, and from whom they received a pecuniary reward for their services. The plaintiff is, therefore, entitled to maintain his action against them, to the extent of any damage he may have sustained by their neglect. He charges a damage in two respects, *first*, by the loss of remedy against *Irving, Smith,* and *Holly*, from whom he received the bill. *Secondly*, by the loss of remedy against *Cranston*, the drawer of the bill. If, as between the plaintiff and *Irving* and Co., he has made the bill his own, and cannot call upon them for the amount, his damage will be to the full amount for which the verdict has been taken. If he still retains a remedy against them, and has only been delayed in the pursuit of such

(a) 5 M. & S. 68.   (b) 1 B. & C. 10.   (c) 10 Ves. 204.

remedy

1834.

VAN WART
against
WOOLEY.

remedy as he might have had against the drawer, a
bankrupt, the amount of his loss has not been enquired
into or ascertained, and is probably much less than the
amount of the bill.

We are of opinion that the plaintiff has not, as
between him and *Irving* and Co., made the bill his own;
that he might, notwithstanding the want of notice of the
non-acceptance, have recovered from them the amount
of the bill in an action for money paid; or if he had
notice of the dishonor before he had bought and sent
the goods which they had ordered him to buy, he might
have returned the bill, and have abstained from ordering or buying the goods. It will have been observed
that *Irving* and Co. sent the bill to the plaintiff without
their indorsement, and payable to his own order. The
counsel for the plaintiff was under the necessity of
arguing this case, as if he were arguing for *Irving*
and Co. in an action brought against them by the
plaintiff; and it was contended that *Irving* and Co.
were entitled to notice of the non-acceptance in this
case, as they would have been by the law-merchant in
the case of a bill indorsed by them to the plaintiff.
But no authority was cited that maintains this proposition. And the case of *Swinyard* and others v.
Bowes is an authority the other way. If a person
deliver a bill to another without indorsing his own
name upon it, he does not subject himself to the obligations of the law-merchant; he cannot be sued on
the bill either by the person to whom he delivers it
or by any other. And as he does not subject himself
to the obligations, we think he is not entitled to the
advantages. If the holder of a bill sell it without his
own indorsement, he is, generally speaking, liable to no

action

action in respect of the bill. If he deliver it without his indorsement upon any other consideration, antecedent or concomitant, the nature of the transaction, and all circumstances regarding the bill, must be inquired into, in order to ascertain whether he is subject to any responsibility. If the bill be delivered, and received as an absolute discharge, he will not be liable; if otherwise, he may be. The mere fact of receiving such a bill does not shew it was received in discharge, *Bishop* v. *Rowe* (a) and *Swinyard* and others v. *Bones*, before mentioned. Then what are the facts of this particular case? *Irving* and Co., residing in *America*, had employed the plaintiff, residing at *Birmingham*, to purchase hardware for them in *England* by commission. By accepting this employment he became, as between him and them, their agent. They then send him the bill in question as a further remittance on account of their order for hardware. The bill is drawn upon persons residing in *London*; the plaintiff therefore could not have been expected to present the bill himself: it must have been understood that he was to do this through the medium of some other person. He employed for that purpose persons in the habit of transacting such business for him and others, and upon whose punctuality he might reasonably rely. In doing this, we think he did all that was incumbent upon him as between him and *Irving* and Co.; that he is personally in no default as to them, and is not answerable to them for the default of the persons whom he employed under such circumstances. In the course of the argument, the situation of *Irving* and Co. was compared

(a). 3 M. & S. 362.

to that of a guarantee. The decisions that have taken place in actions brought against a guarantee warrant the proposition that has been before mentioned, viz. that the nature of the transaction, and the circumstances of the particular case, are to be considered and regarded. Thus, in *Warrington* and another v. *Furbor* (a), where a commission of bankrupt had issued against the acceptor before the bill became due, a presentment for payment to him was held unnecessary to charge the guarantee. *Phillips* v. *Astling* (b) stood upon different grounds : the bill was not presented for payment when it became due, as it ought to have been; two days afterwards notice that it remained unpaid was given to the drawers, for whom the defendant was guarantee, but no notice was then given to the defendant. The drawers and acceptor continued solvent : for many months after the bill was dishonored; and it was not until they had become bankrupts that payment was demanded of the defendant. Under these circumstances, because the necessary steps were not taken to obtain payment from the parties to the bill while they continued solvent, the Court of C. P. held the guarantee to be discharged. In *Holbrow* v. *Wilkins* (c), the acceptors were known to be insolvent before the bill fell due; and some days after that fact was known the plaintiffs wrote to the defendant, and desired him to accept a new bill, which he refused. The bill was not presented for payment when due, nor any notice of the non-payment given to the defendant. The bill would not have been paid if presented; and it did not appear that the defendant sustained any damage by reason of

(a) 8 *East*, 242.   (b) 2 *Taunt*. 206.   (c) 1 *B. & C*. 10.

the

the want of presentment or notice; and this Court held the guarantee not to be discharged. These decisions shew that cases of this kind depend upon the circumstances peculiar to each. In the present case it does not appear that *Irving* and Co. have sustained any damage by the want of notice of the non-acceptance of the bill. *Cranston*, the drawer, was not entitled to such notice; he had no right to draw, and he sustained no prejudice. He had become bankrupt some weeks before notice of the non-acceptance could have reached *Irving* and Co.: nothing appears to shew that they have lost any remedy that they might have had either against him or his estate, if they could ever have had any: but even this does not appear affirmatively; the circumstances under which they received the bill not being disclosed; and possibly they may have received it upon the terms of being accountable only in case it should be accepted, and not otherwise.

I come now to advert to the supposed loss in respect of *Cranston* the drawer of the bill. I have already observed that the amount of this loss has not been inquired into or ascertained. Perhaps it may be merely nominal; but even if it be so, the plaintiff was entitled to a verdict for nominal damages. In order, therefore, to do justice between these parties, the cause must be again submitted to a jury to ascertain the amount of this loss (it being clearly understood that the plaintiff is entitled to a verdict), unless the parties can agree upon the amount, and correct the present verdict accordingly, which it is highly desirable for them to do.

A rule was accordingly drawn up for a new trial.

DYSON *against* WOOD.

TRESPASS for breaking and entering the plaintiff's dwelling-house, and seizing and taking away divers chairs and other household furniture, &c. Plea, as to the breaking and entering the dwelling-house that our lord the now king was, and still is, seised in right of his duchy of *Lancaster*, of the liberty and franchise of the honor of *Pontefract*, in the county of *York*, with the appurtenances; and that from time whereof, the memory of man is not to the contrary until the time of the passing of an act of the 17 *G. 3. c.* 15., a court baron had been used to be holden in and for the said honor for the suitors of the court, for the recovery of debts and damages not exceeding 40s. arising within the said honor, and after the passing of that act of parliament for the recovery of debts and damages not exceeding five pounds, arising within the honor. The plea then stated a judgment recovered in the same court for 1*l.* 9s. 11d.; and that defendant prosecuted and sued out upon the said judgment, according to the custom of the said court, a precept directed to the chief bailiff and his deputies, commanding him to levy the sum so awarded. It then justified breaking and entering the house for the purpose of taking the chairs, &c., under the precept. Replication that there was not any memorandum of the proceedings, or of the said supposed judgment remaining in the said court baron in the plea mentioned. General demurrer and joinder. The case was argued by

Milner in support of the demurrer, and *Blackburn* contrà. By the former it was contended, that the fact put

Trespass for breaking and entering plaintiff's dwelling-house. Defendant justified under a judgment recovered in a court baron, and a precept issued thereon. Replication, that there was not any memorandum of the proceedings, or of the said supposed judgment, remaining in the said court baron: Held, upon general demurrer, that the replication was bad, inasmuch as it put in issue an immaterial fact. Dubitante Littledale J.

in issue was immaterial, and therefore ground of general demurrer. A court baron is not a court of record, and a judgment obtained in it is not entitled to greater weight than a foreign judgment, which is not a record, *Walker* v. *Whitter*, 1 *Doug*. 1. Now, if the defendant had taken issue on this replication and had brought into court a memorandum of the proceedings, it could not have been read in evidence. The steward must have been called as a witness to prove the proceedings. The only mode of reviewing the proceedings is by writ of false judgment, and in that case they are not removed, but the writ is directed to the steward, and he certifies the proceedings to the court above. Of common right, all pleas in the court baron ought to be determined by wager of law, 2 *Inst*. 143. That court could only decide otherwise by custom. The steward may take a note or memorandum of the proceedings for his own convenience, but that note or memorandum not being the judgment itself, or even evidence of it, an issue tendered upon the fact whether there was such a memorandum or note is immaterial, and therefore ground of general demurrer. On the other hand it was contended, that it was essential in inferior courts, that there should be a memorandum of the proceedings, and that the writ of false judgment, which is in the nature of a writ of error from the court below, *Jentleman's* case (a), could have no operation, unless there were such a memorandum; and that at all events, the objection being that the traverse was immaterial, could only prevail upon special demurrer; and *Hawe* v. *Plamer*, 1 *Saund*. 14. n. 2. was cited in support of that position. Some stress was laid upon the 28th clause of the 17 *G*. 3. *c*. 15., but the court held that it it did not affect the question.

(a) 6 *Coke*, 11.

ABBOTT

ABBOTT C. J. I am of opinion that this replication is bad upon general demurrer, because it tends to put in issue a fact which is so immaterial, that if a verdict were found upon that issue for the plaintiff, he would not be entitled to judgment. It appears by the plea, that a court baron had existed from time immemorial within the honour of *Pontefract*, the jurisdiction being by custom limited to 40s., but subsequently enlarged by the 17 *G. 3. c. 15. s. 27.*, to sums not exceeding 5l. That statute, however, does not alter the nature of the court. It is not a court of record, and it is not necessary to enquire whether it be the duty of the steward to make an entry of the proceedings, but supposing that to be so, and he neglect to do his duty, I cannot say that the judgment has absolutely no effect. Giving the largest construction to the words of the replication, they may be considered to import that no memorandum exists or ever was made, and if so, the steward might be guilty of a misdemeanour by his neglect. But if he do so neglect his duty, that ought not deprive a party of his judgment. For the question, whether judgment was given for him in such a court is a matter of fact, the entry would merely give him a facility of proof which he would not otherwise have. In pleas of judgments recovered in the superior courts, the allegation is, that there is not remaining any record of such judgment, and that allegation imports that no such judgment was ever given; for the question whether it was or was not given is to be decided by the court on inspection of the record, and not by a jury. But a judgment may be proved as a fact, and by other evidence than a written memorandum; and that being so, the effect of this replication is not to deny that judgment was given in the court below, but merely that it is not capable of being verified by a particular species of proof.

1824.

DIXON against WOOD.

It

It is therefore insufficient, and judgment must be for the defendant.

BAYLEY J. I think that the replication is bad. The plea is, that a judgment was obtained in the court baron, and that the party sued out execution thereon. The proper question to be raised upon such a plea is, whether the defendant did in fact obtain such judgment. Instead of that the plaintiff says, that there was no memorandum of the said judgment remaining in the said court; he does not say that it was not remaining there at the time when the precept issued. That perhaps, however, might be ground only of special demurrer, but I think that the replication is bad in substance, because it does not appear that there was any distinct obligation in the officer of the court to take a written memorandum of all the proceedings there; and even if that did appear, the effect of it only would be, that if the officer neglected his duty, he might be punished on that account. The suitor, however, ought not to lose the benefit of the judgment on that account.

HOLROYD J. I think that this replication is bad upon general demurrer. The plea alleges as a fact to be tried by a jury, that the defendant obtained a judgment in the court baron, for that fact is alleged without any verification, or without any prout patet by the memorandum or entry. The plaintiff in his replication does not, in express terms or by necessary implication, deny that the judgment was so obtained; and whatever is not denied must be taken to be admitted. The effect of the replication therefore is, that the plaintiff admits

that

that a judgment has been obtained, but denies that there is any memorandum or written minute of it. Now that circumstance may make it more difficult to prove the judgment afterwards, but it is no answer to the plea, because it does not deny the fact of a judgment having been obtained, but only asserts that it cannot be proved by a particular species of evidence. It does not even allege that there is no evidence of the judgment, but only that there is no evidence of that particular species; for if a memorandum had been made, and it had been destroyed by fire, it might be proved by parol evidence. Even in cases of removal by writ of false judgment, no original entry is removed; but it is the duty of the steward to make up a statement of such of the proceedings as may give the necessary information to the superior court. If he has no written memorandum of the proceedings, he may supply the defect from his own memory.

LITTLEDALE J. The plaintiff certainly was not bound to reply de injuria generally, although he might have done so, but he was at liberty to select a particular fact and put it in issue. The question is, whether he has put any fact properly in issue. I incline to think that the replication is good upon general demurrer, although it would be bad upon special demurrer. I think that the substance of the replication is, that no judgment ever was obtained. It is certainly true, that the usual mode of proceeding in courts baron is by wager of law. But still I think that the steward should make an entry that the defendant came and waged his law. If it was the duty of the steward, we should presume that he did so, and then the plaintiff, by denying that any such memoran-

dum

dum was made, may be considered as denying that any judgment was obtained. But on special demurrer it would clearly have been bad.

Judgment for defendant.

Wednesday,
November 17th.

The King *against* The Inhabitants of LAMPETER.

An order of removal was made, and suspended on the same day, by reason of the infirmity of the pauper. She lived three years afterwards, and no notice of the order of removal was served on the parish to which she was to be removed under the order, until after the death of the pauper: Held, that notice of the order not having been served within a reasonable time, the order of removal was a nullity.

AN order was made by two justices, dated the 14th of *May* 1821, for the removal of *Gwen Rees*, widow, from the parish of *Lampeter*, in the county of *Cardigan*, to the parish of *Llanfairclydoge*, in the same county, the execution of which order was on the same day suspended, because it appeared to the justices that it would be dangerous for the pauper to travel, by reason of infirmity of old age. By another order of the 16th of *February* 1824, the same justices, reciting, that the pauper *Gwen Rees*, was then dead, and that it had been duly proved to them upon oath, that the sum of 12*l.* 13*s.* 6*d.* had been incurred by the suspension of the order of removal, directed the churchwardens and overseers of the poor of the parish of *Llanfairclydoge*, in the county of *Cardigan*, to pay the said charges to the churchwardens and overseers of the poor of the parish of *Lampeter*, or to such of them as should demand the same. On the said 16th *February* 1824, the appellants were, for the first time, served with the order of removal, and with the other orders hereinbefore mentioned; and on the same day payment was demanded of the sum of 12*l.* 13*s.* 6*d.*, as the expences incurred by the suspension. Against the order of removal the parish of *Llanfairclydoge* appealed. Upon the hearing of the appeal at the last

Easter

Easter quarter sessions for the county of *Cardigan*, the court decided that, the pauper being dead, and the order of removal and suspension not having been executed, or any service made of them in the pauper's lifetime, nor after the pauper's death, until the demand of payment, the order of removal became a nullity and inoperative, and they accordingly precluded the respondents from giving evidence in support of the order of removal and of the adjudication of settlement in the appellant parish, and quashed the order, subject to the opinion of this Court.

Taunton and *Oldnall Russell* in support of the order of sessions. The question in this case is, whether a parish can recover the charge incurred by the suspension of an order of removal by the virtue of the 35 *G. 3. c.* 101. *s.* 2., where the pauper dies before removal, and until after his death no notice of the order and suspension has been served upon the parish to which he was ordered to be removed. There is not any express decision on the point; but it was alluded to by *Bayley* J. in *Rex* v. *Chagford* (a), where an order of removal was suspended, and before any removal took place, an estate descended to the pauper, whereby he became irremovable; and it was held by the sessions, and afterwards by this Court, that the expence incurred by the suspension of the order could not be recovered, as the order was not served until after the descent of the estate. *Bayley* J. says, " Besides, in the present case, a very long period has elapsed during which this order remained suspended, and no notice of it was given to the opposite party.

(a) 4 B. & A. 235.

G g 4   Now

1824.

The King
against
The Inhabit-
ants of
Lampeter.

Now if that notice had been given (and there are no words in the act that supersede the necessity of it), it might have enabled the other parish to have made prompt enquiry, and to have ascertained the fact relative to the settlement of the pauper. I think, therefore, that this affords an additional reason for holding that the sessions have come to a right conclusion in this case.". So here the evidence of the pauper, which would have been very material in determining the place of her settle-. ment, has been lost. Again, the burthen of payment is cast on different persons by this long delay; the inhabitants of a parish are to bear the current expences of supporting the poor; but in this case new inhabitants would be charged with the expences incurred before, they came into the parish. The 49 G. 3. c. 124. s. 2. enacts, that where an order of removal is suspended, the time of appealing shall be computed from the time of serving the order, and not from the time of making the removal; which shews that the legislature contemplated a service of the order before it was carried into execution. *Rex* v. *St. Mary-le-bone* (a) is the only instance where a suspended order appears to have been served after the death of the pauper; the Court did not indeed decide that the order was thereby rendered of no avail; that point was not touched upon; but they held that the order to pay the expences was a grievance against which an appeal was given by the 3 *W. & M. c.* 11. *s.* 9.

R. V. *Richards* contrà. In *Rex* v. *St. Mary-le-bone,* the order of removal was suspended, and the pauper

(a) 13 *East,* 51.

died

1824.

The King
against
The Inhabit-
ants of
LAMPETER.

died before any removal took place, and before the order was served or notice of it given. If the want of service or notice during the life of the pauper had rendered the order void, that would have disposed of the case, and the Court would not have entered into any discussion as to whether the order for payment of the expences incurred by the suspension of the former order, was or was not a grievance within the 3 *W. & M.* c. 11. The judgment, however, was upon the latter point; it was held to be a grievance for which an appeal would lie. The whole proceeding towards a removal could not, therefore, have been deemed a nullity, and the service after the death of the pauper must have been considered a good service.

ABBOTT C. J. I am of opinion that the decision of the court of quarter sessions is right. The case of *Rex* v. *St. Mary-le-bone*, at the utmost, only decided that the death of the pauper during the suspension of an order of removal did not make the order void, and that the subsequent order for the payment of costs was a grievance on the parish to which the removal was directed to be made, and therefore that an appeal lay against such an order; but no question arose in that case as to the necessity of serving notice of the order of removal, or of the order suspending it. That question now comes before the Court for the first time. The legislature has not fixed any precise time for that purpose. It is manifest, however, from the 49 *G.* 3. *c.* 124. *s.* 2. that the legislature considered that such an order might be served before the removal; and if a suspended order may be served, and reason and convenience require that it should be served before removal, the service must be within

1824.

The King
against
The Inhabit-
ants of
LAMPETER.

within a reasonable time. I am clearly of opinion that a period of three years having elapsed between the time when the order of removal was made and the death of the pauper, and no notice of the original order, or of the order for the suspension of it, having been given during that period, the order was not served within a reasonable time, and consequently the order of sessions must be confirmed.

BAYLEY J. The decision in *Rex* v. *St. Mary-le-bone* is perfectly consistent with the opinion now delivered by my Lord Chief Justice. In that case, the pauper died before the parish sought to be charged could have had any opportunity of appealing against the order of removal. They were bound to appeal to the next practicable sessions after the order of removal was made. Now the orders of removal and suspension were made on the 3d of *July*, and the pauper died on the 11th of *July*. The 35 G. 3. gave magistrates the power of suspending orders of removal, and gave the costs of such suspension; and it was decided in the case cited, that an order for costs consequent upon such order of removal being suspended, was a grievance to be appealed against within the meaning of the statute 3 *W. & M.* c. 11. s. 9. It is perfectly consistent with that decision to hold that there should not be an indefinite power of delaying the service of the order. It is just, that the parish sought to be charged should have an opportunity of investigating, within a reasonable time, whether they are liable to the burden so sought to be thrown upon them. By the delay of three years, the opportunity of examining the pauper has been lost, and the expence incurred in supporting the pauper may be

thrown

thrown upon a number of persons who were not inhabitants of the parish during that period.

1824.

The King
against
The Inhabit-
ants of
Lampeter.

LITTLEDALE J. concurred.

Order of sessions confirmed.

The KING *against* The Churchwardens and
Overseers of the Poor of CHRIST's Parish in
YORK.

*Wednesday,
November* 17th.

TWO justices made an order for the removal of
 William Huby, Jane, his wife, and Ann, their daughter,
from the township of *Saint Mary Gate*, in the North
Riding of the county of *York*, to *Christ's Parish*, in
the city of *York* ; and, upon appeal, the sessions confirmed that order, subject to the opinion of this Court
on the following case: The father of the pauper was
settled in *Christ's Parish*, and the pauper lived with his
parents till he was about ten years old, when he went to
Mr. *Francis Peacock* for meat and clothes, as long as he
had a mind to stop. *Peacock* then lived at *Craike*, was
a wood-carrier, and had two farms. The pauper was to
do what he could, and what he was bid. He staid
rather more than two years in *Peacock's* service in the
parish of *Craike*, and was supplied with meat and
clothes. The pauper's father did not hire his son to
Peacock, and believed the bargain was only for meat
and clothes. The Court being of opinion that such
service in *Craike* was not sufficient to give the pauper a
settlement there, confirmed the order as aforesaid.

*A. B., at ten
years of age,
went to C. D.
for meat and
clothes as long
as he had a
mind to stop ;
he was to do
what he could,
and what he
was bid. A. B.
remained two
years with C. D.
upon these
terms : Held,
that there was
no yearly hir-
ing, and there-
fore no settle-
ment gained by
the service.*

Tindal, in support of the order of sessions. The
pauper gained no settlement in the parish of *Craike*,
first,

first, because the pauper being an infant of only ten years of age, and the sessions having found that his father was no party to any contract of hiring him to *Peacock*, he cannot be considered as sufficiently sui juris to make any contract capable of giving his master that control over him which must exist between a master and his hired servant. It must be presumed that he was taken into *Peacock's* service from charity, and that is insufficient to give a settlement, *Rex v. Weyhill*. (a) Secondly, the justices must find a contract of hiring, which is not done in the present case, and without which this Court cannot draw the presumption of a hiring, *Rex v. Seacroft*. (b) Thirdly, this was no hiring for a year, but only at the will of the parties, which is insufficient.

Nolan and *Alexander* contrà. First, it is established that an infant may contract without the concurrence of his father if it be for his benefit; and here it is clearly so, because the master engages to supply him with meat and clothes in return for his services, although of an age not exceeding ten years. Nor is the case of *Rex v. Weyhill* any authority for the Court's presuming that he was taken from charity, because there the fact of being so taken was expressly found, whilst here no such finding appears. Secondly, the court of quarter sessions are not required to find a hiring, *Rex v. Chertsey* (c), *Rex v. Worfield*. (d) Cases have occurred where that could not be done, and yet this court has held a settlement to have been gained, *Rex v. Holy Trinity*. (e)

(a) *Burr. S.C.* 491.   (b) *2 M. & S.* 472.
(c) *2 T. R.* 39.   (d) *5 T. R.* 506.
(e) *Cald.* 101.

There

There need not be any stipulation for wages to be paid in money, *Rex* v. *Worfield*. Thirdly, this was a conditional hiring for a year. It was a general hiring which after a year's service is equivalent to an express hiring for a year; and it was subject to a condition that if at any time the pauper should be desirous of quitting the service, he might do so. But no advantage having been taken of that condition, the contract remained at the termination of the service as though no such condition had existed; and a settlement was consequently gained, *Rex* v. *Sidney* (a), *Rex* v. *New Winsor* (b), *Rex* v. *Atherton* (c), *Rex* v. *St. Ebbs* (d), *Rex* v. *Putney* (e), *Rex* v. *Byker*. (f) The power which the pauper had of quitting at any time is only what would have been implied; dict. per Lord *Ellenborough* C. J. in *Rex* v. *Mitcham* (g), and cannot therefore alter the case. The cases that seem to militate against this view of the case are all distinguishable. In *Rex* v. *Elstack* (h) there was an express reservation of weekly wages; and so also in *Rex* v. *Dedham*. (i) In *Rex* v. *Bradninch* (k) there was an agreement to live with the master by the week.

ABBOTT C. J. It must be admitted that a general hiring is a hiring for a year, unless something appear to rebut the presumption. Here the pauper might have

1824.

The King
against
Camwr's
Parish in York.

(a) *Burr. S. C.* 1.   (b) *Burr. S. C.* 19.
(c) *Burr. S. C.* 205.   (d) *Burr. S. C.* 289.
(e) 2 *Bott.* 191. *pl.* 234. (f) 2 *B. & C.* 720.
(g) 12 *East*, 351.   (h) 2 *Bott.* 203. *pl.* 264.
(i) *Burr. S. C.* 655.   (k) *Burr. S. C.* 662.

left at any time, and that completely negatives the idea of there having been a hiring for a year.

BAYLEY J. In *Rex* v. *Trowbridge*, which was decided in 1816, but is not reported, it was held that a hiring "for as long time as the pauper pleased" was a hiring at will, excluded any presumption of a yearly hiring. This is a similar case, and I am therefore of opinion that no settlement was gained under the service stated.

LITTLEDALE J. concurred.

Rule discharged.

Alexander v. Barker 2 C. & Jerv. 133

GARRETT *against* HANDLEY.

Assumpsit that in consideration that plaintiff would advance a sum of money to *A. B.*, defendant promised that provision should be made for repaying the plaintiff. At the trial, it appeared that the defendant had given to the plaintiff the guarantee stated in the declaration and that the latter was a partner with two other persons in a banking house, and that the firm had advanced the money, and charged *A. B.* in account with the same: Held, that the averment in the declaration, that the plaintiff had advanced the money, was not supported by the proof, there being no evidence to shew that the money had been advanced to the plaintiff by the firm, and by him to *A. B.*

ASSUMPSIT upon a guarantee. The first count of the declaration stated that, on the 12th *February* 1818, in consideration that the plaintiff, at the request of the defendant, would advance to one *T. Gibbons* the sum of 550*l.* to enable him to discharge immediately the sum of 550*l.*, for which he had become security for one other *T. Gibbons*, the defendant promised plaintiff that provision should be made for repaying him, the said first-mentioned sum of 550*l.* under a certain arrangement then going on for the settlement of all the concerns of the said first-mentioned *T. Gibbons*. Averment that the plaintiff did immediately after the making of

that

that promise, to wit, on the said 12th *February*, advance and pay, and cause to be advanced and paid, to the said first-mentioned *T. Gibbons* the said sum of 550*l.* for the purpose aforesaid; breach, that defendant had not made provision for the repayment. At the trial before *Abbott* C.J. at the *Middlesex* sittings after last *Hilary* term, the following facts appeared: The plaintiff was a junior partner in the firm of *Bodenham, Phillips,* and *Garrett,* of *Hereford,* bankers. The defendant was an attorney, and in the year 1818, and for some time previously, had been professionally concerned for one *T. Gibbons,* Esq., who had contracted to purchase some landed property of his cousin, a Mr. *T. Gibbons,* but had not paid any part of the purchase-money. The latter being indebted to one *Woodhouse* in a considerable sum of money, prevailed on his cousin *T. Gibbons* Esq. to join him in giving a warrant of attorney to *Woodhouse* for securing the debt due to him. The money not being paid to *Woodhouse* at the time stipulated, he sent an execution to the sheriff of *Herefordshire* against the goods of the two *Gibbonses.* *T. Gibbons* Esq. then applied to the plaintiff *Garrett* to advance him a sum of money to enable him to discharge the execution. The plaintiff agreed to advance it on the defendant's guaranteeing the re-payment, which he consented to do, and on the 2d *February* 1818, addressed the following letter to the plaintiff: " Sir, I understand from Mr. *Gibbons* that you have had the goodness to consent to advance 550*l.* to discharge immediately a like sum for which he became security for his cousin, Mr. *T. Gibbons,* upon my assurance, which I hereby give, that provision shall be made for repaying you this sum under the arrangement now

now going on for the settlement of all Mr. *Gibbons's* concerns." In consequence of the assurance given in this letter the sum necessary to discharge the execution, viz. 574*l.*, was, on the 18th *February* 1818, advanced by *Bodenham* and Co. on account of *T. Gibbons* Esq., by debiting him with that sum, and transferring it to the credit of *W. Pattcshall,* at that time the under-sheriff of *Herefordshire,* in his account with *Budenham* and Co. *T. Gibbons* Esq. had an account with *Bodenham* and Co., and at the time when the guarantee was entered into he owed them 1138*l.*, including the sum of 574*l.*; and this latter sum was charged to *Gibbons,* and it was then carried to a separate account. It was objected by the defendant's counsel, that the money was advanced by the partners, and not by *Garrett* alone on his own individual account, and therefore that the averment in the first count of the declaration was not sustained by the evidence. The Lord Chief Justice directed a nonsuit to be entered, on the ground that the action was brought in the name of *Garrett* only, whereas the money was advanced by *Bodenham* and Co. A rule nisi to set aside the nonsuit, and for granting a new trial, was obtained in last *Easter* term, against which

Jervis and *Tindal* were to have shewed cause; but the Court called upon the

Attorney General and *Campbell* to support the rule. They contended, that as it appeared by the letter of guarantee that *Garrett* had consented to advance the money, and that the guarantee was given to him on the supposition that he was to make the advance, it was therefore fairly to be collected from the evidence that

Bodenham

Bodenham and Co. had lent to their partner, the plaintiff, the money which he had so consented to advance to *Gibbons;* and that he afterwards advanced it, on his own account, in furtherance of that agreement.

ABBOTT C. J. My learned brothers agree with me in opinion that the nonsuit was right. The letter of the defendant is an engagement on his part to be answerable to the plaintiff for an advance of money to be made by him. It is addressed to the plaintiff alone, and takes no notice of his partners. If the plaintiff had borrowed the money of his partners, and had then advanced it to *Gibbons,* it would have been competent for him to have maintained this action. But upon the evidence, the contrary appears to have been the fact. If the plaintiff had borrowed the money of his partners he would have been made debtor to them in the partnership account; but he was not. *Gibbons* was made their debtor in the books, and the sum advanced was entered as an item in the account which previously existed between them and *Gibbons.* That was abundant evidence to shew that the money was lent by the partnership, and not by the plaintiff; and therefore I think that the declaration is not sustained by the proof, and that the nonsuit was right.

Rule discharged.

1824.

GILL *against* CUBITT and Others.

Where a bill
of exchange
was stolen
during the
night, and
taken to the
office of a dis-
count broker
early in the
following
morning by a
person whose
features were
known, but
whose name was
unknown to the
broker, and the
latter being sa-
tisfied with the
name of the
acceptor, dis-
counted the bill,
according to
his usual prac-
tice, without
making any
enquiry of
the person who
brought it;
Held that, in
an action on
the bill by the
broker against
the acceptor,
the jury were
properly direct-
ed to find a
verdict for the
defendant if
they thought
that the plaintiff
had taken the
bill under cir-
cumstances
which ought to
have excited the
suspicion of a
prudent and
careful man;
and they having
found for the defendant, the Court refused to disturb the verdict.

DECLARATION by the plaintiff as indorsee of a
bill of exchange, bearing date the 19th of August
1823, drawn by one *R. Evered* and accepted by the defendants. Plea, general issue. At the trial before
Abbott C. J., at the *London* sittings after *Hilary* term
1824, the plaintiff proved the hand-writing of the acceptors, and indorser. The defendant then proved,
that on the 20th of *August* a letter containing the bill
in question and two others, was inclosed in a parcel
and delivered at the *Green Man and Still* coach office,
and booked for *Birmingham*. The parcel arrived at
Birmingham by the coach, but the letter containing
the bills had been opened, and the bills taken out of it.
On the following day the drawer advertised the loss of
the bills in two newspapers. The plaintiff, who was a
bill broker in *London*, then proved by his nephew, who
assisted him in his business, that the bill was brought
to his office between the hours of nine and ten, on the
morning of the 21st of *August*, by a person having a
respectable appearance, and whose features were familiar
to the witness, but whose name was unknown to him.
He desired that the bill might be discounted for him,
but the witness at first declined so to do, because the
acceptors were not known to him. The person who
brought the bill then said, that a few days before he
had brought other bills to the office, and that if enquiry was made, it would be found that the parties

whose

whose names were on this bill were highly respectable. He then quitted the office and left the bill, and upon enquiry the witness was satisfied with the names of the acceptors. The stranger returned after a lapse of two hours and indorsed the bill in the name of *Charles Taylor*, and received the full value for it, the usual discount and a commission of two shillings being deducted. The witness did not enquire the name of the person who brought the bill, or his address, or whether he brough it on his own account or otherwise, or how he came by the bill. It was the practice in the plaintiff's office not to make any enquiries about the drawer or other parties to a bill, provided the acceptor was good. Upon this evidence the Lord Chief Justice told the jury, that there were two questions for their consideration; first, whether the plaintiff had given value for the bill, of which there could be no doubt; and, secondly, whether he took it under circumstances which ought to have excited the suspicion of a prudent and careful man. If they thought that he had taken the bill under such circumstances, then, notwithstanding he had given the full value for it, they ought to find a verdict for the defendant. Then the Lord Chief Justice, after stating the evidence and commenting upon the practice in the plaintiff's office of discounting bills for any persons whose features were known to him, but whose names and abode were unknown, without asking any questions; asked the jury what they would think if a board were affixed over an office with this notice, " Bills discounted for persons whose features are known, and no questions asked." The jury having found a verdict for the defendants, a rule nisi for a new trial was obtained in *Easter* term last, upon the ground that the plaintiff having paid a valuable consideration for the bill, was entitled to recover its value; and, secondly, that the case had been put too strongly to the jury, when it was compared to the case of a public notice given by a broker that he would discount all bills without asking questions.

Scarlett and *Parke* now shewed cause. Where a bill or note has been acquired by theft, and afterwards comes to the possession of a holder for valuable consideration, it is incumbent upon him when he brings an action, not only to shew that he paid that consideration, but also that he used due diligence to ascertain, before he took the bill or note, whether the party bringing it to him came by it honestly. Unless he does this he cannot be said to have taken it bonâ fide, although he may have paid the full value for it. It is true, that in *Lawson* v. *Weston* (a), Lord *Kenyon* was of opinion, that it was sufficient for a person who discounted such a bill, to shew that he paid value for it, but the propriety of that decision has always been doubted. If it is to be laid down as a rule, that a party in possession of a stolen bill or note may obtain the value of it without being subjected to any enquiry, it will give a great facility to the disposal of property so acquired, and operate as an encouragement to fraud and theft. It is desirable that the rule laid down should have the effect of preventing parties, who are either guilty or cognizant of such fraud, from profiting by it. Then if that be the correct rule upon the subject, the Lord Chief Justice was well war-ranted in the observations he made to the jury, and their verdict is supported by the evidence. The plaintiff

(a) 4 *Esp.* 56.

took

took the bill from a person whose features were known to him, but of whom he knew nothing else, and made no enquiry as to how he came by the bill; and it was in evidence that he always conducted his business in this mode. Surely that is like the case of a person giving a public notice, " Bills discounted for persons whose features are known, and no questions asked."

Gurney and *F. Pollock*, contrà. A party who has paid the full value for a bill which has been lost or stolen, is entitled to recover the amount from the acceptor. The circulation of negotiable paper would be greatly impeded if it were laid down as a rule, that a party discounting a bill was bound to investigate the title of the person from whom he receives it. In the case of *Lawson* v. *Weston* (a), the plaintiffs, who were bankers, had discounted the bill in the usual course of their business for a person who brought it to their shop, but who was unknown to them. It was contended by the defendant, that although a person might pay a bill, to which he was a party, to one who had come dishonestly by it, by reason of the personal liability attached to his name on the bill, a banker or any other should not discount a bill for a person unknown without using due diligence to enquire into the circumstances, as well respecting the bill as of the person who offered to discount it. But Lord *Kenyon* said, that to adopt the principle of the defence to the full extent stated, would be at once to paralize the circulation of all the paper in the country, and with it all its commerce. The circumstance of the bill having been lost, might have been material if they

(a) 4 *Esp.* 56.

H h 3

could

could bring knowledge of that fact home to the·plaintiffs. They might or might not have seen the advertisement and it would be going great length to say, that a banker was bound to make enquiry concerning every ·bill brought to him to discount, it· would apply as well to a bill for 10*l.* as for 10,000*l.*" In that case, therefore, the very point now raised was made and overruled by Lord *Kenyon,* and although the bill was of the amount of 500*l.*, the parties acquiesced in that decision. The principle acted upon in that case had been previously adopted in *Miller* v. *Race* (*a*), *Grant* v. *Vaughan* (*b*), and *Peacock* v. *Rhodes.* (*c*)   At all events, the· case was put too strongly to the jury by my Lord Chief Justice. It was not·like the case of a public notice, ·that all bills would· be discounted for persons whose features were known, and no questions would be asked.   That mode of putting it excited an undue prejudice against the plaintiff, and the case ought to be submitted to a second jury.

ABBOTT C. J.   If we thought that, upon reconsideration of the evidence, another jury ought to come.to a different conclusion,· we would send the case down to another trial.   But being of opinion, that the proper conclusion has been drawn from the evidence, we think that this rule ought to be discharged.   I. agree with the counsel for the plaintiff, that this case is hardly distinguishable from *Lawson* v. *Weston.* .If there is any distinction it is, that in this case the plaintiff's clerk said it was not usual with the plaintiff to ask any questions, or to make any enquiry if bills were brought

. (*a*) 1 *Burr.* 452.   (*b*) 3 *Burr.* 1516.   (*c*) *Doug.* 611.

to

1824.

Gray
city
against
Cooper.

to them, by persons whose features they supposed themselves to be, acquainted with, provided they were satisfied with the names of the acceptors. I cannot help thinking, that if Lord *Kenyon* had anticipated the consequences which have followed from the rule laid down by him in *Lawson* v. *Weston*, he would have paused before he pronounced that decision. Since the decision of that case, the practice of robbing stage-coaches and other conveyances of securities of this kind, has been very considerable. I cannot forbear thinking, that that practice has received encouragement by the rule laid down in *Lawson* v. *Weston*, by which a facility has been given to the disposal of stolen property of this description. I should be sorry if I were to say any thing, sitting in the seat of judgment, that either might have the effect, or reasonably be supposed to have the effect of impeding the commerce of the country by preventing the due and easy circulation of paper. But I am decidedly of opinion, that no injury will be done to the interests of commerce, by a decision that the plaintiff cannot recover in this action. It appears to me to be for the interest of commerce, that no person should take a security of this kind from another without using reasonable caution. If he take such security from a person whom he knows, and whom he can find out, no complaint can be made of him. In that case he has done all any person could do. But if it is to be laid down as the law of the land, that a person may take a security of this kind from a man of whom he knows nothing, and of whom he makes no enquiry at all, it appears to me that such a decision would be more injurious to commerce than convenient for it, by reason of the encouragement it would afford to the purloining,

stealing,

stealing, and defrauding persons of securities of this sort. The interest of commerce requires that *bonâ fide* and real holders of bills, known to be such by those with whom they are dealing, should have no difficulties thrown in their way in parting with them. But it is not for the interest of commerce that any individual should be enabled to dispose of bills or notes without being subject to enquiry. I think the sooner it is known that the case of *Lawson* v. *Weston* is doubted, at least by this Court, the better. I wish doubts had been cast on that case at an earlier time. If that had been done, this plaintiff probably would not have suffered. Coming to the facts of this case, they are these, that the young man, acting according to the course which the plaintiff when he was present followed, gave money for this bill to a person of whom, though he supposed he knew him, he really knew nothing. This is done at a very early hour, between nine and ten in the morning on the day after the bill was lost. I cannot help saying that that practice, in the plaintiff's business of a bill broker, is a practice inconvenient for the reasons I have already given. It seems to me, that it is a great encouragement to fraud, and it is the duty of the court to lay down such rules as will tend to prevent fraud and robbery, and not give encouragement to them. For these reasons, notwithstanding all the unfeigned reverence I feel for every thing that fell from Lord *Kenyon*, by whom *Lawson* v. *Weston* was decided, I cannot think the view taken by that learned lord at that time was a correct one; and that being so, I am of opinion that this rule ought to be discharged.

BAYLEY

1824.
Gill
against
Cuart.

BAYLEY J. I agree that the way in which my Lord Chief Justice put this case for the consideration of the jury, by asking what would be the case if a man were to put over his shop, " Bills discounted for strangers, if they have good names on them, without any questions being asked," was a very strong way of putting the case for their consideration. But I think it was no more than the facts of this case warranted, and that he was putting as a general proposition, that which exactly squared with the particular facts of this case. If a man commonly dealt in that way, (and it appeared to be the plaintiff's habit as a broker,) it would warrant such an advertisement as that which was described. If in general that was not the plaintiff's course and habit, then in this particular instance he deviated from his general course. In this case a party goes to a shop between nine and ten in the morning to get a bill discounted, the clerk does not know his name; he thinks he knows his features; he does not know where he lives; he knows nothing at all about him. The bill is left for two hours, and at the expiration of that time the party comes back again; and the clerk then has the opportunity of asking names, and whether he came on his own account, or from any and what house. No question of that description is put to him. Under these circumstances, I think it was the duty of my Lord Chief Justice to put it to the consideration of the jury whether there was due caution used by that party in that particular instance. If there was not due caution used, the plaintiff has not discounted this bill in the usual and ordinary course of business, or in that way in which business properly and rightly conducted would have required. But it is said that

that the question usually submitted for the consideration of the jury, in cases of this description, up to the period of time at which my Lord Chief Justice's direction was given, has been whether the bill was taken bonâ fide, and whether a valuable consideration was given for it. I admit that has been generally the case; but I consider it was parcel of the bona fides whether the plaintiff had asked all those questions which, in the ordinary and proper manner in which trade is conducted, a party ought to ask. I think from the manner in which my Lord Chief Justice presented this case to the consideration of the jury, he put it as being part and parcel of the bona fides; and it has been so put in former cases. In the case of *Miller* v. *Race*, 1 Burr., Lord *Mansfield* says: " Here an innkeeper took the note bonâ fide in his business from a person who made the appearance of a gentleman. Here is no pretence or suspicion of collusion with the robber. For this matter was strictly inquired and examined into at the trial; and is so stated in the case that he took it for a full and valuable consideration, in *the usual course of business.* Indeed if there had been any collusion, or any circumstance of unfair dealing, the case had been much otherwise." Now, the question which my Lord Chief Justice has put to the consideration of the jury, whether a party uses due caution or not, is, in other words, putting to them, whether he took it in the usual course of business; for the course of business must require, in the usual and ordinary manner of conducting it, a proper and reasonable degree of caution necessary to preserve the interest of trade. The next case, in order of time, is *Grant* v. *Vaughan.* Mr. Justice *Wilmott* there says:

says: " The note appears to have been taken by him fairly and bonâ fide in *the course of trade*, and even with the greatest caution. He made inquiry about it, and then gave the change for it; and there is not the least imputation or pretence of suspicion that he had any notice of its being a lost note." That learned judge did not consider the question of bona fides to be merely whether the note was taken by a party without having any real suspicion in his own mind, but whether he had taken it in the usual course of trade, and with caution. In *Peacock* v. *Rhodes*, a shopkeeper at *Scarborough* took from a perfect stranger a bill of exchange. The latter bought certain goods in the way of the plaintiff's trade. Lord *Mansfield* says: " The question of *mala fides* was for the consideration of the jury. The circumstance that the buyers and the drawers were strangers to the plaintiff, and that he took the bill for goods on which he had a profit, were grounds of suspicion very fit for their consideration. But they have considered them, and have found it was received in the *course of trade*, and therefore the case is clear." Then if in that case those were questions fit for the consideration of a jury, as part and parcel of the question of bona fides, is it not also a fit and proper question for their consideration, (when the point to be decided is whether a man has acted bona fide or not,) whether he has inquired with that degree of caution which, in the ordinary course of trade, a prudent trader ought to use. That was the question propounded by my Lord Chief Justice in his direction to the jury; and they have exercised their judgment on it. I think the question was a fit question for their decision, and I think their

decision

1821.

Gurr
against
Curry.

decision was one with which we are not at liberty to quarrel. On the contrary, it appears to me to be material for the interests of trade, to lay down as a rule that a party cannot in law be considered to act bonâ fide, or with due caution and due diligence, if he takes a bill of exchange from a person whose features alone he knows, without knowing what his name is, where he lives, or whether he is a person with whom he has been in the habit of trading. If we were to say that in this instance there had been due caution, it would certainly be giving a great facility to the disposal of bills of exchange which have been lost or stolen, by persons who have found or dishonestly obtained them. For these reasons it appears to me that my Lord Chief Justice took the right view of this case; that it was consistent with the doctrine laid down in former cases; and that the decision of the jury was warranted by the evidence.

HOLROYD J. I think the rule was correctly laid down to the jury by my Lord Chief Justice, and that there is no ground for granting a new trial. A party who discounts a bill which has been stolen is bound to shew, not only that a good consideration was really and bonâ fide given for the bill (although that of itself would tend to the establishing of the other point requisite for him to shew), but he must also make it appear to the satisfaction of a jury that he actually took it bona fide. If he takes it with a view to profit arising from interest or commission, under circumstances affording reasonable ground of suspicion, without inquiring whether the party of whom he takes it came by it honestly

or

or not, or if he takes it merely because it is drawn
upon a good acceptor, then he takes it at a risk (or
what ought, in the contemplation of a reasonable man,
to be a risk), whether the bill be stolen or not: he
takes it at his peril. I cannot agree with the doctrine
laid down in *Lawson* v. *Weston*. The question whether
a bill or note has been taken bonâ fide involves in
it the question whether it has been taken with due
caution. It is a question of fact for the jury, under
all the circumstances of the case, whether a bill has
been taken bonâ fide or not; and whether due and
reasonable caution has been used by the person taking
it. And if a bill be drawn upon parties of respect-
ability capable of answering it, and another person
discounts it merely because the acceptance is good,
without using due caution, and without inquiring how
the holder came by it, I think that the law will not,
under such circumstances, assist the parties so taking
the bill, in recovering the money. If the bill be taken
without using due means to ascertain that it has been
honestly come by, the party, so taking on himself the
risk for gain, must take the consequence if it should turn
out that it was not honestly acquired by the person of
whom he received it. Here the person in possession of
the bill was a perfect stranger to the plaintiff, and he
discounted it, and made no inquiry of whom the bill
had been obtained, or to whom he was to apply if the bill
should not be taken up by the acceptor. I think those
circumstances tend strongly to shew that the party who
discounted the bill did not choose to make inquiry, but
supposing the questions might not be satisfactorily
answered, rather than refuse to take the bill, took the
risk in order to get the profit arising from commission
and

and interest. I am therefore of opinion that the direction of my Lord Chief Justice to the jury was correct in point of law, that they have drawn the proper conclusion, and that there is no ground for granting a new trial.

Rule discharged.

HAMERTON *against* STEAD.

TRESPASS for breaking and entering a mill, dwelling-house, and close of plaintiff, ejecting him therefrom, and keeping him out of possession for a long space of time. Plea, liberum tenementum. Replication, that before the said time when, &c., to wit, on, &c., defendant demised the premises to plaintiff, as tenant from year to year, by virtue of which demise plaintiff entered, and was possessed of the premises, and continued so possessed until and at the said time when, &c. Rejoinder, that after the making of the said demise in the replication-mentioned, and before the said time when, &c., the said tenancy, and the estate and interest of the plaintiff in the demised premises, in which, &c., wholly ended and determined. Surrejoinder, that the tenancy, &c., did not end and determine in manner and form alleged in the rejoinder. At the trial before *Garrow* B. at the last Spring assizes for *Salop*, it appeared that on the 1st of *May* 1810, the premises in question were demised by the defendant to the plaintiff, as tenant from year to year, and he continued so to hold them until the 25th of *September* 1815, when notice was given to him to quit on the 1st of *May* then next. On the 10th of *October* 1815,

by

by an agreement in writing, made between the defendant
of the one part, and the plaintiff and one *Moore* of the
other part, defendant agreed to let and demise unto
plaintiff and *Moore* the premises in question, to hold
them unto plaintiff and *Moore* from the 1st of *November*
then next, for seven years thence next ensuing, at a
yearly rent of 159*l*., payable half yearly on the 1st of
May and 1st of *November*.   Plaintiff and *Moore* thereby
agreed to pay the rent and all taxes, except the landlord's property tax; and defendant agreed to put all the
premises in tenantable repair as soon as conveniency
would permit.   And the plaintiff and *Moore* further
agreed to keep the premises in repair, and leave them
so at the end of the term; and lastly, it was further
agreed that a lease should be forthwith drawn, in which
the usual covenants were to be inserted, and particularly
that the lessees should not let, set, or assign the premises, or any part thereof, without the lessor's consent
in writing.   The lessees took possession under this
agreement, and *Moore* continued to occupy the premises
jointly with *Hamerton* until *April* 1816, and then quitted.
In *June* the same year, defendant not being able to get
any rent, a negociation was entered into respecting the
surrender of the premises, but that proved fruitless; and
defendant having obtained the keys, took and retained
possession of the mill and other premises.   For the defendant it was objected that the new agreement in *October* 1816 was a lease, and put an end to the original
tenancy of the plaintiff; or, at all events, if it was only
an agreement for a lease, yet that the agreement, together with the fact of *Moore's* having been let into possession, by virtue of it, as a joint occupier with the
plaintiff, worked a surrender in law of the old tenancy.
                                                      The

The learned Judge reserved the point, and a verdict having been found for the plaintiff, a rule to enter a nonsuit was obtained in Easter term; and now

W. E. Taunton shewed cause. The issue on the pleadings certainly was, whether the tenancy of the plaintiff had or had not determined at the time when the alleged trespass was committed. There was no actual surrender of his interest, nor was there a surrender in law. The instrument dated on the 30th of October 1815 was not a lease, but merely an executory agreement for a lease, and a subsisting tenancy is not put an end to by such an agreement for a new tenancy, *Roe* v. *Archbishop of York.* (a) It is unnecessary to state particularly the various cases on this point, such as *Goodtitle* v. *Way* (b), *Doe* v. *Clare* (c), *Tempest* v. *Rawlings* (d), *Roe* v. *Ashburner* (e), *Doe* v. *Smith* (f), and *Dunk* v. *Hunter* (g), the principle resulting from them is, that where an agreement to let is entered into, but it appears to have been the intent of the parties that something further should be done to insure the interests of either party, such an instrument is not a present lease, but a mere contract for a lease to be granted in future. Here, it is plain that the lessor intended to reserve a right of re-entry if the tenants assigned without leave in writing; but the instrument before the Court would not give that right. The lease was, moreover, to contain the usual covenants, and they are not inserted in the agreement.

(a) 6 East, 86.　　　　(b) 1 T. R. 732.
(c) 2 T. R. 739.　　　 (d) 13 East, 18.
(e) 5 T. R. 163.　　　 (f) 6 East, 530.
(g) 5 B. & A. 322.

Campbell

Campbell (with whom was *Oldnall Russell*), contrà. The old tenancy of the plaintiff had determined by surrender before the time when the alleged trespass was committed. If the instrument executed on the 10th of *October* 1816 be a lease, then there is no doubt that the acceptance of it amounted to a surrender of the plaintiff's former interest. Now, by that instrument a present interest passed, or at all events an interest from the 1st of *November* following, and wherever an instrument gives a right to the possession and profits of land it is a lease. It is said that it does not contain the usual covenants, but the agreement to pay rent and taxes and to repair, are the usual covenants in such leases. The clause at the end respecting the making of a lease, does not prevent the original instrument from operating as a lease if such was the intent of the parties. [*Bayley* J. It contains a stipulation, that the defendant should put the premises in repair as soon as convenience would allow, might it not have been a sufficient ground for afterwards refusing to accept the lease, that the premises had not been repaired?] Then supposing it to be only an agreement for a lease, yet the effect of that, coupled with the fact of possession having been taken by *Moore* together with the plaintiff, was to determine the former tenancy and operate as a surrender. (He was then stopped by the Court.)

Abbott C. J. In *Roe* v. *The Archbishop of York*, the occupation by virtue of the new lease took place under a mistaken idea, that it was a good and valid lease; and when that was discovered to be void, the Court very properly held that it should not operate as a surrender

of

of the former lease. Here, there is nothing to shew that the defendant refused to grant such a lease as was contracted for; and we find, in fact, that a new contract was made to let the premises to two persons instead of one, and that both entered and occupied. The lessor might then have sued both for the rent, although no distress could have been made. It frequently happens, that persons enter and occupy at a rent to be fixed in future. In such cases no distress can be made, but an action may be brought for the rent on a quantum valebat. It seems to me, therefore, that in the present case the old tenancy was determined, and a new joint tenancy by the plaintiff and *Moore* created by that which was done under the agreement with the plaintiff's concurrence.

BAYLEY J. It is clear since the passing of the statute of frauds, that a subsisting term cannot be surrendered unless by writing or by operation of law. But if a sole tenant agrees to occupy, and does occupy jointly with another, that puts an end to the former sole tenancy. The case of *Roe* v. *The Archbishop of York* does not apply to this case, for here the agreement connected with the joint occupation by *Moore* and the plaintiff, made them both tenants and therefore operated as a surrender of the separate tenancy of the latter.

HOLROYD J. I think that an agreement for a fresh lease would not put an end to a former tenancy, unless a new tenancy were actually created. But taking the document in question not to amount to a lease, yet the entry and holding by *Moore* and the plaintiff together under it, created a new tenancy either from year to

year

year or at will; and that, according to *Mellow* v. *May* (a), would terminate the old holding. Perhaps, until a lease was executed, it might not be considered that the two held at the rent mentioned in the agreement, but still it might be a holding under the agreement. For, as was said by my Lord Chief Justice, there might be an occupation on a quantum valebat until the execution of the lease, and although no distress for rent could be made, yet still a tenancy would exist. For these reasons it appears to me, that the sole tenancy of the plaintiff had terminated, and that a nonsuit must be entered.

LITTLEDALE J. I am of opinion that the former tenancy of the plaintiff was put an end to by the agreement for a new lease, and the occupation by *Moore* and the plaintiff jointly in pursuance of that agreement. It is unnecessary to say, whether the instrument in question is or is not a lease, for where parties enter under a mere agreement for a future lease they are tenants at will; and if rent is paid under the agreement, they become tenants from year to year, determinable on the execution of the lease contracted for, that being the primary contract. But if no rent is paid, still before the execution of a lease the relation of landlord and tenant exists, the parties having entered with a view to a lease and not a purchase. I therefore concur in thinking that a nonsuit must be entered.

Rule absolute.

(a) *Moore,* 656.

The KING *against* The Inhabitants of GREAT
· WIGSTON in the County of LEICESTER. ·

An infant
bound himself
apprentice for
seven years,
and served
three of them;
having then
quarrelled with
his master, the
latter offered to
sell him the re-
mainder of his
time for 6d.
The infant paid
the money, and
went away and
bound himself
to another mas-
ter in another
parish: Held,
that the infant
had no power
to dissolve the
first apprentice-
ship; the se-
cond binding
was therefore
invalid, and no
settlement
could be gained
by service
under it.

BY order dated the 3d day of *February* 1823, *John
Stanyan*, his wife *Mary*, and their child *Olive*, were
directed to be removed from the parish of *Saint Margaret*, in the borough of *Leicester*, to the parish of
Great Wigston in *Leicestershire*. On appeal the sessions
confirmed the order, subject to the opinion of this court
on the following case. The pauper, when he was eleven
years of age, was bound apprentice to *John Humberston*,
of the parish of *Great Wigston*, for the term of seven
years. The indenture was executed by the master, the
pauper, and *John Bullivant*, the grandfather of the
pauper, the pauper's father being a soldier abroad. The
grandfather paid a premium of 7*l.* to *Humberston*. The
pauper served *Humberston* under this indenture for
between three and four years at *Wigston*, when some
disagreement taking place between them, *Humberston*
agreed to sell the pauper the remainder of his time for 6*d.*
The pauper accordingly paid *Humberston* the 6*d.*, and
left him on the same day. The indenture had never
been in the possession of any of the parties, but had
been kept for all the parties, by the person who prepared it, and no application was made for it to be
delivered up. The grandfather was not a party to the
agreement for parting entered into between the pauper
and his master, and was not even privy to it. A few
days after the pauper left *Humberston* he bound himself
apprentice to *Thomas Waine*, of the parish of *Saint
Mary*,

Mary, in the borough of *Leicester*, for seven years, and served him under the indenture for five years, and resided during the whole of that time in that parish.

Phillipps and *Humfrey* in support of the order of sessions. The second binding was bad, for there was no legal termination of the first apprenticeship. It was by deed and could not be dissolved by parol, *Rex* v. *Bow.* (a) *Rex* v. *Skeffington.* (b) One of the parties to the binding, viz. the grandfather, was not a party even to the parol agreement to dissolve it. *Rex* v. *Austrey* (c) shews that all must join. The dissolution was by an infant, who is incapable of making a bargain to his prejudice. Here the dissolution must be taken to have been prejudicial to him; the case is therefore very different from *Rex* v. *Mountsorrel.* (d) The second binding being invalid, the pauper could not gain a settlement by the service under it, and was properly removed to the place where he served under the first binding.

Marriott and *Simons* contrà. *Rex* v. *Mountsorrel* is directly in point. There the dissolution was by parol, and by an infant apprentice. *Rex* v. *Skeffington* was decided on the ground that the binding was originally invalid, and no agreement was there made for the dissolution of the apprenticeship. *Rex* v. *Austrey* was the case of a parish apprentice who was no party to the deed, it was therefore clear that he had no power to dissolve the contract. The grandfather here had no right to interfere, the father of the apprentice being alive.

(a) 4 *M. & S.* 585.   (b) 3 *B. & A.* 382.
(c) *Burr. S. C.* 441.   (d) 5 *M. & S.* 497.

I i 3   ABBOTT

ABBOTT C. J. I am of opinion that the order of sessions was right. It is a general rule of law that an infant cannot do any act to bind himself unless it be manifestly for his benefit. Binding himself an apprentice has been considered such an act, and therefore it has been held that an infant is competent to make such a contract. If then it is for the benefit of the infant to bind himself an apprentice, it is impossible to say generally, that it is for his benefit to dissolve such a connexion; such a position involves a contradiction. That being the general rule, we must inquire whether in the particular instance it is for the advantage of the infant to dissolve his apprenticeship. In the case of *Rex* v. *Mountsorrel*, the master had absconded, and the infant could no longer derive instruction or support from him. Under those circumstances the Court thought that the dissolution of the relation of master and apprentice was beneficial to the latter, for unless that had been done the apprentice must have remained unemployed and uninstructed. Here no facts are stated whence we can infer that it was for the infant's benefit to put an end to the apprenticeship; this case therefore falls within the general rule, and the first binding not being dissolved, the second was necessarily invalid, and the service under it could not confer a settlement.

BAYLEY J. The decision of the court of quarter sessions upon this point was perfectly correct. The only error that they have committed was in sending for our opinion a case upon which no reasonable doubt could be entertained.

HOLROYD J. concurred.

Order of sessions confirmed.

The King *against* The Inhabitants of LUTTER-WORTH.

UPON an appeal against an order of two justices for the removal of *Mary Hickley*, wife of *William Hickley*, a soldier, and their son *Francis*, aged six months, from the parish of *Lutterworth* to the parish of *Huncote*, both in the county of *Leicester*, the sessions quashed the order, subject to the opinion of this court on the following case: *William Hickley*, a poor child of the parish of *Broughton Astley*, was bound apprentice by the churchwardens and overseers of that parish, with consent of two magistrates, by indenture dated 19th *January* 1807, to *Benjamin Elliott*, of *Huncote*; and he served him in *Huncote* under that indenture for the term of his apprenticeship. At the time when the pauper was bound out the parish of *Broughton Astley* formed part of the incorporation of the house of industry at *Ullesthorpe*, in the said county, under the provisions of the 22 G. 3. c. 83. *George Lakin* was appointed guardian of the poor of *Broughton Astley* at Easter 1803, by two magistrates. That appointment is in existence; but though *George Lakin* continued to act as guardian for *Broughton Astley* for several years afterwards, and was acting in that capacity at the time the boy was bound out, he was not made a party to the indenture, nor can any subsequent appointment be found.

Marriott and *Simons*, in support of the order of sessions. The indenture of apprenticeship in this case

Where a parish has united with others for the support of the poor according to the provisions of the 22 G. 3. c. 83., and a guardian has been appointed, the churchwardens and overseers may nevertheless bind poor children apprentices, and it is not necessary that the guardian should sign the indentures.

was

was invalid for want of the signature of the guardian of the poor. That signature is made necessary by the 72 G. 3. c. 83. By the seventh section of that act every guardian of the poor is invested with " all the powers and authorities given to overseers of the poor by any other act or acts of parliament, and shall to all intents and purposes, except with regard to the making and collecting of rates, be an overseer of the poor for the parish or township for which he shall be so appointed guardian." After pointing out certain acts to be done by the guardian, that section proceeds to enact, that in all cases where such guardian of the poor shall be appointed as aforesaid, neither the churchwardens or overseers of the poor shall interfere or intermeddle in the care and management of the poor." In this parish a guardian had been appointed in 1803, and as he continued to act as such, it must be presumed that he was regularly re-appointed down to the time when the pauper was bound; it was not therefore competent to the churchwardens and overseers to interfere, and bind the pauper as an apprentice. The 20 G. 3. c. 36. is to be kept in view in deciding this case. It enacts "that where guardians of the poor are appointed, persons to whom any poor children are bound apprentices shall receive them according to the indentures to be executed by the directors and acting guardians of the poor for the binding of such poor children, in like manner as persons are now obliged by the laws in being to receive and provide for poor children appointed to be bound apprentices by churchwardens and overseers of the poor, with the assent of two justices." The thirtieth section of the 22 G. 3. c. 83. provides for the support of poor children until they are of sufficient age to be bound

appren-

apprentices, and enacts that when they arrive at such age, they shall be so placed out at the expence of the parish to which they belong, " according to the laws in being." Now the 28 G. 3. c. 86. was a law then in being, made for the purpose of compelling persons to receive apprentices bound out by guardians of the poor; and that provides for binding by the guardians, and not by the overseers.

Phillipps and *Humfrey* contrà.   It does not distinctly appear by the case that there was a guardian of the poor appointed for the parish to which the pauper belonged at the time of the binding.   That should have been made quite clear, as this is an attempt to defeat a settlement.   But even supposing that there was a guardian, still he was not the proper person, or, at all events, not the only person capable of binding poor children apprentices.   There is not any clause in the 22 G. 3. c. 83. making it necessary for the guardian to sign the indentures.   That statute points out several things which the guardians must do, but does not specify the binding of apprentices.   It is true that the seventh section gives them all the powers which belong to overseers of the poor; that may enable them to bind apprentices, but does not take away the jurisdiction of the overseers.   The latter part of the section which says that the churchwardens and overseers shall not interfere where there are guardians, applies only to the "care and management of the poor," and not to binding apprentices.   If any doubt existed as to the meaning of that section, it would be removed by section 30., which says that where guardians are appointed they shall provide for poor children until they arrive at a sufficient

age

1821.
———
The King
against
The Inhabit-
ants of
Lutterworth.

age to be put into service; and that then they shall be placed out according " to the laws in being;" not " according to this act." The 43 *Eliz. c. 2.* was the law in being relating to and, except in some particular cases, regulating the binding of apprentices; and the pauper was bound according to that law; it was therefore a valid binding, and he gained a settlement by the service under it.

ABBOTT C. J. I am of opinion that the binding stated in this case was a valid binding, and that the pauper, by serving under it, gained a settlement in *Hincote.* The seventh section of the 22 *G. 3. c. 83.* is calculated to raise a doubt upon the point, for it excludes the interference of the churchwardens and overseers in the care and management of the poor where guardians are appointed. If there were nothing else in the act to guide us, it might be difficult to say that they could interfere in binding parish apprentices. But in subsequent parts of that statute various powers are expressly given to guardians of the poor, and by the thirtieth section they are authorised to provide for poor children until they arrive at a proper age to be placed out, when they are to be bound out according to the laws then existing. One of these laws was the 43 *Eliz. c. 2,* directing that parish apprentices shall be bound out by the churchwardens and overseers of the poor. And it is better that a binding should take place by several churchwardens and overseers, than by a single guardian of the poor.

BAYLEY and HOLROYD Js. concurred.

Order of sessions quashed.

KEENE *against* DEEBLE.

ASSUMPSIT for goods sold and delivered. The defendant was held to bail for 28*l.*, and paid 2*l.* into Court. The cause was entered for trial, but before it was called on, the cause and all matters in difference were referred to a barrister, with power to examine the parties, and call for books, &c. The costs of the cause and reference to abide the event. The arbitrator awarded to the plaintiff 1*l.* 19*s.* in addition to the 2*l.* paid into court. A rule was afterwards obtained to tax the costs for the defendant under the 43 G. 3. c. 46. s. 3.

Rolland shewed cause. The defendant having paid money into Court, cannot claim the benefit of that statute, *Butler* v. *Brown* (a), *Davey* v. *Renton* (b). The money must be recovered by verdict, or at all events by judgment of the Court, in order to bring the case within the statute. Besides, this was not a reference of the cause alone, but of all matters in difference, and the costs were to abide the event; that is the legal event of the award, not the event of a subsequent application to this Court.

Crowder, contrà. In *Butler* v. *Brown* and *Davey* v. *Renton*, the plaintiff took out the money which had been paid into Court, and so the cause ended. It has never been decided, that a defendant by paying money into

---

Where a defendant was arrested and holden to special bail for 28*l.*, and paid 2*l.* into court, and afterwards the cause, before it came on for trial, and all matters in difference were referred to an arbitrator, who had power to examine the parties, and call for books, &c., and it was agreed that the costs should abide the event, the arbitrator having awarded to the plaintiff the sum of 1*l.* 19*s.*, a motion was made to allow the defendant his costs: Held, that this was not a case within the 43 G. 3. c. 46. s. 3., and that the defendant was not entitled to costs.

(a) 1 B. & B. 66.   (b) 2 B. & C. 711.

Court

Court loses the benefit of the 43 G. 3. c. 46. s. 3., unless the plaintiff consents to accept it and put an end to the suit. Nor does it make any difference that the cause was referred, *Neal* v. *Porter* (a), *Burns* v. *Palmer*. (b) [*Bayley* J. In those cases a verdict was taken, upon which judgment was afterwards entered, the money was therefore recovered in the action.] In *Robinson* v. *Bloam* (c), there was merely a reference to the master, and no verdict or judgment. In *Payne* v. *Acton* (d), the verdict was taken subject to a reference, and there *Dallas* C. J. refused a rule, to tax the defendant's costs, on the merits, and not on the ground that it could not be done after a reference.

ABBOTT C. J. Upon an attentive perusal of the act in question, I am of opinion that this case does not come within its meaning. It is manifest that the legislature contemplated a recovery by verdict, whereupon judgment should afterwards be entered. The words are, "in all actions to be brought in *England* or *Ireland* wherein the defendant shall be arrested and held to special bail, and wherein the plaintiff shall not recover the amount of the sum for which the defendant in such actions shall have been so arrested and held to special bail, such defendants shall be entitled to costs of suit, to be taxed according to the custom of the Court, provided it shall appear to the satisfaction of the Court that the arrest was without reasonable or probable cause." In all the cases cited for the defendant where costs were given to the defendant after the cause had been referred, the awards were made under references at Nisi Prius; in each

(a) *Tidd's Pr.* 1018. sixth edit.   (b) *Tidd's Pr.* 1018.
(c) 5 B. & A. 661.   (d) 1 B. & B. 278.

of

1824

Kirk
against
Dibble

of them, a verdict was taken, and then the arbitrator was, mately substituted for the jury, in fixing the amount for; which judgment was to be entered. *Robinson* v. *Elsam* was not a case of that description, it was an action by an attorney suing for the amount of his bill, and the Court ordered it to be referred to the master by virtue of a power vested in them, which is very different from a reference by consent of the parties. In the present case the cause was stopped in its progress, by an agreement to refer all matters in difference, and it was made a part of the rule that the costs should abide the event of the award. I am of opinion, that money awarded on such a reference is not money *recovered* within the meaning of the act, and that this rule must be discharged.

BAYLEY J. I think that the money awarded in this case cannot be considered as money recovered in the action. It was awarded upon a reference of the action and all matters in difference. The parties might have made a special provision for the costs, but by the rule they agreed that they should abide the event of the award.

HOLROYD J. concurred.

LITTLEDALE J. I think that the word *recovered* as used in this statute bears the technical legal sense, recovered by the consideration and judgment of the Court. This is made plain by the subsequent part of the clause, for after providing for the taxation of costs, it goes on to direct how execution shall issue. " And the plaintiff. shall, upon such rule or order being made as aforesaid, be disabled from taking out any execution for the sum
recovered

recovered in any such action, unless the same shall exceed, and then in such sum only as the same shall exceed, the amount of the taxed costs of the defendant in such action." I am not prepared to say, that a sum recovered by judgment entered up in pursuance of a reference after verdict is not within the act. But here, the cause was referred before it came on for trial. Not only the cause, but all matters in difference were referred, and the arbitrator had power to examine the parties and call for their books. Not only were different matters put under investigation, but a different mode of proceeding was allowed, and different media of proof were rendered admissible by such an agreement. At the trial the defendant's evidence could not have been received; before the arbitrator it was admissible, and might possibly operate to reduce the plaintiff's damages. When, therefore, parties by their agreement take a cause out of the ordinary course of investigation, I think that they take it out of the operation of the statute. It was farther agreed that the costs should abide the event; that, as it appears to me, means the legal event, following in ordinary cases without the interposition of the Court. But it is not necessary to give any decided opinion as to that; upon the other grounds I am satisfied that this rule ought to be discharged.

Rule discharged.

la Cokeam . Kila 2 Cotton 191

LANG and Others *against* ANDERDON.

ASSUMPSIT on a policy of assurance, on goods by ship or ships at and from *Demerara* to *London*, warranted to sail from *Demerara* on or before the 1st of *August* 1823. Plea, non-assumpsit. At the trial before *Abbott* C. J., at the *London* sittings after last *Hilary* term, the following facts were given in evidence. Goods covered by the policy were loaded on board the snow *Iris*, burthen 200 tons, in the river at *Demerara*, opposite the town. Vessels of the size of the *Iris* always take in their cargoes near the same place, and clear out there. The mouth of the river is about two miles below the town, and there is a shoal which commences about three miles further out, and extends for six miles. Large vessels take in part of their cargo in the river, then go to the outside of the shoal, and complete their loading. Their papers are in the mean time left at the custom-house, and are delivered to them when their loading is completed, if no irregularity appears. The *Iris* having completed her cargo, and obtained clearances, the captain, on the 1st of *August*, unmoored, and sailed down beyond the mouth of the river; the tide being low he then anchored, and did not cross the shoal until the 3d of *August*, when the pilot was discharged. On the 8th of the same month the vessel and cargo were lost by perils of the sea. It was contended for the defendant, that the warranty " to sail from" *Demerara* was the same

Goods were insured at and from *Demerara* to *London* in ship or ships warranted to sail from *Demerara* on or before the 1st of *August* 1823. Small ships take in and discharge the whole of their cargoes in the river of *Demerara*; but there is a shoal off the coast about ten miles out at sea, and large ships usually discharge and take in part of their cargoes on the outside of the shoal. Goods covered by the policy were laden on board a small vessel that completed her cargo in the river, and on the 1st of *August*, the captain having obtained his clearance, set sail, proceeded down the river, and about two miles out to sea, and then anchored, the tide being low. On the 3d of *August* he

crossed the shoal, and on the 8th the vessel was lost by perils of the sea: vessel sailed from *Demerara* on the 1st of *August* within the meaning of the policy, and that the warranty was thereby satisfied. Held, that the vessel sailed from *Demerara* on the 1st of *August* within the meaning of the policy, and that the warranty was thereby satisfied.

as

as to " depart," and that this warranty was not satisfied by merely dropping down the river. That the vessel did not quit *Demerara* until the 3d of *August*, when she passed the shoal where larger ships complete their cargoes. The Lord Chief Justice left it to the jury to say whether the vessel did sail from *Demerara* on the 1st of *August*, and they found for the plaintiffs. In *Easter* term a rule nisi for a new trial was obtained, and on a former day in this term

The *Attorney-General*, *Gurney*, and *Kaye* shewed cause. The only question in this case is, whether the ship sailed within the time limited by the policy. If the warranty had been " to sail," omitting " from *Demerara*," it would certainly have been satisfied; for, in order to satisfy such a warranty, it is sufficient if there is a bonâ fide commencement of the voyage, although the vessel does not clear the port on the day specified. But it will be said, that the words " sail from *Demerara*" are equivalent to " depart," and bring this case within *Moir v. The Royal Exchange* (a), where it was held, that a vessel had not *departed* until she had cleared the port. The distinction between sailing and departing is very refined, and it would be still more so between " sailing" and " sailing from." But, admitting the distinction to exist, still the warranty was satisfied, the ship proceeded beyond the river on the 1st of *August*, and came to an anchor in the open sea, although within the shoal. There was no evidence to shew that the port extended to the outer side of the shoal, no duties were proved to have been ever collected there. The only argument on the other side must be, that the shoal is

(a) 5 *M. & S.* 461. 6 *Taunt.* 241.

within

within the port, because large vessels take in part of
their cargo on the outside of it; but that is not so; the
underwriters on such ships being supposed to know the
course of the trade, quasi give a licence to large ships
to stop at the outside of the shoal for a part of their
cargoes. Suppose a vessel going *to Demerara*, with a
policy *to Demerara*, were to stop at the outside of the
shoal to discharge part of her cargo, and a loss were to
happen there by some of the perils insured against, it
could not be contended that she had arrived at *Demerara*, and that the policy was at an end. But, at all
events, it was a question of fact, whether the vessel sailed
from *Demerara* on the 1st of *August*, and the jury found
that she did.

  Scarlett, Campbell, and *F. Pollock,* contrà. The question in this case is a question of law, resulting from facts
which are not disputed. It is assumed on the other
side, that this was a warranty to sail from the *port* of
Demerara, but no port is mentioned, nor is any town
mentioned in the policy. *Demerara* is a province. According to the argument on the other side a policy on a
ship at and from *Demerara* would never attach on a
ship which did not go within the bar or shoal; but
surely, under such policies, that must in law be considered to be a part of *Demerara*, where ships usually
take in a part of their cargoes. Suppose a policy on
the ship and cargo *at Demerara*, and a loss had happened on the 2d of *August*, when the *Iris* was within
the shoal, would not the loss have been covered by the
policy? If so, she had not then sailed from *Demerara*.
In the case of a large vessel about to cross the shoal,
and then stop for a part of her cargo, there would be no

doubt; and it would be very inconvenient if a different construction should prevail, according to the size of the vessel, particularly when the policy, as in the present case, is on goods by ship or ships. Take the case of a ship insured at and from *Jamaica*, warranted to sail on or before a certain day. If she bonâ fide commenced her voyage before that day the warranty would be satisfied. But suppose the warranty to be to " sail from *Jamaica*," then, if she commenced her voyage, and sailed from one port to another for convoy, and so did not quit *Jamaica* within the time prescribed, the policy would be vacated. " To sail from," implies an exclusion; it means, to depart; and to satisfy it the ship must be beyond the limits of the place from which she is to sail; *Moir* v. *The Royal Exchange.*

Cur. adv. vult.

The judgment of the Court was now delivered by
ABBOTT C. J. This was an action on a policy on goods by ship or ships at and from *Demerara* to *London*, warranted to sail from *Demerara* on or before the 1st of *August* 1823. The only question was, whether the warranty was complied with.

The ship having taken in all her cargo and obtained her clearance, sailed from the town, which is on the bank of the river, about one at noon, the 1st of *August*, passed the fort, which is at the point of the mouth of the river, and anchored the same day about two miles beyond the fort. She anchored there by advice of the pilot, and he being unwilling to sail again at the night tide, she lay there for about twenty-four hours, and then proceeded on her voyage, upon which she was afterwards lost. There is a shoal about ten or twelve miles

from

1824.

LAKE
against
ANDERSON.

from the fort, at the outside whereof large inward bound vessels heavily laden usually anchor and put out part of their cargo; and large vessels outward bound usually anchor and complete their cargo. The pilots usually leave vessels outward bound after passing this shoal. Upon these facts, it was contended at the trial, and again before the Court on the motion, that the words *sail from* were of the same import as *depart*, and that this vessel had not sailed from *Demerara* on the 1st of *August* within the meaning of this warranty.

It is clear that a warranty to sail, without the word *from*, is not complied with by the vessel's raising her anchor, getting under sail, and moving onwards, unless at the time of the performance of these acts she has every thing ready for the performance of the voyage, and such acts are done as the commencement of it, nothing remaining to be done afterwards. This appears from the case of *Bond* v. *Nutt* (a), and was so decided in *Ridsale and Others* v. *Newnham.* (b) And if it had been necessary for the ship in question to take in a part of her cargo at the outside of the shoal, she would not only not have *sailed from Demerara* within the meaning of this warranty, but would not even have *sailed* within the meaning of the other warranty to which I have alluded. It was contended that the words " from *Demerara*" must have the same sense in every case, and must therefore be construed to mean " sail from the outside of this shoal," that is, from the place at which some vessels take or unload a part of their cargo, for otherwise one vessel might be said to sail from *Demerara* before she had arrived at that part of the sea from which another

(a) Camp. 601. (b) 3 M. & S. 456.

K k 2

vessel

vessel must depart before she could be said to have sailed from *Demerara* ; and that this might even have been the case with regard to two ships on board whereof goods were insured by this policy. And if that part of the sea which lies at the outside of the shoal was, in a popular or general sense, part of *Demerara,* this argument would prevail. But the fact appears to be otherwise. For, whether we take *Demerara* to be the name of a province, as it is, or of the river, which is sometimes called the river *Demerara,* though perhaps more properly the river *of Demerara,* we think no person speaking in popular language would say that a ship, being at the outside of this shoal, at a distance of ten or twelve miles from land, was at *Demerara.* It would rather be said, she was lying off *Demerara.*

. The terms of a policy are, to use the language of . Lord *Ellenborough* in *Robertson* v. *French* (a), to be understood in their plain, ordinary, and popular sense, unless they have generally in respect of the subject-matter, as by the known usage of trade, or the like, acquired a sense distinct from the popular sense of the same words, or unless the context evidently shews that they must be understood in some other special and peculiar sense.

It appears in the present case, that large vessels heavily laden usually anchor at the outside of this shoal, and take in part of their cargo there. In the case of such a ship, therefore, goods so laden may be considered as laden at *Demerara* by reason of the usage; and in such a case, the ship would not be said to have sailed

(a) 4 *East,* 130.

until

until she had completed her lading and quitted that part of the sea. In the case of such a ship, the taking part of her cargo there will be like the taking in a part at the outside of the bar at *Oporto*, which was held to be within the protection of a policy, by reason of the usage, in *Kingston* v. *Knibbs*. (a) But the proper effect of such a usage will not extend beyond the instances that fall under the usage. In the case of *Moir* v. *The Royal Exchange Assurance Company* (b), which was on a policy of insurance, at and from *Memel*, warranted to depart on or before the 15th of *September*, the ship having taken her cargo and clearance, began to sail on her voyage, and proceeded some way down the river before the 15th of *September*, but was obliged by change of weather to come to an anchor within the limits of the port of *Memel*, and to remain there until after the 15th. And the Court of Common Pleas considering departure, to mean departure *from the port of Memel*, held, (as this Court had previously done,) that the warranty was not complied with. But Lord Chief Justice *Gibbs* said, if the warranty had been " to sail," he should have been of opinion that the ship had sailed. Yet, if another ship had performed the same manœuvres and sailed in company to the same spot, intending to wait there for her clearance or other necessary papers, such a ship could not have been said to have sailed within the meaning of the warranty. If, in the present case, the outside of this shoal had been part of the port of the ship's departure, or in any popular and general sense a part of *Demarara*, we should, (as I have before intimated,) have thought the warranty not complied with; but we cannot say the warranty has not

(a) 1 *Campb.* 508; n.   (b) 6 *Taunt.* 241.

K k 3   been

been complied with in this case, merely because it would not have been complied with in the case of some other ship, which might have intended to take a part of her cargo at the outside of this shoal. And our decision has not the effect of attributing two meanings to the name *Demarara*, but is only in conformity to the authorities and distinctions as to the meaning of the word " sail ;" and to that extension, which may be given to the words of a policy by usage in particular instances.

Rule discharged.

The KING, on the Prosecution of JOHN SMITH, *against* JOSIAH TAYLOR.

Indictment
charged that
defendant on,
&c., in the
second year of
the reign of the
present king,
kept a gaming
house. Plea,
that on, &c., in
the fourth year
of the reign of
the present
king, defendant
was arraigned
upon an indict-
ment, which
charged that
defendant on

INDICTMENT charged that the defendant being an idle and evil disposed person, &c. on the 20th of *April*, in the second year of the reign of *George* the Fourth, and on divers other days and times, between that day and the day of the taking of this inquisition with force of arms, at, &c. a certain common gaming-house, for his lucre and gain, unlawfully and injuriously did keep and maintain, and in the same common gaming-house, on the said 20th day of *April* in the year aforesaid, and on the said other days and times, there, un-

the 18th of *January*, in the fifty seventh year of the reign of the late king, and on divers other days and times between that day and the day of taking the inquisition, kept a gaming house, &c , to the nuisance of the subjects of our said lord the king, and against the peace of our said lord the king, &c. The plea then averred the identity of the offences described in the two indictments, and the acquittal of the defendant." Upon demurrer to this plea, concluding with a prayer of judgment of respondeas ouster, it was held that the plea was bad, because the indictment upon which the acquittal was alleged to have taken place, on the face of it, charged an offence committed in the reign of the late king ; and it was not competent to the defendant to shew by averment that it was for the same offence as that charged in the indictment before the Court, because that would be in effect to contradict the record : Held, secondly, that the crown was entitled to final judgment, notwithstanding the form in which demurrer concluded. Semble, that such an indictment must conclude contra pacem domini regis.

lawfully

lawfully and injuriously, did cause and procure divers
idle and ill disposed persons to frequent and come
together to game and play; and the same idle and ill
disposed persons to be and remain in the same common
gaming-house, and to game and play together on the
said 20th day of *April* in the year aforesaid, and on the
other days and times aforesaid, at, &c., did unlawfully
and injuriously procure, permit, and suffer, by means
whereof divers noises, disturbances, and breaches of
the peace were there occasioned and committed to the
great encouragement of idleness and dissipation, to the
great damage and common nuisance of all the liege
subjects of our said lord the king, and against the peace
of our said lord the king, his crown and dignity.   Defendant by his plea demanded judgment of the said indictment, he having theretofore by a jury of the country
in due form of law been acquitted of the premises in the
said indictment charged: and for plea said, that theretofore, to wit, at the general quarter session of the peace
of our lord the king, begun and holden at the Guildhall in the city and liberty of *Westminster*, in and for
the county of *Middlesex*, on *Wednesday* the 15th day of
October, in the fourth year of the reign of *George* the
Fourth, before, &c. justices, &c.; on *Monday* the 20th day
of the same month of *October*, he, the said *Josiah Taylor*,
was duly arraigned upon a certain indictment before
them, to wit, at the general session of the peace of our
said lord the king, holden in and for the said county of
Middlesex, on *Monday* the 8th of *September*, in the fourth
year aforesaid, duly presented and found by a certain
grand jury of the said county of *Middlesex*, for that he,
the said *Josiah Taylor*, being an idle and evil disposed
person, and not intending to gain his livelihood by

Kk 4   honest

honest labour; on the 18th day of *January, in the 57th year of the reign of our late Sovereign Lord* George *the Third*, and on divers other days and times, between that day and the day of the taking of that inquisition, with force and arms, at, &c. a certain common gaming-house there situate for his lucre and gain, unlawfully and injuriously did keep and maintain; and in the same common gaming-house, on the said 18th day of *January* in the year aforesaid, and on the said other days and times there, unlawfully and injuriously did cause and procure divers idle and ill disposed persons to frequent and come together to game and play; and the said idle and evil disposed persons to be and remain in the same common gaming-house, and to game and play together on the said 18th day of *January* in the year aforesaid, and on the said other days and times aforesaid, at, &c. there, did unlawfully and injuriously procure, permit, and suffer, by means whereof divers noises, disturbances, and breaches of the peace were there occasioned and committed, to the great encouragement of idleness and dissipation, to the great damage and common nuisance of all the liege subjects of our said lord the king, and *against the peace of our said lord the king, his crown and dignity.* The plea then stated the acquittal of the defendant upon the indictment, and averred the identity of the defendant, and the offences described in the two indictments. And this, &c. wherefore defendant prayed judgment of the Court, whether our said lord the king ought further to prosecute, impeach, or charge him on account of the premises in the said present indictment contained and specified, and whether he ought further to answer thereto, and that he might be dismissed the Court without day. Demurrer praying judgment of respondeas ouster, and joinder in demurrer.

The

The case was argued at the sittings after *Trinity* term.

Chitty in support of the demurrer.   This plea of autrefois acquit is bad, because the indictment set out in it, and upon which the acquittal is alleged to have taken place, was one upon which no sentence could have followed, inasmuch as it charges the defendant with an offence committed in the reign of the late king, and concludes against the peace of the present king, and *Hawkins's Pleas of the Crown, B.2. c.25. s.92.*, and *Rex* v. *Lookup* (a), are authorities to shew that such an indictment is bad.   If the indictment was intended to have comprised offences in both reigns, it ought to have concluded against the peace of the late and the present king, *Winter's* case. (b)   Besides, it is quite clear, that the offences charged in the two indictments are not the same.   In the first indictment the offence is alleged to have been committed in the reign of the late king, and in the present indictment it is charged to have been committed in the reign of the present king.   They cannot, therefore, be the same offences; and it is not competent to the defendant to shew the contrary by averment.

...

Curwood, contrà.   The averment contra pacem is unnecessary, and may be rejected as surplusage.   Secondly, there is a sufficient averment that some of the acts charged were committed in the reign of the present king, and that being so, the acquittal upon that indictment is a good answer to the present.   The object of the averment contra pacem was to shew to whom the forfeiture accrued from the peace having been broken:

(a) *Burr.* 1901.   (b) *Yelv.* 66.

In

1824.

The King
against
Taylor.

In ancient times, in indictments for offences committed
within a county palatine, or liberty, it was usual to lay
the offence against the peace of the lord of the franchise, because the thing forfeited belonged to him. The
stat. 27 *Hen.* 8. c. 24. enacts, that no person shall have
power to pardon but the king; and that in indictments
for offences committed in counties palatine or liberties,
whereby any thing shall be supposed to be done against
the peace, it shall be supposed to be done against the
king's peace only, and not against the peace of any other
person. In the *Queen* v. *Wyat* (a) such an averment
was held unnecessary, in an indictment against a constable for neglecting his duty, and so in an indictment
for a nuisance for not repairing a highway, or even if the
nuisance be a misfeazance, 2 *Roll. Abr.* tit. *Indictment,
Chose de Form* G. Or in an indictment of homicide by
misadventure, or in self-defence, *Co. Entr.* 253. 254., or
in an indictment for perjury upon statute, *Co. Entr.* 253.
In *Rastall's Entries* there are numerous indictments for
felony and other offences without such an averment.
Assuming it, however, to be essential, there is sufficient upon the face of the indictment, to shew that the
offences were committed in the time of the present
king; for by the caption the indictment appears to have
been found in the 4th year of the reign of the present king, and the offences are charged to have been
committed on a day in the reign of the late king, and
on divers other days and times between that day and
the day of taking the inquisition. Now the words
divers other days and times may include an offence committed in the reign of the present king, and that they do
so is manifest, because the offences are laid to have
been committed against the peace of our said lord the

(a) 1 *Salk.* 380.

king.

king. Those words must refer to the present king, in whose reign the indictment was found.

ABBOTT C. J. I am of opinion that this plea cannot be supported, and that there must be judgment for the crown. A plea of autrefois acquit must shew, that the defendant was legitimo modo acquietatus, viz. that he was acquitted upon an indictment sufficient to induce punishment if he had been convicted, and charging the same offence; and if it appears manifestly to the Court, on looking at the two indictments, that the offences charged cannot be the same, it is quite clear, that the defendant cannot, by averment, shew that they are the same, because he would thereby contradict the record. Now I think that it clearly appears, upon comparing the two indictments, that the offences charged in them are not the same. It is not necessary to decide, in this case, whether the averment "contra pacem domini regis" be necessary or not in such an indictment. I am strongly inclined to think that it is, for the reasons stated by Serjeant *Hawkins, b. 2. c. 25. s. 92.*, viz. that the offence is a breach of the law, and in that respect tends to the disturbance of the peaceable and quiet government of the king over his people, and also because it is to be found in the greater number of precedents; and it is very desirable to adhere to the old forms of pleading. Assuming, however, that the first indictment was good, I am of opinion that it did not cover the offence with which the defendant now stands charged upon this record. The first indictment states, that the defendant, on the 18th day of *January*, in the 57th year of the reign of the late king, and on divers other days between that day and the taking of the inquisition, committed the offence. The indictment, therefore, distinctly charges

an

an offence to have been committed in the reign of the late king, and the words " on divers other days and times" do not necessarily import that any offence was committed on any day not in the reign of the late king. They may include offences committed in either reign : a limit, however, is afterwards put upon that allegation, by the averment, that all the offences were committed against the peace of our said lord the king; for as some of the offences are distinctly charged to have been committed in the time of the late king, they must have been committed against the peace of that king; and, therefore, the words " our said lord the king" must refer to the late king, and not to the present; and that, too, is the grammatical construction of the words. That being so, it appears by the plea, that the defendant has been acquitted, upon an indictment which charged him with an offence committed in the reign of the late king. The present indictment charges him with an offence committed in the reign of the now king. These are two distinct offences; the plea is therefore bad, and there must be judgment for the crown.

BAYLEY J. I think that " contra pacem domini regis" is an essential allegation in such an indictment as the present, for the reasons given by Serjeant *Hawkins.* It is unnecessary, however, to decide that question. I am also clearly of opinion, that the plea is no answer to the present indictment, unless the party was put in hazard by the first; and I think, also, that the plain construction of the first indictment is, that it comprised offences committed in the reign of the late king only, and that being so, the offences are not the same, and the plea cannot be supported.

. HOLROYD

HOLROYD J. I think that the averment of contra pacem is necessary, in such an indictment as the present; but I am clearly of opinion that the prosecutor, on the trial of the former indictment, ought to have been confined to the proof of offences committed in the reign of the late king; and, therefore, the two indictments charge different offences.

The Court entertaining some doubt whether they ought to pronounce final judgment for the crown or judgment of respondeas ouster, directed the case to be re-argued on that point. On a former day in this term,

Chitty contended that final judgment might be entered against the defendant. The plea of autrefois acquit is a plea in bar, and not in abatement. (a) If it had been a plea in abatement, it may be admitted that the proper judgment would be respondeat ouster, although if issue be taken on a plea in abatement in misdemeanor, and found against the defendant, the judgment is final, *Rex* v. *Gibson* (b), *Eichorn* v. *Le Maitre* (c); so also the judgment on demurrer to a plea in bar in misdemeanor is final, *Bowen* v. *Shapcott*. (d) If the plea had been autrefois convict, or a pardon, and had been held bad on demurrer, it is clear that the defendant could not claim a right to plead over. In felony, the party indicted may plead over after judgment against him on such a plea; but that is said to be in favorem vitæ (e), and the rule does not apply to cases of misdemeanor, *Regina* v. *Goddard*. (f)

(a) 2 *Hale's P. C.* 241.
(b) 8 *East*, 107.
(c) 2 *Wils.* 367.
(d) 1 *East*, 541.
(e) 2 *Hale's P. C.* 239. 247.
(f) 2 *Ld. Raym.* 920.

Brodrick

Brodrick contra. No decision has been cited, nor indeed can any such be found, to shew that the defendant in this case is to be concluded by the judgment given against him on demurrer. There are indeed dicta in some degree applicable, but none expressly on the point now presented to the Court. In felony, a party is allowed to plead over after issue on a plea in abatement found against him; so also after judgment against him on demurrer to a plea of autrefois acquit, *Rex* v. *Vandercomb and Abbott* (a), *Rex* v. *Coogan.* (b) It is said that this is in favorem vitæ; but the privilege is allowed in all cases of felony, whether clergyable or not, and many misdemeanors are more heavily punished than clergyable felonies. It is therefore reasonable that the practice in misdemeanors should be assimilated to that in felonies, rather than to the course taken in civil cases, where a party may plead double. Even in civil cases, if a plea in abatement be demurred to, and judgment given for the plaintiff, the defendant may plead over; the reason of which is said to be, " because every man shall not be presumed to know the matter of law, which he leaves to the judgment of the Court, *Eichorn* v. *Le Maitre* (c), *Bowen* v. *Shapcott.* (d) That reasoning applies equally to a demurrer to a plea in bar. In some cases of pleas to the jurisdiction which cannot strictly be called pleas in abatement, for they go to bar the proceeding altogether, the judgment on demurrer is respondeat ouster. Thus, in *Rex* v. *Johnston* (e) such a judgment was given, although the defendant pleaded to the jurisdiction of all courts in this country; and *The*

(a) 2 *Leach,* 708. 2 *East, P. C.* 519.   (b) 1 *Leach,* 448.
(c) 2 *Wils.* 367.   (d) 1 *East,* 542.
(e) 6 *East,* 583.

Earl

Earl of Devonshire's case (a) is to the same effect. An attempt has been made to assimilate this plea to pleas of autrefois convict or pardon, but there is a plain and very important distinction. Those pleas involve a confession of the offence charged, and therefore if the party so pleading fails in his attempt to set up a legal bar to the proceeding, the judgment is very properly final, for there is no question of fact to be tried. This plea, on the contrary, contains an implied denial of the offence; and if the defendant, by a formal error in pleading, has lost the benefit of a defence in law, it is but reasonable that the question of fact should be tried before he is subjected to punishment. It must be admitted that in *Regina* v. *Goddard*, Lord *Holt* said, "a man could not plead over in any case but treason or felony, and not in case of a misdemeanor;" but that dictum was not necessary to the case; no question as to pleading over was then before the Court; and it certainly is not accurate to the full extent; for a man may clearly plead over after demurrer to plea in abatement to an indictment for misdemeanor. The judgment in this case then cannot be final unless it is to be held that a man is to be punished as guilty because he has pleaded informally a defence in law, although his plea does not involve an admission of guilt, but is directly repugnant to it, and which the demurrer confesses to be true in fact.

Cur. adv. vult.

ABBOTT C.J. now delivered the judgment of the Court.

(a) 11 *St. Tr.* 1354.

This

This case came originally before the Court on a demurrer to a plea of autrefois acquit, and after argument the Court held the plea to be bad. It has come again before the Court in the present term, on the question what judgment ought to be given, whether a judgment that the defendant do answer over or a final judgment.

The indictment is for a misdemeanor, viz. the keeping a common gaming-house. The entry of the demurrer concludes with a prayer that the defendant do answer over to the indictment. The Court, however, is not bound by the prayer with which any part of the pleadings in bar may conclude, but is to give such judgment upon a plea in bar as by law ought to be given. This was settled, after argument and consideration, in the case of *Le Bret* v. *Papillon*, (a), confirmed afterwards by the case of *The King* v. *Shakespeare*. (b) If the demurrer in this case had concluded by prayer of a judgment that the defendant be convicted, yet the Court would only have given a judgment to answer over, if the latter had been the proper judgment. We are therefore to consider the question as a matter of law, entirely independent of the particular prayer that has been entered upon the record.

Now the plea in this case is a plea not in abatement, but in bar. The distinction between such pleas in civil actions is well known. If a plea in abatement be held bad on demurrer, the judgment is, that the defendant do answer over; but if a plea in bar be held bad on demurrer, the judgment is general against the defendant. For it is a general rule in civil actions at least, that a defendant is not to plead a second plea in bar after a first shall have been determined against him. If he might do this he might also plead a third, a

(a) 4 *Burr*, 502.　　　(b) 10 *East*, 83.

fourth

fourth, &c., and there would be no end to the proceed-

ing. It is to be seen whether this rule applies also to
an indictment for a misdemeanor. Another rule in
civil actions is, that if issue be joined on a plea in
abatement, and the verdict pass against the defendant,
the jury who pronounce that verdict assess the damages
also, and the judgment against the defendant is final, no
further plea being allowed. The same rule holds also
in the case of a plea in abatement to an indictment for
a misdemeanor, if issue be joined thereon, and found
against the defendant, *Rex* v. *Gibson.* (a)   In this
respect, therefore, the analogy between actions and
misdemeanors is established by express decision.   In
felonies the rule is otherwise.   There, " if a man
plead any plea to an indictment or appeal of felony,
that does not confess the felony, he shall yet plead over
to the felony, *in favorem vitae ;* and that pleading over
to the felony is neither a waiver of his special plea, nor
makes his plea insufficient for doubleness.   And, therefore, if he pleads any matter of fact to the writ or indictment, or pleads autrefois convict or autrefois acquit, he
shall plead over to the felony; and although he doth it
not upon his plea, but his plea be found or tried
against him, yet he shall not be thereby convict without
pleading to the felony, and trial thereupon." *2 Hale's
P. C. c. 33.* The same learned author afterwards adds,
that if he plead a plea that confesses the fact, as a release in an appeal, *in his opinion* he may, if he please,
plead over to the felony not guilty; and, accordingly,
he says it was held by *Markham* in 7 *Ed.* 4. 15. *a,* though
he refers to two later authorities to the contrary.   If a

_____

(a) 8 *East*, 107.

man pleads the king's pardon, he shall not need to plead over to the felony," because it suits not with his plea; and yet if the pardon upon a demurrer, or upon advisement of the Court, be adjudged insufficient, the party shall not be thereupon convict, but shall be put to plead to the felony, and be tried for it; the pleading of the pardon is a kind of confession of the fact; but ·yet *in favorem vitae* the party shall be put to answer the felony. *Hale* ubi supra.

The reason of the rule in these cases is expressly mentioned by the learned author, and by all other writers on the subject, — in favor of life. And these passages also shew that there is not any distinction ·between pleas which contain an admission of guilt, and ·those·which may import a denial of guilt; but the rule is ·the same in both cases, ·because the reason extends ·alike to both. It is well known that there is no felony ·at the common law, except petty larceny, upon which ·judgment of death may not be given; nor any mis- ·demeanor upon which such judgment can be given: ·and therefore the reason of the rule will not apply to the case of a misdemeanor. And if the reason does not apply, the rule ought not to be extended to misde- ·meanors. And, accordingly, in 2 *Lord Raymond*, 921. Lord Chief Justice *Holt* plainly declared his opinion ·that a man could not plead over in any case but in treason or felony, and not in case of a misdemeanor. It is true that this point was not then in judgment before the Court; but, nevertheless, the opinion of so great a ·judge·is entitled to very great respect. The only case supposed to be a decision in favor of the present is that of *The Earl of Devonshire* in *Howel's State Trials*, vol. 11. col. 1353. I should be sorry to consider that case as an

authority

authority for any thing; but upon examination it will not be found applicable to the present question. The plea of the Earl was not properly a plea in bar, for he pleaded that no peer of parliament could be called upon to answer, before any court inferior to the court of parliament, for any misdemeanor during the sitting of parliament or the usual time before or after a prorogation, that the information was filed during the time of privilege; and he concluded by praying judgment, whether the Court would or ought to take cognizance of the plea aforesaid (that is of the information) during the usual time of privilege. Upon this peculiar plea, (which is in the nature of a temporary plea to the jurisdiction,) supposing the privilege to be disallowed, the proper, or at least the most lenient judgment would be that the Earl should answer to the information; and this was the judgment actually given. This case, therefore, cannot be considered as an authority to the point in question. And as the reason of the rule in cases of felony does not apply to misdemeanors, and it has been decided that the rule of civil actions applies to misdemeanors in case of issue joined on a plea in abatement; we think the rule in civil actions, and not the rule in felony, applies to the present case; and, consequently, the judgment against the defendant must be final.

Judgment for the crown.

The KING *against* The HULL Dock Company.

By a statute of
the 9 & 10 *W.* 3.,
the poor of the
town of *King-
ston-upon-Hull*
are placed un-
der the ma-
nagement of a
corporation
established by
that act, and
are to be main-
tained by mo-
ney to be levied
" by taxation
of every inha-
bitant, and of
all lands,
houses, tithes
impropriate,
appropriation of
tithes, and all
stocks and es-
tates in the
said town in
equal propor-
tions, according
to their respec-
tive worths and
values." Upon
an appeal
against a rate
made by virtue
of this act, it
appeared that
it omitted,

UPON an appeal by the *Hull* Dock Company against
a rate made for the relief of the poor of the town
of *Kingston-upon-Hull*, the sessions amended the rate
by inserting the names of certain persons therein, and
confirmed the rate so amended, subject to the opinion
of this Court, on a case of which the following is the
substance. The rate was duly made, but it was contended, on behalf of the appellants, that certain persons (named in the case) ought to have been assessed, in
respect of property hereinafter mentioned, and that they
were improperly omitted from the rate, and also that a
deduction ought to have been made from the sum upon
which the dock company were assessed, in respect to
the amount of the poor-rate with which they were
chargeable. The poor of the parishes of the *Holy
Trinity* and *St. Mary*, which two parishes comprise the
whole of the town of *Hull* and the precinct of *Myton*,
adjoining and belonging to the town, are under the management of a corporation, which was created by an

first, persons not resident in *Hull*, but having stock in trade there which had produced a
specified profit in the last year; secondly, a tenant of houses which he underlet at a specified
profit, the undertenants being rated, but excused from paying on account of poverty;
thirdly, owners and part owners of ships registered at *Hull*, and trading to and from that
port, and within the port at the time when the rate was made. Some of these persons were
resident in *Hull*, others were not. Some profits had been derived from the ships in the
preceding year, but the appellants could not shew the amount: Held, that the act in question made all personal property rateable, whether the owner were or were not resident in
Hull, and that consequently the first and third classes of persons ought to have been included
in the rate, and that it was not incumbent on the appellants to shew the amount of profit
made by the ships, for that it being established they were profitable, they ought not to have
been altogether omitted: secondly, that the tenant of houses underlet, as before mentioned,
was not liable to be rated. The *Hull* Dock Company were rated at the full amount of
their profits, without first making any deduction for the poor-rate: Held, that this was
wrong, that the " worth and value" could only be the profits, minus the outgoings, and
that, therefore, supposing other property to be rated at a rack rent, the poor-rate should
have been calculated upon such a sum as would, together with the rate, make up the whole
amount of profits.

act

act of parliament, passed in the 9 & 10 *W*. 3., and is
called by the name of the " Governor, deputy-governor,
assistants, and guardians of the poor, in the town of
Kingston-upon-Hull ;" and by that statute, after authorising the said corporation to erect workhouses, it is
enacted, " that it shall and may be lawful for the said
corporation, from time to time, to set down and ascertain
what weekly, monthly, or other sums shall be needful
for the maintenance of the poor in the said hospital or
hospitals, workhouse or workhouses, house or houses
of correction, or within the care of the said corporation,
so that the same do not exceed what hath been paid in
the said town towards the maintenance of the poor
thereof in any one of the three last years, and so as
such poor of the said respective parishes in the said
town as are unable to work or get their living be
weekly provided for thereout; to the intent that no
other levy or assessment may be made for any other
maintenance or allowance to any of the poor of the said
respective parishes, or any of them, upon the said inhabitants; and shall and may under their common
seal, certify the same unto the mayor, recorder, and
aldermen of the said town for the time being. Which
said mayor, and any six of the aldermen, or any eight
of the aldermen without the mayor, may, and are hereby
required from time to time to cause the same to be
raised and levied by taxation of ' every inhabitant, and
of all lands, houses, tithes impropriate, appropriation of
tithes, and all stocks and estates' in the said town and
the lordship of *Myton* adjoining and belonging to the
said town, in equal proportions according to their respective worths and values; and in order thereunto the
said mayor and any six of the said aldermen, or any

L l 3   eight

eight of the said aldermen without the mayor, shall have power, and are hereby required indifferently to proportion out the said sum and sums upon each parish and precinct within the said town, and by their warrants under the hands and seals of the major part of them, to authorise and require the churchwardens and overseers of the poor of each respective parish and precinct to assess the same respectively, and after such assessments made and returned, the said mayor and six aldermen, or any eight of the aldermen without the mayor, are hereby empowered to approve, confirm, or alter such assessments as to them shall seem just and reasonable: and the said assessments by warrants under their hands and seals to authorise the said churchwardens and overseers to demand, gather, and receive." Pursuant to this statute, the mayor and aldermen in *July* 1823 issued their warrants to the proper officers of the several wards into which the town of *Hull* is divided, and of the precincts of *Myton*, authorising and directing them to make assessments within their respective wards and precincts upon every inhabitant, and upon all lands, houses, tithes impropriate, appropriation of tithes, and all stocks and estates within the same, against which assessment the Dock Company appealed, on the ground of the omission of the persons hereinafter mentioned. The case then mentioned several persons not resident in *Hull*, but having either shops or counting-houses there, and stock in trade, of which a clear profit, the amount of which was specified, had been made in the year then last past. One case was stated, of a lessee of houses which he underlet at a profit, which was specified, and one of the owner of houses which he let at rents specified; the occupiers of these

houses

houses were rated, but excused from payment on the ground of poverty. A long list followed of persons owners or part owners of ships, but the shares of each person were not specified, which were registered at *Hull*, and usually traded to and from that port, and were within the town of *Hull* at the time when the rate was made. One part owner at least of each ship was resident within the town, others were not, but had counting-houses there, others were neither resident nor occupied counting-houses in the town. The said several ships respectively made several voyages from and to *Hull* in the course of the then last year, and the owners made a profit thereof respectively, but the particular amounts of such profits did not appear. None of the persons above mentioned were rated in respect of the several descriptions of property enumerated. In addition to the several persons whose cases are above specified, notice of appeal had been given to divers other persons having stock in trade within the ward aforesaid, and who were not assessed or rated to the relief of the poor, and it being proved that they derived a profit from their stock and were resident in *Hull* in the ward aforesaid, and the respondents admitting at the hearing of the appeal that such last mentioned persons ought to be added to the rate, the court of quarter sessions accordingly ordered the said rate to be amended, by inserting the names of those persons in the rate, reserving for the opinion of this Court the question whether the said persons whose cases are above particularly specified, ought to have been assessed in respect of the property also above particularly specified. The appellants in this case are assessed in respect of the profits arising from dock dues and wharfage

L l 4   rates

rates received by them. Their net profits for the year amount to 8900*l.*, after making a fair allowance in respect of repairs and all other expences incidental to and necessary for making the property profitable, but without making any deduction in respect of the sum with which they are chargeable to the poor-rate, and which, according to the present assessment, amounts to 2225*l.* If the amount with which they are so chargeable as poor's-rate ought to be deducted, then their net profits would amount only to 6675*l.*, or thereabouts. The Dock Company are assessed as upon profits amounting to 8900*l.*, and not as upon profits amounting to 6675*l.* only, no deduction being allowed in respect of the poor's-rate.

Marryat and *Coltman* in support of the order of sessions. The words of the 9 & 10 *W.* 3., by which act the management of the poor at *Hull* is regulated, are somewhat different from those used in the 43 *Eliz.* *c.* 2., but the acts being made in pari materiâ, must have a similar construction. Now, it was decided very soon after the passing of the 43 *Eliz. c.* 2., that the owners of personal property are not rateable unless resident within the parish where the property lies, Sir *Anthony Earby*'s case. (*a*) It must be admitted, that the words " stocks and estates" in the 8 & 9 *W.* 3. mean personalty, but as the owners of those stocks were not resident, the persons comprised in the first class mentioned in the case were properly omitted from the rate: Neither is there any pretence for rating the landlords of houses the tenants whereof were rated, but excused from paying on the

(*a*) 2 *Bulst.* 354.

ground

ground of poverty. Sir *Anthony Earby's* case shews that the occupier and not the landlord is to be rated, and there is nothing in the 9 & 10 *W.* 3. to alter that general rule. With respect to the ships, it certainly appears that part owners of some of them were resident in *Hull*, and it must be conceded that ships are rateable, *Rex* v. *White* (a); but in order to make personal property rateable, the owner must be resident, and the property must be profitable. This case does not state what shares belonged to the resident part-owners, and it does state that the amount of the profits was not shewn. The appellants were bound to shew not only that rateable property was omitted, but also the amount at which it should have been rated, *Rex* v. *Topham* (b), *Rex* v. *Ringwood.* (c) It was the duty of the sessions to amend the rate if improperly made, *Rex* v. *Ambleside.*(d), but they could not do that without evidence of the profits arising from the property omitted. Lastly, the Dock Company were liable to be rated at the whole amount of their net profits. The deduction claimed has never been allowed in cases of canals, nor was it made in *Rolls* v. *Gell* (e), where the produce of lot and cope for a lead mine was rated; nor in *Rex* v. *Agar* (f), which was a rate on the profits of a methodist chapel.

Scarlett, Tindal, and *Archbold* contrà. This case does not depend upon the 43 *Eliz. c.* 2., but upon the 9 & 10 *W.* 3., which was passed to regulate the management of the poor in this particular place. It must therefore be assumed, that when the legislature used

(a) 4 T. R. 771.
(b) 12 *East*, 546.
(c) *Cowp.* 326.
(d) 16 *East*, 380.
(e) *Cowp.* 451.
(f) 14 *East*, 256.

different

different words, they intended them to receive a construction different from that which had been put upon the former statute. Stocks are expressly made rateable, and nothing is said about inhabitancy: it is clear, then, that personal property was intended to be rated, whether the owner were or were not resident within the town. There may perhaps be a difficulty in maintaining that the landlords of houses are rateable; but that point is of little importance.. With respect to the ships, it may not be very easy to ascertain the quantum of profit, but that is not a sufficient ground for omitting them, nor were the justices bound to amend the rate; they ought to have quashed it; for it would be very unreasonable to impose upon the appellants the necessity of proving at how much each of a very large class of persons ought to have been rated. As to the deduction claimed, it is clear that the Dock Company were rated too high. They should be rated at the sum for which the docks would let. The annual value of land is made up of the rent, and the outgoings, of which the poor-rate is a considerable one; and, therefore, when land is rated according to the rent, the poor-rate is, in effect, first deducted from the value; it should, therefore, in like manner, have been deducted from the profits of the docks.

ABBOTT C. J. We are all of opinion that the local act is to be construed by itself. It is probable that the legislature would take into its consideration all the circumstances of the case, and adapt its language to those circumstances. There is not, therefore, any ground for surprize, if we should find property made rateable in

Hull

Hull which is not so elsewhere. As to the case generally,

Cur. adv. vult.

The judgment of the Court was now delivered by

ABBOTT C.J. This was an appeal against a rate by the *Hull* Dock Company. The grounds of appeal were, that some persons were improperly omitted, and that a deduction ought to have been made, from the sum at which the company were rated, to the extent of the poor rate they were compellable to pay. The poor rate in *Hull* is raised under an act of parliament of the 9 & 10 W. 3., which directs " that it shall be levied by taxation of every inhabitant, and of all lands, houses, tithes impropriate, appropriations of tithes, and all stocks and estates, according to their respective worths and values;" and the cases of persons improperly omitted were reduced to certain classes, viz. first, persons residing out of *Hull*, but occupying counting-houses or shops within the town of *Hull*, and having stock in trade by which they made a specified profit; secondly, owners or part owners of ships registered at the port of *Hull*, and trading to and from it, and making profit yearly, though the amounts of such profit did not appear, such owners being in some instances resident in *Hull*, and in other instances not; and, thirdly, a lessee of houses underlet by him at an advanced rent to persons who were rated, but on account of their poverty were excused from paying their rates; and if any one of these three classes was improperly omitted, the rate was pro tanto wrong. The rate had originally omitted certain other persons resident in *Hull*, and having stock in trade there yielding

ing

ing profit, but it was conceded at the sessions that those persons ought to be added to the rate, and they were added accordingly. The case, therefore, as to omissions is confined to the three sets of cases I have mentioned; and we are of opinion that the first and second classes were liable to be rated, and were improperly omitted; but that the lessee in the third case was not liable, and that the omission as to him was right. It was urged upon the argument that though the local act 9 & 10 *W. 3.* used different language from the 43 *Eliz. c. 2.*, yet that it ought to be construed as if the language in both had been the same; but the Court intimated their opinion to the contrary in the progress of the discussion; and they see no reason, upon further consideration, to change that opinion. The 43 *Eliz.* uses language applicable generally to the kingdom at large. The 9 & 10 *W. 3.* having in its view the town of *Hull* only, would naturally suit its expressions to the state and circumstances of that place; and where we find a deviation from the language in the stat. of *Elizabeth*, the presumption is that the deviation was intended, and that a different system was thought better for *Hull*, and that the language proper for such system was therefore used. We are therefore to consider it the intention of the statute 9 & 10 *W. 3.* that the rates should be raised by taxation of every inhabitant, and of all lands, houses, tithes impropriate, appropriations of tithes, and all stocks and estates within the town. It was most properly admitted by Mr. *Coltman*, upon the argument that "stocks and estates" must include all stock in trade and personal property. "Stocks" could have no other meaning, and "estates" placed as it is in the clause must extend to personal estates. This statute, there-

fore,

fore, has these two effective words, which are not to be
found in the statute of *Elizabeth*, and these two words
remove from this case all distinction between residents
and non-residents.   Under the statute of *Elizabeth* there
was no word applicable to personal property; and it
was only on the ground of his being *an inhabitant* that
any owner of personal property could be rated for that
property, because there was no word in that statute to
include him, except the word *inhabitant*.   Under
that statute, therefore, there was necessarily a distinction between residents and non-residents, because
the resident would be rateable for his personalty within
the place, the non-resident not.   The distinction, however, under that statute applied only to those kinds of
property which the statute did not specify; for the
occupier of lands, houses, &c. and whatever the
statute enumerated was rateable, whether he were resident or not.   In this statute, 9 & 10 *W.* 3., what was
defective in this respect in the statute of *Elizabeth* is
supplied; the rate is to be not only upon every inhabitant, but upon all stocks and estates.   Lands, houses,
and tithes are all rateable according to the general
principles of rating, whether the occupier be resident
or not; and it is impossible upon this act to say that
lands within the town shall be rated, but that stocks
and personalty within the town shall not.   The stocks
and personalty are not rateable elsewhere, they have all
the benefit of the town, and there can be no reason
therefore why, when there are words sufficient to include them, they should not be included.   We are,
therefore, of opinion that the stock in trade, and ships
yielding profit, are liable to be rated.   It was pressed
upon us in the argument, that as the appellants had not
made

made out what was each ship's profit, they had not given to the sessions the means of amending the rate; and that the appeal, therefore, as to the ships, could not be supported; but, besides that this is evading the question upon which it is obvious the sessions wished for the opinion of the Court, it is founded upon a misapprehension of the duties of the parish officers, and of an appellant. Where property is rateable it is the duty of the officers to include it in the rate, and to take what means they can to ascertain its value. It is not for them to omit it altogether, and to cast upon the appellant, what is properly their duty, the burthen of proving its value. In the case of a single omission the difficulty upon the appellant might not be very great; but where all the property of a given description is omitted, the difficulty might be excessive. Before the 41 Geo. 3. c. 23. (U.K.) the omission of a single individual who ought to have been included compelled the sessions to quash the whole rate; and so as he was rateable at all, the extent to which he was rateable was not in question. The statute 41 G. 3. requires the sessions to amend or alter a rate appealed against, without quashing it; but with this proviso, that if the sessions shall think it necessary for the purpose of giving relief to the appellant, to quash the rate, they may do so; and when a rate contains so many omissions that it can hardly be expected of an appellant that he should have evidence to shew the extent to which each person omitted ought to be rated, and where the investigation before the sessions would be likely to exhaust more time than they could reasonably be required to give up, we think it would not be an improper exercise of their discretion to quash the rate, and make the officers do in

the

the end what they ought to have done at the beginning.
Another answer is, that the sessions do not appear to us
to have made this a ground upon which they wish for
our opinion.

As to the question of the lessee whose under-tenants
have been excused from poverty, the point was not
much pressed upon us in the argument, and we think
the lessee not liable. The statute 9 & 10 *W. 3.* imposes
the rate indeed upon the lands, &c. without mentioning
either occupier or owner; but as this is a burthen commonly falling on the occupier, and rarely imposed upon
the owner, we think the owner not compellable to bear
it. The owner fixes his rent upon the supposition that
this is his tenant's burthen, and without very clear
words to shew that such was the intention, we think we
cannot make the landlord surety for the tenant. As to
the question whether the rate upon the company should
be according to the full amount of their profits, without
making any deduction for the sum they are liable to
pay for poor-rate, we think the rate ought not to be so
made. This property is to be charged according to its
worth and value, in like manner and in the same proportion as other real property is charged in the same
rate. If other real property is charged only at three-
fourths, or any other part of its value, after making deductions of the same nature as those which have been
made in the case of the company, the company ought to
be charged in the same proportion. If other real property is charged according to the rack rent actually paid
by the occupier, and according to a rent so estimated
where the occupier is not a tenant at such rent, there
will even in those cases be a virtual allowance in respect
of the poor-rate, such a rent being in reality a part only

of

of the worth or value of the land. The whole worth or value is made up of what is paid in-rent and what in rates and other outgoings. Land intrinsically worth 40*l.* a year, can only pay a rent of 30*l.*, if it is to pay 10*l.* per annum in other ways; and in estimating a rent both landlord and tenant look to the value of the thing on the one hand and to the outgoings on the other, and the outgoings must be deducted from the value before the rent can properly be fixed. Whatever, therefore, the rate is according to the rent, which is generally the case, an allowance is virtually made for the poor-rate, and if this rate is made according to the rent, the company should have the allowance. The mode of estimating the allowance is a different thing. That suggested in the case is clearly wrong; for if 1125*l.* the present rate, is deducted from the 8900*l.*, the rate upon 6675*l.* only will leave part of the rateable proportion of 8900*l.* free from rate. The allowance must be so made, that the sum upon which the annual rates are made, may, with the amount of the rates, make up the 8900*l.* This sum, according to the present rate, will be 7190*l.*, and the sum to be paid by the company will be 1780*l.* The process of calculation must be adapted to the amount of the rates; it is sufficient for us to propound the rule, leaving the process of calculation to others.

Upon the whole, therefore, the poor-rates omitted, except the leases of houses and lands, by him, must be put upon the rate; the rate payable by the Dock Company must be reduced to 1900*l.*; and the leases must be sent down to the sessions, that they may introduce the proper cases, if they find it practicable, or that they may quash the rate if it fail.

Order of sessions confirming the rate, quashed.

RAYER *against* COOKE.

A RULE nisi had been obtained for reversing the outlawry in this case, upon the defendant's putting in bail in the alternative. The action was debt upon bond, and in the bond the defendant was described as of *Wortham Dale Farm*, in the parish of *Lifton*, in the county of *Devon*. The bond bore date about twelve years before the action was commenced, and about the same time the defendant had sold *Wortham Dale Farm* to the plaintiff, which, however, he had continued to rent of him for two or three years after the sale. He had then removed from the parish, and for seven years his principal residence had been in the parish of *Georgeham*, fifty miles from *Lifton*, but in the same county. The affidavits for the rule stated, that the defendant was possessed of several houses in *Southwark*, which had required his personal attendance occasionally in *London*: the affidavits against it disclosed a great many shifts practised by the defendant in the avoidance of process in *London* and *Middlesex* in other suits than the present, and also a secreting of himself in his dwelling-house in *Georgeham* to avoid service of the process in this suit; but they shewed also that the plaintiff had attempted to serve his process on defendant in the parish of *Georgeham*; that the sheriff about the same time had executed a fi. fa. on his stock in the same parish. The plaintiff's attorney and agent swore expressly that they did not consider *Georgeham* to be the last permanent place of residence of the defendant, nor did they know in what

Marginal note: Where the third proclamation was made at the door of the church of the parish of which the defendant was described to be in the writ, and in the bond upon which the action was brought, but where he did not reside at the time when the proclamation was made, the Court reversed the outlawry as for want of proclamations, and ordered bail to be taken to pay the condemnation money.

part of the county his last place of residence was. The third proclamation under the outlawry was made at the church-door of the parish of *Lifton*.

Marryat now shewed cause. The defendant seeks to reverse the outlawry on the ground that the third proclamation was not made at the place prescribed by the statute of *Elizabeth*. If that allegation is correct, the case must be considered as if no proclamation had been made, *Waters* v. *Taylor* (a), and then it is quite clear that bail must be given to satisfy the condemnation money.

Coleridge contrà. It is impossible to distinguish the case of a proclamation made at a wrong time, from one where it is made at a wrong place. It appears, however, that in *Waters* v. *Taylor*, bail was given in the alternative, and therefore the court must have considered the making of the proclamation at the wrong time as a mere irregularity, because if there was no proclamation the recognizance of bail ought to have been taken to satisfy the condemnation money. Besides, in this case there has been an abuse of the process of the Court, because the proclamation has been made at a place distant fifty miles from that where the defendant resided, and the plaintiff by using due diligence might have ascertained the defendant's residence. In *Hely* v. *Hewson* (b), the Court reversed the outlawry on motion, on the ground that the outlaw was a prisoner pending the writ of exigent. That decision, as explained by *Lawrence* J. in *Beauchamp* v. *Tomkins* (c), proceeded on the ground that their process was abused, for the defendant was in the country, and by due diligence might

(a) 2 B. & C. 353.   (b) Barnes, 321.   (c) 3 Taunt. 143.

have

have been found. In *Hesse* v. *Wood* (a), where the outlawry was reversed because the defendant was beyond
seas at the time when the outlawry took place, it was
held that the recognizance was to be taken in the alternative.

ABBOTT C. J. It appears to me that this case is distinguishable from those which have been cited by the
defendant. There was no objection in those cases that
the proclamation required by the statute of *Elizabeth*
had not been made. Here the objection is, that although
the proclamations were in fact made, yet that the third
proclamation was made in the county and at the parish
of which the defendant was described to be in the writ
and in the bond, but not in that parish where he resided
at the time when the outlawry took place. This undoubtedly would have been a good outlawry before the
statute of the 31 *Elizabeth*, *c.* 3. That statute enacts,
that a writ of proclamation shall be awarded and made
out of the same court having day of teste and return as
the said writ of exigent shall have, directed and delivered of record to the sheriff of the county where the
defendant at the time of the exigent so awarded shall be
dwelling, and that the sheriff of the county unto whom
any such writ of proclamation shall be directed, shall
make three proclamations, the third to be *at or near to
the most usual door of the church or chapel of that town or
parish where the defendant shall be dwelling.* Now, in
this case, the sheriff instead of making the third proclamation in the parish where the defendant dwelt,
made it in the parish of which he was described to be
in the writ and in the bond which he executed, and the

(a) 4 *Taunt.* 691.

M m 2   question

question is, whether the defendant who now applies to set aside the outlawry, is entitled to have that done except on the terms of giving bail to pay the condemnation money. If the plaintiff or his attorney had done this wilfully in order to prevent the defendant from knowing it, the Court might, at their discretion, have allowed bail to be taken in another form, but I cannot collect that from the affidavits. It appears that the defendant was constantly moving from place to place, and that it must have been a matter of great difficulty to ascertain his residence. That being so, I think that as the third proclamation was not made in the place where according to the provisions of the statute of *Elizabeth* it ought to have been made, it is to be considered as if no such proclamation had been made. I think, therefore, that the recognizance of bail must be taken to pay the condemnation money.

HOLROYD J. If this be a case within the statute of *Elizabeth*, it is quite clear that the Court have no discretionary power, but must order bail to be taken to pay the condemnation money. Now here the objection is, that the proclamation was not made at the place where the statute of *Elizabeth* requires it to be made. Then it must be considered as if no such proclamation had been made as is required by that statute. I think also upon the facts disclosed in the affidavits, that there was not any want of due diligence on the part of the plaintiff or the party employed by him to ascertain where the defendant resided.

LITTLEDALE J. Where an outlawry is to be reversed for irregularity, the Court may, in its discretion, order

bail

bail to be taken in the alternative, but where it is to be reversed on the ground that the provisions of the statute of *Elizabeth* have not been complied with, then the Court are bound to order bail to be taken to pay the condemnation money. Now I think this case strictly within the statute of *Elizabeth*, because the third proclamation not having been made at the place required by that statute, it must be considered as if no such proclamation had been made.

Rule absolute on defendant's putting in bail to answer the condemnation money.

NEALE *against* WYLLIE.

Monday,
Nov. 29th.

COVENANT. The declaration stated a demise by indenture, in 1804, of certain premises by plaintiff to one *Finch*, for eighteen years, wanting seven days, if one *Eliz. Coppock* should so long live; and a covenant to repair and leave the premises in repair at the expiration of the term. That the interest of *Finch* vested in defendant by assignment; that defendant during the term suffered the premises to be out of repair; and so left them at the expiration of the term in 1822. By reason whereof plaintiff afterwards, to wit, on, &c. was forced and obliged to pay, and did pay to the said *Eliz. Coppock*, (by whom the premises had been demised to plaintiff for a longer term before he granted the lease to *Finch*,) the sum of 10*l.*, as and for damages for the bad state of repair of the premises; and also 100*l.* for the costs of an action brought against him by *Eliz. Coppock* to recover those damages, and whereby also he

Where the tenant, under a lease containing a covenant to repair, underlet the premises to one who entered into a similar covenant, and the original lessor brought an action on this covenant in the first lease, and recovered : Held, that the damages and costs recovered in that action, and also the costs of defending it, might be recovered as special damages in an action against the undertenant for the breach of his covenant to repair.

M m 3　　　　　　　　　　was

was put to the further expence of 100*l.* in defending that action. The defendant suffered judgment by default. On the execution of the writ of enquiry the plaintiff proved that the premises were left out of repair at the expiration of the defendant's term, as alleged in the declaration. He then proved that he was tenant of the premises to Mrs. *Coppock*, under a lease granted to him in 1801, in which there was a covenant to repair; and that he paid 10*l.* damages, and 57*l.* costs, in an action brought by Mrs. *Coppock* on that covenant; and also that the costs of the defence amounted to 48*l.* The jury assessed the damages at 10*l.*, the sum recovered by Mrs. *Coppock.* In this term *Abraham* obtained a rule nisi to set aside that inquisition, and have a new writ of enquiry executed.

Hutchinson shewed cause, and contended that the defendant was not liable to pay the costs of the action brought by Mrs. *Coppock* against the present plaintiff. The defendant was not assignee of the original lease, but an under-lessee, so that there was not any privity between him and Mrs. *Coppock;* nor was there any covenant by the defendant to indemnify the plaintiff against any costs or damages which he might sustain in any action brought against him for not repairing the premises. The plaintiff might, if he had thought fit, have repaired the premises, and then no action could have been brought against him; he ought not, therefore, to recover the costs of such an action as special damages.

Abraham contrà, was stopped by the Court.

. *Per*

Per Curiam. The defendant by taking an assignment of the lease granted to *Finch* bound himself by the covenant to keep the premises in repair during the term thereby granted, and so to deliver them up at the expiration of the term. The premises were suffered to be out of repair, in consequence whereof an action was commenced against the present plaintiff, and he has alleged as special damage, resulting from the defendant's breach of covenant, that he was compelled to pay damages and costs in that action, and was also put to considerable expence in defending it. If he could not recover those damages and costs against this defendant he would be without redress for an injury sustained through the neglect of the defendant, and not in consequence of his own default; for during the term he could not enter and repair the premises without rendering himself liable to be treated as a trespasser. For these reasons we think that the jury assessed the damages upon erroneous grounds, and that a new writ of enquiry must be executed.

Rule absolute.

1824.

NEALE
against
WYLLIE.

STEPHENS *against* WESTON and GRIFFITHS.

Monday,
Nov. 29th.

IN *September* 1822, defendant *Weston* distrained for rent upon a farm of which the plaintiff was tenant; the distress not producing sufficient to pay the arrears, *Weston*, on the 8d of *October*, brought an action against *Stephens* for the balance, which was tried at the *Hereford* Spring assizes 1823, when the plaintiff obtained a verdict

Where an application is made to set off costs and damages in one action against those recovered in a cross action, an attorney has a lien on the judgment obtained

by his client against the opposite party, to the extent of his costs of that cause only.

M m 4   for

for 385l. 10s.; and the costs were subsequently taxed at
48l., making together 493l. 10s. In *November* 1822,
Stephens brought an action against *Weston* and three
other persons employed by him in making the distress;
and at the Spring assizes 1823, obtained a verdict. The
damages and taxed costs in that action amounted to the
sum of 208l. 10s., which was paid on the 3d of *November*
1823. In *November* 1822, *Stephens* brought an action
against *Weston* and three other persons, *Harris*, *Cole*, and
the defendant *Griffiths*, for taking possession of his farm
under an order of justices made as upon a vacant possession; and he also appealed against that order. This
action was tried, and the appeal heard at the Spring
assizes 1823, when *Stephens* recovered against *Weston*,
Harris, and *Cole*; but *Griffiths* was acquitted, and restitution of the farm was ordered upon the appeal. The
farm was restored to him on the 1st of *April*; and the
costs of the action of trespass being taxed amounted,
together with the damages, to 88l. 10s., which were
paid on the 5th *November* 1823. *Stephens*, in *April*
1823, commenced the present action against *Weston*
and *Griffiths* for a continuation of the trespass in keeping possession of the farm from the 16th *September*
1822, until the 1st of *April* 1823. During that time
Griffiths held the farm as tenant to *Weston* under a
promise of indemnity. The defendants suffered judgment by default, which was signed on the 10th of *July*,
and a writ of enquiry was executed on the 15th of *September*, when the damages were assessed at 160l. The
defendant *Weston* died on the 16th of *October*. In
Michaelmas term an application was made to the Court,
with the consent of the personal representatives of the
defendant *Weston*, to set off the amount of the damages

                                              and

and costs in this action against the damages and costs in the cause in which *Weston* was plaintiff, and in which he had recovered 438l. 10s.; and a rule was made by which it was referred to the Master to ascertain the amount of the lien of the plaintiff's attorney on the judgment obtained in this cause; and that the damages and costs in this action should be set off against the damages and costs in the action of *Weston* v. *Stephens*, subject to the amount which the Master should find to be the attorney's lien. The Master was of opinion that the plaintiff's attorney had a lien on the judgment for all business transacted for the plaintiff in the causes, wherein the parties were virtually the same, and which arose out of the same grievance; and he taxed all the bills of costs in the various causes before enumerated as between attorney and client. The costs in this particular cause were taxed at 76l. 10s.; and the Master found that the lien of the plaintiff's attorney on the judgment in this case amounted to 188l. 17s. 11d.

Marryat now shewed cause. This court have laid it down as a general rule, that the equitable claims of the parties to a suit are not to prejudice the lien of the attorney. In this case it is quite clear, that if the damages and costs in this action had been paid to the plaintiff's attorney he would have been entitled to retain them for his general balance; and if that be so, and the defendants in this action are entitled to set off the amount of the judgment obtained by them against the damages and costs in this action, the plaintiff's attorney will be deprived of the general lien which he otherwise would have had. In *Harrison* v. *Bainbridge*, decided in this court last *Easter* term, where the Court allowed the

1824.

Saunders
against
Winson.

the costs in equity to be set off against a judgment at law, the Lord Chief Justice said that it must be subject to the *general* lien of the attorney.(a)

W. E. Taunton, contrà, was stopped by the Court.

ABBOTT C. J. The only authority cited to shew that an attorney has a general lien on a judgment obtained by his client against the opposite party is a dictum attributed to me in *Harrison* v. *Bainbridge*. It is to be observed, that in that case the question was not whether the lien was general or special, but whether the costs of a bill in equity, which had been dismissed, might be set off against the judgment in an action brought for the same cause, and the Court decided that they might subject to the lien of the attorney; and it is said that I used the expression, " subject to the *general* lien of the attorney." If I did, it certainly was an inaccurate expression. It is to be observed, however, that that case was referred to the Master to ascertain the amount of the attorney's lien; and that it is still pending before the Master, who now awaits the decision of the Court in this case before he makes his report. Independently of that supposed expression of mine, there is no authority for saying that an attorney is entitled to claim a general lien on such a judgment. In *Middleton* v. *Hill* (b) the costs in error were considered as costs in the cause. In the present case the attorney claims a lien not merely for the costs in this particular cause, but for costs incurred in other causes in which the damages and costs have been paid. So that the effect of allow-

(a) See this case reported in 2 *B. & C.* 800., where the expression *general* lien does not occur:

. (b) 1 *M. & S.* 240.

1824.

Stephens
against
Weston.

ing such a lien would be to make the present defendant pay such costs twice over, which certainly would not be consistent with justice. Another question is, whether the present plaintiff is entitled to a lien for the costs of the appeal. Now, it does not appear upon the affidavits whether that appeal was necessary in order to enable the plaintiff to bring the action of trespass. If that were so, perhaps it might be considered as parcel of the cause, as the writ of error was in the case of *Middleton* v. *Hill*. I think it sufficient to answer all the purposes of justice, to lay it down as a rule, that when a party seeks to set off judgments in different actions, the attorney shall have a lien for his costs in the particular cause only; and I think that that is the only lien which an attorney is by law entitled to insist upon.

BAYLEY J. This is an application to the equitable jurisdiction of the Court. In the Common Pleas, the attorney's lien for his costs is held to be subject to the equitable claims of the parties in the cause; but in this court, parties are not allowed to set off judgments until the attorney's bill for the costs in the particular cause has been discharged. I am not aware of any authority to shew that an attorney in such a case has a general lien; and I think that the case of *Middleton* v. *Hill* is an authority to shew that his lien is confined to the costs in the particular cause. In that case, it was held that the lien of the plaintiff's attorney upon the debt and costs recovered in the cause after affirmance upon writ of error, must be satisfied before the defendants were entitled to set them off against a judgment recovered by them in another cause against the plaintiffs; and that costs in error were costs in the cause. It was objected that the costs to be

allowed

allowed to the plaintiff's attorney ought not to include the costs in error; but the Court held that the costs in error were costs in the cause; for the plaintiff was not in full possession of his judgment until the writ of error was determined. Now, if the attorney had been entitled to a general lien, that question could not have arisen. It is clear, therefore, that it was considered both by the counsel and the Court in that case, that the attorney had a lien for his costs in the particular cause only.

HOLROYD J. Although an attorney has a general lien, as against his own client, it by no means follows that he has a general lien so as to affect the rights of other persons. Where an attorney has been at the expence of obtaining a judgment, it is perfectly consistent with justice that the debt due to him for costs should be paid to him out of that debt of which he has been the means of procuring payment to his client; but it is sufficient for all the purposes of justice, to say that the attorney shall have a lien on the judgment so obtained against the opposite party for the costs in that particular cause.

LITTLEDALE J. concurred.

Rule absolute.

SYKES *against* SYKES and Another. (a)

CASE. The declaration alleged that the plaintiff, before and at the time of committing the grievances complained of, carried on the business of a shot-belt and powder-flask manufacturer, and made and sold for profit a large quantity of shot-belts, powder-flasks, &c., which he was accustomed to mark with the words " *Sykes* Patent," in order to denote that they were manufactured by him, the plaintiff, and to distinguish them from articles of the same description manufactured by other persons. That plaintiff enjoyed great reputation with the public, on account of the good quality of the said articles, and made great gains by the sale of them, and that defendants, knowing the premises, and contriving, &c., did wrongfully, knowing, and fraudulently, against the will and without the licence and consent of the plaintiff, make a great quantity of shot-belts and powder-flasks, and cause them to be marked with the words " *Sykes* Patent," in imitation of the said mark so made by the plaintiff in that behalf as aforesaid, and in order to denote that the said shot-belts and powder-flasks, &c. were of the manufacture of the plaintiff; and did knowingly, wrongfully, and deceitfully sell, for their own lucre and gain, the said articles so made and marked as aforesaid, *as and for* shot-belts and powder-flasks, &c. of the manufacture of the plaintiff; whereby plain-

Where a manufacturer had adopted a particular mark for his goods, in order to denote that they were manufactured by him : Held, that an action on the case was maintainable by him against another person who adopted the same mark for the purpose of denoting that his goods were manufactured by the plaintiff, and who sold the goods so marked as and for goods manufactured by the plaintiff. The declaration stated that defendant sold the goods as and for goods manufactured by the plaintiff ; it appeared in evidence that the persons who bought the goods of the defendant knew by whom they were manufactured, but that the defendant used the plain-

tiff's mark. and sold the goods so marked in order that his customers might, and in fact they did, resell them as and for goods manufactured by the plaintiff : Held, that this evidence supported the declaration.

(a) This case ought to have appeared in an earlier day in this term, but it was unavoidably postponed.

tiff

tiff was prevented from selling a great quantity of shot-belts, powder-flasks, &c., and greatly injured in reputation, the articles so manufactured and sold by the defendants being greatly inferior to those manufactured by the plaintiff. Plea, not guilty. At the trial before *Bayley* J., at the last *Yorkshire* assizes, it was proved that some years since the plaintiff's father obtained a patent for the manufacture of the articles in question. In an action afterwards brought for infringing the patent, it was held to be invalid, on account of a defect in the specification ; but the patentee, and afterwards the plaintiff, continued to mark their articles with the words " *Sykes* Patent," in order to distinguish them as their manufacture. The defendants afterwards commenced business, and manufactured articles of the same sort, but of an inferior description, and sold them at a reduced price to the retail dealers. They marked them with a stamp, resembling as nearly as possible that used by the plaintiff, in order that the retail dealers might, and it was proved that they actually did sell them again, as and for goods manufactured by the plaintiff; but the persons who bought these articles from the defendants, for the purpose of so reselling them, knew by whom they were manufactured. It further appeared, that the plaintiff's sale had decreased since the defendants commenced this business. It was contended for the defendants, that the plaintiffs could not maintain this action, for that one of the defendants being named *Sykes*, he had a right to mark his goods with that name, and had also as much right to add the word " patent" as the plaintiff, the patent granted to the latter having been declared invalid. The learned Judge overruled the objection, as the defendant had no right so to mark his goods *as and for* goods manufac-

20   tured

tured by the plaintiff, which is the allegation in the declaration. It was then urged that the declaration was not supported by the evidence, for that it charged that the defendants sold the goods as and for goods made by the plaintiff, whereas the immediate purchasers knew them to be manufactured by the defendants. The learned Judge overruled this objection also, and left it to the jury to say, whether the defendants adopted the mark in question for the purpose of inducing the public to suppose that the articles were not manufactured by them but by the plaintiff, and they found a verdict for the plaintiff. And now

Brougham moved for a rule nisi for a new trial, and renewed the second objection taken at the trial, and contended, that the facts proved did not support the declaration. The allegation should have been, not that defendants sold the goods as and for goods made by the plaintiff, but that they sold them to third persons, in order that they might be resold, as and for goods manufactured by the plaintiff.

ABBOTT C. J. I think that the substance of the declaration was proved. It was established most clearly, that the defendants marked the goods manufactured by them with the words " *Sykes* Patent," in order to denote that they were of the genuine manufacture of the plaintiff; and although they did not themselves sell them as goods of the plaintiff's manufacture, yet they sold them to retail dealers, for the express purpose of being resold, as goods of the plaintiff's manufacture. I think that is substantially the same thing, and that we ought not to disturb the verdict.

Rule refused.

The KING *against* TUCKER.

Where the
magistrates at
a special petty
session dismiss
an application
under the
3 G. 4. c. 33.
s. 2., not on
the merits but
on a mistaken
notion of the
law, an appeal
lies to the
general quarter
sessions.

ON the 4th of *November* 1823, two corn stacks, the
property of *Tucker*, were wilfully set on fire in the
hundred of *Winterstoke*, in the county of *Somerset*, by
some person unknown. The damages sustained amounting to 30*l.* *Tucker* gave the notice required by the
3 G. 4. c. 33. s. 2. (*a*), and in pursuance thereof a special

(*a*) This section enacts, " That where the loss, injury, or damage,
claimed or alleged to have been sustained, shall not exceed in amount the
sum of 30*l.*, it shall and may be lawful for the party or parties damnified
or injured, and he, she, and they are hereby directed within one calendar
month next after such damage or injury shall have been sustained, to give
notice in writing to the high constable of the hundred, &c. in which such
loss, injury, or damage shall have been suffered or sustained, of such
riotous or tumultuous assembly having taken place, and the nature and
amount of the loss, injury, or damage sustained, and of his, her, and their
intention of calling upon the inhabitants of such hundred, &c. to make
good such loss, injury, or damage; and the said high constable is forthwith to give notice in writing thereof to the magistrates residing in or
acting for such hundred, &c., who shall thereupon appoint a special petty
session to be holden within thirty days next after the receipt of such notice,
of all the magistrates residing in or acting for such hundred, &c., to hear
and determine of any complaint which may be then and there brought
before them, for or on account of any such damage or injury having been
sustained by or through the means aforesaid; and the party or parties so
damnified and injured, is and are hereby directed to give notice, or cause
a notice in writing to be placed on the church or chapel doors, or most
conspicuous place of the parish, township, or place in which such loss, &c.
shall have been sustained, on two successive *Sundays* next preceding the
day of holding such special petty session, of the intent and purpose for
which such special petty session is to be held."

By sect. 7. it is enacted, " That if any person or persons in *England*
shall think himself, herself, or themselves aggrieved by any thing done in
pursuance of this act, such person or persons may appeal to the justices of
the peace at their next general quarter sessions of the peace to be holden
for such county."

17   *petty*

petty sessions was holden on the 9th of *December* 1823, by *S. T. W., T. W.*, and *R. P.*, justices acting for the hundred of *Winterstoke*, to hear the complaint. Having heard the evidence the justices dismissed the complaint, on the ground that they had no power to grant relief, as it had not been proved to them that any riot or tumultuous assembly existed when the offence was committed, or that the persons who committed it were armed with swords, fire-arms, or other offensive weapons, or had their faces blacked, or were in disguised habits. *Tucker* entered an appeal at the general quarter sessions holden for the county, on the 12th of *January*, 1824. The justices at sessions dismissed the appeal, on the ground that they had not jurisdiction to hear it. In *Easter* term a rule was obtained, calling upon the justices of the county of *Somerset*, to shew cause why a mandamus should not issue, commanding them to hear the appeal, upon notice of that rule to be given to the said justices, *or some of them.* The rule was served upon those justices alone who heard the original complaint at the special petty sessions, and upon the high constable of the hundred. No cause was shewn and the rule was made absolute, and the mandamus was served upon the same justices. At the *Midsummer* quarter sessions it was objected against the appeal, that the rule nisi for the mandamus was not properly served, and thereupon the justices refused to hear the appeal. In this term a rule nisi was obtained to quash the writ of mandamus, quia improvide emanavit; and now the court called upon

Barnard to support the rule. The rule-nisi for the mandamus ought to have been served upon some justices for the county besides those who heard the original complaint. It was not probable that they would interfere to prevent the appeal from being heard, however clear it might be that the sessions were not authorised to hear it. (The officers of the crown office stated, that the rule was served according to the usual practice of that office.) Still the writ of mandamus ought not to have issued, for the justices at sessions had no power to hear the appeal. By the 3 G. 4. c. 33. s. 7., an appeal is given to any person aggrieved by any thing *done* in pursuance of that act. In this instance nothing was done by the justices in petty sessions. They heard the statement and evidence, but thinking that the complainant had not established a case within the act, they refused to make any order and dismissed the complaint. There was nothing then to appeal against. What was called an appeal was more properly an application to the justices at quarter sessions to exercise an original jurisdiction, which is not given to them by the statute. This is analogous to orders of removal in which the sessions have not any original jurisdiction. Nor have they any such jurisdiction to make a poor rate. So also, until the 3 *Car.* 1. c. 4., they could not make original orders of filiation, although an appeal was given by the 18 *Eliz.* c. 3.: nor can they entertain an appeal where an information for a penalty has been dismissed. There must be some act *done*, in order to give them jurisdiction.

ABBOTT C. J, I am of opinion that we ought not to quash this writ. It appears that the rule to shew cause was served according to the general practice adopted in the crown office, and therefore the justices cannot allege as a ground of complaint, that they had

not

not an opportunity of shewing cause against it. But still, if the writ commanded them to do that which by law they have no power to do, it would be the duty of this Court to quash it. The observation is perfectly correct, that with respect to orders of removal or of filiation under the 18 *Eliz. c. 3.*, or poor rates or proceedings to recover penalties, the sessions cannot entertain an appeal unless some order has been made. But the authority given by the 3 *G. 4. c. 33.* is special and peculiar. The party injured is, within one month after the injury has been sustained, to give notice of the injury to the high constable, and that he intends to call upon the inhabitants of the hundred to make good the loss. The high constable is to give notice to the justices residing in or acting for the hundred, who, within thirty days, are to hold a special petty sessions to hear the complaint; and the party injured is also to affix a notice to the church door on two *Sundays* next before the holding of the petty sessions. The application for relief cannot then be made to this or that justice at the pleasure of the party, but in such a manner as that all the justices acting for the division may attend. The application must be made within a certain time, notices are to be given, and the petty sessions must be held within thirty days. The party cannot, therefore, renew his application for relief if the complaint is dismissed, nor can this Court issue a mandamus to the special petty sessions. The question then is, whether a dismissal of the complaint, not on the merits, but on a mistaken notion of law, is not under such circumstances to be considered as an act done, against which an appeal lies by the seventh section of the act. I think that it is, but my opinion is founded on the peculiar

N n 2   provisions

provisions and language of the act, and must not be considered as a precedent in any other case.

> Rule discharged and peremptory mandamus awarded.

C. F. Williams and *Jeremy* were to have opposed the rule.

The KING *against* The Justices of LINCOLNSHIRE.

An appeal against an order of bastardy cannot be entered at the quarter sessions, unless there be such notice and recognizance as is required by the 49 G. 3. c. 68. s. 7.

$D.$ F. JONES in *Trinity* term had obtained a rule, calling upon the justices of the county of *Lincoln* to shew cause why a mandamus should not issue, directing them to enter as of the last *Easter* general quarter sessions, the appeal of *John Ulyatt* against an order of two justices adjudging *Ulyatt* to be the reputed father of a bastard child, and to cause continuances to be entered until the next general quarter sessions, and then to hear and determine the appeal. The order was made upon the 14th of *January*, and the next general quarter sessions of the peace for the county took place on the 27th of *April*. No notice of appeal was given nor any recognizance entered into to try the appeal at that sessions, but an application was made to the justices assembled at that sessions to enter the appeal then, and to adjourn it to the next sessions; but the justices refused to receive the appeal, for want of notice and recognizance. The affidavits in support of the rule stated it had been the practice to receive such appeals without notice, and to adjourn them to the following sessions, but that was denied by the affidavits on the other side. It appeared, further, that notice of appeal was given for the adjourned sessions at *Spalding*, which were held on the 6th of *May*.

Balguy

· *Balguy* now shewed cause, and relied on the 49 G. 3. c. 68. s. 7., which enacts, that no appeal in any case relating to bastardy is to be *brought, received, or heard,* unless notice be given according to that act, ten days before the next general quarter sessions, and recognizance · entered into within three days after such notice, *Ulyatt* having omitted to give such notice and enter into such recognizance, the court below had no jurisdiction even to enter the appeal, and no notice or recognizance intended for any *adjourned* sessions to be holden for any division of the county would be sufficient under this act.

D. F. Jones, in support of the rule, admitted, that though all the other provisions of the statute 49 G. 3. c. 68. had reference to an extended liability of the reputed father in point of expence, yet the terms of the seventh section were general, " no appeal in any case relating to bastardy." But he contended, that inasmuch as it appeared upon his affidavits that it had been the practice of those sessions to enter the appeal at the next sessions, and to hear it at the subsequent sessions, the prohibitory words of the statute would be satisfied by holding, that the appeal could not be *heard and decided* at the next general quarter sessions, unless the notices and recognizances were given in time for such sessions. At all events notice and recognizance having been, in fact, given in time for the sessions to be held by adjournment at *Spalding* for another division of the county, *Ulyatt* was entitled to have the appeal received and heard, *Rex* v. *Coystan.* (a)

(a) 1 Sid. 149.

N n 3

Per

1814.

The King
against
The Justices of
Lincolnshire.

Per Curiam. No alleged practice can prevail against the positive words of the act, " that no appeal shall be brought, received, or heard." The justices, therefore, had no power to enter or receive the appeal. And as to the *Spalding* sessions, they appear to be only *adjourned* sessions, whereas the words of the act are, " the next general quarter sessions of the peace for the county." The notice and recognizance were clearly too late, and this rule must be discharged.

Rule discharged.

Monday,
November 29th.

PATTERSON, on the Demise of GRADRIDGE and Others, *against* EADES.

An ejectment brought in an inferior court on a lease executed and sealed on the premises, which were within the jurisdiction of that court, may be removed into this court by certiorari, if there be any ground for believing that it cannot be impartially tried in the inferior court.

THIS was an ejectment brought in the court of the mayor, recorder, and bailiffs of the city of *Winchester*, on a lease executed and sealed on the premises by the lessors of the plaintiff. The defendant having removed the cause by certiorari to this court, a rule had been obtained to take the certiorari and return off the file on an affidavit stating the execution of the lease on the premises which lay within the city of *Winchester*, and that the plaintiff intended to proceed to trial in the court below as soon as the recorder (a barrister), should be present to preside, which was expected to be before the next assizes. The affidavits in answer stated, that the defendant was apprehensive that the cause would not be fairly and impartially tried in the town court, by reason of the deputy town clerk being, as the defendant believed, the attorney of the lessors of the plaintiff, and having the impanelling of the jury.

Jeremy

Jeremy now shewed cause, and relied on the facts stated in the affidavits.

W. E. Taunton in support of the rule. The distinction is, whether a lease had or had not been sealed on the premises. In the former case, the practice is for the Court to award a procedendo, because the land is local property within the jurisdiction of the court below, in the latter not. *Runnington on Ejectment,* 151, 152. *Sellon's Pract.* 2d edit. vol. ii. 138., *Allen* v. *Burneye* (a), and *Jones* v. *Davies.* (b) Besides, the lessors of the plaintiff will be delayed, if the trial of the cause should stand over until the assizes.

ABBOTT C. J. This is a cause commenced in a court of inferior jurisdiction, and the defendant is entitled to his writ of certiorari. The rule relied on is only to be found in *Sellon's Practice;* and that book, though a very valuable one, has been published too many years to be relied on as being an authority at the present day in all cases. The defendant's apprehension of not having a fair trial is a sufficient ground for his suing out a certiorari. The present case is essentially different from that of *Jones* v. *Davies.*

HOLROYD J. The writ of certiorari is a matter of course; it is like a re. fa. lo. in replevin, and I cannot see why an ejectment should not be removable as well as a replevin. At any rate, the defendant's apprehension is a sufficient ground to justify us in retaining the cause.

Rule discharged.

(a) 2 *Keble,* 119.   (b) 1 *B. & C.* 143.

See Maule v [illegible] 1 C. M. & R. 86

WEATHERBY *against* GORING.

The Court will not, before issue joined, entertain a motion to change the venue in an action on a specialty.

COVENANT on an indenture of apprenticeship.

Before plea *Wightman* moved to change the venue from *London* to *Lancashire*, on an affidavit that the cause of action, if any, arose in that county, and that all the witnesses resided there.

Cresswell shewed cause and contended, that the defendant could not be entitled to change the venue, without making an affidavit of merits; for otherwise, it would not appear that he had any defence, or any witness to examine.

Per Curiam. The motion was made too soon. Until issue has been joined, the Court cannot tell whether the defendant intends to set up any defence to the action, and he cannot be entitled to change the venue in an action on a specialty, unless it appears clearly that he will have some witnesses to examine on the trial of the cause.

Rule discharged.

1824.

INWOOD *against* ROBERT RICHARD MAWLEY, CHARLES MAWLEY, and S. TRESS.

A RULE nisi had been obtained by *Comyn* for setting aside the judgment of non-pros. for irregularity. It appeared that a latitat was issued on the 17th of *June* 1823, returnable on the last day of *Trinity* term; and that a copy was served on the defendant *Tress* on the 18th of *June*, but not upon the other defendants. On the 24th *November* 1823, an alias latitat issued against the defendants returnable on the last day of *Michaelmas* term; and on the 25th of *November*, a copy of this alias latitat was served on the defendant *Robert Richard Mawley*, but the plaintiff's attorney could not effect any service thereof, on the defendant *Charles Mawley* before the return. On the 9th of *February* 1824, a pluries latitat issued against the defendants returnable on the last day of *Hilary* term, which the plaintiff's attorney could not succeed in serving upon *Charles Mawley* in consequence of his absence from *London;* and another pluries writ issued on the 12th *February* 1824 against the defendants; returnable on the 19th of *May* in *Easter* term last past, a copy of which last writ was served upon *Charles Mawley* on the 10th of *May*. An appearance was entered for all the defendants in *Easter* term, which

By the statute 13 Car. 2. c. 2. s. 3., upon an appearance for the defendant by attorney of the term wherein the process is returnable, unless the plaintiff declare before the end of the term then next following after appearance, judgment of non-pros. for want of a declaration may be entered against him: Held, that the statute contemplated such an appearance as would entitle the plaintiff to declare; and, therefore, where a latitat against three defendants having issued, returnable on the last day of Trinity term, but only one of the defendants being served, an alias

issued returnable on the last day of *Michaelmas* term, and one other of the defendants was served with a copy. In *Hilary* term following a pluries latitat issued, returnable on the last day of *Hilary* term, but which was not served on the third defendant, and another pluries issued returnable on the 19th of *May*, in *Easter* term, a copy of which was served on the third defendant. An appearance was entered for all the defendants in *Easter* term, and the plaintiff not having declared in *Trinity* term, the defendant signed judgment of non-pros. : Held, that such judgment was regular, within the stat. 13 *Car.* 2. *c.* 2. *s.* 3,

ended

1824.

Inwood
against
Mawley.

ended on the 31st of *May*. *Trinity* term ended on the 7th of *July*, and on the 9th of *July* the judgment of non-pros. was signed.

E. Lawes shewed cause. There was no appearance upon which the plaintiff could declare until *Easter* term, because, till that time, all the defendants were not in court. In *Brandon* v. *Henry* (a), the defendant was arrested on a bill of *Middlesex* on the 22d *November*, and special bail were put in in *Michaelmas* term and perfected in *Hilary* term, and judgment of non-pros. being signed in *Hilary* vacation was held to be irregular, and the court said that the plaintiff was guilty of no laches in not declaring in *Michaelmas* term, as the defendant was not then fully in court. All the defendants were not in court until *Easter* term. Now the statute must have contemplated such an appearance of the defendants as would entitle the plaintiff to declare against them.

Comyn, contrà. The first writ being joint, and no appearance entered of the term of which such writ was returnable, the statute of the 13 *Car.* 2. stat. 2. c. 2. s. 3. does not apply, and the judgment of non-pros. cannot be entered. That statute enacts, that " upon an appearance entered for the defendant by attorney, of the term wherein the *process* is returnable, unless the plaintiff shall put into the court from whence the process issued his declaration against the defendant, before the end of the term next following after appearance, a nonsuit for want of a declaration may be entered against him."

(a) 3 B. & A. 514.

Now

Now here, no appearance has been entered for the defendants, of the term when the first process was returnable, and, therefore, the statute does not apply to this case. In *Holmes* v. *White,* cited in *Prigmore* v. *Bradley (a),* the Master reported that a non-pros. could never be signed, unless bail were filed in the term in which the writ was returnable.

ABBOTT C. J.   I think that the appearance directed by the statute to be entered for the defendant must be an available appearance. In *Brandon* v. *Henry,* the court seemed to consider that the plaintiff was entitled to one clear term to declare in after the defendant was fully in court.   Here, the appearance was entered for all the defendants in *Easter* term.   There was no appearance before, so as to entitle the plaintiff to declare.   The plaintiff could not declare until that time, and he was bound to declare only in *Trinity* term.   The judgment of non-pros. was not signed until after *Trinity* term; it is therefore regular, and this rule must be discharged.

Rule discharged.

(a) 6 *East,* 314.

Andrew Duncan *against* Henry Thwaites
and Others.

Declaration for a libel stated, that the plaintiff was taken before a justice to answer a charge of

DECLARATION stated that plaintiff was a person of good fame, and that he had not been guilty, or until the time of the committing of the said several grievances

having assaulted *A. B*, and that the said charge was proceeded upon, and, in part, heard, and witnesses were examined concerning the same, of which *A. B.* was one, and the further examination was adjourned to a future day; that at the time of publishing the libel no bill of indictment had been preferred against the plaintiff in respect of the charge, nor any trial had, and the subject matter of the charge was undetermined, yet that defendants, intending to hinder and obstruct the course of justice, and to prevent the plaintiff from having a fair trial, maliciously published in a newspaper, on the 10th *July*, the following libel: " One *A. D.*, of &c., underwent a long examination on a charge of having indecently assaulted a female child only thirteen years old   The evidence of the child herself, and her companion, *A. D* 's own cousin, displayed such a complication of disgusting indecencies, that we cannot detail it.   It is right, however, that we should say that the accused denied the principal facts alleged, and that the children made some slight variation in their evidence."   The same count charged the defendants with publishing another libel on the 18th *July*, stating that " *A. D.*, who was charged a week ago with attempting to violate the person of a girl of thirteen, was again examined, but no further evidence was heard, and he was ordered to enter into a recognizance for 200*l.*, and all the witnesses were bound over to prosecute."   There were other counts setting out the libels, but making no reference to any proceeding before a magistrate.   Plea, first, not guilty; secondly, that on, &c., at, &c., before *J. H.*, justice, the plaintiff did undergo a long examination, &c. (repeating the libel) and that afterwards, to wit, on the 1st day of *July*, at the public office, *Bow-street*, the plaintiff was again examined, &c. (repeating the second libel.)   The plea then stated that the supposed libels contained no other than true, fair, just, and correct report and account of the proceedings which took place on the 8th and 15th days of *July* respectively, at the said public office, *Bow-street*, and were published by the defendants, with no scandalous, defamatory, unworthy, or unlawful motive whatever, and that the proceedings therein reported took place publicly and openly at the police office, and the reports or accounts thereof composing the said supposed libels, were printed and published in the said newspapers as public news of such public proceedings, and with no other intent, and for no other object or purpose whatsoever: Held, upon demurrer, that this plea was bad, inasmuch as it was no justification of the publication of slanderous matter, that it contained a correct report of the proceedings which took place in the course of a preliminary inquiry before a magistrate.

The third plea was, that the several matters and things in the supposed libels contained were true: Held, that this plea was bad, because it was uncertain whether it meant that the report in the newspaper was a true report of the proceedings, or that the facts mentioned in it were true; and if the latter were the meaning, then the plea was, much too general.

The fourth plea to the whole declaration stated, that the supposed libel was nothing more than a fair, true, and correct report of proceedings which took place publicly and openly before the justice at the public office: Held, that this plea was bad, because it was no answer to those counts which did not allege that any proceedings had taken place before a justice.

The fifth plea which was pleaded to the counts containing the libel of the 10th of *July* was,

grievances by the defendants as thereinafter mentioned, been suspected to have been guilty of indecently assaulting female children, or of attempting to violate the persons of female children, or of attempting feloniously to ravish and carnally know any female against her will, or any other such crime; and that the plaintiff, before and at the time of the committing of the said several grievances by the several defendants as thereinafter mentioned, was and still is a solicitor of the High Court of Chancery. By means of which said several premises the plaintiff had not only obtained the good opinion, &c. but also, in the way of his aforesaid profession, was honestly acquiring great gains, &c., to wit, at, &c. And that before the printing and publishing the respective false, scandalous, malicious, and defamatory libels in this first count, to wit, on the 8th day of *July* 1823, to wit, at, &c. the plaintiff was taken and brought before *Thomas Halls*, Esq., being then and there one of the justices of our lord the present king for *Westminster* and *Middlesex*, to answer a charge, complaint, and accusation against the plaintiff, for having assaulted *Ann Chandler*, and behaved in an indecent manner towards her; and the plaintiff being so taken and brought before the said justice, the said charge was, to wit, on the 8th day of *July* in the year aforesaid, to wit, at, &c. proceeded upon, and in part heard and examined into before the said justice, and certain witnesses were heard and examined concerning the said charge, of which said witnesses so heard and examined the said *Ann Chandler* was one, and the further inquiry and ex-

1824.

DUNCAN
against
THWAITES.

was, that the plaintiff on the 8th of *July* was before the justice, and underwent a long examination, as in the second plea, and upon that occasion the mother of *A. C.* deposed as follows. (The plea then set out the depositions verbatim, and by them it appeared that the libel complained of did not contain a full, fair, and accurate report of what passed at the police office, and on that ground, it was held that this plea was clearly bad.)

The sixth plea which was pleaded to the libel of the 15th of *July*, alleged that the plaintiff was examined at the police office, and ordered to enter into recognizances, as in the libel mentioned: Held, that this plea was good, inasmuch as the publication of the 15th of *July* contained no statement of the evidence, nor any comment upon the case, but merely stated the result of what the justice had thought fit to do.

The seventh plea was, in substance, the same as the fifth, and held bad for the same reasons. The eighth being similar to the sixth, was held good.

amination

amination concerning the said charge was adjourned by
the said justice to a future day; * but at the time of
printing and publishing the false, scandalous, malicious,
and defamatory libel in this count mentioned, no bill of
indictment had been preferred against the plaintiff for
or in respect of the said charge, nor had any trial of the
plaintiff by a jury of the country been had or taken
place for or in respect of the said charge, and the subject-matter of the said charge was then undecided and
undetermined, to wit, at, &c. ; yet the defendants well
knowing the premises, but contriving and intending
wrongfully unlawfully, and maliciously to hinder and
obstruct the due course and proceedings of the administration of law and justice, and to hinder and prevent
the plaintiff from having a fair and impartial trial in
respect of the said charge, and to influence, inflame, and
prejudice the minds of the liege subjects of our said lord
the king against the plaintiff, and to make it be believed
that he, the plaintiff, had been, and was guilty of having
indecently assaulted a female child, and to injure the
plaintiff in his aforesaid good name, fame, and credit,
and also in his said profession and business of a solicitor,
and to subject him to the pains and punishment to
which persons, who are guilty of indecently assaulting
females, are liable by the laws of this kingdom, and to
vex, harrass, oppress, impoverish, and ruin him, the
plaintiff, heretofore, and before any bill of indictment
was preferred against the plaintiff for the said supposed
offence, and before any trial of the plaintiff was had by
a jury of the country for the said supposed offence, and
whilst the subject-matter of the said charge was undecided and undetermined, * to wit, on the 10th day of July
1823, to wit, at, &c. unlawfully, wrongfully, maliciously,
                                                    and

and injuriously did print and publish, and cause to be
printed and published, in a certain newspaper called the
Morning Herald, a certain scandalous, malicious, and
defamatory libel, of and concerning the plaintiff, and of
and concerning the said charge, and of and concerning
the said proceeding upon, and in part hearing, investigating, and examining of the said charge before the
said justice, containing therein divers scandalous, malicious, and defamatory matters and things of and concerning the plaintiff, and of and concerning the said
charge, and of and concerning the said proceeding before, and in part hearing, investigating, and examining
the said charge before the said justice, according to the
tenor and effect following : that is to say, " One Mr.
Andrew Duncan of *New Inn*, (meaning the said plaintiff,)
underwent a long examination on a charge of having
indecently assaulted a female child of only thirteen years
old, (meaning the said *Ann Chandler*,) the evidence of
the child herself, (meaning the said *Ann Chandler*,) and
her companion Mr. *Duncan's* (meaning the said plaintiff's) own cousin of the same age, displayed such a complication of disgusting indecencies that we cannot detail
it. It is right, however, that we should say the accused
(meaning the said plaintiff) denied the principal facts
alleged, and that the children made some slight variation
in their evidence. Eventually the accused (meaning the
said plaintiff) was admitted to bail himself in 100*l.*, and
two sureties in 50*l.* each for his appearance again (meaning the appearance of the said plaintiff) on *Tuesday*
next." Then followed eleven other counts on the same
libel, not materially differing from the first. Thirteenth
count, that before the respective printing and publishing
the respective scandalous, malicious, and defamatory
libels

libels in this thirteenth count mentioned, to wit, on the 8th day of July 1823, to wit, at, &c. the plaintiff was taken and brought before the said *Thomas Halls, Esq.*, being then and there one of the justices of our lord the present king, for *Westminster* and *Middlesex*, to answer a charge, complaint, and accusation against the plaintiff, for having assaulted one *Ann Chandler* and behaved in an indecent manner towards her; and the plaintiff being so taken and brought before the said justice, and before the respective printing and publishing the respective scandalous, malicious, and defamatory libels in this thirteenth count mentioned, the said charge, complaint, and accusation was, to wit, on the 8th day of July in the year aforesaid, to wit, at, &c. proceeded upon, and in part heard and examined into before the said justice, and certain witnesses were heard and examined touching and concerning the said charge, and the further enquiry and examination concerning the said charge was adjourned by the said justice to a future day. And whereas heretofore, to wit, on the said 15th day of July in the year aforesaid, to wit, at, &c. the said charge was further proceeded upon before the said *Thomas Halls* the said justice; [The inducement then proceeded as in the first count from the * to the * in p. 558.] to wit, on the 16th day of July 1823, at, &c. unlawfully, wrongfully, and maliciously, and injuriously, did print and publish in a newspaper, called the *Morning Herald* a certain other scandalous, malicious, and defamatory libel of, and concerning the plaintiff, and of, and concerning the said charge, and of, and concerning the said proceedings thereupon, containing the indictable scandalous, malicious, and defamatory matters and things of and concerning the plaintiff, and of, and concerning the said above set forth in their evidence, and several said charge, and of and concerning the said proceedings thereupon, according to the tenor and effect following : that is to say, " *Andrew Duncan* the attorney, (meaning the said plaintiff,) who was charged a week ago with attempting to violate the person of a girl of thirteen named *Ann Chandler*, (meaning the said *Ann Chandler*,) was again examined, but no further evidence was heard, and he (meaning the said plaintiff) was ordered to enter into recognizances to the amount of 200*l.* for his appearance at the sessions, and all the witnesses were bound over to prosecute." There then followed eleven other counts founded on this libel of the 16th of *July*. The inducement at the commencement of this declaration applied to the first twenty-four counts. There then followed twelve counts, of which some were founded on the first libel, and others on the second, to which the inducement did not apply.

Plea first, general issue. Second plea, as to publishing the several libels in the declaration mentioned, that before any of the said several times when, &c. to wit, on the 8th day of *July* 1823, at the public police office at *Bow Street*, in the county of *Middlesex*, before the said *Thomas Halls*, so being such justice as aforesaid, the plaintiff did undergo a long examination on a charge of having indecently assaulted a female child of only thirteen years old, to wit, one *Ann Chandler*, and attempting to violate the person of the said *Ann Chandler*, and the evidence of the child herself, and her companion the plaintiff's own cousin of the same age, did upon that occasion then and there display a complication of disgusting indecencies, although the plaintiff then and there denied the principal facts alleged, and the children made some slight variation in their evidence, and eventually

1824.
PERRY
against
THRAKEN.

the plaintiff was on that occasion then and there admitted to bail himself in 100*l.* and two sureties in 50*l.*
each, for the appearance of him, the said plaintiff, again
on *Tuesday* then next following. And that afterwards,
to wit, on *Tuesday* the 15th day of *July* in the year
aforesaid, at the said public office in *Bow Street* aforesaid, the plaintiff was again examined before the said
Thomas Halls, so being such justice as aforesaid, touching the said charge; but no further evidence was heard,
and he, the said plaintiff, was then and there ordered by
the said justice to enter into recognisances to the
amount of 200*l.* for his appearance at the sessions, and
all the witnesses were bound over to prosecute. And
that the said several supposed libels in the said declaration mentioned, contained and contain no other than
a true, fair, and just report and account of the proceedings which took place on the said 8th and 15th days
of *July* respectively, at the said public police office,
Bow Street, aforesaid, on the respective occasions aforesaid, and were printed and published by the defendants
in the said newspaper called the *Morning Herald,* with
no scandalous, malicious, or defamatory, unworthy, or
unlawful motive whatever; and that the said proceedings therein reported as aforesaid, took place as aforesaid, publicly and openly at the said police office, and
the said reports or accounts thereof composing the said
supposed libels, were so printed and published as aforesaid, in the said newspaper as public news of such
public proceedings, and, with no other intent, and for
no other object or purpose whatsoever, to wit, &c.

Third plea, that the several matters and things in
the said several supposed libels contained, were and are
true.

Fourth plea, that the said supposed libels respectively
were,

were, and consisted of nothing more than fair, true, and correct reports in the said newspaper called the *Morning Herald*, of proceedings which took place publicly and openly before the said *Thomas Halls*, so being such justices as aforesaid, at the public police office at *Bow Street* aforesaid; and this, &c.

" Fifth plea, as to printing and publishing, and causing to be printed and published, the several supposed libels in the said declaration mentioned, which contain all or any part of the following words or matter: (that is to say) "One Mr. *Andrew Duncan*, of *New Inn*, underwent a long examination on a charge of having indecently assaulted a female child of only thirteen years old, the evidence of the child herself, and her companion, Mr. *Duncan's* own cousin, of the same age, displayed such a complication of disgusting indecencies that we cannot detail it. It is right, however, that we should say the accused denied the principal facts alleged; and that the children made some slight variation in their evidence. Eventually, the accused was admitted to bail himself in 100*l*. and two sureties in 50*l*. each for his appearance again on *Tuesday* next;" the said defendants say, that the said last mentioned several supposed libels were, and are several copies only of one and the same supposed libel printed and published by the said defendants in several copies of the said public newspaper called the *Morning Herald* of *Thursday* the tenth day of *July* 1823 aforesaid; and that, before that time, to wit, on the said 8th day of *July* in that year, the said plaintiff had been, and was in due course of law examined and brought to the public police office in *Bow Street* in the county of *Middlesex*, before *Thomas Halls*, Esq., one of the Justices for *Westminster* and *Middlesex*, to answer a certain charge or complaint

made

1824.

Duncan
against
Thwaites.

made by one *Ann Chandler* the younger, against him
the said plaintiff, for having indecently assaulted her the
said *Ann Chandler* ; she, the said *Ann Chandler*, then
and there being a female child of only thirteen years old,
and the said plaintiff did then and there undergo a long
examination on that charge, and on that occasion then
and there publicly in the presence of the said plaintiff
before the said justice, *Ann Chandler* the elder, the
mother of the said *Ann Chandler*, did make oath and
depose as follows: that is to say, (This plea then set out
verbatim the depositions taken before the magistrate, by
one of which, made by a surgeon, it appeared that *Ann
Chandler* had several times answered in the negative
to certain questions put by him, to which she answered
in the affirmative before the magistrate.) And that the
plaintiff then and there, on the occasion aforesaid, denied the principal facts alleged against him as aforesaid,
and was eventually admitted to bail, himself in 100*l.* and
two sureties in 50*l.* each, for his appearance again on
Tuesday then next before the said justice, to answer the
said charge or complaint, to wit, at *London* aforesaid,
in the parish, &c. aforesaid. Wherefore the said defendants printed and published, and caused to be printed
and published, the said supposed libels in the introductory part of this plea mentioned, in copies of the
said public newspaper called the *Morning Herald* of the
said 10th of *July*, as and for, and the same being a true,
fair, just, and correct report and account of the said
proceedings which so took place on the said 8th day of
July in the year aforesaid, at the said police office on the
occasion aforesaid, and the said report or account thereof,
composing the said last mentioned supposed libels, was
so printed and published as aforesaid, in the said copies
of the said newspaper, as public news of the said last
                                              mentioned

1824.

mentioned proceedings, and with no other intent, and for no other object or purpose whatsoever, to wit, at, &c.

Sixth plea, as to the printing and publishing, and causing to be printed and published, the said several supposed libels in the said declaration mentioned, which contain all or any part of the following matter: that is to say, "Andrew Duncan the attorney, who was charged a week ago with attempting to violate the person of a girl of thirteen, named Ann Chandler, was again examined, but no further evidence was heard, and he was ordered to enter into recognizances to the amount of 200l. for his appearance at the sessions, and all the witnesses were bound over to prosecute." The said defendants by like leave, &c. here say, that the said last mentioned several supposed libels were, and are copies only of one and the same supposed libel, printed and published by the said defendants in several copies of the said public newspaper, called the Morning Herald, of Tuesday the 16th day of July 1823 aforesaid; and that after the said proceedings at the said public police office in the last preceding plea mentioned, had taken place as in that plea is mentioned, and which did actually take place as is therein stated and set forth; and before the said 16th day of July 1823, to wit, on the 15th day of July in that year, the said Andrew was publicly examined at the said police office before the said justice, respecting the said charge or complaint in the said last plea mentioned, but no further evidence was on that occasion heard respecting the said charge or complaint; and he, the said Andrew, was then and there ordered by the said justice to enter into recognizances to the amount of 200l. for his appearance at the sessions of the peace to be holden in and for the said county of Middlesex, to answer the said charge

O o 3

or

1824.

DUNCAN
against
THWAITES.

or complaint. And all the witnesses so examined as in the said last plea mentioned, were bound over to prosecute for the same at such sessions, to wit, at, &c. Wherefore the said defendants printed and published, and caused to be printed and published, the said supposed libels in the introductory part of this plea mentioned, in copies of the said public newspaper called the *Morning Herald*, of the said 16th day of *July*, as and for, and the same being a true, fair, just, and correct report and account of the said proceedings, which so took place on the said 15th day of *July* at the said police office on the occasion last aforesaid; and the said report or account thereof, composing the said last mentioned supposed libels, was so printed and published in the said newspaper as public news of the said last mentioned proceedings, and with no other intent, and for no other object or purpose whatsoever, to wit, at, &c.

The seventh plea was pleaded to a part only of the supposed libel of the 10th of *July*, in all other respects it resembled the fifth plea.

The eighth plea varied in like manner from the sixth. To these pleas the plaintiff demurred, and assigned several special causes, most of which are noticed in the argument.

Patteson, in support of the demurrer. The second plea is clearly bad, inasmuch as the libel does not profess to be an account of every thing which took place at *Bow Street*. It only gives a summary, or what the writer considered the result, of what took place. That being read unless the publication can be assisted by the plea which sets out what actually did take place, the plea is bad, *Lewis* v. *Walter* (a). In that case the libel purported to be a

(a) 4 B. & A. 605.

speech

speech of counsel at the trial of the plaintiff on a
criminal charge; and it stated, after setting out the
speech, that a witness was called who proved all that
had been stated by counsel, and that the defendant was
immediately after that acquitted upon a defect in proving
some matter of form. The plea stated that in fact such
a speech was made, and that the witness called proved
all that had been so stated; but it did not set out the
evidence, or justify the truth of the charges made in the
counsel's speech: and the Court held that the plea was
insufficient. The principle of that decision applies here;
and the second plea is not aided by that which sets out
the depositions. This publication in a newspaper was
circulated throughout the country, but the plea put upon
the record where an action is brought against a party
cannot be so circulated; and it would be of no effect in
taking away the sting of the libel unless published in the
same newspaper. Then, if that be so, none of the pleas
can cure the original defect in the libel, in not having
stated the evidence.

The third plea states that the matters contained in
the libel are true. Now, if the import of that plea
be that the libel contains a correct statement of what
took place at *Bow Street*, it is open to the same objection as the second plea. If, on the other hand, the
import be that the plaintiff is guilty of the charge
brought against him, it is a bad plea, because it ought
to have been more particular, and the facts ought to
have been enumerated, and time and place ought to
have been alleged; *J'Anson* v. *Stuart* (a), *Holmes* v.
Catesby (b), *Jones* v. *Stevens*. (c) This plea is also bad,

(a) 1 T. R. 748. (b) 1 Taunt. 543. (c) 11 Price, 235.

Q o 4   because

1821
DUNCAN
against
THOMAS
WHITWELL

because it is uncertain whether it means that the report was true, or that the charge was true.

The same objection applies to the fourth plea as to the second.

There is another objection also which applies to these three pleas, namely, that the matters alleged amount to the general issue; for, assuming the libels to be a correct account of what took place at *Bow Street*, the pleas do not justify the main charge, but go only to the motive, which is a mere negation of malice, and that might be proved on the general issue only; and the effect of pleading that in bar would be to withdraw the question of malice from the consideration of the jury. *Lewis* v. *Walter*. (a)

The fifth plea, which is confined to the first libel, states all the depositions. One objection to that plea, which applies also to the seventh, is, that it appears upon the face of the plea that the libel does not contain a true account of all that took place, because it does not contain the evidence of the surgeon, which is very material to shew the innocence of the plaintiff. Supposing, however, that the statement of the evidence in the plea can supply the defect in the publication, and that that does contain a true summary of what took place at *Bow Street*, then the question will be raised, whether a party is to be allowed to publish an account of ex parte proceedings at a police office, containing scandalous and defamatory matters against any individual. It has been expressly held, that it is an offence to publish ex parte proceedings at a police office. That was ruled by *Heath* J. in *Rex* v. *Lea* (b), and in *Rex* v. *Fisher* (c) by Lord Ellen-

(a) 4 B. & A. 605.   (b) 5 Esp. 123.   (c) 2 Camp. 563.

borough,

1824.

DUNCAN
v.
THWAITES.

borough, on the ground that such publications have a tendency to pervert the public mind, and to disturb the course of justice, by preventing a fair trial. In *Rex* v. *Fleet* (a) this court granted a criminal information against a party for publishing in a newspaper a statement of the evidence given before a coroner's jury, and the opinions of Lord Chief Justice *Abbott* and Mr. Justice *Bayley* seem to be founded chiefly upon the ground that such a publication had a tendency to prevent a fair trial; and in *Rex* v. *Clement* (b) this court supported a fine imposed upon the editor of a newspaper for publishing proceedings while the parties were still on their trials. All these cases were certainly cases of indictment or information, but no distinction can be taken in this respect between an indictment and an action. The indictment proceeds on the ground that the publication has a tendency to prejudice the public administration of justice, by preventing a fair trial, and that it is therefore unlawful. Now, if a party sustain a special injury thereby, he ought to be allowed to maintain an action. There is, indeed, this distinction between an indictment and an action for a libel, that truth is no justification in the former case, but it is in the latter. The reason of that, however, is, that an indictment lies because the act committed has a tendency to promote a breach of the peace; and therefore truth, as it may produce that effect, is no justification. That distinction might apply to these cases if the publication of *ex parte* proceedings tended to a breach of the peace, but the reason assigned why an indictment lies in such cases is, that the tendency of the publication is to prevent a fair trial. Now, that is injurious to the party whether he be

(a) 1 B. & A. 379.   (b) 4 B. & A. 218.

innocent

innocent or guilty. Besides, here the proceeding did not take place before a tribunal to which the public could claim admittance as of right, *Cox* v. *Coleridge* (a). In that respect these proceedings differ materially from those in a court of justice, which is open to all the world. Then if a party is present at such examination by the permission of the magistrate, he can have no more right to publish any matter which passes there, and which is injurious to an individual, than if it took place in any private room. Besides it appears from what fell from Lord *Kenyon*, in *Rex* v. *Creevey* (b), that even the proceedings of a court of justice cannot be published under all circumstances. *Rex* v. *Mary Carlile* (c) shews that a party is not at liberty to publish any matter which is scandalous and injurious to another, merely because it passes in a court of justice; and so, à fortiori, he cannot publish matter which has passed in a police office, which is not an open court of justice, and where the proceedings are exparte. The publication of them has a necessary tendency to prevent a fair trial in the ulterior stage of the investigation. *Rex* v. *Wright* (d) will probably be cited on the other side, but that was a publication of a report made by the House of Commons; and in *Rex* v. *Creevey* (e) it was held that a speech made in that House cannot lawfully be published if it contains libellous matter. Then as to the policy of such publications. There is indeed one contingent advantage which may arise from them, but that is counterbalanced by numerous inconveniences. The possible advantage is, that by accident, the public

....

(a) 1 B. & C. 37.   (b) 1 M. & S. 273.
(c) 3 B. & A. 167.   (d) 8 T. R. 293.
(e) 1 M. & S. 273.

cation

cation may catch the attention of persons who otherwise
might never hear of such a proceeding, and who might
come forward as witnesses for or against the party
accused; and might, therefore, have a tendency to assist
the administration of public justice.

On the other hand, if reports of this description are to
be published, it will, under all circumstances, be at the
expence of harassing the feelings of every person who is
unfortunately taken up upon any charge. When once
such a charge is published, it is extremely difficult to
take off the effect of it by any counter statement, and it
may possibly meet the eye of thousands who may never
hear that the party accused was ultimately proved innocent or guilty. The inconveniences, therefore, in-
finitely outweigh any good that may arise from such
publications.

E. Lawes, contrà. The question is, whether to publish a true account of the substance of what passed before a magistrate at a police office, respecting a prisoner
there present and charged with an attempt to commit
a rape, published in a newspaper as public news without
comment of any sort, or any malicious or defamatory
motive, be justifiable; and if so, whether the particulars
of the defendant's examination, as well as all the indecencies mentioned in the depositions, must be detailed
in the publication, or whether it is sufficient to state
fairly the substance of what passed before the magistrate.
It may be admitted, that reports of legal proceedings
may be libellous whether *ex parte* or not, but all the
cases in which they have been held to be so libellous, may be reduced to three classes; first, where the
account published has been false or highly coloured,

Waterfield

Waterfield v. The Bishop of Chichester (a); or, secondly, where the narrator has added some comments or opinion of his own reflecting on the court or the party, Stiles v. Nokes (b), Lewis v. Clement (c), Rex v. Fleet (d), Carr v. Jones (e), Rex v. Lee (f), Rex v. Fisher (g); or, thirdly, where he has made the report a vehicle of blasphemy, Rex v. Mary Carlisle, (h) The same doctrine applies to reports of proceedings in parliament, Rex v. Lord Abingdon (i), Rex v. Creevey (k) The publication in question does not contain a false or highly coloured account of the proceedings; nor is it accompanied with comments reflecting on the character of the individual; nor is there any thing immoral or indecent in it; it is not, therefore, within any of the excepted cases, the publication, therefore, not having been prohibited by any express order of the magistrate, is lawful within the general rule, as containing a fair and true account of the proceedings of a court of justice. There is no express authority to shew, that such a publication can be made the subject of a criminal charge, much less that it is the subject of a civil action at the suit of the party accused. In Rex v. Lee (l), the decision of Heath J. was perfectly correct, because the libel contained, besides the depositions, expressions and representations prejudicial to the character of the person accused, and therefore, the evidence offered to shew that the statement of facts was warranted by the depositions before the magistrates was not admissible. It is true that the learned Judge expressed an opinion,

(e) 3 Smith, 491.   (f) 5 Esp. 123.
(g) 2 Campb. 570.   (h) 3 B. & A. 167.
(i) 1 Esp. 228.
(l) 5 Esp. 123.

that

1824.
Duncan
against
Thwaites.

that the publication of exparte evidence before a trial was of itself highly criminal, but that opinion was extrajudicial. In *Rex* v. *Fisher* (a), the publication, instead of merely giving the examination, contained observations prejudicial to the party accused ; and in *Rex* v. *Fleet* (b), the publication contained a comment upon the facts which had occurred, and charged that the civil power had occasioned great mischief and had called out the military unnecessarily.

Assuming, however, that the publication of evidence taken before a magistrate in a preliminary enquiry is an indictable offence, it by no means follows that the party accused can therefore maintain an action against the publisher before any trial has taken place. Here it is alleged, that he never was suspected of the offence charged in the libel. But it appears upon the record that he was suspected, and that in consequence of those suspicions he was examined before a magistrate. There is an averment also that the charge is undetermined. That of itself is an answer to the action. He may or may not be guilty. The defendants have made no charge against him, they have only stated that he had been charged in the legal way before a magistrate. Now, if he be found guilty and the law be put in execution against him, he cannot be said to have sustained any injury by this publication, and if he be acquitted, he will have sustained no injury from it. The only case in which he could sustain injury would be, if he were wrongfully convicted in consequence of the publication ; but he has brought his present action before a trial has taken place, and before he can have sustained

(a) 2 Camp. S.O.   (b) 3 B. & A. 167.
(b) 1 B. & A. 579.   (a) 9 Camb. 570.

any

any injury: the declaration, therefore, does not disclose any sufficient cause of action, and on that ground the defendants are entitled to the judgment of the Court. There is a great distinction between proceedings in a civil action and proceedings by indictment. An indictment for a libel has nothing to do with the character of the person libelled up to the moment of the indictment. The object of it is to prevent a breach of the peace; but in civil actions, the loss of character is the ground of the action. Another distinction is, that to maintain an action the party must have sustained an injury. Thus, though a public nuisance should be a particular inconvenience to a party, it does not follow that he can maintain an action. To do that, his inconvenience must be shewn to be different from that of the rest of the king's subjects, *Iveson v. Moore*. (a) Now, at the time when this action was commenced, the plaintiff had not sustained any particular injury. He had only suffered that inconvenience which is supposed to result to the public from such a publication, viz. the tendency of it to impede the due administration of justice. The third distinction between indictments and civil actions for libels is, that in the former truth is no answer; in the latter it is. But, both in a civil action and in an indictment the libel must contain something more than defamatory matter, there must be an evil intention in the party publishing the libel, and no action can be maintained where there is a total absence of malice in the defendant. In *Carpenter v. Tarrant* (b), the action was for these words, "*Carpenter* would kill *Winckner* gaol and tried for his life, and would have been hanged had it not been for *Leggat*, for breaking open the

(a) 1 Salk. 15.   (b) Cas. Temp. Hardw. 339.

granary

granary of farmer *A.*, and stealing his bacon;" and there *Lee J.* said, " If these words had been only a narrative of what passed at the trial, he might have pleaded it so, and have justified, though at the trial it could only have been given in evidence in mitigation of damages; the true gist of the action with respect to the defendant being, whether he spoke the words falsely and *maliciously.*" But *Curry* v. *Walter* (a) is an authority expressly in point, for the libel contained an account of an application to the Court of King's Bench for a criminal information. Now that was *an exparte* proceeding, and *Eyre* C. J. laid it down, that a bonâ fide report containing the substance of the speech delivered in court was not actionable, and that opinion was afterwards confirmed by the Court of Common Pleas. It is true, that in that case some stress was laid upon the circumstance of the proceeding having taken place in a court of justice which was open to all the world; but in this case although it was in the power of the magistrate to exclude the public, *Cox* v. *Coleridge* (b), *Rex* v. *Borron.* (c) Yet he did not do so, and therefore, in fact, it was an open court. The case of *Curry* v. *Walter* remains uncontradicted by subsequent authorities. It is recognised by Lord *Ellenborough* in *Styles* v. *Nokes* (d), and in *Rex* v. *Fisher,* (e). In *Rex* v. *Wright* (f) it was held, that the printing of a true copy of a report of a committee of the House of Commons, containing a charge, injurious to an individual was not libellous. Upon the same principle, the publication of that which passed before a magistrate cannot be libellous. These two cases are authorities ex-

(a) 1 Esp. 456. 1 Bos. & Pul. 525.   (b) 1 B. & C. 37.
(c) 3 B. & A. 437.   (d) 7 East, 493.
(e) 2 Campb. 570.   (f) 8 T. R. 293.

pressly

pressly in point, and they are only opposed by a few nisi prius dicta.

The argument on the other side assumes, that such a publication will prejudice a fair trial founded on a fair accusation. Now it is to be observed, that if an action will lie for such a publication, it might on the same principle be maintainable in respect of slanderous matter contained in a hand-bill issued for the apprehension of persons suspected of offences, (*Delaney* v. *Jones* (a), is an authority to the contrary,) or for saying that the grand jury had found a true bill against *A. B.* for such an offence. Secondly, it assumes that the hearers will keep the proceedings secret. Thirdly, that what may lawfully be communicated to as many people as the police office will conveniently contain cannot lawfully be communicated to others. Fourthly, that there will be a trial. Now no intention to prosecute is averred in this case, and the case may have been compromised or otherwise abandoned. But, in fact, publications of this sort have a tendency to protect innocent persons by communicating knowledge of the accusation to their friends and enabling them to come forward in their defence. It is also calculated to bring forward witnesses for the prosecution, and to prevent the repetition of crimes and frauds by putting unwary people on their guard. Nor is there any ground for making a distinction between publishing preliminary proceedings and proceedings after a final adjudication has taken place, except where there is an express prohibition, for it is equally important for the public to know every circumstance connected with the administration of justice, whether sentence be pronounced or not.

(a) 4 *Esp.* 191.

In

In order to maintain a civil action for a libel, there must be malice in the defendant. Now here there is a total absence of malice, for wherever there is a fair motive or an interest in the party who utters or publishes the supposed slander, that is sufficient to negative malice; as, for instance, where it is done bonâ fide with a view to obtain information on a subject in which the party is interested, *Delaney* v. *Jones (a)*, or by a suitor in his own defence, *Moulton* v. *Clapham (b)*, cited 1 Barn. & A. 244, or by counsel in defence of his client, where the matter is pertinent, *Brook* v. *Montague (c)*, *Hodgson* v. *Scarlett (d)*, or where the matter is uttered for the purpose of giving information to a party interested, as in the case of the character of a servant, *Edmonson* v. *Stephenson (e)*, *Weatherstone* v. *Hawkins. (f)* So if the matter be uttered by a clergyman instructing his congregation, *Greenwood's* case cited *Cro. Jac.* 90. In all these cases the occasion of uttering the slanderous matter rebuts the presumption of malice; and to apply the same principle to this case, the reporter for a public newspaper has no evil intention, his object is only to give information to the public upon a subject in which they have an interest. Now it is perfectly clear that the public have an interest in the public administration of justice; and whatever is relevant thereto may be lawfully published. Upon this ground criticism upon theatrical performance or literary works is allowed, *Dibdin* v. *Swan (g)*, *Carr* v. *Hood. (h)* In this case, and particularly in the second plea, it is expressly averred that the defendants published the supposed slanderous matter without any malicious motive,

(a) 4 Esp. 191.
(b) ....
(c) Cro. Jac. 90.
(d) 1 B. & A. 232.
(e) Bull. N. P. 8.
(f) 1 T. R. 110.
(g) 1 Esp. 28.
(h) 1 Campb. 355.

and that is admitted by the demurrer. Besides which, circumstances are averred upon the record which would negative malice.

Then as to the objection that the libel only contains the substance of the proceeding, and does not set out the evidence. It is quite clear that if the evidence had been set out it would have been an indictable offence. Besides, it is almost impossible to give a verbatim report of any sort, and if it was it would not give the fair sense of what took place, and the effect of saying that that was necessary would be to prohibit the publication of all such reports in future.

Cur. adv. vult.

The judgment of the Court was now delivered by

ABBOTT C. J. This is an action for the publication of two supposed libels; the defendant has pleaded several special pleas to the declaration, to some of which the plaintiff has demurred.

The demurrer was argued before us at the sittings in *October* last. The declaration contains a great number of counts. It will be sufficient, for the purpose of our present judgment, to consider the counts as divided into two classes, and each class subdivided into two parts or branches. The first class will contain all those counts which are preceded by introductory averment of a proceeding before the justice. The second class will contain all those counts that have no such introduction. The first part or branch of each class will comprise the counts founded on the publication of the 10th of *July*, and the second those founded on the publication of the 16th of *July*. And with this distribution, it will not be necessary to advert particularly to any, except the first

and

and thirteenth counts. The Lord Chief Justice then
read those counts, and proceeded as follows :

The defendant has pleaded the general issue, and also
some pleas of justification, averring the truth of the
facts, that is, of the supposed assault, upon which pleas
issues have been joined.

To the second, third, fourth, fifth, sixth, seventh, and
eighth pleas the plaintiff has demurred. The third plea
alleges very shortly that the several matters and things
in the said several supposed libels contained, were and
are true. Now this plea is evidently bad. It is uncertain whether it be thereby meant to allege that the
report in the newspaper is a true report of certain proceedings, or that the facts mentioned in the report are
true; if the latter be meant, the plea is much too
general.

The fourth plea, which is pleaded to the whole declaration, is as follows: that the said supposed libels
respectively were and consisted of nothing more than
fair, true, and correct reports in the said newspaper
called the *Morning Herald*, of proceedings which took
place publicly and openly before the said *T. Halls*, so
being such justice as aforesaid, at the public police
office at *Bow-street* aforesaid.

Now, as one class of the counts in the declaration
does not allege any proceeding before a justice, it was at
least necessary in a plea to that class, to aver and shew
distinctly that proceedings had taken place before a
justice, and to do this with the formality and certainty
required in pleading; and if the plea be bad as to any
part of the matter to which it is pleaded, it is, according
to general rules, bad for the whole.

The fifth plea is pleaded to the first branch only of
the two classes of counts, or, in other words, to the sup-

posed libel of the 10th of *July*. It alleges that the plaintiff was brought before the magistrate and examined, and that, on that occasion, *Ann Chandler* the mother, *Ann Chandler* the daughter, *Ann Duncan*, and *Lewis Desormeaux* were examined, and that each of them deposed as set forth at large in this fifth plea; and then the plea goes on to allege, " wherefore the defendants published the supposed libel, as and for, and being a true, fair, just, and correct report and account of the said proceedings." But upon the face of the plea itself, it is manifest that it is not a true, fair, just, and correct report and account of the proceedings, for (without noticing other objections) the report wholly omits the deposition of *Desormeaux*, in which he deposes, that to a question proposed by him to the girl *Ann Chandler* as to a material fact, of which, before the justice she swore to the affirmative, she distinctly answered " No, he had not ;" and the same question being put to her over and over again, she always repeated " No."

The sixth plea is pleaded only to the supposed libel of the 15th of *July*, which alleges that the plaintiff was examined at the police office, and ordered to enter into recognizances, and the plea avers that the plaintiff was so examined, and that he was ordered to enter into such recognizances ; and as this libel contains no detail of the evidence, nor any comment upon the case, but nakedly states the result of what the justice thought fit to do, we think this plea good. The eighth plea is good upon the same grounds.

The seventh plea is pleaded to a part only of the supposed libel of the 10th of *July*; in all other respects it resembles the fifth plea, upon which our opinion has been already given.

It

It remains only to consider the second plea, which was very properly considered in the argument for the defendants as the important plea in this cause. That plea states, that on the 8th of *July* 1823, at the public police office *Bow-street*, the plaintiff underwent a long examination before the justice, on the charge of having indecently assaulted and attempted to violate the person of *Ann Chandler*, a female child only thirteen years old, and the evidence of the child herself, and her companion the plaintiff's own cousin of the same age, did upon that occasion display a complication of disgusting indecencies, although the plaintiff denied the principal facts alleged, and the children made some slight variations in their evidence, and eventually the plaintiff was on that occasion then and there admitted to bail, himself in 100*l.*, and two sureties in 50*l.* for his appearance again on *Tuesday* then next following. And that afterwards, on *Tuesday* the 15th day of *July*, at the said public office in *Bow-street* aforesaid, the said plaintiff was again examined before the justice touching the said charge; but no further evidence was heard, and he was ordered by the justice to enter into recognizances to the amount of 200*l.* for his appearance at the sessions, and all the witnesses were bound over to prosecute. And that the said several supposed libels, in the said declaration mentioned, contained and contain no other than a fair and just report and account of the proceedings which took place on the said 8th and 15th days of *July* respectively, at the said public police office *Bow-street* aforesaid, on the respective occasions aforesaid, and were printed and published by the defendants in the said newspaper called the *Morning Herald*, with no scandalous, malicious, or defamatory, unworthy, or unlawful motive whatever;

P p 3   and

and that the said proceedings therein reported as aforesaid, took place as aforesaid, publicly and openly at the said police office, and the said reports or accounts thereof, composing the said supposed libels, were so printed and published as aforesaid, in the said newspaper as public news of such public proceedings, and with no other intent, and for no other object or purpose whatsoever.

This plea is founded upon the supposition that it is lawful for the editors of the public journals to publish accounts of proceedings taking place before justices of the peace by way of preliminary enquiry, and with a view to commit to prison, or otherwise make amenable to justice, persons against whom charges are preferred before the justices; and to do this where the proceeding terminates by commitment or bail, and before the intended trial can take place, provided the proceedings themselves are conducted openly, and the accounts are just and true. This proposition was strongly contended for in the argument on behalf of the defendants, and it was inferred from the supposed legality of such publications, that no action can be maintained by the person thus accused, whose character and reputation may be injured by the publication.

The case was argued before us with much learning on both sides, and all the decisions and opinions of judges that have any bearing on the question were quoted on the one side or the other. It would be an unnecessary employment of the time of the Court to comment upon all these authorities. It may be sufficient to say of them, that there is not any one plainly supporting the affirmative of this proposition, and that there are many expressly declaring the negative. The case approaching nearest, and certainly approaching nearly,

to

to the affirmative, is that of *Currie* v. *Walter*, (a) The case is of great authority in itself, and derives additional weight from the manner in which it is mentioned by Mr. Justice *Lawrence* in the *King* v. *Wright*.

It has not, however, received the sanction of subsequent judges: and it differs in some important facts from the present case. It was an account of a proceeding in this court, a court instituted for final determination, as well as preliminary enquiry, and whose doors are, as they ought to be, open to so many of the public as can be conveniently accommodated within its walls. The proceeding now in question was before justices of the peace, and was of a kind which they may lawfully conduct *in private* whenever they think fit to do so. That proceeding terminated by a refusal of the application, and not by putting the subject into a train for further inquiry and trial. The proceeding in question terminated in the first instance by holding the accused to bail for his future appearance before the justices, and finally by holding him to bail to take his trial before a jury. Such a trial therefore might be expected at the time of each of the publications.

This court has on more than one occasion within a few years been called upon to express its opinion judicially on the publication of preliminary and ex parte proceedings, and has on every occasion delivered its judgment against the legality of such proceedings, as was done by Mr. Justice *Heath* in the year 1804, in the case of *The King* v. *Lee.* (b) Other judges have delivered opinions to the same effect, and it is well known that many other persons have lamented the inconvenience and the mischievous tendency of such pub-

(a) 1 *Esp.* 456. and 1 *B.* & *P.* 525.   (b) 5 *Esp.* 123.

lications.

lications. They were within the memory of many persons now living rare and unfrequent, they have gradually increased in number, and are now unhappily become very frequent and numerous; but they are not on that account the less unlawful, nor is it less the duty of those, to whom the administration of justice is entrusted, to express their judgment against them.

I have pointed out some distinctions between the present case and that of *Currie* v. *Walter*; but we wish it not to be inferred from thence that we think the publication of ex parte proceedings even in this court to be a matter allowable by law.

But it was further contended, that even supposing publications of this kind to be so far unlawful as to render their authors amenable to the criminal law, by reason of the public inconvenience and mischief, yet that the party himself could not maintain a civil action in respect of such publications, or at least that the plaintiff was barred of his action in the present case by the denial of malice, which denial was supposed to be admitted by the demurrer. If, however, a plea be bad in law, a demurrer to it admits no fact alleged in it. I take it to be a general rule that a party who sustains a special and particular injury by an act, which is unlawful on the ground of public injury, may maintain an action for his own *special* injury; and if publications like the present tend to prevent or impede the due administration of justice towards persons accused of offences, it is impossible to say that the individual whose trial may be affected by them, does not sustain a special and peculiar injury even in that view, and he certainly sustains an injury to his character of the same nature as the injury to any other person by any other species of defamation. I take it to be also a general rule that an

act

act unlawful in itself and injurious to another is considered both in law and reason to be done malo animo toward the person injured: and this is all that is meant by a charge of malice in a declaration of this sort, which is introduced rather to exclude the supposition that the publication may have been made on some innocent occasion, than for any other purpose. There are even some acts not in themselves unlawful, but which become so only by reason of their injury to others, which in all civil actions are charged to be maliciously done. Take the common case of an offensive trade; the melting of tallow, for instance; such a trade is not in itself unlawful, but if carried on to the annoyance of the neighbouring dwellings, it becomes unlawful with respect to them, and their inhabitants may maintain an action, and may charge the act of the defendant to be malicious, and no one ever objected to such a charge; though probably in most cases the defendant has no personal malice toward his neighbours, but acts only with a view to his own profit and gain. The publication in question impeaches the plaintiff's character; a publication impeaching private character is actionable, unless the occasion of publishing makes the publication excusable, and where the publication is a violation of the criminal jurisprudence of the country, and there is nothing to call for it, the publication is not excusable.

These observations upon the plea are an answer also to the objections that were taken to the declaration: for if the facts stated in the plea do not furnish a defence, the introductory averments even in those counts that contain such, do not shew that the action is not maintainable.

> Judgment for the plaintiff on the demurrer to the second, third, fourth, fifth, and seventh pleas; for the defendants as to the sixth and eighth.

1824.

DAVIES *against* BINT and Others.

An information
for penalties
under the game
law is not an
information
within the
meaning of the
stat. 48 G 3.
c. 58., whereby,
if the defendant
neglect to ap-
pear and plead,
the prosecutor
is at liberty to
enter an ap-
pearance and a
plea of not
guilty for the
defendant; and
therefore,
where the pro-
secutor had en-
tered an ap-
pearance and a
plea of not
guilty for the
defendant, and
a verdict had
been found
against the de-
fendant, the
Court set aside
such verdict for
irregularity.

THIS was an information brought for recovery of
penalties, for offences committed against the game
laws. A copy of the information had been served upon
each of the defendants pursuant to the 48 G. 3. c. 58.,
and upon the copies there was indorsed a notice, " that
unless the respective defendants should, within eight
days after the delivery thereof, cause an appearance and
plea or demurrer to be entered in the Court of King's
Bench to that information, an appearance and the plea
of not guilty would be entered thereto in their names,
pursuant to the statute in such case made and provided,
and the issue to be joined thereon would be tried at
the next assizes to be holden in and for the county of
Worcester." The defendants having neglected to appear, an appearance and plea of not guilty were accordingly entered for them, and the cause sent down to trial
at the last Summer assizes pursuant to the notice, when
a verdict was found against three of the defendants, and
the other was acquitted. A rule nisi had been obtained
for setting aside this verdict, upon the ground that the
48 G. 3. c. 58. did not apply to informations brought
for penalties on penal statutes, but was confined to indictments and informations for criminal matters; and
that, as the only notice of trial given to the defendants was that indorsed on the copies of the information,
they had, in effect, no notice at all, and the whole proceeding was a nullity.

.. *W. E. Taun-*

W. E. Taunton and Russell now shewed cause. The statute of the 48 G. 3. c. 58. s. 1. recites, that the provisions of the 26 G. 3. c. 77., and the 35 G. 3. c. 96. which were statutes passed to amend the law with regard to the course of proceeding in indictments and informations in the Court of King's Bench, in certain cases relating to the public revenue had been found beneficial, and that it was expedient to extend the same to other cases, and then enacts, that " whenever any person shall be charged with any offence for which he may be prosecuted by indictment or *information* in his majesty's Court of King's Bench, and the same shall be made appear to any judge of the same court by affidavit or by certificate of an indictment or information being filed against such person in the said court for such offence, it shall be lawful for such judge to issue his warrant, &c.; and for want of bail, to commit the d e fendant to the gaol of the county where the *offence* shall have been committed, or where he shall have been apprehended, until he shall have been *acquitted of such offence*, or in case of conviction shall have received judgment for the same." It afterwards enables the prosecutor of such indictment or information to cause a copy thereof to be delivered to such person, or to the gaoler, &c., with notice to plead within eight days, and to cause an appearance and a plea or demurrer to be entered in the said court to such indictment or information; and then if he neglect to cause an appearance and a plea or demurrer to be entered to such indictment or information, the prosecutor is enabled to enter an appearance and a plea of not guilty for him. In this case the proceeding is by information, and therefore falls within the *words* of the statute; and an information

ation on the game laws is an information within the *meaning* of the statute. In 4 *Blackstone's Commentaries, p.* 308. it is expressly stated, "that such informations as are usually brought upon penal statutes, are informations partly at the suit of the king and partly at that of a subject, which inflict a penalty upon conviction of the *offender*, one part to the use of the king and another to the use of the informer, and are a sort of qui tam actions only carried on by a criminal instead of a civil process." Here, the word *offence* is mentioned in the statute, for it speaks of the defendant being acquitted of such offence. The statute 8 *G*. 1. *c*. 19., and the statute of the 5th of *Anne*, speak of the offender and of his conviction. *Hawkins*, in his *Treatise on the Pleas of the Crown, Book* 2. *c.* 26., takes the same distinction as to informations as *Blackstone*, and under the title " informations qui tam," the party sued is spoken of as an offender, and the matter as an offence; and in sect. 64. it is said, that the king may bar the penalty by a pardon or release precedent to the commencement of the suit; and in sect. 66. that the plea is not guilty, and if there be more than one defendant, they ought not to plead that they are not guilty, but severally that neither they nor any of them are guilty. Now the judgment is, that the king or informer shall recover, or that the defendant shall forfeit the sum mentioned by the statute.

The statute 26 *G*.3. *c*.77. *s*.13., which is mentioned in the preamble to the 48 *G*.3. *c*.58., relates to persons charged with obstructing excise officers, rescuing uncustomed goods, or with any offence against any law respecting quarantine; and that statute, as well as the 35 *G*.3. *c*.96., regulates the proceedings in indictments or informations for such offences. Now one of the

statutes

statutes in force prior to the 26 *G.* 3. relating to quarantine was the 26 *G.* 2. *c.* 6. *s.* 3., and by that statute
the master of every vessel was required to make a discovery of certain particulars specified; and in case he
did not make a true discovery, was to forfeit 200*l.*, one
moiety thereof to the king, and the other moiety thereof
to him who would sue for the same by action of debt,
bill, plaint, or *information*, in any court of record, &c.

ABBOTT C. J. It is quite clear that the stat. 48 *G.* 3.
c. 58. does not apply to an information brought for
penalties on the game laws. It enacts, "that when
any person shall be charged with an offence for which
he may be prosecuted by indictment or information in
his majesty's court of K. B." It therefore contemplates
offences over which this court has exclusive jurisdiction
by indictment or information. Now penalties under the
game laws may be recovered by information not only
in this court but in the other courts in *Westminster
Hall.* I think the statute applies only to such offences
as the Court of King's Bench may exclusively entertain
when prosecuted by indictment or information, at the
suit of the king.

Rule absolute.

Curwood and *Carrington* were to have supported the
rule.

WARNE *against* BRYANT.

BY an order of Nisi Prius all matters in difference in
this cause between the parties were referred to an
arbitrator, and, among other things, it was ordered
that the arbitrator should be at liberty, if he should
think fit, to examine the parties to this suit upon oath.
It appeared now by affidavit that the action was brought
to recover the amount of a builder's bill for work and
labour, and materials found. The defendant proved by
an indifferent witness that a verbal agreement was made
between the plaintiff and the defendant, by which the
plaintiff agreed to charge the prime cost for materials
and labour, and to be paid 10*l.* per cent. for profit, and
no more. The plaintiff's attorney admitted that he had
no evidence to disprove such agreement, except that
of the plaintiff himself. The defendant objected to
the plaintiff's being examined in support of his own
case; but, notwithstanding such objection, the arbitrator allowed the plaintiff to be examined in support
of his own case, and awarded a sum to the plaintiff much
exceeding the value of the materials, and 10*l.* per cent.
profit.

Denman moved to set aside the award, on the ground
that the arbitrator had not any power under the terms
of this order to examine a party in support of his own

case;

case; but admitted that he could not find any case in which the point had been decided.

Per Curiam. We think the words of the order of reference are sufficiently large to empower the arbitrator to examine the parties for any purpose, and in any stage of the inquiry; and it seems that our judgment is not fettered by any prior decision. The arbitrator is to exercise his discretion in all cases whether he will allow a party to be examined at all. In practice many cases are referred for the express purpose of having the parties to the suit examined (which cannot be done in a court of law). We think the arbitrator may under an order framed like the present examine a party to the suit even in support of his own case; and that being so, there is no ground for granting this rule.

Rule refused.

CUXON and Another, Assignees of T. SWEET, a Bankrupt, *against* JAMES CHADLEY.

ASSUMPSIT for goods sold by the bankrupt before his bankruptcy. Plea, non assumpsit. At the trial before *Abbott* C. J. at the *London* sittings after *Hilary* term 1824, the following appeared to be the facts of the case: The bankrupt was an upholsterer in *London*, and in *May*, 1822, had sold and delivered to the defendant some plate glasses and frames of the value

J. C. being indebted to S., and R. C. being indebted to S. and also to J. C., it was verbally agreed between the three that S. should transfer the debt due to him from J. C. to the account of R. C.; and

S., in pursuance of such agreement, delivered to *R. C.* an account, in which he (*R. C.*) was charged with the debt due from *J. C.* to *S.*: Held, that *J. C.* was not thereby discharged.

of

of 14l. 1s. Sweet, the bankrupt, and Robert Chadley, the brother of the defendant, had been concerned together in accommodation bills, and in 1822, Robert Chadley was indebted to Sweet for goods. In August 1822, Robert Chadley told Sweet to carry to his Robert Chadley's account the debt due from his brother James to him Sweet. Sweet agreed to do so, and Robert Chadley afterwards informed his brother of what had taken place between him and Sweet. At this time Robert Chadley owed his brother James Chadley 60l. In an account between Robert Chadley and Sweet, made up, by the latter, to Christmas 1822, and entered in a book kept by him, there was the following entry: "December 1st. Your brother's account, 14l. 1s." This entry was in the hand-writing of Sweet, and was so made by him with the assent of Robert Chadley. Sweet never applied to Robert Chadley for the money. It appeared further, that by charging the 14l. 1s. against Robert Chadley, the account between Robert Chadley and Sweet was nearly balanced. Upon this evidence the Lord Chief Justice was of opinion that the defendant was not discharged, and he directed the jury to find a verdict for the plaintiffs, but reserved liberty to the defendant to move to enter a nonsuit if the Court should be of opinion that the plaintiffs were not entitled to recover. A rule nisi having been obtained in last Easter term, ...
. . . .

Marryat and Reader now shewed cause: The defendant James Chadley was originally liable for these goods, and he has never paid for them. There is no evidence to shew that Robert Chadley ever became legally bound to pay his brother's debt, for there was

no

no promise in writing, and a mere verbal promise is void by the statute of frauds. *Robert Chadley*, therefore, never having become bound to pay the debt, there was no sufficient consideration for the bankrupt's discharging *James Chadley*. *Wyatt* v. *The Marquis of Hertford* (a) is a much stronger case. There the plaintiff had done work for the defendant, and after the completion of it sent in his account to the defendant's steward, and accepted from the steward his draft in payment, and gave a receipt for the amount. The draft being dishonored, the plaintiff, without making any representation to the defendant, took from the steward a second draft payable at a future day. The second draft was not paid, and the steward becoming insolvent, the plaintiff applied to the defendant for payment, which was refused; and in that case it was laid down that if one take the security of the agent of the principal, with whom he deals, unknown to the principal, and give the agent a receipt for the money due from the principal, in consequence of which the principal deals differently with his agent on the faith of such receipt, the principal is discharged, although the security fail; but that it would be otherwise if the principal failed to shew that he was injured by means of such false voucher and the omission of the party to inform him of the truth in due time. Now, assuming *Robert Chadley* here to have been the agent of his brother *James Chadley* for the purpose of paying this debt, the latter would still, according to the case cited, continue liable to the bankrupt, unless he could shew that in consequence of the sum due from *James Chadley* having been transferred to *Robert Chad-*

(a) 3 *East*, 147.

ley's account, *James Chadley* had been induced to deal
differently with his brother on the supposition that the
demand had been satisfied. There is no evidence of
that description, therefore *James Chadley* continued liable
for the debt which he had originally contracted.

Gurney and *Holt*, contrà. It must be taken in this
case, that *Sweet*, *Robert Chadley*, and *James Chadley*,
had agreed that the debt due to *Sweet* should be paid
by *Robert*, and that *Sweet* had agreed to take *Robert*
as his debtor instead of *James*. And *Sweet*, acting
upon that agreement, did actually transfer to *Robert's*
account the debt due from *James*. By so doing he
accepted *Robert* as his debtor instead of *James*. The
consideration for *Robert's* engagement was *Sweet's* forbearing to sue his brother, and the relative situation
of the parties was altered, for *James Chadley* was induced to forego any remedy against his brother *Robert*
for the debt due from him, in consequence of its having
been agreed by *Sweet* to accept *Robert* as his debtor.
No formal receipt could be necessary in this case, and
the agreement between the parties amounted, in substance, to an accord and satisfaction. When *Sweet*, in
stating his account with *Robert Chadley* at *Christmas*
1822, entered in his book the following item: " To your
brother's account 14*l.* 1*s.*," he must be considered to
have ratified the previous agreement, which, though
executory before, became thenceforward a satisfaction
and discharge. The stating and rendering an account
is a sufficient consideration for a promise to pay the
balance. By parity of reasoning, it must also be a
sufficient consideration for discharging the debtor from
any item which his creditor, with not only a full
                                                    knowledge

knowledge of the circumstances, but upon the basis of his own previous agreement, thinks proper to expunge from the account. (a)

Cur. adv. vult.

ABBOTT C. J. This case came before us on a motion for a nonsuit. We are of opinion that the rule must be discharged. *Sweet* the bankrupt had sold goods to the amount of 14*l.* to *James Chadley* the defendant. The bankrupt, and *Robert Chadley* the brother of the defendant, were concerned together in accommodation bills, and there was another account between them, in which *Robert Chadley* was debtor to *Sweet*. *Robert Chadley* was also debtor to his brother *James*. About the month of *August* or *September*, *Robert Chadley* spoke to *Sweet* and desired that he would put down the goods which had been sold to *James Chadley* to the account of him, *Robert*. *Sweet* agreed to this, and *Robert Chadley* informed his brother of what had passed between them. Towards the end of the year, when *Sweet* gave in an account of the monies due to him from *Robert*, he put at the end of the account this entry: "*December* the 1st, 1822, your brother's account 14*l.* 1*s.*" This is all that passed. *Sweet* is not proved ever to have said, " I will take you, *Robert*, as my debtor and discharge *James;*" he is not proved ever to have said or done that which would have the effect of discharging *James*. It is contended by the defendant's counsel that this is accord and satisfaction; but, admitting the previous agreement, where is the satisfaction? But I consider the entry made by *Sweet* to mean no more

(a) The case was argued on a former day in this term.

Q q 2

than

than this; I will debit the account of *Robert* for 14*l.* 1*s.*; not, I will discharge *James*, at all events, from this sum. Nor are the dealings of the parties at all varied by this arrangement; the bankrupt's condition is not improved by it, nor the defendant's deteriorated. It amounts at most to an accord, but certainly not to a satisfaction. We cannot say, therefore, that either *Robert* could have been made to pay this money to *Sweet* if he had called for it, or that *James* is discharged from his original obligation to pay the amount of goods sold to him. We, therefore, think the verdict right, and that the rule which has been obtained must be discharged.

Rule discharged.

In the Matter of R. J. ELSAM, an Attorney.

J. FOX devised all his estate, real and personal, to *Richard John Elsam,* to hold to him and his heirs for ever, subject however to a condition that if the said *R. J. Elsam* should happen to die without issue lawfully begotten of his own body, the said estates should go to seven other great-nephews and nieces, to hold to them, their heirs and assigns for ever, as tenants in common; and if any of the devisees over should die in the interim, the children of them so dying should take their parent's share; and for lack of such children, to be divided equally among the survivors; and, after giving legacies to the devisees over, he appointed *R. J. Elsam* sole executor. After the testator's death, the will was laid before a conveyancer, who was of opinion that Mr. *Elsam* took an estate tail, but suggested that it might be argued that the words " if he shall happen to die without issue" referred to the time of his, *Elsam*'s death, and thus gave him a fee-simple, subject to an executory devise, in the event of his leaving no issue living. *Elsam* having applied a large part of the personal estate in paying the pecuniary legacies to the devisees; and knowing that he should be obliged to raise money on the security of the real estate for payment of the testator's debts, and that he could not raise money otherwise than upon annuity at a great expence, while the doubt suggested hung over the title, for the purpose of obtaining the opinion of a court of law upon the construction of the will, instituted an action in the

nature

A special case was stated for the opinion of the Court. The greater part of the statement was fictitious. The Court fined the attorney.

nature of a feigned issue. The parties to it were stated
to be *John Fox*, plaintiff, and *James Dodds*, defendant;
and the action purported to be brought upon an agreement for the sale of certain freehold and copyhold property, and fixtures, by the plaintiff to the defendant.
The cause was tried upon admissions, and a verdict
taken for the plaintiff, subject to the opinion of this
court on a special case. The case set forth the contract for sale by the plaintiff to the defendant; the seisin
of the testator; his will in hæc verba; his death; the
entry of the devisee, *R. J. Elsam ;* that he had suffered
recoveries of the property, and subsequently sold and
conveyed the premises in question to the plaintiff, who
had offered to convey to the defendant, pursuant to the
agreement; but that the defendant had objected to the
title, on the ground that the will contained an executory
devise, which the recoveries had not barred, and the
question was, whether *R. J. Elsam* took an estate tail.
The case was argued at the sittings before this term,
and a doubt occurring whether the transaction were
bonâ fide, the Court required the production of the recoveries suffered by *Elsam ;* the conveyance from him
to the plaintiff; and the alleged contract of sale to the
defendant, with an affidavit of its due execution, and of
its being a bonâ fide transaction. It being admitted
that this could not be done, the Court referred it to the
Master to inquire which of the facts stated in the
special case were truly stated, and to ascertain what
proceedings had taken place in the cause prior to the
engrossment of the record of nisi prius. The Master
reported that the whole of the statement was fictitious,
except the seisin of the testator, and the entry of *Elsam*
as his devisee; and also that no writ was issued in the

cause,

cause, nor was any common bail filed, &c.; and that the only proceeding taken in the cause prior to the engrossment of the record of nisi prius was the entry of the issue.   The defendant now, by affidavit, stated his reasons for wishing to obtain the opinion of the Court speedily, and that he was not actuated by any corrupt or fraudulent motive, and that he had already incurred an expence of 40*l.* in the course of the proceedings.

ABBOTT C. J.   It is impossible to pass over a case of this kind without notice; but as it appears that the party before the Court did not intend any fraud, and that he has already incurred an expense of 40*l.* in the course of these proceedings, the object of the Court, which is to prevent the repetition of such a practice in future, will be answered by ordering him to pay a fine of 40*l.*, and to be imprisoned till that fine be paid.

END OF MICHAELMAS TERM.

C A S E S

ARGUED AND DETERMINED

IN THE

Court of KING's BENCH,

IN

Hilary Term,

In the Fifth and Sixth Years of the Reign of GEORGE IV.

1825.

MAYHEW and Another *against* EAMES and Another.

Monday,
January 24th.

THIS was an action against the defendants, as carriers, brought to recover the value of a parcel of country bank notes sent by their coach from *Downham,* in the county of *Norfolk,* to *London.* At the trial before *Abbott* C. J., at the *London* sittings after last term, the following appeared to be the facts of the case. The plaintiffs were silk warehousemen, residing in *London,* and employed one *Hughes* as their agent to collect their debts in the country. The defendants were coach pro-

An agent employed by a commercial house in London to collect debts in the country, delivered a parcel containing bank notes to a common carrier, to be forwarded to his principals in London, which parcel was lost. The carriers had given notice that they would not be accountable for parcels containing bank notes. The agent had no knowledge of such notice, but the principals had: Held, that it was their duty to have instructed their agent not to send bank notes by that carrier, and that the latter was not responsible.

prietors and owners of a coach running from *Lynn* to the *White Horse, Fetter Lane, London.* On the 10th of *February* 1824, *Hughes,* the agent of the plaintiffs, having collected, in payment of debts due to them, provincial banker's notes to the amount of 87*l.,* inclosed them in a parcel, and upon the parcel he wrote the word " Mourning," and addressed it to the plaintiffs, " *Foster Lane, Cheapside, London.*" *Hughes* then delivered the parcel to one *Wright,* at whose house in *Downham* the coach stopped to change horses, and he paid fór the carriage 1*s.* 2*d.,* ard *Wright* gave him a receipt for the parcel. When the coach arrived, *Wright* delivered the parcel to the coachman, and it was afterwards lost. For the defendants it was proved, that the plaintiffs had frequently received parcels before the 10th of *February* coming by coaches to the *White Horse, Fetter Lane, London,* and the porter who delivered such parcels proved that he had always delivered with them a ticket containing the amount of the charge for carriage and porterage, and a printed notice, " that the proprietors of carriages which set out from that office would not hold themselves accountable for any passenger's luggage, truss, parcel, or any package whatever above the value of 5*l.* if lost or damaged, unless the same were entered as such and paid for accordingly when delivered there, or to their agents in town or country; nor would they be accountable for any glass, china, plate, watches, writings, cash, bank notes, or jewels of any description, however small the value." But there was no evidence to shew that *Hughes* had any knowledge of such notice at the time when he delivered the parcel to *Wright.* Upon this evidence the Lord Chief Justice was of opinion that as the plaintiffs knew that the defendants were not ac-

countable

countable for bank notes, they ought to have desired their agent not to send parcels of that description by any coach of the defendants, and the plaintiffs were nonsuited, with liberty to them to move to enter a verdict for 87*l.*

Denman now moved accordingly. The contract for the safe carriage of the goods was made by the plaintiffs' agent, and there was no evidence to shew that he had any knowledge of the notice given by the defendants, or that he knew that the coach stopped at the *White Horse, Fetter Lane*, or even that *Eames*'s name was on the coach. In making the contract for the carriage of the goods, he must be taken to have trusted to the common law responsibility of carriers.

Per Curiam. At common law, carriers are responsible for the value of the goods they undertake to carry, but they may limit their responsibility by making a special contract, and that is usually done by giving public notice that they will not be accountable for parcels of a given description. In order, however, to shew in any particular case that they are not subject to the common law responsibility, they must prove that the party sending the goods had knowledge of the notice. But the knowledge of the principal is the knowledge of the agent. Now here the agent was employed to transmit bank notes, which are the subject of the present action, and it appears that the plaintiffs themselves had knowledge that the defendants would not be responsible for bank notes, because it is in evidence that many parcels came to them from the defendants, and that the

porter

porter delivered together with such parcels a printed paper containing a notice that "the proprietors of carriages setting out from the *White Horse, Fetter Lane,* would not hold themselves accountable for any glass, china, plate, watches, writings, cash, *bank notes,* or jewels of any description, however small the value." Now when a parcel came to the plaintiffs in this way before, they must have seen the notice, because it was contained in the same paper which they must have looked at in order to ascertain the amount of the charge for carriage and porterage which they had to pay. Then if the plaintiffs knew that parcels would not be accounted for if they contained bank notes, it was their duty to tell their agent not to send any such parcels by any of the coaches coming to the *White Horse, Fetter Lane.* But as the plaintiffs suffered their agent to send notes by those coaches, we think that knowledge of the notice having been brought home to the plaintiffs, the carrier is thereby protected from such loss, although the parcel was sent by an agent.

Rule refused.

JOHN PIDCOCK, GEORGE BARKER, JOHN HENZEY *Tuesday,* *January 25th.*
PIDCOCK, and GEORGE PIDCOCK *against* SAMUEL
HINTON TOWNSEND BISHOP.

ASSUMPSIT by the plaintiffs, manufacturers of pig
iron at *Lightmoor*, in the county of *Salop*, against
the defendant a dealer in iron at *Bankside*, *London*,
upon his guarantee. The guarantee declared upon was
contained in a letter of the 16th *December* 1822, addressed by the defendant to the plaintiffs, and was as
follows:

"At the request of Mr. *Thomas Tickell*, I beg to inform you that I will guaranty you in the payment of
200*l.* value to be delivered to him in *Lightmoor* pig
iron."

At the trial before *Hullock* B., at the *Warwick Lent*
assizes 1824, it was proved on the part of the plaintiffs,
that the defendant gave the above mentioned guarantee,
and that in *February* 1823 the plaintiffs supplied to
Tickell twenty tons of *Lightmoor* pig iron of the value
and price of 82*l.* 10*s.*, that they had applied to him for
payment, but he was unable to pay any part of the
money. On the part of the defendant, *Tickell* proved
that he had formerly been in the iron trade, but had
become bankrupt some time before the transaction out
of which the action arose; that in the beginning of *December* 1822 he applied to *John Pidcock*, one of the plaintiffs, (who managed the business at the *Lightmoor* works),
to supply him with *Lightmoor* pig iron on credit in the
usual way, and told him that if the company would

It was agreed between the vendors and vendee of goods that the latter should pay 10s. per ton beyond the market price, which sum was to be applied in liquidation of an old debt due to one of the vendors. The payment of the goods was guaranteed by a third person, but the bargain between the parties was not communicated to the surety: Held, that that was a fraud on the surety, and rendered the guaranty void.

R r 3   supply

supply him, he would pay him (*John Pidcock*) ten shillings (beyond the price to be paid to the company) for every ton of iron supplied to him, and which ten shillings was to go towards the liquidation of an old debt due from *Tickell* to *John Pidcock*. *John Pidcock* said he must consult his partners, but that he thought they would not consent to supply the iron without a guarantee. It was afterwards agreed between *Tickell* and *John Pidcock* that the iron should be supplied, *Tickell* paying the company the market price, and ten shillings per ton extra to *John Pidcock* in liquidation of his private debt, and also procuring a satisfactory guarantee for the price of the iron. *Tickell* accordingly applied to the defendant, who gave the guarantee, but the agreement he had entered into with *John Pidcock* for the payment of the extra ten shillings per ton was not communicated to the defendant. A bill of parcels was sent with the iron, as follows:

" To 20 tons of *Lightmoor*

pig iron	-	-	£82 10s. to Mr. *Pidcock.*
" Debt	-	-	10 0
			——— total £92 10s."

On the part of the defendant it was contended, that the agreement as to the payment of the ten shillings per ton was a fraud upon the defendant, and that he consequently was not liable upon his guarantee. *Hullock* B. thought this no answer to the action, and a verdict was found for the plaintiffs for 82*l*. 10*s*., but liberty was given to the defendant to move to enter a nonsuit.

In the following *Easter* term *Denman* obtained a rule to shew cause why the verdict should not be set aside and a nonsuit entered, and in this term

Clarke

Clarke and *N. R. Clarke* shewed cause. There was no fraud upon the defendant either practised or intended. There was nothing in the agreement by which he could be prejudiced, or by which the probability of his being called upon to pay for the iron in consequence of his guarantee was increased. The agreement as far as it respected the ten shillings, was merely an arrangement between *J. Pidcock* and *Tickell* for the payment of the debt of the latter by easy instalments. There was nothing to shew that it was not at the time an existing debt, and one upon which *Pidcock* might have sued; for though *Tickell* stated he had been a bankrupt, it did not appear when this debt was incurred, and if it was *before* the bankruptcy, it did not appear that *Tickell* had obtained his certificate, or that the debt had been proved under his commission. If the defendant intended to rely upon the debt having been barred by the bankruptcy, it was for him to prove it. Taking it then to be a debt still due from *Tickell* to *J. Pidcock*, the agreement so far from being prejudicial to the defendant, was, in fact, for his advantage, for if *J. Pidcock* after the supply of the iron had sued *Tickell* and obtained judgment against him, and taken his effects in execution for the whole amount of his debt, *Tickell* would probably have been less able to pay for the iron than if he was allowed to pay his debt by such easy instalments as were stipulated for in the agreement. It was not the agreement, but the previous debts and embarrassed circumstances of *Tickell* which rendered him unable to pay for the iron; the defendant was probably aware of *Tickell's* situation when he gave the guarantee, or if not, and he gave the guarantee without inquiring into it, he must take the consequences of having neglected to

do

do so. The case of *Jackson* v. *Duchaire* (a) was very different from this case; there a person of the name of *Welch*, wishing to assist the defendant, who was entering upon a house which the plaintiff had before occupied, agreed to purchase of the plaintiff for the defendant at the price of 70*l.* the goods left by the former in the house; and it formed part of the consideration which induced *Welch* to furnish the money that the plaintiff agreed to take 70*l.* for the goods, and the Court, therefore, held that a private agreement between the plaintiff and defendant, that 30*l.* more should be paid by the latter, was a fraud upon *Welch*, who had paid the 70*l.* in confidence that that sum was the whole consideration. The plaintiff, therefore, could not recover the 30*l.* But there is nothing in the case to shew that the Court considered the contract between plaintiff and *Welch* for the sale of the goods at 70*l.* void; or that *Welch* could recover back that sum. If in the present case the ten shillings per ton to be paid to J. *Pidcock* had not been to discharge an existing debt, the case of *Jackson* v. *Duchaire* might have been an authority to shew that J. *Pidcock* could not recover that money, but even then it would be no authority for saying that the guarantee was not binding to the extent of the actual price of the iron, and it was never proposed or intended to make the defendant liable beyond that.

Denman and *F. Pollock*, contrà. Although it is attempted to distinguish the present case from that of *Jackson* v. *Duchaire*, they are the same in principle. Wherever a person agrees to pay money *for*, or gua-

(a) 3 T. R. 551.

rantees

rantees the payment of money *by* another, it is a fraud upon that person if the contract in consequence of which he agrees to pay the money, or for the fulfilment of which he consents to become guarantee, is not fully and fairly disclosed to him. Here the contract, the fulfilment of which was guaranteed by the defendant, (which was merely a contract for iron at the market price), was totally different from the contract actually entered into with *Tickell*. If the agreement for the payment of the extra ten shillings per ton had been communicated to the defendant, he might perhaps have refused to become guarantee.

ABBOTT C. J. I am of opinion that a party giving a guarantee ought to be informed of any private bargain made between the vendor and vendee of goods which may have the effect of varying the degree of his responsibility. Here the bargain was that the vendee should pay, beyond the market price of the goods supplied to him, ten shillings per ton, which was to be applied in payment of an old debt due to one of the plaintiffs. The effect of that would be to compel the vendor to appropriate to the payment of the old debt, a portion of those funds which the surety might reasonably suppose would go towards defraying the debt for the payment of which he made himself collaterally responsible. Such a bargain, therefore, increased his responsibility. That being so, I am of opinion that the withholding the knowledge of that bargain from the defendant was a fraud upon him, and vitiated the contract.

BAYLEY

BAYLEY J. It is the duty of a party taking a guarantee to put the surety in possession of all the facts likely to affect the degree of his responsibility; and if he neglect to do so, it is at his peril. It is highly probable that J. Pidcock proved his debt under the commission against Tickell, although that does not appear on the evidence; but, however that may be, the question in this case depends upon the nature of the bargain between Tickell and J. Pidcock. The defendant might reasonably suppose that the iron was to be supplied to Tickell at the market price, but by the bargain Tickell was to pay, beyond the market price of the iron, ten shillings per ton to J. Pidcock, in discharge of an old debt due to him. Now if the plaintiff had apprized the defendant that there was such a subsisting bargain, he would have known that Tickell would not be able to pay for so much of the iron as he otherwise might have done, and might have declined entering into the guarantee. He gave the guarantee under a supposition that Tickell would be at liberty to apply all his funds, except what were necessary for his support, towards payment of the iron supplied at the regular market price, whereas the plaintiff when he accepted the guarantee knew that Tickell was to pay him not only the market price of the iron, but ten shillings per ton on the iron provided, in extinction of an old debt. The concealment of that fact from the knowledge of the defendant was a fraud upon him, and avoids this contract. Where by a composition deed the creditors agree to take a certain sum in full discharge of their respective debts, a secret agreement, by which the debtor stipulates with one of the creditors to pay him a larger sum, is void, upon the ground that

that

that agreement is a fraud upon the rest of the creditors. So that a contract which is a fraud upon a third person may, on that account, be void as between the parties to it. Here the contract to guaranty is void, because a fact materially affecting the nature of the obligation created by the contract was not communicated to the surety.

HOLROYD J. I am also of opinion that the contract of the surety is not binding upon him, by reason of the plaintiff's not having communicated to the surety a secret bargain previously made by him with the vendee of the goods. The effect of that bargain was to divert a portion of the funds of the vendee from being applied to discharge the debt which he was about to contract with the plaintiffs, and to render the vendee less able to pay for the iron supplied to him. The defendant might reasonably suppose that *Tickell* was to pay only the market price of the iron, but the plaintiff knew that he was to pay more, and did not communicate that fact to the plaintiff. The plaintiff and defendant therefore were not on equal terms. The former with the knowledge of a fact which necessarily must have the effect of increasing the responsibility of the surety, without communicating that fact to him, suffers him to give the guarantee. That was a fraud upon the defendant, and vitiates the contract.

LITTLEDALE J. I think that a surety ought to be acquainted with the whole contract entered into with his principal. The surety might fairly suppose that the vendee would be able to pay the market price of the iron out of its produce, when manufactured, and he

gave

1825.

Pidcock
against
Bishop.

gave the guarantee under that supposition; but if he
had known that, besides paying the market price of the
iron, the vendee was also to pay ten shillings per ton in
extinction of an old debt, he would have known that the
vendee would have so much less to appropriate in payment for the iron, and, consequently, that the risk of the
surety would thereby be increased. Besides the object
of a person becoming a surety for another is to render
him a service. But the effect of such a private bargain
as was made in this case would be to defeat the object
of the surety. For if the proceeds of the goods supplied to the vendee are to be applied wholly in discharge
of an old debt, a benefit will be conferred on the vendor
of the goods, and not on the vendee; now that certainly
was not the intention of the surety.

Rule absolute.

Tuesday,
January 25th.

The KING against TAYLOR.

Where a con-
tinuance was
entered from
Trinity to the
first day of Mi-
chaelmas term,
and matter aris-
ing during the
interval was
pleaded after the
first day of Mi-
chaelmas term
by way of plea
puis darrein
continuance,
the Court or-
dered the plea
to be taken off
the file.

INDICTMENT for keeping a gaming-house. Plea
autre fois acquit pleaded in *Trinity* term. Between
Trinity and *Michaelmas* terms the defendant was again
tried and acquitted at the sessions on an indictment for
the same offence. In *Michaelmas* term, on the 19th of
November, and before the prosecutor had replied to the
former plea, the defendant pleaded the last acquittal by
way of plea puis darrein continuance. This plea was
entitled of the term generally. For taking the plea off the
file, a rule nisi having been obtained, on an affidavit
that the acquittal was collusive,

Brodrick

Brodrick shewed cause. The Court cannot exercise the summary jurisdiction which this rule supposes to be vested in them. They are bound to receive pleas puis darrein continuance, *Paris* v. *Salkeld* (a), *Lovell* v. *Eastaff.* (b) And, indeed, this plea is strictly regular, for where issue has not been joined the matter puis darrein continuance may be pleaded of the term generally, and need not be pleaded on the very day to which the continuance is entered. Thus, in *Com. Dig.* tit. *Abatement* (I 24.) it is said, " If any thing happens pending the writ, and *before issue joined*, which goes in bar or proves the writ abated and not abateable only, it may be pleaded, without saying after the last continuance," and 2 *Lutw.* 1178. is cited. The same rule must be applicable after plea and before replication. [*Littledale* J., under the same title there is a case cited from 2 *Jones*, 129. where a plea puis darrein continuance was admitted a week after the term commenced.] The only mode in which the Court can interfere, is by ordering the plea to be entitled of the very day when it was filed, but that must be upon a distinct application for that purpose.

Chitty contrà. It is true that the Court have no discretionary power to receive or reject pleas puis darrein continuance when they are pleaded at a proper time. But pleas of this description may be set aside if pleaded too late, as well as pleas in abatement, which jurisdiction over the latter is frequently exercised. *Willoughby* v. *Wilkins* (c), *Tidd's Prac.* 677. 6th edit.

Cur. adv. vult.

(a) 2 *Wils.* 157.   (b) 5 *T. R.* 554.   (c) 2 *Smith,* 396.

ABBOTT

ABBOTT C. J. now delivered the judgment of the Court. This case came before the Court upon a motion to set aside a plea puis darrein continuance. The indictment was for keeping a common gaming-house. The plea stated, that after the indictment was preferred in this court, another indictment had been preferred at the quarter sessions for the same offence, upon which indictment being brought on for trial, the defendant was acquitted. This plea was pleaded generally as if it referred to the first day of the term. It is clear by the affidavit that it was not put upon the file of this Court until the 19th day of *November*. The prosecutor by his counsel therefore moved to take that plea off the file, contending that a plea puis darrein continuance must be pleaded on that day to which the continuance is made; that is, in this case that it could only be pleaded on the first day of *Michaelmas* term. This is the case of a criminal proceeding. In civil actions, by the indulgence of the Court, four days are allowed; but even if that indulgence was extended to the case of indictments, it would not apply to a case where the plea was not pleaded until long after the first four days of the term. If we consider how the record would have been drawn up in ancient times, and how it should be drawn up in modern times, we shall find that it would stat ethe continuance to be upon the appearance of the attornies for the prosecution and for the defendant, and that would be recorded on the first day of the term. Supposing this entry to have been made, it is quite clear that this plea, coming in after that day, and referring to a matter which took place in vacation, would, on the very face of it, appear to be a bad plea. Now it was said, inasmuch as there was no such entry

on

on this record, this party might come and put his plea on the file at a later time. It is obvious he might do so on the first day of the term; but why wait during almost the whole of that term, if he professes to enter the continuance, from the very last day of the preceding term to the first day of the ensuing term? In the case cited from 2 *Jones*, the party was admitted to plead after the first day of term, which certainly imports that it was not done without the permission of the Court. No doubt, for the furtherance of justice, more especially in a criminal case, if the party by any inadvertence has let slip his time and forborne to plead, the Court would give him leave to do so. In the case of *Lovell* v. *Eastaff*(a), although the defendant did not put his plea in until a later day, yet, on a motion to take that plea off the file, the Court looked to the circumstances of the case, to see if justice required that it should be taken off. In that case the Court refused to allow the plea to be taken off the file; and the reason assigned was, that on the first day of the term, and for several days afterwards, a motion was pending in this court for a new trial, and therefore, until that motion was disposed of, it would have been useless to put on the file that plea which was put on the file immediately after the motion for a new trial was disposed of. The plea was a plea of bankruptcy, and it would have been quite useless to put it on the file earlier. But upon the present occasion, the plea was pleaded without any previous application to the Court. The rule which was obtained

(a) 3 T. R. 554.

to

to set aside the plea is founded upon an affidavit, stating positively that the acquittal, which forms the subject of the plea, had been obtained by fraud and collusion, and that is not denied by the defendant. He has been advised, and no doubt well advised, not to pledge his conscience in contradiction to that which is here alleged. That fact remaining uncontradicted, the question is, if a plea irregularly pleaded should be suffered to stand on the file of the court, when its effect would be, according to an uncontradicted affidavit, to defeat justice, and to prevent the trial of the defendant by means of an acquittal, obtained probably by the defendant's money. For these reasons I do not think the rule ought to be discharged.

Rule absolute.

BARTLETT *against* DOWNES.

The lord of a manor may, by deed, grant the stewardship of the manor and of the courts thereto belonging for the life of the grantee.

A term of 500 years, created in 1712, was upon a sale of the estate in 1785, assigned to attend the inheritance. Upon a subsequent sale in 1795, there was a general declaration in the conveyance, that all persons having outstanding terms should hold them in trust to attend the inheritance, but no particular term was specified: Held, that in support of the grant of the stewardship made in 1821, it was properly left to the jury to say whether they thought the term had been surrendered, and that they were justified in finding that it had.

ASSUMPSIT for money had and received. Plea general issue. At the trial before *Abbott* C. J. at the *Westminster* sittings after *Michaelmas* term, it appeared that the action was brought by the plaintiff, who claimed to be steward of the manor of *Danbury*, in the county of *Essex*, to recover certain fees received by the defendant when acting in that capacity. The plaintiff's right to the office of steward rested on a deed under seal, executed in 1821, by *Rose Ray*, who was then

seised

seised in fee of the manor, by which she " gave and
granted unto the plaintiff the office of steward of the
said manor of *Danbury*, and the holding and keeping of
all courts of what kind soever to the said manor belonging or appertaining, and doing all other acts relating
thereto; and she did thereby make, constitute, and appoint the said plaintiff steward of the said manor, and
of the courts to the same belonging, to have, hold, exercise, and enjoy the office aforesaid, and the holding and
keeping of the said courts, and the doing all other acts
as aforesaid, and receiving the fees and profits to the
said office belonging from thenceforth during the term
of his natural life." *Rose Ray* died on the 20th of
October 1821, having devised the manor of *Danbury* in
fee to *Charles Downes*. *C. Downes* disputed the plaintiff's right to continue steward of the manor, and *E.
Downes* (the defendant) held a court and received certain fees, to recover which this action was brought. For
the defendant it was objected, that the grant by *Rose
Ray* was void, for that she had no power to create a
freehold office. The Lord Chief Justice overruled the
objection, but gave the defendant leave to move for a
nonsuit. The defendant then set up a term supposed to
have been outstanding at the time when *Rose Ray* made
the grant. It appeared that this term, which was for 500
years was created in 1712. In 1785 it was assigned as
a satisfied term to attend the inheritance. In 1798,
when *Robert Ray*, the then husband of *Rose Ray*, purchased the manor of *Danbury*, there was a general
declaration that all persons having any terms in them
should hold them in trust to attend the inheritance, but
no particular term was specified. When the dispute

first arose between these parties, *C. Downes* wrote a letter, admitting that Mrs. *Ray* had a right to appoint, but questioning the fact of her having done so. The Lord Chief Justice left it to the jury to say whether they thought the term was still outstanding or not. They thought that it was not, and found a verdict for the plaintiff for the amount of the fees received by the defendant.

Scarlett now moved for a rule nisi for a nonsuit or new trial. The grant by Mrs. *Ray* to the plaintiff was void. The crown may create a freehold office, but an individual cannot; Mrs. *Ray*, therefore, had no power to grant the office of steward for the life of the grantee so as to bind the future owners of the manor. In the Earl of *Shrewsbury's* case (a) the stewardship of a manor was granted for life, but that was by queen *Elizabeth ;* and in *Owen* v. *Saunders* (b), which was the case of a clerk of the peace, it appeared that the appointment was made by virtue of an act of parliament. (c) Then, secondly, it should not have been left to the jury to say whether the term had been surrendered. In 1785 it was expressly assigned to attend the inheritance ; and in 1793, when Mr. *Ray* purchased the manor, a declaration was made that all outstanding terms should be held in trust to attend the inheritance. No evidence was given of the creation of any term except that of 1712; it must, therefore, be presumed that the deed of 1793 alluded to that term. If so, it must at that time have been in existence, and there was no evidence of any fact whence

(a) 9 Co. 42.   (b) 1 Ld. Raym. 158.   (c) 1 W. & M. st. 1. c. 21. s. 5.

the

the jury could infer that it had been afterwards surrendered or merged.

Cur. adv. vult.

ABBOTT C. J. now delivered the judgment of the
Court. There were two grounds upon which the rule
in this case was moved. The first point was, whether
the appointment of a steward of a manor court beyond
the life of the grantor, could be a good grant. It was
admitted that such a grant by the crown might be good,
but it was contended that such a grant by a subject
could not be good without custom or act of parliament.
In *Littleton*, section 378., where he is writing on the
subject of estates which are held upon conditions in
law, he mentions the case of a grant by deed of the
office of keeper of a park. "If a man grant by his
deed to another the office of parkership of a park, to
have and occupy the same office *for term of his life*,
the estate which he hath in the office is upon condition in law, to wit, that the parker shall well and lawfully keep the park, and shall do that which to such
office belongeth to do, or otherwise it shall be lawful to
the grantor and his heirs to oust him." This is to
shew that a grant of an office of that kind is subject to a
condition in law, namely, that the party shall discharge
the duty of the office, and that upon the violation of
such duty there would be a forfeiture of the office; and
that is said in respect of a grant by a subject. Then
Lord *Coke*, when he comes to comment upon that
section (*a*), introduces among others the very office now
in question. He states, that " where an officer hath

(*a*) 1 *Inst.* 233. b.

no other profit but a certain collateral fee, the grantor may discharge him of his service, the discharge whereof is but labour and charge to him, but he must have his fee;" and in the same page he proceeds: "If a man doth grant to another the office of the stewardship of his courts of his manors, with a certain fee, the grantor cannot discharge him of his service and attendance, because he hath *other* profits and fees belonging to his office which he should lose if he were discharged of his office." Now this is very good authority, or they are instances at least, to say no more of them, to shew that a grant for life of an office of the description now in discussion is a good and valid grant. If the grantor himself cannot discharge the grantee, how can any other person? On what principle shall it be said that a person claiming under the grantor shall be in a different situation from him? In *Harvey* v. *Newlyn* (a) the Court seem to have come to their decision against the plaintiff, because it was not alleged by him that there was any profit belonging to the office; and if so he suffered no injury from being discharged; he was only relieved from certain trouble. The Court say distinctly if profit belonged to the office, and it had been so alleged in the declaration, the grant of the office for life would have been good. That point, therefore, seems to be set at rest upon this authority. Then the next point made was, that I ought not to have left it to the jury to presume any surrender or merging of the outstanding term. I did not direct them as to their finding, but merely left it to them to consider whether they would or would not presume a surrender, having first endea-

(a) *Cro. Eliz.* 859.

voured

voured to explain the nature of the subject. If I ought not to have left it to the jury to consider if such a presumption might not be made from the circumstances which appeared on the trial, then there ought to be a new trial. The plaintiff proved the grant as having been made by this lady just before the execution of her will. The defendant on this evidence was clearly a wrong doer, and he shewed no title; but we will take it that the devisee had thought fit to appoint him steward of the manor and to rescind the appointment of the testator. It appeared that there had been a term originally created in 1712 for a future purpose, and that such purpose was satisfied. Then in 1785 there was a sale of the estate; that term was then outstanding in a trustee for the benefit of the inheritance. In 1793 there was another sale of the estate to the husband of the testatrix, and in one of the conveyances there was a general declaration that all outstanding terms should be for the benefit of the purchaser, but the particular term was not mentioned. Now, if the outstanding term which the defendant set up could prevail, it would prevail to defeat the act of the testatrix in making the grant she made. The general principle upon which a presumption should be allowed I think is this, that that which has been done should be presumed to be rightly done; and if we apply that principle to many cases of right, it must be taken to be so. Applying it to the question of a right of way. If we find the act has been often repeated (for the occasional use of a walk or path across a man's field would be hardly such a use as would establish the right), but if the act must necessarily have been often repeated with the knowledge of the persons acting upon an adverse right, it affords a strong presumption in favour

of

of the right so exercised. The same principle is to be applied to presumptions in the case of light, or of flowing water. In each of these cases there must be a long continuance of enjoyment to warrant the presumption. But upon the question of the surrender of a term the case is somewhat different; for with respect to conveyances you cannot find in the nature of things repeated acts; it is not to be expected. And although that be so, the courts have in many instances for a considerable length of time decided that juries are at liberty, where they find that such a term as this has been set up, and has done the duty for which it was originally created, to presume a surrender of it. In this case there was the letter of *C. Downes*, admitting that Mrs. *Ray* had a right to appoint; whence it might be inferred, as against him, that the term did not exist; I therefore thought the jury might be justified in presuming this outstanding term to have ceased. Here the grant of the office, supposing such a term to be outstanding, would have been void at law, which certainly it was never meant to be. On the contrary, if you presume the term had merged, the grant of the office would be good. In that view of it we are of opinion it might properly be left to the jury to presume a surrender of the term, to give validity and effect to the act of the testatrix in making the grant. For these reasons we are of opinion that the verdict found for the plaintiff ought not to be disturbed.

                                        Rule refused.

DOBELL *against* STEVENS.

CASE for a deceitful representation. The declaration stated that before the time of committing the grievance thereinafter mentioned, defendant kept a public-house, and was possessed of a lease of the house for a certain term of years, and thereupon the plaintiff, at the request of the defendant, on, &c. at, &c. was in treaty with defendant to buy his interest in the said house for a certain sum of money, to wit, the sum of 460*l.*, and also to buy the household furniture and fixtures, and stock in trade, at a valuation; and defendant falsely, fraudulently, and deceitfully pretended and represented to the plaintiff that the returns or receipts for the spirits sold in the said public-house had been and then amounted to the sum of 160*l.* per month; and that the quantity of porter sold in the house amounted to seven butts per month; and that the tap was let for 82*l.* per annum, and two rooms in the public-house for 2"*l.* per annum; and by such representation then and there induced the plaintiff to buy the said lease of the house at the price of 460*l.* The declaration then averred the falsehood of each particular of the statement. At the trial before *Littledale* J. at the *London* sittings after last term, the plaintiff proved that whilst the treaty for the purchase was going on, a representation was made, as stated in the declaration, and that it was false. On the cross-examination of his witnesses it was proved that the defendant's books were in the house at the time of the treaty, and might have been inspected

Where the vendor of a public-house made, pending the treaty, certain deceitful representations respecting the amount of the business done in the house, and the rent received for a part of the premises, whereby the plaintiff was induced to give a large sum for the premises: Held, that the latter might maintain an action on the case for the deceitful representations, although they were not noticed in the conveyance of the premises, or in a written memorandum of the bargain, which was drawn up after these representations were made.

S s 4   by

by the plaintiff; and that they would have shewn the real quantity of spirits and porter sold in the house. The plaintiff, however, did not examine them. A written memorandum of the bargain was afterwards drawn up, and an assignment of the lease was executed; but neither of those instruments contained any mention of the defendant's representation. The learned Judge left it to the jury to say whether the representation was fraudulent, and they found a verdict for the plaintiff.

Gurney now moved for a rule nisi for a new trial. The parol evidence of the defendant's representation was inadmissible in this case. The contract having been reduced into writing the parties must be bound by that, and cannot add to it by evidence of previous conversations, *Pickering* v. *Dowson.* (a) (*Abbott* C. J. In that case *Gibbs* J. says, " if there had been any fraud it would not have been done away by the contract." *Bayley* J. The same view of the point was taken by my Lord Chief Justice in *Kain* v. *Old.* (b)) The fraud there alluded to is some fraudulent conduct whereby the party deceived is prevented from discovering the falsehood of the representation. Here the plaintiff had the means of knowledge within his reach, and neglected to make use of them. In *Powell* v. *Edmunds* (c) it appeared that an auctioneer, at a sale by auction, made a statement not noticed in the conditions of sale, and it was held that parol evidence of that statement had been properly rejected. Lord *Ellenborough* says, " The only question which could be made is, whether if by

(a) 4 *Taunt.* 779.   (b) 2 *B. & C.* 627.   (c) 12 *East,* 6.

the

the collateral representation a party be induced to enter into a written agreement different from such represent-ation, he may not have an action on the case for the fraud practised to lay asleep his prudence." At all events, therefore, the propriety of admitting such evi-dence has been considered very questionable by a high authority, and is a point worthy of further discussion.

Abbott C. J. Whether any fraud or deceit had or had not been practised in this case was peculiarly a question for the jury; nor has any complaint been made against the mode in which that question was presented to their consideration. If then this motion be sustain-able at all, it must be sustainable on the ground that evidence of a fraudulent or deceitful representation could not be received, inasmuch as it was not noticed in the written agreement, or in the conveyance which was afterwards executed by the parties. The case of *Lysney* v. *Selby* (a) is to the contrary of that position, and precisely analogous to the present case. That was an action against the defendant for falsely and fraudulently representing to the plaintiff that certain houses of him (defendant) were then demised at the yearly rent of 68*l.*, to which plaintiff giving credit, bought the houses for a large sum of money, to wit, &c., and an assignment was afterwards executed to him; whereas, in truth and in fact, the houses were at that time demised at the yearly rent of 52*l.* 10*s.*, and no more. After verdict for the plaintiff a motion was made in arrest of judgment, on the ground that it did not appear that the assertion was made at the time of the sale. Lord *Holt* says, "If the vendor gives

(a) 2 *Ld. Raym.* 1118.

in

1825.

Dobell
against
Stevens.

in a particular of the rents, and the vendee says he will trust him, and inquire no further, but rely upon his particular, then if the particular be false an action will lie." Here the plaintiff did rely on the assertion of the defendant, and that was his inducement to make the purchase. The representation was not of any matter or quality pertaining to the thing sold, and therefore likely to be mentioned in the conveyance, but was altogether collateral to it; as was the rent in the case of *Lysney* v. *Selby*. That case appears to me to be exactly in point, and the jury having found that that which was untruly represented was fraudulently and deceitfully represented, I think that we ought not to grant a rule for a new trial.

Rule refused.

*Tuesday,
January 25th.*

HARVEY and Others, Assignees of BANCK and JOSEPH, Bankrupts, *against* ARCHBOLD and Others.

Debt for money had and received. Plea, general issue, and set off for money lent, paid, &c. At the trial, it appeared that the plaintiffs, *A.* and Co. in *England*, con-

D EBT for money paid by the bankrupts, before the bankruptcy, to the use of the defendants, and for money had and received by the defendants to their use. Account stated between bankrupts and defendants. Money had and received by defendants to the use of the plaintiffs as assignees, and on an account stated with

signed goods to the defendants, *B.* and Co. at *Gibraltar*, to be sold on commission. *B.* and Co., as soon as the bills of lading and invoices were delivered to their agents in *London*, advanced, through them, to *A.* and Co. two-thirds of the invoice price of the goods, by bills at ninety days; and for these advances received interest at the rate of 6 per cent., calculated from the date of the bills, which was the usual rate of interest at *Gibraltar*. In an action for the proceeds of the goods : Held, that this could not be considered as a loan of money in *England*, and was not usurious, and that the defendants were entitled to set off the monies so advanced.

Semble, that in an action for money had and received the plaintiff must give evidence of a particular sum to which he is entitled.

them

them in that capacity. Detinue of goods of the value of 100,000*l.* delivered by bankrupts, before their bankruptcy, to defendants, to be re-delivered by them on request. Detinue on a trover of goods to same amount, the property of the bankrupts, before the bankruptcy. Similar count laying the property in plaintiffs, and the trover after the bankruptcy. Plea, general issue, and notice of set-off for work and labour, goods sold and delivered, money lent, paid to the use of the bankrupts, and money had and received by them to the use of defendants before the bankruptcy. At the trial before *Abbott* C. J. at the *London* sittings after *Michaelmas* term, it appeared that the bankrupts in 1821 carried on business in *London* ; the defendants were merchants at *Gibraltar.* *Archbold* generally resided in *England*, but they had no house of business in this country. In 1821, and the following year, the bankrupts consigned large quantities of goods to the defendants at *Gibraltar*, to be sold on commission. The defendants agreed to advance, through *Reid* and Co., their agents in *England*, two-thirds of the invoice price of the goods consigned to them, as soon as the invoices and bills of lading were delivered. The advances were to be made by bills at three months, accepted by *Reid* and Co. The bankrupts were to be charged by the defendants with interest on the money advanced at the rate of 6 per cent. from the date of the bills. In addition to this the defendants were to receive on some consignments 5, and on others 3 per cent. commission for the sales, and 2½ del credere. This was the usual rate of interest and commission at *Gibraltar.* Transactions to a considerable extent took place between the parties according to this agreement. All the advances were made in *England* by bills at

ninety

652

CASES in HILARY TERM

1825.

HARVEY
against
ARCHBOLD.

ninety days, drawn upon *Reid* and Co., who did not, in fact, accept them, but advanced the amount in cash, deducting discount at 5 per cent. At *Gibraltar* bills on *England* at ninety days are considered as cash. The plaintiffs having proved these facts, put in the account-sales rendered by the defendants, but not the account-current between the parties. It appeared by the correspondence that there was a loss on each consignment, but the amount was not specified. It was contended for the defendants, that as no proof had been given that any goods remained in specie, or that any demand of them had been made, the plaintiffs clearly could not recover on the counts in detinue; and that as the defendants had advanced two-thirds of the invoice prices, and there had been a loss upon each consignment, it must be presumed that the advances and commission exceeded the sums received by the defendants from the sales; and the Lord Chief Justice was of this opinion. For the plaintiffs it was contended, that the defendants could not set off the monies advanced, as those advances were tainted with usury, the defendants receiving interest at the rate of 6 per cent., and the agents *Reid* and Co. not actually accepting the bills drawn, but advancing the money, and deducting discount at the rate of 5 per cent. The Lord Chief Justice left it to the jury to say whether it was part of the original bargain between the bankrupts and the defendants that *Reid* and Co. should not accept bills to be at the disposal of the bankrupts, but that they should advance the amount in cash, minus the discount for three months. The jury found that this was not part of the bargain, whereupon the verdict was ordered to be entered for the defendants.

The

The *Attorney General* now moved for a rule nisi for a new trial, contending that the verdict was improperly entered for the defendants. No evidence was given of the amount of the set-off. The plaintiffs, therefore, having proved the amount for which the goods had been sold, were entitled to a verdict. Secondly, the advances made by the defendants were upon usurious terms, and therefore could not legally be set off. Although the jury found that it was not part of the bargain that *Reid* and Co. should always discount the bills, yet, independently of that, the bankrupts were charged with usurious interest. The contract for the advances was made in this country, the money was advanced here, and it did not appear that the defendants ever transmitted money from *Gibraltar* in order to make those advances. The defendants, therefore, were not entitled to take more than 5 per cent. interest, but in fact they took 6 per cent., and calculated it from the date of the bill drawn, and not from the time of its being payable.

ABBOTT C. J. This was an action brought to recover goods placed in the hands of the defendants by the bankrupts before their bankruptcy, and for money had and received to their use. With respect to the former part of the case, it is sufficient to say that there was no proof of any demand of the goods, or that any part of them remained in the hands of the defendants. On the second part of the case the plaintiff gave in evidence the account-sales, but not the account-current, and left the defendants to make out their set-off. It is said that there was no proof of the amount of the set-off. But it was in evidence that two-thirds of the invoice price

was

was advanced by the defendants through their agents in *England*, and that those goods, or by far the greater part of them, were sold at *Gibraltar*, and that a loss was sustained upon each consignment. If so, it appears to me demonstratively that the money advanced in *England*, together with the interest and the commission on the sales at *Gibraltar*, amounted to more than the invoice price of the goods. But even supposing it to be otherwise, to what amount did the plaintiffs establish a claim? Surely they should have given some further evidence of the state of the accounts. I also thought at the trial, that the case must be considered as if the bargain for the advances had been made at *Gibraltar*, and not in *London*; and that under such circumstances interest might lawfully be charged at 6 per cent. from the date of the bills drawn upon *Reid* and Co. But I thought that if it was part of the bargain that the bankrupts were not to have bills accepted by *Reid* and Co. to be disposed of as they pleased, but were to receive the amount of the bills, minus 5 per cent. discount, it would be usurious. The jury, however, found that this was not part of the bargain; and therefore being of opinion that the defendants were entitled to set off the whole of the advances, and that the advances, together with interest and commission, exceeded the monies received by them, I directed the verdict to be entered in their favor; and I still think it was correctly entered for them. Had the finding of the jury been different, I should have thought that the plaintiffs ought to be nonsuited for want of evidence of any particular sum that they were entitled to recover.

BAYLEY

BAYLEY J. I am of opinion that the advances made by the defendants cannot be considered as a loan of money. The substance of the bargain appears to have been that, instead of waiting to make remittances until the proceeds were realized, the defendants should remit by anticipation the probable amount of the net proceeds. The money could only be procured and transmitted from *Gibraltar* upon certain terms, viz. that a bill at ninety days should be considered as cash, and that interest should be paid for the money at the rate of 6 per cent. per annum; and upon those terms the money was paid to the bankrupts by *Reid, Irving,* and Co. This was rather an arrangement for the payment of the proceeds of the goods than a loan of money, and cannot, I think, be called usurious. That being so, I entirely concur in thinking that there ought not to be a new trial.

. LITTLEDALE J. (*a*) concurred.

Rule refused.

(*a*) *Holroyd* J. was in the Bail Court.

1825.

HARVEY
against
ARCHBOLD.

MONTAGUE *against* BENEDICT.

*Wednesday,
January 26th.*

A SSUMPSIT for goods sold and delivered. Plea, general issue. At the trial before *Abbott* C. J., at the *Middlesex* sittings after *Trinity* term, 1824, it ap-

In assumpsit for goods sold, it appeared that the plaintiff, a jeweller, in the course of two

months, delivered articles of jewelry to the wife of the defendant amounting in value to 83*l.* It appeared that the defendant was a certificated special pleader, and lived in a ready furnished house, of which the annual rent was 200*l.*; that he kept no man servant; that his wife's fortune upon her marriage was less than 4000*l.*; that she had, at the time of her marriage, jewelry suitable to her condition, and that she had never worn, in her husband's presence, any articles furnished her by the plaintiff; it appeared also that the plaintiff, when he went to the defendant's house to ask for payment always enquired for the wife and not for the defendant: Held, that the goods so furnished were not necessaries, and that, as there was no evidence to go to the jury of any assent of the husband to the contract made by his wife, the action could not be maintained.

peared

peared that the plaintiff was a working jeweller, and the
defendant a special pleader in considerable practice.
The plaintiff, between the 20th of *October* and the 14th
of *December* 1823, had delivered to the wife of the defendant, at his house in *Guildford-street*, different articles
of jewelry, amounting in the whole to the sum of 83*l.*,
and had received from her on account 34*l.* These
things were usually delivered about twelve o'clock in the
day, and plaintiff never saw any person but the defendant's wife. Upon these facts being proved the defendant's counsel contended that the plaintiff ought to be
nonsuited, because there was no evidence to shew that
the husband had any knowledge that the goods had
been delivered to his wife, and, consequently, no evidence of his assent to the purchase, and *Metcalfe* v.
Shaw (a), *Waithman* v. *Wakefield* (b), *Bentley* v. *Griffin* (c),
were cited. The Lord Chief Justice thought it a question for the jury, whether the articles had been supplied
with the assent of the husband. The defendant proved
that he was married in *September* 1817, and that the
fortune of his wife was less than 4000*l.*, and that she
received, by virtue of her marriage settlement, for her
exclusive use, a sum of 60*l.* annually; that they in-
habited a ready-furnished house in *Guildford-street*, at
the rent of 200*l.* a year; that the furniture of it was not
new or expensive, some of it indeed being very shabby;
that the defendant kept no man-servant; that his wife,
before *October* 1823 had jewelry suitable to her condition, and that she had never, in her husband's' presence, worn any of the articles furnished by the plaintiff.
The defendant usually left his house and went to his

(a) 3 *Campb.* 22.   (b) 1 *Campb.* 120.   (c) 5 *Taunt.* 356.

chambers

chambers about ten o'clock in the morning, and did not
return before five in the evening. When the plaintiff
or his servant called at the defendant's house, they always
asked for his wife, and not for him; and upon one occasion, when the clerk called in *March*, and stated to the
female servant who opened the door, that he called for
the purpose of getting settled a bill for jewelry to the
amount of 80*l*.; the servant expressed her surprise that
the plaintiff had trusted her mistress for such a sum,
and said she was sure that her master knew nothing of
it, and she swore that the clerk replied, "his master was
aware of that." This, however, was denied by the clerk.
The Lord Chief Justice told the jury, that a husband
was not liable for goods supplied to his wife, unless he
gave her an express or implied authority to purchase.
In considering the question of authority, the estate and
degree of the parties was a fit subject for consideration,
and so also was the nature of the articles. There were
some things which it might and must always be presumed the wife had authority to buy, such as provisions
for the daily use of the family over which she presided;
but in this case the articles were not necessary to any
one; the proof was, that the husband never saw them,
and the jury were to say, under these circumstances,
whether the wife of the defendant had any authority
from him to make a contract for the articles in question.
The jury found for the plaintiff to the amount of his bill.
A rule nisi had been obtained for a nonsuit, on the ground
that there was no evidence to be left to the jury of the
husband's assent to the contract; or for a new trial, on the
ground that the verdict was against the weight of evidence.

Platt shewed cause. It was a question for the jury, upon
the evidence, whether the articles provided for the wife of

1825.

Montague
against
Benedict.

the defendant were necessaries suitable to the degree and estate of the husband. The latter is responsible in respect of the contracts made by the wife, for goods suitable to that condition which he suffers her to. hold out to the world. It is not necessary to shew an express assent of the husband to the contract, or that the articles provided were worn in his presence. If they were conformable to the apparent condition of the husband, his assent is to be presumed. Here there was abundant evidence to go to the jury, that the things provided were necessaries suitable to the degree of the husband, for it appeared that he lived in a ready-furnished house, the rent of which was 200*l*. per annum, and that his wife had originally a fortune of 4000*l*., and if they were necessaries suitable to the degree of the husband, then cohabitation was evidence of his assent to the contract made by. his wife. He cited *Morton* v. *Withy*. (a)

Scarlett and *Gurney*, contrà. It appeared upon the trial that the plaintiff, in the course of two months, had delivered to the defendant's wife articles of jewelry amounting to 83*l*., and that before that time she had articles of that description suitable to her degree. The things provided by the plaintiff, therefore, were not necessaries. There was no evidence of any assent (express or implied) of the husband, to the purchase made by the wife. Cohabitation is only primâ facie evidence of such assent, and here it was rebutted by the evidence given on the part of the defendant.

BAYLEY J. It seems to me, that in this case there was no evidence to go to a jury to entitle the plaintiff to a

(a) Skinner, 348.

verdict.

verdict. I take the rule of law to be this: if a man, without any justifiable cause, turns away his wife, he is bound by any contract she may make, for necessaries suitable to her degree and estate. If the husband and wife live together, and the husband will not supply her with necessaries, or the means of obtaining them, then, although she has her remedy in the Ecclesiastical Court, yet she is still at liberty to pledge the credit of her husband for what is strictly necessary for her own support. But whenever the husband and wife are living together, and he provides her with necessaries, the husband is not bound by contracts of the wife, except where there is reasonable evidence to shew, that the wife has made the contract with his assent, *Etherington* v. *Parrott.* (a) Cohabitation is presumptive evidence of the assent of the husband, but it may be rebutted by contrary evidence; and when such assent is proved, the wife is the agent of the husband duly authorised. Then the question is, was there any evidence in this case to warrant my Lord Chief Justice in submitting, as a question for the consideration of the jury, whether the wife had the authority of the husband to make this purchase? It appears, that the wife had originally a fortune under 4000l.; that would yield an income less than 200l. per annum. There was no evidence on the part of the plaintiff to shew that she had a fortune even to that extent; that fact afterwards appeared upon the defendant's evidence. Then is it to be presumed, that a husband working hard for the maintenance of himself and family, keeping no man-servant, and living in a house badly furnished, would authorise his wife to lay out, in the course of six weeks, half of her yearly in-

1825.

MONTAGUE
against
BENEDICT.

(a) *Ld. Ryyki.* 1006.

T t 2

com

come in trinkets? If the tradesman in this case had exercised a sound judgment, he must have perceived that this money would have been much better laid out in furniture for the house, than in decking the plaintiff's wife with useless ornaments, which would so ill correspond with the furniture in the house. I think, at all events, there was gross negligence on the part of the plaintiff, if he ever intended to make the husband responsible. If a tradesman is about to trust a married woman for what are not necessaries, and to an extent beyond what her station in life requires, he ought, in common prudence, to enquire of the husband if she has his consent for the order she is giving; and if he had so enquired in this case, it is not improbable that the husband might have told him not to trust her. But no such enquiry was made; on the contrary, the plaintiff always enquired for the wife, and that is strong evidence to shew that she was the person trusted, and not the husband. On the whole, I think that the plaintiff did not make out, by reasonable evidence, that the wife had any authority to make the purchase in question.

HOLROYD J. I think the plaintiff ought to have been nonsuited. If the plaintiff had made a claim in respect of necessaries provided for the defendant's wife, the case would have stood upon a very different ground; but I think, upon the evidence, it appeared that the things provided were not necessaries. They consisted of articles of jewelry, and the wife had upon her marriage been supplied with a sufficiency of such things, considering her situation in life. Undoubtedly the husband is liable for necessaries provided for his wife, where he neglects to provide them himself. If, however, there be no necessity for the articles provided, the tradesman will not

be

be entitled to recover their value, unless he can shew an express or implied assent of the husband to the contract made by the wife. Where a tradesman takes no pains to ascertain whether the necessity exists or not, he supplies the articles at his own peril; and if it turn out that the necessity does not exist, the husband is not responsible for what may be furnished to his wife without his knowledge. Where a tradesman provides articles for a person whom he knows to be a married woman, it is his duty, if he wishes to make the husband responsible, to enquire if she has her husband's authority or not; for where he chooses to trust her, in the expectation that she will pay, he must take the consequence if she does not. If it turn out that she did act under the authority of her husband, when she gave the orders, he will be liable, but otherwise he will not. If we were to hold that he would, no man in any case would be safe, if the wife chose to say that she had the authority of her husband. I think that the burden of the proof of the assent of the husband lies on the party who provided the goods, and who acted upon the supposed authority. In this case, it appears to me that the proof was to the contrary, and that it negatived all presumption of assent on the part of the husband. I think, therefore, that the plaintiff did not make out a case to entitle him to recover.

LITTLEDALE J. I agree in thinking that a nonsuit must be entered. The husband is not liable in respect of a contract made by his wife without his assent to it, and a party seeking to charge him in respect of such a contract, is bound either to prove an express assent on his part, or circumstances from which such assent is to be

T t 3   implied

implied. Then was there any express assent in this case? So far from that, it appears that no application was made to the defendant for several months after the articles had been delivered; but the plaintiff always called when he knew the defendant was from home, and always asked for the wife. There was, therefore, no express assent of the husband. Then can we say that there was any implied assent? There are many cases in which the assent of the husband may be presumed. In *Comyn's Digest*, tit. *Baron and Feme*, (Q.) it is laid down, that if the wife trades in goods, and buys for her trade when she cohabits with her husband, his assent is to be presumed; and if a wife buy *necessary* apparel for herself, the assent of the husband shall generally be intended. But here the apparel provided consists of articles of ornament of considerable value. It does not appear, considering the defendant's occupation, and his wife's fortune, that articles of jewelry to that amount can be considered as necessary apparel, and one reason is, because the wife had articles of that description provided for her when she married, and there is no evidence to shew that the husband ever saw the wife wearing these articles, and if he did not, then there is nothing to shew any implied assent.

ABBOTT C. J. I entirely agree with the opinion which has been delivered by my learned brothers, and I think the rule for a nonsuit ought to be made absolute. If this decision should have the effect of introducing somewhat more caution into the conduct of those who are to obtain their living by selling their goods and wares, it will be most beneficial. It will occasionally be beneficial to infants, to fathers, to husbands, and to friends; it will also be beneficial to those who

have

have goods to sell, for the experience we have in courts of justice leads us to know, that persons who trade without due caution often find their hopes deceived; they find in the result, that they have parted with goods for which they never can obtain the money. The rule must be made absolute.

Rule absolute for a nonsuit.

Josephs *against* Pebrer.

ASSUMPSIT for work and labour and commission, and for money paid to the use of defendant. Plea, non assumpsit. At the trial before *Littledale* J., at the *London* sittings after last *Trinity* term, it appeared, that in *April* last the defendant had employed the plaintiff, a person carrying on business on the foreign stock exchange, to purchase for him ten shares in an association called " The Equitable Loan Bank Company." The shares had not, at that time been distributed, or in technical language, " come out," and the plaintiff was to buy them for the coming out. He did so, and on the 23d two certificates for the shares were delivered to him, for which he paid 1*l.* as the deposit, and 5*l.* 10*s.* as premium on each share. The certificates were in the following form:

In assumpsit for work and labor, and money expended in the purchase of shares in a concern called the " Equitable Loan Bank Company," it appeared that the company professed to have a capital of 2,000,000*l.*, in shares of 50*l.* each; that a deposit of 1*l.* per share was required on the delivery of certificates for shares to the holders; that the shares were to be transferrable without any restriction, and that the holders were to be subject to such regulations as might be contained in any act of parliament passed for the government of the society, and in the mean time, to such regulations as might be made by a committee of management. No evidence was given as to the particular object or tendency of the company. Held, that, upon this evidence the company was to be considered illegal, and within the operation of the 6 G 1. c. 18., as having transferrable shares, and affecting to act as a body corporate without authority by charter or act of parliament; and that plaintiff consequently could not maintain his action, which arose out of an illegal transaction.

T t 4 " Equitable

" Equitable Loan Bank Company,

Capital two millions sterling, in shares of 50l. each.

(Then followed a list of Presidents, Vice-Presidents, Directors, Auditors, Treasurers, Solicitors, &c. &c.)

No. 16,156 to 16,160 inclusive.

This certificate declares, that the sum of 1l. having been paid as a deposit for each of the above mentioned shares of 50l. each, the holder of this certificate will be entitled to those five shares in the Equitable Loan Bank Company, with all the benefits and emoluments, but subject to the future payments on the shares, and all matters contained in any act of parliament for the regulation of the company; and in the meantime to such conditions, regulations, and orders as the vice-presidents and directors grounding the present committee of management may direct." Signed by two directors. When the certificates were tendered to the defendant, he said that they ought to have been obtained sooner, and refused to accept or pay for them. It was objected for the defendant, that the association was within the 18th and 19th sections of the 6 G. 1. c. 18. and therefore illegal, and that consequently all contracts relating to the purchase of shares were void. Several other objections were also made, but it is unnecessary to notice them, as the case was ultimately decided upon that which is above stated. The learned Judge reserved the point, and the plaintiff obtained a verdict. In *Michaelmas* term a rule nisi to enter a nonsuit was obtained, against which

Marryat and *Andrews* shewed cause, and contended that the association in question did not fall within the meaning of the 6 G. 1. c. 18. It was decided, after much

consider-

consideration, in *Rex* v. *Webb* (a), that the mere creation of transferrable shares does not render a concern illegal. It must tend to the common prejudice of his majesty's subjects. That is a point to be established by evidence. And as the defendant had employed the plaintiff to purchase the shares, it was not incumbent on the plaintiff to prove the legality of the association; the onus of impeaching it was on the defendant.

Gurney and *Chitty* contrà, were stopped by the Court.

ABBOTT C. J. I am of opinion that enough appeared in evidence on the trial of this cause, to shew that the bargain for the shares in question was void by law. Whether from a further explanation of the objects and tendency of the Equitable Loan Association, a different conclusion might or might not be drawn, it is not now necessary to enquire. My decision is founded on the evidence that was given in the cause. A certificate purporting to entitle the holder to certain shares was put in. The particular objects of the association did not indeed appear; but in the opening speech of the plaintiff's counsel, it was stated that the association was founded for the purpose of lending money at 8 per cent. That is a larger rate of interest than the law allows in general, but it would not be illegal to form such an association for the purpose of lending money at that rate. upon certain terms, in the event of its being sanctioned by an act of parliament, or a royal charter of incorporation. But if the projectors go further, and, before the association has been sanctioned either by an act of

(a) 14 *East*, 406.

the

the legislature or by a royal charter, make shares in the
concern transferrable without any restriction, at the mere
will of the holder, and provide that the purchasers
shall render themselves liable to regulations to be
framed by certain persons styling themselves a committee of management or directors, then the association
assumes an unlawful shape. The words of the 6 G.1.
c.18. are large and comprehensive, although not altogether free from obscurity. In the 18th and 19th
sections, the two objects of raising transferrable shares,
and affecting to act as a body corporate, are pointed out
as particularly shewing what the legislature intended to
prohibit. The 18th section begins by reciting, "that
several undertakings or projects of different kinds had
been publicly contrived and practised, or attempted to
be practised, which manifestly tended to the common
grievance, prejudice, and inconvenience of the king's
subjects in their trade or commerce, and other their
affairs; and that persons who contrive or attempt such
dangerous and mischievous undertakings or projects
under false pretences of public good, did presume according to their own devices or schemes to open books
for public subscriptions, and draw in many unwary persons to subscribe therein, towards raising great sums of
money, whereupon the subscribers or claimants under
them did pay small proportions thereof, and such proportions in the whole did amount to very large sums;
which dangerous and mischievous undertakings or projects did relate to several fisheries and other affairs,
wherein the trade, commerce, and welfare of the king's
subjects, or great numbers of them, were concerned and
interested. And that in many cases the said under-
takers or subscribers had presumed to act as if they

were

were corporate bodies, and had pretended to make their shares in stocks transferrable or assignable without any legal authority by act of parliament or by any charter from the crown for so doing," and then enacts, " that all and every the undertakings and attempts described as aforesaid, and all other public undertakings and attempts tending to the common grievance, prejudice, and inconvenience of his majesty's subjects, or great numbers of them, in their trade, commerce, or other lawful affairs; and all public subscriptions, receipts, payments, assignments, transfers, pretended assignments and transfers, and all matters and things whatsoever for furthering any such undertaking or attempt, and *more particularly* the acting or presuming to act as a corporate body or bodies, the raising or pretending to raise transferrable stock or stocks, the transferring or pretending to transfer or assign any share or shares in such stock or stocks, without legal authority either by act of parliament or charter, shall for ever be deemed to be illegal and void, and shall not be practised or in anywise put in execution." The 19th section makes all such undertakings public nusances. Now what was the nature of the association in question? By the certificate which was in evidence it appeared that they professed to have a capital of 2,000,000*l.* in shares of 50*l.* each, consequently there must have been 40,000 shares; and the holder of the certificate was to be entitled to the number of shares specified in it, upon payment of 1*l.* upon each share. That amounts to an express declaration that the shares are to be transferrable at the mere option of the holder, and it was quite uncertain what person would thereafter, as holder of the certificate, become partner in the concern. Again, until

an

an act of parliament could be obtained, the shareholders
were to be subject to such conditions, regulations, and
orders as the vice-presidents and directors, forming the
committee of management, might direct. The members
of the association then took upon themselves to act as a
corporate body, having a select body invested with
power to make bye-laws. But what was the grievance
and prejudice which the association tended to cause to
his majesty's subjects? It appears that these shares,
upon each of which only 1l. was paid, were sold at
5l. 10s. premium, and unless we shut our eyes altogether
to what is going on in the world, we cannot help observing that in other companies and associations the sale
and transfer of shares at enormous premiums is carried
on to a greater extent than was ever known, except at
the period when the statute referred to was passed.
The necessary effect of such a practice is to introduce
gaming and rash speculation to a ruinous extent. In
such transactions one cannot gain unless another loses,
whereas in fair mercantile transactions each party, in
the ordinary course of things, reaps a profit in his turn.
Upon the evidence in this case, then, the association appears to be one of which the effect cannot but be mischievous; and it exhibits two signs and tokens which are
pointed out by the legislature as the signs and tokens of
illegal associations. We say, therefore, that dealing in
these shares was an illegal transaction, and this being
our opinion, every one must observe that the signs of
the times require us to declare it without delay. There
is another point which I shall notice very briefly, as it
was not touched upon in the argument, viz. that traffick-
ing in these shares may very possibly have been illegal
at common law, inasmuch as it was bargaining and

wagering

wagering about an act of parliament to be obtained in future. Upon the whole, I am satisfied that the plaintiff was not in law entitled to maintain his action; the rule for a nonsuit must, therefore, be made absolute.

BAYLEY J. I am clearly of opinion that, upon the evidence given on the trial of this cause, we are bound to say that the association in question is illegal. It presumed to act as a body corporate, and pretended to create transferrable shares in its stocks. It is true that in *Rex* v. *Webb,* the society then brought before the Court was considered legal, although the shares were transferrable; but in that instance they were not transferrable at the mere unrestricted option of the holder. They could not be transferred to any person who would not enter into the original covenants; nor could more than twenty be held by the same person, unless they came to him by operation of law; and the object of the society, which was to supply the inhabitants of *Birmingham,* being shareholders, with bread and flour, virtually limited the transfer of shares to persons residing in that neighbourhood. So in *Pratt* v. *Hutchinson* (a), which was the case of a building company, no person could become a member of the company until he had made himself a party to the partnership articles, nor until he had been proposed and approved by a certain majority of persons present at a meeting of the society. Both those cases are very distinguishable from the present, which manifestly tends to the common grievance of many of his majesty's subjects, and falls within the description of illegal societies given by the 6 *G.* 1. *c.* 18. *s.* 18.

(a) 15 *East,* 511.

HOLROYD

HOLROYD J. I am of opinion that the transaction in question was illegal, and that the association is one of those prohibited by the 6 G. 1. c. 18. But it would have been very different if the project had been, not to constitute the society, or to make the shares transferrable, until the scheme had obtained the authority of an act of parliament or a royal charter.

LITTLEDALE J. It appears to me also that this association is illegal within the 6 G. 1. c. 18. I think that upon the evidence given at the trial we must say that it tends to the common grievance of many of his majesty's subjects. The act of parliament, after pointing out certain things which will be illegal, proceeds: " more particularly the acting as a body corporate, and the raising or pretending to raise transferrable shares." Those are the indicia by which we are to judge whether the society be illegal, and whether it tends to the public grievance or not. In the case cited, evidence was given of the particular objects of the society, which negatived the idea of its being a grievance; and regulations existed somewhat restraining the transfer of the shares. Here nothing of the kind appeared, and we are left to draw our conclusions from the certificate which was given in evidence. For these reasons, I concur in thinking that a nonsuit must be entered.

Rule absolute. (a)

(a) See *Rex* v. *Dodd*, 9 *East*, 516. *Buck* v. *Buck*, 1 *Campb.* 547. *Rex* v. *Stratton*, 1 *Campb.* 549. *n.* *Brown* v. *Holt*, 4 *Taunt.* 587.

1825.

ATKINSON *against* COTESWORTH.

Friday,
February 4th.

ASSUMPSIT on a charter-party, not under seal, whereby it was mutually agreed between the plaintiff, commander of the ship *Agaphea,* then lying in the river *Thames,* and the defendant, that the vessel should take a cargo to *Pernambuco,* and bring a cargo thence to *London* or *Liverpool,* according to the directions of the charterers' agent in the *Brazils,* and deliver the same, on being paid freight, at and after a certain rate therein specified, by a good bill, payable at two months from the day of final discharge. Breach, non-payment of freight. Plea, non-assumpsit. At the trial before *Abbott* C. J., at the *London* sittings after last *Trinity* term, it appeared, that the plaintiff, at the time of making the charter-party, was the commander of the *Agaphea,* whereof *David Hodgins,* then resident in *Ireland,* was owner. Before the vessel returned to *England, Hodgins,* being dissatisfied with the plaintiff, appointed one *Bain* as his agent, to receive the freight, and gave notice to the defendant to pay it to him, which he accordingly did, but before it was paid, the plaintiff demanded that it should be paid to himself and not to *Bain.* Upon these facts the Lord Chief Justice nonsuited the plaintiff, but gave his counsel leave to move to enter a verdict in his favour for 80l., which appeared to be due to him from the owner. In *Michaelmas* term *Gurney* obtained a rule accordingly, and now

Scarlett

Where the commander of a ship entered into a charter party, (not under seal,) whereby the charterer agreed to pay freight generally, without saying to whom: Held, that the owner having demanded and received the freight, the commander could not maintain an action for it against the charterer, although he had given him notice not to pay it to any one but himself.

Scarlett and *Campbell* shewed cause. The plaintiff in this case was merely the agent of the owner, and made the charter-party for his benefit. In the absence of any interference by the owner, he might have claimed the freight from the defendant. But when the owner intervened, and desired the freight to be paid to a third person, the authority of the captain was at an end. He had not any prospective lien for his wages, although, if he had received the money, he might then have set off the sum due for wages, had he been sued by the owner for the money so received. If a factor receives the proceeds of goods sold by him he has a lien on the money, but he cannot claim the proceeds from the vendee, if his principal intervenes, and desires the payment to be made to himself. *Smith* v. *Plummer* (a) is expressly in point.

Gurney and *Chitty*, contrà. The case of *Smith* v. *Plummer* differs materially from the present. It does not appear that any charter-party was executed in that case between the captain and the defendant, the latter therefore had never contracted to pay freight to the captain. In the present case, the plaintiff was the person who chartered the ship to the defendant; and it does not appear on the face of the instrument that he was not owner; the defendant must, therefore, be taken to have contracted to pay the freight to him, and could not exonerate himself from his liability by paying it to a third person.

ABBOTT C. J. I am unable to discover any solid distinction between the present case and that of *Smith* v. *Plummer*. Upon the authority of that case, there-

(a) 1 *B. & A.* 575.

fore,

fore, I am of opinion that the nonsuit was right. The only distinction now pointed out between the two cases is, that in the present instance a charter-party was entered into, and that it does not appear that any such instrument existed in *Smith* v. *Plummer*. Let us suppose that no charter-party was made in that case, then the freight would be made payable generally by the bill of lading, signed by the commander of the vessel. Now the charter-party entered into by this plaintiff and defendant does not specify to whom the freight was to be paid; in that respect, therefore, the case is the same as if the freight had been stipulated for by a common bill of lading. The master of a ship has no prospective lien on the freight, and cannot insist upon having it paid to himself, although a payment to him in the absence of any [notice by the owner to the charterer to withhold it, would be a good and valid payment. For these reasons I think that this rule must be discharged.

1825.

———

ATKINSON
against
COTTSWORTH.

Rule discharged.

see Ashcroft v Bourne 3 B & Ald 684

BASTEN *against* CAREW and Another.

Friday,
February 4th.

TRESPASS for breaking and entering the plaintiff's house and closes, and ejecting him therefrom. Plea, general issue. At the trial before *Abbott* C. J., at the last Summer assizes for *Devon*, the trespass having been

It is not necessary that any information or complaint should be made on oath, in order to justify the interference

of magistrates under the 11 *G*. 2. *c*. 19. *s*. 16.

In trespass against two magistrates for giving plaintiff's landlord possession of a farm as a deserted farm, they produced in evidence a record of their proceedings under that act, which set forth all such circumstances as were necessary to give them jurisdiction, and by which it appeared that they had pursued the directions of the statute: Held, that this was conclusive as an answer to the action.

proved, the defendants, who were justices of the peace,
gave in evidence the record of certain proceedings by
them, under the 11 G. 2. c. 19., which was as follows:
" *Devonshire :* Be it remembered that on, &c., at, &c.,
A. B. complained unto us *J. W. Carew* and *C. O. Or-
mond,* Esquires, two of the justices of our said lord the
king, assigned, &c., that he the said *A. B.* did demise at
rack rent unto *J. Basten,* of, &c., husbandman, a messuage and tenement called, &c., consisting of, &c., situate,
lying, and being at, &c., and that on, &c., there was in
arrear and due unto the said *A. B.,* from him the said
J. Basten, the tenant, of the said demised premises, half
a year's rent thereof, and that he the said *J. Basten* hath
deserted the said demised premises, and left the same
uncultivated and unoccupied, so as no sufficient distress
could be had to countervail the said arrears of rent;
whereupon the said *A. B.* then and there, to wit, on, &c.,
at, &c., *requested* of us the said justices, that a due
remedy should be provided according to the form of the
statute in that case made and provided, which *complaint
and request* by us the aforesaid justices being heard, we
(having no interest, nor either of us having any interest in
the said demised premises), on, &c., did personally go,
&c.," stating the subsequent proceedings in the usual
form; and it was contended, that this record was conclusive
as to the facts stated in it, and a sufficient defence to the
action. The Lord Chief Justice refused to nonsuit the
plaintiff, but gave the defendants leave to move to enter a
nonsuit, if it should eventually become necessary. The
facts were then investigated before the jury, and the defendants obtained a verdict. In *Michaelmas* term the Court
granted a rule nisi for a new trial, on the ground that
the verdict was contrary to the weight of evidence, and

16   also,

also, that the jury had been misdirected, but the defendants had leave to insist upon the matter of law urged for them at the trial, and as the case was decided on that point, it is unnecessary to notice the others.

Pell Serjt., *Tancred*, and *Chitty* shewed cause. The record of the proceedings by the defendants was in the nature of a conviction, and was, therefore, conclusive evidence of the facts contained in it, and a sufficient defence to the action, *Brittain* v. *Kinnaird.* (a) The form of the record is also good, it is precisely the same as that given in *Burn's Justice*, 791., which was upheld by this Court in ex parte *Pilton*.(b) The stat. 11 G. 2. c. 19. s. 16., upon which the proceeding is founded, does not require that the justices should have evidence on oath; it merely speaks of a complaint and request made by the landlord or his bailiff. Besides, if the plaintiff intended to impeach the proceeding, on the ground that the justices had acted without sufficient evidence, he should first have moved for a mandamus to compel them to set out the evidence in their record. But in truth the justices may proceed on their own view, as in cases of forcible entry and detainer. In such cases the consequence is much more serious to the party charged, yet the record merely shews a complaint, and not the evidence upon which the justice proceeds; 2 *Burn's Just.* 456., *Lambard's Eirenarcha*, 146. 149.

Wilde Serjt., contrà. The document given in evidence in this case, and which was called a record, was not really a record, and, therefore, was not conclusive. The proceedings under the 11 G. 2. c. 19. s. 16. are extremely harsh towards tenants, and should therefore be

(a) 1 B. & B. 432.　　　　(b) 1 B. & A. 369.

　　　　strictly

strictly watched. The information as to the arrears of rent and the desertion by the tenant is given ex parte, and without notice to the tenant. The latter, therefore, has not any opportunity of disputing the assertions of the landlord. Upon the information so given the justices view the farm, and affix the first notice required by the statute. The tenant, by this ex parte proceeding, is prevented from afterwards disputing that the rent is in arrear, but must pay the rent or lose possession of the farm. Now it is a general principle of law, that where magistrates act judicially, and have power to bind by their judgment, they must proceed on evidence given under the sanction of an oath. It is not any where stated in that which is miscalled a record, that the information was given on oath, and therefore the contrary must be taken to have been the fact. If that were so, the justices had not jurisdiction, and at all events, as enough does not appear on this document to shew that they had jurisdiction, it cannot be conclusive in their favor.

ABBOTT C. J. It was urged at the trial of this cause, that the record made by the justices of their proceedings, in giving the landlord possession of the farm demised to the plaintiff, was conclusive as an answer to the action. At that time I entertained some doubts upon the point, and therefore refused to direct a nonsuit; for, in that case, had my direction proved erroneous, the parties would have been put to the expence of a second trial. But in the shape which the question now assumes this rule must be discharged, if I ought then to have nonsuited the plaintiff; and upon consideration, I am of opinion that I ought to have done so. It is a general rule and principle of law, that where justices of

18   the

the peace have an authority given to them by an act of parliament, and they appear to have acted within the jurisdiction so given, and to have done all that they are required by the act to do in order to originate their jurisdiction, a conviction drawn up in due form, and remaining in force, is a protection in any action brought against them for the act so done. It has been said, that this doctrine applied to such cases as the present will work great injustice, but that argument was pressed too far. The seventeenth section of the statute gives an appeal to the Judges at the next assize; the tenant may, therefore, have summary redress if any wrong has been done, and the appeal is not attended with any great risk, for if it is dismissed, the amount of the costs to be awarded against the appellant cannot exceed 5l. It has also been said, that a proceeding taken ex parte and without notice, will preclude the tenant from disputing that the rent is in arrear. The record may, indeed, be conclusive upon that point in favor of the justices, but will not protect the landlord. If the rent were not in arrear as alleged, he would be liable to an action on the case, for wrongfully procuring the justices to interfere. There are many cases in which a magistrate acting bonâ fide may be protected, and yet the person upon whose information he has acted may be liable to an action for giving false or malicious information. In the proceeding in question the statute does not direct the justices to make enquiry upon oath; can this Court, then, impose upon them the necessity of doing so; or can we say, that by forbearing so to enquire, or by omitting to state on their record that they did so enquire, they have neglected to take any step made necessary by the statute to originate their jurisdiction? It no where requires an information to be made on oath, or that it shall in that mode be proved that the rent is in arrear: but that "if any tenant holding lands, tenements, or hereditaments at a rack rent, or where the rent reserved shall be full three-fourths of the yearly value of the demised premises, who shall be in arrear for one year's rent(a), shall desert the demised premises, and leave the same uncultivated or unoccupied, so as no sufficient distress can be had to countervail the arrears of rent; it shall and may be lawful to and for two or more justices of the peace of the county, riding, &c. (having no interest in the demised premises) at the *request* of the lessor or landlord, or his or her bailiff or receiver, to go upon and view the same, and to affix on the most notorious part of the premises notice in writing what day (at the distance of fourteen days at least) they will return to take a second view thereof." The justices are, therefore, to determine upon their own view, whether the premises are deserted or not. Suppose the case of a refusal by all the justices of the district to act upon the information and request of the landlord; this is certainly an extreme case and not likely to occur, but if it did, must not this Court direct them to go and view the premises? It is clear, that we cannot require of them to act only where information is given on oath, as the legislature has not made that requisite. The record given in evidence, therefore, shews that they had jurisdiction, and is conclusive in their behalf, leaving to the tenant such other remedy as he may have against the landlord, if he has improperly set the justices in motion by means of false information.

(a) Altered to half a year's rent by the 57 G. 3. c. 52.

BAYLEY

BAYLEY J. A landlord would certainly be liable to an action on the case, for improperly procuring the interference of the magistrates under the statute in question. But this is an action against the magistrates, and the only question is, whether upon the face of their proceedings they appear to have acted within the scope of their jurisdiction. The 11 $G. 2. c. 19. s. 16.$ does not require that any information or complaint shall be made on oath, but that the magistrates shall, at the request of the landlord, go and view the premises, and if they find them in a given state, affix a notice, stating that on a certain day they will return; and then if the rent arrear is not paid, or no sufficient distress is found on the premises, they are to put the landlord in possession. It is said that this measure is extremely harsh, and that the power thus given to the magistrates may be used as an instrument of oppression; but it must be remembered, that magistrates acting corruptly are liable to criminal informations. Then it is assumed that the tenant, the party grieved, is without remedy; but that is not so, he has a manifest right of action against the landlord, if he improperly procures the interference of the magistrates; and it would be most mischievous to subject the magistrates to an action under such circumstances. The tenant has also a summary remedy by appeal to the justices of assize. The record, however, unappealed from, is conclusive as to the magistrates, for it is their duty to act on the *request* of the landlord, and it appears by the record that they did so act, and that they pursued the directions given by the statute.

HOLROYD J. I am of the same opinion. This was an action of trespass against magistrates, who say that

they

they have acted in discharge of a duty imposed by an act of parliament: and the question is, whether their record of the proceedings is conclusive in their favour. It has been objected, that the complaint should have been on oath, but that is not required unless specially directed by the act of parliament. That objection, therefore, cannot avail if the magistrates have acted in the mode pointed out by the statute; and if they have done so, many cases establish that their record is conclusive in this action, although they will be liable to punishment if they have corruptly made it differ from the real facts of the case. The statute 11 G. 2. c. 19. s. 16. gives the magistrates jurisdiction to act at the request of the landlord, and whether his statement be true or false they have power to view the premises and investigate the complaint. They are, therefore, judges of record as has been decided on the statutes of forcible entry. Thus it has been held, " if a justice of peace record that upon his view as a force, which is no force, he cannot be drawn in question either by action or indictment," cited in *Floyd and Barker's* case (a), and in *Greenwell* v. *Burwell* (b); and in 27 *Ass.* 19. there is this passage, " A judge of oyer and terminer, where the jury found and presented a fact to be a trespass, caused their finding to be entered as a felony, and yet could not be punished by indictment or otherwise, because he was a judge of record, and the indictment against him was to defeat his record by averring against what he did as a judge of record," *Salk.* 397. So also in *Strickland* v. *Ward* (c), which was trespass for false imprisonment brought against a magistrate who produced, in answer, a conviction of

(a) 12 Co. 25.   (b) 1 Salk. 397.   (c) 7 T. R. 654. n.

the

the plaintiff for unlawfully returning to a parish, after having been legally removed thence, without bringing a certificate; and also a warrant reciting that conviction, *Yates* J. held that the conviction could not be controverted in evidence; that the justice having a competent jurisdiction of the matter, his judgment was conclusive till reversed or quashed; and that it could not be set aside at Nisi Prius, and the plaintiff was nonsuited. If, indeed, a justice acts without jurisdiction, he is liable to an action of trespass, *Morgan* v. *Hughes.* (a) In *Miller* v. *Seare* (b), (which has since been overruled (c),) it was held that an action would lie against commissioners for committing a bankrupt who did not answer to their satisfaction. Lord Chief Justice *De Grey* held that the commissioners were not judges, but admitted that they would have been protected had they been acting as judges; and he says, " So justices of the peace may be justices of record, when made so by act of parliament, as in case of riots, force, going armed, &c. in which cases their records are not traversable." In this case, I think that the justices were made judges of record, that their record was not traversable, and that it was a conclusive answer to the action. The rule for a new trial must therefore be discharged.

Rule discharged, (d)

(a) *T. R.* 225.   (b) 2 *W. Bl.* 1141.

(c) See *Doswell* v. *Impey*, 1 B. & C. 163.

(d) *Littledale* J. was attending the Admiralty Sessions at the Old Bailey.

SPENCELEY *against* ROBINSON.

By statute
17 G. 3. c. 3.
s. 2. it is en-
acted, " that
overseers of the
poor shall per-
mit inhabitants
of the parish to
inspect rates at
all reasonable
times, and shall
upon demand
forthwith
give copies of
the same to any
inhabitant of
the parish ;"
and by s. 3.
" if any over-
seer shall not
permit an in-
habitant to in-
spect the rate,
or shall neglect
to give copies
thereof as
aforesaid, such
overseer for
every such of-
fence shall for-
feit and pay to
*the party ag-
grieved* the sum
of 20l. : Held,
first, that in
order to entitle
a party to sue
for the penalty
under the sta-
tute, he must
shew that he
has sustained
an injury by
the act of the
overseer :
Held, se-
condly, that
there must be a demand to inspect the rate made at a reasonable time and place ; and,
Semble, that the house of the overseer is the place at which the demand ought to be
made. *(a)*
Thirdly, although the statute says, that copies shall upon demand be *forthwith* given, yet
the overseer is entitled to a reasonable time for making them out.

DEBT on the statute 17 G. 2. c. 8. The declaration
stated, that the plaintiff was an inhabitant of the
township of *Coxwould*, in the North Riding of the county
of *York*, and that the defendant was one of the overseers
of the poor of that township; that on the 26th of *March*
1824, the churchwardens and overseers of the poor of
that township made a rate for the relief of the poor,
which was afterwards duly allowed by two justices; and
that the churchwardens and overseers, after the allowance of the rate, gave public notice thereof in the
church. The declaration then stated, that the plaintiff requested the defendant, as such overseer, to permit him, the plaintiff, to inspect the rate, and tendered
to him one shilling for the same; yet that the defendant neglected and refused to permit the plaintiff to inspect the rate, contrary to the form of the
statute, &c. whereby defendant forfeited 20l. The
second count stated, that the plaintiff at a reasonable
time, to wit, on, &c., at, &c., demanded of the defendant, so being such overseer, a copy of the rate, and was
ready and offered to pay to the defendant, at, and after
the rate of 6d. for every twenty-four names thereof, yet
that the defendant refused to give him the copy.

At the trial before *Bayley* J., at the Summer assizes
for the county of *York*, 1824, the following appeared to

be

(a) See the Case of Parker v. Edwards 7. B & C 374.

1825.

SPENCELEY
against
ROBINSON.

be the facts of the case: The plaintiff was an inhabitant of the township of Coxwould, and the defendant was overseer of that parish. The rate in question was made on the 26th of March, allowed on the 27th, and published on the 28th. About eight o'clock of the 19th of April the plaintiff sent his son to the defendant, to request that he would come to him at his, plaintiff's, house. The defendant went and saw the plaintiff and his attorney; the plaintiff asked the defendant to allow him to inspect the rate, and tendered him 1s. on that account. The defendant said that he durst not allow it, he was ordered not to do it. The plaintiff's attorney then asked him for a copy of the rate. The defendant then went away, and related what had taken place to the Rev. Mr. Newton a magistrate, and stated that he had not shewn the rate, because he was informed that he was not obliged to shew it. Mr. Newton told him that he was, and pointed out the clause in the act of parliament, and advised him to go back immediately and shew the plaintiff the rate, and take a copy of it next morning as early as possible to the attorney. The defendant did return to the plaintiff's house in about two hours after the inspection of the rate had been demanded, and offered to shew him the rate, and the defendant made out a copy that night and delivered it to the plaintiff's attorney early the following morning. The latter said that it was too late, for the plaintiff could not appeal to the next sessions. The defendant said that he would waive all objection to the notice. The defendant, on the 17th of April, had met the plaintiff's attorney in Helmsley market, which is about eight miles from Coxwould, and he then asked him if he had a copy of the rate, for he was employed by the

plaintiff

plaintiff and wished to see one. The defendant said that he should have one if he was entitled to it, and the attorney replied that he should be at Corwould on *Monday* the 19th and should expect to have one. Upon this evidence the learned judge told the jury, that although there was a refusal at one time to permit an inspection of the rate, the question was, whether that refusal was not done away with by what subsequently took place, the defendant within two hours after the refusal having offered to allow the plaintiff to inspect the rate, and having delivered a copy to the plaintiff's attorney early next morning. A party was bound to give an overseer a reasonable time to do what the law required. The learned judge then told the jury, that if they thought that the defendant had complied with the demand in a reasonable time, the defendant was entitled to a verdict. The jury found a verdict for the defendant. A rule nisi was obtained for a new trial in *Michaelmas* term, upon the ground that this verdict was against evidence, and also upon the ground, that the learned judge misdirected the jury, inasmuch as a permission to inspect the rate having been once refused, a right of action vested in the plaintiff.

Scarlett and *Alexander* now shewed cause. The words of the 17 *G. 2. c. 3. s. 2,*, are, that the church-wardens and overseers of the poor shall permit all and every the inhabitants of the parish, township, or place, to inspect every such rate at all seasonable times, paying 1s. for the same, and shall upon demand forthwith give copies of the same, or any part thereof, to any inhabitant of the said parish, township, or place, paying at the rate of 6d. for every twenty-four names. The third

section

section enacts, that if any churchwarden or overseer shall not permit any inhabitant or parishioner to inspect the rate, or shall refuse or neglect to give copies thereof as aforesaid, the churchwarden or overseer for every such offence shall forfeit and pay to the party aggrieved the sum of 20l. The statute creates two offences; the one is not permitting the inhabitant to inspect the rate, the other is the refusing to give copies thereof. The refusal to permit implies a previous request, and it must be made at a reasonable time and a reasonable place. Now, an overseer cannot be expected to carry the rate-book with him, and, therefore, the request to see the rate should have been made at the house of the overseer. Here it was made at the plaintiff's house, when the defendant had not, and could not be expected to have the rate-book with him. Then as to the demand of the copy of the rate, there was no legal demand until the evening of the 19th, for that was the first demand made by an inhabitant of the parish, and a reasonable time must be allowed for the purpose of making out the copy. It appears by the evidence, that a copy was made out by twelve o'clock that night, and delivered early next morning to the plaintiff's attorney. The defendant, therefore, complied with that demand within a reasonable time. Besides, the penalty is given to the party aggrieved. Now the plaintiff was not aggrieved by this act of the defendant, for he might have entered his appeal at the then next sessions, and the justices might have adjourned it to a further sessions under the 17 G. 2. c. 38. s. 4. Besides, by the 41 G. 3. c. 28. s. 5., the parties might in open court have consented to waive any objection to the appeal.

Brougham,

Brougham, contrà. The statute imposes a public duty upon the churchwardens to permit the inspection of the rate, and to give copies, without reference to any injury done to an individual. The question was not submitted to the jury, whether the request was made at a reasonable time and place. The question submitted to them was, whether the demand was complied with within a reasonable time. A refusal was distinctly proved, and that being so, a right of action had vested in the plaintiff, which was not divested by a subsequent offer to allow the plaintiff to inspect the rate. It might have been a question for the jury, whether the acts proved amounted to a refusal to permit an inspection or to give a copy; but upon that point the weight of evidence was in favour of the plaintiff; for it appeared that on the 17th of *April* the defendant had notice that a copy would be required of him on the *19th.*

ABBOTT C. J. My doubt in this case has been, not whether the learned Judge left the proper question to the jury, but whether he ought to have left any question at all to the jury. I think that the plaintiff ought to have been nonsuited. The 17 *G. 2. c. 3. s. 2.* enacts, " that the churchwardens and overseers shall permit all the inhabitants of the parish, township, or place, to inspect every such rate at all seasonable times, paying 1*s.* for the same, and shall, upon demand, *forthwith* give copies of the same, or any part thereof, to any inhabitant of the said parish, township, or place, paying at the rate of 6*d.* for every twenty-four names." The person to whom an inspection is to be allowed, or a copy to be given, must be an inhabitant. The defendant, therefore, was not bound to attend to the request made by the

attorney

attorney of the plaintiff on the 17th. The next clause enacts, " that in case any overseer shall not permit any inhabitant or parishioner to inspect the said rates, or shall refuse or neglect to give copies thereof, such church-warden or overseer, for every such offence, shall forfeit and pay to the party aggrieved 20*l.*" The latter words plainly import that the penalty is to be given to the party who has sustained an injury by the act of the overseer. Now here the plaintiff sustained no injury, for he was not deprived of his appeal by what took place, as it might have been entered at the next sessions, and the justices had power to adjourn it to a subsequent sessions. The question left to the jury was, whether the defendant had, within a reasonable time, complied with the request of the plaintiff to be permitted to inspect the rate, or to have a copy. Before any right of action could vest in the plaintiff, by reason of the defendant's not permitting him to inspect the rate, a request must have been made for such permission at a reasonable time and place. The house of the overseer, 'where he may be fairly supposed to keep the rate-book, must be the reasonable place for making such a request or demand. Now in this case, the overseer, without having any notice that the rate-book is required, is desired to come to the plaintiff's house, and the demand to inspect the rate-book is made at a place where it was known he could not have the book with him. That was an unreasonable place for making the request. I think, therefore, that there was in this case no legal request or demand to inspect the rate-book. Then, as to the copy of the rate; assuming that the demand of a copy made by the solicitor, in the presence of the plaintiff, to have been a demand by the latter, the defendant

fendant

fendant was entitled to a reasonable time to comply with that demand. For although the statute requires the overseer to furnish the copy *forthwith*, that word must receive a reasonable construction, so as to give the overseer an opportunity of making the copy required. Here the copy was made during the night, and delivered the following morning. That demand was complied with in a reasonable time, and the plaintiff ought to have been nonsuited. It has been contended, that the question was not left to the jury, whether the demand was made at a reasonable time and place, but the question submitted to them implied as much, and the learned Judge must be taken to have left to them to say, whether the defendant had, within a reasonable time, complied with a legal demand, viz. a demand made at a reasonable time and place. I think that the direction was right, and that the verdict was right also; but I strongly incline to think that the Judge ought to have nonsuited the plaintiff.

HOLROYD J. It seems to me that the plaintiff is not entitled to recover. I think that the demand to inspect the rate was not sufficient, because it was not made at a reasonable time and place. I think, also, that the plaintiff was not a party grieved, because he did not sustain any injury by the refusal to allow him to inspect the rate. The being an inhabitant does not make him a party grieved. It has been held, under the bankrupt laws, that unless the party be a creditor, he is not a party grieved within the meaning of those statutes.

BAYLEY J. concurred.

Rule discharged.

Chauter ... Dickinson b Lock'r No 112/

DRANT *against* BROWN, Executor of LEGGOTT.

*Tuesday,
February 8th.*

A SSUMPSIT on a special agreement. The declaration stated, that, in consideration that plaintiff
would let to defendant's testator, one *Leggott*, a certain
piece of ground to be dug for clay to make bricks, he
(*Leggott*) undertook not to dig deeper than three feet;
breach, that he had dug five feet deep, and thereby injured the land. Counts on a quan. mer., for suffering
and permitting *Leggott* to dig and carry away a quantity
of clay; for clay bargained and sold to *Leggott*, and by
him accepted, dug, and carried away, for use and occupation of a close by *Leggott*, and on an account stated
between plaintiff and *Leggott*. Plea, general issue. At
the trial before *Bayley* J., at the *York* Summer assizes
1824, a witness proved, that in the month of *March*
1815, the plaintiff and *Leggott*, the testator, met at a
club, when the latter complained that he was likely to
lose a piece of land which he had contracted to rent of
one *Grant*, upon certain terms, for the purpose of dig-
ging clay to make bricks. Plaintiff said, that if that
bargain went off he would let him a piece of land on
the same terms, and put his offer in writing as follows:
" Memorandum, that I, *George Drant*, do hereby offer to
Mr. *J. Leggott* the clay of two acres, two roods, and twenty
perches of land, for the purpose of making bricks, upon
the same conditions as the said *J. Leggott* hath made
with *J. Grant*, the conditions being shewn that now
exist between *J. Leggott* and *J. Grant*, and a price according to quantity being allowed. This agreement to

A. entered into
a written agree-
ment with *B.*
for the hire of
a piece of land
for the purpose
of making
bricks. *C.*
afterwards
made an offer
in writing to
let another
piece of land to
A. upon the
terms contained
in the agree-
ment between
him (*A.*) and
B., and at a
subsequent
time *A.* ver-
bally accepted
this offer. In
an action by *C.*
for a breach of
some of the
terms of this
contract :
Held, that the
written offer
made by *C.* was
admissible in
evidence with-
out being
stamped.

be

be void on the 1st of *April*, if no further arrangements are entered into." Before the expiration of that time the bargain between *Leggott* and *Grant* went off; and at a subsequent meeting before the 1st of *April*, *Leggott* agreed, verbally, with the plaintiff, to take his land upon the terms before offered. The witness heard the terms specified at the time. On his cross-examination, it appeared that the plaintiff's offer was reduced into writing. The plaintiff's counsel had produced the agreement entered into between *Grant* and *Leggott*, in which the terms were specified, and that had an agreement stamp. *Williams*, for the defendant, contended, that they were also bound to give in evidence the written offer made by the plaintiff; he was then required by the other side to produce it, pursuant to a notice given for that purpose; he did so, and it not being stamped, he contended that it could not be read, and that the plaintiff must, therefore, be nonsuited. The learned Judge thought that the document might be read in evidence, although unstamped, and the plaintiff having proved the other allegations in his declaration, obtained a verdict, but the defendants had leave to move to enter a nonsuit, if the evidence of the contract was improperly admitted. In *Michaelmas* term a rule nisi for entering a nonsuit was accordingly obtained, against which

Scarlett and *F. Pollock* shewed cause. The paper containing the terms originally agreed upon between *Grant* and *Leggott*, and that containing *Grant's* proposal, form together but one agreement. It was therefore sufficient to have a stamp upon either, and the first paper being stamped, both were admissible in evidence. But if that were otherwise, still the second paper was

not

not necessary to the plaintiff's case; he shewed that, at the second meeting between the parties, they agreed by parol that the land should be held according to the terms of a written agreement, which written agreement was stamped. The plaintiff's case was therefore complete, without the production of the written proposal made by him.

J. Williams and *Parke* contrà. It may be very true, that the plaintiff gave evidence which would have suf- ficed to prove his case if nothing had been known of the written document; but as soon as it appeared that the bargain made between the plaintiff and *Leggott* was reduced into writing, the parol evidence became insuf- ficient. That document was not a mere proposal, but a memorandum of an agreement to be thereafter com- pleted. Neither was it sufficient to stamp the former agreement between *Grant* and *Leggott*, that was only admissible in evidence by reason of reference being made to it in the subsequent writing. Now, the exception in the stamp act is only where a bargain is contained in several letters, but the document in question was not a letter, but a memorandum of agreement; it ought not, therefore, to have been admitted, and without it the plaintiff could not establish his case.

ABBOTT C. J. I quite agree to the proposition of law laid down for the defendant, that if a bargain made by parol is afterwards reduced into writing, that is the perfection of the agreement. But here the order was reversed; a written proposal was made at the first meeting, but then it was uncertain whether there would or would not be a contract. The fact as to the agree-

X x 2   ment

ment between *Leggott* and *Grant* was first to be ascertained. Then an agreement was made, by parol, that *Leggott* should have the land on certain terms. The writing signed by the plaintiff was a mere proposal, and was never signed by *Leggott*. The plaintiff, therefore, had legally made out his case before that paper was produced, and when produced, it did not shew that there was any written contract.

BAYLEY J. The stamp act only applies to agreements, or minutes or memorandums of agreements; and, therefore, unless the paper in question contained an agreement, or a minute or memorandum of agreement, it did not come within the operation of that statute. That paper contained a mere proposal to let the land, according to the terms contained in another paper which was stamped; and the parties ultimately agreed to those terms by parol. The second paper, therefore, contained neither an agreement, nor a minute, or memorandum of agreement.

HOLROYD J. I am of opinion, that the second paper given in evidence did not require a stamp. A stamp is not necessary to every writing given in evidence to support an agreement, but only to agreements themselves, or minutes, or memorandums of agreements. This was a mere proposal; if it had been accepted by writing, that must have been stamped, but being accepted by parol, the agreement was in law a parol agreement. The evidence was therefore properly admitted, and the rule for a nonsuit must be discharged.

Rule discharged.

LITTLEDALE J. was absent.

STONEHOUSE, Assignee of HARRISON, a Bank-   *Wednesday,*
rupt, *against* READ.   *February 9th.*

ASSUMPSIT for money had and received, and on
an account stated.   At the trial before *Abbott* C. J.,
at the *London* sittings after *Michaelmas* term 1823, a
verdict was taken for the plaintiff for 4000*l.*, subject to
the award of a barrister to whom it was referred to
take all accounts between the parties, with liberty to
state on the face of his award any point of law that either
party might require.   The arbitrator by his award found,
that on a settlement of all accounts between the parties,
the defendant was, and still is, indebted to the plaintiff
as assignee as aforesaid, in the sum of 1772*l.* 13*s.*, and
directed the same to be paid; and that the defendant
should forthwith deliver to the plaintiff a bill of exchange, drawn by the defendant upon and accepted by
the bankrupt for the sum of 1334*l.* 12*s.*   The award
then stated, that it was proved before the arbitrator
that the defendant had, before *Harrison* became bankrupt, accepted bills drawn upon him by the bankrupt to a considerable amount; that the bills had been
paid away to creditors of the bankrupt; that at the time
of his so accepting the bills, the defendant, as the agent

*In an action by
the assignees of
a bankrupt, it
was referred to
an arbitrator to
take accounts
between the
parties, with
liberty to him
to state on the
face of his
award any point
of law that
either party
might require.
The arbitrator
by his award
found the fol-
lowing facts.
The defendant,
before the
bankruptcy,
had accepted
bills drawn
upon him by
the bankrupt.
These bills had
been paid away
to creditors of
the bankrupt.
At the time of
his accepting
the bills the
defendant, as
the agent of the
bankrupt, had
in his hands
money of the
bankrupt to the
full amount of*

the sum for which the bills were drawn, and these funds had not been withdrawn at the
time of the bankruptcy.   After the bills became due respectively, and before the act of
bankruptcy, the holders of the bills, in order *to relieve the defendant from his responsibility
to them,* took from the defendant a composition upon the acceptances, and delivered up
the bills to the defendant; but the bankrupt was not a party to this arrangement.   The
award then stated that, in taking the accounts between the parties, the arbitrator had not
allowed the amount of the sums for which the bills were drawn to be set off by the defendant, but only the amount of the composition: Held, that the defendant was entitled to have
the full amount of the bills allowed him in account.

X x 3   of

of the bankrupt, had in his hands monies of the bankrupt to the full amount of the sum for which the bills were drawn; that these monies had not been withdrawn from the hands of the defendant before the bankruptcy of *Harrison ;* and that after the bills had respectively become due, and before the act of bankruptcy, upon which the commission against *Harrison* was founded, the holders of the bills, *in order to relieve the defendant from his responsibility to them,* consented to take, and did take from the defendant a composition upon the acceptances, and upon payment thereof by the defendant, the bills of exchange were delivered up by the holders of them to the defendant, to which arrangement the bankrupt was not a party. The award further stated, that in taking the account between the parties, the arbitrator thought that the defendant ought not to be allowed to set off the amount of the sums for which the bills were drawn, but the amount of the composition only, and had in his award allowed to him the full amount of the composition actually paid by him; but that if the defendant was entitled to charge in the account against his principal, the bankrupt, or the above named plaintiff as assignee as aforesaid, the amount of the sums for which the compounded bills were drawn, the balance would be in his favor. A rule nisi having been obtained for entering a verdict for the defendant or a judgment of nonsuit,

Marryat and *Comyn* now shewed cause. The defendant may either be considered in the character of agent of the bankrupt, or as the acceptor of the bills. As agent of the bankrupt, he is not entitled to charge him with more money than he actually paid on his account. The agent is bound to do the best he can, consistently

16   with

with his duty, for the benefit of his principal. [*Bayley* J.
Suppose the bill holders to have been induced to take
the composition, on the supposition that *Read* had no
effects of *Harrison* in his possession, and it turned out
afterwards that he had effects to the full amount of the
bills, the creditors would be entitled to treat the composition as void, and to call upon him for the balance.
Therefore, although it may turn out that *Read* ought
not to have the money, yet it may be equally clear that
Harrison ought not to have it.] The defendant, by
seeking to retain beyond the amount which he has paid,
attempts to turn himself into a purchaser of the bills.
Now that cannot be, because whatever he has paid, has
been paid out of the funds of the bankrupt. Secondly,
considering the defendant in his character of acceptor
of the bills, he is in the nature of a surety, and in that
character he cannot charge his principal with more than
he has actually paid.

Scarlett, Gurney, and *Brodrick,* contrà. The defendant was the commercial agent of the bankrupt, and had
funds in his hands belonging to his principal, and accepted bills on his account to the amount of those funds.
Now, the very acceptance of a bill operates as a payment of the debt unless it be dishonored, and the drawer
of the bill be called upon to take it up. Secondly, *Harrison* paid his creditors with these bills. He has, therefore, had full value for them. Thirdly, the composition
was accepted, not in order to confer any benefit on
Harrison, but on *Read,* and it would have the effect of
defeating that object if the bankrupt could call upon *Read*
to pay him the difference between the composition and

X x 4　　　　　　　　the

the full amount of the bills.   If the holder of a bill gives
time to the acceptor without the assent of the drawer,
the latter is discharged.   Here, the holders of the bills
accepted the composition without the knowledge of
Harrison, and he is therefore discharged.   Having had
the full value of them, and being under no liability in
respect of the bills, the bankrupt or his assignee can
have no further claim upon the defendant.   Suppose
the drawer had not been discharged, and the composition
had been made with his consent, he would then have
remained liable for the difference between the composition and the full amount of the bills ; and if he had
paid that difference, he would have been entitled to recover it from the acceptor.   Now it is contended on the
other side, that he is entitled to the same benefit as if
he had actually paid the difference out of his own estate.
As far as the drawer is concerned, it is to him the
same thing as if the acceptor had paid the full amount
of the bills, for the drawer has had the full value of
them, and is under no liability in respect of them.
Suppose the holders of the bills chose to make a gift of
them to the acceptor, could the drawer have claimed
the benefit of the gift so made to the acceptor, and have
called upon him to pay the amount?   Here the holders
did give up the bills to the acceptor upon being paid a
composition.   The giving up of the bills for that composition, in point of legal effect, was a gift to the acceptor of the difference between the composition and
the full amount of the bills.   The latter may be considered to have paid the full amount, and to have had
the difference between that sum and the compostion
returned to him by the holders.   [*Holroyd* J. If it can

14   be

be considered that there was an actual payment of the full amount of the bills by the acceptor, and a gift of part by the holder, there can be no doubt that the defendant is entitled to charge the bankrupt's estate with the whole sum actually paid; but unless that be the effect of what has taken place, I have great difficulty in saying that the defendant can charge the bankrupt for more than he has actually paid. It appears upon the award, that supposing the full amount of the bills to have been paid, there remains a balance due to *Read.* Now, if *Harrison* had not become bankrupt, could *Read* have maintained any action for that balance? If he had paid the full amount of the bills, and that payment exceeded the funds in his hands, *Read* might have maintained such action.] *Read* might have supported such an action, as between him and *Harrison* there was a payment of the full amount of the bills. Suppose the holder gave a month's time to the acceptor, the drawer is discharged, but the holder still has a right of action against the acceptor. Could the drawer, before the month expired, bring an action against the acceptor, on the ground that he had not paid the money according to his undertaking? If, when the month expires, the holder upon receiving 15s. in the pound gives up the bill to the acceptor, that would be an answer to any action at the suit of the drawer. All that the acceptor undertakes is, that the estate of the drawer shall be discharged, that his funds shall be applied in satisfaction of the bill, and that he shall not be called upon to pay. Whether he performs that contract to the drawer by obtaining a gift of the bill from the holder, or by paying him a composition, is wholly immaterial.

ABBOTT

Abbott C. J. I am not at all surprized that the
learned arbitrator should have come to the conclusion
of law upon the facts found which he appears to have
done, for it appeared to me, for some time after I had
perused this award, that the conclusion of law to which
he had come was the right one. On further consideration, however, I am of opinion that that conclusion is
erroneous, and that this award must be set aside. My
opinion is founded upon this single and short point, that
the bankrupt and his assignees have had the full and
entire benefit of the bills accepted by the defendant;
and, having had that, I am of opinion that they are entitled to no more.

Bayley J. In the early part of the discussion of this
case I had upon my mind exactly the same impression
which my Lord Chief Justice had; but during the discussion my opinion has entirely changed. At first I
thought that, as against his principal, the defendant, as
agent, was only entitled to have relief to the extent to
which he had actually paid; and if the composition in
this case had been taken for the purpose of relieving
the bankrupt only, I should have continued of the same
opinion; but it appears from the award that it was taken
for the purpose of relieving *Read* only. Now it may
have been taken either fairly or not fairly, and I shall
consider it under both points of view. If it was taken
fairly, and under a full representation by *Read* to all the
bill-holders of the exact situation in which he stood,
then it would be clear that they must have intended to
relieve him, and him only. The effect of that would be
that they would take from him a composition, say ten
shillings in the pound, upon a secret understanding
                                                    between

between him and them that *Harrison* was to be completely discharged. That would make it, as between *Harrison* and the bill-holders, a payment of twenty shillings in the pound. It must have been intended that *Read* should be effectually discharged by the payment of the ten shillings in the pound, for if *Read* were still to be liable to *Harrison* for the difference, he, and not *Read*, would benefit by the composition. The only persons who would lose by it would be the bill-holders, for they would get their composition only; *Read* would pay ten shillings in the pound, and *Harrison* would be relieved from the payment of twenty shillings in the pound, to which he was liable as drawer; and, in addition to that, would be entitled to claim ten shillings in the pound from *Read.* Assuming, however, that this composition was not made fairly by *Read*, and under a true representation to the bill-holders of the situation in which he stood, it does not vary the case as between *Harrison* and *Read.* The composition may be fraudulent as against the bill-holders; but if it be so, that remits them to their original right, they would then be no longer bound by the receipt of the composition, but would be entitled to call upon *Read* for the difference; and if they are so entitled to call upon *Read* for the difference, he is entitled to have that fund in his possession to answer the call. Whether the composition, therefore, were fair or not, appears to me to be immaterial as between these parties, though it may be otherwise between the bill-holders and *Read.*

HOLROYD J. ' It appears by the award that this composition was made by the defendant, the acceptor of the bills, in order to relieve himself from his responsibility; and

and it appears to have been made by the creditors for his benefit, and not for the benefit of the drawer of the bills. But although that be so, and although the bankrupt's estate has received benefit to the full extent of those bills, yet, inasmuch as the defendant did not actually pay to the amount of the monies in his hands, unless the transaction can be considered as a payment of the whole, and as a gift to him by the holders of the difference between what was actually paid and the amount of the bills, I think there would be great difficulty in supporting the proposition that the defendant is entitled to set off the full amount of the bills. I think, however, that the creditors, by stipulating for so much in the pound, or by taking as a composition a certain sum in lieu of the whole, and giving up the bills to the acceptor, gave the same legal effect to the transaction, as if there had been a payment of the whole to the creditors, and then a gift by the latter of the difference. It amounted, in point of law, to full payment of the bills, and would have given the defendant a right of action against *Harrison*, if the amount of the bills had exceeded the amount of the balance in his hands belonging to the bankrupt. It is true, that the acceptor of a bill, when he has paid it, supposing he had or had not funds in his hands, can only recover from the drawer of the bill so much money as was paid to his use. But taking this transaction to have been in law a payment of the whole amount of the bills, and a gift to the acceptor of the difference, then the latter was entitled to charge the drawer with the whole.

Rule absolute for entering a nonsuit.

The KING *against* The Mayor, &c. of WEST LOOE.

Wednesday, February 9th.

IN *Michaelmas* term the *Attorney General* obtained a rule calling upon the mayor and steward of the borough of *West Looe* to shew cause why a writ of mandamus should not issue, directed to them or other proper officer in that behalf, commanding them, at the next court leet to be holden for the said borough, to enrol and swear *R. Reath* as a resiant and burgess of the said borough. The affidavits upon which the rule was obtained alleged that *R. Reath* is an inhabitant householder in the borough, and had applied at the court leet to be sworn and enrolled as a resiant and burgess, which application was rejected; they then set out a charter granted to the borough by *Ed. 2.*, reciting and confirming a charter, whereby *Richard* Earl of *Poictou* and *Cornwall* granted to *Odo de Treverbyn* " that his borough of *Portbyan*, otherwise *West Looe*, should be a free borough, and that the burgesses of the same borough should be free and quit of all customs. Also, if any one should reside for a year and a day in the same borough without just claim, he should, according to the law of other free burgesses, be quit of all neifty and servitude." Queen *Elizabeth*, in the sixteenth year of her reign, granted another charter to the borough, whereby (after reciting that *Portbyan*, otherwise *West Looe*, was an ancient town, and that the burgesses and inhabitants had immemorially enjoyed several franchises,

Where an inhabitant of a borough applied for a mandamus to the mayor and steward of the borough, to enrol and swear him at the court leet of the borough, as a resiant and burgess, but did not make out an inchoate right in every inhabitant to be a burgess, or that any such connexion existed between the corporation and the court leet, as would make swearing and enrolment at the latter the means of perfecting such right; the Court refused the writ.

as

as well by prescription as by charters theretofore granted to the tenants and inhabitants of the town, and that the town was brought to great decay by reason of the poverty of the inhabitants, and that divers of the inhabitants had petitioned her majesty to make the same inhabitants a body corporate), she granted " that the said borough should thenceforth be a free borough corporate of one mayor and burgesses, being inhabitants of the town aforesaid." The charter then provided that there should be twelve capital burgesses, who were to be the common council, and to make bye-laws, &c.; and further, that in the event of the death of any capital burgess, a new one should be elected, within eight days, by the mayor and capital burgesses. The charter further gave them a court leet to be holden twice a year, at Easter and Michaelmas. The affidavits then alleged that there are no books of record of the borough in existence of an earlier date than 1607, but that there are books in regular succession from 1607 to the present time, except from 1623 to 1641, and that those books contain entries of the proceedings of the several successive borough and leet courts, the elections and swearings of the mayors, and elections, swearings, and dismissals of capital burgesses, &c. &c.; and the swearing the freemen, upon their entry on the resiant rolls, the lists of jurors, two or three constitutions or bye-laws, and all the other corporate affairs. That in these books there are lists (generally annual lists) of the persons who formed the corporation; that these lists, whenever they appear, form part of the proceedings of the leet or law courts, and are thus placed in the books:—

From 1607 to 1624, free tenants, residents, capital burgesses.

1641.

1641. Free tenants, capital burgesses, resiants.

1645. Free tenants, capital burgesses, sensores.

1649. Capital burgesses, free tenants, resiants.

1651 to 1660. Capital burgesses, free tenants, freemen.

1660 to 1672. Capital burgesses free tenants, resiants.

1672. Capital burgesses, free tenants, conventionary tenants.

1675 to 1678. Capital burgesses, free tenants, conventionary tenants or resiants.

1678. Capital burgesses, free tenants, conventionary tenants, vel resiants tenentes. The line through resiants and the word " tenentes" appearing to be written in a different ink, and at a subsequent period.

1679. Capital burgesses, free tenants, free burgesses. And thenceforth the lists thus continue : It was further alleged, that by the parish registers and corporation records it appears that the persons whose names are contained in the said several lists named residents, resiants, sensores, freemen, and conventionary tenants, vel resiants, were all inhabitants of the borough previous to 1676. That at the court leet in *October* 1676, the names of certain persons, not inhabitants · of the borough, were added to the bottom of the resiant list, with the words, " admitted, Jurat. liber." affixed; such list being there styled the list of " convent. tenentes vel 'resiants." That no other mention whatever was made in the records of those non-resident persons than the · mere entry of their names on the resiant roll, although thenceforth they exercised the rights and privileges of freemen or burgesses, together · with the other resiants, by signing· subsequent returns of · members of par-

parliament. That in *May* 1679, all the persons who
were named in the last list of resiants are found in the
same successive order on a list then headed or styled
" Free Burgesses," which list stands in the said book
in the place where the resiant list always theretofore
stood; the term " free burgesses" being then applied
to the same persons, instead of " resiants." The
affidavits then stated, that many persons whose names
appeared on the resiant list joined in the election of
mayors, and sometimes of members of parliament; and
that no one ever took a part in such proceedings until
after his name appeared in that list; and that there did
not appear to be any other mode of making free burgesses except putting them on the resiant list. The
affidavits in answer shewed that, as far as living memory
extends, the usage had been for the mayor and capital
burgesses to assemble on certain days, and elect free
burgesses; and they alleged that there was no tradition
in the borough of any other mode of making free
burgesses. The ancient books of the corporation did
not contain any entries, excepting those already mentioned, of elections either of capital burgesses or free
burgesses. The affidavits also shewed that from 1714
down to the present time the members of parliament for
the borough had always been elected by the mayor and
capital burgesses.

Adam and *Coleridge* shewed cause. It must be contended, in support of this application, that all inhabitants
of the borough of *West Looe* are ipso facto corporators
upon being presented and sworn at the court leet. To
this there are two answers; first, the inhabitants of a
town

town cannot be incorporated; and, secondly, the being
sworn at a court leet cannot affect a corporate office.
But even if those points are considered disputable, still
the affidavits do not shew that the usage of the borough
entitles the applicant to be presented and sworn.   By
the charter of queen *Elizabeth* it is granted that the
mayor and burgesses shall be a body corporate; it did
not incorporate the inhabitants.   But even supposing it
to have incorporated the inhabitants, when the king in-
corporates the inhabitants of a town he does not give to
any person coming to that town power to become a corporator, he specially appoints the first corporators, but
the body must be continued by some mode pointed out
either in the charter, or in a bye-law, the power to
make which is incident to every corporation, *Bro. Abr.
Corp.* pl. 65.   Where the party has an inchoate right
by birth or service, the Court will grant a mandamus to
compel the perfection of that right; but here the applicant has no such right.   Nor does it appear how the
court leet can affect his rights.   It will probably be
urged in support of the rule that all persons upon being
put on the resiant list, exercised the rights of corporators; but the affidavits do not warrant any such
conclusion; and unless that can be established, the
allegations in the affidavits that persons mentioned in
the resiant lists did such and such things, are of no
value whatever: for although inhabitancy is certainly
a part of the corporate character, it is not the whole of
it.   Besides, it appears that the court leet and court
baron were holden together, and whether the persons
named in those lists attended the one court or the
other, or for what purpose they attended, does not
appear.   It is sworn, however, that no entry of any

VOL. III.   Y y   election

election of free burgesses can be found in the corporation books; but neither do they contain any entry of the election of capital burgesses; and as there is no doubt that the latter elections took place, the observation is of no value. If usage be relied on, the usage as to the election of members of parliament is extremely clear, for it is sworn that from 1714 down to the present time those elections have always been made by the mayor and capital burgesses.

The *Attorney-General* and *Merewether*, contrà. That usage is of no avail, for part of the usage was, that non-residents should vote, and that usage has been declared bad by a committee of the House of Commons. (a) The real question is, who were burgesses by prescription within this borough, for they are mentioned in the charter of Queen *Elizabeth*, but no mode of creating them is pointed out. By the other charters, the inhabitants were incorporated, and the only question is, who are the inhabitants in contemplation of law. Now, no one is a legal inhabitant but a freeman, or liber homo, a householder sworn at the leet; until he is sworn, he is not entitled to the privileges of an inhabitant, not being a legalis homo, and upon becoming a legalis homo, he would, under an incorporation of inhabitants, be a member of the corporation. Now, the affidavits shew from the early usage, that the inhabitants were the persons incorporated, for by the lists there set out, and which were extracted from the books of the corporation, it appears, that from 1607 to 1624, that body consisted of free tenants, residents, and capital burgesses, and until the

(a) See the *West Looe* case, p. 224.

year

year 1678, the resiants under various denominations
continued to form one list of corporators. In 1679,
free burgesses were substituted for resiants, and the lists
have been so made out ever since. As soon as persons
were sworn and enrolled on the resiant list, they appear
to have been parties to corporate proceedings, and never
to have been permitted to be so until sworn and enrolled.
And this is corroborated by that which took place in
1676, when non-residents were introduced into the corporation; for that was effected by getting their names
inserted on the list of resiants. As this is an application
with reference to a public right, the applicant is entitled
to the writ as a matter of right; and it is the practice in
this court, if there is a doubt as to the evidence of the
facts alleged in the affidavits, to make the rule absolute,
in order that the evidence may be submitted to a jury;
so also, if the law resulting from those facts, or from the
charters at various times granted to this borough be
doubtful, the applicant ought to have an opportunity of
raising that question on the record.

ABBOTT C. J. I am of opinion that we ought not
to grant the writ prayed for in this case. We are desired to grant a writ of mandamus directed to the mayor
and steward of the borough of *West Looe*, or other
proper officer in that behalf, commanding them at the
next court leet to be holden for the borough, to enrol
and swear *Robert Reath* as a resiant or burgess of the
said borough. If it had appeared on the affidavits
before us, that a resiant when enrolled as such was, in
that capacity and without reference to any other character, entitled to vote at the election of members of
parliament, I should have thought that we were bound

Y y 2   to

1825.

The King
against
Mayor, &c. of
West Looe.

to grant the writ. But it appears that a committee of the House of Commons, which is competent to give the law to us upon this point, has decided the right of voting to be in members of the corporation being inhabitants of the town. (a) There is not, therefore, any ground for a writ commanding that *R. Reath* shall be enrolled a *resiant.* Has he then shewn any right to be enrolled a burgess or member of the corporation? It has been contended that, by the usage and charters, every householder resiant has a right to be enrolled at the court leet as a resiant and corporator. It is said that inhabitancy confers the right, but at the same time it is urged, that the right is confined to householders; if inhabitancy confers the right, what is there so to limit it? This charter is in language very similar to many others. Whether such charters were wisely granted, it is not any part of our duty, nor is it within our power to decide. Our duty is to interpret such charters according to the decisions of our predecessors. An inchoate right to become a member of a corporation may be derived in various well known ways, as by birth, service, or marriage, and then this Court will order that right to be perfected. But an inchoate right, resting solely upon inhabitancy, or upon that and householding, is something perfectly novel. This charter certainly confers no such right. Let us then advert to the usage; that is very obscure, and there appears to have been great negligence in the mode of keeping the books of the corporation; but there is no usage shewn to have existed either before or after the charter of Queen *Eliz.* which can warrant us in saying, that every inhabitant householder has a

(a) *West Looe* case, p. 224.

right

right to be sworn a corporator; and we ought to find a very clear and cogent usage before we interpose our authority for the purpose of establishing a constitution in this borough, unknown to the law and to our experience. It does appear that there are instances of the election of members of the corporation, and that power is incident to a body corporate, if no other mode of keeping up their succession is pointed out by their charter. Much of the argument which has been addressed to us was more properly applicable to the question, whether resiancy confers a right of voting for members of parliament, and with the decision which has taken place on that point we cannot interfere. For these reasons, I think that this rule must be discharged.

BAYLEY J. I quite agree that if a serious doubt exists, either as to matter of fact or of law, the writ ought to be granted; but it is also the duty of the Court to be satisfied of the existence of such a doubt before they interfere. The form of the rule obtained in this case is confused, and I am inclined to think that it was made so intentionally. It is for a mandamus to be addressed to persons filling different characters, and it leaves it doubtful in which character they are to act. The mayor and steward of the borough are also officers of the court leet, and it is left in doubt whether they are required to act as officers of that court or of the corporation. It is, therefore, necessary to consider the question as affecting them in each capacity. The application is to be sworn a resiant or burgess. Now it is to be observed, that the leet does not appear to be a place where the business of the corporation is to be transacted. It may sometimes, for convenience, be transacted at the time and place of

holding

holding the leet, but the charter does not direct that any of the corporation proceedings shall be carried on there, and in many cases that would be impossible. If any one of the capital burgesses dies, an election is to take place within eight days, whether a court leet is or is not holden during that period. The leet, therefore, does not appear to have any connexion with the corporation. If the party applying to us wishes to be sworn at the leet, for any purpose connected with that court, let him attend there, and ask to have the oath of allegiance administered to him. As yet, it does not appear that he has done so; and until he has made such a request, and been refused, we cannot grant a mandamus on that ground. But it is said, that he has certain rights under the charter granted to the corporation, and that there is a connexion between the persons enrolled at the leet as resiants and the members of the corporation; and if this is to be considered as directed to the mayor and steward, as officers of the corporation, then it becomes necessary to consider whether he has any such rights. The charter of Queen *Eliz.* recites a petition from divers of the queen's subjects, inhabitants of the borough (and whether this petition was from all or only some of the inhabitants does not appear material), that the inhabitants might be created a body politic and corporate; and then it grants, that the town of *Portbyan* or *West Looe*, shall be a borough corporate of one mayor and burgesses, being inhabitants of the town. It does not any where state that *all* the inhabitants shall be burgesses, and it provides for the election of a mayor and capital burgesses; but says nothing about common burgesses. Suppose the legal effect of the charter to have been to make all the in-

15

habitants

habitants burgesses, (which, however, I take not to have been the case,) that would not make all persons burgesses who thereafter might become inhabitants of the borough. No mode of supplying new members to the corporation being pointed out, they would have an incidental power to make regulations for that purpose, and they might lawfully do it by election. For these reasons, I think that the applicant has not shewn any such reasonable doubt in this case as would authorise us to grant the writ. The lists of persons attending the leet have been relied on, but it does not appear to me that they are in any way connected with the corporation. I should suppose that they were made for the purposes of the leet only. Then it is urged, that, according to this view, the corporation may elect non-residents, which is contrary to the decision of the committee of the House of Commons; but they have no such power, for the charter imposes the qualification of inhabitancy. For these reasons I concur in thinking that this rule must be discharged.

HOLROYD J. gave no opinion, not having been present during the argument.

LITTLEDALE J. concurred.

Rule discharged.

Wednesday,
February 9th.

BUCKLE *against* BEWES.

The sheriff
having taken
goods in exe-
cution under a
fi. fa., the pro-
ceeds of which
are not suffi-
cient to satisfy
the plaintiff's
claim, cannot
against him
retain any
thing beyond
the poundage
allowed by the
stat. 29 Eliz.
c. 4.

THIS was an action against the sheriff of *Devon*. The
first count of the declaration, after stating in the
common form that the plaintiff had recovered a judgment, and had issued a fieri facias thereon, directed to
the defendant as such sheriff, and that the defendant had
seized goods, and levied money thereon, charged the
defendant with wrongfully retaining a part of the money
levied. The last count was founded on the 29 *Eliz. c.* 4.,
and after alleging the judgment, fieri facias, and levy as
aforesaid, proceeded to state as follows: that " the said
defendant, so being sheriff as aforesaid, not regarding
his duty as such sheriff, nor the statute in such case
made and provided, afterwards, to wit, on, &c. at, &c., by
reason and color of his said office of sheriff, wrongfully,
illegally, and oppressively had, received, and took, indirectly of and from the said plaintiff, for the serving and
executing of the said last-mentioned execution, more and
other consideration and recompence than in the statute
in that case made and provided is limited and appointed
in that behalf, that is to say, by deducting from the monies
so levied, which were before such deduction insufficient
to satisfy the said last-mentioned damages, a large sum of
money, to wit, 50l. 5s. more than in the said statute is
limited and appointed, whereby the said plaintiff is damaged and aggrieved to the amount of that sum of money,
contrary to the form of the statute, &c. The defendant
had suffered judgment by default, and upon the execution of the writ of enquiry, the return to the writ was

given

given in evidence, in which the sheriff stated, that after he had seized the goods, and before the sale, he was served with an injunction out of the Court of Chancery, restraining him from the sale of the goods; that afterwards, upon the injunction being dissolved, he proceeded to the sale of the same, and after deducting the poundage and certain legal payments, he further stated, that he had retained 50*l.* 5*s.*, further part of the proceeds of the sale, for his necessary charges and expences in and about the keeping possession of the goods, from the time when he was served with the injunction to the time of the sale, and that the residue of the money he had ready for the plaintiff." The whole proceeds of the sale were not sufficient to satisfy the amount of damages directed to be levied by the indorsement on the writ of fieri facias. The jury gave nominal damages on the first count, and the sum of 50*l.* 5*s.* on the last count.

Carter, in order to relieve the sheriff, now moved for a rule to shew cause why the assessment should not be set aside, or the sum of 50*l.* 5*s.* be entered as the damages on the first count, and the nominal damages only on the last count, on the ground that the circumstances under which the sheriff had retained the money did not amount to a receiving or taking of the plaintiff within the meaning of the statute.

But *the Court* were of opinion, that as the money levied was not sufficient to satisfy the plaintiff's claim, the retaining of any part which ought to have been paid over to the plaintiff, was an indirect receiving or taking from him, and they refused the rule.

Rule refused.

Hawkins *against* Warre.

In replevin,
defendant
avowed for
rent due upon
a demise at a
certain fixed
rent. Plea,
that plaintiff
did not hold
under defend-
ant at the rent
mentioned in
the avowry, and
issue joined
upon that fact.
At the trial the
defendant, in
order to prove
the holding as
alleged, ten-
dered in evi-
dence certain
unstamped
papers, the
effect of which
was to shew
that the plain-
tiff had paid
rent at the rate
mentioned in
the avowry:
Held, that these
papers were
inadmissible for
want of stamps,
inasmuch as
they were in
effect tendered
to prove the
payment of the

REPLEVIN for growing corn taken in the parishes of *Kingston* and *Broomfield*, in the county of *Somerset*, in certain closes of land and premises there situate, called *Valis' Yards, Broomfield, Broomfield Down,* north part of *Hestercombe Park* and *Broad Meadow.* Defendant avowed for 337*l.* 10*s.* for three quarters of a year's rent due 25th of *March* 1823, upon a demise at 450*l.* payable quarterly. There were other avowries claiming rent, at the rate of 432*l.*, 430*l.*, and 412*l.* per annum. To these avowries the plaintiff pleaded non tenuit modo et formā and riens en arriere. At the trial before *Bosanquet* Serjt. at the *Taunton* Spring Assizes 1824, the defendant proved, in support of the issues on the avowries, the following facts: The plaintiff held part of the lands in question under Mr. *Warre*, the father of the defendant, by a lease for seven years, which expired at *Lady-day* 1815, at the rent of 360*l.* Upon the expiration of this term, the plaintiff continued in possession, and in 1818 a negociation took place for a fresh lease, which negociation was conducted partly through the agency of Mr. *Charter*, who acted as steward to Mr. *Warre.* The

rent; for if they did not prove the payment of the rent they would not support the issue, and would on that ground be inadmissible.

The defendant's steward proved that a lease had been executed by the defendant but not by the plaintiff, the terms of which had been reduced into writing by the assent of both parties, and he stated that to be the final agreement between the parties. The plaintiff, in order to negative this statement, tendered in evidence another unstamped paper in the handwriting of the defendant's steward, the effect of which was to shew that it was subsequently proposed by him that the plaintiff was to hold at a rent different from that mentioned in the lease: Held, that as this paper was not signed by the parties, it did not amount to an agreement or minute of an agreement, but to a proposal only, and therefore that it did not require a stamp, and was properly received in evidence.

draft

draft of a lease was prepared under the instructions of *Charter*. This draft was handed to Mr. *Warre*, who made various alterations therein, in the shape of observations upon the draft, and filled up the blanks which had been left for additional lands, of which the plaintiff had taken possession, and which were to be included in the new lease. After this a meeting of the parties took place, when a further alteration in the draft was made by *Charter*, and the draft as then settled, was stated by *Charter* to have been the final agreement between the parties. The lease was then engrossed, executed by Mr. *Warre*, and taken by *Charter's* servant to the plaintiff, with a bill of charges for preparing the lease, the amount of which bill was shortly afterwards paid by the plaintiff to *Charter*, but the lease was never executed by the plaintiff. The rent reserved by this lease was 450*l.*, with a proviso for abating 20*l.*, if wheat was under ten shillings a bushel; and for deducting a proportional part of the rent, in case the term should cease as to *Higher Volis*, in which Mr. *Warre* had only an estate for life, the immediate remainder being in Mrs. *Warre*. Upon the death of Mr. *Warre*, it was agreed between Mrs. *Warre*, her daughter, the defendant, and the plaintiff, that 18*l.* should be paid to Mrs. *Warre* as the rent of *Higher Volis;* and the different avowries were framed so as to meet a claim for the whole rent of 450*l.*; the deduction of 20*l.*, which would reduce the rent to 430*l*; the deduction of 18*l.* for *Higher Volis*, which would reduce it to 432*l.*, and the two deductions joined, which would bring the rent to 412*l.* To shew the acquiescence of the plaintiff in the terms of the lease, though he had not executed it, the defendant proposed to give in evidence certain unstamped receipts, purporting, that rent had been since paid upon the terms of that demise. These

These receipts had been set forth by the now plaintiff, *Hawkins*, in a schedule to his answer to a bill filed against him for a specific performance; and the papers produced were copies furnished by the now plaintiff, pursuant to an order to that effect. The first, which was tendered and rejected by the learned judge, was in the following form:

Hestercombe, Oct. 28th, 1821.

Mr. *Hawkins*,   Dr. to Miss *Warre*.

For half a year's rent due last *Michaelmas*,				
Oct. 12th	-	-	- £30	0 0
Oct. 28th	-	-	- 70	0 0
Feb. 23d	-	-	- 91	14 0
Disbursements	-	-	4	6 0
According to the price of wheat		20	0 0
		£216	0 0

Received the above, *E. M. T. Warre*.

The plaintiff then, in order to rebut the statement of *Charter*, that the draft of the lease contained the final agreement between the parties, produced an unstamped paper of a subsequent date in the hand-writing of *Charter*, of which the following is a copy: —

" Old rent	-	-	- £360	0 0
Abatement	-	-	- 36	0 0
			324	0 0
To 27 acres	-	- £67 10 0		
To 16 acres of Broadmead	40 0 0			
To B.	-	26 0 0		
			133	10 0
			£457	10 0

450*l.* a

45*0l*. a year from *Michaelmas* 1818, for a term of seven years, Mr. *Warre* undertaking wheat shall be at 10*s*. a bushel, and barley 5*s*., upon the terms of the old lease." It was objected by the defendant's counsel, that this document was not admissible in evidence, on the ground of its not being stamped, and not being shewn to have been authorized or adopted by Mr. *Warre* or the defendant. The learned judge received the evidence, and the jury found a verdict for the plaintiff for 4*l*. 4*s*. the amount of the expences of the replevin bond. In *Michaelmas* term last, *Pell* serjt. obtained a rule nisi for a new trial.

Wilde Serjt. and *R. Bayly* now shewed cause. The receipts offered in evidence by the defendant were properly rejected. They were offered to prove that the plaintiff held under the defendant at the fixed rent mentioned in some of the avowries. Now unless the papers amounted to proof of the payment of the sums mentioned in them, they would not be any evidence of the plaintiff's holding under the defendant at such a rent. The receipts therefore were offered to prove the payment of the rent, and not for a collateral purpose, and, consequently, were properly rejected, *Jacob* v. *Lindsay*. (a) Secondly, the other paper was properly received as evidence of the terms of the negociation then pending. It was not produced as evidence of the actual agreement between the parties. If it had been it would no doubt have required a stamp. But it might properly be received as evidence of an unaccepted proposal although it was unstamped, *Dalison* v. *Stark* (b), *Doe* v. *Cartwright*. (d)

(a) 1 *East*, 460.   (b) 4 *Esp*. 163.   (c) 3 *B. & A.* 326.

Pell

Pell Serjt., *Adam, C. F. Williams*, and *Manning*, contrà. The receipts offered in evidence by the defendant were not for the purpose of discharging the party producing them from the obligation of payment, but for the purpose of establishing the collateral fact that the plaintiff held under the defendant at the rent mentioned in the avowries. Now an unstamped instrument may be receivable in evidence for a collateral purpose: thus upon an indictment for forging an instrument it is receivable in evidence although unstamped, *Rex* v. *Hawkeswood.* (a) So an unstamped check is admissible, for the purpose of identifying property stolen, on an indictment for larceny, *Rex* v. *Pooley* (b), and an unstamped policy may be read in evidence to prove the effecting of a lottery insurance, *Holland* v. *Duffin.* (c) So in an action for bribery against a candidate at an election, an unstamped paper purporting to be a promissory note which had been given by the voter as a cloak for the bribe is evidence to prove the fact of payment, or to confirm the testimony of a witness, *Dover* v. *Maestaer.* (d) Here previously to the affixing of Miss *Warre's* signature, an account had been stated between the parties, for it could make no difference whether the paper set forth a regular debtor and creditor account, charging the rent on one side, and giving credit for the payment, disbursements, and allowances on the other, or exhibited the same items in one column, as was done here, *Jacob* v. *Lindsay.* (e) Secondly, the unstamped memorandum was improperly received, because the question being what was the ultimate agreement between the parties, and this document being pro

(a) 2 *E. P. C.* 955.   (b) 3 *Bos. & P.* 316.
(c) *Peake's C.* 58.   (d) 5 *Esp. N. P.* 92.
(e) 1 *East,* 460.

duced

duced for the purpose of negativing *Charter's* statement, that the lease executed by Mr. *Warre* contained the terms finally agreed on, it was in effect produced as evidence of an agreement.

ABBOTT C. J. I am of opinion that the rule for a new trial must be discharged. This is an action of replevin in which the plaintiff declares that the defendant took the growing corn, and unjustly detained the same. The defendant avows the taking of the corn as a distress for three quarters of a year's rent in respect of premises which the plaintiff held under the defendant as her tenant, by virtue of a demise at a certain fixed rent. The plaintiff pleads to the avowry that he did not hold or enjoy the said closes in which, &c., with the appurtenances, as tenant thereof to the said defendant, by virtue of the said supposed demise, at and under the said rent, payable as in the said avowry mentioned, and issue is joined upon this fact. If the defendant could have established that the plaintiff held under her at the rent mentioned in the avowries, she would have been entitled to a verdict, but otherwise the plaintiff is entitled to the verdict upon these issues. The burden of proof that the plaintiff did so hold under the rent mentioned in the avowries lay on the defendant, and unless the rent was fixed there could be no distress. The mode in which the defendant had attempted to prove that the plaintiff so held under her was by shewing that in a former year the plaintiff had paid her rent equal in amount to that mentioned in some of the avowries, and for that purpose the defendant tendered in evidence certain unstamped papers, by which it would appear (if they were admissible) that the plaintiff in a former year did pay
her

her rent at the rate mentioned in some of the avowries. But taking away the fact that the rent was paid, the papers would only be evidence of a claim having been made by the defendant upon the plaintiff. They are produced, therefore, by the defendant to prove the fact of that sum having been paid by the plaintiff, and it is said, that although such an unstamped instrument cannot be used so as to operate as a discharge to the party producing it, it may be used for the purpose of creating a further charge against another. But by the stamp act 31 G. 3 c. 25. s. 16. which is incorporated in the 55 G. 3. c. 184., " no receipt, discharge, or acquittance, note, memorandum, or writing, shall be pleaded or given in evidence in any court, or admitted in any court to be useful, or available in law or equity as an acknowledgment of any debt, claim, accounts, or demands being paid, settled, &c., unless the same shall be stamped." Now here an unstamped paper was offered in evidence as an acknowledgment of a debt having been paid. I am clearly of opinion that such evidence was not admissible, and that these receipts were properly rejected. The next mode by which the defendant attempted to prove that the plaintiff held under her the premises in question at a fixed rent was by shewing that he had the estate according to the terms of a lease executed by the defendant's father, but not by the plaintiff. *Charter* in his evidence stated that the lease so executed by Mr. *Warre* was the final agreement between the parties. From his evidence, unexplained, it would appear that the terms proposed by Mr. *Warre* in the draft which he had corrected had been accepted by the plaintiff. In order to shew that *Charter* was mistaken in that respect, an unstamped paper in his hand-writing was produced, by which it would appear that he had subsequently proposed

proposed to the plaintiff to pay a different rent from that mentioned in the lease. It was objected that for want of a stamp this paper could not be read because it amounted to an agreement. I am of opinion, however, that it did not contain any agreement between the parties, but a mere proposal made by *Charter* not corresponding with the terms of the lease. It cannot be treated as a contract between the parties, because it was not signed by them. The case is not distinguishable from *Ramsbottom* v. *Tunbridge*. (a) There a written paper delivered by the auctioneer to the bidder, to whom lands were let by auction, containing the description of the lands, the term for which they were let to the bidder, and the rent payable, *but not signed by the auctioneer, or any of the parties*, was held not to be such a minute of the agreement as was required to be stamped. But in *Ramsbottom* v. *Mortley* (b), a similar paper, *signed by the auctioneer*, was held to require a stamp. I think that the paper in this case amounted to no more than if the defendant had said, " I made such and such proposals to the plaintiff." That being so, it required no stamp, and was properly received.

BAYLEY J. I am clearly of opinion that the receipts were properly rejected for the reasons given by my Lord Chief Justice. Then as to the other paper, the 55 G. 3. c. 184. requires that every agreement, or minute or memorandum of agreement shall be stamped. Now I think this paper did not contain any agreement, or minute or memorandum of an agreement, but that it contained only a mere unaccepted proposal. In *Doe*

1825.

Hawkins
against
Warry.

(a) 2 M. & S. 434.   (b) Ib. 445.

v. *Cartwright* (a), upon the letting of premises to a
tenant, a memorandum of agreement was drawn up, the
terms of which were read over, and assented to by him,
and it was then agreed that he should on a future day
bring a surety and sign the agreement, neither of which
he ever did ; it was held that the memorandum was not
an agreement, but a mere unaccepted proposal, and that
the terms of the letting therefore might be proved by parol
evidence. That case is an authority to shew that the
paper produced in evidence did not amount to an
agreement, and that being so, I think it was properly
admitted, and that the rule for a new trial must be
discharged.

Holroyd J. concurred.

Rule discharged.

(a) 3 B. & A. 326.

The King *against* The Justices of St. Alban's.

The appoint-
ment of sur-
veyors of high-
ways under the
15 G. 3. c. 78.
cannot be re-
moved into this
court by cer-
tiorari.

A RULE nisi had been obtained for a certiorari to
    remove an appointment of surveyors of highways
into this Court, in order that the same might be quashed.

Brodrick (with whom was *Platt*,) shewed cause, and
urged as a preliminary objection, that the certiorari
ought not to issue, the words of the 13 G. 3. c. 78.
s. 81. being clear and positive, " that no proceedings to
be had or taken in pursuance of this act shall be quashed
or vacated for want of form, or removed by certiorari,

16   or

or any other writ or process whatsoever, (except as therein before mentioned,) into any of his majesty's courts of record at *Westminster ;*" and the appointment of surveyors was not within the exception. (He was then stopped by the Court.)

Gurney and *Brougham,* contrà. The certiorari is not taken away in this case; for the party has not any right of appeal. The eighty-first section of the high-way act begins by giving an appeal in certain cases to any person aggrieved by any thing done by any justice or justices of the peace or other person in execution of the act; and in a subsequent part the certiorari is taken away. Now it has been held, that where an appeal is not given a certiorari still lies, *Rex* v. *The Justices of the West Riding of Yorkshire* (a), *Rex* v. *Mitchell* (b), and the same cases shew that an appeal does not lie where the act complained of is done at the petty sessions. The appointment of surveyors is within the principle of those decisions, for *s.* 1. of the act orders it to be made at the petty sessions. Besides it may be difficult for any person in particular to say that he is a party aggrieved by the appointment.

Abbott C. J. Supposing that the words of the eighty-first section, taking away the certiorari, are to be confined to cases in which an appeal is given, then the applicant should have made out that no appeal lies against the appointment of surveyors. I think that such an appeal does lie. The words of the act are general, and give an appeal to any person aggrieved by any thing

(a) 5 T. R. 629.   (b) Ib. 701.

Z z 2   done

1825.

The KING
against
The Justices of
St. ALBAN's.

done in pursuance of the act by any justice of the peace or other person. The appointment of surveyors is a thing done in pursuance of the act, and I cannot see the force of the distinction between acts done by justices at the petty sessions or elsewhere; nor has the party grieved any other remedy given by the act. But it is said that no person can say that he is aggrieved. If so, no person can apply to quash the appointment; but in truth every inhabitant is aggrieved by a bad appointment of surveyors. But independently of all question about the appeal, I think that the certiorari is taken away by the general words of the eighty-first section: " No proceedings to be had or taken in pursuance of this act shall be removed by certiorari into any of his majesty's courts of record at *Westminster*," quacunque viâ, therefore the certiorari is taken away, and this rule must be discharged.

Rule Discharged.

PEARSON *against* M'GOWRAN.

In an action brought to recover penalties under the statute of usury, it appeared that the contract was made in one county and the money paid in another. The venue was laid in the county where the contract was made: Held, that it ought to have been laid where the usurious interest was received.

DECLARATION in debt for penalties under the statute of usury. Venue in *Middlesex*. The usurious interest was alleged to have been secured by a bill of exchange accepted by one *Bottrill*, and afterwards paid by him. At the trial before *Abbott* C. J. at the *Middlesex* sittings after last *Trinity* term, the corrupt contract was proved as laid, and it appeared to have been made, and the acceptance to have been given in

Middlesex,

Middlesex, but the bill was paid in *London* to the holders, Messrs. *Currie* and Co., to whom the defendant had indorsed it. Upon this it was objected by the defendant's counsel that the offence was not complete until the payment of the illegal interest, *i. e.* until the bill was paid; and, therefore, that the venue ought to have been laid in *London*, and not in *Middlesex*. The Lord Chief Justice reserved the point, and a verdict was found for the plaintiff, with liberty to the defendant to move to enter a nonsuit. A rule nisi having been obtained for that purpose,

Scarlett now shewed cause. · Where two facts essential to the commission of a misdemeanor are done one in each of two counties, the venue may be laid in either. That rule is laid down by *Ashhurst* J. in *Scott qui tam v. Brest* (a), and was recognised in *Scurry* v. *Freeman* (b), and in *Rex* v. *Burdett.* (c) Now in this case, although it be true that the offence was not complete until the usurious interest was paid, still the corrupt agreement constituted an essential part of that offence, and that was made in *Middlesex*. The venue, therefore, was properly laid in that county.

Denman and *Comyn* contrà. The true rule applicable to this subject is laid down by *Holroyd* J. in *Rex* v. *Burdett* (d), viz. that where a misdemeanor consists of different parts, so much of the charge must be proved to have been committed in the county where the venue is laid as amounts in law to a misde-

(a) 2 *T. R.* 241.   (b) 2 *Bos. & Pul.* 381.
(c) 4 *B. & A.* 95.   (d) 4 *B. & A.* 136.

meanour.

meanor. Then the question is, was any offence committed in *Middlesex?* The statute 12 *Anne*, *st.* 2. *c.*16. *s.*1. enacts that no person shall take directly or indirectly for the loan of any monies above the value of 5*l.* for the forbearance of 100*l.* for a year, and declares all contracts for greater interest void; and then enacts that all persons who shall upon any contract *take, accept, and receive* by way of any corrupt bargain, loan, &c. for the forbearance or giving day of payment for one whole year of money above the rate of 5*l.* per cent. per annum, shall forfeit treble value. The offence, therefore, consists in the taking and receiving more than 5 per cent. interest, and no offence is committed until the usurious interest is taken and accepted, *Fisher q. t.* v. *Beasley* (*a*), *Maddox q. t.* v. *Hammett.* (*b*) In *Bird's* case, 20 *Eliz.*, referred to in *Sir Wollaston Dixie's* case (*c*), the plaintiff shewed the place of the receipt, and not of the contract, and there was judgment for the crown; and the reason assigned was, that the contract is but inducement to the receipt, and it shall be tried where the taking was; therefore it was not necessary to shew the place of the bargain. In *Scurry* v. *Freeman* it was held, that if a draft be given for usurious interest, and a receipt taken for it in one county, and the draft be afterwards exchanged for money in another, the usury is committed in the latter county, and the venue must be laid there. In *Scott* v. *Brest* the offence was held to be committed in the place where the settlement of accounts and the payment of the balance took place.

Cur. adv. vult.

(*a*) *Doug.* 235.   (*b*) 7 *T. R.* 184.   (*c*) 1 *Leon.* 97.

The

The judgment of the Court was now delivered by

ABBOTT C. J. This was an action of debt for penalties under the statute against usury. It appeared in evidence that the corrupt contract was made in *Middlesex*, but the money was paid in pursuance of it in *London*. The venue was laid in *Middlesex*, and the question to be determined is, whether it was properly laid in that county. An opinion was certainly thrown out in the case of *Scott* v. *Brest* that, under such circumstances, the venue might have been laid in either county. But on a careful inspection of the statute 12 *Anne*, *st*. 2. *c*. 16. we think that the action for penalties can only be brought in the county where the offence is completed. After enacting that " every person who shall upon any contract to be made after a certain time *take, accept, and receive* by way or means of any corrupt bargain, &c. above the sum of 5*l.* for the forbearing of 100*l.* for a year, shall forfeit the treble value of the monies lent," it goes on to provide that " the forfeiture shall be, one-half to the queen, her heirs, and successors, and the other moiety to him that will sue for the same in the same county where the offence is committed, and not elsewhere." That brings the case to the single question, what is the offence? We think it consists in the taking and receipt of usurious interest. The corrupt contract is antecedent to, and not a part of the taking. The offence, therefore, was not committed partly in one county and partly in another, although the contract is undoubtedly a material circumstance in the case, because it stamps the illegality of the receipt. This resembles the case of *Rex* v. *Buttery*(a), which was an indictment on the

(a) Cited by *Abbott* C. J. in *Rex* v. *Burdett*, 4 *B.* & *A.* 179.

Z z 4   statute

statute 30 *G. 2. c.* 24. for obtaining money by false pretences. That statute enacts " that all persons who knowingly and designedly by false pretences shall obtain from any person money, goods, &c. with intent to cheat or defraud any person of the same, shall be deemed offenders against law." The language of the statute makes the offence to consist in obtaining the money, and not in using any false pretence whereby money shall be obtained. The indictment was in *Herefordshire*, the false pretence was in *Herefordshire*, but the money was received in *Monmouthshire*. The judges thought the indictment was laid in the wrong county. That comes nearer to the present case than any of those cited at the bar or found by us. Upon that authority, therefore, and upon the language of the statute, we are of opinion that the rule for entering a nonsuit must be made absolute.

Rule absolute.

THOMAS DUFFIELD, Esq. and EMILY FRANCES his Wife *against* AMELIA MARIA ELWES, Widow, FRANCIS CONST and GEORGE LAW, ABRAHAM HENRY CHAMBERS, the Rev. WILLIAM HICKS, Clerk, and GEORGE THOMAS WARREN HASTINGS DUFFIELD, CAROLINE DUFFIELD, MARIA DUFFIELD, ANNE DUFFIELD, and SUSAN ELIZA DUFFIELD, Infants, by G. H. CRUTCHLEY, Esq., their Guardian.

THIS was a case sent by his Honor the Vice-Chancellor for the opinion of this Court. It began by setting out indentures of lease and release and assignment,

G. E., seised of the manor of M. amongst other estates, in fee, conveyed it to trustees and their heirs,

to secure to his wife an annuity for her life, and subject thereto to the use of himself in fee. *G. E.* by his will, duly executed to pass real estates, recited and confirmed that settlement, and then devised to *J. E.* (who died in testator's lifetime), and *A. H. C.* and their heirs, his freehold and copyhold estate in *S.*, and his freehold estate at *H.*, upon the following, amongst other trusts, viz.: in case there should be but one son of his daughter *E. D.* by her husband *T. D.* who should attain the age of twenty-one years, upon trust for such son, his heirs and assigns for ever; and in case there should be two or more sons of Mrs. *D.* who should attain the age of twenty-one years, then in trust for the second of such sons, his heirs and assigns for ever; and in case there should be no son of Mrs. *D.* by the said *T. D.* who should live to attain the age of twenty-one years, then upon trust for such of the daughters, if any, of Mrs. *D.* by *T. D.* as should first attain the age of twenty-one years, or be married under that age with the consent of the trustees or trustee for the time being of that his will, and the heirs and assigns of such daughter for ever. After some pecuniary legacies, the testator proceeded as follows: "And as to, for, and concerning all the rest, residue, and remainder of the property of which I shall be possessed, or to which I shall be entitled at the time of my decease, or over which I have a disposing power, whether the same consists wholly or in part of estates of freehold, copyhold, or for years, money in the funds, upon mortgage, or otherwise out upon security or at interest, debts, or of whatever other nature the same or any part thereof may be, I give, devise, and bequeath the same unto the said *J. E.* and *A. H. C.*, their heirs, &c., upon trust, to sell and convert the same into money, to get in debts, &c., and out of the monies to be so raised, in the first place, to set apart 50,000*l.* three per cent. consols in trust for such son of Mrs. *D.* who, under the trusts of a settlement now intended to be forthwith made, shall become possessed of an estate tail in the manor of *M.*;" the residue to be divided amongst the other children of Mrs. *D.*; and the testator made *J. E.* and *A. H. C.* executors of his will. Sometime after making his will, the testator drew a line across the direction to sell the property devised by the residuary clause; and after making the will, the testator purchased a considerable freehold estate in *W.* and *H.* Testator afterwards made and published a codicil, duly executed, to pass freehold estates, whereby, after reciting the rasure

1825.
———
DUFFIELD
against
ELWES.

rasure before
mentioned, and
that he was
apprehensive
that such ra-
sure, not being
witnessed,
might lead to
litigation, he
declared by
that codicil
that the sole
intention of
such rasure was
to revoke that
part only of the
will whereby he
directed the sale
of his freehold
property. It
then proceed-
ed, " And I

ment, by way of voluntary settlement, dated 6th and 7th
of *October* 1802, made and executed by *George Elwes*.
By the release, expressed to be made between the said
G. Elwes of the first part, the defendant *Amelia Maria
Elwes*, his then wife and now widow, of the second part,
and *J. Elwes* and *R. Wastie*, both since deceased, of the
third part, after reciting that *G. Elwes* was seised in fee
simple of the manor, messuages, farms, lands, and hereditaments thereinafter granted and released, and was also
possessed of the leasehold messuages, lands, tithes, and
premises thereinafter assigned; and that he the said
G. Elwes had by his said wife one daughter, the plaintiff,
E. F. Duffield, then an infant of eleven years, and no
other child, and that he had agreed to make a suitable
provision for his wife and daughter. *G. Elwes* granted,

do hereby direct and appoint that the son lawfully begotten of my daughter Mrs. *D.* who
shall first attain the age of twenty-one years, shall, on attaining such age, change his name
for that of *E.* ; and I give and devise to the said son of my daughter on his attaining the
age of twenty-one years and changing his name to *E.*, all my freehold property, lands,
tenements, and hereditaments, to have and to hold to him, his heirs and assigns for ever."
Testator then appointed a new executor in the room of *J. E.*, then deceased, and did
thereby ratify and confirm the aforementioned will and testament, except as before excepted.
Testator died without again altering his will or codicil, leaving his widow, and Mrs. *D.*,
his only child and heir at law, and heir according to the custom of the manors of which his
copyhold estates were holden, and also his sole next of kin. At the death of testator Mr.
and Mrs. *D.* had and now have five children, one son and four daughters. Upon a case
sent for the opinion of this Court: Held, firstly, that the devise of the freehold part of the
estate at *S.*, and of the freehold farm and estate at *H.*, contained in the will, was not revoked
by the codicil.
    Secondly, That the manor of *M.* did pass under the residuary devise contained in the
testator's will, and that such devise was revoked by the codicil:
    Thirdly, That the manor of *M.* did pass under the codicil to the first son of the plaintiff,
Mrs. *D.*, who shall attain twenty-one years and change his name to *E.*:
    Fourthly, That the estate in *W.* and *H.*, purchased after the testator made his will, passed
under the devise in the codicil to the first son of the plaintiff, Mrs. *D.*, who shall attain
twenty-one years and change his name to *E.*:
    Fifthly, That the surplus rents and profits of the said copyhold estates at *S.*, and of the
said freehold estate at the same place, and of the said freehold farm and estate at *H.*,
after providing for the maintenance of the devisee thereof, belong to *A. H. C.*, the surviving
trustee under the will of the testator, until a first son of the said plaintiff, Mrs. *D.*, shall
attain twenty-one years, or in failure of such son, till a daughter shall attain that age, or be
married with consent, according to the will:
    Sixthly, That the intermediate rents and profits of such of the testator's freehold estates as
are effectually devised by his codicil to the son of the plaintiff, Mrs. *D.*, who shall first
attain twenty-one years and change his name to *E.*, until such events take place, belong
to *A. H. C.*, the surviving trustee under the will of the testator.

                                                        bargained,

bargained, &c. unto the said *J. Elwes* and *F. Wastie*,
their heirs and assigns for ever, all that the manor of
Marcham, in the county of *Berks*, with its rights, members, and appurtenances, together with the several lands,
tenements, rents, and hereditaments belonging or reputed
to belong to the said manor, and thereinafter mentioned,
comprising, among other lands and hereditaments in
possession therein described, the capital messuage or
manor house, gardens, and park, situate at *Marcham*,
and the reversion of certain other lands, after the termination of certain subsisting terms of 1000 years therein,
situate within the parish of *Marcham* but not within the
manor of *Marcham*, and certain other premises therein
described, to hold unto them the said *J. Elwes* and
F. Wastie, their heirs and assigns for ever, to the uses
and upon the trusts thereinafter mentioned. First, to
levy, out of the issues and profits, and pay to the defendant *Amelia M. Elwes*, an annuity of 800*l.*, during
the joint lives of her and her daughter, if the daughter
so long continued to live with her; but if the daughter
died or ceased to live with her, then to raise and pay to
A. M. Elwes an annuity of 400*l.* for her life; various
other trusts were then specified; but in case his daughter
should die unmarried in the lifetime of the settler, or
should marry without his consent, then subject to the
annuity of 400*l.* to *A. M. Elwes*, to the use of himself
in fee. The deed then contained an assignment of certain leasehold premises to the same uses. By indentures
of lease and release, dated 14th and 15th *October* 1807,
and executed by *G. Elwes*, made between himself of the
first part, and *J. Elwes* and *F. Wastie* of the second
part, reciting the former deeds, and that he had since
bought

bought a mansion-house and other premises in *Marcham*, he conveyed the same, and all household goods, furniture, &c. to *J. Elwes* and *F. Wastie*, upon the same trusts and to the same uses before mentioned. In *February* 1810, the plaintiff *Emily Frances Duffield*, the only child of the said *George Elwes*, and then a minor, intermarried with the plaintiff *Thomas Duffield*, without the consent of her father *George Elwes*. The said *George Elwes* did no act subsequently to affect his interest in the manor of *Marcham* before the date of his will, and at the date of that will he was seised in fee simple of other freehold estates in the counties of *Berks, Surrey, Middlesex*, and *Suffolk*. He was also seised in fee simple of some copyhold estate, and was possessed of a very large personal estate, consisting of leaseholds for years, monies in the funds, and other particulars. By his will, dated 1st *March* 1811, duly executed and attested to pass freehold estates, the said *George Elwes* first willed, that his debts, funeral and testamentary expences, should be paid as thereinafter mentioned; and after reciting that by a settlement made previous to the testator's marriage with his wife, the defendant *A. M. Elwes*, she would be entitled to the dividends of a sum of 3 per cent. consolidated bank annuities therein mentioned, for her life, in case she survived the testator, in the nature of a jointure and in lieu of dower; and that the same bank annuities were by the said settlement directed to be in trust after the decease of the testator and his said wife, for the child or children of their marriage, the will proceeded in the following words: " And whereas, under and by virtue of the limitations contained in a certain indenture of settlement, bearing date on or about the 7th day

of

of *October*, in the year 1802, and expressed to be made
between me *George Elwes* of the first part, my said wife
A. M. Elwes of the second part, and *J. Elwes* and
F. Wastie of the third part, my wife is entitled, for her
life, to an annuity or yearly rent charge of 400*l.*, issuing
and payable out of the manor of *Marcham*, in the
county of *Berks*, and divers freeholds and leasehold messuages, farms, lands, tenements, and hereditaments, in
the several parishes or places of *Marcham*, *Frilford*,
Cotwell, and *Garford*, and elsewhere, in the county of
Berks. Now I do, by this my will, ratify and confirm the
said jointure and annuity to my said wife. The testator
then bequeathed to his dear daughter the plaintiff, Mrs.
Duffield, and her assigns for her life, his leasehold messuage or dwelling-house, with the appurtenances, situate
in *High-street*, *Mary-le-bone*, and declared that the same
should, after her decease, fall into the residue of his personal estate thereinafter devised; and he gave and bequeathed to his said daughter all his carriages, horses,
household furniture, and goods, plate, linen, china, stock
of wine, and other liquors which should be in and about the
said messuages or dwelling-house, or in or about any other
house or houses which he might inhabit at the time of his
decease; and the testator then gave and bequeathed unto
his brother the said *J. Elwes* (who died afterwards in the
testator's lifetime) and the defendant *A. H. Chambers*, and
their heirs, all that the testator's freehold and copyhold
farm and estate, situate, lying, and being in *Southwood Park*,
in the county of *Suffolk*, which he had lately purchased
from *J. Pytches* Esquire (the copyhold part whereof
he recited that he had already surrendered to the uses
of his will), and also all that his freehold farm and estate
at *Haverhill*, in the county of *Essex*, to, for, and upon
such

such trusts, as were in and by his said will expressed and declared thereof; that is to say, in case there should be but one son of his daughter, the plaintiff Mrs. *Duffield*, by her husband, the plaintiff *Thomas Duffield*, who should attain the age of twenty-one years, upon trust for such son, his heirs and assigns for ever; and in case there should be two or more sons of Mrs. *Duffield* by the said *Thomas Duffield*, who should attain the age of twenty-one years, then in trust for the second of such sons, his heirs and assigns for ever; and in case there should be no son of Mrs. *Duffield*, by the said *Thomas Duffield*, who should attain the age of twenty-one years, then upon trust for such of the daughters, if any, of Mrs. *Duffield*, by the said *Thomas Duffield*, as should first attain the age of twenty-one years, or be married under that age with the consent of the trustees or trustee for the time being of that his will, and the heirs and assigns of such daughter for ever. But if there should not be any son of Mrs. *Duffield* by the said *Thomas Duffield*, who should attain twenty-one, nor any daughter who should attain that age, or be married, and the said *Thomas Duffield* should die, leaving the said testator's daughter, Mrs. *Duffield*, him surviving, then upon the same trusts for the benefit of the children, as well sons as daughters of Mrs. *Duffield*, by any second husband with whom she might happen to intermarry, as were therein before declared concerning the said freehold and copyhold farms and estates, for the benefit of the children of Mrs. *Duffield*, by the said *Thomas Duffield*. But if there should not be any son of Mrs. *Duffield* by such after taken husband who should attain twenty-one, nor a daughter who should attain that age, or be married with such consent as aforesaid, then upon

trust

trust for the said *J. Elwes* in fee.   The testator then bequeathed to the *J. Elwes* and *A. H. Chambers* such a sum in the public stocks of *Great Britain*, as would produce a certain annual sum to be paid to several persons for their lives; the principal sum after their deaths to fall into the residue.   The will then proceeded in the words following, that is to say, "and as to, for, and concerning all the rest, residue, and remainder of the property of which I shall be possessed, or to which I shall be entitled at the time of my decease, or over which I have a disposing power, whether the same consist wholly or in part of estates of freehold, copyhold, or for years, money in the funds, upon mortgage, or otherwise out upon security, or at interest debts, or of whatever other nature the same or any part thereof may be, I give, devise, and bequeath the same and every part thereof unto the said *J. Elwes* and *A. H. Chambers*, their heirs, executors, administrators, and assigns*, upon trust that they the said *J. Elwes* and *A. H. Chambers*, or the survivor of them, or the heirs, executors, administrators, or assigns of such survivor do, and shall, with all convenient speed, after my decease, sell, dispose of, and convey all and singular my freehold, copyhold, and leasehold estates, with the appurtenances either together or in parcels, and either by public auction or private contract, as to him or them shall seem best, unto any person or persons who shall be willing to become and be the purchaser or purchasers thereof, or of any part thereof, for the most money and best prices that can be reasonably had or gotten for the same, and to make and execute all such deeds, surrenders, conveyances, assignments, and assurances in the law as shall be necessary or proper for perfecting the sale and transfer thereof; and also do

and

and shall make sale of and convert into money all such
part and parts of my personal estate and effects as shall
not consist of money, and call in and compel payment
of all such parts thereof as shall consist of money out
upon mortgage or other security, at interest or otherwise, and also get in all debts which shall be due and
owing to me at the time of my decease in such manner
as they shall think expedient.°" And the testator, after
declaring that the receipts of the said *J. Elwes* and *A. H.
Chambers* should be good discharges, directed that the
said *J. Elwes* and *A. H. Chambers*, and the survivor of
them, his executors, administrators, and assigns, should
stand possessed of and interested in the monies to arise
or be gotten in by the means aforesaid or otherwise,
under or by virtue of that his will upon trust, in the first
place, from and immediately after his decease *to satisfy*
and discharge all such debts as should be due and
owing by him to any person or persons whomsoever at
the time of his decease, or which should afterwards
become due; and in the next place to pay his funeral
and testamentary expences, and then to pay the several
legacies and bequests which he had given or bequeathed,
or should give or bequeath by that his will, or by any
codicil or codicils thereto; and after full payment and
satisfaction thereof in trust forthwith to lay out and invest such a portion of the residue of the monies to arise
and be produced by the means aforesaid in the purchase
of so much and such sum of three per cent. consolidated
bank annuities in the names of the said *J. Elwes* and
A. H. Chambers, or of the survivor of them, his executors,
administrators, or assigns, as the yearly dividends thereof
would amount to the sum of 1000*l.*, and upon trust during the natural life of Mrs. *Duffield*, to pay the dividends

14   of

of the said 3 per cent. consolidated bank annuities so
to be purchased, to Mrs. *Duffield,* for her separate use;
and the said testator directed, that the said 3 per cent.
consolidated bank annuities so to be purchased as last
aforesaid, should from and after the decease of his
daughter Mrs. *Duffield,* fall into and be taken as part
of his personal estate, and be disposed of in manner
thereinafter declared thereof." The will then declared,
that as to the then residue of the monies to arise and be
produced by the sales thereinbefore directed to be made
of the testator's real and personal estate; the trustees
should be possessed thereof upon trust, to invest the
same in the purchase of parliamentary stocks, or upon
real securities at interest, in the names of the trustees,
upon the trusts thereinafter expressed, viz. in case there
should be only one child of Mrs. *Duffield,* by the said
Thomas Duffield, in trust, to pay, assign, transfer, or
assure the said stocks, funds, or securities, and the dividends and interest thereof, unto such only child, on
his attaining the age of twenty-one years, if a son, or on
her attaining that age or being married with the consent
in writing of the trustees for the time being of his will,
if a daughter; and in case there should be but two or
three children of Mrs. *Duffield* by the said *Thomas
Duffield,* then upon trust for such two or three children,
equally to be divided between them, share and share
alike; the shares of sons to be paid or assured to them
on attaining twenty-one, and the shares of daughters to
be paid or assured to them on attaining twenty-one, or
being married with such consent as aforesaid. Then
followed a clause of survivorship among such children,
in case of sons dying under twenty-one, or daughters
dying before twenty-one or marriage; and a proviso

for the children of a son dying under twenty-one, leaving lawful issue, to take their father's share. The will then proceeded as follows : " And my will is, that in case there shall be four or more children of the said Mrs. *Duffield*, by the said *Thomas Duffield*, that the said *J. Elwes* and *A. H. Chambers*, and the survivor of them, his executors, &c., shall stand and be possessed of the said stock, funds, and securities, and the dividends, interest, and annual proceeds thereof upon trust; in the first place to purchase with a competent part thereof, or otherwise to set apart thereout the sum of 50,000*l.* 3 per cent. consolidated bank annuities, and to stand possessed thereof, and of the dividends, interest, and annual proceeds thereof, in trust for such son of the said Mrs. *Duffield*, by the said *Thomas Duffield*, who under the trusts of a settlement now intended to be forthwith made, shall become possessed of an estate tail in the said manor of *Marcham*, and the messuages, farms, lands, tenements, and hereditaments which shall be comprised in the same settlement; and subject to the payment or setting apart of the said sum of 50,000*l.* 3 per cent. consolidated bank annuities, my will is, that the said *J. Elwes* and *A. H. Chambers*, and the survivor of them, his executors, &c., shall stand and be possessed of the then residue of the said stock, funds, and securities, and the dividends, interest, and annual proceeds thereof, upon trust for such four or more children, exclusive of such son as last aforesaid of the said Mrs. *Duffield* by the said *Thomas Duffield*, equally to be divided between them, share and share alike, and to be paid, assigned, transferred, or assured to them respectively, at the same time or times, and with such benefit of survivorship amongst them, and in such manner in all respects as is hereinbefore directed and declared of and concerning the said

18   stocks,

stocks, funds, and securities, and the dividends, interest, and annual proceeds thereof, in the event of there being only two or three children of the said Mrs. *Duffield*, by the said *Thomas Duffield.*" The will then provided, that in case the said *Thomas Duffield* should die, leaving the plaintiff, Mrs. *Duffield*, surviving him, and without having issue by her, or if he should leave issue by her, and all such issue being sons should die under twenty-one, and without lawful issue, or being daughters should die under that age, and without having been married with such consent as aforesaid, then the said trustees should from and after such the decease of the said *Thomas Duffield*, and such failure of issue as aforesaid, stand possessed of the stocks, funds, and securities, in or upon which the monies to arise and be produced from the residue of the testator's real and personal estate thereinbefore devised, under the trusts thereinbefore declared thereof, should be laid out or invested, upon trust to pay the interest and dividends thereof, from time to time, during the life of Mrs. *Duffield*, to such persons as she should in writing appoint, and in default of appointment upon trust, to pay the said interest and dividends to herself for her separate use. The will then made similar provision for the children of Mrs. *Duffield* by any second husband. And in case of the decease of the plaintiff Mrs. *Duffield*, without leaving any issue of her body, who by virtue of the trusts of that his will should become entitled to the said stocks, funds, or securities, and the dividends, interest, and annual proceeds thereof, then the testator gave, bequeathed, and disposed of the same stocks, funds, and securities, and the dividends, interest, and annual proceeds thereof, in manner therein-mentioned;

3 A 2   that

that is to say, he then gave certain sums to charitable
purposes; and as to, for, and concerning all the then
residue of the said stocks, funds, and securities, and the
interest, dividends, and annual proceeds thereof, he
gave and bequeathed the same and every part thereof
unto the said *J. Elwes*, his executors, administrators,
and assigns, for his and their own use and benefit; and
to be paid, assigned, transferred, and assured to him
and them accordingly. And the testator further willed,
that his trustees should by and out of the rents, issues,
and profits of the said freehold and copyhold estates
by that his will first devised, and by and out of the part
or share of and in the said stocks, funds, and securities,
and the dividends and interest thereof, to which any child
or children of the plaintiff Mrs. *Duffield*, by the said
Thomas Duffield, or by any after taken husband, should
be presumptively entitled, pay and apply for the maintenance and education of any such child or children
in the meantime, and until his, her, or their share
or portion, shares or portions, should become payable,
such yearly sum and sums of money, as to the trustees should seem meet; and the testator empowered
his trustees from time to time, when necessary, to alter
and vary the securities upon which the monies arising
from the said residue of his real and personal estate
thereinbefore bequeathed, should, under the trusts thereinbefore declared thereof, be invested: and he also empowered the trustees for the time being of his will, during
the minority of such child of Mrs. *Duffield*, as by virtue
of the limitations thereinbefore contained, should be
presumptively entitled to the said freehold and copyhold
estates first thereinbefore devised, to demise or lease all
or any part of the said freehold and copyhold estates,

15   for

for any term not exceeding twenty-one years, in possession, and with such clauses and restrictions as therein mentioned; and the testator appointed the said *J. Elwes* and the defendant *A. H. Chambers* joint executors of that his will, and he thereby revoked all former and other wills by him at any time heretofore made; and declared that to be his last will and testament.

Some time after the making of his will the testator drew two cross lines with his pen over a part of his will, between the * in p. 711. and the * in p. 712., and which contained the direction for the sale of his residuary freehold, leasehold, and copyhold estates. The testator, after making his will, and before his codicil, purchased considerable estates in fee simple, consisting of the manor of *Withersfield*, with the perpetual advowson of the rectory of *Withersfield*, and about 1283 acres of freehold land, situate in the parishes of *Withersfield* and *Haverhill* aforesaid, in *Suffolk;* and he was seised thereof at the times of making his codicil and of his death. He afterwards made and published a codicil to his will, bearing date the 3d of *March* 1821, duly executed and attested, to pass freehold estates; the codicil was verbatim as follows: " Having some short time back drawn my pen through the first fifteen lines of the sixth sheet of my last will and testament, dated on or about the 1st day of *March*, in the year of our Lord 1811, and being apprehensive that such rasure not being witnessed might lead to litigation, I *George Elwes* do declare, by this my codicil to the said will, that the sole intention of such rasure was and is to revoke that part only of the aforesaid will whereby I direct the sale of my freehold property, which sale I accordingly do hereby revoke; and I do hereby direct and appoint, that the son law-

fully

fully begotten of my daughter *E. F. Duffield*, who shall first attain the age of twenty-one years, shall, on attaining such age, change his name for that of *Elwes;* and I give and devise to the said son of my daughter aforesaid, on his attaining the age of twenty-one years, and changing his name to *Elwes*, all my freehold property, lands, tenements, and hereditaments, to have and to hold to him my said grandson,.his heirs and assigns for ever. Also, I give and bequeath to my wife *A. M. Elwes*, for and during the term of her natural life, my dwelling-house, situate and being on the terrace in *High-street*, in the parish of *Mary-le-bone*, and.I also give unto my said wife the contents of the said house: and I do hereby nominate and appoint the Reverend *William Hicks* of *Whittington* rectory, in the county of *Gloucestershire*, to be my executor, in the room of my late brother *John Elwes*, Esquire, deceased. And I do hereby ratify and confirm the afore-mentioned will and testament, dated as aforesaid, except as is before excepted." *George Elwes*, the testator, never after the making of his will made any settlement whatever of the manor of *Marcham*, or of any other part of his property. On the 2d of *September* 1821 the testator *George Elwes* died, without revoking or altering his will, save as aforesaid, and without revoking or altering his codicil, leaving the defendant, *A. M. Elwes*, his widow, and the plaintiff, *E. F. Duffield*, his daughter and only child, and heir at law, and heir according to the custom of the manors whereof his copyhold estates were holden, and also his sole next of kin. The plaintiffs, Mr. and Mrs. *Duffield*, at the testator's death, had and now have living five children, namely, their eldest child and only son, the defendant, *G. T. W. H.*
                                                         Duffield,

Duffield, now of the age of ten years, and four younger children, the infant defendants, *C. Duffield, M. Duffield, A. Duffield,* and *S. E. Duffield. John Elwes,* one of the executors and trustees named in the will, died before the testator; the other executor and trustee therein named survived him, being the defendant, *A. H. Chambers.*

Upon the hearing of this cause before the Vice-Chancellor, his Honor directed this case to be made for the opinion of the Judges of this court, upon the following questions.

First, Whether the devise of the freehold part of the estate at *Southwood Park,* and of the freehold farm and estate at *Haverhill* contained in the will is revoked by the codicil?

Second, Did the manor of *Marcham* pass under the residuary devise contained in the testator's will; and if it did, was such devise revoked by the codicil?

Third, Did the manor of *Marcham* pass under the codicil to the first son of the plaintiff *E. F. Duffield,* who shall attain twenty-one years, and change his name to *Elwes,* or to whom does the same belong?

Fourth, Does the estate at *Withersfield* and *Haverhill,* purchased after the testator made his will, pass under the devise in the codicil to the first son of the plaintiff *E. F. Duffield,* who shall attain twenty-one years and change his name to *Elwes,* or does it go to the residuary devisee under the joint operation of the will and codicil, or does it descend to the testator's heir at law?

Fifth, To whom belong the surplus, rents, and profits of the said copyhold estates at *Southwood Park* and of the said freehold estate at the same place, and of the said freehold farm and estate at *Haverhill* (if the devise of such estates contained in the will was not revoked by

3 A 4   the

the codicil), after providing for the maintenance of the devisee thereof, until a first son of the said plaintiff *E. F. Duffield* shall attain twenty-one years, or in failure of such son till a daughter shall attain that age, or be married with consent according to the will?

Sixth, To whom do the intermediate rents and profits of such of the testator's freehold estates as are effectually devised by his codicil to the son of the plaintiff *E. F. Duffield*, who shall first attain twenty-one years and change his name to *Elwes*, until such events take place, belong? This case was argued at the sittings after last *Easter* term by

Tindal for the plaintiffs. To the first question the court must say that the devise of the freehold part of the estate at *Southwood Park*, and of the freehold farm and estate at *Haverhill*, is not revoked by the codicil.

If the words, " all my freehold property, lands, tenements, and hereditaments," in the codicil, had stood alone and unexplained, they would have been sufficient to revoke the former devise, because there would have been a new disposition of that property inconsistent with the old one. But they are restrained by other parts of the codicil, and the court will look to the whole of it in order to discover the real intent of the testator. General words in a release have been controlled by the recital, *Thorpe* v. *Thorpe* (a), and the same rule of construction has been applied to the condition of a bond, *Lord Arlington* v. *Berricke* (b), and to the operative part of a grant by deed poll, *Oliver* v. *Daniel* (c); and if this has been so generally the case as to deeds à

(a) 1 *Ld. Raym.* 255.   (b) 2 *Saund.* 411.

(c) 1 *Mer.* 500., and see Lord *Cholmondeley* v. *Clinton*, 2 *Mer.* 345.

fortiori,

1825.

DUFFIELD
against
ELWES.

fortiori, the same principle should be applied to wills. The intention of the testator is extremely clear; he had made a will, and having drawn a pen through part of it, he makes a codicil, and therein states that where he had drawn a pen through the will he meant to cancel it. That shews that he intended all the other parts to remain uncancelled. He then proceeds to make a disposition of his property, and certainly uses very comprehensive words; but the fair construction of them is, that they were intended to apply to that property only as to which the will had been cancelled. The last words of the codicil put this beyond doubt, for by them the testator ratifies and confirms the aforementioned will and testament, except as is before excepted. Now the devise of *Southwood* and *Haverhill* is not before excepted, unless by implication, and if the testator had intended not to confirm the devise of those estates, he would have said, " except in those respects in which a different disposition is hereby made." [*Bayley* J. *Southwood Park* is stated to be part freehold and part copyhold, there is nothing to shew a revocation as to the copyhold.] That is a strong argument to shew that he did not intend to revoke the devise of any part of *Southwood Park*, as that would have the effect of dividing it.

Then as to the second question: the manor of *Marcham* did not pass under the residuary devise. In dealing with a residuary clause as to personalty, the courts incline to put a large construction upon the words, in order that the testator may not die intestate as to any part, but the rule as to realty is different, for the heir at law is not to be disinherited, unless by express devise or necessary implication; and in this, as in all other cases, the intention of the testator is to be looked to.

Now

1825.

Duffield
against
Elwes.

Now as a testator can only devise what real property he has at the time of making his will, and not what he has at the time of his death, every devise of real property, though in form it may be residuary, is, in substance, specific, *Howe* v. *Lord Dartmouth* (a), *Milner* v. *Slater* (b), *Lamb* v. *Bland.* (c) If then the manor of *Marcham* was intended to pass under the residuary clause, it passed as a specific devise, and this absurdity follows; the testator devises that manor to be sold, and a certain portion is to be thereby raised in trust for the grandson, who by virtue of a settlement then intended to be made would be seized of an estate-tail in this very same manor. [*Bayley* J. The settlement was to be made immediately, whereas the will would not operate until his death.] He speaks of the settlement as of a thing to be in operation at the same time as his will. Now an act done after the making of a will which is inconsistent with it, has been held to operate as a revocation (d), à fortiori therefore, any thing in the will itself inconsistent with a particular devise, must suffice to shew that such a devise was not within the scope of the testator's intentions. Again, in the will the testator refers to the settlement made on his wife before her marriage, and by which an annuity for her life was charged on the manor of *Marcham*, and he confirms that annuity; but the residuary clause directs that all the property mentioned in it shall be sold. [*Bayley* J. The estate might be sold subject to the annuity].

As to the third question: the manor of *Marcham* did not pass under the codicil, but belongs to the

(a) 7 *Ves.* 147.   (b) 8 *Ves.* 305.
(c) 2 J. & W. 404.   (d) 1 *Saund.* 278 a.   6 *Cruise*, 118.

testator's

testator's heir at law.   This question involves two others; first, whether the words in the codicil, " all my freehold property, lands, tenements, and hereditaments," were intended to operate on any other property than that affected by the erasure in the will.   Secondly, whether the codicil is such a republication of the will as to make it speak from the time when the codicil was executed, so as to include the manor of *Marcham* in the residuary clause.   The argument on the fourth question will embrace these two points; and the decision of that question will dispose of the third, unless a distinction can be taken between lands purchased after the making of the will and before the codicil, and lands which at the time of making the will the testator did not intend to pass by it, but to include them in a settlement; the idea of making which he afterwards abandoned before the making of the codicil.   There does not appear to be any ground for such a distinction; the two questions, therefore, may be coupled together.   As to the fourth question then: the estates of *Withersfield* and *Haverhill* descended to the testator's heir at law.   It must be admitted on the authority of *Goodtitle* v. *Meredith* (a) and *Hulme* v. *Heygate* (b) that the codicil would be such a republication of the will as to make after-purchased lands pass by the residuary clause.   But in this case the residuary clause in the will was itself revoked so far as extends to the real estate by the drawing a line through the power of sale before the codicil was made.   And where a codicil can be shewn to relate only to the republication of part of a will it will not pass after

(a) 2 M. & S. 5.   (b) 1 Mer. 285.

purchased

purchased estates, *Strathmore* v. *Bowes.* (*a*)   Now **the**
principal object of the testator was to explain by **his**
codicil the erasure that he had made in his will, and **to**
provide for the disposition of that property as to which
he had revoked the will; and in *Thellusson* v. *Wood-
ford* (*b*) *Buller* J. says, that " slight circumstances are
sufficient to qualify and restrain general words."   At all
events, the meaning of the testator is very doubtful, and
it is difficult for any person to decide whether this property passed by the will or the codicil; and the heir at
law is entitled to the benefit of that doubt.

As to the fifth question : the rents and profits therein
mentioned belong to the customary heir of the copyhold,
and the heir at law of the freehold respectively.   This
depends on the nature of the devise of the *Southwood* and
Haverill estates to a son or daughter of Mrs. *Duffield*.
It is an executory devise, and until it vests the surplus
rents go to the heir at law, unless they are disposed of
by the residuary clause.   *Boraston*'s case (*c*) will probably
be cited contrà ; but that was a devise to *A.* for eight years,
remainder to the testator's executors until *H.* attained
twenty-one, then to him in fee; but here there was no
person in esse answering the designation in the will.
The time at which, and the person in whom the estate
would vest, were both uncertain.   It is, therefore, a devise of a future interest in lands not to take effect at the
testator's death, but limited to arise and vest upon a
future contingency; which is the definition commonly
given of an executory devise.(*d*)   *Doe* v. *Moore* (*e*),

(*a*) 2 B. & P. 500.   (*b*) 4 Ves. 325.
(*c*) 3 Co. 19.   (*d*) See Fearne, 381. 4th edit.
(*e*) 14 East, 601.

                                        Bromfield

Bromfield v. *Crowder* (a), *Doe* v. *Nowell* (b) are all distinguishable, for in none of them was there the double
doubt which has been shewn to exist in the present case.
It is manifest that the testator did not at the time of
making his will think of any particular person as answering the description in the will; for the terms which he
uses are all negative, and not positive; which proves
clearly that he contemplated the possibility of there
being no person to answer the description given.
And again, in the clause giving a leasing power to the
trustees, he speaks of the child *presumptively* entitled,
which is not the language of a person meaning to give
a vested interest. This case is hardly to be distinguished
from *Bullock* v. *Stones.* (c)   That was a devise of a real
and personal estate to the first son of *A.* when he shall
attain twenty-one.   *A.* had no son at the date of the
will or the testator's death: held, that as to the real
estate it was a good executory devise.   If the devise in
question be an executory devise, the rents and profits in
the mean time until it vests, belong to the heir at law,
Hopkins v. *Hopkins* (d), *Stanley* v. *Stanley* (e), unless the
residuary clause is sufficient to pass them.   That they
are not included in that clause is plain, for every thing
there given is in trust to sell; now he could not have
intended these surplus rents to be sold.   Neither do
they pass by the codicil, for such surplus rents and
profits will not pass where there is an executory devise,
unless by the words " rest and residue," which are not
found in the codicil, *Gibson* v. *Lord Montfort.* (*f*)   The

(a) 1 *N. R.* 313.   (b) 1 *M. & S.* 327.
(c) 2 *Ves.* sen. 521.   (d) 1 *Ves.* sen. 268.   1 *Atk.* 581.
(e) 16 *Ves.* 496.   (*f*) 1 *Ves.* sen. 491.

inter-

intermediate rents mentioned in the sixth question go to the heir at law, on the same grounds as the surplus rents already discussed. Besides, the argument on the residuary clause in favor of the son of Mrs. *Duffield* does not apply to these rents, for the devise to him is by the codicil which had previously revoked that clause.

Dampier for *G. T. W. H. Duffield,* only son of the plaintiffs. The devise mentioned in the first question is revoked by the codicil. It appears to have been the general intention of the testator not to die intestate as to any part of his property; and the words of the codicil are sufficiently comprehensive to carry that intention into effect. He also had certain particular intents, the first of which was, that all his property should be divested out of the son of Mr. and Mrs. *Duffield* if he neglected to take the name of *Elwes.* But if *Southwood* and *Haverill* do not pass by the codicil, that intent may be defeated, for then the son will be able to take and hold those estates without taking the name of *Elwes.*

Secondly, the manor of *Marcham* did pass by the residuary clause of the will. The argument against this, founded on the circumstance of its being charged with an annuity, is of no weight, for the vendee would take it subject to that charge. This devise, however, was revoked by the codicil, and by the same instrument the manor of *Marcham* passed to the first son of *E. F. Duffield* who shall attain the age of twenty-one years and change his name to *Elwes,* which is the third question proposed. The circumstances of the testator and his family had varied much between the date of the will and the codicil. Ten years had elapsed, and he

had

had not made the settlement mentioned in the will. At
the date of the will his daughter had no children; at
the date of the codicil she had five, one son and four
daughters, and in the interval the testator had bought
new estates. Under these circumstances the codicil was
made, and it appears to have a three-fold operation; it
revokes the former residuary devise, disposes of all the
property not included in the will or afterwards purchased, and in all other respects confirms the will. The
codicil may be read thus: " Whereas I have disposed
by my will of all but the manor of *Marcham* to be sold,
I now revoke that, and give all, without exception, to
my grandson." The codicil contains no exception;
and to say that the manor of *Marcham* did not pass is,
in effect, to say that the codicil without an exception
had no greater effect than the will with an exception.
It was excepted out of the will for the purpose of being
settled; that intention was abandoned before the date of
the codicil; the reason for the exception was, therefore,
at an end. An argument has been drawn from the
words of the codicil as to the intention of the testator;
now he does not state that the sole intent of the codicil
was to revoke the residuary clause, but that the sole intent of the *rasure* was to do that, and then he proceeds
to make a new disposition of his property.

Fourthly, the estates at *Withersfield* and *Haverhill*, purchased after the testator made his will, pass under the devise in the codicil. All the circumstances which tend to
shew an intent to pass, by the codicil, lands excepted out
of the will, shew also an intent to pass after-purchased
property. The devise in the residuary clause of the
will is for sale only, the codicil revokes the power of
sale, which is the same in effect as revoking the devise.
The

The residuary clause may, therefore, be read as if no mention of freeholds were made in it, and if so the codicil cannot make it, by republication, pass the after-purchased freeholds. But those estates pass by the codicil itself, there are no words to describe a particular part of the testator's lands, no words of reference, nothing to restrain or qualify the meaning of the general expression, " all my freehold property, lands, tenements, and hereditaments." The case of *Lord Strathmore* v. *Bowes* certainly resembles this, except as to one point, and upon that point the decision proceeded. There the codicil contained words of reference which explained the testator's meaning. The case was thus: testator devised all his freehold and copyhold manors, messuages, tenements, and hereditaments whatsoever in trust; he afterwards purchased other lands, and then made a codicil reciting that he had devised all his freehold and copyhold manors, &c. (as in the will); he then revoked the devise in trust, as far as concerned some of the trustees, and proceeded: " I do hereby give and devise my *said* lands, &c. and do hereby make and declare this codicil to be part of my last will." And it was held that the after-purchased lands did not pass.

The fifth question relates to the intermediate profits of the *Southwood* and *Haverhill* property. The sixth to the same profits of the after-purchased lands; and as this question is the more simple, it may be convenient to take it first. All the cases from *Baraston's* case down to *Warter* v. *Hutchinson* (a) shew that words seemingly of condition precedent, may be, by intent of the testator, words of condition subsequent, such as may affect the

(a) 1 *B. & C.* 721.

pos-

possession, but not the interest, *Trodd* v. *Downes* (a),
Bromfield v. *Crowder*, *Doe* v. *Moore*. It is relied on
for the plaintiffs that in this codicil there is no persona
designata, but that is not necessary, *Doe* v. *Nowell*,
Driver v. *Frank* (b), where those who took a vested interest under similar words were not alive at the death of
the testator; and in the latter case *Dampier* J. says, " It
has always been an object with courts of law and equity
to vest interests as soon as the words of the instruments
will admit of it. The words *from and immediately after*
point out the time when the party shall come into possession, and whether the devise be immediate or in remainder makes no real distinction." As to the negative
words in the codicil, they were equally strong in *Doe* v.
Underdown (c), but did not prevent the estate from
vesting. The case of *Bullock* v. *Stones*, cited for the
plaintiffs, is rather an authority in favor of their son,
for there, as soon as a grandson was born, he took the
rents and profits from the heir at law. *Stanley* v.
Stanley proves that the suspension of the conveyance
is of no consequence, and that the particular mention
of the time of possession shews the interest to be vested
before. It must be admitted that if there were no
grandson the rents and profits would belong to the heir
at law, *Hopkins* v. *Hopkins*. If the eldest grandson
does not take a vested interest, this inconvenience might
follow. If he were to marry and have issue, and die
before twenty-one, his issue would not take, but the
second grandson; and the property would thereby go
away from the testator's heir; which event actually happened in *Denn* v. *Bagshaw*. (d)

(a) 2 *Atk.* 294.   (b) 3 *M.& S.* 25.
(c) *Willes*, 293.   (d) 6 *T. R.* 512.

VOL. III.   3 B   The

The fifth question is in effect the same, for it is not altered by the substitution of a second grandson for the first. The event by which an estate is to be determined cannot affect the clause by which it is to be vested. If the estate is divested out of one and given to the other, each takes during his interest and title, *Co. Lit.* 11. *b. n.* 4. The hæres factus is in the place of the hæres natus.

Patteson for the infant daughters of the plaintiffs. These parties are not interested in the first question, for they can only claim under the residuary clause. The second question must be decided in the affirmative, for the manor of *Marcham* did pass under that clause, although it was afterwards revoked by the codicil. It appears that the testator intended to make a settlement of *Marcham*; but it appears also, that he did not wish to die intestate as to any part of *his* property; and, therefore, it is probable that he meant the residuary clause to operate upon *Marcham*, unless he should make the proposed settlement. There is not then, in supposing *Marcham* to be included, any such absurdity as was contended on behalf of the plaintiffs. The testator not having made the settlement, and wishing to revoke the trust for sale, in his residuary clause, probably meant the property devised by the codicil, to the eldest son of his daughter, to be an equivalent for the 50,000*l.* 3 per cents. mentioned in the residuary clause; and this view of the question confirms the argument, that the codicil was intended to pass that property alone, as to which a former devise had been revoked. This furnishes an answer to the 3d question, that the manor of *Marcham* did pass by the codicil. The 4th question must receive a different answer; for

as

as the codicil confirms the will with the exception of those parts to which the revocation applied, the after purchased estates now pass by the will; the revocation could not apply to them, for at the time of the revocation the will had no operation as to those estates, *Goodtitle* v. *Meredith.* (a)

The 5th and 6th questions are more important for the daughters. It has already been fully argued, that the devise to the grandson is executory, and if so, the surplus and intermediate rents either go to the heir at law or pass by the residuary clause. The words of that clause are clearly sufficient to embrace those rents, for the testator includes every thing over which he had a disposing power. Now it cannot be denied, that he had power to dispose of these rents, and if the words are sufficient to pass the property, it is for the heir at law to shew that the testator did not intend it to pass. Little can be added to the argument as to the executory devise, but it is to be observed, that in every case where the devise has been held to give a vested interest, the party in whom it vested was either named or pointed out, and where pointed out, it will be found that he answered the whole description given in the will. Here the person was not named, nor can the son of the plaintiffs answer the whole description, until he attains the age of twenty-one years, and takes the name of *Elwes.* The circumstance of there being a grandson living at the date of the codicil is against him, for if the testator had contemplated him in particular as the object of his bounty, no doubt he would have named him.

Cur. adv. vult.

(a) 2 M. & S. 5.

The

The Judges afterwards sent the following certificate:

This case has been argued before us by Counsel. We have considered it, and are of opinion,

1st. That the devise of the freehold part of the estate at *Southwood Park*, and of the freehold farm and estate at *Haverhill*, contained in the will, is not revoked by the codicil.

2d. That the manor of *Marcham* did pass under the residuary devise contained in the testator's will, and that such devise was revoked by the codicil.

3d. That the manor of *Marcham* did pass under the codicil to the first son of the plaintiff, *Emily Frances Duffield*, who shall attain twenty-one years, and change his name to *Elwes*.

4th. That the estate of *Withersfield* and *Haverhill*, purchased after the testator made his will, passed, under the devise in the codicil, to the first son of the plaintiff, *Emily Frances Duffield*, who shall attain twenty-one years, and change his name to *Elwes*.

5th. That the surplus rents and profits of the said copyhold estates at *Southwood Park*, and of the said freehold estate at the same place; and of the said freehold farm and estate at *Haverhill*, after providing for the maintenance of the devisee thereof, belong to *A. H. Chambers*, the surviving trustee under the will of the testator, until a first son of the said plaintiff, *E. F. Duffield*, shall attain twenty-one years; or in failure of such son, till a daughter shall attain that age, or be married with consent, according to the will.

6th. That the intermediate rents and profits of such of the testator's freehold estates as are effectually devised by his codicil to the son of the plaintiff, *E. F. Duffield*, who shall first attain twenty-one years, and change

his

his name to *Elwes*, until such events take place, belong to *A. H. Chambers*, the surviving trustee under the will of the testator.

1825.

DUFFIELD
against
ELWES.

> J. BAYLEY.
> G. S. HOLROYD.
> J. LITTLEDALE.

PRICE *against* VARNEY.

Thursday,
February 10th.

A RULE had been obtained, calling upon the plaintiff to shew cause why it should not be referred to the Master, to take an account of the rents and profits received by the plaintiff out of an estate of the defendant in his possession under an elegit, and why the plaintiff should not give up possession to the defendant, if it should be found that all the monies due to him had been received. It appeared that the original judgment obtained by the plaintiff was for 43*l.* 10*s.* He then issued an elegit, and brought ejectments to get possession of the lands. The defendant's affidavit shewed that much more than 43*l.* 10*s.* had been received. The plaintiff swore that the receipts were not sufficient to satisfy the original judgment, and the costs of the elegit and ejectments.

The Court referred it to the master to take an account of the rents and profits of an estate received by the plaintiff, who was in possession by virtue of an elegit, and ordered that the plaintiff should give up possession if it appeared that all the monies due to him had been received.

Brodrick shewed cause. Hitherto the mode of getting back possession of lands taken under an elegit, has been by ejectment, by *scire facias ad computandum,* or by application to a court of equity. And the latter is the most reasonable, for at law an account of the value at which the land is estimated by the sheriff only can be taken,

1825.

Price
against
Varney.

taken, whereas in equity it is of the actual proceeds, and there interest is allowed upon the debt, *Godfrey* v. *Watson* (a), *Earl of Bath* v. *Earl of Bradford.*(b)

Per Curiam. The plaintiff's possession is by virtue of an execution issuing out of this Court, and the proposed reference is only to take an account of the monies received under that execution. No doubt the master will allow every thing that is reasonable, and if any difficulties occur in taking the account he will present them to the Court.

Rule absolute.

(a) 3 *Atk.* 517.   (b) 2 *Ves. sen.* 589.

Saturday,
February 19th.

WILSON *against* EDWARDS.

In tort, a party
suing out bail-
able process
jointly against
several, may
declare sepa-
rately against
one of them.

A RULE having been obtained, calling on the plaintiff to shew cause why the declaration should not be set aside for irregularity with costs, on the ground that the plaintiff sued out bailable process jointly against the defendant and one *Thompson*, but had declared separately against the defendant alone.

Comyn shewed cause on an affidavit stating that the bailable process had been sued out against the defendant and *Thompson* under a Judge's order, the cause of action being a violent *assault and battery* committed by the two; and he contended, that the rule as to joining all the defendants in the declaration against whom bailable process has issued, applied only to cases of *contract* and not to cases of *tort*.

D. F. *Jones*

D. F. Jones in support of the rule, insisted that the rule was not confined to cases of contract, but that in all cases of bailable process the declaration must, as to the joinder of parties, agree with the affidavit to hold to bail, and with the process. *Lewin* v. *Smith* (*a*), *Stables* v. *Ashley.* (*b*)

Per Curiam. It does not appear to have been ever decided, that the rule in question is applicable to actions of tort, and on principle we think that it is not. The present rule must therefore be discharged.

Rule discharged. (*c*)

(*a*) *4 East,* 589.   (*b*) 1 *B. & P.* 49.
(*c*) See *Spencer* v. *Scott,* 1 *B. & P.* 19. *Chapman* v. *Eland,* 2 *N. R.* 82. *Thompson* v. *Cotter,* 1 *M. & S.* 55. *Jonge* v. *Murray,* 1 *Marsh.* 274.

- *The Apothecaries Company* v. *Merrion 12 ad 4th, 642*

CAVE *against* MASEY.

A RULE nisi for quashing the writ of error, or for leave to take out execution, notwithstanding the writ of error, had been obtained on an affidavit stating that the defendant had, in *Michaelmas* term, obtained time to plead on the terms of giving judgment of that term.

Where a defendant obtained time to plead on the terms of giving judgment of the term, and afterwards brought a writ of error, the Court quashed the writ.

D. F. Jones shewed cause. The affidavit in support of the rule does not contain sufficient grounds for the motion. The Court do not act upon conjectures as to the writ of error being brought for delay, but refuse to interfere unless there be a distinct admission by the party, that the writ of error is for delay. As to the

3 B 4   circum-

1825.

Cave
against
Masey.

circumstance of the defendant having obtained time to plead in *Michaelmas* term, on the terms of giving judgment of that term; it is true, that a writ of error, if brought at that time, would have been returnable in *Michaelmas* term, yet the Court has never quashed a writ of error merely on the ground of such a calculation of time. The plaintiff should have objected to the defendant's being allowed time to plead, unless under the express stipulation that no writ of error should be brought.

J. Williams, contrà, was stopped by the Court.

Per Curiam. This appears to us to be a case for quashing the writ of error. The defendant obtained time to plead in *Michaelmas* term, on the terms of giving judgment of that term, which must mean an available judgment. If a writ of error had been brought, then the writ of error would have been returnable last term. By this breach of engagement, unless we quashed the writ of error, the defendant would gain a term.

Rule absolute.

— See Moulditch. v. Swinfen 2 Bing NC 712

---

*Saturday,
February 12th.*

PLUNKETT *against* BUCHANAN.

Where a party, seeking to reverse an outlawry, does not appear in person, but by attorney, it must appear by affidavit that the attorney acts at the instance of the outlaw.

D. F. *JONES* (with whom was *Bompas*) shewed cause against a rule for reversing an outlawry on payment of costs, and on the defendant's putting in and perfecting bail, in the alternative of satisfying the judgment or rendering the defendant; and he took a preliminary objection, that it did not appear on the affidavits
in

in support of the rule that the application was made at
the instance and by the authority of the outlaw. Before
the statute 5 *W. & M. c.* 18. *s.* 3. the party outlawed must
have appeared *in person*, and though by that statute he
may appear *by attorney*, yet at least it must be distinctly
shewn by affidavit that the attorney is duly authorised
by him to make the application. He was then stopped
by the Court.

F. Pollock and *Tindal,* in support of the rule, contended that it was not necessary that any such authority
should appear on affidavit. They received their instructions from an attorney, who must be taken to have
made the application with the privity and in obedience
to the directions of the outlaw.

The Court, however, were clearly of opinion, that
where the party did not appear in person, it should be
expressly stated in the affidavits that the attorney was
authorised by him to make the application on his behalf.

Rule discharged.

END OF HILARY TERM.

1825.

[handwritten annotation]

LAIDLER *against* ELLIOTT. (a)

In case against an attorney for negligence, it appeared that the plaintiff in H. T. 4 G. 4. obtained final judgment against H., who surrendered in discharge of his bail on the day preceding the essoign day of E. T., but notice of the surrender was not given until two days afterwards. H. not having been charged in execution in E. T. was superseded, and discharged out of custody by a Judge of K. B.: Held, that the present action could not be maintained, for that H. was improperly superseded, inasmuch as the

CASE against an attorney for negligence. The declaration stated that in *Hilary* term 3 & 4 G. 4. plaintiff recovered a judgment in K. B. against one *Hall* for 272*l.*; that whilst that suit was depending, to wit, in E. T. 3 G. 4., certain persons became bail for *Hall*; that after the recovery of the said judgment, viz., on the 12th of *April* 1823, *Hall* rendered in discharge of his bail, and was thereupon committed to the custody of the Marshal at the suit of the said plaintiff, and there continued until superseded as hereinafter mentioned; that the plaintiff employed the now defendant as his attorney in that suit; and the said *Hall* being so surrendered and committed as aforesaid, he, the said *Hall*, by the rule and practice of the Court of K. B. ought to have been charged in execution at the suit of the plaintiff, in order to prevent his being discharged out of the said custody without first paying off or making satisfaction to the plaintiff for the said damages, costs, and charges, of all which premises defendant had

two terms allowed by the rule of court, H. T. 26 G. 3. for charging a prisoner in execution, are to be calculated from the time of giving notice of the surrender, which in this case was not done until after the legal commencement of E. T.: Held, secondly, that even if H. had been properly superseded, still the present defendant would not have been liable to an action for negligence, the meaning of the rule of court being obscure.

(a) In pursuance of the king's warrant, issued ten days before the end of *Hilary* term, three of the Judges of this court sat, as on former occasions, on the 14th of *February* and the following days until *Saturday* the 19th of *February* inclusive; and on *Monday* the 11th of *April* and the following days until *Saturday* the 16th inclusive. During that period this and the following cases were argued.

15

notice,

notice, yet defendant wholly neglected to charge *Hall*
in execution as aforesaid, by means whereof he was, on
the 16th of *May*, in the fourth year of the reign aforesaid, discharged out of the custody of the marshal, the
damages and costs aforesaid being wholly unpaid,
whereby the plaintiff hath been prevented from obtaining those damages and costs. Plea, not guilty. At the
trial before *Bayley* J. at the last Summer assizes for
Northumberland, it appeared that the plaintiff recovered a
judgment against *Hall*, and that the latter surrendered
in discharge of his bail, as alleged in the declaration.
That surrender was on *Saturday* the 12th of *April*, the
essoign day of *Easter* term was the 13th, and notice of
the surrender was not given until the 14th of the same
month. In *Trinity* term 4 G. 4., *Hall* applied to one of
the Judges of this court to be discharged out of custody,
on the ground that, according to the rule of court of
Hilary term 26 G. 3. (a) he ought to have been charged
in execution before the end of *Easter* term. (b) The
defendant's agent attended and opposed the application,
but an order was made for *Hall's* discharge, and the
Court refused to grant a new ca. sa. which the defendant applied for on the ground that *Hall* had been improperly discharged. Soon after *Hall* was discharged,
the defendant wrote to the plaintiff, saying that it never

(a) That rule, as far as it relates to this matter, is as follows: "In
case of a surrender in discharge of bail after trial had or final judgment
obtained, unless the plaintiff shall cause the defendant to be charged in
execution within two terms next after such surrender, and due notice
thereof, of which two terms the term wherein such surrender shall be
made shall be taken to be one, in case no writ of error shall be depending
or injunction obtained for stay of proceedings, the prisoner shall be discharged out of custody by supersedeas."

(b) See *Neil* v. *Lovelace*, 8 *Taunt.* 674.

was his intention to charge *Hall* in execution, because he feared he would take the benefit of the insolvent act. Some evidence was given to shew that *Hall's* friends would have paid a part of the debt in order to procure his liberation, if he had been detained in custody. Upon this evidence it was urged for the defendant that the discharge of *Hall* was not warranted by the rule of court, 26 *G.* 3., or at all events that the practice was so doubtful that the defendant's mistake respecting it was not such negligence as gave his client a right of action. The learned Judge reserved these points, and the plaintiff having gained a verdict, *Brougham,* in *Michaelmas* term, obtained a rule nisi to enter a nonsuit, and now

Alderson (with whom was *Scarlett*) shewed cause. The defendant ought to have charged *Hall* in execution before the end of *Easter* term. That was decided by *Best* J. at chambers; and that decision was confirmed by the refusal of this Court to grant a new ca. sa. [*Bayley* J. The rule of court is obscure, and perhaps the calculation should be made from the giving of the notice.] The words " due notice" are omitted in the second branch of the rule, and therefore, although notice of the surrender must be given, yet the time within which the prisoner is to be charged in execution is to be computed from the surrender, and not from the giving of the notice. Then, secondly, it is true that in *Pitt* v. *Yalden* (a) the Court held that a mistake as to a nice point of practice was not sufficient to give a right of action against an attorney; but, in order to bring himself within that case, the defendant should have shewn

(a) 4 *Burr.* 2060.

that

that his conduct was founded on a mistake as to the
practice. Here it did not appear that the defendant
was misled by the obscurity of the rule of court, for in
his letter to the plaintiff he declared that he never intended to charge *Hall* in execution; which makes this
case resemble that of *Russell* v. *Palmer.* (a)

Wightman contrà. The defendant put the right construction upon the rule of court. That requires that a
defendant having surrendered, and given due notice
thereof, shall be superseded unless he is charged in
execution within two terms after the surrender. That
must mean a surrender whereof notice has been given,
Rex v. *Sheriff of London.* (b) At all events, the meaning of the rule is very doubtful, and it appeared in
evidence that the defendant was misled by it, and he did
all in his power to detain *Hall,* for he opposed his discharge in the first instance, and afterwards applied to
the Court for a fresh ca. sa. That is a sufficient answer
to the action, *Baikie* v. *Chandless* (c), *Pitt* v. *Yalden.* (d)

BAYLEY J. I am of opinion that a nonsuit must be
entered in this case. It was an action against an attorney for negligence, in not charging a defendant in
execution in due time, whereby the plaintiff alleged that
he lost the fruits of his judgment. At the trial two
points were made for the defendant; first, that the prisoner in the former action was improperly superseded;
secondly, that even if the supersedeas was proper, still
the defendant was not guilty of such negligence as entitled the plaintiff to maintain this action. Now it was

(a) 2 *Wils.* 325.   (b) 1 *Price,* 338.
(c) 3 *Campb.* 17.   (d) 4 *Burr.* 2060.

decided

decided in the case of *Pitt* v. *Yalden*, which case occurred after the decision of *Russell* v. *Palmer*, that a mere
mistake will not give a right of action against an attorney,
but it must be shewn that there has been in his conduct
crassa negligentia, or lata culpa. Upon the authority
of that case, I should have thought that the negligence
in this case was not sufficient to constitute the foundation of an action, even supposing the supersedeas to
have been proper. But upon that point, I think that a
mature consideration of the rule of court is sufficient to
shew that the prisoner was not supersedeable. It appeared in evidence that *Hall*, the defendant in the
original action, was rendered on *Saturday* the 12th of
April; the next day was the essoign day of *Easter* term,
and notice of the render was given on the 14th. The
render, then, was of *Hilary* vacation, but notice of it
was not given until after the legal commencement of
Easter term; and the question is, whether *Hilary* term
is to be reckoned as one of the two within which the
present defendant was bound to charge *Hall* in execution. I am of opinion that it was not, but that
Easter term was the first, so that the prisoner might
have been charged in execution at any time before the
end of *Trinity* term. In the latter branch of the rule,
the word " notice" is certainly omitted; but as in the
former part of it that word is coupled with " surrender,"
I think that the surrender afterwards spoken of must
mean " notified surrender." Unless, therefore, the
interval between the essoign day and the full term is to
be considered as part of the preceding vacation, the
prisoner was discharged within two terms after notice
was given of his surrender. That it cannot be so considered is plain from the course of practice which formerly

merly prevailed; for until times comparatively modern, one of the Judges always went down to court on the essoign day, for the purpose of opening the term and hearing the essoigns; that day is therefore a part of the term. That being so, I am of opinion that the prisoner was not supersedeable at the end of *Easter* term; the present defendant, therefore, was not guilty of negligence in not having charged him in execution before that time, and consequently this action cannot be maintained.

HOLROYD J. I agree in thinking that *Hall* was not supersedeable. The surrender meant, in the rule of court referred to, is a notified surrender, and the calculation of the imprisonment is to be made from that time. I also think that the essoign day is to be considered as a part of the term. It appears that a bill filed against the warden of the *Fleet* in vacation, is filed as of the preceding term, but a bill filed on the essoign day, or between that and the full term, is filed as of that, and not of the preceding term. As to the other principle, I am of opinion that there must be crassa negligentia to make an attorney liable to an action according to the decision in *Pitt* v. *Yalden*, which case was decided after much consideration.

LITTLEDALE J. I think that it was not necessary to charge *Hall*, the defendant in the original suit, in execution until the end of *Trinity* term. The time within which a defendant is to be so charged does not begin to run until notice of his surrender has been given. Then notice not having been given until the 14th of *April*, the day after the essoign day of *Easter* term, I
think

1825.

LAIDLER
against
ELMES.

think that *Hall* was not effectually superseded until *Easter* term. Original writs are returnable in fifteen days of *Easter*, which is the essoign day. That shews it to be a part of the term. Formerly the first day of term was the essoign day, the second day was the day of exceptions, on the third the sheriff returned his writs into court, and on the fourth, all things being prepared for business, the full court sat, whence it has usually been considered as the first day of term. But even if the rule in question were to be differently construed, I quite agree that the defendant was not guilty of that *crassa negligentia* which is necessary to give a right of action. A nonsuit must therefore be entered.

Rule absolute.

POUCHER *against* NORMAN.

ASSUMPSIT on a promissory note, and for work and labour. Plea, non-assumpsit, and notice of set off. At the trial before *Alexander* C. B. at the Summer assizes for the county of *Cambridge*, 1824, the plaintiff proved the defendant's hand-writing to the promissory note, and also, business done by the plaintiff as a conveyancer for the defendant. It appeared that the plaintiff was not an attorney or a barrister, but he had taken out the certificate required by stat. 44 G. 3. c. 98. s. 14. It was however objected that he could not recover amount of his bill for business done as a conveyancer. The defendant gave evidence of a set off. The Lord C. B. told the jury that he was of opinion that the plaintiff was not entitled to recover any thing in respect of his demand for business done, and he left it to the jury to find for the plaintiff or defendant according as they thought upon the evidence that the amount of the set off proved, did or did not exceed the plaintiff's demand upon the promissory note. The jury found for the defendant. A rule nisi for a new trial was obtained in last *Michaelmas* term, on the ground that the plaintiff was entitled to recover the amount of his bill for conveyancing, and also on the ground that the verdict was against evidence. The Lord C. B. reported to the court that he was of opinion that the verdict was against the evidence, and now *Storks* was heard against the rule, and *Dover* contrà. The former cited *Jenkins* v. *Slade*, sittings after *Easter* term 1824, in which *Best* C. J. ruled at nisi prius that a certificated conveyancer could not maintain an action for his fees.

Per Curiam. There must be a new trial in this case. One part of the plaintiff's claim, viz. that for business done was wholly withdrawn from the consideration of the jury, because the Lord C. B. was of opinion that the plaintiff could not maintain any action to recover that sum. The general rule is, that any man who bestows his labour for another, has a right of action to recover a compensation for that labour. There are two exceptions to that rule, viz. physicians and barristers. The law supposes them to act with a view to an honorary reward. In the other degrees of those professions parties may recover for their services. An attorney may recover for conveyancing. So a surgeon may recover for attendance. Then if that be so, there is nothing to take a conveyancer, who is not a barrister, out of the general rule of law by which a man who bestows his labour for the benefit of another has a right of action for a reasonable compensation for his labour. The rule for a new trial must therefore be made absolute.

Rule absolute.

Ewer and Another, Assignees of Ray and Another, *against* Ambrose and John Baker.

Assumpsit for money had and received. Plea, that the promises in the declaration mentioned were made by the defendant jointly with *A. B.* and issue thereon. *A. B.* was called as a witness by the defendant, to prove a partnership, but he proved the contrary; the defendant then tendered in evidence an answer of *A. B.* to a bill filed in chancery, in which *A. B.* swore that up to a certain time he was a partner with the defendant: Semble, that this answer was not admissible in evidence, because the only effect of it was to discredit *A. B.* the defendant's own witness; but,

Held, that it was competent to the defendant, after *A. B.* had denied the partnership, to prove the existence of it by other witnesses.

ASSUMPSIT for money had and received, and on an account stated. *John Baker* suffered judgment by default, and afterwards died, and his death was suggested on the roll. Plea in abatement by *Ambrose*, that the promises were made by him jointly with *John* and *Samuel Baker*. Replication that they were made jointly by defendant and *J. Baker*, and not by the three, and issue thereon. At the trial before *Gaselee* J. at the Summer assizes for the county of *Suffolk*, 1824, the defendant called *Samuel Baker*, the alleged joint contractor, to prove the plea in abatement. He denied that he ever was a partner, but he admitted that articles of partnership were prepared, but not executed, by which he was to have been a partner; that he drew checks in the name of the firm, and received large sums from the bankrupts, who were defendant's bankers, on account of the firm: the profits were divided between *Ambrose* and *John Baker*. The witness lived on the premises where the business was carried on. The defendant's counsel, in order to prove that *S. Baker* was a partner, proposed

posed

posed to read in evidence an answer in Chancery of
John and *S. Baker* to a bill filed against them by
Ambrose in 1821, for a dissolution of the partnership and an account. The learned Judge inclined to
think that the evidence was not admissible, on the
ground that it was produced in order to contradict the
defendant's own witness; but, in order to prevent the
cause coming down again, he received it, reserving
liberty to the plaintiffs, in case the verdict should be
against them, to move the Court to enter the verdict
for them. By the answer it appeared that in 1816,
Samuel Baker had become a partner with his father
John Baker and *Ambrose*, and that that partnership continued down to the time when the answer was filed in
April 1821. The defendant then called two other witnesses, to prove that *Samuel Baker* was a partner. This
evidence was objected to on the ground that the defendant could not contradict his own witness. One of them
stated that on the 13th of *April*, 1820, *Ambrose* and the
two *Bakers* met him, by appointment, to discuss the
state of the partnership; that they all three took a part,
and he said that he, the witness, had borrowed money
to enable *Ambrose* to increase his capital, and to enter
into partnership with *John Baker* and *Samuel Baker*.
The other witness stated that he had done business with
the firm of *Baker* and *Ambrose*, and that it consisted of
Ambrose, *John Baker*, and *Samuel Baker*, and that he
considered *Samuel Baker* to be a partner as well as the
others. The learned Judge left it to the jury to find
for the plaintiff or defendant according as they gave
credit to *Samuel Baker*'s answer in Chancery, or to his
testimony given in court. They found a verdict for
the defendant. A rule nisi having been obtained in

Michael-

Michaelmas term to enter a verdict for the plaintiff, on the objections taken at the trial,

Storks and *Dover* now shewed cause. *Alexander* v. *Gibson* (a) is an authority to shew that if a witness proves facts in a cause which make against the party who calls him, the party may call other witnesses to contradict him as to those facts. In such case the facts are evidence in the cause, and the other witnesses are not called directly to discredit the first witness, the impeachment of his credit is incidental and consequential only.

Rolfe contrà. The effect of the answer was to impeach the credit of the witness called by the defendant, and upon whose credit he rested his case. Now that was clearly inadmissible. The same observation applies to the other witnesses. They were called to prove the fact of *Samuel Baker* being a partner, he himself having disproved it. At all events, if the answer was admissible, the positive testimony of *Samuel Baker* that he was not a partner is much stronger than the evidence of the other witnesses, who merely believed him to be a partner.

BAYLEY J. There have been cases in which, when a witness called to make out a substantive case disproved that case, the party calling him has been allowed to prove it by other witnesses. But those were cases where a witness was forced upon the party by law; as, for instance, a subscribing witness to a deed or will. Thus in *Lowe* v.

_____

(a) 2 Camp. 555.

Joliffe,

1825.

EWER
against
AMBROSE.

Joliffe (*a*), the subscribing witnesses to a will swore to the testator's insanity, yet the plaintiff was allowed to examine other witnesses in support of his case, to prove that the testator was sane. So in *Pike* v. *Badmering*, cited in 2 *Strange*, 1096, where the three subscribing witnesses to a will denied their hands, the plaintiff was permitted to contradict that evidence. This case differs from those, inasmuch as the witness was not forced on the party, but I have no doubt that if a witness gives evidence contrary to that which the party calling him expects, the party is at liberty afterwards to make out his own case by other witnesses. (*b*) I doubt, however, whether the defendant was at liberty to put in the answer in Chancery of the witness in order to discredit him. It was competent to the plaintiff in cross-examination to have asked the witness if he had sworn, in his answer in Chancery, contrary to the fact he was then deposing to; and if he had said that he had not, then the plaintiff, in order to discredit him, might have given the answer in evidence; but he could not do so without putting the preliminary question to him. But I think the defendant ought not to have been permitted so to discredit his own witness. The present impression of my mind therefore is, that the answer ought not to have been received in evidence. At all events, I think there ought to be a new trial, because the answer of itself was not evidence of any fact, and it was left to the jury to consider whether they would credit the testimony given by the witness at the trial, or that given in his answer in Chancery. I think, however, that the evidence of *Wing* and *Spark* was admissible to prove the

(*a*) 1 *Black.* 365.   (*b*) *Richardson* v. *Allan*, 2 *Stark.* 334.

fact

fact of the partnership, and that it ought to have been left to the jury to consider whether they were not satisfied from their evidence, coupled with the other facts of this case, that there was an ostensible partnership between the two *Bakers* and *Ambrose*.

HOLROYD J. I also think there ought to be a new trial. I take the rule of law to be, that if a witness proves a case against the party calling him, the latter may shew the truth by other witnesses. But it is undoubtedly true, that if a party calls a witness to prove a fact, he cannot, when he finds the witness proves the contrary, give general evidence to shew that that witness is not to be believed on his oath, but he may shew by other evidence that he is mistaken as to the fact which he is called to prove. It may admit of doubt whether the answer were admissible at all. It certainly was not admissible to prove generally that the witness was not worthy of any credit. It might, perhaps, be admissible if the effect of it were only to shew that, as to the particular fact sworn to at the trial, the witness was mistaken. But if its effect were only to shew that the witness was not worthy of credit, then it was not admissible, and then, coupled with the evidence given by *Wing* and *Sparks*, the jury might perhaps fairly have come to the conclusion, that there was an ostensible partnership. It is unnecessary to decide whether the answer was admissible, because I am clearly of opinion that it was not admissible to prove substantively the partnership. But it is a very different question, whether it was not evidence to destroy the credit of the witness as to the particular fact to which he swore. Now, the learned Judge considered the answer as if it were substantive evidence of the fact

of

of the partnership. At most it was only evidence to
destroy the credit of the witness as to the particular fact
sworn to; and that being so, I think the case was not
properly presented to the jury, and that there ought to
be a new trial.

LITTLEDALE J.   Where a witness is called by a party
to prove his case, and he disproves that case, I think
the party is still at liberty to prove his case by other
witnesses.   It would be a great hardship if the rule
were otherwise, for if a party had four witnesses upon
whom he relied to prove his case, it would be very
hard, that by calling first the one who happened to disprove it, he should be deprived of the testimony of
the other three.   If he had called the three before the
other who had disproved the case, it would have been
a question for the jury upon the evidence whether they
would give credit to the three or to the one.   The order
in which the witnesses happen to be called ought not
therefore to make any difference.   It may be a doubtful
question, whether the answer in Chancery was properly
received to prove a different state of facts from that
which the witness had sworn to at the trial.   At all
events it could only be admissible to contradict the particular fact to which the witness had then sworn; and
whether it was admissible in the latter point of view, it
is not necessary to decide.

Rule absolute for a new trial. (a)

(a) In Bull. N. P. 297., the rule as to the right of a party to contradict
his own witness is thus laid down.   " A party never shall be permitted to
produce general evidence to discredit his own witness;" and the reason of
the rule follows, "for that would be to enable him to destroy the witness if
he spoke against him, and to make him a good witness if he spoke for him,

3 C 4   with

which this means is to be had of destroying the credit of the witness
him." The expression "general evidence", in the rule itself, seems to
imply that a party may discredit his own witness by evidence of particular
facts, ex gr. as in the present case, by shewing that he has on some former
occasion given on oath a different account of this transaction. But the
reason of the rule extends to the exclusion of all evidence which is offered,
merely for the purpose of discrediting the witness, and which would not
have been otherwise admissible, because not tending to prove or disprove
the issue joined. And this construction is fortified by the passage in
Bull. N. P. which next follows, and explains the rule above cited. "But
if a witness prove *facts in a cause* which make against the party who called
him, yet the party may call other witnesses to prove that those facts were
otherwise; for such facts are *evidence in the cause*, and the other witnesses
are not called directly to discredit the first witness, but the impeachment
of his credit is incidental and consequential only." In the present case,
the answer in Chancery of *St. Baker* was not *evidence of any fact in the
cause*; it would seem therefore that it was not admissible for the purpose
of contradicting him.

Doe on the Demise of Lawrence and Others
against Shawcross.

EJECTMENT on a demise of the 10th of May 1824.
At the trial before *Hullock* B., at the Summer
assizes for the county of *Lancaster* 1824, it appeared
that the defendant was tenant under a lease of the
premises in question, by which the rent was made payable at *Lady-day* and *Michaelmas*, and in which there
was a proviso for re-entry on non-payment of rent for
thirty days, and that half a year's rent due at *Lady-*
day 1824, was in arrear, without any formal demand
without any for such non-payment,

for the non-payment thereof, such landlord or lessor may, without any formal
demand or re-entry, serve a declaration in ejectment for the recovery of the demised premises, which service shall stand in the place and stead of a demand and re-entry; clearly
that by this statute the service of the declaration in ejectment is substituted for the demand
of rent, which at some time must have been made, upon the happening the forfeiture
accrued in case of non-payment, and therefore that it was no ground of nonsuit in ejectment that the declaration was served on a day subsequent to the day on which the forfeiture
was laid, that being after the rent became due; because the title of the lessor must be taken
to have accrued on the day when the forfeiture would have accrued or obtained by non-
payment of the rent.

day

day 1824, was in arrear, and that there was no sufficient distress on the premises; but the declaration in ejectment was served on the 14th of *May* 1824. It was objected by the defendant's counsel, that as the service of the declaration in ejectment was on a day subsequent to the day of the demise, and as no forfeiture could have accrued before the day when the declaration was served, the lessor of the plaintiff could have no title before that day, and, therefore, that he ought to be nonsuited. The objection was without discussion acquiesced in by the plaintiff's counsel, and the plaintiff was non-suited. Upon further consideration, however, the learned Judge thought that he ought not to have yielded to the objection, and he gave leave to the plaintiff to move to set aside the nonsuit. A rule nisi having been obtained for that purpose,

Cross Serjt. and *Starkie* now shewed cause. In order to have entitled the plaintiff to recover at common law, there must have been a demand of the precise rent due on the 20th day after it had become due according to the terms of the lease. The statute 4 *Geo.* 2. c. 28. s. 2. enacts, "that in all cases between landlord and tenant, as often as it shall happen that one half year's rent shall be in arrear, and the landlord or lessor to whom the same is due hath right by law to re-enter for the non-payment thereof, such landlord or lessor shall and may without any formal demand or re-entry, serve a declaration in ejectment for the recovery of the demised premises, which service shall stand in the place and stead of a demand and re-entry." Now before the statute, the day of the demise in the declaration of ejectment could not have been laid before the 24th of *April*,

because

1822.
——
Doe dem.
Litwallert
against
Shawcross.

because until that time no forfeiture had accrued, and since the statute, when no demand of the rent has been made, it cannot be laid before the day when the declaration in ejectment is served, because the forfeiture then accrues, and before that time the lessor of the plaintiff has no title. The nonsuit, therefore, was right, because it appeared at the trial that the demise to the nominal plaintiff was made before the landlord had any title.

F. Pollock contrà, was stopped by the Court.

BAYLEY J. I am of opinion that the nonsuit must be set aside. The statute 4 G. 2. c. 28. was passed in 1731, and from that time until the trial of this cause it never has been contended that the day of the demise in the declaration must be the very day when the declaration in ejectment is served. It is clear that it could not be after that day, because it would then appear upon the proof that the nominal plaintiff had no title at the time of the service. The same objection would have applied in *Doe* v. *Fuchau* (a), for in that case the day of the demise was on the 2d of *May*, and the declaration was served on the 6th of *June*. The statute says, "that the service of the declaration in ejectment shall stand in the place of the demand and re-entry." Now that must mean in the place of a legal demand made on the day on which it ought to have been made by common law. It appears clearly from the subsequent part of the clause, that that is the meaning of the statute. It enacts, "that if it shall be proved upon the trial that

(a) 15 *East*, 286.

half

half a year's rent was due before the said declaration was served, and that no sufficient distress was to be found on the demised premises, countervailing the arrears then due, and that the lessor or lessors in ejectment had power to re-enter, then, and in every such case, the lessor or lessors in ejectment shall recover judgment and execution in the same manner as if the rent had been legally demanded, and a re-entry made." Now, before the statute, the plaintiff could not have recovered in ejectment, unless a demand had been made on the 30th day after the rent had become due, according to the terms of the lease; and when the declaration in ejectment is served, the parties are in the same situation as if such a demand had been made at common law. The title of the lessor of the plaintiff must be taken to have accrued at that time, which in this case would have been on the 24th of *April.* According to the argument, it must be an essential part of the plaintiff's case to prove the day when the declaration in ejectment was served, but such proof is not rendered necessary by the statute. The plaintiff is entitled to recover upon proving that half a year's rent was due before the declaration in ejectment was served, that no sufficient distress was found upon the premises, and that he had a power to re-enter. I am of opinion that the true construction of the statute is that which has been put upon it for ninety-five years, viz. that it substitutes the service of the declaration in ejectment for the demand of rent, which at common law must have been made upon the day when the forfeiture was to accrue in case of its not being paid.

HOLROYD

1825.

Doe dem.
LAWRENCE
against
SHAWCROSS.

HOLROYD J. The effect of the statute is to dispense with the necessity of a demand by the landlord, and not to put the tenant in a worse situation than he would have been in if he had tendered the rent when it ought to have been paid. The service of the declaration in ejectment is substituted for the demand which was required to be made at common law. At common law there could have been no legal title in the landlord until that demand had been made. The statute is beneficial to the tenant as well as to the landlord. It relieves the latter from the necessity of making a demand with all the precision required at common law, and the tenant incurs no forfeiture until the declaration in ejectment is served upon him, and if at that time he is ready to pay the rent, although he did not tender it when it was due, it gives him the same benefit as if he had tendered it at that time. The statute says, that in case certain things be proved at the trial (and all of them were proved in this case), the lessor in ejectment shall recover judgment in the same manner as if the rent had been legally demanded and a re-entry made. Now, applying the statute to this case, the lessor of the plaintiff is entitled to recover in the same manner as if the rent had been legally demanded on the 24th of *April,* and if it had been demanded on that day, it is quite clear that the lessor of the plaintiff would have been entitled to recover in this case, although the day of the demise in the declaration was prior to the day when the declaration in ejectment was served.

LITTLEDALE J. I am of the same opinion.

Rule absolute.

1825.

Doe dem.
Colclough
v.
Hulse.

DOE on the Demise of T. COLCLOUGH and ALICE, his Wife *against* HULSE.

EJECTMENT of *Michaelmas* term 4 G. 4. on a demise of the 2d of *December* 1817. At the trial before *Littledale* J. at the last Summer assizes for *Stafford*, the following appeared to be the facts of the case. The wife of the lessor of the plaintiff was the widow of *William Booth*, who died in *April* 1803, and devised all his real and personal estate to his wife for her life, and she claimed the property in question as part of that real estate. The title of *William Booth* was as follows. *Mary Mason* being seised in fee under the will of her father, *T. Mason*, of an undivided moiety of his real estate, died on the 17th of *December* 1793, and by her will devised her moiety to *W. Booth, Ann Booth* and *Sarah Bill*, formerly *Booth*, the three children of her sister *Margaret Booth*, as tenants in common, but *Sarah Bill* having died in the life-time of *Mary Mason*, she, before her death, made another will, by which she intended to devise her moiety to *W. Booth, Ann Booth*, and *Sarah Bill*, the infant daughter of *Sarah Bill*, formerly *Sarah Booth*. But this will was never executed. By deed of the 11th of *January* 1794, between *W. Booth* and *Ann Booth*, reciting the unexecuted will

A. being seised in fee of an undivided moiety of an estate, devised the same (by will made some years before her death) to her nephew and two nieces as tenants in common; one of the nieces died in the lifetime of A. and left an infant daughter. A. by another will, intended to have devised the moiety to the nephew and surviving niece and the infant daughter of the deceased niece, but this will was never executed. After A.'s death, the nephew and surviving niece covenanted to carry the unexecuted will into execution, and to convey one-third of the moiety to a trustee upon

trust to convey the same to the infant if she attained twenty-one, or to her issue if she died under twenty-one and left issue, or otherwise to the nephew and niece in equal moieties. No conveyance was executed in pursuance of the deed. The rents of the third were received by the trustee for the use of the infant during her lifetime. An ejectment having been brought by the devisee of the nephew more than twenty years after his death, but less than twenty years after the death of the infant; it was held that there was no adverse possession until the death of the infant, and that the ejectment was well brought.

of

of *Mary Mason*, they, in pursuance of and in obedience to the intention of *Mary Mason*, did covenant for
themselves, their heirs, executors, and administrators,
and to and with each other, that the unexecuted will of
Mary Mason should be established, carried into effect
and confirmed; and that they would at any time thereafter grant, convey, and assign the estate of *Mary Mason*
as therein mentioned: viz. one-third part to *W. Booth*,
his heirs, &c.; another third part to *Ann Booth*, her
heirs, &c.; and the remaining third part to *Thomas
Bill*, his heirs, &c. upon trust to convey, assure, and
assign that share to *Sarah Bill*, for her sole and separate use and benefit, at her age of twenty-one years,
or unto her issue in like manner in case she should die
before that time leaving issue, and in case she should
die before the age of twenty-one years without issue,
then to convey the said share to *W. Booth* and *Ann
Booth*, equally, share and share alike, as tenants in common, and not as joint tenants. *W. Booth* afterwards
sold his third share of the moiety to two persons, who
again sold it to *Ann Booth*. So that she became seised
of two-thirds of that moiety. *W. Booth* died on the
25th *April* 1803, and by his will devised all his real
estate to his wife, *Alice Booth* for her life, and after her
decease, unto his son *Hugh Booth* and his daughter,
equally to be divided between them as tenants in common. *Sarah Bill*, the infant child of *Sarah Bill*, died
on the 2d *December* 1804, her father having died before
her. It appeared in evidence that the wife of the lessor
of the plaintiff had never received any part of the rents
of the property in question. They were received during
the life-time of *Thomas Bill* by him and by *Ann Booth*,
and after his death *Ann Booth* continued to receive the

rents,

rents, and upon *Hugh Booth's* coming of age she accounted to him for part. *Hugh Booth* sold the property now claimed to the defendant, and suffered a recovery, and levied a fine as of *Trinity* term, 1822; but the wife of the lessor of the plaintiff made an entry to avoid the fine on the 21st of *October* 1823. At the trial it was objected for the defendant, that there having been no receipt of the rents for twenty years by the lessors of the plaintiff, or those under whom they claimed, the title was barred. On the other hand it was contended, that there could be no adverse possession until the death of *Sarah Bill*, the infant, in *December* 1804, and that the ejectment having been commenced in *Michaelmas* term 1823, was in time. The learned Judge nonsuited the plaintiff, but reserved liberty to him to move to enter a verdict. A rule nisi having been obtained for that purpose,

W. E. Taunton shewed cause. One-third of the moiety of *M. Mason* having, by reason of the death of her niece *Sarah Bill*, become a lapsed devise, descended to *W. Booth*, the heir at law of the testatrix. He then was seised of two-thirds of her moiety, and *Ann Booth* of the other third. They agreed to carry into effect the unexecuted will of the testatrix, and to convey the third to a trustee for the use of the infant. No conveyance was however executed. The legal estate in the third, which was intended to go to the infant *Sarah Bill*, continued in *W. Booth* until his death in 1803, when it passed by his will to his wife for life. She never was in possession of that third; the rents were received by *Ann Booth*, and she accounted for them to the trustee of the infant during her life. The title of *Alice Booth* therefore

therefore accrued more than twenty years before the ejectment was brought, and her claim is barred.

Campbell contrà. The possession and receipt of the rents of the third by *Ann Booth* during the lifetime of the infant, was consistent with the title of *W. Booth* and of his widow, and that possession was with their permission. They were bound by covenant to allow the rents to be received for the use of the infant. The legal estate may have been in *W. Booth*, but the equitable estate was in the infant. A court of equity would have compelled *William* and *Ann Booth* to execute a conveyance of the third to a trustee for the use of the infant. At all events the rents were rightfully received by *Ann Booth* during the lifetime of the infant.

BAYLEY J. It seems to me that there was not any adverse possession for a sufficient period of time to bar the plaintiff's title to recover in ejectment, because I think the adverse possession began to run only from the death of *Sarah Bill*, on the 2d of *December* 1804. After the deed by which *W. Booth* and *Ann Booth* agreed to confirm the will of *Mary Mason*, *W. Booth* had no right to take for his own use any part of the rents and profits of that third. Those rents and profits according to that deed were to enure to the benefit of *Sarah Bill*. When she died without issue, the interest created by that instrument for the benefit of her and her issue ceased, and of the third which was the subject of that instrument, one moiety passed to *Ann Booth*, and the other moiety would have returned to *W. Booth*, had he been living, but as he was dead, it passed under his will to his widow, the lessor of the plaintiff. Notwithstand-

ing

ing the deed of 1794, *W. Booth* had a vested interest expectant upon the death of *Sarah Bill,* under age, without issue, and that interest passed under his will to his widow. I am therefore of opinion that a verdict ought to be entered for that share, which is one-sixth of the moiety.

HOLROYD J. It was proved at the trial that *Thomas Bill* received the rents of this third of the moiety as long as he lived. After his decease *Ann Booth* received the rents. So long as *Sarah Bill* lived *W. Booth* or his representatives would have been guilty of a breach of covenant if they had prevented the rents being received for her use. The possession of the third by her trustee so long was consistent with the covenant of *W. Booth,* which was binding upon his heir or devisee. There was therefore no adverse possession until the death of *Sarah Bill,* and consequently the ejectment was brought in time. The rule for entering a verdict for the plaintiff must therefore be made absolute.

Rule absolute.

786

1825.

Jones against Williams.

By charter, the
aldermen,
bailiffs, and
burgesses had
power to elect
two of the bur-
gesses to be
aldermen of a
borough for one
whole year, and
they were to
have power and
authority to
execute by
themselves, or
in their absence
by their depu-
ties, the office
of aldermen of
the borough.
The charter
then contained
clauses by
which it was
provided that
in the event of
the death or
removal of any
alderman, a
new one might
be elected, who,
during the re-
mainder of the
year, should
execute the
office by him-
self or his de-
puty. It was
then Provided,
that in the ab-
sence of any of
the aldermen

TRESPASS and false imprisonment. Plea, not
guilty. At the trial before *Park* J. at the Summer assizes for the county of *Salop*, 1824, it appeared
that the plaintiff had been convicted under the statute
4 *G.* 4. *c.* 34. *s.* 3. by the defendant, a deputy alderman of the borough of *Denbigh*, for absenting herself from her service before the end of the year for
which she had contracted to serve, and had been committed to the house of correction at *Ruthin*, in the
county of *Denbigh*, for one calendar month. It was objected that the defendant was entitled to notice under
the statute 24 *G.* 2. *c.* 44. *s.* 1., and the question was
whether the defendant was a justice of the peace for
the borough of *Denbigh*. By the charter of *Denbigh* it
was granted that the aldermen, bailiffs, and capital burgesses of the borough for the time being, or the major
part of them, of which one of the aldermen and one of
the bailiffs were to be two, being assembled from time
to time, might and should have power and authority
yearly, on, &c. to elect two, out of the number of the
burgesses of the borough, who should be aldermen of
the said borough for one whole year then next ensuing;

for the time being, the bailiffs and capital burgesses might elect one or more of the burgesses to supply the vacancy or vacancies. These substituted aldermen had no power to appoint deputies. There then followed a clause which directed that the aldermen for the time
being, during the time they should remain in their offices, should be justices of the peace
within the borough: Held, that this charter did not enable the aldermen elected for the
year to delegate their office of justice of the peace, and therefore that a deputy alderman was
not a justice of the peace for the borough.

Quære whether, since the statute 27 *H.* 8. *c.* 24. *s.* 2., the crown can delegate to a subject
the power of appointing a justice of the peace?

and

and they, after they were so elected and nominated
aldermen of the borough, were to take the oaths before
the steward or his deputy; or if there were no steward.
at the time of such election and nomination, before their
immediate predecessors, and in the presence of ten
capital burgesses of the said borough for the time being
to execute their office well and faithfully; and they were
to have power and authority to execute by themselves,
or in their absence, by *their deputies*, the offices of
aldermen of the said borough for one whole year then
next ensuing, and until some other should in due form
be elected and sworn to the offices of alderman; and
if it should happen that either of the aldermen of the
borough for the time being should die or be displaced
from his office, that then and so oft it should be lawful
for the surviving alderman and the bailiffs and capital
burgesses of the borough for the time being, or the
major part of them, to elect or place in another of the
number of the burgesses of the said borough for alderman of the said borough; and that he being so elected
and placed in might have and exercise the said office.
for the remainder of the said year, and until one or
more were duly chosen and sworn to the said office,
(the corporal oaths to be so first taken in form aforesaid,)
by himself or themselves, or his or their deputies, in his or
their absence, and so toties quoties, as often as such an accident should happen. There then followed a proviso that
the aldermen, bailiffs, and burgesses of the said borough,
on the major part of them, from time to time, and at all
times thereafter, should and might have power and
authority for electing and nominating, and that they
should and might elect the welfare of the said borough
requiring it, and when it should be necessary and re-

quisite,

quisite, out of the number of the capital burgesses of the borough aforesaid, one or two other alderman or aldermen, in the absence of the former alderman or aldermen and bailiffs, or one or more of them; any thing to the contrary in any wise notwithstanding. And that he or they, after they were so elected and nominated as aforesaid to be alderman or aldermen of the borough aforesaid, before they were admitted to execute those offices, should take, as aforesaid, their corporal oaths in due form that they would execute their offices well and faithfully so long as he or they should continue in the said office or offices. By another clause the aldermen of the borough for the time being, during the time they should remain in their offices, were to be keepers and justices of the peace in the said borough, liberties, and precincts of the same, &c. The charter also contained a non-intromittas clause, and then nominated the first aldermen, &c.

Upon this evidence it was argued, first, that the crown could not give to other persons the power of making a justice of the peace; and, secondly, assuming that it had that power, it had not conferred it by the language of this charter, for the charter only enabled the aldermen to execute by themselves or their deputies the office of aldermen of the borough, and the office of justice of the peace, though annexed by the charter to that office, was of itself a distinct office, and the charter did not enable the alderman to appoint another person as deputy justice. The learned Judge, however, was of opinion that as one clause of the charter enabled the aldermen to appoint a deputy to the office of aldermen, and a subsequent clause made the aldermen for the time being justices of the peace for the borough,

borough, the two clauses were to be construed together, and as giving to the alderman a power of appointing a deputy to do all that he was authorized to do by the charter, and, among other things, to execute the office of justice of the peace, consequently that the deputy was a good justice, and entitled to notice. The plaintiff was therefore nonsuited. *Godson* in last *Michaelmas* term obtained a rule nisi to set aside that nonsuit on two grounds; first, that the defendant had no right to exercise the functions of a justice of the peace; and, secondly, if he had, still he was only a deputy to a justice of the peace, and not named in 24 *G.* 2. *c.* 44. *s.* 1. requiring the notice. On the first point, he urged that the king could not by charter grant to any person a power of making a judicial officer; and, consequently, that a man who was a judicial officer himself could not make a deputy. He cited *Comyn's Digest, Officer, D.* 2. *The King* v. *The Mayor of Gravesend* (a), and contended that the king being the fountain of justice could alone make justices of the peace, *Comyn's Digest, Justices* (*A.* 1.), 27 *H.* 8. *c.* 24. *s.* 2. & 6. But, admitting that the king had the power, yet he had not by this charter exercised it, for it could only be done by express words, which were not in this charter; and that it did not follow, without express words, that an alderman should be a justice of the peace, *Reg.* v. *Langley.* (b) And further, that no inconvenience could arise to the borough, as there was a proviso for electing aldermen in the absence of those elected annually under the charter.

W. E. Taunton and *Campbell* now shewed cause. By the charter the alderman had power to appoint a deputy

(a) 2 *B.* & *C.* 602.   . (b) 2 *Ld. Raym* 1029.

3 D 3   to

to execute all the duties which the principal could execute. The charter nominates two persons to sustain
the characters of aldermen and justices of the peace for
the borough, and it contains a non-intromittas clause.
In the absence of the two aldermen, according to the
argument on the other side, there would be no person
competent to execute the office of justice of the peace
within the borough. It is true that a judicial officer,
without an express power, cannot appoint a deputy; but
here there is such an express power. The charter says
that the aldermen shall have power and authority to
execute by themselves or their deputies the office of
aldermen. Now the deputy is to act as alderman, and
to exercise all the powers which the charter confers on
the alderman. If the clause by which the aldermen are
made justices of the peace of the borough had preceded the clause enabling them to appoint a deputy, it
could not be doubted that a deputy would have been a
good justice of the peace. Then a different intention
cannot be inferred from the order in which the clauses
stand in the charter. The deputy is to exercise the
office of alderman of the borough, and the acting as a
justice of the peace is parcel of that office. Now, if a
judicial office be granted tenendum per se vel deputatem,
he may make a deputy; as the Recorder of *London*,
Molins v. *Werley* (a), *Com. Dig.* tit. *Officer, D. 2.*; and
a deputy not only succeeds to all the functions of his
principal, and has power to do any act which the principal may do, but the law will not even sanction a sub-
division of the duties of the office. So that if a
principal makes a deputy covenant that he will not do
any thing which the principal may do, the covenant is

(a) 1 *Esp.* 76.

void

void and repugnant, *Parker* v. *Kett* (a), *Com. Dig.* tit.
Officer, *D.* 3. Here, therefore, it being a part of the
office of alderman to exercise the duties of a justice of
the peace within the borough, the deputy had the like
power.

Godson contrà, was stopped by the Court.

BAYLEY J. The question here turns partly on the
power of the crown to delegate the power to a subject
to make a justice of the peace, and partly on the construction of the charter. Supposing the crown to have
the power to delegate such an authority, the language
used ought to be extremely clear and express in order
to effectuate such an object. The present impression
on my mind is, that that power is superseded by the
statute 27 *H.* 8. *c.* 24. *s.* 2., by which it is enacted,
" that no person shall have any power or authority to
make any justices of eyre, justices of assize, justices of
peace, or justices of gaol delivery; but that all such
officers and ministers shall be made by letters patent
under the king's great seal, in the name and by the
authority of the king's highness, and his heirs, kings of
this realm, in all shires, counties, counties palatine, and
other places of this realm, *Wales*, and marches of the
same, or in any other his dominions, at their pleasure
and wills, in such manner and form as justices of eyre,
justices of assize, justices of peace, and justices of gaol
delivery be commonly made in every shire of this
realm; any grants, usages, prescriptions, allowances,
act or acts of parliament, or any other thing or things

(a) 1 *Salk.* 96.

to

to the contrary thereof notwithstanding." And section 6. contains a proviso " that all cities, boroughs,
and towns corporate which have liberty, power, and
authority to have justices of peace shall still have and
enjoy their liberties and authorities in that behalf after
such like manner as they have been accustomed, without any alteration by occasion of this act." I do not
find any clause relating to a corporation to be thereafter created. The words of the act however are very
general, and when we consider the power given to justices of the peace, and the talent and integrity required
in executing the office, a certain discretion ought to be
exercised in selecting persons fit for the office. In *Com.
Dig.* tit. *Justice of the Peace*, it is laid down, that none
but the king can make justices of the peace, for which
Dalton, s. 10. is cited, and that the king cannot grant a
power to another to make them. It has been said that
the Recorder of *London* and the justices of great sessions in *Wales*, have power to appoint deputies for certain purposes, but that is by act of parliament. The
charter of *London*, which requires that the Recorder
shall execute his office by himself or his sufficient deputy, is confirmed by act of parliament. So by stat.
34 & 35 *Hen.* 8. *c.* 26. the *Welch* judges might execute
their office by themselves or their sufficient deputies,
and that power is now limited by the 13 *G.* 3. *c.* 51. *s.* 3,
to the purpose of calling or adjourning any court and
receiving certain motions, and taking and proclaim-
ing fines, and arraigning recoveries. (*a*) Assuming that
the king had the power to enable a person to delegate
the office of justice of the peace to another, I cannot

(*a*) *Oldnall's Welch Practice*, p. 4.

1825.

JONES
against
WILLIAMS

say, looking at the language of this charter, that the king intended to exercise that power. The position of the clauses in the charter is of material assistance in guiding our judgment. By one clause, the aldermen, bailiffs, or capital burgesses for the time being are to have power every year to nominate two of the burgesses who shall be aldermen of the borough for one year next ensuing, and after they are so elected aldermen, before they are admitted to execute that office, they are to take the oaths before the steward, or if there be no steward, before the aldermen and ten burgesses, to execute their office well and faithfully, and after this oath so taken, they are to have power and authority to execute by themselves, or in their absence, by their deputies, the office of *aldermen* of the borough for one whole year next ensuing. The deputies are to exercise the powers of aldermen. Now the powers of aldermen vary in different boroughs. The powers of a justice of peace do not necessarily belong to the office of alderman. There then follow clauses for making new aldermen in the event of the death or removal of any alderman elected for the year, and they are to take the oaths and perform the office by themselves or *their deputies*. Another clause enables the corporation to elect additional aldermen to act in the absence of the other aldermen; but those additional aldermen have not any power of appointing deputies. There are therefore two descriptions of aldermen, first, those originally elected for the year, and those elected on their death or removal, and they may execute their offices by themselves or by their deputies; secondly, aldermen elected in the absence of the aldermen chosen for the year, and these substituted aldermen have not any

power

power to appoint deputies. The charter then provides that the aldermen for the time being during the time they shall remain in office, shall be justices, of the peace for the borough. It does not, say, that the deputies of the aldermen shall be justices. The aldermen are to take certain oaths, the deputies are not required to take any oaths. The aldermen are to be chosen out of the burgesses. The charter does not require that the deputy should be a member of the corporation. Considering, therefore, that this charter creates two descriptions of aldermen, and that one of them only has the power of exercising the office of alderman by deputy; and that in the event of the absence of the aldermen, others may be elected in their stead, and that those substituted aldermen have the power of executing the office of justice of the peace within the borough, so that no inconvenience can arise from the deputy not having that power, and that the words of the charter will be fully satisfied by holding that the alderman has a power to appoint a deputy to exercise all his corporate powers only, I am of opinion that the language of this charter is not sufficiently clear to shew an intention on the part of the crown to delegate to the aldermen for the time being a power of appointing deputy justices of the peace. The rule for a new trial must therefore be made absolute.

Holroyd J. I think that the deputy had not vested in him the office or power of a justice of the peace. By the charter two persons are constituted justices of the peace, to continue so until others are appointed. The office of justices of the peace is annexed to that of alderman. Then there is a further power that other aldermen

may

1825.

Jochs
against
WILLIAMS.

may be appointed to act in the absence of those first
elected. The charter, after giving this power, states that
the aldermen for the time being shall and may exercise
the office of justices of the peace, but it does not follow
that that office is part of the office to which it is annexed. I do not know that a person qua alderman has
vested in him any known duties, but the duties are
generally defined by the charter. The powers of aldermen are to be exercised only on members of the corporation, they are to exercise only corporate powers,
but a justice exercises powers which are not corporate,
and not confined to members of the corporation. Generally speaking, where there is a power by charter to
appoint a deputy, the latter has all the powers of his
principal, but then those would be corporate powers.
But that is very different from the present case, for
here one office is annexed to the other. I think too
we are to take into consideration that the legislature
has confined to the king generally the power of making
justices, and that we ought not, unless the language of
the charter be clear and express, to infer that the king
meant to delegate that power to others. The deputy
does not become an alderman, but he has all the corporate powers only which were annexed to the officer
who is an alderman. That being so, I am of opinion
that the defendant was not a justice of peace, and consequently that he was not entitled to notice of action
under the statute 24 G. 2. c. 44. The rule for a new
trial must therefore be made absolute.   **Rule absolute.**

WILLIAMS *against* Lord BAGOT.

(In Error.)

Upon error from an inferior court, it appeared by the record that in an action of debt, a summons and attachment issued at the same time, and were returnable at the same time; and neither of them was served personally on the defendant. At the return of these writs the plaintiff declared, and at a subsequent court had judgment by default, the defendant never having appeared, and no appearance having been entered for him. The recorder of the inferior court certified this to be the practice of the court according to immemorial custom: Held, that the custom to declare against a defendant before entry of appearance by him or by some person for him, was bad in law.

Semble, That the method to issue a summons and attachment at the same time was also bad.

UPON a writ of error the following record was sent from the court of the lordship of *Ruthin.*

Lordship of *Ruthin* otherwise *Dyffryn Clwyd.* Pleas of the court of our lord the king, in and for the lordship or dominion of *Dyffryn Clwyd,* with the town of *Ruthin,* in the county of *Denbigh,* held at *Ruthin* in the lordship aforesaid, the 2d of *November* 1822, according to the use and custom of the same lordship, hitherto used and approved from time whereof the memory of man is not to the contrary, before *R. H. Jones,* Esq., chief steward of the said court.

Be it remembered, that heretofore, to wit, on the 7th day of *September,* in the year of our Lord 1822, at the court of the lordship or dominion aforesaid, holden at *Ruthin* aforesaid, in and for the lordship aforesaid, and within the jurisdiction of the same court, before *R. H. Jones,* steward of the said court, came The Right Honorable *William* Lord *Bagot,* by *J. Jones* his attorney, and then and there made and levied his certain plaint against *John Williams,* Gent. in a plea of debt of 4000l. an affidavit that the sum of 2000l. and upwards was then due and unsatisfied from the said *J. Williams* to the said Lord *Bagot,* having been first duly made and filed

John Williams, Gent. summoned to be

in

in the said court of the said lordship or dominion, which said plaint and affidavit are as follows:

In the lordship court of *Ruthin*, otherwise *Dyffryn Clwyd*, 7th *September* 1822. The Right Honorable *William Lord Bagot* complains against *John Williams*, Gent., in a plea of debt of 4000*l.* *John Jones*, plaintiff's attorney, by distringas oath for 2000*l.* and upwards.

: In the lordship court of *Ruthin*, otherwise *Dyffryn Clwyd*. *Thomas Turner* of *Bagot's Park*, in the parish of *Abbotts Bromley*, in the county of *Stafford*, Gentleman, maketh oath and saith, that *John Williams*, now or late of *Pool Park*, in the parish of *Llanfwrog*, in the said lordship of *Ruthin*, and within the jurisdiction of this court, gentleman, is justly and truly indebted unto the Right Honorable *William Lord Bagot*, in the sum of 2000*l.* and upwards of lawful money, for money had and received by the said *John Williams*, to and for the use of the said Lord *Bagot* ; and this deponent further saith, that no offer or tender hath been made to pay the said sum of 2000*l.*, or any part thereof, either to the said Lord *Bagot* or to this deponent, or any other person on the behalf of the said Lord *Bagot*, in any note or notes of the governor and company of the bank of *England* expressed to be payable on demand.

. And upon this the said *William Lord Bagot* prays the process of the same court, to be made to him thereupon against the said *John Williams* in the plea aforesaid, and it is granted to him, and so forth; and upon this a certain summons is issued by the said court as follows:

Lordship of *Ruthin* otherwise *Dyffryn Clwyd*. To *John Williams*, Gent. You are hereby summoned to be and appear at the next court to be held and kept in and for the said lordship, to answer The Right Honorable
William

William, Lord Bagot in a plea of debt of 4000*l.* whereof you have this summons, dated the 18th day of September 1822.

From *Edward Jones* recorder thereof, *John Jones* attorney, *John Maddocks*, and *Thomas Turner* bailiffs.

By distringes.

Which said summons is thereupon delivered to the said *Thomas Turner* and *John Maddocks*, to be by them, or one of them, served upon the said defendant according to the custom of the said court; and upon this a certain precept or attachment is, according to the custom of the court, issued by the same court as follows:

Lordship of *Ruthin* otherwise *Dyffryn Clwyd*. Between The Right Honorable *William Lord Bagot*, plaintiff, and *John Williams*, defendant, in a plea of debt of 4000*l.* It is commanded on the part and behalf of the Lady of the said lordship, to all and singular the bailiffs and ministers there, and also to *Thomas Turner* and *John Maddocks*, *Robert Jones* and *John Jones*, for this time especially appointed, that you, some or one of you, attach the said defendant by his goods or chattels if found within the said lordship, and them safely keep; so that the defendant be and appear by good and sufficient sureties, at the next court to be held for the said lordship, before the steward of the lordship aforesaid, to answer to the above named plaintiff in the plea above mentioned, and have you there this precept. Witness, *Rudd Jones*, Esq. chief steward of the said lordship at *Ruthin*, the 7th day of *September* 1822, before *Edward Jones*, recorder thereof. Issued 18th *September* 1822. Oath for 4000*l.* thereupon. Which said attachment is thereupon delivered to

to

to the said *Thomas Turner* and *John Maddocks*, to be
by them, or one of them, executed according to such
custom. At which said court, to wit, at the court of
the said lordship holden at *Ruthin* aforesaid, in the
county of *Denbigh* aforesaid, and within the jurisdiction
of the said court, on the 21st day of *September*, in the
said third year of the reign of our said lord the king,
before *R. H. Jones*, Esq., steward of the said court, comes
the said *William Lord Bagot*, by *John Jones* his attorney,
and offers himself against the said *John Williams*, in the
plea of the said plaint. And the said *Thomas Turner*
being such bailiff as aforesaid, now informs the same
court here upon oath, that he did on the 18th day of
September in the same year, summon the said *John
Williams*, by delivering a true copy of the said summons
to the wife of the said *John Williams* in his dwelling-
house, within the jurisdiction of the same court, according to the tenor of the said summons, and by shewing
to her, then and there, the original summons. And he
further informs the said court upon oath, that he did,
on the said 18th day of *September* in the year aforesaid,
in all things execute the said precept of attachment so
to him directed, by then shewing to the said wife of the
said defendant in his said dwelling-house, the said writ
or precept of attachment, and delivering her a true copy
thereof, and by virtue thereof, within the jurisdiction
aforesaid, taking possession of the goods and chattels of
the said Defendant, according to the usage and custom
of the said court; and that the same continue in the
custody of the said *Thomas Turner*. At which same
court, to wit, at the court of the lordship aforesaid, held
at *Ruthin* in and for the said lordship, and within the
jurisdiction of the same court, on the aforesaid 21st day
of

800

of September, in the said third year of the reign of the said lord the now king, before R. H. Jones, Esq. steward of the said lordship, comes the said William Lord Bagot, by John Jones his attorney, and thereupon the said William Lord Bagot declares against the said John Williams in the plea of the said plaint, in manner and form following: that is to say,

In the lordship court of Ruthin, otherwise called Dyffryn Clwyd, in the county of Denbigh. For the Right Honourable William Lord Bagot, plaintiff, against John Williams, Gentleman, defendant, in a plea of debt of 4000l., and hereupon the said plaintiff, by John Jones his attorney, complains; for that whereas the said defendant, on the 30th day of July, in the year of our Lord 1822, at Ruthin, in the said county of Denbigh, and within the jurisdiction of this court, did grant money to pay to the said plaintiff, the said sum of 4000l. of lawful money of Great Britain, whensoever afterwards he, the said defendant, should be thereunto requested; nevertheless the said defendant, although oftentimes afterwards thereunto requested, hath not yet paid to the said plaintiff the said sum of 4000l., or any part thereof, but the same to him to pay hath hitherto refused, and still doth refuse; wherefore the said plaintiff saith he is damnified, and hath sustained damage to the value of 4000l., and therefore he brings his suit, and so forth; pledges to prosecute, John Doe and Richard Roe; And the said John Williams, although solemnly called and afterwards by the crier of the surveyor, &c. came not; whereupon a day given to the said plaintiff to appear in the said plaint against the said defendant, &c. And thereupon the said lordship, &c. And thereupon the said plaintiff

aforesaid here, and within the jurisdiction of the same
court, to wit, at, &c., on the 5th day of *October* now
next ensuing. The same day is given to the said
William Lord Bagot, to be there and so forth. At
which same next court, to wit, at the court of the said
lordship, holden before the said *R. H. Jones*, steward
of the said lordship as aforesaid, and within the jurisdiction of the same court, to wit, at, &c., on the said
5th day of *October* in the year aforesaid, comes the said
William Lord Bagot, by his attorney aforesaid, but the
said *John Williams*, though as aforesaid solemnly called,
cometh not, whereby the said *William Lord Bagot* remains therein undefended against the said *John Williams*,
therefore it is considered according to the custom of
this court, that the said *William Lord Bagot* do recover
against the said *John Williams* his said debt, and also
6l. 18s. for his damages which he has sustained, as well
on occasion of the detaining his said debt, as for his
costs and charges by him about his suit in this behalf
expended, by the court here adjudged to the said
William Lord Bagot, and with his assent. And the
said *John Williams* in mercy and so forth. And, thereupon, by a certain verification duly made on the part
and behalf of the said *William Lord Bagot*, by the oath
of the said *Thomas Turnor*, sworn before *Edward Jones*,
Esq., recorder of the said court of the said lordship,
and duly filed in the said court, it is manifest, and
made manifest to the said court, that the sum of 2400l.
of lawful money of *Great Britain*, besides the ordinary
costs of suit, is still due and unpaid to the said *William
Lord Bagot*, and thereupon it is commanded to *Thomas
Turnor, John Maddocks*, and other bailiffs, that they, or

some or one them, of the goods and chattels of the said
John Williams, if found in the said lordship and jurisdiction, chuse to be made, as well the said debt of 4000*l.*,
as also the said sum of 6*l.* 18*s.*, which, to the said *William
Lord Bagot*, in the said court was awarded for his said
costs and damages as aforesaid, and whereof the said
John Williams was convicted as aforesaid; and that they
have the said money at the next court to be holden for
the said lordship, to be rendered to the said *William
Lord Bagot*, for the debt, damages, and costs aforesaid,
and that they have there this precept. And the said
writ was then and there indorsed by the said court to
levy the sum of 3406*l.* 18*s.*, being the amount of the
said sum so as aforesaid verified, and of the costs and
damages to as aforesaid by the said court awarded to
the said *William Lord Bagot*. And afterwards, at the
said court, to wit, at the said court of the said lordship,
holden before the said *R. H. Jones*, steward of the said
lordship as aforesaid, and within the jurisdiction of the
same court, to wit, at *Ruthin* aforesaid, in the county
aforesaid, on the 2d day of *November* in the third year
aforesaid, come the said *Thomas Turnor* and *John
Maddocks*, and inform the court, that, by virtue of
the said writ, they have caused to be made, of the goods
and chattels aforesaid of the said *John Williams*, the sum
of 1416*l.*, which money they have ready before the
steward of the said lordship, at the day and place within
contained, to render to the said *William Lord Bagot*,
in part of his debt and costs in the said writ mentioned.
And they further certify, that the said *John Williams*
has not any other or more goods or chattels within the
said lordship, whereof they can cause to be made the

A cer-   residue

residue of the said debt and costs aforesaid, according
to the exigency of the said writ.

The answer of *Thomas Turner* and *John Maddocks.*

R. H. Jones.

The following errors were then assigned: That by
the record it appears that a summons and also an
attachment issued out of the lordship court on one and
the same day in the same suit; and that the two processes are inconsistent with each other, and cannot by
law be issued together. That the process against the
person and against the goods of the said *John Williams*
issued out of the lordship court at one and the same
time. That inconsistent processes, one bailable, the
other not bailable, were issued at one and the same
time. That process of attachment was issued against
the goods of *John Williams* before any process of summons against him was returnable. That two inconsistent processes were served upon *John Williams* at the
same time. That no appearance was ever entered in
the said lordship court by or for the said *John Williams*
at the suit of the said Lord *Bagot* in the plaint aforesaid, nevertheless Lord *Bagot* proceeded to declare and
sign judgment against the said *John Williams*, he not
having appeared or being in any manner brought into
or before the said lordship court. That in the record
aforesaid there is no entry of any appearance by or for
the said *John Williams* in the said suit, whereas by the
law of the land, an appearance must be entered by or
for the defendant, in order to warrant a plaintiff in declaring against him, and signing judgment for want of
a plea.   Common errors.   Joinder in error.

A certiorari then issued, commanding the recorder of the lordship court of _____ to certify the practice of that court, with all things touching the same; to which the following answer was sent. "The court of the lordship of _____, &c. is, and from time immemorial hath been holden before the steward, who officiates as judge thereof once every fourteen days, that is, on every alternate _Saturday_; and, by the custom and usage of the court from time immemorial, a creditor may, for a debt amounting to or exceeding 40s. at any intervening time between the holding of the said court, and after having duly made and filed an affidavit that a sum of money is justly due to him from a debtor, he, by his attorney, may levy his plaint against such debtor as of the preceding court day, which the recorder of the court enters in the court-book under the style and title of the next preceding court-day; whereupon a summons from the recorder to the defendant issues, according to such usage and custom, whereby the defendant is summoned to appear at the court to be holden next immediately after the date of the summons, to answer the plaintiff in a plea of debt, and is tested the day it is issued; and at the same time a writ of attachment, according to such usage and custom, is issued under the hand and seal of the recorder, tested before the steward on the next preceding court-day (dated in the margin the day and year on which it is actually issued), whereby the bailiffs therein specially appointed are commanded to attach the defendant by his goods and chattels, if found within the lordship, and them safely keep, so that the defendant be had to appear by good and sufficient sureties at the next court to be held for the lordship before the steward of that lordship, to

answer

1825.

WARREN
against
Lord H. &c.

answer to the plaintiff therein named in the plea therein mentioned, which is tested on the preceding court-day. The summons bears, in the margin, the name of the particular bailiff to whom the writ of attachment is directed, and who is appointed to serve the summons and execute the attachment, which service and execution are, according to such usage and custom, effected within the limits and jurisdiction of the same court, either by shewing the original summons and attachment to the defendant, and giving a copy of the summons to him, personally, and taking possession of his goods and chattels equal in value to the debt sworn to and costs; or by shewing the original summons and attachment to the defendant's wife in his dwelling-house, and by giving her a copy of the summons in his dwelling-house, and taking possession of such his goods and chattels. If the defendant, according to the exigency of the writ of attachment, gives sufficient sureties to appear and satisfy the plaintiff, if the latter should obtain a verdict or judgment in the said plaint, the condemnation money, being debt, damages, and costs, then the goods and chattels so taken or attached are immediately given up and restored to the defendant. The defendant is, however, at liberty to appear and proceed to trial without putting in such bail, if he chooses to permit his goods and chattels to remain in the custody of the bailiff to abide the event of the suit. At the next court holden in and for the lordship, after the service of the summons and seizure under the attachment, the bailiff informs the court, upon oath, of the time and manner of such service and seizure, and the plaintiff is then at liberty, at the same court, to file his declaration against the defendant; and if the defendant has not previously caused an appearance to be

entered

entered for him, he is then and there solemnly called in
open court by the recorder, and afterwards by the
crier of the court, to appear to the plaint, and plead to
the plaintiff's declaration; and, in case of default, a day
is given to appear and plead until the following court;
and if the defendant does not appear and plead previous to such following court, he is again in like manner
called at such following or third court, to appear and
plead; and if the defendant should still make default,
and neglect to appear, then at such third court judgment by default is given, according to such usage and
custom, for the plaintiff against the defendant for the
amount of the debt, and for the costs and damages sustained by the plaintiff by reason of the defendant's detaining the debt; and that afterwards an affidavit of
verification on oath is made by, or on behalf of the
plaintiff of the amount of the debt justly and truly due
from the defendant, and unsatisfied, to the plaintiff, and
execution is thereupon awarded by the court, indorsed
to levy for the amount of the debt so sworn to, and
costs taxed by the recorder of the court."

The case was now argued by

Patteson, for the plaintiff in error. The certificate
certainly appears to have been framed so as to support
the record, and if the custom alleged in the certificate
be good in law the judgment must be affirmed. But
the custom is not good; for, first, the process was
erroneous, and, secondly, custom cannot authorize a
plaintiff to declare against a party who is not in court.
First, as to the process, it appears that the plaint was
levied between the 7th of September 1823, and the 21st,
as of the 7th. A summons issued on the 16th, tested

the

the same day, returnable on the 21st; the attachment
issued on the same day, tested the 7th, and was
made returnable on the same day, and the officer returned that both were executed on the same day. Now
that, in effect, is the same as if the attachment had
issued without a previous summons; but it is a general
rule that that cannot be done in inferior courts. Previous summons means a summons returnable before the
attachment issues, for the latter issues for non-compliance with the summons, *Com. Dig. Court* (P. 8),
Marpole v. Barnett (a), *Murphy v. Fitzgerald* (b), *Titley
v. Foxell* (c). And, in *Com. Dig.* tit. *County* (C. 9.) the
rule is thus given: "Process in the county court shall
be by summons, attachment, and distress infinite, in all
personal actions by plaint or justicies, except in trespass.
In trespass it shall be by attachment and distress infinite," [*Bayley* J. Are there any cases which shew
that this can be assigned for error?] In *Moravia v.
Sloper* (d) it appears to have been considered that it
might, for there *Willes* C. J. cites a dictum of *Powell* B.
in *Gwinne v. Poole* (e), that a capias, in the first instance,
in inferior courts is erroneous, and not void; and he
dissents from that position not on the ground that the
process was not erroneous, but that it was void. And in
Prat v. Dixon (f) the judgment of an inferior court, in an
action of debt, was reversed on error, because it appeared
by the record that the defendant below was attached in
the first instance, and not summoned; and the same
point was ruled in *Ward v. Elleum* (g). But, secondly,

(a) *Willes*, 38. n.   (b) *Willes*, 38. n.
(c) *Willes*, 688.   (d) *Willes*, 30.
(f) *Willes*, [...]

3 E 4

with the process.   Here there was no personal service,
and no appearance was entered.

The ... does not apply to inferior courts, and they may still be governed by their own customs. If that statute had such application, the proceeding by foreign attachment in the mayor's court would be affected by it. Yet there a judgment may be obtained against the garnishee, although the defendant in the original action has never been actually summoned, and that defendant is bound by the judgment. It is certainly reasonable that the defendant ought to appear, and have an opportunity of answering the plaintiff's declaration before judgment is given; but here he had such opportunity, for the process was served on his wife at his dwelling-house; it must therefore be presumed to have come to his hands, as in the action of ejectment. There is not in this case the same apparent hardship as in some parts of the practice of the superior courts, ex. gr. the fixing of bail by suing out two writs of mes. &c., of which it is unnecessary to give them any notice, *Silitoe v. Wallace* (a); *Clark v. Bradshaw* (b). [Littledale J. The certificate of the practice of this court does not agree with the record. The certificate states, that after the declaration the defendant must be called to *appear and plead*; the record states that he was called, not that he was *called to appear and plead*; now a mere calling of the defendant gives no notice of a declaration having been filed, but that notice is given by a call to appear and plead.] Then as to the other objection made to the process, that ... was no ground of error, but merely an irregularity which is cured by the statute of jeofails. The record would ... if it had been served with a ... with the process. There ... was no personal service ... and ...

precludes... est after the plaint... [Holroyd J.] Yet they justify by pleading, with a latter process... est, but this is very different... received any notice of... to... in the law to support the custom. In... the terms of...

BAYLEY J. I have no doubt that the custom stated in the certificate is bad in law. This was an action in a court of record, and a final judgment there is conclusive against all parties and privies; and it is contrary to common justice that a party should be concluded unheard. In ordinary actions of debt there is first a summons, and upon the return of that a distress. There is not in general any attachment in actions of debt. Here there was an attachment concurrent with the summons, and that is alleged to be according to the custom of the court. Perhaps the custom might render the proceeding valid, but it is not necessary to decide that point. It seems to me to be a fatal objection that the plaintiff declared in the absence of the defendant, and that final judgment was given against the latter although he had never appeared. It is unnecessary to go beyond the facts of the present case in order to judge of the reasonableness of the custom. Only seventeen days elapsed between the issuing of the process and final judgment; the process issued on the 18th of *September*, returnable on the 21st. It was not served personally on the defendant, but on his wife, at his dwelling-house, that being within the jurisdiction of the court. It is not alleged as part of the custom that the process so served must be brought to the hands of the defendant. As the custom exists, the party was called, and did not appear, and at the next, fourteen days afterwards, final judgment was given against him, and by that it is the goods are con-

by   clusively

clusively bound. It is very possible that in the short interval of seventeen days the defendant may not have received any notice of the action. There is no analogy in the law to support this custom. In all the forms of the superior courts it is alleged that the party comes, and in all personal actions his personal appearance is recorded. If he does not appear, then the plaintiff may proceed by summons and distress infinite, or by outlawry where a capias lies. In certain cases the plaintiff may enter an appearance for the defendant by virtue of the 12 G. 1. c. 29., but then the defendant must have been personally served with the process. That statute extends to inferior courts, but the plaintiff below could not avail himself of it, inasmuch as the defendant had not been personally served. For these reasons I am of opinion that the judgment of the court below must be reversed, and I also agree in thinking that the record varies from the practice certified in the manner pointed out by my brother *Littledale*.

HOLROYD J. I am of the same opinion upon that point, and also upon the general question; for it appears to me that the custom certified is bad. In personal actions it must appear that the person of the defendant has been brought into court. In real actions first the petit cape issues, upon which the issues of the land sought to be recovered are taken; if the defendant does not appear to that process, the grand cape goes, upon which the land itself is taken; but this does not affect the defendant's person. In the superior courts the summons is the first process in debt or covenant; in trespass an injury having been done, an attachment issues in the first instance. The party is then attached

... This is undoubtedly the course of practice in the superior courts, and if the right of declaring in the absence of the defendant, which is now contended for, can be supported on any legal principle, it is singular that it should not be within the power of the highest courts in the country.

...

1824.

[illegible] against Lord [illegible]

it be sufficient in this case to say taliter processum est. That is sufficient where the proceedings of the court below are brought in collaterally; but here we are examining the record itself. For these reasons I think that the judgment must be reversed.

Judgment reversed.

J. [illegible] and Another against W. Moxsy, Survivor of J. Moxsy, deceased.

Where the tenant of certain premises underlet a part by deed, and the original landlord distrained for rent upon the under-tenant: Held, that assumpsit would not lie by the latter against his lessor upon an implied promise to indemnify him against the rent payable to the superior landlord.

THE first count in the declaration in substance stated that the defendant *W. Moxsy* and one *J. Moxsy* in his life-time held a certain messuage and premises in, &c., as tenants thereof to one *C. Whitmore*, for a term, a part of which, viz. nine years, was unexpired, at a rent of 40*l.* a-year; and that so holding the premises, on the 24th *October* 1815, they, by indenture, demised a part of the said messuage to the plaintiffs for the term of nine years, at the yearly rent of 30*l.* That in consideration of the premises, the defendant promised and undertook to the said plaintiffs to indemnify and save them harmless from and against the said yearly rent payable to the said *C. Whitmore*; and assigned as a breach that the defendant did not save them harmless, but that they were obliged to pay two years' ground rent to *C. Whitmore* for the years ending *Lady-day* 1822, and *Lady-day* 1823. At the trial before *Abbott* C. J., at the *London* sittings after *Hilary* term 1824, a verdict was taken for the plaintiffs for the sum of 8[illegible], subject to the opinion of the Court upon the following case: On the 29th of *September* 1806, *C. Whitmore* demised

the

.1825.

_____
Somerset against Moxon.

the premises in the declaration mentioned to one W.
Vaughn, for the term of twenty years from Michaelmas
preceding, with the usual covenants, at the yearly rent
of 40l. In the year 1815, one Wilkinson, the assignee of the said term, assigned his interest in the premises to the defendant and to J. Morsy deceased.
During the time they were in possession, viz. on the
24th of October 1815, the defendant and J. Morsy by
indenture, granted an under-lease of a part of the said
premises to the plaintiffs, from the then last Michael-
day, for the term of nine years, at the yearly rent of 8l.,
free from all parochial and parliamentary taxes, with
covenant for the payment of the rent, for quiet enjoyment, and other usual covenants; but the lease did not
contain a covenant that the lessors would indemnify the
lessees against the claim of C. Whitmore, the ground land-
lady. The plaintiffs regularly paid their rent to their
lessors up to Midsummer 1821. The two following quarters, namely, the Michaelmas and Christmas quarters, they
paid to one Wade, to whom they understood the defendant and J. Morsy had assigned all their interest in the
lease which they held under C. Whitmore. After the last
payment to Wade, who lived in the other part of the in
part demised messuage, left the same, and could not be
found. On the following quarter-day, namely, Lady-
day 1822, Mr. Whitmore, the agent of C. Whitmore,
claimed 10l. 5 year's ground rent, and three constitu-
tionland-tax, which the plaintiffs, under a threat of
distress, were compelled to pay. In March following
another year's ground rent became due, for which C. Whitmore actually distrained on the plaintiff, together with
a year's redeemed land-tax; this the plaintiff was also
obliged to pay, making altogether, including the odd-

Curwood   pences

quences of distress, 83l. 5s. 4d., leaving upon a balance 34l. 18s. 7d. claimed to be due to the plaintiffs from defendant, after deducting the 30l. yearly rent due from plaintiffs, and some other trifling items, being the sum taken by the verdict. The defendant paid the rent and taxes up to *Midsummer* 1821. One *J. Watson* being called as a witness on the part of the defendant, and required under a subpoena duces tecum for that purpose, to produce an assignment of the said term, alleged to be executed by the defendant, after the death of *J. Many*, to *Wade*, in *July* 1821, declined to produce it unless he was ordered so to do by the Lord Chief Justice; and he demurred, on the ground that it was deposited with him by *Wade* as a collateral security, and the production of it might be injurious to his interest. The Lord Chief Justice ruled that *Watson* was not bound to produce the assignment. *Wade* had never paid rent to *C. Whitmore*, but he was in possession of the original lease from *C. Whitmore* to *Nooght*, which was produced by him at the trial, and duly proved by the subscribing witness.

The questions for the opinion of the Court were,

First, whether the Lord Chief Justice should have directed the witness to produce the assignment from *Many* to *Wade*?

Secondly, if the Court should be of opinion that the witness ought not to have been required to produce the assignment, whether, under the above circumstances the plaintiffs are entitled to recover?

Thirdly, if the Court should think that the witness ought to have been directed to produce the assignment, the assignment to be considered in evidence, and whether in that case the plaintiffs are entitled to recover? To

Curwood

Chitwood for the plaintiffs. Even supposing that the Lord Chief Justice ought to have insisted upon the production of the assignment to *Wade*, still the plaintiffs would be entitled to recover. It is true, that the assignee of a lease, who again assigns his interest, is not responsible to the lessor for any breach of covenant committed while the lease is vested in him; but this is a very different case. The defendant and *J. Manny* were original lessors of part of the premises to the plaintiffs, and could not get rid of their responsibility by assigning their lease of the whole. It is stated that the under lease contained no covenant to indemnify. That is so; but by implication of law a promise arose on their part that they would indemnify the plaintiffs against all payments, save the annual rent of 20l.

Per Curiam. It is unnecessary to decide whether or not the Lord Chief Justice was right in refusing to order the production of the assignment to *Wade*, for it is perfectly clear, that no action of assumpsit can in this case be maintained on any implied promise. The parties made an express contract by deed, that excludes any implied contract. If the plaintiffs were interrupted in the quiet enjoyment of the premises, covenant would lie on the demise, *Com. Dig.* tit. *Covenant* (A. 4.) Upon this view of the case the first and second questions proposed to us become immaterial, and a nonsuit must be entered.

               Judgment of nonsuit.(d)

Campbell was to have argued for the defendant.

(d) As to the right to compel *Watson* to produce the assignment, see 5 Bark. &c. No. 1792, and the cases there collected.

Gibsy and Another against Lloyd.

DECLARATION upon a policy of insurance on goods, as per annexed statement, valued at 2800l., on the ship *Aimwell*, at and from *Liverpool* to *Jamaica*. By a memorandum, horses were *warranted free of jettison and mortality*. The declaration then stated that the defendant subscribed the policy for 200l.; that three horses, parcel of the goods valued in the statement, had been shipped at *Liverpool* on board the *Aimwell*; that the plaintiffs were interested, and then averred a loss of the horses by perils of the sea. At the trial before *Abbott* C. J., at the *London* sittings, the jury found a special verdict, stating the following facts: the order for effecting the insurance, that the three horses mentioned in the declaration were parcel of the goods valued in the statement; the payment of the premium; the subscription of the defendant; the shipment of the horses; the interest of the plaintiffs in the goods, and amongst these, of the three horses; the sailing of the vessel; and that on, &c. at, &c. the said vessel having the said three horses on board thereof, together with the other goods in the said order mentioned, the said horses (which were between decks) being at that time in good safety, and properly secured in stalls, with slings and halters, and having sufficient partitions between them, and also a person to attend to take charge of them; and the said vessel being in every respect seaworthy, sailed from the

A policy was effected on horses warranted free from mortality and jettison. In the course of the voyage, in consequence of the agitation of the ship in a storm, the horses broke down the partitions by which they were separated, and by their kicking bruised and wounded each other so much that they all died: Held, upon special verdict, that this was a loss by a peril of the sea, and that the plaintiff was entitled to recover. It was found in the special verdict that a certain usage with respect to such policies prevailed amongst the underwriters subscribing policies at *Lloyd's* coffee-house in *London*, and merchants and others effecting policies there, and that the policy in question was effected at *Lloyd's* coffee-house, but it was not found that the plaintiff was in the habit of effecting policies at that place: Held, that this usage was not sufficient to bind the plaintiff.

1828.
Gerard
against
Lawson

port of *Liverpool* aforesaid on her said voyage; and that during the night of that day the wind came on to blow very hard, with excessive squalls, and the gale continued with excessive squalls. The said three horses, by the labouring of the vessel, broke their slings, and one of them, by kicking, broke down the partition between it and the next horse, in consequence of which the remaining partition, by the kicking of the two horses which were thus brought together, was also broken down, and the three horses having then nothing to support them, were unable to stand, on account of the great rolling of the vessel; and that by their kicking they bruised and that each other so much, that about eight in the morning of the 26th two of them were found dead, having their necks broken; and being otherwise excessively bruised; and that the third was in a dying state, and in about an hour and a half afterwards it also died from the wounds and bruises it had received; and that the slings having been broken in the manner above mentioned, they could not for some time be replaced or repaired on account of the state of the weather, and from the danger of going amongst the horses, which were then loose and unsupported; and that the death of the horses was not occasioned by the neglect or default of the plaintiffs or their servants, or of the master or mariners of the vessel, in the shipping, stowing, or taking care of the horses, but was owing to the circumstances set forth in manner aforesaid. The special verdict then stated that the vessel afterwards arrived at *Jamaica* with the residue of the goods, and that the defendant had notice of the loss, and was called upon to pay his proportion of the loss, but refused so to do; and that, according to the usage and custom among insurers or underwriters

who

who were in the habit of subscribing policies of marine
insurance at Lloyd's coffee-house in London, and merchants and others effecting such policies of insurance
there, with such insurers or underwriters, there were,
before and at the time of effecting the policy in the declaration mentioned, two descriptions of policies for insuring live stock on board ships on voyages from the ports
of the United Kingdom to Jamaica and elsewhere; one
containing an exception from the perils insured against,
on a warranty of freedom from mortality; another not
containing any such exception or warranty, and which
latter description of policies usually contained words
expressly including the risk of mortality; that for, instance, by policies of the first description the premium
has been much lower, in some instances four or five,
in others six or eight times less, than for insurance
by policies of the latter description, and has been
usually the same as has been paid at the time upon
inanimate goods. And that, in case of insurances by
policies of the first description, that is, policies containing such exception of losses by mortality, the assured
have not claimed from the underwriters, and the underwriters have not paid to the assured, or been considered
liable to pay, a loss by the mortality of cattle in any
case where the vessel, on board which such cattle were,
arrived safe; but it had always been usual on policies
of the latter description, to claim and pay a loss by
mortality of cattle, in all cases where such loss had occurred, although the vessel arrived safe; and that on
policies of each of the descriptions before mentioned, if
the vessel had been lost on her voyage and the animals
drowned, the underwriters aforesaid had been in the
habit of paying to the assured.   The special verdict

3 F 2   further

further stated, that the policy of Insurance in the declaration mentioned was effected at Lloyd's coffee-house aforesaid, and was then and there signed and subscribed by the defendant, who was an insurer and underwriter there, and merchants and others .... there with such underwriters ....

This case was now argued by *Parke* for the plaintiffs, and *Campbell* for the defendant; and there were two questions, first, whether by the words of this policy the underwriter was liable for the loss accruing from the death of the animals. The arguments upon this point were in substance the same as those urged in *Lawrence v. Aberdein.* (a)

The other question was, whether, assuming that case to be well decided, the usage found by the special verdict did or did not shew, that it was the intention of the parties to the contract, that the underwriter should be exempted. It was contended for the defendant, that the usage was sufficient to explain the meaning of the parties, and to control the ambiguous language of the policy. *Pelly v. The Royal Exchange Assurance Company* (b), *Noble v. Kennoway* (c), *Ougier v. Jennings* (d), *Vallance v. Dewar* (e), and *Palmer v. Blackburn* (f) were cited; and it was urged that the usage clearly shewed that it was not intended that the underwriters should be liable for a loss of this description .... at Lloyd's Coffee .... that they had knowledge of ....

For the plaintiffs it was contended, that the usage found was not sufficient to bind the plaintiff. The facts at Lloyd's Coffee-house ....

it would have given .... on the ....

(a) 3 B. & A. 107.   (b) ....
(c) Doug. 510.   (d) 1 Camp. 505.
(e) 1 Camp. 503.   (f) 1 Bing. 61.

stated

1825.

Great
against
Lloyd

stated were merely evidence, from which the jury might
have drawn a conclusion that there was a usage. The
usage found was confined to insurers or underwriters
in the habit of subscribing policies at Lloyd's Coffee-
house, and merchants and others effecting such policies
there with such underwriters; but it was not found
that the plaintiffs were in the habit of effecting policies
at that place. There was nothing, therefore, to shew
that the plaintiffs had any knowledge of such a usage.
Now the principle upon which usage is received as
evidence to explain the ambiguous language of a
policy is, that the parties to it are supposed to contract with a knowledge of that usage. Here it does
not appear that the plaintiffs had any knowledge of the
usage, and they cannot be supposed to have contracted
with reference to it.

All the Court were of opinion, that the usage found
in this case was not sufficient to take it out of the rule
laid down in *Lawrence* v. *Aberdein* (a), inasmuch as it
was not found to be the general usage of the whole
trade in the city of *London*, but only in one house
where policies were usually effected by private individuals. If there had been any evidence to shew that
the plaintiffs were in the habit of effecting policies
at *Lloyd*'s Coffee-house, the jury ought to have found
that they had knowledge of the usage which prevailed
there. A court of law does not know judicially what
proportion of the policies effected in *London* are effected
at *Lloyd*'s Coffee-house; and even if that had been found,
it would only be evidence of the usage in *London*, and

(a) 5 B. & A. 107.

the

the jury ought to have found the fact of an existing usage : here there was no usage found sufficient to bind the plaintiffs.

As to the other point, the whole court were of opinion, that this case fell within the decision in the case of *Lawrence* v. *Aberdein*, and *Abbott* C. J., *Bayley* J., and *Holroyd* J., said, that they thought that case properly decided, and that they had heard nothing to induce them to alter the opinion which they had then formed. *Littledale* J. said, he doubted whether he should have concurred in the decision in the case of *Lawrence* v. *Aberdein*, but that he thought this case was not distinguishable from it.

Judgment for the plaintiffs.

IRESON *against* PEARMAN, Gent., One, &c.

ASSUMPSIT against an attorney for negligence. Plea, the general issue. At the trial before *Hullock* B. at the *Warwick* Spring assizes 1824, the jury found a verdict for the plaintiff, with 600*l.* damages. The defendant having moved for a new trial, the Court directed the facts to be stated in a special case.

The plaintiff had contracted for the purchase of an estate, consisting of freehold lands and premises, at the sum of 3400*l.*, from one *Joseph Burbidge*, who had contracted to sell the same to the plaintiff in fee. And in

In an action for negligence against an attorney who was employed by a purchaser to inspect the title to an estate, it appeared that by indentures of lease and release of the 9th and 10th of October 1796, the estate had been conveyed to T. M., the father of the vendor's wife, and to J. C.,

to hold unto the said *T. M.* and *J. C.*, and their heirs and assigns, to the use and behoof of the said *T. M.* and *J. C.*, and the heirs and assigns of the said *T. M.* for ever, the estate of *J. C.* being used only in trust for the said *T. M*, his heirs and assigns. *T. M.* devised the estate to his daughter and to the heirs of her body, but in case she died without leaving any issue of her body living at her decease, then to his nephew *T. M.*, and his heirs for ever. The daughter afterwards, by bargain and sale of the 11th of *February* 1814, conveyed the estate to one *J. W.*, to the intent that he might become tenant of the freehold for the purpose of suffering a recovery, and a recovery was suffered in pursuance of such deed. The daughter afterwards, by deeds of lease and release of the 4th and 5th *March* 1814, executed upon her marriage, reciting that she was seised in fee simple of the estate, conveyed the same to two trustees in trust for her and her husband and their issue, and in default of issue, to such person as she should appoint. The marriage was afterwards solemnised, and the daughter died without issue, and devised the estate in fee to her husband, who survived her. The husband having contracted to sell the estate to the plaintiff, in pursuance of that contract, delivered an abstract of his title to the defendant, as attorney to the vendee, and this abstract contained the deeds of the 9th and 10th of *October* 1796, but it omitted to state certain indentures of lease and release of the 25th and 26th *February* 1814, whereby *J. C.* conveyed the estate vested in him unto the daughter of *T. M.* in fee, but an abstract of these deeds was delivered by the vendor's solicitor to the defendant four months before the conveyance of the estate was executed. The defendant laid before counsel a case containing an abstract of the deed of the 11th of *Feb.* 1814, and of the recovery suffered in pursuance of it, of the deeds of the 4th and 5th *March* 1814, and of the will of the daughter of *T. M.*, but omitting altogether the deeds of the 9th and 10th *October* 1796, and it further stated that *T. M.* was seised in fee of the premises. The opinion of counsel was, that the vendor had a good title, but that opinion would not have been given if the deeds of lease and release of the 9th and 10th *October* 1796, or those of the 25th and 26th *February* 1814 had been stated. The plaintiff afterwards, being advised that his title was incomplete, paid a sum of money to *T. M.*, the devisee in remainder, for a confirmation of his title: Held, first, that the recovery suffered by the daughter of *T. M.* was invalid, because at that time the legal estate for life was in *J. C.*, and she was only equitable tenant for life with a legal remainder in tail, and therefore that the title was bad.

Held, secondly, that upon these facts a jury were warranted in finding the defendant guilty of negligence so as to make him liable in this action.

the

the year 1808 the plaintiff employed the defendant as his attorney to inquire into and inspect the title of Burbridge to this estate. By indentures of lease and release of the 9th and 10th of October 1766 respectively, the estate in question was conveyed to Thomas Malin the father of Wagstaff, late wife of the said Burbridge, the vendor, and to one John Caldecott, to hold unto the said T. Malin and J. Caldecott, and their heirs and assigns, to the only proper use and behoof of the said T. Malin and J. Caldecott, and the heirs and assigns of the said T. Malin for ever, (the estate of the said J. Caldecott being used only in trust for the said T. Malin, his heirs and assigns). Malin, by his will of the 1th April 1807, gave and devised the said estate to his daughter Elizabeth Malin, and to the heirs of her body; but in case she died without leaving any issue of her body lawfully begotten, and living at her decease, then he gave and devised the estate to his nephew Thomas Malin, and to his heirs for ever. E. Malin, the daughter, afterwards married one Wagstaff, and after his death, on the 11th of February 1814, by indenture of bargain and sale of that estate duly inrolled, the said E. Wagstaff therein described as only child and devisee in tail generally, under the last will and testament of T. Malin deceased, granted, bargained, sold, and confirmed the said estate to one J. T. Whittle, to hold to Whittle, his heirs and assigns, to the intent that he might become a tenant of the freehold, against whom a good and perfect recovery might be suffered; whereupon J. Downer was to be defendant, the said E. Wagstaff vouchee, to the use of E. Wagstaff, her heirs and assigns for ever. A recovery on this deed was suffered in Hilary term, 54 G. 3, whereby the said J. Downer

J. Dawson was demandant, J. T. Wratislaw tenant, E. Wagstaff vouchee, and E. F. Martin common vouchee of the said estate.

B. Wagstaff, by indentures of lease and release, and settlement, of the 4th and 5th March 1814, of four parts, and made between the said E. Wagstaff of the first part, J. Burbidge of the second part, J. Drayson, and W. Dexter of the third part, and J. Dawson and J. T. Wratislaw of the fourth part; after reciting that the said E. Wagstaff was seised in fee simple of the said estate, and that a marriage was intended to be had between said E. Wagstaff and J. Burbidge, the same was limited and assured to the said J. Drayson and W. Dexter, in trust for the said E. Wagstaff and J. Burbidge, and the issue of said marriage; and in default of issue to such person as she should appoint by deed, or by her last will and testament in writing direct, limit, or appoint. The marriage between J. Burbidge and E. Wagstaff was afterwards duly solemnized, and she died without issue, leaving the said J. Burbidge her surviving, having by her will of the 28th of August 1815, made under the said power, given, devised, and bequeathed the said estate, to the use of her husband, J. Burbidge, his heirs, executors, administrators, and assigns for ever. J. Burbidge, after the death of his wife, having contracted to sell the estate to the plaintiff in fee, in pursuance of such contract an abstract of his title, as vendor, containing sixty-five brief sheets, was sent by the vendor's attorney to the defendant as attorney for the vendee, containing amongst other things, the deeds of the 9th and 10th of October 1796, and the defendant received the same in that character; but in that abstract the vendor's attorney wholly omitted to state certain indentures of lease and release, dated the 25th and 26th of February

1814,

1814, made between J. Caldecott of the one part, and E. Wagstaff of the other part, whereby J. Caldecott conveyed the said estate vested in him unto the said E. Wagstaff, to hold unto the use of E. Wagstaff, her heirs, and assigns; but an abstract of those deeds was delivered by the vendor's solicitor to the defendant on the 27th March 1818. The conveyance and assignment of the estate to the plaintiff were executed on the 24th July 1818. J. Caldecott is still living. The defendant, in the course of the said employment, after such receipt, instead of sending the original abstract, or a complete copy thereof, for the consideration and advice of counsel, prepared and sent to R. Preston, Esq., the counsel whom he consulted, a case, as and for an abstract, containing only eight brief sheets, being part of the abstract of sixty-five brief sheets, commencing the account of title with the will of T. Malin. The abstract of sixty-five sheets included sixty years' title. The abstract of eight brief sheets contained an abstract of the will of the said T. Malin, of the deed of the 11th of February 1814, of the recovery of Hilary term, 54 G. 3., of the deeds of the 4th and 5th March 1814, and of the will of Elizabeth Burbidge, of the 28th of August 1815, and omitted altogether to mention the deeds of the 9th and 10th October 1796. Upon occasions of this sort, it is most usual for the vendee's attorney to send to the counsel whose opinion he takes the original abstract as he receives it from the vendor's attorney, but the practice is not always so. At the end of the said case of eight brief sheets, the defendant stated the following case, and laid the same before Mr. Preston viz. "Case, Thomas Malin, the testator (in p. 1.) was seised in fee of the premises described in p. 4. to be situate in Woolcott, in the parish

parish of *Grandborough* (he having purchased the same),
subject to a mortgage which he made thereon for 2000
years, for securing 2400l. and interest, 1000l. of which
was due at his decease, the residue having been repaid
by him. Mr. T. *Ireson* has purchased the premises described in p. 4., of Mr. *Burbidge*, the devisee under his
wife's will: you will please to advise whether Mr. *Burbidge* can make a good title to the said premises to Mr.
Ireson, and by what means." Upon which case Mr.
Preston gave the following opinion: " A good title may
be made by Mr. *Burbidge* and his mortgagee to Mr.
Ireson. The conveyance should be made by indentures
of lease and release from Mr. *Burbidge*, and by an assignment of the residue of the term of 2000 years, to
attend the inheritance. Judgments, if any, of which
there is notice and crown debts against Mr. *Burbidge*,
are incumbrances. The widow (if any) of *Thomas
Malin* is dowable." In consequence of the omission of
the deeds of the 9th and 10th of *October* 1795, Mr.
Preston gave the opinion above stated, which opinion he
would not have given if those deeds had been set out in
the case or abstract laid before him; and he stated,
that if the deeds of the 25th and 26th *February* 1814
had been set out in the case, that also would have made a
difference in his opinion. Under these circumstances,
the plaintiff being advised that his title was incomplete,
paid 700l. to *Thomas Malin*, the devisee, in remainder,
under the will of *T. Malin* the testator, for confirmation
of his title, who, accordingly, in consideration thereof, in
February 1822 executed to the plaintiff certain deeds of
lease and release for that purpose. The plaintiff also
paid on this occasion the attorney whom he employed
in procuring this confirmation, two several sums of 170l.

and

and ... for his ... trouble, ... expence ... relating
thereto. The case was argued by ... on
that an equitable estate cannot, in suffering a recovery,
... E. Thomson for the plaintiff. The recovery was
inoperative, because *Caldecott*, who had a prior estate of
freehold, did not join in it; and consequently the fine
was defective. Secondly, the defendant, by not laying
the whole abstract before counsel, but taking upon himself to judge what the title was, was guilty of a degree
of negligence of which the law will take notice. As to
the first point, it is quite clear that *John Caldecott* was,
by survivorship, seised of a prior legal estate of freehold;
for, by the deeds of the 9th and 10th of *October* 1796, the
estate were conveyed to *Thomas Mills* and *John Caldecott*, habendum to them, their heirs, and assigns, to the
only proper use and behoof of them and the heirs and
assigns of *Mills* for ever. Upon the death of *Mills*,
therefore, *Caldecott* was seised of a legal estate of freehold for life, and *Mills*'s daughter had an equitable
estate for life, with the legal remainder in tail under her
father's will. Now it is a well established rule that, in
order to suffer a valid recovery, the whole estate must
be either legal or equitable; and therefore, although a
recovery suffered by a cestui que trust in tail who is in
possession under the trustee, will effectually bar that
estate tail, and the equitable reversion depending thereon,
although there be no legal behoof to the *præcipe*,
Champernowne v. *North* (a), yet such recovery will not
affect a legal remainder, *Robinson* v. *Cuming*. (b) In
the same case, ... the recovery ... which ...,
10th of *October* 1796, were not executed by the statute;
and if that be so, then ... took ... legal estate for ...

(b) 1 *Atk.* 475. *Forrester*, 167. (c) 1 *Bro. Cha. Ca.* 73.

party

1825.

Pascoe
against
Pascoe.

the land, for this seemed the intent of the parties by the limitation of the use. Assuming that the statute does apply to this case, the estate tail of Mrs. *Wagstaff* was equitable, at all events during the life of *Caldecott.* The conveyance is to *Malin* and *Caldecott* for life, remainder to the heirs of *Malin.* The estate tail to Mrs. *Wagstaff* continued equitable until it was destroyed. . There was an equitable tenant to the præcipe, and an equitable contingent remainder until the recovery was suffered. It might have been different if Mrs. *Wagstaff* had out-lived *Caldecott,* and then suffered the recovery; for her equitable estate tail would then have been at an end. But here she acquired the fee during the life of *Caldecott;* and *Doe* v. *Selby* (a) shews that the happening of an event may alter the nature of an estate.

Supposing the estate legal, and that the statute of uses applies, and that the use to *Malin* in fee was executed by the statute, and that Mrs. *Wagstaff* consequently had the legal estate tail, still the remainder to *T. Malin* was a contingent, and not a vested remainder, and was destroyed by the destruction of the preceding particular estate (viz. Mrs. *Wagstaff's* estate for life), before it vested. The remainder to *T. Malin* was contingent on the determination of the estate tail in a particular manner, viz. by the failure of issue of Mrs. *Wagstaff* during her life. The particular estate on which this contingent remainder depends has been destroyed, first, by the operation of the bargain and sale; 2dly, by the operation of the recovery considered as operating by way of estoppel; 3dly, by the merger of the particular estate in the reversion in fee. First, the bargain and sale put the estate tail in abeyance, *Co. Litt.* 331 a.

(a) 2 B. & C. 926.

But

But assuming that the whole estate tail passes to the bargainee, and that he takes a base fee, still it is not the same estate which was in the bargainor. The estate in the bargainee is defeasible two ways; first, by failure of issue in the tenant in tail; secondly, by the entry of the issue. But the estate in Mrs. *Wagstaff* is determinable one way only, therefore it is not the same estate. Now it must be the same estate, in point of quantity, to support the contingent remainder. *Fearne's Cont. Rem.* 338. Here the bargain and sale by the tenant in tail effects an alteration in the quantity of the estate, because the estate is defeasible by a different mode of determining it, viz. by entry of the issue in tail. The alienee has a base fee, not co-extensive with the estate tail. Secondly, the particular estate has been destroyed by the operation of the recovery; *Wratislaw* and Mrs. *W.* suffered a common recovery. This passed the interest of the parties by estoppel; *Shep. Touchstone,* 48., 10 *Modern,* 45., *Godbolt,* 147.; and the destruction of the particular estate destroys the remainder. A recovery by tenant for life will bar a contingent remainder, *Goodright* v. *Dunham* (a), *Goodtitle* v. *Billington* (b); but a conveyance by bargain and sale, or lease and release, by tenant for life will not. A conveyance by recovery, though void, as against the remainder man, must operate in some different way from a conveyance by lease and release. The distinction is, that a feoffment and recovery give a tortious fee, and not merely the part of the inheritance, which was rightful and in the bargainor. It may be said, that the tenant in tail being only tenant in tail in remainder, a tortious fee could not be created by the

(a) 1 *Doug.* 264.   (b) 2 *Doug.* 753.

recovery

recovery of such tenant in tail, part of the rightful fee being in *Childcot*, the tenant for life.[?] But the recovery and the subsequent extinction of the tenant for life then operated with no power to destroy the contingent remainder. This common recovery is the security of the fee by mercantile vigilant claimant, and he recovers the whole fee, and not that party only which the recoveree had. The recoverer had a right to have an estate in fee against Mrs. *W.* The only person who could contest it at that time was the tenant for life. But he, on the 25th and 26th of February 1814, conveyed to Mrs. *W.* in fee; therefore she has a fee simple in possession good against every body, except the issue in tail. Nobody could enter upon her possession. If she had had issue, such issue after her death would have taken the wrongful fee, and been remitted by law to the rightful estate tail (a). In that case the contingent remainder, if it had depended upon any other contingency, would have revested.

Thirdly, the contingent remainder is destroyed by the merger of Mrs. *W.*'s estate tail in the fee. She was tenant in tail by devise, with reversion in fee by descent from her father. So long as her tenancy in tail remained unaltered, there was no merger; 2 *Cruise's Digest*, tit. IV. s. 42. p. 429. The statute De Donis protects it. But here, the tenancy in tail is converted into a base fee by the bargain and sale and by the recovery, and a base fee will merge, 2 *Prest. Conv.* 240. [illegible]

But if the title was defective, still an attorney is liable only for *crassa* negligentia; *Pitt v. Yalden* (b), *Baikie v. Chandless* (c). There was not in this case that species of negligence. The defendant laid the case before counsel, in
_____
[in remainder; a torturous fee could not be created in the]
(a) Co. Litt. 333. b.   (b) 4 Burr. 2060.   (c) 3 Camp. 17.

order to obtain his opinion, whether the vendor could make a good title. An attorney is not bound to lay an abstract before counsel in every case; he may exercise his own discretion on the title. If he gives the best opinion he can, and shews a reasonable degree of knowledge, he is not liable, even if that opinion be erroneous; he does not warrant the title. Besides, the deeds of the 25th and 26th of *February* 1814 were not contained in the abstract of the title, so that he had not an opportunity of laying them before his counsel; and the recital in the deeds of the 4th and 5th of *March* 1814, that Mrs. *Wagstaff* was seised in fee, removed any suspicion that *Malin* had died before *Caldecott*. At all events this was a voluntary exposure of his title by the plaintiff, which the remainder man could not compel him to shew. The defendant's only object could be to save expence to his client.

Cur. adv. vult.

BAYLEY J. This was an action against the defendant, who was an attorney, employed on behalf of the purchaser of an estate. An abstract of the title was delivered to him by the vendor, and he from that assumed that one *Thomas Malin* was seised in fee. The title depends on the deeds of 1796, which conveyed the estate to *Malin* and *Caldecott*, habendum to them and their heirs and assigns, to the use and behoof of *Malin* and *Caldecott*, and the heirs and assigns of *Malin* for ever. The legal effect of those deeds was to give to *Caldecott* and *Malin* an estate for life as joint tenants, with an inheritance in fee vested in *Malin*. *Malin*, by will, devised the estate to his daughter in tail. She, in 1814, suffered a recovery, and the validity of the title depends on the validity

lidity or invalidity of that recovery. The other question
was, whether there was that species of negligence in the
defendant which will make him liable in this action.
Caldecott survived *Malin*, and his life estate continued at
law, and the devise by *Malin* to his daughter would
only convey the estate tail, expectant upon the determination of *Caldecott's* life estate. In *Caldecott's* lifetime
Malin's daughter suffered a common recovery, and in
order to do that, she made a conveyance of the estate to
J. Wratislaw, in order to make him a tenant to the præcipe. At that time she had no legal estate in her, except a remainder in tail, expectant on the determination
of *Caldecott's* life estate; and if there was not a good
tenant to the præcipe, the recovery is bad. Then what
was the situation of the daughter? *Caldecott* was tenant
for life, and trustee for her and her heirs in tail; she
had an equitable estate pur autre vie, so long as *Caldecott*
lived, and a legal remainder in tail. Now a recovery
may be suffered by a legal or an equitable tenant in tail;
but then the person having the legal or equitable estate
for life must be tenant to the præcipe, except in the instance of the case provided for by the stat. 14 G. 2. c. 20.
as to leases for lives. Here there was no concurrence of
the tenant for life. The recovery was therefore suffered
by a person at law having only a remainder in tail, and
that was clearly an invalid recovery. It is true, that
the party who made the tenant to the præcipe in this
case had a preceding equitable estate for life. But it is
established by *Shapland* v. *Smith*, and *Salvin* v. *Thornton*,
that an equitable estate for life and a legal remainder in
tail will not unite, so as to make a good recovery; and
that in order to make a good tenant to the præcipe,
there should be a legal estate for life, with a legal re-

3 G 2   mainder

mainder in tail, or an equitable estate for life with an equitable remainder in tail. This is broadly laid down in *Shapland* v. *Smith*. But it has been contended, that although this recovery be void, the plaintiff has sustained no injury, because the estate tail upon which *Malin's* contingent remainder depended was destroyed, and therefore that the remainder was destroyed. The answer to that is, that the conveyance by the daughter to the tenant to the præcipe, could convey no more than she had; and, therefore, that it did not displace the remainder. Then it was said that the conveyance by *Caldecott* to her destroyed the contingent remainder. But the recovery could have no previous operation, therefore *Caldecott's* conveyance to her might make her tenant in tail in possession, but could not have the effect of destroying the remainder. *Doe* v. *Jones* (a) is an authority to shew that no act by a remainder man in tail can destroy the estate tail, it can only be done by tenant in tail in possession. The plaintiff, therefore, having sustained damage by reason of this defect of title, the remaining question is, whether the defendant was guilty of negligence? The court is not bound in this case to say whether there was negligence, but only whether there was evidence to justify the jury in finding that the defendant was guilty of negligence; and we are of opinion that there was. In stating the case laid before Mr. *Preston*, the defendant assumed that *Malin* was tenant in fee, instead of setting out the deeds, which would have shewn that *Caldecott* had an estate for life. Now, although it may not be part of the duty of an attorney to know the legal operation of conveyances, yet it is his duty to take care not to draw wrong conclusions from the deeds laid be-

(a) 1 *B. & C.* 258.

fore

fore him, but to state the deeds to the counsel whom he consults, or he must draw conclusions at his peril. It therefore appears to us, that, in omitting those deeds, and erroneously describing *Malin* as tenant in fee, there was negligence in the defendant. There is another circumstance from which negligence may be inferred. The defendant received the abstract in *February* 1818, and that contained no notice of the deeds whereby *Caldecott* conveyed to Mrs. *Wagstaff*; but they were supplied to him before any conveyance was made, and he never enquired of Mr. *Preston* whether those deeds made any difference in his opinion; and they undoubtedly would; for if *Malin* was seised in fee, how could *Caldecott* have any thing to convey? For these reasons we are of opinion, first, that the title is defective; and, secondly, that there was evidence before the jury sufficient to justify them in coming to the conclusion that the defendant was guilty of a species of negligence sufficient to make him liable in this action. The judgment of the Court must, therefore, be for the plaintiff.

Judgment for the plaintiff.

NOCKELS *against* CROSBY, MITCHELL, and Another.

ASSUMPSIT for money had and received. Defendant pleaded the general issue, and paid 252*l*. 11*s*, into court. At the trial before *Abbott* C. J. at the *London* sittings after *Hilary* term 1824, a verdict was found for the plaintiff for 47*l*. 15*s*., subject to the opinion of the Court upon the following case: The defendants were the directors of a scheme called the " *British* Metropolitan Tontine." A printed paper was circulated with their authority, stating (amongst other things) that to effect the objects of the scheme it was proposed to receive subscriptions of ten shillings a week from each member for the period of one year, viz. from the 1st of *January* 1821, to the 1st of *January* 1822, and that the total amount of such year's subscription should be deemed a share, and all such shares form one capital or joint stock of the company, with benefit of survivorship; that the amount of the subscriptions would be vested in the names of the trustees, and from time to time laid out in government or other securities, the net proceeds and interest of which would be equally divided among all surviving shareholders twice in every year; that members were to subscribe their names to the company's rules and regulations at the time of opening their subscriptions, or at any subsequent convenient

be laid out at interest, and to enure to the benefit of the survivors; the subscribers were to be governed by regulations made by the directors, and at the end of a year, shares were to be issued and to be transferrable: Held, that this was not an undertaking within the operation of the bubble act.

time,

time, and to abide thereby; that the management of the company was vested in eight directors; and that at the expiration of the year every subscriber would receive a shareholder's ticket, which would be saleable or transferrable. The above was the paper referred to in the following agreement, which was signed by the plaintiff and several other persons: " We whose names are hereunder subscribed do hereby consent and agree to, and with the present and any future directors of the *British* Metropolitan Tontine as follows: first, we do each of us agree to become subscribers thereto, and to take such numbers of shares upon such life or lives as is or are set forth against our respective names; secondly, we do acknowledge the plan or prospectus hereto annexed to contain the nature and intent of the said Tontine, so far as the same is therein expressed, and do ratify the same in every respect, and agree to abide thereby; thirdly, we do agree to ratify and confirm all rules, laws, and regulations passed, or which shall at any time hereafter pass, for the further promotion, direction, management, and carrying into effect the said Tontine, and to sign any deed or deeds to that effect; fourthly, we do agree to pay our subscriptions for one year." An account was opened with *Glyn* and Co., bankers in *London*, entitled " *British* Metropolitan Tontine." The plaintiff paid two sums of money, amounting together, to 308*l.* 6*s.*, to the aforesaid account at Messrs. *Glyn* and Co's. Various other subscribers to the Tontine paid sums of money to the said account, amounting in the whole, with the plaintiff's payments, to 737*l.* 10*s.* 6*d.* In the books of the Metropolitan Tontine the following resolutions are entered:

3 G 4 "General

" General resolutions of the 19th *January* 1821.

" First, that the books of the Tontine be opened to receive subscriptions, and that no less than 2*l.* per share shall be received in the first instance, being for the first monthly subscription.

" Secondly, that the affairs and entire management of the concerns of the Tontine be vested in eight directors, any three of whom to be a sufficient quorum for the purpose of transacting business.

" Thirdly, that *James Pope* be appointed secretary and solicitor to the directors of the Tontine, and that for such secretaryship he be paid such yearly salary as the present or any future directors may think fit.

" Fourthly, that all monies to be received under or in virtue of the Tontine be paid into the hands of the treasurer or treasurers thereof, and that no monies be drawn for or paid by the treasurer or treasurers unless by draft, to be signed by not less than three of the directors.

" Fifthly, that the directors do, as often as occasion may require, place out at interest, in the names of the trustees, in government or other securities all sums of money remaining in the hands of the treasurer."

" 30th *August* 1822.

" Resolved by a quorum of the directors present that, there not being a sufficient sum subscribed to warrant the further prosecution of the scheme, the subscribers have returned to them the amount of the subscriptions less the expences attending the same, and that such expences be ascertained at another meeting of the directors to be held at the secretary's house the 6th of *September* next."

" *Old*

" *Old Bethlem*, 6th *September* 1822.

" Resolved by a quorum of the directors present that the expences attending the prosecuting the scheme of the Tontine do amount to the sum of 3*l.* 19*s.* 7*d.* per share, and that each subscriber do have the amount of his subscription returned, less the said 3*l.* 19*s.* 7*d.* per share."

On the 27th of *May* 1822, the plaintiff wrote to the directors, requesting to have his money returned immediately, and said, he understood it was to be returned subject to some small charge, and he did not then make any objection to the charge.

On the 25th of *July* 1822, he again wrote and complained of the delay in returning his money; and that he had "been put off from time to time in consequence of charges attending the concern."

In *September* 1822 several checques signed by the defendants were drawn on *Glyn* and Co. for different sums, amounting in the whole to the said sum of 737*l.* 10*s.* 6*d.*, which checques were paid by them from the money paid into the aforesaid account. One of such checques for 252*l.* 11*s.* was made payable to the plaintiff or bearer, and placed by the defendants in the hands of Mr. *Pope*, the secretary, with instructions to deliver it to the plaintiff; but the plaintiff refused to accept the same in satisfaction of his claim; and the said Mr. *Pope*, without the knowledge or authority of the said defendants, paid the said checque into his own private account at the bank of *England*, through which the same was presented to and paid by *Glyn* and Co. Previous to the commencement of the present action the plaintiff had sued G. C. *Glyn*, one of the partners in the banking-house of *Glyn* and Co., for the money sought to be recovered in this action, but

but had afterwards discontinued that suit. On the trial, Mr. *Pope*, the secretary of the Metropolitan Tontine, being called as a witness for the defendants, stated, that the expences of the institution amounted to 3*l.* 19*s.* 7*d.* a share making 47*l.* 15*s.* on the plaintiff's twelve shares; that the expences consisted in stationery, printing, advertisements, postages, and 75*l.* paid to the witness for his trouble; that he explained this to the plaintiff, and offered him the balance, 252*l.* 11*s.*, which he refused; that none of the money was appropriated to their own use by any of the defendants. He further stated, that the money paid by the subscribers was not laid out at interest, but remained in the hands of the bankers with whom the account was opened, and that the defendant, *George Mitchell*, and the witness alone caused the prospectus to be put forth, and prosecuted the scheme themselves. That the defendant, *Crosby*, was not a subscriber, and that he attended one meeting only when the checques were signed.

Campbell, for the plaintiff. The plaintiff is entitled to recover back the whole sum advanced. The consideration upon which it was paid failed; the money was, therefore, in the hands of the defendants money had and received to the plaintiff's use. It will, perhaps, be urged as a defence, that the scheme was within the bubble act, 6 *G.* 1. *c.* 18.: but first it was not so; and even if the Court should think it was, still the scheme was abandoned, and never carried in any degree into effect. The illegality of it, therefore, cannot alter the present plaintiff's rights. This was not within the bubble act, it was not to carry on any wild trading speculation, which manifestly tended to the prejudice of the subscribers,

subscribers, but was a mere association to contribute money with a benefit of survivorship. But even if this were otherwise, the plaintiff would be entitled to recover. When a person sues to recover back money paid on a consideration that has failed, then it is money had and received to his use, and the nature of the consideration is out of the question: *Farmer* v. *Russell.* (a) If money paid to a stakeholder on an illegal wager is paid over, it cannot be recovered back; but the rule is otherwise if the money has not been paid over, *Cotton* v. *Thurland* (b), *Smith* v. *Bickmore.* (c) Here, the defendants took no steps towards the performance of the contract upon which the money was paid in. It remained wholly unproductive from *January* 1821 till *August* 1822, when the scheme was abandoned; the plaintiff is therefore entitled to recover back the whole sum advanced. [*Holroyd* J. Suppose five persons enter into partnership, and contribute 1000*l.* each, they afterwards find the concern a losing one, and put an end to it, can any one maintain an action against the others for his share?] Perhaps not; but this is a different case; at most it was only a proposed partnership, and nothing was done towards carrying it into effect; and it is most fit that those persons who proposed the scheme should bear the expences. Besides, the directors had no power to make a resolution to deduct the expences out of the monies contributed; they had power to make resolutions for carrying on the concern, but not for the abandonment of it; the plaintiff, therefore, was not bound by the resolution in question.

(a) 1 B. & P. 296.　　　(b) 5 T. R. 405.　　　(c) 4 Taunt. 474.

E. *Lawes*

E. Lawes contrâ. The defendants are clearly entitled to deduct the money in dispute from the amount paid in by the plaintiff. They did not warrant that the concern would answer, but only proposed that it should be tried, and the abandonment of the scheme was with the plaintiff's assent. That appears from his letters, which were written before the resolution to put an end to the concern was made. They also shew that he agreed to pay his proportion of the expences, for he alludes to the proposed deduction of part of his money to pay those expences, and does not object to it. But it does not appear that the defendants ever received any of the plaintiff's money; they only gave an order to *Pope*; and he received, and now has the money. If that were not so, still this action could not be maintained. All the shareholders were jointly interested in the funds of the concern, and the defendants have never stated any account, or bound themselves to pay over any sum to the plaintiff. [*Bayley* J. *Crosby* was not interested in the money.] Then the action was improperly commenced against him. In the next place, this scheme falls within the 6 G. 1. c. 18. s. 18. That act is not confined to trading speculations; and here books were opened for public subscriptions; small sums were collected, amounting in the whole to a large sum, the shareholders acted as a corporation, having agreed to be bound by the resolutions and bye-laws of the directors, and the shares were to be transferrable. It is therefore precisely similar to that which was determined to be illegal in *Josephs* v. *Pebrer*. (a) [*Bayley* J. It might be intended to make the shares transferrable,

(a) *Ante*, 639.

but

but in fact no shares were ever issued.] The intent to make them so was, together with the other circumstances, in itself illegal, and the whole transaction being illegal, no right of action can arise out of it. [*Littledale* J. It seems to be nothing more than an agreement by the subscribers to be joint tenants of the money subscribed.]

BAYLEY J. I am of opinion that the plaintiff is entitled to recover the whole sum which he advanced. There is no difficulty in some of the points urged, viz. that the money was not received by the defendants, or that it was drawn out and applied with the concurrence of the plaintiff. The money was originally paid by the plaintiff into the hands of certain persons, who, for the purposes of this concern, were the bankers of the defendants, and it was paid upon a prospect that it should be in the bankers' hands in furtherance of a continuing scheme. It was afterwards drawn out by the defendants, and it was their duty to see to the proper application of it. If they had paid the whole to the plaintiff, or according to his directions, of course he could not complain; but if they applied a part of it without his assent, and in a mode which the law did not warrant, the plaintiff clearly has a right to recover, unless it can be shewn that he was party to a scheme within the 6. G. 1. c. 18. The scheme was not within that statute, unless it was formed for the purpose of carrying on some mischievous project or undertaking, and unless we can predicate of it that it was likely to tend to the common grievance, prejudice, and inconvenience of his majesty's subjects, or great numbers of them in their trade, commerce, or other lawful affairs. The cases of *Rex* v.
Webb

Webb (a) and *Pratt* v. *Hutchinson* (b) were decided on that principle. I think that we cannot assume, as a matter of law, that this scheme was within the description before given. It is true that a large sum, made up of many small payments, was to be collected; but that was not to be invested in any general speculation, but merely to enure to the benefit of the survivors. Primâ facie the principal effect of the scheme would be to encourage the saving of money. But this action might be maintained even if the scheme were within the act, for it proved abortive, and no transferrable shares were ever created, and the period had not arrived at which it would have been within the operation of the statute. The defendants then having possession of the plaintiff's money, applied it without his express assent. Do they shew any matter of law sufficient to justify that application of it? The scheme was set on foot by *Pope* and the defendants, and the prospectus was circulated with their assent. On all projects some expence must be incurred before many members join the concern. Upon whom should that fall? Undoubtedly, if the scheme proves abortive, it should fall upon the original projectors, and not upon those who advance their money on the faith of its going on. The plaintiff did nothing to render himself liable to the expences, and it was the duty of the defendants within a reasonable time to lay out in securities the money received. They never did so, but kept it for eighteen months in their bankers' hands, and appear to have acted throughout as if they thought the undertaking must fail. For these reasons, I think that the plaintiff is entitled to the whole of the money

(a) 14 *East*, 406.   (b) 15 *East*, 511.

which

which he advanced; and it is also observable that, by the third resolution of the directors, *Pope* was to have such annual salary as the defendants should fix; they never fixed any; it is therefore questionable whether that would not of itself be sufficient to prevent them from deducting that part of the money sought to be retained which was paid to Mr. *Pope.*

HOLROYD J. At the commencement of the argument I entertained great doubts upon this question, but am now satisfied that the plaintiff is entitled to recover. There is not sufficient in the case to warrant the payment of any part of the money detained to *Pope*; for even supposing the concern to have gone so far as to authorise the appointment of a salary to him, still in point of fact none was appointed. It appeared to me at first that this was very like the case of a partnership, which I put during the argument; but here the concern was never really set agoing; and I think that the expences incurred in setting a scheme on foot are not to be paid out of the concern unless they are adopted when it is actually in operation. In the present case a very small sum was collected, and that was not invested in government or other securities, which, by the prospectus, were to be the only source of profit. No tontine could exist until the money was laid out. All the steps taken were therefore only preparatory to carrying the project into effect, and as it never was carried into effect, I think that the plaintiff is entitled to have back the whole of the money that he advanced.

LITTLEDALE J. I also am of opinion that the plaintiff is entitled to recover upon this general principle, that

if

if persons set a scheme afoot, and assume to be the directors or managers, all the expences incurred before the scheme is in actual operation must, in the first instance, be borne by them. When it is in operation, the expences and charge of management should be borne by the concern, and then it may be fair that the preliminary expences should be paid in the same way; for then the subscribers have the benefit of them. The prospectus put forth by these defendants stated that the money subscribed was to be placed out at interest. The plaintiff's sole object in paying the money must have been to have it so placed out, but during eighteen months it remained idle at the bankers. Suppose there had been no subscribers, then the projectors must have paid all the expences. If, then, one person only subscribes, are all those expences to be cast upon him? The hardship and injustice would be monstrous; yet that would be the consequence in such a case were we now to hold that the plaintiff was liable to a proportion of the expences incurred by these defendants. With respect to the supposed partnership, it is plain that there could be none until the money was laid out in execution of the proposed scheme. I am therefore clearly of opinion that the plaintiff was entitled to recover.

Postea to the plaintiff.

1825.

THOMAS *against* THOMAS and Others.

THE following case was sent by the Vice Chancellor, for the opinion of this Court:

John Thomas made his will, duly executed and attested to pass freehold estates by devise, in the words following: "I, John Thomas, do make and declare this my will and testament in manner and form following. First, I charge all and singular my real and personal estate, with the payment of all my debts; then I give, devise, and bequeath unto my brother Richard Thomas, for and during the term of his natural life, an annuity or clear yearly rent or sum of 25L, free of all taxes and other deductions, parliamentary or otherwise, to be issuing and payable out of certain lands therein mentioned and described, to be paid and payable by equal half-yearly payments, at the days therein mentioned. Also, I give, devise, and bequeath unto my beloved wife, Maria Lætitia Thomas, all my real estates, (and which he enumerated by name,) for and during the term of her natural life, or long as she shall remain my widow. Also, I give, devise, and bequeath unto my wife the use and benefit of all interest of money arising from my personal estate, either in bonds, mortgages, or simple contract debts; and also the use and benefit of the household furniture of Llanvaughan, together with the stock, crop, and implements of husbandry, &c. that I shall be possessed of at the time of my decease, for and during her natural life, or as long as she remains my widow; and immediately after her decease, or in case of her marriage,

A., by will, charged all his real and personal estate with the payment of his debts, and then, after giving an annuity for life to his brother, payable out of his lands, devised to his wife all his real and personal estate for the term of her life, or as long as she should remain his widow, and immediately after her decease, or in case of her marriage, which ever should first happen, then he directed all his real and personal estate to be divided according to the statute of distributions in that case made and provided; Held, that by this will there was not any devise to any person of the real estates of the testator after the death or second marriage of the widow.

VOL. III.   3 H   which

which ever shall first happen; then my will is, that all my real and personal estate be divided *according to the statute of distribution in that case made and provided.*" The testator was at the time of making his will, and from thence until and at the time of his death, seised and possessed of the real estates therein specifically mentioned and devised to his wife during her life or widowhood, and of no other real estate. The testator died shortly after the date and execution of his will, without having revoked or altered the same, leaving *M. L. Thomas,* his widow, and *James Thomas, Charles Lloyd Thomas, Richard Thomas,* and the Rev. *Thomas Seth Jones Thomas,* his four brothers, and only next of kin respectively surviving him; and the said *James Thomas* was the eldest brother and the heir at law of the testator. Upon the death of the testator, *M. L. Thomas,* his widow, entered into possession of his real estates, and continued unmarried and in possession thereof, and in receipt of the rents and profits until the time of her death. The testator's brothers having died leaving children surviving them, the suit in Chancery was between the son of the eldest brother (the heir at law of the testator) and the children of the other brothers, who claimed as next of kin, and the representatives of the widow. The question for the opinion of this Court was, whether by the will of *John Thomas,* the testator there was any devise of his real estates after the death or second marriage of his widow, *M. L. Thomas,* and to whom,

Tindal for some of the next of kin. There are two questions; first, whether the real estate passed by the residuary clause; secondly, when it vested. The devise is

sufficient

sufficient to pass the real estate after the death or second marriage of the widow, and the next of kin of the testator are entitled to the property. It is a well established principle, that no formal words are necessary to express the testator's intention in a will; it is sufficient if the intention can be collected from the whole will. It may be said that there is no sufficient designatio personæ, because there is no statute of distribution applicable to real estate, and, therefore, there is no statute " in that case made and provided;" but the Court will take notice that there is a statute of distribution, and will reject the other words as surplusage. If there had been a statute applicable to the distribution of real estate, there would have been no necessity for the devise. The clear intention of the testator through the whole will was, that his real and personal estate should go together as one fund. He charges all and singular his real and personal estates with his debts. Secondly, he gives to his wife all his real estates, by a certain description; for the case finds that he had no other than those devised to her; and he gives her also all the interest and profits of his personal estate. Then comes the devise in question; there he has clearly the same object in view, for it includes the real and personal property. It is clear that the testator knew there was a statute for distribution of personal property, and the words *in that case made and provided*, are merely words of description of that statute, and may be rejected, if the Court see that they are used by mistake. In *Smith* v. *Campbell* (a) Sir *W. Grant* held, that a gift to the testator's nearest relations in his native

---

(a) *Coop. Rep. in Ch.* 275.

3 H 2   country,

country, *Ireland*, included sisters in *America*. If the objection of the heir at law is available he must maintain, not only that the testator was labouring under a mistake, and supposed that there was a statute which applied to the distribution of land, but he must go further, and shew that this mistake was the very ground and reason that he made such devise; that he would not have so devised it unless he had thought that there was such a statute. Now that is absurd; for if there had been such a statute the devise was unnecessary. There is no objection in point of law to this devise, on the ground that the words apply strictly to personalty, provided there be a sufficient designation of the person who is to take the realty; for the courts in many cases have interpreted words, (which would apply in their strict sense to personalty only,) according to the intention of the parties to apply to realty, *Doe* v. *Roper* (a), *Doe* v. *Langlands* (b), *Doe* v. *Trout.* (c) In *Pyot* v. *Pyot* (d), a person devised her real estate to trustees, in trust for her daughter *Martha*, with a proviso, that if she died before twenty-one, or marriage, then in trust to convey all the residue of her estate, both real and personal, unto her nearest relation of the name of *Pyot*, and to his or her heirs, executors, administrators, and assigns. The daughter died under age and unmarried. Lord *Hardwicke* was of opinion, that the word *relation* was to be taken as nomen collectivum, as much as kindred or heirs; and he said that the case differed from all that had been cited, because the personal estate was involved in the same devise with the real; and had that been a

(a) 11 *East*, 518.   (b) 14 *East*, 571.
(c) 15 *East*, 594.   (d) 1 *Ves. sen.* 335.   6 *Cruise Dig.* 185.

bequest

bequest of the personal estate only, all those who were of the name of the *Pyot*, in an equal degree, and were of the nearest stock to the testatrix, would have taken by virtue of the statute of distributions; and if it was clear who should take the personal estate, it naturally inferred whom the testatrix meant should take the real, there being but one intent as to both; and this of the personal was a proper key to explain how the real estate was intended to go. Now that case in principle very much resembles the present, and is an authority to shew that where the real and personal estate are tied together, the devise of the personal estate is a key to explain how the real estate is intended to go. And the case of *Doe* v. *Over* (a) is decisive. There the testator devised all such property as he should be possessed of at his decease (except his freehold estates) to his wife, to be her sole property. And he gave to her all his freehold estates during her natural life, and at her decease to be equally divided amongst *the relations on his side ;* and it was held, that all those in the maternal as well as in the paternal line, who at the time of the testator's death would have been entitled to the personal estate under the statute of distributions, were entitled to take. It is clear that the testator did not mean to die intestate as to his real property; and as the personal property is devised in such a way that it may pass, the real must be governed by it. As to the second point, the devise vested at the testator's death; or in other words, the devisees are those persons who would have taken the personal estate at the time when the will took effect, viz. at the death of the testator. *Doe* v. *Over* (a) is an

(a) 1 *Taunt.* 263.

3 H 3   authority

authority in point for this also. In *Doe* v. *Sheffield* (a)
the devise was to the sisters of *J. H.* (generally) their
heirs, &c. as tenants in common, and not as joint
tenants; and it was held, that one of three sisters of
J. H., who alone survived at the time of the devise
made, and who also survived the testator, was entitled
to take the whole; and even if she had only been entitled to part, still that the residue would not have
gone to the heir at law, as in case of a lapsed devise
but to the residuary legatee.

Stephen, for others of the next of kin. The argument
on behalf of the heir at law must proceed on the as-
sumption that the will is to be read as if the words had
been, that "the real and personal estate should be divided
according to law;" but the will says that they are to be
divided according to the statute of distribution; it does
not apply to the personal estate only, but specifically
directs the real estates to be divided also. The words
"statute of distribution" cannot be struck out of the will.
[*Bayley* J. Suppose the widow to have married again,
and only one person entitled to the personal estate as
next of kin, would the widow have taken the fee in a
moiety of the real estate?] No; for as she has an
estate for life, or during her widowhood, the true construction is, that the next of kin would take according
to the statute of distribution; her estate is not capable
of enlargement except by words, which would admit of
no other construction. [*Bayley* J. She may take the
whole in one case and one half in the other.] It would
be absurd to say that the widow took more than a life.

(a) 13 *East*, 526.

estate,

estate, because then, in the event of her death, her moiety would go to her representatives, for whom the testator could have no interest in providing; for the devise must be construed so as to take effect at the death of the testator.

Barnewall, for the representative of the widow, relied upon the arguments already urged to shew that the real estate passed, and contended, that if it did, then the representative of the widow was entitled to the same share of the real estate as the widow would have taken of the personal estate, under the statute of distribution. The estate cannot be distributed according to the statute of distribution, unless the widow takes her share. Where the devise has been to the relations or next of kin, it has been held, that the widow did not come within that description, *Davis* v. *Bailey* (a), *Worseley* v. *Johnson* (b), and *Garrick* v. *Lord Camden.* (c) But here the estate is to be distributed according to the statute of distribution. Those cases, therefore, are not in point. *Doe* v. *Lawson* (d) is an authority to shew that the estate must be divided amongst those who would have taken it at the time of the testator's death, and not at the time of the death of the widow. There, *A.* devised to his natural son, and in case of his marriage with certain persons, or his dying without issue, then to his nephew for life, and after his decease amongst such persons and his and their heirs, as shall appear and can be proved to be his next of kin, in such proportions as they would, by virtue of the statute of

(a) 1 *Ves.* sen. 85.   (b) 3 *Atk.* 757.
(c) 14 *Ves.* 572.   (d) 3 *East*, 278.

distributions,

distributions, have been entitled to his personal estate
if he died intestate; it was held, that the distribution
was to be made amongst those who were the testator's
next of kin at the time of his death, although the
nephew to whom a prior life estate was given was one
of them. That case is in point. The widow, therefore, at the time of the death of the testator became
entitled to a life estate in the whole realty, and a remainder in fee in a portion of it.

Peake Serjt. The real estate did not pass by the
clause in question. It is a rule too well established to
require any authority to support it, that an heir at law
is not to be disinherited except by express words or
necessary implication; and here there are neither express words nor such necessary implication. As far as
intention can be collected from such inapt and informal
words as are here joined, it would seem that the testator
did not intend to disinherit his heir at law. After
giving his wife every thing for her life, or as long as she
remained his widow, the testator proceeds: " And after
her decease, or in case of her marriage, whichever shall
first happen, then my will is, that all my real and personal estate be divided according to the statute of distribution in that case made and provided." It is not
merely " the statute of distribution," but " the statute
of distribution *in that case made and provided.*" It is
plain that the testator did not know the meaning of the
words he made use of, for there is no statute of distribution applicable to real estate. It is not improbable
that he might think the descent of real estate, as well as
the distribution of personalty, was regulated by statute;
and then the words " the statute of distribution in that

case

1825.

THOMAS
v.
THOMAS

case made and provided" meant no more than that it should go in such course as the law provided; that is, his real estate to his heir at law, his personalty amongst his nearest of kin in a course of distribution, and why should he be supposed to alter the disposition of the law in the one case more than in the other? The word " *divided*" does not necessarily imply that both estates shall be divided into separate parts, but is satisfied by dividing or separating them from each other, and then letting them go as the law directs. In the case of *Piggott* v. *Penrice* (a), the testator devised in these words: " I make my niece *G.* executrix of all my goods, lands, and chattels. The testator had no terms, but only freehold estate, and yet the lands were held not to pass. When pressed that the word lands must mean something, the Lord Chancellor said that word would be satisfied by the rents which might be due at the testator's death. In answer to the argument that the testator has treated the two funds as one, and has disposed of them together, it is to be observed that he has only done so as far as was necessary for the purposes he had immediately in view. The amount of the personalty is not stated in the case, it is plain that the testator thought it might not be sufficient to answer all his debts, and therefore for the security of his creditors, but for no other purpose, he has made the whole of his property, real as well as personal, liable to the payment of his debts. This can form no reason for supposing that he meant the whole to go together afterwards. As little does the devise to his wife afford such a supposition. He wished to enable her to live in

(a) *Prec. in Ch.* 471.

the

the same way as he lived himself, and therefore bequeathed to her during her life the use of his household furniture, &c.; and gives her the same means that
he possessed himself of keeping up the establishment.
That was his only object for so uniting the two pro-
perties during her life-time; but it never can be inferred
from thence that after her death, when he appears to
have no particular wishes or predilections, that he should
wish the whole to be parcelled out and divided as personal property. In the case of *Pyot* v. *Pyot* the two
funds were united for the express purpose of providing
for one person, namely, the nearest relation of that
name. Can it be supposed that any man could have so
absurd an intention as to cut a small estate into a great
number of parcels, which would render his bounty useless to any one? And that would be the case if the estate
was to be divided into as many shares as the personal.
If he had intended that all his relations should take, he
would have ordered the estate to be sold, and the
money produced by the sale to be divided amongst
them. In any other view of the case his meaning is so
uncertain that it cannot be necessarily implied what that
meaning was; and if there is not a reasonable implication what his intention was, the heir at law is equally
entitled to take on account of the uncertainty. It is
sufficient for him that the whole is uncertain. It rests
on the other side to shew what the testator's intention
was. In *Doe dem. Hayter* v. *Joinville* (a), where the
devise was, " to my brother and sister's family," this
Court held it void for uncertainty.

(a) 3 *East*, 172.

Tindal

Tindal in reply. The difficulty is not removed by
supposing that the testator thought that there was a
statute applicable to the distribution of real property, as
well as one to personal; for then he would have used
the word "*statutes*," in the plural. The construction
put on the word divide is insufficient also. The testator
clearly contemplated a division both of the personal and
real estates, and not merely a division of one from the
other. One is a remote, and not an obvious construction; the other is clear, and therefore to be preferred. *Piggott* v. *Penrice* has been cited to shew the
anxiety of the courts to satisfy the words of a will, and
not to make a party die intestate, so as to defeat the·
intent. It is clear the words were insufficient to pass
the land. *Doe* v. *Joinville* is not in point. If in that
case there had been a devise to the next of kin it
would have done, but the doubt there was as to the·
proportions. It was not clear which family was intended. In *Wright* v. *Atkins* (a) the Lord Chancellor·
expressed doubts whether the cases could be supported
in which the word "*family*" had been held to be too
indefinite. The devisees take the fee immediately.
Those who represent the devisees when the will took
effect, viz. at the death of the testator, are the persons
to take, and that does not help the widow, because the
testator did not intend her to take any thing not specifically given to her.

BAYLEY J. I cannot think that any great stress is to
be laid on the circumstance of the testator's having
charged his real and personal estate with the payment.

1825.

THOMAS
against
THOMAS.

(a) 1 *Turner's Ch. Ca.* 156.

of

of his debts, nor of his having given the whole to his wife for life. It is not thence to be inferred that when he comes to divide his property he intended that aliquot parts of his real and personal estate should be kept together. In order to pass the real estate it ought to be clear on the face of the will what is to pass, and to whom. If the words are insufficient to designate the property intended to be passed, or the persons intended to take, then the real estate will not pass, not because the heir is any favorite of the law, but because the devise is insufficient. Then the question is, whether there are words clearly shewing to whom the realty is to go. If the testator had said, " I give my real estate to be divided according to the statute of distribution," the intention would have been clearly expressed. But, taking the whole together, the testator manifestly used words he did not understand. Probably he thought that there was one statute applicable both to the distribution of real and personal estate, and that he meant his property to be divided according to law. My present opinion is, that the will therefore operates as a bequest of the personal property, but that it does not affect the real estate. We will consider the case, and send our opinion.

Cur. adv. vult.

The following certificate was afterwards sent:

This case has been argued before us by counsel, and we are of opinion that, by the will of *John Thomas*, the testator, there was not any devise to any person or persons of his real estates after the death or second marriage of his widow, *Maria Letitia Thomas*.

J. Bayley.

G. S. Holroyd.

J. Littledale.

The Earl of FALMOUTH *against* RICHARDSON and Another.

TRESPASS for taking the plaintiff's goods. The defendants justified as commissioners under a private inclosure act, 5 G. 3. c. 100., for inclosing lands lying in several parishes and townships, and the general inclosure act 41 G. 3. c. 109. The plea alleged, that by the 54th section of the private act it was enacted, " that as well the fees and payments to the commissioners, as also the charges and expences incident to and attending the soliciting, obtaining, and passing of that act; and of the surveying, planning, dividing, allotting, and inclosing of the said open and common field, lands, &c.; and of preparing, making, and depositing the awards of the said commissioners, and of all other plans, maps, &c., directed by the commissioners to be prepared and made out; and all other costs, charges, and expences whatsoever, in anywise attending the execution of that and the general inclosure act, or any of the powers, authorities, provisoes, or declarations therein contained, should be borne and defrayed at such times as the said commissioners should by any writing or writings under their hands to be affixed, &c. (in certain places and at certain specified times) order and direct, but subject to the regulations, proportions, and restraint thereinafter mentioned, that is to say, that so much of the said costs, charges, and expences as should be incurred previous to and up to the

The tenth section of the general inclosure act, 41 G. 3. c. 109., does not give to commissioners any power to make private roads, but only to set them out, and say in what proportions they shall be made by the owners of allotments, and therefore where a private enclosure act gave the commissioners power to raise money to pay the expence of carrying into execution that or the general enclosure act : Held, that they could not make and levy a rate to pay for making private roads.

the time of the passing of the act; and all such other
costs, charges, and expences as should thereafter be incurred, which should relate to or affect the said parishes
and townships jointly, should be paid by the several
proprietors of estates and other persons within the said
several parishes and townships respectively, to whom
allotments should be made by virtue of that act, in proportion to the value of the lands to be allotted to them
respectively, to be ascertained by the said commissioners; and that from the time of the passing of that
act, the commissioners should keep a general account
of all costs, charges, and expences jointly affecting the
said parishes and township; and also a separate account
of all such costs, charges, and expences as separately
relate to or affect the said parishes and townships; which
last mentioned costs, charges, and expences should be
paid by the proprietors of estates, and other persons
in the said parishes and townships respectively, to whom
allotments should be made by virtue of that act, in proportion to the value of the lands to be allotted to them
respectively, to be ascertained by the said commissioners;
and in case any person or persons should refuse or neglect
to pay his, her, or their share or proportion of such
charges and expences within the times, and to such person or persons as the said commissioners should appoint,
then and in such case the said commissioners should
cause the same to be levied and recovered in manner
directed by the said recited act." The plea then stated,
that the commissioners set out certain private roads pursuant to the 41 G. 3. c. 109. s. 10., and afterwards made
their award, whereby they directed that certain persons
should bear the expence of making and keeping those
roads in repair. That the commissioners afterwards
                                                          made

made a rate for that purpose, and because the plaintiff refused to pay his share, they issued a warrant and distrained his goods. Replication, that the rate was made for the sole purpose of defraying the expences of making the said private roads so set out and appointed as aforesaid in *W.* meadow (part of the lands to be inclosed), and that the rate was solely and exclusively made upon the owners of land in that meadow. Rejoinder, that making the private roads was part of the costs attending the execution of the 41 *G. 3. c.* 109. and 51 *G. 3. c.* 100. Demurrer and joinder.

Campbell in support of the demurrer. The question turns on the construction of the general inclosure act 41 *G. 3. c.* 109. *s.* 10., for there is nothing in the private act relating to roads. By that section it is enacted, " that the commissioners shall set out and appoint private roads, and that the same shall be made, and at all times for ever thereafter, be kept in repair by and at the expence of the owners and proprietors for the time being, of the lands to be divided and inclosed in such proportions as the commissioners shall by their award order and direct." The 54th section of the private act 51 *G. 3. c.* 100. gives the commissioners power to raise money for the payment of their expences, and of all costs, charges, and expences whatsoever attending the execution of that or the general inclosure act. The making of private roads is not, however, any thing done in execution of the act, it is rather in execution of the award of the commissioners. They cannot, therefore, make a rate to defray the expence of making such roads.

Taunton

Taunton contra. The case of *Haggerstone v. Dugmore* (a), shews that the commissioners have power to levy a rate to defray the expence of making roads under the powers of the general inclosure act. That case certainly related to public roads, but the principle is applicable to private roads also. By section 10 of the 41 G. 3. c. 109. the commissioners are to set out the private roads, and to direct by whom and in what manner they are to be made. The act cannot be said to be fully executed until the roads are completed, the expence of making them is, therefore, incurred in execution of that section of the act, and if so, the commissioners had full power to make the rate in question.

BAYLEY J. This case has been put upon the true ground, for the simple question is, whether the expence of making private roads is incurred in execution of the 51 G. 3. c. 100., or of the 41 G. 3. c. 109. The former act does not mention private roads, we must, therefore, inquire whether the general inclosure act gives the commissioners power to make private roads. Their authority respecting them, whatever that may be, is given by the 10th section. The 8th section directs that the commissioners shall set out public roads, they are to make a map of them, and give certain notices, and if any objections are made, the commissioners, together with a justice of the district, are finally to determine the matter. By the 9th section, surveyors are to be appointed to make the roads, and power is expressly given to the commissioners to levy money to pay the expence of making them. Then follows the 10th section, as to

(a 1 B. & A. 82.

private

private roads. The commissioners are to set them out and give notices in like manner as in the case of public roads, but then it proceeds, " and the same shall be made and at all times for ever thereafter, be supported and kept in repair by and at the expence of the owners and proprietors for the time being, of the lands and grounds directed to be divided and inclosed, in such shares and proportions as the commissioner or commissioners shall in and by his or their award order and direct." There is no power of appointing a surveyor of those roads, or of raising money to pay for making them, but they are to be made by the owners of the allotments, and at their expence. It is manifest that no rate could be made for future repairs, and " making and repairing" are put in conjunction in this section. I am, therefore, of opinion, that the commissioners were not acting within the scope of their authority when this rate was made, and consequently that it cannot be supported.

HOLROYD J. concurred.

Judgment for the plaintiff.

1825.

HODGSON *against* JAMES ANDERSON.

A. being in-
debted to *B.* ;
and *C.*, who
was resident in
the *West Indies,*
being indebted
to *A.*, the latter
proposed to as-
sign to *B.* the
debt due to
him from *C.*,
and to this pro-
posal *B.* as-
sented. *A.*
then, by letter
directed the
agents of *C.* in
this country,
" As soon as
they should
have funds be-
longing to *C.* in their hands, to pay to *B.* on his (*A.*'s) account, the amount of *C.*'s debt,"
and added that he would credit *C.* for the amount, *having received his order to that effect.*
The agents of *C.* *verbally* promised to pay *B.* as soon as they should have funds in their
hands belonging to *C.* *A.* afterwards gave an order to another creditor, authorising *C.* to
pay to such creditor the amount of the debt due to him (*A.*), and *C.* entered into an obligation to pay the same to such creditor, but there was a clause annexed to the obligation,
stating that it had been alleged that a payment had been made by some person to *A.* on
account of *C.*, and it was declared, that should such payment be proved to have been made,
the amount should be deducted. The creditor to whom this order was given demanded
payment of the debt from *C.* on his arrival in this country, but the latter refused to
pay it, on the ground that his agents were liable to pay it to *B.*, and the same was in fact
afterwards paid to *B.* :

Held, that although a creditor has a right to insist on payment to himself or to his
appointee, yet having once given an order for the payment of his debt to a third person, he
has no right to revoke that order, provided there be a pledge by the person to whom the
authority is given that he will pay the debt according to the authority.

Held, further, that the expression in *A.*'s letter, " that he would credit *C.* for the
amount, having received his order to that effect," was evidence as against *A.*, that he had
at that time received such an order from *C.*, and therefore that *C.* had expressly assented
to the order given by *A.* that the debt due from *C.* to *A.*, should be paid to *B.*

Held, also, that even if that were not so, still there was sufficient to imply the assent of
C., that the debt due from him to *A.* should be applied in discharge of the debt due from
A. to *B.*, inasmuch as it was expressly stipulated by *C.* in the obligation he entered into
to pay the debt to another, that any sum paid by any person on account of that debt to *A.*
should be deducted.

Held, also, that it was not necessary that the promise to pay *B.* should be in
writing, inasmuch as it was a promise by *C.* to pay his own debt, and not that of
another.

ASSUMPSIT for 443*l.* 17*s.* 11*d.*, being the balance
of an account between the plaintiff and defendant,
and interest thereon, from the 1st of *October* 1819. The
defendant paid 300*l.* into court. Plea, general issue,
and notice of set-off. The particular of this set-off was
the sum of 203*l.* 5*s.* 10*d.*, paid on the 11th of *April* 1822,
by the agents of the defendant to the Commercial Banking
Company of *Scotland*, at the request and on the order in
writing of the plaintiff, and in pursuance of an undertaking and liability to pay the same to the Banking
Company for the plaintiff, according to such request and

order,

order, made and entered into long before the time of payment. At the trial before *Abbott* C. J., at the *London* sittings after *Hilary* term 1823, the jury found a verdict for the plaintiff for the sum of 209*l.* 15*s.* A rule nisi for a new trial having been made in *Easter* term 1823, the court directed a special case to be stated for their opinion.

The defendant resided for many years in *Trinidad* until *August* 1821. Prior to the year 1816 he became indebted to the plaintiff in a larger amount than the sum set off by him in this action. The plaintiff was a shareholder in the Commercial Banking Company of *Scotland*, and that company discounted bills for him. Early in 1816 the Company discounted for the plaintiff a bill drawn by him for 270*l.*, and accepted by one *Dickson.* On the 19th *March* 1816 the plaintiff was informed by the secretary to the company that the bill had been dishonored. On the 22d of the same month the plaintiff wrote to the secretary in answer, that both he and Mr. *Dickson* required time to meet their engagements, that they could not retire the bill, and that he, the plaintiff, had mentioned his situation to Mr. *Robert Anderson* of *Edinburgh*, the defendant's brother, and a director of the company, and added, " I also mentioned to my friend, Mr. *Robert Anderson*, that as his brother in *Trinidad* was indebted to me nearly 400*l.*, I would, if he pleased, give him a receipt for the returned bill with charges on his brother's account, which would secure the payment, as that gentleman had considerable property in *Edinburgh*, and as he a few months back referred me to Mr. *Anderson* and Mr. *Rhind*, his attornies, for a settlement of my demand. I trust the company will be induced to accede to our proposal, or that Mr.

Anderson

Anderson will take the bill as a payment from his brother to me." To this proposal Mr. *Anderson* did not accede, and by a letter of the 4th *November* 1816, the secretary again pressed the plaintiff for payment of the bill, who, on the 8th of *November* 1816, returned the following answer: " I propose to grant you my promissory note, at seven months from this date, including interest and charges, you holding Mr. *Dickson's* acceptance till this is paid, and my commercial bank share receipt also, as a collateral security, which I will send you as soon as I have your permission, and know the amount of charges. I had flattered myself my very old friend, *Robert Anderson,* one of your company, would have assumed the amount of Mr. *Dickson's* acceptance on account of a debt, nearly 150*l.* more than this bill, due me by his brother; but this I fear *is* not agreeable; but if the company wish, I will make an assignment of this debt to them in addition, should it be required." On the 19th of *November* the secretary wrote to the plaintiff as follows: " I am directed to acquaint you that the proposal made in your letter of the 8th instant is acceded to; you will please, therefore, immediately hand in your promissory note at seven months, dated the 8th instant, for 291*l.* 19*s.,* being the amount of the former bill, interest, and expences, as noted on the other side. As your share of stock is assigned to us by the contract of copartnery, in security of debts, you need not send us the receipt. Mr. *Anderson* says the debt you mention as due by his brother is as you state, but there is no money of his forthcoming at present to meet it, and that he shall, if necessary, pay to us, when he has funds, on your order : you will please, therefore, hand us a letter addressed to Mr. *Anderson* and Mr. *Rhind,*

desiring

desiring them to pay us the sum due as soon as they are in funds." On the 23d of *November* 1816, the plaintiff wrote to the secretary to the company, and inclosed in the letter his own promissory note for 291*l.* 19*s.* at seven months, and the following note addressed to *Anderson* and *Rhind.* " As soon as you may have funds belonging to *James Anderson* of *Trinidad,* I will thank you to pay, on my account, to the Commercial Banking Company in your city, 291*l.* 19*s.*, being the amount of my promissory note, in favor of *E. Robertson,* Esquire, or any part of the same, advising me the amount, and I will credit Mr. *J. Anderson, having received his order to this effect,* as he is indebted to me more than this order." This note was delivered to Messrs. *Anderson* and *Rhind,* and they *verbally* promised the banking company to pay them according to the terms of the order, as they should have funds of the defendant in hand; and this promise was never retracted. On the 29th of *January* 1820 the plaintiff wrote a letter to *A. Hill,* of *Trinidad,* enclosing an abstract of his account with the defendant, balanced to the 1st of *October* 1819; the amount of this balance was 443*l.* 17*s.* 11*d.* In this letter was also enclosed a power of attorney to enable *Hill* to recover the same; and he then informed *Hill,* that as *Loughnan* and Co. had a considerable demand against him, he had agreed that *Hill* should remit *Loughnan* and Co. the amount he should recover from that debt, and the plaintiff accordingly begged that *Hill* would comply therewith, and remit *Loughnan* and Co. whatever sums he might recover." The plaintiff executed no other assignment to *L.* and Co. of the debt owing by the defendant than this letter. On the same day *Loughnan* and Co.

wrote

wrote to one *Lockhart,* requesting him to direct *Hill* to recover the amount from Dr. *Anderson* the defendant. *Hill* applied to the defendant in *Trinidad,* and he and his son entered into the following obligation. " *Trinidad,* 11th *June* 1821. We do hereby promise to pay, or cause to be paid, unto *H. S. Hill,* or to his order, as attorney of *A. Loughnan* and Co., *London,* being a debt assigned to them by *John Hodgson* of *London,* and due by the undersigned *James Anderson,* the sum of 488*l.* 6*s.* 3*d.* sterling, with interest on the sum of 443*l.* 17*s.* 11*d.* sterling from this date, on or before the 1st day of *March* 1822 ; and for assuring the due payment thereof, we bind ourselves and each of us, our heirs, executors and assigns, each in solidum unto the said *H. S. Hill* or his order, to and for the use of the said *A. Loughnan* and Co. And whereas it hath been alleged, that a payment of 300*l.* has been made on account of this debt by some person to *John Hodgson* on account of *James Anderson ;* it is therefore hereby declared, that should such payment be proved by the said *J. Anderson* to have been made to the said *John Hodgson* by some person on account of the said *J. Anderson,* on or before the 1st day of *March* 1822, that then the said 300*l.* and interest thereon shall be deducted." On the 15th *June* the secretary to the company wrote to the plaintiff, and informed him that the promissory note which was due the 6th instant had been returned under protest from *London,* and informing the plaintiff that the company declined renewing it without some additional security. The plaintiff replied that he could not procure such security, nor pay the note, and directed his share in the bank to be sold for the benefit of the company.

company. According to these instructions the plaintiff's share in the bank was sold, and purchased by the company at the price of 140*l.* The company also received the dividends due to the plaintiff in respect of his share, and thus the debt due from the plaintiff to the company, which had increased to 346*l.* 19*s.* 1*d.* was reduced to 198*l.* 1*s.* 9*d.* On the 10th *May* 1821 the secretary, by letter to the plaintiff, acknowledged the receipt of Mr. *G. Rolfe's* acceptance for 196*l.* 7*s.* 6*d.* The defendant arrived in *Edinburgh* in *August* 1821, and *Loughnan* and Co. then wrote to him, demanding payment of the debt due from him to the plaintiff, and which had been assigned to them as above mentioned, which produced the following letter from the defendant to *L.* and Co., dated the 24th of *August* 1821. " I had the honor of receiving yours of the 17th inst., and have made the necessary inquiries into the business alluded to in your letter. The case is this, the Commercial Bank of *Edinburgh* hold a bill of Mr. *John Hodgson's* for 196*l.* sterling on Mr. *G. Rolfe's* acceptance, due in *November* next, which my brother and father-in-law, (*Anderson* and *Rhind,*) as my attornies, are security for to the bank for the above sum, on account of the debt I owe Mr. *John Hodgson.* If Mr. *Hodgson,* as I suppose he will, pays the bill when due in *November,* I shall then of course owe you the full amount of my account transferred by Mr. *Hodgson* to your house. If, however, the Commercial Bank come upon me for it, it will then, of course, be deducted from the amount due to Mr. *Hodgson* by me, and transferred to you by him." The bill drawn upon and accepted by *Rolfe* was not paid when due. On the 27th *March* 1822 the defendant wrote to *Loughnan* and Co., stating that 203*l.* 1*s.* 7*d.* was due from the plaintiff to the bank,

3 I 4   and

and that he the defendant must pay that sum to the
company. Upon the 30th of the same month *Loughnan* and Co. wrote to the defendant, giving him notice
not to pay to the Banking Company the debt due from him
to the plaintiff. On the 11th of *April* following, the defendant's agents paid the debt due to the Banking Company, under an indemnity from the company; no engagement was entered into by the defendant's agents with
the company beyond the verbal assurance given by them
on the plaintiff's order being communicated to them.
On a former day during these sittings, the case was
argued by

Kaye for the plaintiff. The defendant being indebted
to the plaintiff, and the plaintiff to the Commercial
Banking Company, the plaintiff appointed *Anderson* and
Rhind as agents to pay his debt to the company when
they should have received money to his use from the
defendant; and the company had notice of this. It is
the same thing as if a merchant said to his clerk, " when
my debtor pays me, do you pay my creditor out of the
sum received from my debtor," and that order had been
communicated to the creditor. This is a mere naked
authority, revocable until executed, or at least until the
funds are in some way appropriated to the use of the
creditor. This, however, only applies to the question
as between the plaintiff, *Anderson* and *Rhind*, and the
Commercial Banking Company. But Dr. *Anderson* is
the defendant on this record; and the fallacy of the
argument on the other side is in supposing that *Anderson* and *Rhind* are the defendant's agents in this transaction, instead of the plaintiff's; they had neither
instructions nor authority from the defendant on the
subject,

subject, and he was in utter ignorance of the arrangement until his return to this country in 1821. The
question, whether if the funds came into the hands of
Anderson and *Rhind* from the defendant to the use of
the plaintiff, he, the plaintiff, could revoke his order,
does not arise. The real question is, whether Dr.
Anderson was compelled to place funds in the hands of
A. and *Rhind;* and if not, whether having done so
after notice not to pay the money over to them, he is
not answerable in this action. The defendant had never
been in any way a party to the negotiations between the
plaintiff, *Anderson* and *Rhind,* and the Commercial
Banking Company; but was in *Trinidad,* and ignorant
of them up to the year 1820, when he assented to the
assignment of the debt due to the plaintiff *Hodgson* made
by him to *Loughnan* and Co. The defendant had no notice
of the order of *Nov.* 23, 1816, and therefore cannot be
affected by it, nor can he set it up as a defence to this
action. Had he known of that order he would not have
assented to the assignment to *Loughnan* and Co. He
had no authority from the plaintiff to pay the Commercial
Banking Company. The company could never have
brought an action against the defendant, nor against *Anderson* and *Rhind* his agents, even if one of the latter firm
had not been a partner in the Commercial Bank. This
is not like the case put by *Buller* J. in *Tatlock* v.
Harris (a), " if *A.* owes *B.* 100*l.*, and *B.* owes *C.* 100*l.*,
and the three meet, and it is agreed that *A.* shall pay *C.*,
B.'s debt is extinguished." There there is an absolute
assignment, and the assent of the debtor. Here the
order is conditional, and the debtor does not give his

(a) 5 *T. R.* 180.

assent.

assent. Besides, this is an assignment of a chose in action, and the defendant having assented to the assignment of the debt, due from him to the plaintiff, to *Loughnan* and Co., notice from the latter not to place the funds in *Anderson* and *Rhind's* hands was the same as if the notice came from the plaintiff. Besides, the words in the order " I will credit Mr. *J. Anderson*, having received his order to this effect," cannot mean that the defendant, who was then at *Trinidad*, had ordered him, the plaintiff, to pay his (the plaintiff's) own debt to the Banking Company, but that the plaintiff had received an order from his debtor to demand payment from *A.* and *Rhind*, who were the defendant's attornies in *Edinburgh*. And it is clear from the plaintiff's letter of the 22d *March* 1816, to the secretary to the Bank, that he, the plaintiff, had received such an order.

Cameron for the defendant. First, from the expressions in the plaintiff's letter it must be taken, as against him, that the defendant was a party to the assignment, which is then an assignment of a chose in action with the assent of all the parties concerned, and therefore valid and binding upon them all. In the letter to *Anderson* and *Rhind*, dated *November* 23. 1816, the plaintiff directs them to pay the Commercial Banking Company, and then adds, " I will credit Mr. *J. Anderson* (the defendant), having received his order to this effect." It is to be observed that the plaintiff makes this assertion in the course of a correspondence in which he is seeking to obtain a benefit to himself, and which he obtained upon the faith of this assertion. It is therefore too late for him now to affirm that the defendant was no party to the assignment. Secondly, supposing that the defendant was not a party

to

to the assignment, it may still be irrevocable by the assignor. It is true that at law a chose in action cannot be assigned, but the meaning of that proposition is, that the debtor of one man shall not be made the debtor of another without his own consent; but there is no rule of law which prevents a man from making an assignment of a debt which shall not be revocable by himself. It is also true that a court of law cannot, except upon an application to its equitable jurisdiction, take notice that the plaintiff and defendant on the record are not the real plaintiff and defendant in the action, but wherever such an assignment can be fairly brought before the court, in pleading or in evidence, as affecting the rights of the parties on the record, the court will take notice of it, and will do justice accordingly, *Mouldsdale* v. *Birchall.*(a)   Then if there was nothing in point of law to prevent this plaintiff from assigning irrevocably, neither can there be any doubt that it was his intention to do so; he calls it an assignment throughout the correspondence, and offers it as part of the consideration upon which he was asking for time upon his bills, which would be absurd if he meant to reserve to himself the power of revoking it; for though a consideration depending on a contingency may be worth something, yet a consideration depending upon a contingency, the contingent event being in the power of him from whom the consideration moves, is worth absolutely nothing. Then this is an authority coupled with an interest, and as such could not be revoked, *Walsh* v. *Whitcomb* (b), *Watson* v. *King* (c), *Drinkwater* v. *Goodwin.* (d)   In

(a) 2 Bl. Rep. 820.   (b) 2 Esp. 565.
(c) 4 Camp. 272.   (d) Cowp. 251.

Fisher

Fisher v. *Miller* (a) the distinction was taken between an appropriation and a mere order to pay, and the decision turned upon the distinction, which is equally applicable to the present case. Moreover there has not really been any revocation in fact, for *Loughnan* and Co. are strangers to the transaction, and it is only from them that the defendant had any notice of a revocation. The assignment here was complete from the first, there were four parties consenting to it: the plaintiff who made it, the Commercial Bank who accepted it, *Anderson* and *Rhind*, who promised to pay when they should have funds of the defendant, and the defendant, who is represented by the plaintiff himself to have authorized the transaction, against whom therefore the Bank might have maintained a special assumpsit if he had refused to pay. The case is not affected by the statute of frauds, for this was not a promise by the defendant to pay with his own money the debt of another, but to pay his own debt with his own money.

Cur. adv. vult.

The judgment of the Court was now delivered by

BAYLEY J. This is an action to recover the balance of an account, and the only question is, whether a payment by a debtor to a third person in pursuance of an order given by the creditor, was good so as to operate as a payment to the plaintiff. It appeared that in *March* 1816, the plaintiff and one *Dickson* were indebted to the Commercial Banking Company of *Scotland*, on a bill of exchange of which the plaintiff was the drawer,

(a) 1 *Bing.* 150.

and

and *Dickson* the acceptor. After the bill had become due, a proposal was made by the plaintiff to the company, that a debt, due to him from the defendant, a brother of one of the directors of the company, to a larger amount, should be taken by the Banking Company, and that the debt due from the defendant to the plaintiff should be liquidated pro tanto. That proposal was not acceded to at that time, but it was renewed by the plaintiff in *November* 1816, and he then offered to make a regular assignment of the debt to the company. They were disposed to accede to this proposal, as appears by their letter of the 19th of *November* 1816, and on the 23d of *November* the plaintiff sent the banking company an order on *Anderson* and *Rhind*, who were agents for the defendant, directing them, as soon as they should have funds belonging to the defendant, to pay on account of the plaintiff to the Commercial Banking Company 291*l.* 19*s.* or any part of the same, and the plaintiff says, " that he will credit the defendant for the amount, *having received his order to that effect.*" Now that was a distinct authority from the plaintiff to *Anderson* and *Rhind* to apply the debt due to him from *James Anderson*, the defendant, in discharge of the 291*l.* 19*s.* That order was communicated to *Anderson* and *Rhind*, the defendant's agents, and they verbally promised the company to pay them according to the terms of the order, as soon as they should have funds in their hands belonging to the defendant, and that promise was never retracted. There was, therefore, an order by the plaintiff, that the money due to him from the defendant should be applied in discharge of 291*l.* 19*s.*, and there was an assent to that order by the agents of the defendant. There can be no doubt that a creditor has a right

to

to insist on payment to himself, or to such person as he thinks fit. Whether he can retract an order once given, it is not necessary to decide, because I am of opinion that a creditor is not at liberty to withdraw the authority, provided there is a pledge by the person to whom the authority is given that he will make the payment according to the authority. The question therefore arises, whether there was a legal obligation on the agents to pay this money to the Commercial Banking Company as soon as it came into their hands. There was a verbal promise by the agents of the defendant; but it may be said that that would not bind the defendant. It was insisted for the defendant, that the expression in the plaintiff's letter of the 23d of *November* 1816, addressed to *Anderson* and *Rhind*, " I will credit Mr. *J. Anderson*, having received his order to that effect," was evidence of *J. Anderson's* assent to the order. For the plaintiff it was said, that it was no more than a direction to pay *if* he should receive an order, but I think the fair import of that expression is, that he the plaintiff had before that time received an order from the defendant. Ample time had elapsed since the original proposal was made to have enabled him to procure such an order, and the grammatical construction imports that he had received such an order. If he had not received such an order, then it would only be a conditional security, and indeed no security at all, until the defendant *Anderson* assented to it. And if it had not then been understood by the Commercial Banking Company, that the order had been given, they would have required the assent of the defendant, and the proffered assignment. It appears to me, therefore, that the defendant had made himself liable to the company,

because

because there was evidence of an express assent on his part to the assignment; but if that were not so, there would still be sufficient to imply the assent of the defendant to the arrangement. It appears from the correspondence, that the plaintiff authorized a Mr. *Hill* to collect the money, and remit it to *Alexander Loughnan* and Co., and when that was received in *June* 1821, upon a communication between Mr. *Hill* and the defendant, the latter undertook to pay the debt before the first of *March* 1822, but, there was a reserve, or qualification applying to the transaction in question, and to the security given by the plaintiff, and the assent of the defendant. There is a memorandum, that as it had been alleged that a payment of 300*l.* had been made on account of this debt by some person to the plaintiff on account of the defendant, it was declared, that, should such payment be proved by the defendant to have been made to the plaintiff by some person on account of the defendant, on or before the 1st of *March* 1822, then the said sum of 300*l.* should be deducted. There is nothing stated in the case to which that can apply but the transaction in question, and if it does apply to that, then the implication necessarily arises, that the defendant had assented that that part of the debt due from him to the plaintiff, should be applied in discharge of the debt due from the plaintiff to the banking company; and if he did so assent, then he was legally bound to pay it. In *Tatlock* v. *Harris*, *Buller* J. lays it down, that if *A.* owes *B.* 100*l.* and *B.* owes *C.* 100*l.*, and the three meet, and it is agreed between them that *A.* shall pay *C.* the 100*l.*, *B.*'s debt is extinguished, and *C.* may recover the sum against *A.* So in this case upon payment by *Anderson* to the company, *Hodgson*'s debt would be discharged pro

pro tanto. We are of opinion, that a promise in writing, in order to make it obligatory on *Anderson* so to apply the money, was not necessary, because this was not an agreement to pay money which a party by law was not obliged to pay, but there was a full and adequate consideration for the payment. The debt existed, and it was the debt of the defendant, and the only question was, to whom it was to be paid. There was also a consideration moving from the bank, viz. their forbearing to sue the plaintiff. We are, therefore, of opinion, that the defendant assented to the order; that when he assented to it, he was legally bound to pay the money in pursuance of it, and that that payment was a discharge of the debt in question, notwithstanding the subsequent order in favor of *Loughnan* and Co. And as to them they are not injured, for there was a qualification in the agreement to pay them; that in the event of its being proved before *March* 1822, that part of the money had been already applied to a different destination, there should be a deduction pro tanto. Before that time *L.* and Co. were informed of the obligation to pay the banking company. They were, therefore, promptly apprised of the real situation in which they stood. This was a good payment in point of law to the plaintiff, and binding upon him. I am, therefore, of opinion, that the rule for a new trial must be made absolute.

Rule absolute.

The KING *against* SOPER and CAMFIELD.

INDICTMENT stated, that before the making of the order thereinafter mentioned, a certain friendly society, called "The Society of Brotherly United Philanthropists," had long been established and existed at *Greenwich*, in the county of *Kent*, under and by virtue of the statute of the 33 *G. 3. c. 54.*, the rules, orders, and regulations of which society had, long before the making of the said order, according to the directions of the 35 *G. 3. c. 111.*, been duly exhibited, confirmed, deposited, and filed of record; and that one *James Margetts*, before the making of the order thereinafter mentioned, had been duly admitted a free member of the society, and that although he had not infringed any of the said rules, orders, and regulations, yet that he had been wrongfully, and contrary to the rules, orders, and regulations of the society, expelled the society, and deprived of certain relief and maintenance which he was entitled to from the stewards of the society for the time being; and that *Margetts* thinking himself and being aggrieved *thereby,* did on, &c., at, &c., make complaint thereof to two justices, against the defendants, *Soper* and *Camfield,* and before the justices took his corporal oath of the truth of the said complaint, and deposed to the truth of his said complaint, that *Soper* and *Camfield,* (they then being stewards of the society), were duly sum-

By the friendly society act, stat. 33 *G. 3. c. 54. s. 15.*, it is enacted, that if any member of the society shall think himself aggrieved by any thing done by any such society, two justices may, on complaint upon oath of such member, summon the presidents or stewards of the society, and the justices are to hear and determine the matter of such complaint, and to make such orders *therein* as to them shall seem just: Held, that the jurisdiction of the magistrates was confined strictly to the subject matter of the complaint, and therefore where it appeared that a party had complained to the justices that he had been deprived of relief to which he was en-

titled, and the justices awarded not only that the steward should give him such relief, but also that the party should be continued a member of the society, it was held that the latter part of the order was illegal, inasmuch as the expulsion of the party was no part of the complaint.

3 K   moned

moned to appear before the justices, and that being
so summoned, they did afterwards personally appear
and answer, and shew cause against the *said* complaint and matters required of them in the said summons, and that the justices thereupon, afterwards, to wit,
on, &c., at, &c., hearing what was alleged and proved
before them concerning the premises by both parties,
made their order in writing, whereby they ordered that
Margetts should be continued a member of the said
society. The indictment then stated, that *Soper* and
Camfield had notice of the order, and were requested to
continue *Margetts* a member of the said society, but that
they unlawfully and contemptuously refused so to do.
Plea, not guilty. At the trial before *Alexander* C. B.,
at the Summer assizes for the county of *Kent*, 1824, the
only proof of the complaint made by *Margetts* to the magistrates was contained in the order which was produced
in evidence by the prosecutor. That order recited that
Margetts, a free member of the society, personally complained upon his oath before the justices, that he, *Margetts*, had, for the space of sixteen days, to wit, between,
&c. been sick and infirm, and had been unable to follow
his trade, and that *Soper* and *Camfield*, the stewards of the
society, refused to pay him 1*l*. 0*s*. 6*d*., the arrears of allowance to which he was entitled as a sick member of the
society, for the last nine days of that period, at the rate of
16*s*. a week, against the form of the statute; the order then
recited, that the justices did issue a summons, requiring
the stewards to appear before them on the day of the
date of the order, to answer to the *said* complaint; and
upon the appearance of the stewards before them, in
pursuance of the summons, the justices had that day
proceeded peremptorily to hear and determine in a sum-

mary

mary way the matter of the *said* complaint, according to the true purport and meaning of the rules, orders, and regulations of the society, and according to the statute; and that upon such hearing they were satisfied that *Margetts* had not infringed any of the said rules, orders, and regulations, and that the sum of 16*s.* was then due to him from the said society for the arrears of his allowance as a sick member thereof; and they therefore ordered *Soper* and *Camfield* forthwith to pay to *Margetts* the sum of 16*s.*, and also the further sum of 11*s.* for the costs which *Margetts* had been put unto by reason of the stewards refusing to pay him the said allowance; and they further ordered, that *Margetts should be continued a member of the society*. It was objected for the defendants, that that part of the order which directed that *Margetts* should be continued a member of the society was illegal and void, because the justices had power only by the 33 *G. 3. c. 54.* to adjudicate upon the matter of the complaint before them, and it appeared by the recital in the order that the expulsion was no part of the matter of complaint. The Lord Chief Baron overruled the objection, and the defendants, *Soper* and *Camfield* were found-guilty. A rule nisi was obtained in last *Michaelmas* term upon the objection taken at the trial, and also upon the ground that the allegations in the indictment were not supported by the evidence, inasmuch as the allegations in the indictment were that *Margetts* had made complaint to the justices, first, that he had been expelled from the society; and, secondly, that he had been deprived of the relief which he was entitled to from the stewards of the society for the time being; and the proof was that he had only complained of his having been deprived of relief.

Campbell was now heard against the rule, and *C. Law* in support of it.

BAYLEY J. I am of opinion that the rule for a new trial ought to be made absolute. It is our duty to look at the indictment to see whether the charge contained in it was supported by the proof given at the trial; if it was not, then the defendants were entitled to an acquittal. The indictment states that *Margetts* had been expelled the society, and had been deprived of certain relief to which he was entitled, and that thinking himself, and being aggrieved *thereby*, he made complaint *thereof* to two justices, and took his oath before them, and deposed to the truth of the *said* complaint. The indictment therefore alleges a complaint to have been made involving two propositions, viz. first, that *Margetts* had been expelled from the society; and, secondly, that he had been deprived of relief. The proof was, that the complaint made was confined to one of those propositions, viz. that *Margetts* had been deprived of relief; and the indictment does not charge any disobedience of the order of the justices in that respect. It then proceeds to state that the stewards were summoned, and that they personally appeared and answered to and shewed cause against the complaint and matters required of them in the said summons, and that the justices afterwards made their order that *Margetts* should be continued a member of the society. Now that allegation imports that the stewards were summoned to answer and did answer the complaint, consisting of two branches, mentioned in the former part of the indictment. It appears, however, by the proof contained in the recital of the order, that they were summoned to

                                                    answer

answer one ground of complaint only. I therefore
think that these allegations were not made out in proof,
and that the defendants were entitled to an acquittal on
that ground. The indictment then states that the justices proceeded to order that *Margetts* should be continued a member of the society. A question therefore
arises whether the order was a valid order, because
if it was not, the defendants were not bound to obey it,
and consequently are not indictable for disobeying it.
The statute 33 *G.* 3. *c.* 54. *s.* 15. enacts, that if any
member of the society shall think himself aggrieved by
any thing done by any such society or person acting
under them, two justices, upon complaint upon oath of
such person, may summon the presidents or stewards of
the society, or any one of them, if the complaint be
made against the society collectively, and the justices are
to hear and determine in a summary way the *matter of
such complaint*, and to make such order *therein* as to
them shall seem just. The statute therefore confines
the jurisdiction of the magistrates to the subject matter
of the complaint before them. They cannot therefore
adjudicate upon any matter not comprehended in the
complaint made on oath before them. Now in this case
the only matter of complaint before the justices was,
that *Margetts* had been deprived of the relief to which
he was entitled. The justices have not only determined
that matter of complaint, but they have further ad-
judicated that *Margetts* should be continued a member
of the society, and that was not a matter brought before
them upon oath. Upon the ground therefore, first, that
the allegations in the indictment were not supported by
the proof, and, secondly, that that part of the order
which directs that *Margetts* should be continued a

3 K 3   member

member of the society was illegal, I think that the defendants were entitled to an acquittal, and that the rule for a new trial must therefore be made absolute.

·HOLROYD J. I also think that the ·rule for a new trial ought to be made absolute, because the allegations in the indictment were not ·supported by ·the· evidence given at the trial, and the verdict was therefore wrong, and the defendants were entitled to an acquittal. I also think that the justices had power only to· adjudicate upon the subject matter of complaint ·brought· before them. If the complaint had embraced ·the two propositions which the indictment supposes it ·to· have embraced, the justices would have been guilty of ·no excess of jurisdiction; but here the expulsion of Margetts was no part of the complaint before the magistrates, and the defendants were not summoned to answer for having expelled him. I therefore think that the magistrates acted unlawfully when they ordered that Margetts should be continued a member of the society, and that the defendants were not bound to obey that part of the order. Upon the ground, therefore, that the allegations in the indictment were ·not supported by proof, and that the defendants were not bound by law to obey the order made by the magistrates, I think that there ought to have been an acquittal, and consequently that the rule for a new trial ought to be made absolute.

· LITTLEDALE J. concurred.

Rule absolute.

The Queen v. Shaw D. 2 B. 419 1825.

CHATFIELD, Clerk, *against* RUSTON.

REPLEVIN. Avowry by the defendant, as overseer of the poor of the parish of *Chatteris*, in the county of *Cambridge*, that he seized and took the Plaintiff's goods and chattels by authority of the 43 *Eliz. c. 2.* Plea in bar, that by an act of the 49 *G. 3.*, entitled " An act for inclosing lands in the parish of *Chatteris*, in the isle of *Ely*, in the county of *Cambridge*," it was, amongst other things, recited, that it was convenient that all the tithes, both great and small, arising and renewing as well out of, in or upon the said open fields, commonable lands, commons and low grounds, by the said act intended to be divided and allotted, as also out of, in or upon such of the homesteads, gardens, orchards, and inclosures within the said parish, as were liable to the payment of tithes in kind, should be abolished and extinguished, and that in lieu thereof, an *adequate compensation* should be made to the impropriator of the impropriate rectory of *Chatteris* for the time being, and to the vicar of the vicarage of *Chatteris* for the time being, by an allotment in manner thereinafter mentioned, so far as respected the said open fields, lands, commons, and low grounds, and by an annual corn rent as thereinafter mentioned, so far as respected the said homesteads, gardens, orchards, and inclosures; and it was by the said act, among other things, enacted, that the said commissioners should make a valuation of all the tithes, both great and small, arising or renewing out of, in or upon the said homesteads, gardens, orchards, and in-

Where a private enclosure act (reciting that it was expedient that the tithes in the parish should be extinguished, and an adequate compensation should be made to the vicar), enacted that the commissioners should, in a certain mode, ascertain what yearly sum the tithes were worth, and that there should be issuing and payable to the vicar out of the lands, such yearly sum, " free and clear of all rates, taxes, and deductions whatsoever;" Held, that the vicar was not rateable to the poor in respect of the yearly sum so ascertained and paid to him.

3 K 4   closures,

closures, and to inquire of the clerks of the market, or of the inspectors of corn returns at *Wisbeach*, in the isle of *Ely*, what had been the average price of good marketable wheat in the said market during the term of fourteen years next preceding the first day of *January*, in the year of our Lord 1809, and should, in and by their award, ascertain and set forth what quantity of such wheat, according to the average price aforesaid, would be equal in value to all the tithes arising, renewing, and due or payable out of, or for the said homesteads, gardens, orchards, and inclosures, according to the valuation to be made as aforesaid; and that there should be issuing and payable to the said impropriator and vicar respectively, such several yearly rents or sums of money, *free and clear from all rates, taxes, and deductions whatsoever*, out of the said homesteads, gardens, orchards, and inclosures respectively, as should be equal in value to the quantity of wheat so to be ascertained as aforesaid; which said rents or sums of money should for ever afterwards be payable to the said impropriator and vicar respectively, in such proportions and manner as should be set forth in the said award of the said commissioners, by equal quarterly payments in every year. The plea then averred, that the commissioners made such valuation of the tithes, and ascertained the quantity of wheat equal to them in value; and that the commissioners duly made their award according to the provisions of the act, and proceeded thus. "And the plaintiff further saith, that he, the said plaintiff, after the passing of the said act, and the making of the said award, and long before, and at the said time when, &c. was, and from thence hitherto hath been, and still is vicar of the vicarage of the parish of *Chatteris* aforesaid; and

and

and so being vicar as aforesaid, at the said time when, &c., was, and from thence hitherto hath been, and still is, by virtue of the award of the said commissioners, intitled to the said yearly corn rent, so in and by the said award set forth, ascertained, and directed to be paid to the said vicar for the time being, free and clear from all rates, taxes, and deductions whatsoever. And the said plaintiff further saith, that the said goods and chattels in the said declaration mentioned, were seized, taken, and detained at the said time when, &c., by the said defendant as overseer of the poor of the parish of *Chatteris*, and as a distress for a certain sum of money, to wit, the sum of 76*l.* 3*s.* 9*d.*, rated and assessed on the 25th day of *November*, in the year of our Lord 1823, upon the said plaintiff, for and in respect of the said corn rents so ascertained and directed to be paid to the said plaintiff as aforesaid, in and by a certain rate and assessment, made and assessed according to the statutes in that case made and provided for, and towards the relief of the poor of the said parish of *Chatteris*, and which said sum the said plaintiff had, before the taking and detaining the said goods and chattels on demand, refused to pay, to wit, at *Chatteris* aforesaid, in the county aforesaid. Demurrer and joinder.

Tindal in support of the demurrer. The plain object of the legislature was, to give the vicar a compensation for the tithes and nothing more. The statute begins by reciting, that he is to have an *adequate compensation*, and then specifies the mode in which it is to be calculated and paid. It does not appear to have been intended to place the vicar in a better situation than he was before, nor to repeal the 43 *Eliz. c.* 2., unless that effect

effect is to be given to the words, " free and clear of rates, taxes, and all deductions." Those words will be satisfied by a decision, that the money is to be paid free from all deductions, payable in the first instance by the tenant of the lands, *ex. gr.* the land tax, for which the vicar would be liable to the tenant but for this exemption. By the statute of 43 *Eliz. c. 21*, the rate is not upon the tithe itself, but on the parson in respect of the tithe, and now it will be on him in respect of that which he receives in lieu of tithe, *Lowndes* v. *Horne* (a) In *Rex* v. *Lambeth* (b) it was laid down, that where a parson suffers a tenant to retain his tithes, he is nevertheless liable to poor rate, so also where there is a composition real or modus. It thence follows, that he is rateable in respect of the payments secured by this act. It is called a rent, and strictly rents are not rateable, but the nature of the rent must be considered. A ground rent is not rateable only because the occupier of the premises is rated in respect of the whole produce of the land, which is not the case in the present instance.

Marryat contrà. The exemption in this statute protects the vicar from the burden to which, but for that, he would have been liable. By this act a certain rent is payable for a certain number of years, during which no variation can be made in it. The act, therefore, operates as a lease of the tithes. Now where a parson makes a lease he ceases to be rateable, although the land is otherwise, where he merely by parol allows the tenant of the land to retain the tithes. *Rex* v. *Lambeth*, cited from [ ],

(a) 2 Bl. 1252.   (b) 3 T. R. 525.

is

is also reported in 8 *Mod.* 61., and by that report it appears, that the parson let the tithes, and that the lessee allowed the occupiers of the land to retain, and the court held, that the farmers of the tithe were to be rated; but they add, " It is true it might be otherwise if an under lease had been made thereof." The case of *Lowndes* v. *Horne* is very different from this. Here the act says, that there shall be a certain sum of money issuing out of the inclosed lands by way of rent, and that it shall be paid to the vicar, " free and clear from all rates, taxes, and deductions whatsoever," which last term did not exist in the act upon which *Lowndes* v. *Horne* was decided. The word " rates" was probably used to denote parochial burthens and " taxes," parliamentary imposts. In *Rex* v. *Toms* (a) it appeared, that a private act of parliament for settling the rights of the vicar of *St. Michael's, Coventry*, authorised the making an assessment in a certain mode. A subsequent section gave an option to the parish officers to raise yearly for him, in lieu thereof, a sum not exceeding 300*l.*, and not less than 280*l.*, which was to be paid to him " clear of all taxes, deductions, charges, and expences whatsoever, parochial, parliamentary, or otherwise howsoever;" and it was held, that although the claims of the vicar were satisfied by the former mode, and the clause and appointing that mode did not contain any express exemption, yet that the vicar was not liable to be rated in respect of the money so raised. An exemption in terms similar to those found in this act of parliament has in several cases been held sufficient to exempt property from poor rates; *Rex* v. *Calder Navigation* (b), *Rex* v.

(a) *Doug.* 401.   (b) 1 *B. & A.* 263.

Hull

Hull Dock Company. (a) No doubt the commissioners, in making their valuation of the rent, would take the exemption into consideration.

Tindal, in reply. It is not stated as a fact that the commissioners did take the exemption into consideration, and it cannot, therefore, be assumed that they did so. It is plain, that the words " free and clear of all rates and taxes," cannot be construed in their largest sense, for they would not have exempted the parson from the property-tax, had that now existed. The real meaning appears to be, that the money shall be free of all rates, &c., payable by the tenant. As to *Rex* v. *Toms,* there the assessment for the vicar was to be made by the churchwardens, amongst others; it would, therefore, have been somewhat absurd for the same persons first to fix what he should receive, and then call upon him to pay part back for the poor rates.

BAYLEY J. Under the statute 43 *Eliz. c. 2.* a parson or vicar is expressly made liable to be rated to the poor, and it is not necessary to shew that they occupy lands, &c. in the parish. But the question in the present case is, whether the act now before us exempts the vicar from such rates. That act was a matter of bargain between the parishioners, owners of lands, and the vicar. The act operates on the whole parish, and each proprietor of lands in the parish will derive a benefit from it; for their land will, of course, bring a higher rent, in consequence of being exonerated from tithes. After the provision for the extinguishment of tithes, comes that for

(a) 1 *T. R.* 219.

raising

raising and paying a certain sum of money to the vicar; but that is to be " free and clear of all rates, taxes, and deductions whatsoever." Those words must have some meaning. It is urged that they mean free from all rates and taxes payable by the tenant, but no such rates are pointed out, nor any such tax except the land tax. That meaning, therefore, will not satisfy the words of the statute. The act could not pass without the assent of the vicar, his rights being affected by it, and he would, probably, and not unreasonably, insist upon having a specific annual income, free from all deductions. I feel great difficulty in restraining the meaning of the words used in this act; they are large enough to exempt the vicar from all rates and taxes. I think, therefore, that they are sufficient to exonerate him from the payment now sought to be imposed.

HOLROYD J. I am of the same opinion. By the statute in question the tithes payable to the vicar were abolished, and an adequate compensation provided for them. It appears to have been intended that the compensation should be free from all rates and taxes, for the sum fixed is not only to be issuing out of the lands, but also to be payable to the vicar. That must mean, that he is to receive and keep the whole sum. According to the argument for the defendant the vicar would be no way benefited by the words " free and clear of all taxes," &c.; but I think they cannot be considered as inoperative, and that the vicar is entitled to the exemption which he claims.

Judgment for the plaintiff.

Doe dem. Beach *against* The Earl of Jersey.

Devise of all my *Briton Ferry* estate, and all the land, &c of which it consists; and then all my *Penline Castle* estate, which, as well as my *Briton Ferry* estate, lies in the county of *Glamorgan*. The jury found a special verdict, stating the will of the father of the devisor, and

A T the trial of this cause before *Dallas J.* at the *Hereford* Spring Assizes 1816, a bill of exceptions was tendered as to the admission of evidence offered on the part of the defendant, objected to on that of the plaintiff, and received by the learned Judge. After the usual statement of the pleadings and of the evidence received at the trial without objection, the bill of exceptions goes on to state the evidence objected to, in the following words. "And the counsel learned in the law for the said *George* Earl of *Jersey*, the said then defendant, proposed and offered to prove and give in evidence on

deeds of lease and release executed upon the marriage of the devisor, and certain schedules thereto annexed, purporting to contain a particular account of the several parishes and tenements comprehended in the estate of the devisor's father. Under the head of the *Brecon* estates was a parish called *Lywell*, which contained the messuage for which the ejectment was brought, and under the head of *Glamorganshire* estates was a parish called *Briton Ferry*.

The jury further found that the tenements in the county of *Brecon*, together with the manor and tenements in the county of *Glamorgan*, had been known by the name of the *Briton Ferry* estate for divers, to wit, fifty years before the death of the devisor. Held, that this was consistent with the other findings, especially the descriptions and names of the tenements in the county of *Brecon*, and of the manors and tenements in the county of *Glamorgan*, in the indenture and schedules found in the special verdict, inasmuch as the whole of an estate might be known by one name, and each of its parts by its own particular name: Held also, that it was not sufficiently found that the tenements and manors in the said county were so known by name by the devisor, the expression, divers, to wit, fifty years before the death of the devisor, being too loose and indefinite, as it did not denote any particular number of years, but duly divers years, nor import that the number of years, whatever it was, was a period immediately preceding the death of the devisor. At the trial the defendant offered to give in evidence account books of former stewards of the devisor and her predecessors, owners of the lands devised, in which the stewards charged themselves with the receipt of various sums of money on account of the said owners, and amongst others the following entry: " B F. estate, in the county of B.," and also it was given in evidence that the lands and tenements mentioned in the declaration, together with the lands and tenements in the schedules respectively contained, had all gone by the name of the B. F. estate, and such of the said lands, &c. as were in the county of B. extended over twelve parishes, and contained above 4000 acres of land. Held, that the words " my B. F. estate with all the manors, advowsons, &c. thereto belonging," denoted a property or estate known to the testatrix by the name of her B. F. estate, and not an estate locally situate in a parish or township of B. F.; and that the questions arising upon any particular tenement, was properly a question of parcel or no parcel; and, consequently, that the matters offered to be given in evidence were admissible, and ought to have been received.

the

1825.

Doe dem.
BRACH
against
The Earl of
JERSEY.

the part and behalf of the said Earl, the said then defendant, certain books, being stewards' account books, kept and made out by former stewards, now deceased, of the said *Louisa Barbara Vernan* and her predecessors, owners of the said lands, tenements, and hereditaments, containing particulars thereof, in which the said stewards charged themselves with the receipt of various sums of money on account of the said owners, and among other particulars the entry following, to wit, ' *Briton Ferry* estate, in the county of *Brecon ;*' and also proposed and offered to prove and give in evidence, that the lands and tenements in the said declaration mentioned, together with the lands, tenements, and hereditaments in the said schedules respectively contained, had all gone by the name of the *Briton Ferry* estate; and that such of the said lands, tenements, and hereditaments as were in the county of *Brecon*, extended over twelve parishes, and contained above 4000 acres of land."

The jury found a special verdict, upon which this Court in *Easter* term 1818 (*a*) gave judgment for the defendant. A writ of error having been brought, the question was fully discussed before the House of Lords, and in the course of the present session the following questions were put to the Judges :—

First, Whether all the several matters which it appears by the bill of exceptions were offered to be proved and given in evidence on the part of the defendant, and which it so appears it was insisted by the counsel of *John Doe* were inadmissible, and ought not to be received in evidence, were matters admissible, and

(*a*) 1 *B. & A.* 550.

which

1825.

Ber dem.
Bennet
against
The Earl of
Jersey.

which ought to have been received in evidence, regard
being had to the fact, that none of the particulars of
the evidence proposed to be given appear to have been
stated or required to be stated, in order to prove that
all the lands and tenements had gone by the name of
the *Briton Ferry* estate.

Second, Whether the finding in the special verdict
that the tenements in " the county of *Brecon*, together
with the manors and tenements in the county of *Glamorgan*, had been known by the name of the *Briton
Ferry* estate, and by no other name, for divers, to wit,
fifty years before the death of *Louisa Barbara Vernon*,
(who died in the year 1786), is consistent with the other
findings contained in the special verdict, and especially
with the descriptions and names of the tenements in the
county of *Brecon*, and of the manors and tenements in
the county of *Glamorgan*, in the several indentures and
the schedules thereunto annexed, found and set forth
in the said special verdict and in the will of *Louisa
Barbara Vernon* therein also found and set forth, and
which indentures and will appear to have been respectively executed within fifty years before the death of
the said *Louisa Barbara Vernon*.

Third, Whether upon the whole matter contained
in the special verdict, it ought to have been left to the
jury to find whether the tenements in the county of
Brecon, together with the manors and tenements in the
county of *Glamorgan*, were known by the testatrix by
the name of the *Briton Ferry* estate, or by that name
and that name only, for fifty years or some other period
before she executed her will and codicil in 1785; and
whether, upon the whole matter contained in the special
verdict, it is sufficiently found that the said tenement,
manors,

manors, and tenements in the said counties were so known by name by the testatrix.

Fourth, Whether regard being had to the matters contained in the special verdict and the will and codicil therein set forth, the second son of *George Bussey Villiers*, Earl of *Jersey*, took any and what estate in the tenements in the parish of *Lywell*, in the county of *Brecknock*, mentioned in the declaration.

The following answers of the Judges to these questions, were delivered by the Lord Chief Justice of the Court of King's Bench.

ABBOTT C. J. All the Judges, except the Lord Chief Baron and Mr. Justice *Littledale*, who were not present at the argument, have conferred upon the questions proposed, and have agreed upon answers thereto.

To the first question.

We are of opinion that the words " all that my *Briton Ferry* estate, with all the manors, advowsons, messuages, buildings, lands, tenements, and hereditaments thereunto belonging, or of which the same consists," found in the will of this testatrix, in which mention also is made of her *Penline Castle* estate, denote a property or estate known to the testatrix by the name of her *Briton Ferry* estate, and not an estate locally situate in a parish or township of *Briton Ferry*, and, consequently, that a question arising upon any particular tenement, is properly a question of parcel or no parcel; and we therefore think, the several matters offered to be proved and given in evidence on the part of the defendant were admissible, and ought to have been received. We think the object for which such evidence was offered was ob-

1825.

Doe dem.
Hanson
against
The Earl of
Jersey.

1825.

Doe dem.
Brace
against
The Earl of
Jersey.

vious, and must have been understood by the judge and the counsel on each side, without being specially stated or required to be so.

To the second question.

We are of opinion that the finding in the special verdict that the tenements in the county of *Brecon*, together with the manors and tenements in the county of *Glamorgan*, were known by the name of the *Briton Ferry* estate, and by no other name for divers (*a*), to wit, fifty years before the death of *Louisa Barbara Vernon*, is consistent with the other findings in the special verdict: In the will of Lord *Mansell*, and also in the deeds of 1740, mentioned in the special verdict, it was necessary to describe and name the particular tenements, because the will gave certain tenements only, and not the whole estate in trust for sale; and the deeds of 1740 were intended as an execution of that trust and a sale under it. The deeds of 1757 were a settlement on a marriage, and in such settlements, as well as other conveyances, it is usual to describe the parcels and enumerate the particulars of the estate intended to be settled; and we think a description and enumeration of particulars by situation and names is not inconsistent with a name of the whole, as composing an aggregate mass. The whole of an estate may be known by one name, and each of its parts by its own particular name.

To the third question.

We are of opinion that it is not sufficiently found that the said tenements and manors in the said counties were

(*a*) No point having been made on this finding in the Court of King's Bench, it was stated in the report of the case, 1 *B. & A.* 550, that the jury found that the tenement had been known by that name for fifty years; but in fact the words in the special verdict were for divers, to wit, fifty years.

1825.

Doe dem.
Beach
against
The Earl of
Jersey.

so known by name by the testatrix. In truth, it is not found that they were so known by name to any person at the time of making the will. The expression divers to wit, fifty years before the death of *Louisa Barbara Vernon*, is much too loose and indefinite. That expression denotes only divers years and not fifty, or any other particular number of years, nor does it plainly import that the number of years, whatever it be, was a period immediately preceding the death; so that it will not be inconsistent with this finding that the period should have had its commencement after the making of the will; or should have terminated, and the name have become obsolete and fallen into disuse long before the making of the will. This point was not in any manner suggested or noticed in the court below.

To the fourth question.

The special verdict being in our opinion imperfect, we are not able to say whether regard being had to the matters therein contained, the second son of *George Bussey Villers*, Earl of *Jersey*, did or did not take any estate in the tenements in the parish of *Lywell*, mentioned in the declaration in this cause.

The House of Lords awarded a venire de novo.

ACTION ON T...

1 Where there, ...

END OF HILARY TERM.

2 The right to light is acquired by ...
... where the party who uses ...
joy at the same time, that ...
act to shew an intention or resuming the enjoyment within a
reasonable time. And that ...
where in case by a reversioner for
obstructing lights, it appeared that
the plaintiff's messuage was ... ancient house, and that adjoining to
it there had formerly been a building, in which there was an ancient
window next the lands of the defendant, and that the former owner
of the plaintiff's premises, about
seventeen years before, had pulled
down this building, and erected a ...
... site together with a ...

... Where a manufacturer had adop-
... a particular mark for his goods,
in order to denote that they were
manufactured by him ; Held, that
an action on the case was maintainable by him against another
person who adopted the same mark
for the purpose of denoting that
the goods were manufactured by
the ..., and were sold ...

INDEX

PRINCIPAL MATTERS.

ACTION ON THE CASE.

1. Where there are mutual dealings between two parties, and items known to be due on each side of the account, an arrest for the amount of one side of the account without deducting what is due on the other, is malicious and without probable cause. *Austin* v. *Debnam, T. 5 G.* 4. Page 139

2. The right to light is acquired by enjoyment, and may be lost by a discontinuance of the enjoyment, unless the party who ceases to enjoy at the same time does some act to shew an intention of resuming the enjoyment within a reasonable time. And, therefore, where in case by a reversioner for obstructing lights, it appeared that the plaintiff's messuage was an ancient house, and that adjoining to it there had formerly been a building, in which there was an ancient window next the lands of the defendant, and that the former owner of the plaintiff's premises, about seventeen years before, had pulled down this building, and erected on its site another with a blank wall,

ACTION ON THE CASE.

next adjoining the premises of the defendant; and this latter, about three years before the commencement of the action, erected a building next the blank wall of the plaintiff, who then opened a window in that wall in the same place where the ancient window had been in the old building; it was held, that he could not maintain any action against the defendant for obstructing the new window; because, by erecting the blank wall, he not only ceased to enjoy the light, but had evinced an intention never to resume the enjoyment. *Moore* v. *Rawson, T. 5 G.* 4. Page 332

3. Where a manufacturer had adopted a particular mark for his goods, in order to denote that they were manufactured by him: Held, that an action on the case was maintainable by him against another person who adopted the same mark for the purpose of denoting that his goods were manufactured by the plaintiff, and who sold the goods so marked as and for goods

3 L 3   manu-

manufactured by the plaintiff. *Sykes* v. *Sykes and Another,* M. 5 G. 4.   Page 541

4. Where the vendor of a public house, made pending the treaty, certain deceitful representations respecting the amount of the business done in the house, and the rent received for a part of the premises, whereby the plaintiff was induced to give a large sum for the premises: Held, that the latter might maintain an action on the case for the deceitful representations, although they were not noticed in the conveyance of the premises, or in a written memorandum of the bargain which was drawn up after the representations were made. *Dobell* v. *Stevens,* H. 5 & 6 G. 4.   623

5. In an action for negligence against an attorney who was employed by a purchaser to inspect the title to an estate, it appeared that by indentures of lease and release of the 9th and 10th of *October* 1796, the estate had been conveyed to *T. M.,* the father of the vendor's wife, and to *J. C.* to hold unto the said *T. M.* and *J. C.,* and their heirs and assigns to the use and behoof of the said *T. M.* and *J. C.* and the heirs and assigns of the said *T. M.* for ever, the estate of *J. C.* being used only in trust for the said *T. M.,* his heirs and assigns: *T. M.* devised the estate to his daughter, and to the heirs of her body, but in case she died without leaving any issue of her body living at her decease, then to his nephew *T. M.,* and his heirs for ever. The daughter afterwards by bargain and sale of the 11th of *February* 1814, conveyed the estate to one *J. W.* to the intent that he might become tenant of the freehold for the purpose of suffering a recovery, and a recovery was suffered in pursuance of

such deed. The daughter afterwards by deeds of lease and release of the 4th and 5th of *March* 1814 executed upon her marriage, reciting that she was seised in fee simple of the estate, conveyed the same to two trustees in trust for her and her husband and their issue, and in default of issue to such person as she should appoint. The marriage was afterwards solemnized, and the daughter died without issue, and devised the estate in fee to her husband, who survived her. The husband having contracted to sell the estate to the plaintiff in pursuance of that contract, delivered an abstract of his title to the defendant as attorney to the vendee, and this abstract contained the deeds of the 9th and 10th of *October* 1796, but it omitted to state certain indentures of lease and release of the 25th and 26th of *February* 1814, whereby *J. C.* conveyed the said estate vested in him unto the daughter of *T. M.* in fee, but an abstract of these deeds was delivered by the vendor's solicitor to the defendant four months before the conveyance of the estate was executed. The defendant laid before counsel a case containing an abstract of the deed of the 11th of *February* 1814, and of the recovery suffered in pursuance of it, of the deeds of the 4th and 5th of *March* 1814, and of the will of the daughter of *T. M.,* but omitting altogether the deeds of the 9th and 10th of *October* 1796, and it further stated that *T. M.* was seised in fee of the premises. The opinion of counsel was, that the vendor had a good title, but that opinion would not have been given if the deeds of lease and release of the 9th and 10th of *October* 1796, or those of the 25th and 26th of *February* 1814 had been stated.

stated. The plaintiff afterwards being advised that his title was incomplete, paid a sum of money to *T. M.* the devisee, in remainder for a confirmation of his title: Held, first, that the recovery suffered by the daughter of *T. M.* was invalid, because at that time the legal estate for life was in *J. C.*, and she was only equitable tenant for life with a legal remainder in tail, and therefore that the title was bad:

Held, secondly, that upon these facts a jury were warranted in finding the defendant guilty of negligence, so as to make him liable in this action. *Ireson* v. *Pearman, Gent. one, &c., H. 5 & 6 G. 4.* Page 799

ADVERSE POSSESSION.

See EJECTMENT, 5.

AGREEMENT.

See LANDLORD AND TENANT, 3. 5. STAMP, 1, 2.

ALLUVION.

See LAND GAINED FROM THE SEA.

ANCIENT LIGHT.

See ACTION ON THE CASE, 2.

ANNUITY.

1. By deed, reciting the grant of two distinct annuities to *A.* and *B.* during the life of the grantors and the survivor, it was witnessed that *C.* covenanted with *A.* and *B.* and their executors to pay the annuities, or either of them, when the grantors should make default in payment. *A.* died: Held, that the interest in the annuities being several, the covenant was also several, and that the annuity granted

to *A.* being in arrear, his executor might maintain an action against *C. Withers, Executor of Barker,* v. *Bircham, T. 5 G. 4.* Page 254

2. *A.* and *B.* by deed, (reciting that *C.* had left them estates in strict settlement, with remainder over on failure of issue male, to *D.*,) out of their regard to *D.*, and considering that *C.* had made no other provision for him, agreed with *D.*, his executors and administrators, to pay him an annuity for twenty-one years, if *A.* and *B.*, or the survivor of them should so long live; and in case of the death of *D.* within the term, to his child or children, if any, in such proportions as *D.* should appoint, or in default of appointment, to all of them equally; and if there should be no child, to his then wife, so long as she should remain a widow. *D.* covenanted with *A.* and *B.*, their executors, &c., that in case he or his heirs should come into possession of the said estates under the will of *C.*, then that he, *D.*, his heirs, executors, or administrators, should pay to the executors or administrators of *A.* and *B.*, or the survivors of them, all sums of money received by him, his children, or wife, for or on account of the annuity. *D.*, his wife and child, died within the term, and it was held that the deed did not operate as the grant of an annuity for the term of twenty-one years absolutely, but that it was determinable by the death of the grantee, his children and wife, and therefore that *D.'s* administrator was not entitled to claim payment of the annuity. *Barford, Administrator,* v. *Stuckey, T. 5 G. 4.* 308

3. Where, in covenant against the executors of *A. B.*, plaintiff declared that *A. B.* covenanted with him and two others, that his executors, &c. should pay to them an

3 L 4

an annuity for the use of a third
person, and averred that the other
two never sealed the deed: Held,
on demurrer, that all joint covenantees who may sue, must sue,
and that the declaration was bad,
inasmuch as it did not appear that
any of the covenantees had not
assented to the deed, although
they did not seal it.

Quære, Whether the declaration
would have been sufficient if it had
averred that the two covenantees
not joined had refused to assent to
the deed. *Petrie v. Bury.* T.
5 G. 4. Page 853

APPEAL.

1. Where the magistrates at a special petty session dismiss an application under the 3 G. 4. c. 3. s. 2,
not on the merits, but on a mistaken notion of the law, an appeal
lies to the general quarter sessions.
The King v. Tucker, M. 5 G. 4.
544

2. An appeal against an order of
bastardy cannot be entered at the
quarter sessions, unless there be
such notice and recognizance as is
required by the 49 G. 3. c. 68. s. 7.
*The King v. The Justices of Lin-
colnshire,* M. 5 G. 4. 548

APOTHECARIES.

1. Where an apothecary, in an action to recover the amount of his
bill, produced in evidence a certificate, purporting to be granted
by the court of examiners of the
Apothecaries Company, and bearing twelve signatures, purporting
to be the signatures of the persons
constituting that court, of which
signatures he proved one, and gave
other evidence to shew that the
document was genuine, and that
he obtained it from the court of
examiners: Held, that this was

sufficient, and that he was not
bound to prove the hand-writing
of each member of the court of
examiners who had subscribed the
certificate. *Walmsley v. Abbott,*
T. 5 G. 4. Page 218

4. By an order of Nisi Prius, it
was referred to an arbitrator, with
liberty to him, if, &c.

ARBITRAMENT.

1. By an order of reference, the
award was to be delivered to the
parties, or if they were either of
them were dead before the making
of the award, to their respective
personal representatives on or before a given day, with liberty to
the arbitrator to enlarge the time
for making his award. The plaintiff died before the award was
made, and after his death, the arbitrator enlarged the time for
making the award: Held, that the
award made within the enlarged
time was good. *Tyler v. Jones,
Gent., one, &c.,* T. 5 G. 4. 444

2. Where a cause was referred to
two arbitrators specially named,
together with a third, to be chosen
by them, and the award of any
two was to be binding; and they
agreed that each should name one
person, and that the right of selecting one of those so named
should be determined by lot:
Held, that this mode of appointing the third arbitrator was bad,
and a sufficient ground for setting
aside the award. *Young v. Miller,* M. 5 G. 4. 407

3. Where a defendant was arrested
and holden to special bail for 28l.,
and paid 26 into court, and afterwards the cause, before it came on
for trial, and all matters in difference were referred to an arbitrator, who had power to examine
the parties, and call for books, &c.,
and it was agreed that the costs
should abide the event, the arbitrator having awarded to the plaintiff the sum of 11l. 19s. a motion
was

...was made to allow the defendant his costs; Held, that this was not a case within the 43 G. 3. c. 46. s. 3., and that the defendant was not entitled to costs. *Keene* v. *Deeble*, M. 5 G. 4. Page 491

4. By an order of Nisi Prius a cause was referred to an arbitrator, with liberty to him, if he should think fit, to examine the parties to the suit: Held, that the arbitrator might examine a party to the suit in support of his own case. *Warne* v. *Bryant*, M. 5 G. 4. 590

ARREST.

Where there are mutual dealings between two parties, and items known to be due on each side of the account, an arrest for the amount of one side of the account without deducting what is due on the other, is malicious, and without probable cause. *Austin* v. *Debnam*, T. 5 G. 4. 139

ASSETS.

See HEIR.

ASSUMPSIT.

1. A. being the occupier of a farm, quitted the same on the 25th of *March* 1821, and was succeeded in the possession by B. A. had sown forty acres with wheat, and it appeared that at a meeting between A. and B. in *February* 1821, A. asked B. if he would take the forty acres of wheat at 200l., telling him, if he did not, he should not have the farm. B. said that he would take it. A person present then valued the dead stock, and having so done, asked to whom he was to value it; B. said it was to be valued to him, and then promised to pay A. for the wheat and the dead stock on a given day, and he did pay a sum of money on account. B. afterwards had possession of the farm, the growing wheat, and the dead stock: Held, that in indebitatus assumpsit for crops bargained and sold, and goods sold and delivered, the contract for the dead stock was distinct from any contract for the sale of the growing wheat and the possession of the farm, and, therefore, that A. was entitled to recover to that amount: Held, also, by *Bayley* and *Holroyd* Js., *Littledale* J. dissentiente, that as B. had had the growing wheat, and made a part payment on account, A. was entitled in this action to recover the remainder of the price agreed to be paid for it. *Mayfield* v. *Wadsley*, T. 5 G. 4. Page 357

2. A. agreed to give a horse, warranted sound, in exchange for a horse of B. and a sum of money. The horses were exchanged, but B. refused to pay the money, pretending that A.'s horse was unsound: Held, that it might be recovered on an indebitatus count for horses sold and delivered. *Sheldon* v. *Cox*, M. 5 G. 4. 420

3. In assumpsit by two co-trustees for money had and received to their use, the defendant produced a receipt for the money given by one of the plaintiffs: Held, that this was not conclusive, and that evidence was properly admitted to shew that the giving of the receipt was a fraudulent transaction, and that the money had not been paid. *Skaife and Curis* v. *Jackson*, M. 5 G. 4. 421

4. A. and Co., resident in *America*, employed B., resident at *Birmingham*, in this country, to purchase and ship goods for them. On account of such purchases they sent to B. a bill drawn by C., in *America*, on D., in *London*, but did not

not indorse it. *B.* employed his bankers to present the bill for acceptance. *D.* refused to accept, but of this the bankers did not give notice until the day of payment, when it was again presented and dishonoured. Before the bill arrived in this country *C.* became bankrupt, and he had not either when the bill was drawn, or at any time before it became due, any funds in the hands of *D.*, the drawee. In an action by *B.* against the bankers for neglecting to give him notice of the non-acceptance of the bill: Held, that inasmuch as *A.* and Co. not having indorsed the bill, were not entitled to notice of the dishonor, and still remained liable to *B.* for the price of the goods sent to them, and the drawer was not entitled to notice, as he had no funds in the hands of the drawee, *B.* could not recover the whole amount of the bill, but such damages only as he had sustained in consequence of having been delayed in the pursuit of his remedy against the drawer. *Van Wart* v. *Woolley, Lewis, Moilliet, and Gordon, M. 5 G. 4.* Page 439

5. In assumpsit for goods sold, it appeared that the plaintiff, a jeweller, in the course of two months delivered articles of jewelry to the wife of the defendant, amounting in value to 83*l.* It appeared that the defendant was a certificated special pleader, and lived in a ready furnished house, of which the annual rent was 200*l.*; that he kept no man servant; that his wife's fortune upon her marriage was less than 4000*l.*; that she had at the time of her marriage jewelry suitable to her condition; and that she had never worn in her husband's presence any articles furnished her by the plaintiff; it appeared also, that the plaintiff

when he went to the defendant's house to ask for payment, always enquired for the wife, and not for the defendant: Held, that the goods so furnished were not necessaries, and that as there was no evidence to go to the jury of any assent of the husband to the contract made by his wife, the action could not be maintained. *Montague* v. *Benedict, H. 5 & 6 G. 4.* Page 631

6. In assumpsit for work and labour, and money expended in the purchase of shares in a concern called "The Equitable Loan Bank Company;" it appeared that the company professed to have a capital of 2,000,000*l.*, in shares of 50*l.* each; that a deposit of 1*l.* per share was required on the delivery of certificates for shares to the holders; that the shares were to be transferrable without any restriction; and that the holders were to be subject to such regulations as might be contained in any act of parliament passed for the government of the society, and in the mean time to such regulations as might be made by a committee of management. No evidence was given as to the particular objects or tendency of the company: Held, that upon this evidence the company was to be considered illegal, and within the operation of the 6 G. 1. c. 18. as having transferrable shares, and affecting to act as a body corporate without authority by charter or act of parliament, and that plaintiff consequently could not maintain his action, which arose out of an illegal transaction. *Josephs* v. *Pebrer, H. 5 & 6 G. 4.* 639

7. A certificated conveyancer may maintain an action to recover a compensation for business done. *Pouchez* v. *Norman, H. 5 & 6 G. 4.* 744

8. Where

8. Where the tenant of certain premises underlet a part by deed, and the original landlord distrained for rent upon the under-tenant : Held, that assumpsit would not lie by the latter against his lessor upon an implied promise to indemnify him against the rent payable to the superior landlord. *Schleucker* v. *Monsy, H. 5 & 6 G. 4.* Page 789

9. Where a scheme for establishing a tontine was put forth, stating that the money subscribed was to be laid out at interest, and after some subscriptions had been paid to the directors, in whom the management of the concern was vested, but before any part of the money was laid out at interest, the directors resolved to abandon the project : Held, that each subscriber might in an action for money had and received, recover the whole of the money advanced by him, without the deduction of any part towards the payment of the expences incurred. By the scheme it appeared that the money subscribed was to be laid out at interest, and to enure to the benefit of the survivors ; the subscribers were to be governed by regulations made by the directors, and at the end of a year shares were to be issued, and to be transferrable : Held, that this was not an undertaking within the operation of the statute *6 G. 1. c. 18. Nockells* v. *Crosley and Others, H. 5 & 6 G. 4.* 814

ATTORNEY.

See ACTION ON THE CASE, 5. LIEN, 1. PLEADING, 40. PRACTICE.

1. The court will order an attorney's bill to be taxed, though it consists merely of a charge for drawing a warrant of attorney and attending a defendant respecting it. *Wilson*

Gent. one, &c. v. *Gutteridge, T. 5 G. 4.* Page 157

2. Where an application is made to set off costs and damages in one action against those recovered in a cross action, an attorney has a lien on the judgment obtained by his client against the opposite party, to the extent of his costs of that cause only. *Stephens* v. *Weston and Griffiths, M. 5 G. 4.* 535

3. A special case was stated for the opinion of the Court. The greater part of the statement was fictitious. The Court fined the attorney. *In the Matter of Elsam, an Attorney, M. 5 G. 4.* 597

AUTREFOIS ACQUIT.

See PLEADING, 31.

AWARD.

See ARBITRAMENT.

BAIL.

See PRACTICE.

BANKRUPT.

1. A debt contracted in *England* by a trader residing in *Scotland* is barred by a discharge under a sequestration issued in conformity to the *54 G. 4. c.137.* in like manner as debts contracted in *Scotland. Sidaway* v. *Hay, T. 5 G. 4.* 12

2. The assignee of a bankrupt is not liable to the messenger under the commission for fees due to him before the choice of the assignee. *Burwood* v. *Felton, T. 5 G. 4.* 43

3. Where a private act of parliament, entitled " An act to enable a certain insurance society *to sue* and be sued in the name of their secretary," enacted that they might commence all *actions and suits* in his name as nominal plaintiff: Held, that this did not enable the secretary to petition, on behalf of the society,

society, for a commission of bankruptcy against their debtor. *Guthrie* v. *Fisk*, F. 5 G. 4. . . . Page 178

4. Declaration in sci. fa. stated that " R. So (the plaintiff in the original motion), because Bankrupt, whereupon commission was duly awarded against him; and E. F., R. B., and ... T. (the plaintiffs in the sci. fa.) were duly chosen assignees of the estate and effects of the said R. C. under the commission, and now on behalf of the said E. F., R. B., and J. T. his assignees as aforesaid, we have been informed, &c.:" Held, that this was good (defendant not having demurred to it), without an express averment that an assignment of the bankrupt's effects was made; for that the expression " assignees as aforesaid" might mean " persons to whom an assignment has been made;" and the 5 G. 2. c. 30. s. 26. having directed the choice of assignees to be followed up by an assignment of the effects to the persons chosen, the Court might presume that such an assignment was made.

Semble, that the objection would have been fatal if made the ground of special demurrer. *Fletcher* v. *Pogson*, F. 3 G. 4. . . . 192

5. The Court will order an exoneretur to be entered on the bail piece in all cases where the defendant is entitled to be discharged out of custody; and therefore where a defendant obtained his certificate under a commission of bankruptcy before trial, and did not plead it *puis darrein continuance*, the Court relieved the bail on motion.

The defendant had become bankrupt thrice, and had not paid 15s. in the pound to his creditors under the second commission: Held that the third commission was not therefore void, but voidable only; *Reed* v. *Mayfield*, F. 5 G. 4. . . . 222

B. and C. carried on the business of bankers in copartnership. A. advanced large sums of money to the concern, which he raised by selling out stock, and he took of ... bonds for 18,000l. from B. and C. conditioned for the replacing of 9000l. 3 per cent. consols by each, being their respective proportions of the stock sold by A. The stock not being replaced, A. brought actions, and recovered judgments on the bonds. A. afterwards retired from the concern, and at that time 20,000l. 3 per cent. consols was due to him, by the deed of dissolution B. and C. covenanted to replace it by four instalments, and that if they failed to do so, A. might resort to the judgments recovered on the bonds; and further, that he should have a lien on certain specified securities for that debt; and also as an indemnity against partnership debts which they covenanted to pay. One instalment was replaced when due, but B. and C. having failed to replace the second, a new agreement (not under seal) was entered into, whereby it was agreed that the transaction should be considered as a loan of money from the first, and that the sum produced by the sale of the 15,000l. 3 per cent. which remained due, which was 10,000l. should be the debt, and should bear regard at a future day with 5 per cent. interest. The value of 15,000l. 3 per cent. consols at the date of this last agreement was 9437l. Before any suit of the 10,000l. was paid, B. and C. became bankrupts, and at the taking of the commission of two or one of the three remaining days fixed by the deed of dissolution for replacing of the stock had passed. Held, that this second agreement was void for usury; but that the deed upon which the whole transaction originally rested remained subsisting, and that A. might

A. might

A. might prove, under the commission against *B.* and *C.* for the 15,000*l.* 3 per cent. consols, the value of the two instalments due before the bankruptcy, to be ascertained by the price of consols on the days when those sums respectively became due, the value of the third to be taken at the price of consols on the day when the commission issued, with a rebate for the interval between that day and the day fixed for the re-transfer of that instalment; and further, that *A.* still had the lien given by the deed. *A.* having paid certain old partnership debts after he left the concern: Held, secondly, that he might prove for those also. Whilst *A.* remained in the bank he received interest upon his advances, without any deduction for property tax: Held, thirdly, that no deduction was to be made in respect of that from the sum to be proved by him, inasmuch as it did not appear that the bankrupts had accounted to government for the property tax on the monies so paid. *Parker v. Ramsbottom and Others, T. 5 G. 4.* Page 257

7. By lease the lessor demised to the lessee a colliery and all the engines, machinery, and other implements, effects, and things, then lying on or about the colliery, or used or employed therewith, and mentioned in a certain inventory and valuation then made, habendum for 21 years, at a certain rent therein mentioned. The lease contained a proviso for re-entry in case the rent should be in arrear for the space of thirty days, and also a proviso, that, on the expiration or other sooner determination of the demise, the lessee should leave and yield up to the lessor all engines, machines, effects, and things belonging to and used by the said colliery; and that an inventory and valuation should three months previous thereto, be made and taken by two indifferent persons to be appointed by the parties respectively, or by an umpire; and such inventory should be compared with the then present inventory and valuation, and that the difference in the value of the engines &c. should be paid by the landlord or tenant to the other, according as it was greater or less than the value at the time of the letting. The tenant entered and, occupied the colliery, machinery &c., and failing in the payment of the rent, the lease became forfeited, and the landlord recovered a judgment in ejectment in *Trinity* term 1818, but did not execute his writ of possession until the 9th of *November* 1819. On the following day the tenant committed an act of bankruptcy. The lease having become forfeited by the act of the tenant, no inventory or valuation of the machines and other effects and things, belonging to the collieries, was made three months before the determination of the demise: Held, however, as the tenant by his own act had determined the lease, and had thereby rendered it impracticable for the landlord to have a valuation made three months before the determination of the demise, that the latter was entitled without any such valuation having been made, to recover the possession of the fixtures, machinery, and other effects used in the colliery upon the determination of the demise by such forfeiture; and that he was entitled to demand such possession even of, using machinery erected by the tenant during the term, in the ... Held, secondly, that the tenant never had, under this demise, the ... possession, either ... disposition of the fixtures, or moveable articles, within

within the meaning of the 21 *Jac.*1. c. 19., but a mere qualified right to use them during the term; and if they had been in his possession, &c., within the meaning of the statute, that would have ceased when the landlord resumed possession on the 9th of *November*.

During the intermediate time between the recovery of the judgment in *Trinity* term 1818, and the execution of the writ of hab. fac. poss. on the 9th of *November* 1819, the bankrupt continued to work the colliery, and to have the use of the machinery and implements: Held, that during this period, the bankrupt had not the order or disposition of the machinery and implements, within the meaning of the statute of *James*. *Storer and Others, Assignees,* v. *Hunter, T.* 5 *G.* 4.   Page 968

3. *A.*, a merchant in *London*, ordered goods to be made by *B.*, a manufacturer in the country. The goods were made to order, but before they were forwarded to *A.*, *B.* committed an act of bankruptcy, and afterwards shipped the goods, having previously, but after the act of bankruptcy, drawn upon *A.* a bill of exchange for a larger sum than the price of the goods ordered, which bill *A.* accepted, not then knowing that *B.* had committed an act of bankruptcy. The goods having afterwards come to the possession of *A.*, it was held, that the assignees were entitled to recover them, because, the property in them remained in the bankrupt, both at the time when the act of bankruptcy was committed, and when the bill was accepted by *A.*, and therefore, this was not a payment protected by the 1 *Jac.* 1. c. 15. s. 14.; because, *A.* was not a debtor of *B.* at the time when the acceptance was given. *Bishop and Others, As-*

signees, v, *Crawshay and Others.* *M.* 5 *G.* 4.   Page 415

BARON AND FEME.

1. A woman divorced a mensa et thoro for adultery, and living separate and apart from her husband cannot be sued as a feme sole. *Lewis* v. *Lee, T.* 5 *G.* 4.   291

2. In assumpsit for goods sold, it appeared that the plaintiff, a jeweller, in the course of two months delivered articles of jewelry to the wife of the defendant, amounting in value to 83*l.* It appeared that the defendant was a certificated special pleader, and lived in a ready furnished house, of which the annual rent was 200*l.*; that he kept no man servant; that his wife's fortune, upon her marriage, was less than 4000*l.*; that she had at the time of her marriage jewelry suitable to her condition, and that she had never worn, in her husband's presence, any articles furnished her by the plaintiff; it appeared also that the plaintiff, when he went to the defendant's house to ask for payment, always enquired for the wife, and not for the defendant: Held that the goods so furnished were not necessaries, and that, as there was no evidence to go to the jury of any assent of the husband to the contract made by his wife, the action could not be maintained. *Montague* v. *Benedict, H.* 5 & 6 *G.* 4.   681

BASTARDY, ORDER OF.

See APPEAL, 2.

BILL OF EXCHANGE.

1. Where a bill of exchange was given for the principal money lent and interest to accrue due on a usurious contract, and before the bill became due, the lender advanced

vanced a further sum of money, on the general credit of the borrower, which enabled the latter to pay the bill, it was held the payment of the usurious interest was complete as soon as the bill was paid. *Wright* v. *Laing, T. 5 G. 4.* Page 165

2. Certain bills of exchange, drawn upon and accepted by the *E. I.* Company in favor of *W. H.* in *India*, were afterwards indorsed to *D.* and *C.* by an agent for *W. H.*, under a supposed authority given by a power of attorney, which was seen and inspected by the acceptors; *D.* and *C.* indorsed the bills to *B.* and *Co.* their bankers, in order that the latter might, as their agents, present them for payment when due; *B.* and *Co.* put their names on the back of the bills presented them for payment, and received the amount, which they soon after paid over to their principals. It was afterwards discovered that the power of attorney given by *W. H.* did not authorise his agent to indorse the bills, and the administrator of *W, H.*, in an action against the acceptors, recovered the amount of them. The acceptors then brought an action against *B.* and *Co.*, and declared on a supposed undertaking by them, that they, as holders, were entitled to receive the amount of the bills. The jury found that the plaintiffs paid the bills on the faith of the power of attorney, and not of the indorsement by the defendants, and that the latter paid over the money before they had notice of the invalidity of the first indorsement: Held, that, under these circumstances, the plaintiffs could not recover against the defendants.

Semble, that an indorser does not impliedly warrant the validity of prior indorsements. *The East India Company v. Tritton and Others, T. 5 G. 4.* 980

3. Certain bills of exchange purporting to have, amongst others, the indorsement of *H.* and *Co.* bankers of *Manchester*, were presented for payment in *London*, at a house where the acceptance appointed them to be paid; payment being refused, the notary who presented them, took them to the plaintiff, the *London* correspondent of *H.* and *Co.*, and asked him to take up the bills for their honor. He did so, and struck out the indorsements subsequent to that of *H.* and Co., and the money was paid over to the defendants, the holders of the bills. The same morning, it was discovered that the bills were not genuine, and that the names of the drawer, acceptor, and *H.* and Co. were forgeries. Plaintiff immediately sent notice to the defendant, and demanded to have the money repaid. This notice was given in time for the post, so that notice of the dishonor could be sent the same day to the indorsers: Held, that the plaintiff having paid the money through a mistake, was entitled to recover it back, the mistake having been discovered before the defendant had lost his remedy against the prior indorsers: Held, secondly, that the rights of the parties were not altered by the erasure of the indorsements, that having been done by mistake, and being capable of explanation by evidence. *Wilkinson and Others v. Johnstone and Others, M. 5 G. 4.* Page 428

4. *A.* and Co., resident in *America*, employed *B.*, resident at *Birmingham* in this country, to purchase and ship goods for them. On account of such purchases they sent to *B.* a bill drawn by *C.* in *America* on *D.* in *London*, but did not indorse it. *B.* employed his bankers to present the bill for acceptance. *D.* refused to accept; but of this the

the bankers did not give notice until the day of payment, when it was again presented and dishonored. Before the bill arrived in this country, C. became bankrupt, and he had not either when the bill was drawn, or at any time before it became due, any funds in the hands of D., the drawee. In an action by B. against the bankers for neglecting to give him notice of the non-acceptance of the bill: Held, that inasmuch as A. and Co. not having indorsed the bill, were not entitled to notice of the dishonor, and still remained liable to B. for the price of the goods sent to them, and the drawer was not entitled to notice, as he had no funds in the hands of the drawee; B. could not recover the whole amount . of the bill, but such damages only as he had sustained in consequence of having been delayed in the pursuit of his remedy against the drawer. *Van Wart* v. *Woolley and Others*, M. 5 G. 4.   Page 439

6. Where a bill of exchange was stolen during the night, and taken to the office of a discount broker early in the following morning, by a person whose features were known, but whose name was unknown to the broker, and the latter being satisfied with the name of the acceptor, discounted the bill, according to his usual practice, without making any enquiry of the person who brought it: Held that, in an action on the bill by the broker against the acceptor, the jury were properly directed to find a verdict for the defendant, if they thought, that the plaintiff had taken the bill under circumstances which ought to have excited the suspicion of a prudent and careful man; and they having found for the defendant, the Court refused to disturb the verdict. *Gill* v. *Cubitt and Others*, M. 5 G. 4.   466

BOND.

1. Where a foreign prince gave bonds, whereby he declared himself and his successors bound to every person who should for the time being, be the holders of the bonds for the payment of the principal and interest in a certain manner: Held, that the property in those instruments passed by the delivery, as the property in bank notes, exchequer bills, or bills of exchange payable to bearer; and that consequently an agent in whose hands such a bond was placed, for a special purpose, might confer a good title by pledging it to a person who did not know that the party pledging was not the real owner. *Georgier* v. *Mieville and Another*, T. 5 G. 4.   Page 45

2. A. B. seised of lands in fee simple at the time of her death, in the possession of a tenant from year to year, died, leaving C. D. her heir at law. No rent was ever paid to him, it being supposed that the lands passed to a devisee under the will of A. B. After the death of C. D., his son and heir at law brought ejectment and recovered the lands. In debt against the son as heir of C. D., on a bond given by the latter, to which the son pleaded no assets by descent from his father, it was held that the father was seised *in fact* of the lands in question, that they descended from him to his son, and were therefore assets in the hands of the latter, liable to the bond debt. *Bushby and Another, Executors,* v. *Dixon,* T. 5 G. 4.   Page 298

CARRIER.

1. The driver of a van passing to and from *London* and *York,* is a carrier within the meaning of the 3 *Car.* 1. c. 4., and liable to be convicted in the penalty of 20s. for

for travelling on the Lord's day.
Ex parte 'Middleton, *T. 5 G. 4.*
               Page 164

2. An agent employed by a commercial house in *London* to collect debts in the country, delivered a parcel containing bank notes to a common carrier, to be forwarded to his principals in *London*, which parcel was lost. The carriers had given notice, that they would not be accountable for parcels containing bank notes. The agent had no knowledge of such notice, but the principals had: Held, that it was their duty to have instructed their agent not to send bank notes by that carrier, and that the latter was not responsible. *Mayhew and another* v. *Eames and Another*, *H. 5 & 6 G. 4.*   601

CERTIORARI.

1. An ejectment brought in an inferior court on a lease executed and sealed on the premises, which were within the jurisdiction of the court, may be removed to this Court by certiorari, if there be any ground for believing that it cannot be impartially tried in an inferior court. *Patterson dem. Gradridge* v. *Eades*, *M. 5 G. 4.*   550

2. The appointment of surveyors of highways, under the 13 *G. 3. c.* 78., cannot be removed into this Court by certiorari. *The King* v. *The Justices of St. Alban's*, *H. 5 & 6 G. 4.*   698

CHARTER-PARTY.

Where the commander of a ship entered into a charter-party (not under seal), whereby the charterer agreed to pay freight generally, without saying to whom: Held, that the owner having demanded and received the freight, the com-

mander could not maintain an action for it against the charterer, although he had given him notice not to pay it to any one but himself. *Atkinson* v. *Cotesworth*, *H. 5 & 6 G. 4.*   Page 647

CHURCHWARDENS.

See SETTLEMENT BY APPRENTICESHIP.

COMMITMENT.

See CONVICTION, 2.

COMPOSITION.

1. A tenant conveyed his interest in leasehold premises to trustees for the benefit of his creditors, by deed containing a proviso, that if all and every of the creditors should refuse to execute or consent to the deed within six months from the date thereof it should be void: Held, that the non-execution of the deed by a particular creditor, was not evidence of a refusal by him to execute or assent, but that it was incumbent on a party seeking to avoid the deed to shew a positive refusal to execute or assent to the deed. *Holmes* v. *Love and Tucker*, *T. 5 G. 4.*   242

2. In an action by the assignee of a bankrupt, it was referred to an arbitrator to take accounts between the parties, with liberty to him to state on the face of his award any point of law that either party might require. The arbitrator by his award found the following facts. The defendant, before the bankruptcy, had accepted bills drawn upon him by the bankrupt. These bills had been paid away to creditors of the bankrupt. At the time of his accepting the bills the defendant, as the agent of the bankrupt, had in his hands money of the bankrupt to the full amount of

3 M   the

the sum for which the bills were drawn, and these funds had. not been withdrawn at the time of his bankruptcy. After the bills became due respectively, and before the act of bankruptcy, the holders of the bills, in order to relieve the defendant from his responsibility to them, took from the defendant a composition upon the acceptances, and delivered up the bills to the defendant; but the bankrupt was not a party to this arrangement. The award then stated, that in taking the accounts between the parties, the arbitrator had not allowed the amount of the sums for which the bills were drawn to be set off by the defendant, but only the amount of the composition : Held, that the defendant was entitled to have the full amount of the bills allowed him in account. *Stonehouse, Assignee, v. Read, H. 5 & 6 G. 4.* Page 669

CONVEYANCER.

See Assumpsit, 7.

CONVICTION.

1. The driver of a van passing to and from *London* and *York*, is a carrier within the meaning of the 3 *Car.* 1. *c.* 4., and liable to be convicted in the penalty of 20s. for travelling on the Lord's day. *Ex parte Middleton, T. 5 G. 4.* 164

2. In an action against a magistrate for false imprisonment, the plaintiff proved a commitment for a certain alleged offence. The defendant proved a conviction of the plaintiff for an offence different from that recited in the commitment : Held, that this conviction was no justification of the imprisonment.

The defendant, in order to deprive the plaintiff of his costs under the 43 G. 3. c. 141., tendered evi-

dence to shew that the offence mentioned in the conviction had actually been committed by the plaintiff : it was held, however, that that statute applied only to cases where convictions had been quashed, and, therefore, that the evidence was not admissible for that purpose. Quære, whether it was admissible in mitigation of damages. *Rogers* v. *Jones, M. 5 G. 4.* Page 409

COPYHOLD.

1. The Court will grant a mandamus to admit a copyholder claiming by descent. *The King* v. *The Masters, Keepers, Wardens, and Commoners of the Brewers' Company, T. 5 G. 4.* 172

2. Semble, that coparceners are entitled to be admitted to copyhold tenements as one heir, and upon the payment of one set of fees. *The King* v. *The Lord of the Manor of Bonsall, and Adam Wolley, Steward of the said Manor, T. 5 G. 4.* 173

CORPORATION.

1. Where a charter does not require the members of a corporation to be resident, the Court will not grant a mandamus commanding the corporation to meet and consider of the propriety of removing from their offices non-resident corporators, unless their absence has been productive of some serious inconvenience.

An alderman is not bound to reside within the borough, unless that is necessary to the discharge of the duties of his office, or required by the charter. *The King* v. *The Mayor and Aldermen of the Borough of Portsmouth, T. 5 G. 4.* 152

2. In an action for the breach of a bye law, restraining persons from exercising

exercising trades within the limits of a corporate city, unless they become freemen, the Court will compel the corporation to allow the defendant to inspect the bye law in the corporation books. *Harrison and Another v. Williams*, T. 5 G. 4.   Page 162

3. Where an inhabitant of a borough applied for a mandamus to the mayor and steward of the borough, to enrol and swear him at the Court leet of the borough as a resiant and burgess, but did not make out an incboate right in every inhabitant to be a burgess, or that any such connexion existed between the corporation and the court leet as would make swearing and enrolment at the latter the means of perfecting such right, the Court refused the writ. *The King v. The Mayor, &c. of West Looe*, H. 5 & 6 G. 4.   677

4. By charter, the aldermen, bailiffs, and burgesses had power to elect two of the burgesses to be aldermen of the borough for one whole year, and they were to have power and authority to execute by themselves, or in their absence by their deputies, the office of aldermen of the borough. The charter then contained clauses by which it was provided, that in the event of the death or removal of any alderman, a new one might be elected, who, during the remainder of the year, should execute the office by himself or his deputy. It was then provided, that in the absence of any of the aldermen for the time being, the bailiffs and capital burgesses might elect one or more of the burgesses to supply the vacancy or vacancies. These substituted aldermen had no power to appoint deputies. There then followed a clause, which directed that the aldermen for the time being, during the time they should remain in

their offices, should be justices of the peace within the borough: Held, that this charter did not enable the aldermen elected for the year to delegate their office of justice of the peace, and, therefore, that a deputy alderman was not a justice of peace for the borough.

Quære, whether since the statute 27 H. 8. c. 24. s. 2., the crown can delegate to a subject the power of appointing a justice of the peace. *Jones v. Williams*, H. 5 & 6 G. 4.   Page 762

COSTS.

See CONVICTION, 2.

1. Where a defendant was by a Judge's order allowed to go to trial upon certain terms, upon payment to the plaintiff of a certain sum of money and the costs incurred up to the date of the order; and the plaintiff consented to the trial proceeding on those terms before the costs had been paid: Held, that the defendant having obtained a verdict, was bound to pay those costs, and could not set them off against those afterwards taxed for him on the postea. *Aspinall v. Stamp*, T. 5 G. 4.   108

2. The inhabitants of a town, not within any hundred, are not entitled to be re-imbursed the expences which they incur in defending actions brought against them on the 57 G. 3. c. 19. s. 38., to recover the damages done by tumultuous assemblies. *Rex v. The Justices of King's Lynn*, T. 5 G. 4.   147

3. If a defendant removes an indictment here by certiorari, giving the usual recognisance under statute 5 W. & M. c. 11., and be found guilty and die before the day in bank, his bail are liable to pay the costs. *Rex v. Turner*, T. 5 G. 4.   160

4. Where

4. Where a defendant was arrested and holden to special bail for 28*l*., and paid 2*l*. into court, and afterwards the cause before it came on for trial, and all matters in difference were referred to an arbitrator, who had power to examine the parties and call for books, &c. and it was agreed that the costs should abide the event; the arbitrator having awarded to the plaintiff the sum of 1*l*. 19*s*., a motion was made to allow the defendant his costs: Held, that this was not a case within the 43 *G*. 3. *c*. 46. *s*. 3., and that the defendant was not entitled to costs. *Keene* v. *Deeble*, M. 5 *G*. 4.   Page 491

5. Where an application is made to set off costs and damages in one against those recovered in a cross action, an attorney has a lien on the judgment obtained by his client against the opposite party, to the extent of his costs of that cause only. *Stephens* v. *Weston and Griffiths*, M 5. *G*. 4.   535

COURT BARON.

See PLEADING, 29.

COURT.

Upon error from an inferior court, it appeared by the record that in an action of debt, a summons and attachment issued at the same time, and were returnable at the same time; neither of them was served personally on the defendant. At the return of these writs the plaintiff declared, and at a subsequent court had judgment by default, the defendant never having appeared, and no appearance having been entered for him. The recorder of the inferior court certified this to be the practice of the court according to immemorial custom: Held, that the custom to declare against a defendant before entry of appearance by him, or by some person for him, was bad in law.

Semble, that the custom to issue a summons and attachment at the same time was also bad. *Williams* v. *Lord Bagot*, (*in Error*), H. 5 & 6 *G*. 4.   Page 772

COVENANT.

1. By deed, reciting the grant of two distinct annuities to *A*. and *B*. during the life of the grantors and the survivor, it was witnessed, that *C*. covenanted with *A*. and *B*. and their executors, to pay the annuities, or either of them, when the grantors should make default in payment: *A*. died: Held, that the interest in the annuities being several the covenant was also several, and that the annuity granted to *A*. being in arrear, his executor might maintain an action against *C*. *Withers, Executor*, v. *Bircham and Another, Executors*, T. 5 *G*. 4.   254

2. *A*. and *B*. by deed (reciting that *C*. had left their estates in strict settlement, with remainder over on failure of issue male to *D*.), out of their regard to *D*. and considering that *C*. had made no other provision for him, agreed with *D*., his executors and administrators, to pay him an annuity for twenty-one years, if *A*. and *B*. or the survivor of them should so long live; and in case of the death of *D*. within the term, to his child or children, if any, in such proportions as *D*. should appoint, or in default of appointment, to all of them equally; and, if there should be no child, to his then wife, so long as she should remain a widow. *D*. covenanted with *A*. and *B*. their executors, &c., that in case he (or his heirs should come into possession of the said estates under the will of *C*., then

then that he *D.*, his heirs, executors, or administrators, should pay to the executors or administrators of *A.* and *B.*, or the survivors of them, all sums of money received by him, his children, or wife, for and on account of the annuity. *D.*, his wife and child died within the term, and it was held, that the deed did not operate as the grant of an annuity for the term of twenty-one years absolutely, but that it was determinable by the death of the grantee, his children, and wife, and, therefore, that *D.*'s administrator was not entitled to claim payment of the annuity. *Barford, Administrator, v. Stuckey, T. 5 G. 4.*
             Page 308

3. Where, in covenant against the executors of *A. B.*, plaintiff declared that *A. B.* covenanted with him and two others, that his executors, &c. should pay to them an annuity for the use of a third person, and averred that the other two never sealed the deed: Held, on demurrer, that all joint covenantees who may sue must sue, and that the declaration was bad, inasmuch as it did not appear that any of the covenantees had not assented to the deed, although they did not seal it.

Quære, whether the declaration would have been sufficient if it had averred that the two covenantees not joined, had *refused* to assent to the deed? *Petrie* v. *Bury and Another, Executors, T. 5 G. 4.* 353

4. Where the tenant, under a lease containing a covenant to repair, underlet the premises to one who entered into a similar covenant, and the original lessor brought an action on this covenant in the first lease, and recovered: Held, that the damages and costs recovered in that action, and also the costs of defending it, might be recovered as special damages in an action against the undertenant for the breach of his covenant to repair. *Neale* v. *Wyllie, M. 5 G. 4.*   Page 533

CUSTOM.

Upon error from an inferior court, it appeared by the record, that in an action of debt a summons and attachment issued at the same time, and were returnable at the same time: neither of them was served personally on the defendant. At the return of these writs the plaintiff declared, and at a subsequent court had judgment by default, the defendant never having appeared, and no appearance having been entered for him. The recorder of the inferior court certified this to be the practice of the court, according to immemorial custom: Held, that the custom to declare against a defendant before entry of appearance by him, or by some person for him, was bad in law:

Semble, That the custom to issue a summons and attachment at the same time was also bad. *Williams* v. *Lord Bagot* (*In Error*) *H. 5 & 6 G. 4.*   772

DEBT.

A debt contracted in *England* by a trader residing in *Scotland* is barred by a discharge under a sequestration issued in conformity to the 54 *G.* 3. *c.* 137., in like manner as debts contracted in *Scotland. Sidaway* v. *Hay, T. 5 G. 4.*   12

DEED.

See PLEADING, 15.

1. Where *B.* being indebted to *A.* procured *C.* to join with him in giving a joint and several promissory note for the amount, and afterwards having become further indebted, and being pressed by *A.*

for further security by deed (reciting the debt, and that for a part a note had been given by him (B) and C., and that A. having demanded payment of the debt B. had requested him to accept a *further* security), assigned to A. all his household goods, &c. as a *further* security, with a proviso that he should not be deprived of the possession of the property assigned until after three days' notice: Held, that this deed did not extinguish or suspend the remedy on the note, but that A. might, notwithstanding the deed, sue C. at any time. *Twopenny and Boys* v. *Young*, T. 5 G. 4. Page 208

2. A. and B., by deed (reciting that C. had left them estates in strict settlement, with remainder over on failure of issue male to D.) out of their regard to D., and considering that C. had made no other provision for him, agreed with D., his executors and administrators, to pay him an annuity for twenty-one years, if A. and B. or the survivor of them should so long live; and in case of the death of D. within the term, to his child or children, if any, in such proportions as D. should appoint, or in default of appointment, to all of them equally; and if there should be no child, to his then wife, so long as she should remain a widow. D. covenanted with A. and B., their executors, &c., that in case he or his heirs should come into possession of the said estate, under the will of C., then that he, D., his heirs, executors, or administrators, should pay to the executors or administrators of A. and B., or the survivor of them, all sums of money received by him, his children, or wife, for and on account of the annuity. D. his wife and child died within the term, and it was held, that the deed did not operate as the grant

of an annuity for the term of twenty-one years absolutely, but that it was determinable by the death of the granted, his children, and wife; and, therefore, that D.'s administrator was not entitled to claim payment of the annuity. *Burford, Administrator*, v. *Stuckey*, T. 5 G. 4. Page 308

3. T. C., possessed of lands for the residue of a long term of years, by indenture of three parts, dated November 1st, 1771, between T. C. of first part, J. W. and T. L. of second part, and E. K. of third part, in consideration of an intended marriage between T. C. and E. K., "and for the considerations mentioned and expressed in a certain indenture of three parts, intended to bear date after the date thereof, and made between T. C. S. H., and J. H. of the first part, W. C. and J. K. of the second part, and E. K. of the third part, and for other good considerations," assigned the said lands to J. W. and T. L. for the residue of the said term, upon trust to permit and suffer T. C., his executors, &c., to receive the rents for his own use until the solemnization of the intended marriage, and afterwards to permit T. C. to receive the rents for his life, and afterwards to permit the wife to receive the rents for her life, and upon other subsequent trusts. By indenture of three parts, dated November 2d, 1771, between T. C., S. H., and J. H. of the first part, W. C. and J. K. of the second part, and E. K. of the third part, T. C. enfeoffed W. C. and J. K. of the lands mentioned in the deed of November 1st, 1771, upon certain trusts. The deed contained a power of attorney to deliver seisin, and a memorandum of livery of seisin was indorsed upon it. T. C. continued in possession of the lands

lands from the 1st of *November* 1771 till the time of his death in 1809. In ejectment against the executor of *T. L.*, who survived *J. W.*: Held, that the term "assigned to *J. W.* and *T. L.*" was not destroyed by the feoffment, because it did not appear that they ever assented to it. *Doe dem. of Maddock and Others*, v. *Lynes* and Another, T. 5 G. 4. Page 388

DEVISE.

1. *G. E.* seised of the manor of *M.*, amongst other estates in fee, conveyed it to trustees and their heirs, to secure to his wife an annuity for her life, and subject thereto to the use of himself in fee. *G. E.* by his will duly executed to pass real estates, recited and confirmed that settlement, and then devised to *J. E.* (who died in testator's lifetime) and *A. H. C.* and their heirs, his freehold and copyhold estate in *S.* and his freehold estate at *H.* upon the following, amongst other, trusts; viz. in case there should be but one son of his daughter *E. D.* by her husband *T. D.* who should attain the age of twenty-one years, then upon trust for such son, his heirs and assigns for ever; and in case there should be two or more sons of Mrs. *D.* who should attain the age of twenty-one years, then in trust for the second of such sons, his heirs and assigns for ever; and in case there should be no son of Mrs. *D.* by the said *T. D.* who should live to attain the age of twenty-one years, then upon trust for such of the daughters, if any, of Mrs. *D.* by *T. D.* as should first attain the age of twenty-one years, or be married under that age with the consent of the trustees or trustee for the time being of that his will, and the heirs and assigns of such daughter for ever. After

some pecuniary legacies, the testator proceeded as follows: "And as to, for, and concerning all the rest, residue, and remainder of the property of which I shall be possessed, or to which I shall be entitled at the time of my decease, or over which I have a disposing power, whether the same consists wholly or in part of estates of freehold, copyhold, or for years, money in the funds, upon mortgage, or otherwise out upon security, or at interest, debts, or of whatever other nature the same or any part thereof may be, I give, devise, and bequeath the same unto the said *J. E.* and *A. H. C.*, their heirs, &c. upon trust to sell and convert the same into money, to get in debts, &c., and out of the monies to be so raised, in the first place, to set apart 50,000*l.* 3 per cent. consols, in trust for such son of Mrs. *D.* who under the trusts of a settlement now intended to be forthwith made, shall become possessed of an estate tail in the manor of *M.*;" the residue to be divided amongst the other children of Mrs. *D.*; and the testator made *J. E.* and *A. H. C.* executors of his will. Some time after making his will, the testator drew a line across the direction to sell the property devised by the residuary clause; and after making the will, the testator purchased a considerable freehold estate in *W.* and *H.* Testator afterwards made and published a codicil, duly executed to pass freehold estates, whereby, after reciting the rasure before mentioned, and that he was apprehensive that such rasure, not being witnessed, might lead to litigation, he declared by that codicil that the sole intention of such rasure was to revoke that part only of the will whereby he directed the sale of his freehold property. It then proceeded: "And

3 M 4   I do

I do hereby direct and appoint that the son lawfully begotten of my daughter Mrs. *D,* who shall first attain the age of twenty-one years, shall, on attaining such age, change his name for that of *E.*; and I give and devise to the said son of my daughter, on his attaining the age of twenty-one years, and changing his name to *E.,* all my freehold property, lands, tenements, and hereditaments, to have and to hold to him, his heirs and assigns for ever." Testator then appointed a new executor in the room of *J. E.* then deceased, and did thereby ratify and confirm the above-mentioned will and testament, except as before excepted. Testator died without again altering his will or codicil, leaving his widow and Mrs. *D.* his only child and heir at law, and heir according to the custom of the manors of which his copyhold estates were holden, and also his sole next of kin. At the death of testator, Mr. and Mrs. *D.* had and now have five children,— one son and four daughters. Upon a case sent for the opinion of this Court: Held, firstly, that the devise of the freehold part of the estate at *S.,* and of the freehold farm and estate at *H.* contained in the will, was not revoked by the codicil.

Secondly, that the manor of *M.* did pass under the residuary devise contained in the testator's will, and that such devise was revoked by the codicil.

Thirdly, that the manor of *M.* did pass under the codicil to the first son of the plaintiff, Mrs. *D.* who shall attain twenty-one years, and change his name to *E.*

Fourthly, that the estate in *W.* and *H.* purchased after the testator made his will, passed under the devise in the codicil to the first son of the plaintiff Mrs. *D.* who shall attain twenty-one years; and change his name to *E.*

Fifthly, that the surplus rents and profits of the said copyhold estates at *S.* and of the said freehold estate at the same place, and of the said freehold farm and estate at *H.,* after providing for the maintenance of the devisee thereof, belong to *A. H. C.,* the surviving trustee under the will of the testator, until a first son of the said plaintiff Mrs. *D.* shall attain twenty-one years, or in failure of such son, till a daughter shall attain that age, or be married with consent according to the will.

Sixthly, that the intermediate rents and profits of such of the testator's freehold estates as are effectually devised by his codicil to the son of the plaintiff Mrs. *D.* who shall first attain twenty-one years, and change his name to *E.* until such events take place, belong to *A. H. C.* the surviving trustee under the will of the testator. *Duffield* v. *Elmes,* H. 5 & 6 G. 4.
Page 705

2. *A.* by will charged all his real and personal estate with the payment of his debts; and then, after giving an annuity for life to his brother, payable out of his lands, devised to his wife all his real and personal estate for the term of her life, or as long as she should remain his widow; and immediately after her decease, or in case of her marriage, whichever should first happen, then he directed all his real and personal estate to be divided according to the statute of distributions in that case made and provided. Held, that by this will there was not any devise to any person of the real estate of the testator after the death or second marriage of the widow. *Thomas* v. *Thomas and Others.* H. 5 & 6 G. 4. 295.

3. Devise of all my *Briton Ferry* estate,

estate, and all the land, &c. of which it consists; and then all my *Penline Castle* estate, which, as well as my *Briton Ferry* estate, lies in the county of *Glamorgan*. The jury found a special verdict, stating the will of the father of the devisor, and deeds of lease and release executed upon the marriage of the devisor and certain schedules thereto annexed, purporting to contain a particular account of the several parishes and tenements comprehended in the estate of the devisor's father. Under the head of the *Brecon* estates was a parish called *Lywell*, which contained the messuage for which the ejectment was brought, and under the head of *Glamorganshire* estates was a parish called *Briton Ferry*.

At the trial the defendant offered to give in evidence account books of former stewards of the devisor and her predecessors, owners of the lands devised, in which the stewards charged themselves with the receipt of various sums of money on account of the said owners, and amongst others the following entry: "*B. F.* estate, in the county of *B.*," and also to give in evidence that the lands and tenements mentioned in the declaration, together with the lands and tenements in the schedules respectively contained, had all gone by the name of the *B. F.* estate, and such of the said lands, &c. as were in the county of *B.* extended over twelve parishes, and contained above 4000 acres of land: Held, that the words "my *B. F.* estate, with all the manors, advowsons, &c. thereto belonging," denoted a property or estate known to the testatrix by the name of her *B. F.* estate, and not an estate locally situate in a parish or township of *B. F.*; and, consequently,

that the questions arising upon any particular tenement, was properly a question of parcel or no parcel; and that the matters offered to be given in evidence were admissible, and ought to have been received. *Doe dem. Beach* v. *The Earl of Jersey, H. 5 & 6 G. 4.*

Page 870

DIVORCE.

See BARON AND FEME, 1.

EJECTMENT.

1. Defendant enclosed a small piece of waste land by the side of a public highway, and occupied it for thirty years without paying any rent; at the expiration of that time, the owners of the adjoining land demanded 6*d.* rent, which the defendant paid on three several occasions. In ejectment: Held, that this, in the absence of other evidence, was conclusive to shew that the occupation of defendant began by permission, and entitled the plaintiff to a verdict. *Doe dem. Jackson* v. *Wilkinson, M. 5 G. 4.*
413

2. An ejectment brought in an inferior court on a lease executed and sealed on the premises, which were within the jurisdiction of that court, may be removed into this court by certiorari, if there be any ground for believing that it cannot be impartially tried in the inferior court: *Patterson dem. Gradridge and Others* v. *Eades, M. 5 G. 4.* 550

3. By 4 G. 2. c. 28. s. 2, it is enacted, that in all cases between landlord and tenant, as often as it shall happen that one half year's rent shall be in arrear, and the landlord or lessor to whom the same is due, hath right by law to re-enter for the non-payment thereof, such landlord or lessor shall and may, without any formal demand or re-entry,

essary, serves a declaration in ejectment for the recovery of the demised premises, which service shall
stand in the place and stead of a
demand and re-entry: Held, that
by this statute the service of the
declaration in ejectment is substituted for the demand of rent,
which at common law must have
been made upon the day when the
forfeiture accrued, in case of non-
payment, and therefore that it was
no ground of nonsuit in ejectment
that the declaration was served on
a day subsequent to the day on
which the demise was laid, that
being after the rent became due:
because the title of the lessor must
be taken to have accrued on the
day when the forfeiture would have
accrued, at common law by non-
payment of the rent. *Doe dem.
Lawrence and Others* v. *Shawcross*,
H. 5 & 6 G. 4.   Page 752

4. *A.* being seised in fee of an undivided moiety of an estate, devised
the same (by will made some years
before her death) to her nephew
and two nieces as tenants in common; one of the nieces died in the
lifetime of *A.* and left an infant
daughter. *A.* by another will, intended to have devised the moiety
to the nephew and surviving niece,
and the infant daughter of the deceased niece, but this will was
never executed. After *A.'s* death,
the nephew and surviving niece
covenanted to carry the unexecuted will into execution, and to
convey one-third of the moiety to
a trustee upon trust to convey the
same to the infant if she attained
twenty-one, or to her issue if she
died, and if twenty-one and left
issue, or otherwise to the nephew
and niece in equal moieties. No
conveyance was executed in pursuance of the deed. The rents of
the third were received by the
trustee for the use of the infant

during her lifetime. An ejectment
having been brought by the devisee of the nephew more than
twenty years after his death, but
less than twenty years after the
death of the infant, it was held
that there was no adverse possession until the death of the infant,
and that the ejectment was well
brought. *Doe dem. Colclough* v.
Hulse, H. 5 & 6 G. 4.   Page 757

ELEGIT.

See PRACTICE.

EVIDENCE.

1. Where in an action to a false return to a *fieri facias*, the declaration
stated that the plaintiff in *Trinity*
term 2 G. 4. by the judgment recovered, &c. " as appears by the
record," and the proof was of a
judgment in *Easter* term 3 G. 4.:
Held, that this was no variance,
for that the averment, "as appears
by the record," was surplusage,
and might be rejected, inasmuch
as the judgment was not the foundation of, but mere inducement to
the action. *Stoddart* v. *Palmer*,
T. 5 G. 4.   2

2. *A.* employed *B.*, his agent, to import goods from a foreign country.
Upon the arrival of the goods *B.*,
who resided in *London*, transmitted
to *A.*, who resided in the country,
the invoice, but delivered the bill of
lading to a warehouse keeper in
order to get the goods entered and
warehoused. In the warehouse
keeper's books they were described as the property of *B.* By the
bill of lading the goods were to
be delivered to the order of the
shipper or his assigns, and it was
indorsed by the shipper in blank.
B. had no authority from *A.* to
sell the goods, but after they had
been standing in his name in the
warehouse keeper's books nearly
five

five months, B. sold them. Held,
in an action of trover brought by
A. against the purchasers, that
upon these facts the jury ought to
have been directed that A. was
entitled to recover, inasmuch as
B. had no authority to sell, or at
least, that it ought to have been
submitted as a question of fact to
the jury, whether A. had by his
conduct enabled B. to hold himself out to the world, as having the
apparent property as well as the
possession. *Dyer* v. *Pearson and
Others*, T. 5 G. 4.   Page 38

3. Where an inquisition found that a
piece of land had in times past
been covered with the water of the
sea, but was then and had been
for several years past by the sea
left, and the commissioners caused
the same to be seised into the king's
hands. The defendant filed a traverse, stating that he was seised in
fee of the manor of *North Thoresby* cum *North Cotes*, and the demesne lands thereof; and that the
same piece of land mentioned in
the inquisition, by the slow, gradual, and imperceptible projection,
allution, subsidence and accretion
of ooze, soil, sand, and other matter, being slowly, gradually, and
by imperceptible increase, in long
time cast up, deposited, and settled
by and from the flux and reflux of
the tide upon and against the extremity of the said manor, hath
been formed, &c., and thereby
became parcel of the demesne
lands of the manor; without this,
that the land was left by the sea
as found by the inquisition. The replication by the Attorney General
traversed that the land was formed as alleged in the inducement to
the defendant's traverse, and joined issue on the traverse taken by
the defendant. Issue was also
joined on the traverse taken by the
Attorney General. It appeared by

the evidence, that the land in
question had been formed gradually by ooze and soil deposited by
the sea; and that the increase
could not be observed when actually going on, although a visible
increase took place every year,
and in the course of fifty years a
large piece of land had been thus
formed. Held, first, that upon this
evidence the land could not be
said to have been left by the sea;
secondly, that it was formed by
the slow, gradual, and imperceptible projection, &c. of ooze, soil,
and sand, as alleged in the inducement to the defendant's traverse,
and that both issues were properly
found for him. *The King* v. *Lord
Yarborough*, T. 8 G. 4.   Page 91

4. In an action for a libel, the defendant cannot, either in bar of
the action, or in mitigation of
damages, give in evidence other
libels published of him by the
plaintiff, not distinctly relating to
the same subject.

Declaration stated, that plaintiff
was an attorney, and had been
employed as vestry clerk in the
parish of *A.*, and that, whilst he
was such vestry clerk certain prosecutions were carried on against
B. for certain misdemeanors, and
in furtherance of such proceedings,
and to bring the same to a successful
issue, certain sums of money belonging to the parishioners were
appropriated and applied to the
discharge of the expences incurred
on account of the said proceedings, yet defendant intending, &c.,
to injure the plaintiff in his profession of an attorney, and to cause
him to be esteemed a fraudulent
practiser in his said profession,
and in his office as vestry clerk,
and to cause it to be suspected
that the plaintiff had fraudulently
applied money belonging to the
parishioners, did, &c.,
falsely

falsely and maliciously published of and concerning the plaintiff, and of and concerning his conduct in his office of vestry clerk; and of and concerning the matters aforesaid, the libel, &c. It appeared on the production of the libel at the trial, that the imputation was, that the plaintiff had applied the parish money in payment of the expences of the prosecution after it had terminated: Held, that this was no variance, because it did not alter the character of the libel; the fraud imputed to the plaintiff being the same, whether the money was misapplied before or after the proceedings had terminated; and that the allegation that the libel was published of and concerning the matters aforesaid, did not make it necessary to prove precisely that the libel did relate to every part of the matter previously stated. May, Gent. one, &c. v. Brown, T. 5 G. 4. Page 113

5. Declaration for a libel stated that the plaintiff was an attorney, and that the defendant intending to injure him in his good name, and in his said profession of an attorney, published a libel of and concerning the plaintiff; and of and concerning him in his said profession. At the trial, the plaintiff failed in proving that at the time of the publication of the libel he was an attorney: Held, that this was not a fatal variance between the allegation and the proof, the words of the libel being actionable, although not used with reference to the professional character of the plaintiff. Lewis v. Walter, T. 5 G. 4. 108

6. Where in case for not carrying away tithe-corn, the plaintiff alleged that it was lawfully and in due manner set out: Held, that this allegation was satisfied by proof, that the tithe was set out according to an agreement be-

tween the parties, although it varied from the mode prescribed by the common law.

Whether the whole crop has been left on the ground for a reasonable time after the tithe has been set out, in order that the tithe owner may compare the tenth part with the other nine, is a question for the jury; and not for the Court. Facey v. Hurdom, T. 5 G. 4. Page 213

7. Where an apothecary, in an action to recover the amount of his bill, produced in evidence a certificate, purporting to be granted by the court of examiners of the Apothecaries' Company, and bearing twelve signatures, purporting to be the signatures of the persons constituting that court, of which signatures he proved one, and gave other evidence to shew that the document was genuine, and that he obtained it from the court of examiners : Held, that this was sufficient, and that he was not bound to prove the hand writing of each member of the court of examiners who had subscribed the certificate. Walmsley v. Abbot, T. 5 G. 4. 218

8. Assumpsit for money had and received. Plea, a judgment recovered for want of a plea for 4000l. in an inferior court in Wales for the same causes of action. Replication that the causes of action were not the same, and issue joined thereon. At the trial it appeared that the defendant had received on account of the plaintiff, and as his steward, different sums of money at different times, and that on the investigation of the accounts, the plaintiff found that there was due to him a much larger sum than that for which he had declared in the inferior court, but that he had proceeded for the smaller sum, under the belief that the

the defendant had no available property beyond that amount, defendant in that action suffered judgment by default, and plaintiff verified for 3400*l.* : Held, that all the sums which the plaintiff knew the defendant had received at the time when he commenced the action in the inferior court, were to be considered as causes of action in respect of which he had declared and recovered the judgment. *Lord Bagot v. Williams, T. 5 G. 4.*
Page 285

9. A tenant conveyed his interest in leasehold premises to trustees for the benefit of his creditors by deed, containing a proviso that if all and every of the creditors should refuse to execute or consent to the deed within six months from the date thereof, it should be void: Held that the non-execution of the deed by a particular creditor was not evidence of a refusal by him to execute or assent, but that it was incumbent on a party seeking to avoid the deed to shew a positive refusal to execute or assent to the deed. *Holmes v. Love and Tucker, T. 5 G. 4.* 242

10. By the Black Act, 9 *G. 1. c. 22.* any person who shall unlawfully and *maliciously* kill, maim, or wound any cattle, or cut down or otherwise destroy any trees, planted in any avenue, or growing in any garden, orchard, or plantation for ornament, shelter, or profit, shall be adjudged guilty of felony, and the inhabitants of the hundred, are to make satisfaction to the persons damnified by the cutting down or destroying any trees which shall be committed by any offenders against the act: Held, that in order to make the malicious destruction of trees a felony within this statute, the act done must proceed from a malicious motive towards the owner of

the trees, and, therefore, where an action was brought against the hundred by a party damnified, in consequence of his plantation having been destroyed by fire, and it appeared that the fire had commenced at the distance of a mile from his plantation, and in adjoining grounds belonging to a different proprietor, it was held, that there was not any evidence that the act was done from motives of malice towards the plaintiff, and therefore, that no offence had been committed against the statute, and that the action, consequently, was not maintainable against the hundred. *Curtis, Bart, and Another, v. Hundred of Godley, T. 5 G. 4.*
Page 248

11. The right to light and air is acquired by enjoyment, and may be lost by a discontinuance of the enjoyment, unless the party who ceases to enjoy, at the same time does some act to shew an intention of resuming the enjoyment, within a reasonable time. And, therefore, where in case by a reversioner for obstructing lights, it appeared that the plaintiff's messuage was an ancient house, and that adjoining to it, there had formerly been a building, in which there was an ancient window, next the lands of the defendant; and that the former owner of the plaintiff's premises, about seventeen years before, had pulled down this building, and erected on its site another with a blank wall adjoining the premises of the defendant; and this latter, about three years before the commencement of the action, erected a building next the blank wall of the plaintiff, who then opened a window in that wall, in the same place where the ancient window had been, in the old building; it was held that he could not maintain any action against the defendant

defendant for obstructing the new window; because, by erecting the blank wall, he not only ceased to enjoy the light, but had evinced an intention never to resume the enjoyment. *Moore* v. *Rawson*, *T. 5 G. 4.* Page 862

14. A. being the occupier of a farm, quitted the same on the 25th of *March* 1821, and was succeeded in the possession by B. A. had sown forty acres with wheat, and it appeared that at a meeting between A. and B. in *February* 1821, A. asked B. if he would take the forty acres of wheat at 900l., telling him, that if he did not, he should not have the farm. B. said that he would take it. A person present then valued the dead stock, and having so done, asked to whom he was to value it; B. said that it was to be valued to him, and then promised to pay A. for the wheat and the dead stock on a given day, and he did pay a sum of money on account. B. afterwards had possession of the farm, the growing wheat, and the dead stock: Held, that in indebitatus assumpsit for crops bargained and sold, and goods sold and delivered, the contract for the dead stock was distinct from any contract for the sale of the growing wheat and the possession of the farm, and, therefore, that A. was entitled to recover to that amount: Held, also by *Bayley* and *Holroyd* Js., *Littledale* J. dissentiente, that as B. had had the growing wheat, and had made a part payment on account, he was entitled in this action to recover the remainder of the price agreed to be paid for it. *Mayfield* v. *Wadsley*, T. 5 G. 4. Page 357

18. F. C. possessed of lands for the residue of a long term of years, by indenture of three parts, dated *Nov.* 1st, 1771, between F. C. of

first part, J. W. and T. L. of second part, and E. K. of third part, in consideration of an intended marriage between T. C. and E. K. and for this consideration mentioned and expressed in a certain indenture of three parts, intended to bear date after the date thereof, and made between T. C., S. H., and J. H. of the first part, W. C. and J. K. of the second part, and E. K. of the third part; and for other good considerations," assigned the said lands to J. W. and T. L. for the residue of the said term, upon trust to permit and suffer T. C., his executors, &c. to receive the rents for his own use until the solemnization of the intended marriage, and afterwards to permit T. C. to receive the rents for his life, and afterwards to permit the wife to receive the rents for her life, and upon other subsequent trusts. By indenture of three parts, dated *November* 2d, 1771, between T. C., S. H., and J. K. of the first part, W. C. and J. K. of the second part, and E. K. of the third part, T. C. enfeoffed W. C. and J. K. of the lands mentioned in the deed of *November* 1st, 1771, upon certain trusts. The deed contained a power of attorney to deliver seisin, and a memorandum of livery of seisin was indorsed upon it. T. C. continued in possession of the lands from the 1st of *November* 1771, till the time of his death in 1809. In ejectment against the executor of T. L. who survived J. K.: Held, that the term assigned to J. W. and T. L. was not destroyed by the feoffment, because it did not appear that they even assented to it. *Doe* v. *Lynes*, T. 5 G. 4. Page 388

14. In an action against a magistrate for false imprisonment, the plaintiff proved a commitment for a certain

certain alleged offence. The defendant proved a conviction of the plaintiff for an offence differing from that recited in the commitment: Held, that this conviction was no justification of the imprisonment, because it appeared that the offence mentioned in the conviction was different from that recited in the commitment. The defendant, in order to deprive the plaintiff of his costs under the 48 G. 3. c. 141, tendered evidence to shew that the offence mentioned in the conviction had actually been committed by the plaintiff: it was held, however, that that statute applied only to cases where convictions had been quashed, and, therefore, that the evidence was not admissible for that purpose. *Quære*, whether it was admissible in mitigation of damages. *Rogers v. Jones*, M. 5 G. 4. Page 409

15. Defendant enclosed a small piece of waste land by the side of a public highway, and occupied it for thirty years, without paying any rent; at the expiration of that time the owner of the adjoining land demanded 6d. rent, which defendant paid on three several occasions. In ejectment: Held, that this, in the absence of other evidence, was conclusive to shew that the occupation of defendant began by permission, and entitled the plaintiff to a verdict. *Doe dem. Jackson v. Wilkinson*, M. 5 G. 4. 413

16. In assumpsit by two co-trustees for money had and received to their use, the defendant produced a receipt for the money given by one of the plaintiffs: Held, that this was not conclusive, and that evidence was properly admitted, to shew that the giving of the receipt was a fraudulent transaction, and that the money had not been paid. *Snaife and Caris v. Jackson*, M. 5 G. 4. 421

17. In case for words defendant suffered judgment by default. At the execution of the writ of enquiry the plaintiff offered no evidence, and the jury assessed the damages at 40l. Held, that it was not incumbent on the plaintiff to give any evidence, and that the jury, under such circumstances, were bound to give nominal damages only. *Tripp v. Thomas*, M. 5 G. 4. Page 427

18. Assumpsit, in consideration that plaintiff would advance a sum of money to A. B., defendant promised that provision should be made for repaying the plaintiff. At the trial it appeared that the defendant had given to the plaintiff the guarantee stated in the declaration, and that the latter was a partner with two other persons in a banking-house, and that the firm had advanced the money, and charged A. B. in account with the same: Held, that the averment in the declaration that the plaintiff had advanced the money was not supported by the proof, there being no evidence to shew that the money had been advanced to the plaintiff by the firm, and by him to A. B. *Garrett v. Handley*, M. 5 G. 4. 462

19. Where a manufacturer had adopted a particular mark for his goods, in order to denote that they were manufactured by him: Held, that an action on the case was maintainable by him against another person who adopted the same mark, for the purpose of denoting that his goods were manufactured by the plaintiff, and who sold the goods so marked as and for goods manufactured by the plaintiff. The declaration stated that defendant sold the goods as and for goods manufactured by the plaintiff; it appeared in evidence that the persons who bought the goods of the defendant knew by whom they

they were manufactured, but that
the defendant used the plaintiff's
mark, and sold the goods so marked
in order that his customers might,
and in fact they did, resell them as
and for goods manufactured by the
plaintiff: Held, that this evidence
supported the declaration. *Sykes
v. Sykes and Another, M. 5 G. 4.*
Page 541

20. A term of 500 years created in
1712 was, upon a sale of the estate
in 1785, assigned to attend the inheritance. Upon a subsequent sale
in 1793, there was a general declaration in the conveyance, that
all persons having outstanding
terms should hold them in trust to
attend the inheritance, but no particular term was specified: Held,
that in support of the grant of the
stewardship of the manor made in
1821, it was properly left to the
jury to say whether they thought
the term had been surrendered,
and that they were justified in finding that it had. *Bartlett v. Downes,
H. 5 & 6 G. 4.* 616

21. In assumpsit for goods sold, it
appeared that the plaintiff, a jeweller, in the course of two months,
delivered articles of jewelry to the
wife, amounting in value to 83*l*. It
appeared that the defendant was a
certificated special pleader, and
lived in a ready-furnished house, of
which the annual rent was 200*l*.;
that he kept no man servant; that
his wife's fortune upon her marriage was less than 4000*l*.; that she
had, at the time of her marriage,
jewelry suitable to her condition,
and that she had never worn in her
husband's presence any articles
furnished her by the plaintiff; it
appeared, also, that the plaintiff,
when he went to the defendant's
house to ask for payment, always
enquired for the wife and not for
the defendant: Held, that the
goods so furnished were not necessaries, and that, as there was no

evidence to go to the jury of any
assent of the husband to the contract made by his wife, the action
could not be maintained. *Mont-
gue v. Benedict, H. 5 & 6 G. 4.*
Page 631

22. In trespass against two magistrates for giving plaintiff's landlord
possession of a certain deserted
farm, they produced in evidence a
record of their proceedings under
that act, which set forth all such
circumstances as were necessary to
give them jurisdiction, and by
which it appeared that they had
pursued the directions of the statute: Held, that this was conclusive as an answer to the action.
*Basten v. Carew and Another, H.
5 & 6 G. 4.* 649

23. By statute 17 G. 3. c. 3. s. 2. it is
enacted, "that overseers of the
poor shall permit inhabitants of the
parish to inspect rates at all seasonable times, and shall upon demand
forthwith give copies of the same to
any inhabitant of the parish;" and
by s. 3., "if any overseer shall not
permit an inhabitant to inspect the
rate, or shall neglect to give copies
thereof as aforesaid, such overseer,
for every such offence, shall forfeit
and pay to *the party aggrieved* the
sum of 20*l*.: Held, first, that in
order to entitle a party to sue for
the penalty under the statute, he
must shew that he was sustained an
injury by the act of the overseer.

Held, secondly, that there must
be a demand to inspect the rate
made at a reasonable time and
place; and

Semble, That the house of the
overseer is the place at which the
demand ought to be made. *Brand-
ly v. Robinson, H. 5 & 6 G. 4.*
648

24. A. entered into an agreement
with B. for the hire of a piece
of land for the purpose of making
bricks. B. afterwards made an
offer in writing to let and he a piece
of

of land to A. upon the terms contained in the agreement between him (A.) and B.; and at a subsequent time A. verbally accepted this offer. In an action by C. for a breach of some of the terms of this contract: Held, that the written offer made by C. was admissible in evidence without being stamped. *Drant, Executor of Brown v. Leggott, H. 5 & 6 G. 4.* Page 665

25. In replevin defendant avowed for rent due upon a demise, at a certain fixed rent. Plea, that that plaintiff did not hold under defendant at the rent mentioned in the avowry, and issue joined upon that fact. At the trial, the defendant, in order to prove the holding as alleged, tendered in evidence certain unstamped papers, the effect of which was to shew that the plaintiff had paid rent at the rate mentioned in the avowry: Held, that these papers were inadmissible for want of stamps, inasmuch as they were in effect tendered to prove the payment of the rent; for if they did not prove the payment of the rent, they would not support the issue, and would on that ground be inadmissible.

The defendant's steward proved that a lease had been executed by the defendant but not by the plaintiff, the terms of which had been reduced into writing by the assent of both parties, and he stated that to be the final agreement between the parties. The plaintiff, in order to negative this statement, tendered in evidence another unstamped paper, in the handwriting of the defendant's steward; the effect of which was, to shew that it was subsequently proposed by him that the plaintiff was to hold at a rent different from that mentioned in the demise. Held, that as this paper was not signed by the parties, it did not amount to an agreement

Vol. III.

or minute of an agreement, but to a proposal only, and, therefore, that it did not require a stamp, and was properly received in evidence. *Hawkins v. Warre, H. 5 & 6 G. 4.* Page 690

26. Assumpsit for money had and received. Plea, that the promises in the declaration mentioned were made by the defendant, jointly with A. B., and issue thereon. A. B. was called as a witness by the defendant to prove a partnership, but he proved the contrary; the defendant then tendered in evidence an answer of A. B. to a bill filed in chancery, in which A. B. swore, that, up to a certain time, he was a partner with the defendant: *Semble,* That this answer was not admissible in evidence, because the effect of it was to discredit A. B., the defendant's own witness: but

Held, That it was competent to the defendant, after A. B. had denied the partnership, to prove it by other witnesses. *Ewer and Another, Assignees, v. Ambrose and Baker, H. 5 & 6 G. 4.* 746

27. By the friendly society act, stat. 33 G. 3. c. 54. s. 15., it is enacted, that if any member of the society shall think himself aggrieved by any thing done by any such society, two justices may, on complaint upon oath of such member, summon the presidents or stewards of the society, and the justices are to hear and determine the matter of such complaint; and to make such orders *therein* as to them shall seem just: Held, that the jurisdiction of the magistrates was confined strictly to the subject matter of the complaint, and therefore where it appeared that a party had complained to the justices that he had been deprived of relief to which he was entitled, and the justices awarded not only that the steward

3 N

steward should give him such relief, but also that the party should be continued a member of the society, it was held that the latter part of the order was illegal, inasmuch as the expulsion of the party was no part of the complaint. *The King v. Soper and Another*, H. 5 & 6 G. 4.   Page 857

28. Devise of all my *Briton Ferry* estate, and all the land, &c. of which it consists ; and then all my *Penline Castle* estate, which, as well as my *Briton Ferry* estate, lies in the county of *Glamorgan*. The jury found a special verdict, stating the will of the father of the devisor, and deeds of lease and release executed upon the marriage of the devisor and certain schedules thereto annexed, purporting to contain a particular account of the several parishes and tenements comprehended in the estate of the devisor's father. Under the head of the *Brecon* estates was a parish called *Lywell*, which contained the messuage for which the ejectment was brought, and under the head of *Glamorganshire* estates was a parish called *Briton Ferry*.

The jury further found, that the tenements in the county of *Brecon*, together with the manor and tenements in the county of *Glamorgan*, had been known by the name of the *Briton Ferry* estate for divers, to wit, fifty years before the death of the devisor : Held, that this was consistent with the other findings, especially the descriptions and names of the tenements in the county of *Brecon*, and of the manors and tenements in the county of *Glamorgan*, in the indenture and schedules found in the special verdict, inasmuch as the whole of an estate might be known by one name, and each of its parts by its own particular name : Held also,

that it was not sufficiently found that the tenements and manors in the said county were so known by name by the devisor, the expression, divers, to wit, fifty years before the death of the devisor, being too loose and indefinite, as it did not denote any particular number of years, but only divers years, nor import that the number of years whatever it was, was a period immediately preceding the death of the devisor. At the trial the defendant offered to give in evidence account books of former stewards of the devisor and her predecessors, owners of the lands devised in which the stewards charged themselves with the receipt of various sums of money on account of the said owners, and, amongst others the following entry: "*B. F.* estate, in the county of *B.*," and also to give in evidence that the lands and tenements mentioned in the declaration, together with the lands and tenements in the schedule respectively contained, had all gone by the name of the *B. F.* estate, and such of the said lands, &c. as were in the county of *B.* extended over twelve parishes, and contained above 4000 acres of land: Held, that the words " my *B. F.* estate, with all the manors, advowsons, &c. thereto belonging," denoted a property or estate known to the testatrix by the name of her *B. F.* estate, and not an estate locally situate in a parish or township of *B. F.*, and consequently, that the questions arising upon any particular tenement, was properly a question of parcel, or no parcel ; and, consequently, that the matters offered to be given in evidence were inadmissible, and ought to have been received. *Doe dem. Beach v. The Earl of Jersey*, H. 5 & 6 G. 4.   Page 870

EXE-

EXECUTION.

See PRACTICE, 22.

EXECUTORS AND ADMINIS-TRATORS.

See ANNUITY, 1, 2, 3. COVENANT, 1, 2, 3. PLEADING, 21.

FACTOR.

1. A. and Co., merchants at *Rio Janeiro*, consigned cottons to B. in this country for sale, and sent bills of lading, which shewed that the cottons were sent on account and risk of the consignors. B. employed C. and D., brokers at *Liverpool*, to effect the sales, which they did; some at a credit of ten days, and bills at three months; others for cash in one month. C. and D. made large advances to B., and received the proceeds of the cottons when due. Before that time B. had become bankrupt. In an action by A. and Co. against C. and D. for money had and received: Held, that the latter were not entitled to retain for the advances made by them to B., for that he was a factor for sale only, and had no authority to pledge the goods, and that the plaintiffs were entitled to recover the net proceeds, deducting such sums only as B. could have retained. A. and Co., when they consigned the cottons to B., requested him to make remittances in anticipation of sales: Held, secondly, that this request did not give B. any special authority to pledge the goods. *Queiroz and Others v. Truman and Others, T. 5 G. 4.*   Page 342

FALSE IMPRISONMENT.

See CONVICTION, 2.

FEOFFMENT.

See DEED, 3.

FORFEITURE.

See LANDLORD AND TENANT, 2.

FORGERY.

See BILL OF EXCHANGE, 3.

FRAUDS, STATUTE OF.

See PAYMENT, 4.

1. Where goods of the value of 144*l.* were made to order, and remained in the possession of the vendor at the request of the vendee, with the exception of a small part which the latter took away: Held, that there was no acceptance of the residue of the goods within the statute of frauds, sect. 17. *Thompson v. Maceroni, T. 5 G. 4.*   Page 1

2. A. knowing that B. was a horse-dealer, made a verbal bargain on a *Sunday* for the purchase of a horse. The price, which was above 10*l.*, was specified, and B. warranted the horse to be sound. It was not delivered until the following *Tuesday*, when the money was paid: Held, that there was not any complete contract until the delivery of the horse, and consequently that the contract was not void within the stat. 29 Car. 2. c. 7. s. 2. But assuming it to be void, held, secondly, in an action for breach of the warranty, that the purchaser having no knowledge of the fact that the vendor was exercising his ordinary calling on the *Sunday*, had not been guilty of any breach of the law, and therefore was entitled to recover back the price of the horse. *Blossome v. Williams, T. 5 G. 4.*   232

3. A. being the occupier of a farm,

3 N 2   quitted

quitted the same on the 25th of *March* 1821, and was succeeded in the possession by *B*. *A*. had sown forty acres with wheat, and it appeared that at a meeting between *A*. and *B*. in *February* 1821, *A*. asked *B*. if he would take the forty acres of wheat at 200*l*., telling him, that if he did not, he should not have the farm. *B*. said that he would take it. A person present then valued the dead stock, and having so done, asked to whom he was to value it; *B*. said that it was to be valued to him, and then promised to pay *A*. for the wheat and the dead stock on a given day, and he did pay a sum of money on account. *B*. afterwards had possession of the farm, the growing wheat, and the dead stock: Held, that, in indebitatus assumpsit for crops bargained and sold, and goods sold and delivered, the contract for the dead stock was distinct from any contract for the sale of the growing wheat and the possession of the farm, and therefore that *A*. was entitled to recover to that amount: Held, also, by *Bayley* and *Holroyd* Js., *Little-dale* J. dissentiente, that as *B*. had had the growing wheat, and had made a part payment on account, *A*. was entitled in this action to recover the remainder of the price agreed to be paid for it.

Where a plaintiff had recovered a verdict for a sum of money composed of several items, some of which he was not in strict law entitled to recover under the declaration in that action, but which he would be clearly entitled to recover by declaring in a different form, the Court will not reduce the damages. Per *Abbott* C. J. *Mayfield* v. *Wadsley*, T. 5 G. 4.   Page 357

4. A hogshead of wine in the warehouse of the *London* Dock Company was sold for 13*l*. and a delivery order given to the vendee. There was no contract in writing: Held, that the acceptance of the delivery order by the vendee was not an actual acceptance of the wine within the statute of frauds. *Bentall* v. *Burn*, M. 5 G. 4.   Page 423

FREIGHT.

Where the commander of a ship entered into a charter-party (not under seal), whereby the charterer agreed to pay freight generally, without saying to whom: Held, that the owner having demanded and received the freight, the commander could not maintain an action for it against the charterer, although he had given him notice not to pay it to any one but himself. *Atkinson* v. *Cotesworth*, H. 5 & 6 G. 4.   647

FRIENDLY SOCIETIES.

By the friendly society act, stat. 33 G. 3. c. 54. s. 15., it is enacted, that if any member of the society shall think himself aggrieved by any thing done by any such society, two justices may, on complaint upon oath of such member, summon the presidents or stewards of the society, and the justices are to hear and determine the matter of such complaint, and to make such orders *therein* as to them shall seem just: Held, that the jurisdiction of the magistrates was confined strictly to the subject-matter of the complaint, and therefore where it appeared that a party had complained to the justices that he had been deprived of relief to which he was entitled, and the justices awarded not only that the steward should give him such relief, but also that the party should be be continued a member of the society, it was held that the latter part of the order was illegal, inasmuch as the expulsion of the party was no part of the complaint. *The King v. Soper and Another,* H. 5 & 6 G. 4. 　　　Page 857

GAME.

See INFORMATION, 1.

GUARANTY.

It was agreed between the vendors and vendee of goods, that the latter should pay 10*s.* per ton beyond the market price, which sum was to be applied, in liquidation of an old debt due to one of the vendors. The payment of the goods was guaranteed by a third person, but the bargain between the parties was not communicated to the surety : Held, that that was a fraud on the surety, and rendered the guaranty void. *Pidcock and Others v. Bishop,* H. 5 & 6 G. 4. 　　　605

GUARDIAN OF THE POOR.

See SETTLEMENT BY APPRENTICESHIP, 3.

HEIR.

A. B. seised of lands in fee simple at the time of her death, in the possession of a tenant from year to year, died leaving *C. D.* her heir at law. No rent was ever paid to him, it being supposed that the lands passed to a devisee under the will of *A. B.* After the death of *C. D.,* his son and heir at law, brought ejectment and recovered the lands. In debt against the son as heir of *C. D.* on a bond given by the latter, to which the son pleaded no assets by descent from his father; it was held that the father was seised, *in fact,* of the lands in question, that they de-

scended from him to his son, and were therefore assets in the hands of the latter, liable to the bond debt. *Bushby and Another, Executors, v. Dixon,* T. 5 G. 4. 　　　Page 298

HIGHWAY, SURVEYOR OF.

See CERTIORARI, 21.

HUNDRED, ACTION AGAINST.

1, The inhabitants of a *town* not within any hundred are not entitled to be reimbursed the expences which they incur in defending actions brought against them on the 57 G. 3. c. 19. *s.* 38., to recover the damages done by tumultuous assemblies. *The King v. The Justices of King's Lynn,* T. 5 G. 4. 　　　147

2. By the black act, 9 G. 1. c. 22., any person who shall unlawfully and *maliciously* kill, maim, or wound any cattle, or cut down or otherwise destroy any trees planted in any avenue, or growing in any garden or orchard, or plantation for ornament, shelter or profit, shall be adjudged guilty of felony, and the inhabitants of the hundred are to make satisfaction to the persons damnified by the cutting down or destroying any trees which shall be committed by any offenders against the act: Held, that in order to make the malicious destruction of trees a felony within this statute, the act done must proceed from a malicious motive towards the owner of the trees ; and, therefore, where an action was brought against the hundred by a party damnified in consequence of his plantation having been destroyed by fire, and it appeared that the fire had commenced at the distance of a mile from his plantation, and in adjoining grounds belonging to a different

ferent proprietor it was held, that
there was not any evidence that
the act was done from motives of
malice towards the plaintiff; and,
therefore, that no offence had been
committed against the statute, and
that the action consequently was
not maintainable against the hundred. *Curtis v. The Hundred of
Godley, T. 5 G. 4.*   Page 248

INCLOSURE ACT.

1. The tenth section of the general
inclosure act, 41 G. 3. c. 109., does
not give to commissioners any power
to make private roads, but only to
set them out, and say in what proportions they shall be made by the
owners of allotments; and, therefore, where a private inclosure act
gave the commissioners power to
raise money to pay the expence of
carrying into execution that or the
general inclosure act: Held, that
they could not make and levy a
rate to pay for making private
roads. *The Earl of Falmouth v.
Richardson, H. 5 & 6 G. 4.*   837

2. Where a private enclosure act (reciting that it was expedient that
the tithes in the parish should be
extinguished, and an adequate
compensation should be made to
the vicar), enacted that the commissioners should, in a certain
mode, ascertain what yearly sum
the tithes were worth, and that there
should be issuing and payable to
the vicar out of the lands, such
yearly sum, "free and clear of all
rates, taxes, and deductions whatsoever:" Held that the vicar was
not rateable to the poor in respect
of the yearly sum so ascertained
and paid to him, *Chatfield v.
Ruston, H. 5 & 6 G. 4.*   863

INDICTMENT.

Indictment charged that the defend-

ant, on, &c. in the second year of
the reign of the present king, kept
a gaming house. Plea, that on,
&c. in the fourth year of the reign
of the present king, defendant
was arraigned upon an indictment
which charged that defendant, on
the 18th of *January*, in the fifty-
seventh year of the reign of the
late king, and on divers other days
and times between that day and
the day of taking the inquisition,
kept a gaming house, &c. to the
nuisance of the subjects of our said
lord the king, and against the
peace of our said lord the king, &c.
The plea then averred the identity
of the offences described in the
two indictments, and the acquittal
of the defendant. Upon demurrer
to this plea, concluding with a
prayer of judgment of respondeas
ouster, it was held that the plea
was bad, because the indictment
upon which the acquittal was alleged to have taken place, on the
face of it, charged an offence committed in the reign of the late
king; and it was not competent to
the defendant to shew by averment,
that it was for the same offence as
that charged in the indictment before the court, because that would
be in effect to contradict the record:

Held, secondly, that the crown
was entitled to final judgment, notwithstanding the form in which the
demurrer concluded.

Semble, that such an indictment
must conclude contra pacem domini regis. *The King v. Taylor,
M. 5 G. 4.*   Page 502

INFERIOR COURT.

See EJECTMENT, 3. PLEADING, 29.
45.

INFORMATION.

1. An information for penalties under
the game law is not an information
within

within the meaning of the stat.
48 G. 3. c. 58.; whereby, if the defendant neglect to appear and plead, the prosecutor is at liberty to enter an appearance and a plea of not guilty for the defendant; and, therefore, where the prosecutor had entered an appearance and a plea of not guilty for the defendant, and a verdict had been found against the defendant, the Court set aside such verdict for irregularity. *Davis* v. *Bint and Others, M. 5 G. 4.*   Page 586

2. It is not necessary that any information or complaint should be made on oath, in order to justify the interference of magistrates under the 11 G. 2. c. 19. s. 16. *Basten* v. *Carew, H. 5 & 6 G. 4.*   649

INQUIRY, WRIT OF.

In case for words, defendant suffered judgment by default. At the execution of the writ of enquiry, the plaintiff offered no evidence, and the jury assessed the damages at 40*l.*: Held, that it was not incumbent on the plaintiff to give any evidence, and that the jury were not, under such circumstances, bound to give nominal damages only. *Tripp* v. *Thomas, M. 5 G. 4.*   427

INSURANCE.

1. Goods were insured at and from *Demerara* to *London* in ship or ships warranted to sail from *Demerara* on or before the 1st of *August* 1823. Small ships take in and discharge the whole of their cargoes in the river of *Demerara*; but there is a shoal off the coast, about ten miles out at sea; and large ships usually discharge and take in part of their cargoes on the outside of the shoal. Goods covered by the policy were laden

on board a small vessel that completed her cargo in the river, and on the 1st of *August,* the captain having obtained his clearance, set sail, proceeded down the river, and about two miles out to sea, and then anchored, the tide being low. On the 3d of *August* he crossed the shoal, and on the 6th the vessel was lost by perils of the sea: Held, that the vessel sailed from *Demerara* on the 1st of *August* within the meaning of the policy, and that the warranty was thereby satisfied. *Lang and Others* v. *Anderdon, M. 5 G. 4.*   Page 495

2. A policy was effected on horses warranted free from mortality and jettison. In the course of the voyage, in consequence of the agitation of the ship in a storm, the horses broke down the partitions by which they were separated, and by their kicking, bruised and wounded each other so much that they all died: Held, upon special verdict, that this was a loss by a peril of the sea, and that the plaintiff was entitled to recover. It was found in the special verdict that a certain usage with respect to such policies prevailed amongst the underwriters subscribing policies at *Lloyd's* coffee-house in *London,* and merchants and others effecting policies there; and that the policy in question was effected at *Lloyd's* coffee-house, but it was not found that the plaintiff was in the habit of effecting policies at that place: Held, that this usage was not sufficient to bind the plaintiff. *Gabay and Another* v. *Lloyd, H. 5 & 6 G. 4.*   793

JOINDER OF ACTION.

See PRACTICE 25.

JOINT STOCK COMPANY.

1. In assumpsit for work and labour and

and money expended in the purchase of shares in a concern called the "Equitable Loan Bank Company." It appeared that the company professed to have a capital of 8,000,000l. in shares of 50l. each; that a deposit of 1l. per share was required on the delivery of certificates for shares; that the holders; that the shares were to be transferrable without any restriction, and that the holders were not to be subject to such regulations as might be contained in any act of parliament passed for the government of the society, and in the mean time to such regulations as might be made by a committee of management. No evidence was given as to the particular objects or tendency of the company:— Held, that, upon this evidence the company was to be considered illegal, and within the operation of the 6 G.1. c.18. as having transferrable shares, and, affecting to act as a body corporate without authority by charter or act of parliament, and that plaintiff consequently could not maintain his action, which arose out of an illegal transaction. *Josephs v. Pebrer, H. 5 & 6 G.4.* . . . . . Page 639

2. Where a scheme for establishing a tontine was put forth, stating that the money subscribed was to be laid out at interest, and after some subscriptions had been paid to the directors in whom the management of the concern was vested, but before any part of the money was laid out at interest, the directors resolved to abandon the project: Held, that each subscriber might, in an action for money had and received, recover the whole of the money advanced by him, without the deduction of any part towards the payment of the expenses incurred within. latter was entitled relief.
By the scheme it appeared that

the money subscribed was to be laid out at interest, and to ensure to the benefit of the survivors; the subscribers were to be governed by regulations made by the directors, and at the end of a year shares were to be issued and be transferrable: Held, that this was not an undertaking within the operation of the bubble act. *Nockells v. Crosby and Others, H. 5 & 6 G.4.* . . . . . Page 814

Held, that the claim was not enure thereto . . . . . .

1. It is not necessary that any information or complaint should be made on oath, in order to justify the interference of magistrates under 11 G.2. c.19. s.6.

In trespass against two magistrates for giving plaintiff's landlord possession of a farm as a deserted farm, they produced in evidence a record of their proceedings under that act, which set forth all such circumstances as were necessary to give them jurisdiction, and by which it appeared that they had pursued the directions of the statute: Held, that this was conclusive as an answer to the action. *Basten v. Carew and Another, H. 5 & 6 G.4.* 649

2. By charter, the aldermen, bailiffs, and burgesses had power to elect two of the burgesses to be aldermen of the borough for one whole year, and they were to have power and authority to execute by themselves or in their absence by their deputies, the office of aldermen of the borough. The charter then contained clauses by which it was provided, that in the event of the death or removal of any alderman, a new one might be elected, who, during the remainder of the year, should execute the office by himself or his deputy. It was then provided, that in the absence of any

any

dany of the aldermen for the time being, the bailiffs and capital burgesses might elect one or more of the burgesses to supply the vacancy. These substituted aldermen had no power to appoint deputies. There then followed a clause, which directed that the aldermen for the time being, during the time they should remain in their offices, should be justices of the peace within the borough: Held, that this charter did not enable the aldermen elected for the year to delegate their office of justice of the peace, and therefore that a deputy alderman was not a justice of the peace for the borough.

Quære, whether since the statute 27 H. 8. c. 24. s. 2. the crown can delegate to a subject the power of appointing a justice of the peace. *Jones* v. *Williams*, H. 5 & 6 G. 4. Page 762

LANDLORD AND TENANT.

1. *A.* let apartments in his dwelling house to *B.*, at a rent payable half yearly. *B.* took possession at *Michaelmas* 1822, and at *Lady-day* 1823 paid half a year's rent. In *June* of that year *B.* left the apartments without giving any notice to quit, but at *Michaelmas* 1823 he paid half a year's rent. At *Lady-day* 1824, *A.* demanded another half year's rent, which *B.* refused to pay: Held, that from these facts the law would not imply a taking from year to year. *Wilson* v. *Abbott*, T. 5 G. 4. 88

2. By lease the lessor demised to the lessee a colliery, and all the engines, machinery, and other implements, effects, and things then lying on or about the colliery, or used or employed therewith, and mentioned in a certain inventory and valuation then made, habendum for twenty-one years, at a certain rent therein mentioned. The lease contained a proviso for re-entry in case the rent should be in arrear for the space of thirty days, and also a proviso that on the expiration or other sooner determination of the demise, the lessee should leave and yield up to the lessor all engines, machines, effects, and things belonging to and used in the said colliery, and that an inventory and valuation should three months previous thereto be made and taken by two indifferent persons to be appointed by the parties respectively, or by an umpire, and such inventory should be compared with the then present inventory and valuation, and that the difference in the value of the engine, &c. should be paid by the landlord or tenant to the other according as it was greater or less than the value at the time of the letting. The tenant entered and occupied the colliery, machinery, &c. and failing in the payment of the rent, the lease became forfeited, and the landlord recovered a judgment in ejectment in *Trinity* term 1818, but did not execute his writ of possession until the 9th of *November* 1819. On the following day the tenant committed an act of bankruptcy. The lease having become forfeited by the act of the tenant, no inventory or valuation of the machines and other effects and things belonging to the collieries was made three months before the determination of the demise: Held, however, as the tenant by his own act had determined the lease, and had thereby rendered it impracticable for the landlord to have a valuation made three months before the determination of the demise, that the latter was entitled without any such valuation having been made, to

to resume the possession of the fixtures, machinery, and other effects used in the colliery, upon the determination of the demise by such forfeiture, and that he was entitled to resume such possession even of new machinery erected by the tenant during the term.

Held, secondly, that the tenant never had, under this demise, the possession, order, or disposition of the fixtures, or moveable articles within the meaning of 21 Jac. 1. c. 19. but a mere qualified right to use them during the term; and if they had been in his possession, &c., within the meaning of the statute, that would have ceased when the landlord resumed possession on the 9th of November.

During the intermediate time between the recovery of the judgment in Trinity term 1818, and the execution of the writ, hab. fac. poss. on the 9th of November 1819, the bankrupt continued to work the colliery, and to have the use of the machinery and implements: Held, that during this period the bankrupt had not the order or disposition of the machinery and implements, within the meaning of the statute. of James, Storer and Others, Assignees, v. Hunter, T. 5 G. 4. Page 368

8. Tenant from year to year, entered into an agreement during a current year, for a lease to be granted to him, and A. B., entered and occupied jointly with him; Held, that by this agreement and the joint occupation under it, the former tenancy was determined although the lease contracted for, was never granted. Hamerton v. Steadman, M. 5 G. 4. 478

4. Where the tenant, under a lease containing a covenant to repair, underlet the premises to one who entered into a similar covenant, and the original lessor brought

an action on this covenant in the first lease, and recovered: Held, that the damages and costs recovered in that action, and also the costs of defending it, might be recovered, as special damages in an action against the undertenant for breach of his covenant to repair. Neale v. Wyllie, M. 5 G. 4. Page 533

5. A. entered into a written agreement with B. for the hire of a piece of land for the purpose of making bricks; C. afterwards made an offer, in writing, to let another piece of land to A. upon the terms contained in the agreement between him (A.) and B., and at a subsequent time A., verbally, accepted the offer. In an action by C. for a breach of some of the terms of this contract: Held that the written offer made by C. was admissible in evidence, without being stamped. Drant v. Brown, Executor of Leggott, H. 5 & 6 G. 4. 665

6. By 4 G. 2. c. 28. s. 2. it is enacted that in all cases between landlord and tenant, as often as it shall happen that one half year's rent shall be in arrear, and the landlord or lessor to whom the same is due, hath right by law to re-enter for the non-payment thereof, such landlord or lessor shall and may, without any formal demand or re-entry, serve a declaration in ejectment for the recovery of the demised premises, which service shall stand in the place and stead of a demand and re-entry: Held, that by this statute the service of the declaration in ejectment is substituted for the demand of rent, which, at common law, must have been made upon the day when the forfeiture accrued in case of non-payment, and therefore that it was no ground of nonsuit in ejectment that the declaration was served on a day subsequent to the day on which

which the demise was laid, that
being after the rent became due;
because the title of the lessor must
be taken to have accrued on the
day when the forfeiture would have
accrued at common law by non-
payment of the rent. *Doe* d.
Laurence and Others v. *Shatcross*,
H. 5 & 6 G. 4.   Page 752

7. Where the tenant of certain premises underlet a part by deed, and
the original landlord distrained for
rent upon the undertenant: Held
that assumpsit would not lie by the
latter against his lessor upon an
implied promise to indemnify him
against the rent payable to the
superior landlord. *Schlencker* v.
Moxsy, H. 5 & 6 G. 4.   789

LAND GAINED FROM THE SEA BY ALLUVION.

See EVIDENCE, 3.

LEASE.

See LANDLORD AND TENANT, 8.

LIBEL.

1. Declaration for a libel purporting
to contain an account of a proceeding which had taken place before a magistrate, respecting a
matter in which he was merely
asked for advice, and not called
upon to act in his magisterial capacity. The libel itself alleged that
A. B. and C. D. stated the matter
charged to the magistrate, a great
part of which was not actionable
when spoken, but became so when
written. Plea, that A. B. and
C. D. did go before the magistrate
and make the statement set forth
in the libel, and that it contained
a correct account of the proceedings before the magistrate, and that
the facts charged in it were true.
The jury found that the matters
contained in the libel were not

true, but that it contained a correct account of the proceedings
which had taken place before the
magistrate. Held, first, that, as
the matter brought before the magistrate, was not brought before
him in his judicial character, or in
discharge of his magisterial functions, the defendant could not justify the publication on the ground
of its being a correct report of the
proceedings which had taken place
before the magistrate.

Held, secondly, that it was no
justification that the defendants,
when they published the libel,
mentioned the names of the parties
who stated the matter of the libel
to the magistrate, because as to
part of the slanderous matter no
action would lie against the party
who stated it to the magistrate;
it had become actionable merely
from its having been published by
the defendants in print, and therefore, by stating the names of the
persons from whom they heard it,
they gave the plaintiff no right of
action against them.

Held, thirdly, that in order to
justify the repeating of slander, it
was necessary that the party repeating it should, at the time of
repeating it, offer himself as a witness to prove the uttering of the
slander, and therefore that, as the
defendants did not state that they
themselves heard the slander uttered by A. B. and C. D. but
merely stated that A. B. and C. D.
had said so and so, the plea was
bad. *M'Gregor* v. *Thwaites*, T.
5 G. 4.   Page 24

2. In an action for a libel the defendant cannot, either in bar of the
action, or in mitigation of damages,
give in evidence other libels published of him by the plaintiff, not
distinctly relating to the same subject. Declaration stated that plaintiff was an attorney, and had been
employed

employed as vestry clerk in the parish of A., and that, while he was such vestry clerk, certain prosecutions were carried on against B. for certain misdemeanors, and in furtherance of such proceedings, and to bring the same to a successful issue, certain sums of money belonging to the parishioners were appropriated and applied to the discharge of the expences incurred in and about of the said proceedings, yet, defendant intending, &c., to injure the plaintiff in his profession of an attorney, and to cause him to be esteemed a fraudulent practiser in his said profession, and in his office as vestry clerk, and to cause it to be suspected that the plaintiff had fraudulently applied money belonging to the parishioners, &c., &c., &c., falsely and maliciously published of and concerning the plaintiff, and of and concerning his conduct in his office as vestry clerk, and of and concerning the matters aforesaid, the libel, &c. It appeared on the production of the libel at the trial, that the imputation was, that the plaintiff had applied the parish money in payment of the expences of the prosecution after it had terminated: Held, this was no variance, because it did not alter the character of the libel, the fraud imputed to the plaintiff being the same, whether the money was misapplied before or after the proceedings had terminated; and that the allegation that the libel was published of and concerning the matters aforesaid did not make it necessary to prove precisely that the libel did relate to every part of the matter previously stated. ... Held, &c. ... Page 113

3. Declaration for a libel stated that the plaintiff was an attorney, and that the defendant intending to injure him in his good name, had

The

in his said profession of an attorney, published a libel of and concerning the plaintiff, and of and concerning him in his said profession. At the trial the plaintiff failed in proving that at the time of the publication of the libel he was an attorney: Held, that this was not a fatal variance between the allegation and the proof, the words of the libel being actionable, although not used with reference to the professional character of the plaintiff. Bevis v. Walter, I. C. & P. 4. .... Page 138

4. Declaration for a libel stated, that the plaintiff was taken before a justice to answer a charge of having assaulted A. B., and that the said charge was proceeded upon, and, in part, heard, and witnesses were examined concerning the same, of which A. B. was one, and the further examination was adjourned to a future day; that at the time of publishing the libel no bill of indictment had been preferred against the plaintiff in respect of the charge, nor any trial had, and the subject matter of the charge was undetermined; yet that defendants, intending to hinder and obstruct the course of justice, and to prevent the plaintiff from having a fair trial, maliciously published in a newspaper, on the 10th July, the following libel: "One A. D., of, &c., underwent a long examination on a charge of having recently assaulted a female child only thirteen years old. The evidence of the child herself, and her companion, A. D.'s own cousin, displayed such a complication of guilt, as we cannot detail. We observe, however, that we should say that the accused denied the principal facts alleged, and that the children made some slight variation in their evidence." The same count charged the defendants

ants

...ants with publishing another libel on the 18th July, stating that "A. D., who was charged a week ago with attempting to violate the person of a girl of thirteen, was again examined, but no further evidence was heard, and he was ordered to enter into a recognizance for 200l.; and all the witnesses were bound over to prosecute." There were other counts setting out the libels, but making no reference to any proceeding before a magistrate. Plea, first, not guilty; secondly, that on, &c., at, &c., before J. H., justice, the plaintiff did undergo a long examination, &c., (repeating the libel); and that afterwards, to wit, on the 15th day of July, at the public office, Bow-street, the plaintiff was again examined, &c. (repeating the second libel)). The plea then stated that the supposed libels contained no other than a true, fair, just, and correct report and account of the proceedings which took place on the 8th and 15th days of July respectively, at the said public office, Bow-street, and were published by the defendants, with no scandalous, defamatory, unworthy, or unlawful motive whatever, and that the proceedings therein reported took place publicly, and openly at the police office, and the reports, on account thereof, composing the said supposed libels, were printed and published in the said newspapers as public news of such public proceedings, and with no other intent or form other than object or purpose whatever. Held, upon demurrer, that this plea was bad, inasmuch as it was no justification of the publication of slanderous matter, that it contained a correct report of the proceedings which took place in the course of a preliminary inquiry before a magistrate.

The third plea was, that the several matters and things in the supposed libels contained were true: Held, that this plea was bad, because it was uncertain whether it meant that the report in the newspaper was a true report of the proceedings, or that the facts mentioned in it were true; and if the latter were the meaning, then the plea was much too general.

The fourth plea to the whole declaration, stated that the supposed libel was nothing more than a fair, true, and correct report of proceedings which took place publicly and openly before the justice at the public office: Held, that this plea was bad; because it was no answer to those counts which did not allege that any proceedings had taken place before a justice.

The fifth plea, which was pleaded to the counts containing the libel of the 10th of July, was, that the plaintiff on the 8th of July was before the justice, and underwent a long examination, as in the second plea, and upon that occasion the mother of A. C. deposed as follows. The plea then set out the depositions verbatim, and by them it appeared that the libel complained of did not contain a full, fair, and accurate report of what passed at the police office; and upon that ground, it was held that this plea was clearly bad.

The sixth plea, which was pleaded to the libel of the 15th of July, alleged that the plaintiff was examined at the police office, and contained an entering into recognizances as in the libel mentioned: Held, that this plea was good, inasmuch as the publication of the 15th of July contained no statement of the evidence, nor any statement upon the case, but simply stated the result of what the justice had thought fit to do, nor did injure him in...

The

The seventh plea was, in substance, the same as the fifth, and held bad for the same reasons. The eighth being similar to the sixth, was held good. *Duncan* v. *Thwaites*, M. 5 G. 4.   Page 556

LIEN.

1. Plaintiff having contracted to purchase an estate of B., had the deeds of conveyance prepared at his own expense, and sent them to B. for execution. B. executed and gave them to a servant to be sent back. The servant delivered them to defendant, an attorney, who had a demand upon B. for business done in his profession. No directions were given to defendant to retain the deeds until the purchase money should be paid. Some necessary parties refused to execute the deeds, and plaintiff having abandoned the contract, demanded the deeds from the defendant, who refused to deliver them up, claiming to have a lien for his demand against B. In trover for deeds and stamped pieces of parchment: Held, that the plaintiff was entitled to recover the deeds at all events, in a cancelled, if not in an uncancelled state. *Littledale* J. dubitante. *Esdaile* v. *Oxenham*, T. 5 G. 4.   225

2. A., B., and C. carried on the business of bankers in copartnership. A. advanced large sums of money to the concern, which he raised by selling out stock, and he took separate bonds for 18,000l. from B. and C. conditioned for the replacing of 9000l. 3 per cent. consols by each, being their respective proportions of the stock sold by A. The stock not being replaced, A. brought actions, and recovered judgments on the bonds. A. afterwards retired from the concern, and at that time 20,000l. 3 per cent. consols was due to him by

the deed of dissolution, B. and C. covenanted to replace it by four instalments, and that if they failed to do so, A. might resort to the judgments recovered on the bonds, and further, that he should have a lien on certain specified securities for that debt, and also as an indemnity against partnership debts which they had covenanted to pay. One instalment was replaced when due, but B. and C. having failed to replace the second, a new agreement (not under seal) was entered into, whereby it was agreed that the transaction should be considered as a loan of money, from the first, and that the sum produced by the sale of the 15,000l. 3 per cents. which remained due, which was 10,083l., should be the debt, and be repaid at a future day with 5 per cent. interest. The value of 15,000l. 3 per cent. consols at the date of this last agreement, was 8437l. Before any part of the 10,083l. was paid, B. and C. became bankrupts; and at the issuing of the commission two out of the three remaining days fixed by the deed of dissolution for the retransfer of stock had passed. Held, that the second agreement was void for usury, but that the deed of dissolution remained binding, and that A. might prove under the commission against B. and C. for the 15,000l. 3 per cent. consols, the value of the two instalments before the bankruptcy to be ascertained by the price of consols on the day when these sums respectively became due; the value of the third to be taken at the price of consols on the day when the commission issued, with a rebate for the interval between that day and the day fixed for the retransfer of those instalments, and further, that A. still had the lien given by the deed.

A. having

A. having paid certain old partnership debts after he left the concern: Held, secondly, that he might prove for these also.

Whilst *A.* remained in the bank he received interest upon his advances, without any deduction for property tax: Held, thirdly, that no deduction was to be made in respect of that from the sum to be proved by him, inasmuch as it did not appear that the bankrupts had accounted to government for the property tax on the monies so paid. *Parker v. Ramsbottom and Others,* T. 5 G. 4.   Page 257

8. Where an application is made to set off costs and damages in one action against those recovered in a cross action, an attorney has a lien on the judgment obtained by his client against the opposite party, to the extent of his costs of that cause only. *Stephens v. Weston and Griffiths,* M. 5 G. 4.   535

LIMITATIONS, STATUTE OF.

1. Assumpsit for goods sold and delivered, and on the money counts. Pleas, general issue and the statute of limitations. Defendant paid money into court generally: Held, that such payment did not take the case out of the statute. *Long v. Greville,* T. 5 G. 4.   10

2. *A.* being seised in fee of an undivided moiety of an estate, devised the same (by will made some years before her death) to her nephew and two nieces as tenants in common: one of the nieces died in the lifetime of *A.* and left an infant daughter. *A.* by another will intended to have devised the moiety to the nephew and surviving niece, and the infant daughter of the deceased niece, but this will was never executed. After *A.*'s death, the nephew and surviving

niece covenanted to carry the unexecuted will into execution, and to convey one-third of the moiety to a trustee upon trust, to convey the same to the infant if she attained twenty-one, or to her issue if she died under twenty-one and left issue; or otherwise to the nephew and niece in equal moieties. No conveyance was executed in pursuance of the deed. The rents of the third were received by the trustee for the use of the infant during her life time. An ejectment having been brought by the devisee of the nephew more than twenty years after his death, but less than twenty years after the death of the infant; it was held that there was no adverse possession until the death of the infant, and that the ejectment was well brought. *Doe dem. Colclough v. Hulse,* H. 5 & 6 G. 4.   Page 757

LORD'S DAY.

See VENDOR AND VENDEE, 5.

MAGISTRATE.

See CONVICTION, 2. JUSTICES.

MALICIOUS ARREST.

See ARREST, 1.

MANDAMUS.

1. Where a charter does not require the members of a corporation to be resident, the Court will not grant a mandamus commanding the corporation to meet and consider of the propriety of removing from their offices non-resident corporators, unless their absence has been productive of some serious inconvenience. An alderman is not bound to reside within the borough, unless this is necessary

to the discharge of the duties of
his office, or required by the charter. *The King* v. *The Mayor and
Aldermen of the Borough of Portsmouth, T. 5 G. 4.* Page 132

2. The Court will grant a mandamus
to admit a copyholder claiming
by descent. *The King v. The
Masters, Keepers, Wardens, and
Commoners of the Brewers' Company, T. 5 G. 4.* 172

3. Semble, that coparceners are entitled to be admitted to copyhold
tenements as one heir, and upon
the payment of one set of fees.
*The King v. The Lord of the Ma-
nor of Bonsall, and Adam Wolley,
Steward of the said Manor, T.
5 G. 4.* 173

4. Where an inhabitant of a borough
applied for a mandamus to the
mayor and steward of the borough,
to enrol and swear him at the
court leet of the borough as a
resiant burgess, but did not make
out an inchoate right in every inhabitant to be a burgess, or that
any such connexion existed between the corporation and the
court leet as would make swearing
and enrolment at the latter the
means of perfecting such right,
the Court refused the writ. *The
King v. The Mayor, &c. of West
Looe, H. 5 & 6 G. 4.* 677

MONEY HAD AND RECEIVED.

See ASSUMPSIT. PLEADING.

OUTLAWRY

See PRACTICE, 16. 27.

OVERSEER.

1. By stat. 55 G. 3. c. 137. s. 6.,
churchwardens, or overseers of the
poor, either in his own name, or in
the name of any other person,
shall supply for his own profit any

goods, materials, or provisions for
the use of any workhouse, or otherwise for the support or maintenance of the poor in any place for
which he shall be appointed overseer, during the time he shall retain such appointment, nor shall
be concerned directly or indirectly
in supplying the same, or in any
contract or contracts relating
thereto, under the penalty of
100l. : Held, that an overseer who
supplied coals indirectly for the
use of the poor was not liable to
any penalty, unless he did it with
a view to his own profit. *Skinner
v. Bucket, T. 5 G. 4.* Page 6

2. Declaration on the 55 G. 3. c. 137.
s. 6., stated that defendant being
an overseer of the poor of the
parish of *A.*, supplied for his own
profit, provisions for the support
of the poor of the said parish,
" whereby, and by force of the
statute in such case made and
provided, he forfeited for his said
offence 100l., and thereby and by
force of the statute an action hath
accrued," &c. On motion in arrest of judgment : Held, that the
declaration was bad for want of
an allegation, that the act done
was " against the form of the
statute," and the judgment was
arrested. *Wells v. Iggulden, T.
5 G. 4.* 166

3. By stat. 17 G. 3. c. 3. s. 2. it is
enacted, " that overseers of the
poor shall permit inhabitants of the
parish to inspect rates at all seasonable times, and shall upon demand
forthwith give copies of the same to
any inhabitant of the parish," and
by sect. 3, " if any overseer shall
not permit an inhabitant to inspect
the rate, or shall neglect to give
copies thereof as aforesaid, such
overseer for every neglect thereof
shall forfeit and pay to the person
aggrieved the sum of 40l. : Held,
first, that inhabitants entitled to

III

... to ... for the penalty ... under the statute, he must shew that he has sustained an injury by the act of the contravener ... ... that there must be a demand ... import the ... that the ... a reasonable time and place ... Semble, that the house of the ... is the place at which the demand ought to be made. 3dly, Although the statute says that copies upon demand shall be forthwith given, yet the owner is entitled to a reasonable time for making them out. *Spinaslop v. Robinson, H. 5 & 6 G. A. Page 858*

PARTNERSHIP.

See USURY, 2.

PAYMENT.

1. When a person has two demands upon another, one arising out of a lawful contract, the other out of a contract forbidden by law, and the debtor makes a payment which is not specifically appropriated by either party at the time of payment, the law will appropriate it to the debt recognised by law; and therefore, where distinct sums of money were due, one for goods sold, the other for money lent on a usurious contract, and a payment was made which was not specifically appropriated to either debt by debtor or creditor, it was held that the law would afterwards appropriate such payment to the debt for goods sold. Where a bill of exchange was given for the principal money lent, and interest to accrue due on an usurious contract, and before the bill became due, the lender advanced a further sum of money on the general credit of the borrower, which enabled the latter to pay the bill, it was held that the ...

payment of the residue instead was completed as soon as the bill of exchange was paid ... *Wright v. Laing, T. 5 G. 4.* Page 335

2. W. C. being indebted to B. and R. C. being indebted to J. C., it was verbally agreed between the three that C. should transfer his debt due to him from J. C. to the account of B. C. and ... in pursuance of such agreement, delivered to D. a certain account, in which a (the G.) being charged with the debt due from J. C. to D.: Held, that C. was not thereby discharged. C. on ... and ... Assignees ... *Chadham, M. 5 G. 4.* ... 592

3. In an action by the assignee of a bankrupt, it was referred to an arbitrator to take accounts between the parties, with liberty to him to state on the face of his award any point of law that either party might require. The arbitrator by his award found the following facts. The defendant, before the bankruptcy, had accepted bills drawn upon him by the bankrupt. These bills had been paid away to creditors of the bankrupt. At the time of his accepting the bills, the defendant, as the agent of the bankrupt, had in his hands money of the bankrupt to the full amount of the sum for which the bills were drawn, and these funds had not been withdrawn at the time of the bankruptcy. After the bills became due respectively, and before the act of bankruptcy, the holders of the bills, in order to release the defendant from his responsibility to them, took from the defendant a composition upon the acceptances, and delivered up the bills to the defendant; thus the bankrupt remained no party to this arrangement. The award ...

... between the parties, this arbitrator ... had not allowed the amount of the ... sued ... for which the bills were ... drawn ... be set off by the defend- ant, but only the amount of the composition. Held, that the de- fendant was entitled to have the whole amount of the bills allowed on his account. *Stokehouse* v. *Reed*, 5 B. & C. ... Page 669

... being indebted to B., and C., who was resident in the West Indies, being indebted to him, the latter proposed to assign the debt due to him from C. to B.; and to this proposal B. assented. A. ... them by a letter directed the agents of C. in this country, "as soon as they should have funds belonging to C. in their hands, to pay B. on his (A.'s) account, the amount of C.'s debt," and added, that he would credit C. for the amount, *having received his order to that effect*. This order was communicated to the agents of C., and they *verbally* promised to pay B. as soon as they should have funds in their hands belonging to C. A. afterwards gave an order to another creditor, authorising C. to pay to such creditor the amount of the debt due to him. A. and C. entered into an obligation to pay the same to such creditor, but there was a clause annexed to the obligation, stating that it had been alleged that a payment had been made on account of the debt by some person to A. on account of C., and it was declared, that should such payment be proved to have been made by C., the amount should be deducted. The credi- tor to whom this order was given demanded payment of the debt from C. on his arrival in this country, but the latter refused to ... that his ... were liable to pay it to B., and ... afterwards paid to B.

Held that although a creditor in having a right to insist on payment to himself, or to his appointee, yet to having once given an order for the payment of his debt to a third per- son, he had no right to revoke that order, provided there be a pledge by the person to whom the autho- rity is given, that he will pay the debt according to that authority.

Held further, that the expres- sion in A.'s letter, that he would credit C. for the amount, having received his order to that effect, was evidence against him, that he had at that time received such an order from C., and, therefore, that C. had expressly assented to the order given by A., that the debt due from C. to A. should be paid to B.

Held, also, that even if that were not so, still there was sufficient to imply the assent of C., that the debt due from him to A. should be applied in discharge of the debt due from A. to B., inasmuch as it was expressly stipulated by C. in the obligation he entered into, to pay the debt to another, that any sum paid by any person on ac- count of that debt to A. should be deducted.

Held, also, that it was not ne- cessary that the promise to pay the debt of A. should be in writ- ing, inasmuch as it was a promise by A. to pay his own debt, and not that of another. *Hodgson* v. *An- derton*, H. 5 & 6 G. 4. Page 842

PAYMENT OF MONEY INTO COURT.

See PRACTICE, 2.

PENAL ACTION.

See OVERSEER, USURY.

PLEADING.

Where, in an action, ... false return to a fieri facias, the declar- ation

…tion stated that the plaintiff in *T— v. G—*, by the judgment recovered, &c. "as appears by the record," and the proof was of a judgment in *Easter* term 3 G. 4.: Held, that this was no variance; for that the averment, "as appears by the record," was surplusage, and might be rejected, inasmuch as the judgment was not the foundation of, but mere inducement to the action. *Stoddart* v. *Palmer*, T. 5 G. 4. Page 2

2. A debt contracted in *England* by a trader residing in *Scotland*, is barred by a discharge under a sequestration issued in conformity to the 54 G. 3. c. 137, in like manner as debts contracted in *Scotland*. *Sidaway* v. *Hay*, T. 5 G. 4. 12

3. Declaration for a libel purporting to contain an account of a proceeding which had taken place before a magistrate, respecting a matter in which he was merely asked for advice, and not called upon to act in his magisterial capacity. The libel itself alleged that *A. B.* and *C. D.* stated the matter charged to the magistrate, a great part of which was not actionable when spoken, but became so when written. Plea, that *A. B.* and *C. D.* did go before the magistrate and make the statement set forth in the libel, and that it contained a correct account of the proceedings before the magistrate, and that the facts charged in it were true. The jury found that the matters contained in the libel were not true, but that it contained a correct account of the proceedings which had taken place before the magistrate: Held, first, that as the matter brought before the magistrate was not brought before him in his judicial character, or in the discharge of his magisterial functions, the defendant could not

…justify the publication as the ground of its being an accurate report of the proceedings which had taken place before the magistrate. Held, secondly, that it was no justification that the defendants, when they published the libel, mentioned the names of the parties who stated the matter of the libel to the magistrate, because as to that part of the slanderous matter no action would lie against the party who stated it to the magistrate, it had become actionable merely from its having been published by the defendants in print, and therefore by stating the names of the persons from whom they heard it, they gave the plaintiff no right of action against them.

Held, thirdly, that in order to justify the repeating of slander, it was necessary that the party repeating it should, at the time of repeating it, offer himself as a witness to prove the uttering of the slander, and therefore that, as the defendants did not state that they themselves heard the slander uttered by *A. B.* and *C. D.*, but merely stated that *A. B.* and *C. D.* had said so and so, the plea was bad. *M'Gregor* v. *Thwaites*, T. 5 G. 4. Page 24

4. *A.* let apartments in his dwelling-house to *B.*, at a rent payable half-yearly, *B.* took possession at *Michaelmas* 1822, and at *Lady-day* 1823 paid half a year's rent. In *June* of that year *B.* left the apartments without giving any notice to quit; but at *Michaelmas* 1823, he paid half a year's rent. At *Lady-day* 1824 *A.* demanded another half year's rent, which *B.* refused to pay: Held, that from these facts the law would not imply a taking from year to year. *Wilson* v. *Abbot*, T. 5 G. 4. 88

5. Where an inquisition found that a piece of land had in times past been covered with the materials the sea,

sea, but was then, and had been for several years past, by the sea left, the commissioners caused the same to be seized into the king's hands. The defendant filed a traverse, stating that he was seised in fee of the manor of *North Thoresby cum North Cotes*, and the demesne lands thereof; and that the same piece of land mentioned in the inquisition, by the slow, gradual, and imperceptible projection, alluvion, subsidence, and accretion of ooze, soil, sand, and other matter, being slowly, gradually, and by imperceptible increase in long time cast up, deposited, and settled, by and from the flux and reflux of the tide upon and against the extremity of the said manor, hath been formed, &c., and thereby became parcel of the demesne lands of the manor; without this, that the land was *left* by the sea, as found by the inquisition. The replication by the Attorney-General traversed, that the land was formed as alleged in the inducement to the defendant's traverse, and joined issue on the traverse taken by the defendant. Issue was also joined on the traverse taken by the Attorney-General. It appeared by the evidence, that the land in question had been formed gradually, by ooze and soil deposited by the sea, and that the increase could not be observed when actually going on, although a visible increase took place every year, and in the course of fifty years, a large piece of land had been thus formed : Held, first, that upon this evidence the land could not be said to have been *left* by the sea ; secondly, that it was formed by the slow, gradual, and imperceptible projection, &c. of ooze, soil, and sand, as alleged in the inducement to the defendant's traverse, and that both issues were

properly found for him. *The King v. Lord Yarborough*, 1, 5 G. 4.

Page 91

6. Declaration stated that plaintiff was an attorney, and had been employed as vestry clerk in the parish of *A.*, and that, whilst he was such vestry clerk, certain prosecutions were carried on against *B.* for certain misdemeanors, and in furtherance of such proceedings, and to bring the same to a successful issue, certain sums of money belonging to the parishioners were appropriated and applied to the discharge of the expences incurred on account of the said proceedings. Yet defendant, intending, &c. to injure the plaintiff in his profession of an attorney, and to cause him to be esteemed a fraudulent practiser in his said profession and in his office as vestry clerk, and to cause it to be suspected that the plaintiff had fraudulently applied money belonging to the parishioners, on, &c., at, &c., falsely and maliciously published, of and concerning the plaintiff, and of and concerning his conduct in his office as vestry clerk, and of and concerning the matters aforesaid, the libel, &c. It appeared, on the production of the libel at the trial, that the imputation was, that the plaintiff had applied the parish money in payment of the expences of the prosecution *after* it had terminated : Held, that this was no variance, because it did not alter the character of the libel, the fraud imputed to the plaintiff being the same; whether the money was misapplied before or after the proceedings had terminated ; and that the allegation, that the libel was published of and concerning the *matters aforesaid*, did not make it necessary to prove precisely that the libel did relate to every part of the

the matter previously stated, *May, Gent, One, &c.* v. *Brown, T.* 5 G. 4
Page 118

7. Declaration for a libel, stated that the plaintiff was an attorney, and that the defendant, intending to injure him in his good name, and in his said profession of an attorney, published a libel of and concerning the plaintiff, and of and concerning him in his said profession. At the trial the plaintiff failed in proving that, at the time of the publication of the libel, he was an attorney: Held, that this was not a fatal variance between the allegation and the proof; the words of the libel being actionable, although not used with reference to the professional character of the plaintiff. *Lewis* v. *Walter, T.* 5 G. 4.
138

8. Where there are mutual dealings between two parties, and items known to be due on each side of the account, an arrest for the amount of one side of the account, without deducting what is due on the other, is malicious, and without probable cause. *Austin* v. *Debnam, T.* 5 G. 4.
139

9. When a person has two demands upon another, one arising out of a lawful contract, the other out of a contract forbidden by law, and the debtor makes a payment which is not specifically appropriated by either party at the time of payment, the law will appropriate it to the debt recognised by law; and therefore, where distinct sums of money were due, one for goods sold the other for money lent on a usurious contract, and a payment was made which was not specifically appropriated to either debt by debtor or creditor, it was held that the law would afterwards appropriate such payment to the debt for goods sold. Where a bill of exchange was given for the

principal money lent and interest, to accrue due on an usurious contract, and before the bill became due, the lender advanced a further sum of money on the general credit of the borrower, which enabled the latter to pay the bill, it was held, that the payment of the usurious interest was complete as soon as the bill was paid. *Wright and Another, Assignees,* v. *Laing, T.* 5 G. 4.
Page 165

10. Declaration on the 55 G. 3. c. 137. s. 6. stated that defendant being an overseer of the parish of *A.*, supplied for his own profit provisions for the support of the poor of the said parish, " whereby and by force of the statute in such case made and provided, he forfeited for his said offence 100l., and thereby and by force of the statute an action hath accrued," &c. On motion in arrest of judgment: Held, that the declaration was bad, for want of an allegation that the act done was against the statute," and the judgment was arrested. *Wells* v. *Iggulden, T.* 5 G. 4. 186

11. Declaration in sci. fa. stated that *R. S.* (the plaintiff in the original action) became bankrupt, whereupon a commission was duly awarded against him and *E. H., R. B.,* and *J. T.* (the plaintiffs in the sci. fa.) were duly chosen assignees of the estate and effects of the said *R. S.,* under the commission, and now on behalf of the said *E. F., R. B.,* and *J. T., as assignees as aforesaid,* we have been informed, &c.: Held, that this was good (defendant not having demurred to it) without an express averment that an assignment of the bankrupt's effects was made; for that the expression " assignees as aforesaid," might mean " persons to whom an assignment has been made;" and the 5 G. 2. c. 30. s. 26. having directed the choice of assignees

3 O 3

signees to be followed up by an assignment of the effects to the persons chosen, the court might presume that such an assignment was made.

Semble, That the objection would have been fatal if made the ground of special demurrer. *Fletcher* v. *Rogers, T. 5 G. 4.* Page 192.

12. The master of a ship which was injured by the perils of the sea, put into the *Mauritius*, and there abandoned the ship and cargo, which were afterwards sold under an order of the Vice-Admiralty Court there, and the proceeds paid into that court. The cargo was not damaged or perishable, nor was there any pressing necessity for the sale of it. The owners of the cargo brought an action on the case against the owners of the ship for wrongfully selling the cargo instead of carrying it to *London*, according to their contract, with a count in trover, and recovered a general verdict for the value of the ship and freight, which was one-fifth of the value of the cargo. They also sent out a power of attorney to an agent at the *Mauritius* to procure from the Vice-Admiralty Court there the proceeds of the sale which had been paid in. The agent demanded them, but they had been previously remitted to the High Court of Admiralty in this country. In an action for money had and received against the purchaser of the goods: Held, first, that the captain had not any authority to sell the cargo, although acting *bona fide*, and under the orders of the Vice-Admiralty Court; secondly, that the recovery against the owners of the ship was no answer to the present action; thirdly, that the proceeds of the sale at the *Mauritius* not having been paid when demanded, the plaintiffs were in the same situation as if no

such demand had been made, and therefore entitled to recover the value of the goods from the defendant. *Morris and Another* v. *Robinson, T. 5 G. 4.* Page 196

13. Where *B.* being indebted to *A.*, procured *C.* to join with him in giving a joint and several promissory note for the amount, and afterwards having become further indebted, and being pressed by *A.* for further security, by deed (reciting the debt, and that for a part a note had been given by him *B.*) and *C.*, and that *A.* having demanded payment of the debt, *B.* had requested him to accept a *further* security, assigned to *A.* all his household goods, &c. as a *further* security, with a proviso, that he should not be deprived of the possession of the property assigned until after three days' notice: Held, that this deed did not extinguish or suspend the remedy on the note, but that *A.* might, notwithstanding the deed, sue *C.* at any time. *Twopenny and Boys* v. *Young, T. 5 G. 4.* 208

14. Where, in case for not carrying away tithe corn, the plaintiff alleged that it was " lawfully and in due manner" set out: Held, that this allegation was satisfied by proof, that the tithe was set out according to an agreement between the parties, although it varied from the mode prescribed by the common law. *Facey* v. *Hurdom, T. 5 G. 4.* 213

15. Plaintiff having contracted to purchase an estate of *B.* had the deeds of conveyance prepared at his own expence, and sent them to *B.* for execution. *B.* executed and gave them to a servant to be sent back. The servant delivered them to defendant an attorney, who had a demand upon *B.* for business done in his profession. No directions were given to defendant to

to retain the deeds, until the purchase money should be paid. Some necessary parties refused to execute the deeds, and plaintiff having abandoned the contract, demanded the deeds from defendant, who refused to deliver them up, claiming to have a lien for his demand against B. In trover for deeds and stamped pieces of parchment: Held, that the plaintiff was entitled to recover the deeds at all events, in a cancelled, if not in an uncancelled state, *Littledale J. dubitante, Esdaile* v. *Oxenham*, T. 5 G. 4. Page 225

16. Assumpsit for money had and received. Plea, a judgment recovered for want of a plea for 4000l. in an inferior court in *Wales*, for the same causes of action. Replication that the causes of action were not the same, and issue joined thereon. At the trial it appeared that the defendant had received on account of the plaintiff, and as his steward, different sums of money at different times, and that on the investigation of the accounts, the plaintiff found that there was due to him a much larger sum than that for which he had declared in the inferior court, but that he had proceeded for the smaller sum under the belief that the defendant had no available property beyond that amount, defendant in that action suffered judgment by default, and plaintiff verified for 3400l. Held, that all the sums which the plaintiff knew the defendant had received at the time when he commenced the action in the inferior court, were to be considered as causes of action, in respect of which he had declared and recovered the judgment. *Lord Bagot* v. *Williams*, 4, 5 G. 4. 235

17. By the Black Act, 9 G. I. c. 22, any person who shall unlawfully and maliciously kill, maim, or wound any cattle, or cut down, or otherwise destroy any trees planted in any avenue, or growing in any garden, orchard, or plantation for ornament, shelter, or profit, shall be adjudged guilty of felony, and the inhabitants of the hundred are to make satisfaction to the persons damnified by the cutting down or destroying any trees which shall be committed by the offenders against the act: Held, that in order to make the malicious destruction of trees, a felony within this statute, the act done must proceed from a malicious motive towards the owner of the trees, and therefore, where an action was brought against the hundred by a party damnified in consequence of his plantation having been destroyed by fire, and it appeared that the fire had commenced at the distance of a mile from his plantation, and in adjoining grounds belonging to a different proprietor, it was held, that there was not any evidence that the act was done from motives of malice towards the plaintiff, and therefore, that no offence had been committed against the statute, and that the action, consequently, was not maintainable against the hundred. *Curtis, Bart. and Another*, v. *The hundred of Godley*, T. 5 G. 4. Page 248

18. By deed reciting the grant of two distinct annuities to A. and B. during the life of the grantors and the survivor, it was witnessed that C. covenanted with A. and B. and their executors, to pay the annuities, or either of them, when the grantors should make default in payment: Held, that the interest in the annuities being several, the covenant was also several, and that the annuity granted to A. being in arrear, his executor might maintain an action against C. *Withers Executors* v. *Bircham and Another*,

Another. Executor, T. 5 G. 4.
Page 254
19. A woman, divorced a mensa et thoro, for adultery, and living separate and apart from her husband cannot be sued as a feme sole. Lewis v. Lee, T. 5 G. 4. 291

20. A. B., seised of lands in fee simple at the time of her death, in the possession of a tenant from year to year, died, leaving C. D. her heir at law. No rent was ever paid to him, it being supposed that the lands passed to a devisee under the will of A. B. After the death of C. D., his son and heir at law brought ejectment, and recovered the lands. In debt against the son, as heir of C. B., on a bond given by the latter, to which the son pleaded no assets by descent from his father: Held, that the father was seised, in fact of the lands in question, and that they descended from him, to his son, and were, therefore, assets in the hands of the latter, liable to the bond debt. Bushley and Another, Executors, v. Dixon, T. 5 G. 4. 298

21. By fiction of law, all judgments are supposed to be recovered in term, and to relate to the first day of the term; but in practice judgments are frequently signed in vacation, and where the purposes of justice require that the true time when the judgment was obtained should be made appear. A party may shew it by averment in pleading; therefore in an action against an executor for breaches of covenant, him, an indenture made by his testator, the defendants having pleaded, in chief plene administravit and a retainer for a simple contract debt, upon which issues were taken, and joined, and then nis darrien continuance. A judgment recovered upon a bond of the testators, after the last continuance being the last day of Trinity

and where it was the second day of August, and of Trinity term preceding, to which plaintiff replied, that the defendants had notice of the bond before the commencement of the action. Held, upon demurrer to the replication, that the plea was well pleaded, and was an answer to the action. Leighton and Ashton v. Cnbes and Others, Executors, T. 5 G. 4. Page 317

22. A. and Co., merchants at Rio Janeiro, consigned cottons to B. in this country for sale, and sent bills of lading, which shewed that the cottons were sent on account and risk of the consigners. B. employed C. and D., brokers at Liverpool, to effect the sales, which they did; some at a credit of ten days, and bills at three months; others for cash in one month. C. and D. made large advances to B., and received the proceeds of the cottons when due. Before that time B. had become bankrupt. In an action by A. and Co. against C. and D. for money had and received: Held, that the latter were not entitled to retain for the advances made by them to B., for that he was a factor for sale only, and had no authority to pledge the goods, and that the plaintiffs were entitled to recover the net proceeds, deducting such sums only, as B. could have retained. A. and Co. when they consigned the cottons to B. requested him to make remittances in anticipation of sales. Held, secondly, that this request did not give B. any special authority to pledge the goods. Davison and Others v. Trimmer and Others, T. 5 G. 4. 342

23. Where in covenant against the executors of A. B., plaintiff declared that A. B. covenanted with him and with others, that his executors, &c. should pay to them an annuity for the use of a third person,

holden

to person, and averred that the other two never sealed the deed: Held on demurrer, that all joint covenantees who may sue, must sue, and that the declaration was bad, inasmuch as it did not appear that any of the covenantees had not assented to the deed, although they could not seal it.

Quære, whether the declaration would have been sufficient if it had averred that the two covenantees not joined had refused to assent to the deed. *Petrie v. Bury*, T. 5 G. 4. Page 353

24. A. being the occupier of a farm quitted the same on the 25th of March 1821, and was succeeded in the possession by B. A. had sown forty acres with wheat, and it appeared that at a meeting between A. and B. in February 1821, A. asked B. if he would take the forty acres of wheat at 200l., telling him that if he did not, he should not have the farm. B. said that he would take it. A person present then valued the dead stock, and having so done, asked to whom it was to value it; B. said that it was to be valued to him, and then promised to pay A. for the wheat and dead stock on a given day, and he did pay a sum of money on account. B. afterwards had possession of the farm, of the growing wheat, and the dead stock; Held, that in indebitatus assumpsit for crops bargained and sold, and goods sold and delivered, the contract for the dead stock was distinct from any contract for the sale of the growing wheat, and the possession of the farm, and, therefore, that A. was entitled to recover to that amount: Held, also, by Bayley and Holroyd Js., Littledale J. dissentiente, that as B. had had the growing wheat, and had made a part payment on account, A. was entitled in this action to recover the remainder of the price agreed to be paid for it.

Where a plaintiff has recovered a verdict for a sum of money composed of several items, some of which he was not entitled in strict law to recover under the declaration in that action, but which he would be clearly entitled to recover by declaring in a different form, the Court will not reduce the damages. *Per Abbott C. J. Mayfield v. Wadsley*, T. 5 G. 4. Page 357

25. A. agreed to give a horse, warranted sound, in exchange for a horse of B.'s and a sum of money. The horses were exchanged, but B. refused to pay the money, pretending that A.'s horse was unsound: Held, that it might be recovered on an indebitatus count for horses sold and delivered. *Sheldon v. Cox*, M. 5 G 4. 420

26. In assumpsit by two co-trustees for money had and received, to their use the defendant produced a receipt for the money given by one of the plaintiffs: Held, that this was not conclusive, and that evidence was properly admitted to shew that the giving of the receipt was a fraudulent transaction, and that the money had not been paid. *Skaife v. Jackson*, M. 5 G. 4. 421

27. Certain bills of exchange purporting to have, amongst others, the indorsement of H. and Co. bankers, of Manchester, were presented for payment in London, at a house where the acceptance appointed them to be paid. Payment being refused, the notary who presented them took them to the plaintiff, the London correspondent of H. and Co., and asked him to take up the bills for their honor. He did so, and struck but the indorsements subsequent to that of H. and Co., and the money was paid over to the defendants, the holders

... holders of the bills. ... morning it was discovered that the bills were not genuine, and that the names of the drawer, acceptor, and ... and &c. were ... Plaintiff immediately ... notice to the defendant, and ... ... have the money re- ... ... notice was given in ... for the ... so that notice ... of the dishonor could be sent the ... day to the indorsee. Held, that the plaintiff having paid the money through a mistake, was en- titled to recover it back, the mis- take having been discovered before the defendant had lost his remedy against the prior indorsees. Held, secondly, that the rights of the parties were not altered by the erasure of the indorsements, that having been done by mistake, and being capable of explanation by evidence. *Wilkinson and Others v. Johnson and Others, M. 5 G. 4.* Page 428

28. A. and Co., resident in *America*, employed B., resident at *Birming-ham*, in this country, to purchase and ship goods for them. On ac- count of such purchases, they sent to B. a bill drawn by C. in *America* on D. ... but did not in- dorse it. B. employed his bankers to present the bill for acceptance. D. refused to accept, but ... this ... the bankers did not give notice ... the day of payment, when it ... again presented and disho- noured. Before this bill arrived in this country ... became bankrupt, ... Held, that neither when the bill was ... due ... be- ... became due ... the ... D. ... the drawee ... an action by B. against the bankers for neglecting to give due notice of the dishonour of the bill ... Held that ... Co. ... having indorsed the bill were ... notified his dishonour ...

... for any ... and still remained liable to B., for the price of the goods sent ... them; and the drawees not ... entitled to notice, ... had no funds in the hands of the drawee; ... could not recover the whole amount of the bill, but such da- mages only as he had sustained in consequence of having been de- layed in the pursuit of his remedy against the drawee. *Vane West v. Woolley and Others, M. 5 G. 4.* &c. &c. Page 439

29. Trespass for breaking and enter- ing plaintiff's dwelling-house. De- fendant justified under a judgment recovered in a court baron, and a precept issued thereon. Repli- cation, that there was not any memorandum of the proceedings, or of the said supposed judgment, remaining in the said court baron: Held, upon general demurrer, that the replication was bad, inasmuch as it put in issue an immaterial fact.

Dubitante *Littledale J.* *Dyne v. Wood, M. 5 G. 4.* 449

30. Assumpsit, that in consideration that plaintiff would advance a sum of money to A. B., defendant pro- mised that provision should be made for repaying the plaintiff. At the trial, it appeared that the defendant had given to the plain- tiff the guarantee stated in the de- claration, and that the latter was a partner with another person in a banking-house, and that the firm had advanced the money, and charged A. B. in account with the same. Held, that the words in the declaration that the plaintiff had advanced the money, were not as supported by the proof, there being ... the money ... had been advanced to the plaintiff by the firm. Held by him too. B. *&c. Girlett and Hamilton, M. 5 G. 4.* ... and also the costs of defend- ... Indictment charged that defend- ant

and on, &c., in the second year of the reign of the present king, kept a gaming-house. Plea, that on, &c. in the fourth year of the reign of the present king, defendant was arraigned upon an indictment, which charged that defendant on the 16th of January, in the fifty-seventh year of the reign of the late king, and on divers other days and times between that day and the day of taking the inquisition, kept a gaming house, &c., to the nuisance of the subjects of our said lord the king, and against the peace of our said lord the king, &c. The plea then averred the identity of the offences described in the two indictments, and the acquittal of the defendant. Upon demurrer to this plea, concluding with a prayer of judgment of respondeas ouster, it was held that the plea was bad, because the indictment upon which the acquittal was alleged to have taken place, on the face of it, charged an offence committed in the reign of the late king; and it was not competent to the defendant to shew by averment that it was for the same offence as that charged in the indictment before the Court, because that would be in effect to contradict the record. Held, secondly, that the crown was entitled to final judgment, notwithstanding the form in which demurrer concluded. Semble, that such an indictment must conclude contra pacem domini regis. The King v. Taylor, M. 5 G. 4. . . . . Page 502

82. Where the tenant under a lease containing a covenant to repair, underlet the premises to one who entered into a similar covenant, and the original lessor brought an action on this covenant in the first lease, and recovered. Held, that the damages and costs recovered in that action, and also the costs of defending, might be recovered as special

damages in an action against the under-tenant for the breach of his covenant to repair. Neale v. Wyllie, M. 5 G. 4. . . . . Page 533

83. Where a manufacturer had adopted a particular mark for his goods, in order to denote that they were manufactured by him: Held, that an action on the case was maintainable by him against another person who adopted the same mark for the purpose of denoting that his goods were manufactured by the plaintiff, and who sold the goods so marked, as and for goods manufactured by the plaintiff.

The declaration stated that defendant sold the goods as and for goods manufactured by the plaintiff; it appeared in evidence that the persons who bought the goods of the defendant knew by whom they were manufactured, but that the defendant used the plaintiff's mark, and sold the goods so marked, in order that his customers might, and in fact they did, resell them as and for goods manufactured by the plaintiff: Held, that this evidence supported the declaration. Sykes v. Sykes and Another, M. 5 G. 4. 541

84. Declaration for a libel stated that the plaintiff was taken before a justice to answer a charge of having assaulted A. B., and that the said charge was proceeded upon, and, in part heard, and witnesses were examined concerning the issue, of which A. B. was one, and the further examination was adjourned to a future day; that at the time of publishing the libel no bill of indictment had been preferred against the plaintiff in respect of the charge, nor any trial had; and the subject matter of the charge was undetermined; yet that defendant, intending to hinder and obstruct the course of justice, and to prevent the plaintiff from having a fair

a fair trial, maliciously published in a newspaper, on the 10th July, the following libel: "One A. D., of, &c., underwent a long examination on a charge of having indecently assaulted a female child only thirteen years old. The evidence of the child herself, and her companion, A. D.'s own cousin, displayed such a complication of disgusting indecencies, that we cannot detail it. It is right, however, that we should say that the accused denied the principal facts alleged, and that the children made some slight variation in their evidence." The same count charged the defendants with publishing another libel on the 18th July, stating that A. D., who was charged a week ago with attempting to violate the person of a girl of thirteen, was again examined, but no further evidence was heard; and he was ordered to enter into a recognizance for 200l., and all the witnesses were bound over to prosecute. There were other counts setting out the libels, but making no reference to any proceeding before a magistrate. Plea, first, not guilty; secondly, that on, &c., at, &c. before J. H., justice, the plaintiff did undergo a long examination, &c.; and that afterwards, to wit, on the 15th day of July, at the public office, Bow-street, the plaintiff was again examined, &c. (repeating the second libel.) The plea then stated that the supposed libels contained "no other than a true, full, just, and correct report and account of the proceedings which took place on the 8th and 10th days of July respectively, at the said public office, Bow-street, and were published by the defendants, with no scandalous, defamatory, unworthy, or unlawful motive whatsoever, and that the proceedings therein reported took place publicly and openly at the police office,

office, and the reports or accounts thereof composing the said supposed libels, were printed and published in the said newspapers as public news of such public proceedings, and with no other intent, and for no other object or purpose whatsoever: Held, upon demurrer, that this plea was bad, inasmuch as it was no justification of the publication of slanderous matter, that it contained a correct report of the proceedings which took place in the course of a preliminary inquiry before a magistrate.

The third plea was, that the several matters and things in the supposed libels contained were true: Held, that this plea was bad, because it was uncertain whether it meant that the report in the newspaper was a true report of the proceedings, or that the facts mentioned in it were true; and if the latter were the meaning, then the plea was much too general.

The fourth plea to the whole declaration, that the supposed libel was nothing more than a fair, true, and correct report of proceedings which took place publicly and openly before the justice at the public office: Held, that this plea was bad, because it was no answer to those counts which did not allege that any proceedings had taken place before a justice.

The fifth plea which was pleaded to the counts containing the libel of the 10th of July was, that the plaintiff on the 8th of July was before the justice, and underwent a long examination, as in the second plea, and upon that occasion the mother of A. C. deposed as follows. (The plea then set out the depositions verbatim, and by them it appeared that the libel complained of did not contain a full, fair, and accurate report of what passed at the police office, and on that ground, it was held that this plea was clearly bad.

The sixth plea which was pleaded to the libel of the 15th of July, alleged that the plaintiff was examined at the police office, and ordered to enter into recognizances, as in the libel mentioned: Held, that this plea was good, inasmuch as the publication of the 15th of July contained no detail of the evidence, nor any comment upon the case, but merely stated the result of what the justice had thought fit to do.

The seventh plea was, in substance, the same as the fifth, and held bad for the same reasons. The eighth being similar to the sixth, was held good. *Duncan v. Thwaites*, M. 5 G. 4. Page 556

35. Where a continuance was entered from *Trinity* to the first day of *Michaelmas* term, and matter arising during the interval was pleaded after the first day of *Michaelmas* term, by way of puis darrein continuance, the Court ordered the plea to be taken off the file. *The King v. Taylor*, H. 5 & 6 G. 4. 612

36. Debt for money had and received. Plea, general issue, and set-off for money lent, paid, &c. At the trial, it appeared that the plaintiffs, *A.* and *Co.*, in *England*, consigned goods to the defendants, *B.* and *Co.* at *Gibraltar*, to be sold on commission, *B.* and *Co.*, as soon as the bills of lading and invoices were delivered to their agents in *London*, advanced, through them, to *A.* and *Co.*, two-thirds of the invoice price of the goods, by bills at ninety days; and, for these advances received interest at the rate of 6 per cent. calculated from the date of the bills, which was the usual rate of interest at *Gibraltar*. In an action

for the proceeds of the goods: Held, that this could not be considered as a loan of money in *England*, and was not usurious, and that the defendants were entitled to set off the monies so advanced.

Semble, That in an action for money had and received, the plaintiff must give evidence of a particular sum to which he is entitled. *Harvey and Others, Assignees, v. Archbold and Others*, H. 5 & 6 G. 4. Page 626

37. In assumpsit for goods sold, it appeared that the plaintiff, a jeweller, in the course of two months, delivered articles of jewelry to the wife of the defendant amounting in value to 83l. It appeared that the defendant was a certificated special pleader, and lived in a ready furnished house, of which the annual rent was 200l.; that he kept no man servant; that his wife's fortune upon her marriage was less than 4000l.; that she had, at the time of her marriage, jewelry suitable to her condition, and that she had never worn, in her husband's presence, any articles furnished her by the plaintiff; it appeared also, that the plaintiff, when he went to the defendant's house to ask for payment, always enquired for the wife and not for the defendant. Held, that the goods so furnished were not necessaries, and that, as there was no evidence to go to the jury of any assent of the husband to the contract made by his wife, the action could not be maintained. *Montague v. Benedict*, H. 5 & 6 G. 4. 631

38. Where the commander of a ship entered into a charter party (not under seal), whereby the charterer agreed to pay freight generally, without saying to whom; Held, that the owner, having demanded and

had received the freight, the commander could not maintain an action for it against the charterer,
although he had given him notice
not to pay it to any one but himself. *Atkinson* v. *Cotesworth*, *H.
5 & 6 G. 4.* .... Page 647

39. It is not necessary that any information or complaint should be
made on oath in order to justify
the interference of magistrates
under the 11 *G. 2. c. 19. s. 16.* In
trespass against two magistrates
for giving plaintiff's landlord possession of a farm, as a deserted
farm, they produced in evidence a
record of their proceedings under
that act, which set forth all such
circumstances as were necessary
to give them jurisdiction, and by
which it appeared that they had
pursued the directions of the statute: Held, that this was conclusive as an answer to the action.
Basten v. *Carew*, *H. 5 & 6 G. 4.*
.... 649

40. By stat. 17 *G. 3. c. 3. s. 2.* it is
enacted " That overseers of the
poor shall permit inhabitants of the
parish to inspect rates at all seasonable times, and shall, upon demand,
forthwith give copies of the same to
any inhabitant of the parish; and
by s. 3. 4. if any overseer shall not
permit an inhabitant to inspect the
rates, or shall neglect to give copies
thereof as aforesaid; such overseers for every such offence, shall
forfeit and pay to the party aggrieved the sum of 20l.: Held,
that in order to entitle a
party to sue for the penalty under
the statute, he must shew that he
has sustained an injury by the act
of the overseer. *Spencely* v. *Robinson*, *H. 5 & 6 G. 4.* 658

41. In an action brought to recover
penalties under the statute of
usury, it appeared that the contract was made in one county, and
the money paid in another. The

venue was laid in the county where
the contract was made: Held, that
it ought to have been laid where
the noxious interest was received.
Pearson v. *M'Gowran*, *H. 5 &
6 G. 4.* .... Page 760

42. In tort, a party suing out bailable process jointly against several, may declare separately against
one of them. *Wilson* v. *Edwards*,
H. 5 & 6 G. 4. 764

43. In case against an attorney for
negligence, it appeared that the
plaintiff in *H. T. 4 G. 4.* obtained
final judgment against *H.*, who
surrendered in discharge of his
bail on the day preceding the essoign day of *E. T.*, but notice of
the surrender was not given until
two days afterwards. *H.* not having been charged in execution in
E. T. was superseded, and discharged out of custody by a Judge
of *K. B.*: Held, that the present
action could not be maintained,
for that *H.* was improperly superseded, inasmuch as the two terms
allowed by the rule of court
H. T. 26 G. 3. for charging a prisoner in execution, are to be calculated from the time of giving
notice of the surrender, which, in
this case was not done until after
the legal commencement of *E. T.*:
Held, secondly, that even if *H.*
had been properly superseded,
still the present defendant would
not have been liable to an action
for negligence, the meaning of the
rule of court being obscure. *Lud-
ler* v. *Elliott*, *H. 5 & 6 G. 4.* 758

44. By 4 *G. 2. c. 28. s. 2.* it is enacted,
that in all cases between landlord
and tenant, as often as it shall
happen that one half year's rent
shall be in arrear, and the landlord
or lessor to whom the same is due,
hath right by law to re-enter for
the non-payment thereof, such
landlord or lessor shall and may,
without any formal demand or re-
entry

... a declaration in ejectment for the recovery of the demised premises, which service shall extend in the place and stead of a demand and recovery: v Held, that this statute the service of the declaration in ejectment is substituted for the demand of rent, which at common law must have been made upon the day when the forfeiture accrued in case of nonpayment; and, therefore, that it was no ground of nonsuit in ejectment, that the declaration was served on a day subsequent to the day on which the demise was laid, that being after the rent became due, because the title of the lessor must be taken to have accrued on the day when the forfeiture would have accrued at common law by nonpayment of the rent. Doe d. *Lawrence and Others v. Shawcross*, H. 5 & 6 G. 4. Page 752

45. Upon error from an inferior court, it appeared by the record that in an action of debt, a summons and attachment issued at the same time, and were returnable at the same time; and neither of them was served personally on the defendant. At the return of these writs the plaintiff declared, and at a subsequent court had judgment by default; the defendant never having appeared, and no appearance having been entered for him. The recorder of the inferior court certified that to be the practice of the court according to immemorial custom. Held, that the custom to declare against a defendant before entry of appearance by him or by some person for him, was bad in law. ... Held, that the custom to issue a summons and attachment at the same time, was also bad. *William v. Lord Paget (in Error)*, H. 5 & 6 G. 4. Page 772

46. Where the tenant of certain premises (under demise out of part by deed, and the original landlord distrained for rent upon the under-tenant: Held, that a sum unpaid would not die by the latter against his lessor, upon an implied promise to indemnify him against the rent payable to the superior landlord. *Schlencker v. Moxey*, H. 5 & 6 G. 4. Page 589

47. In an action for negligence against an attorney, who was employed by a purchaser to inspect the title to an estate, it appeared that by indenture of lease and release of the 9th and 10th of October 1796, the estate had been conveyed to T. M., the father of the vendor's wife, and to J. C., to hold unto the said T. M. and J. C. and their heirs and assigns, to the use and behoof of the said T. M. and J. C. and the heirs and assigns of the said T. M. for ever, the estate of J. C. being used only in trust for the said T. M., his heirs and assigns. T. M. devised the estate to his daughter and to the heirs of her body, but in case she died without leaving any issue of her body living at her decease, then to his nephew T. M. and his heirs for ever. The daughter afterwards by bargain and sale of the 11th of February 1814, conveyed the estate to one J. W., to the intent that he might become tenant of the freehold, for the purpose of suffering a recovery, and a recovery was suffered in pursuance of such deed. This daughter afterwards by deeds of lease and release of the 4th and 5th March 1814 ... upon her marriage, reciting that she was seised in fee simple of the estate, conveyed the same to trustees in trust for her and her husband and their issue, and in default of his upon such persons as she should appoint. The marriage was afterwards

wards solemnized, and the daughter died without issue, and devised the estate in fee to her husband, who survived her. The husband having contracted to sell the estate to the plaintiff, in pursuance of that contract, delivered an abstract of his title to the defendant, as attorney to the vendee, and this abstract contained the deeds of the 9th and 10th of *October* 1796, but it omitted to state certain indentures of lease and release of the 25th and 26th *February* 1814, whereby *J. C.* conveyed the said estate vested in him unto the daughter of *T. M.* in fee; but an abstract of these deeds was delivered by the vendor's solicitor to the defendant, four months before the conveyance of the estate was executed. The defendant laid before counsel a case containing an abstract of the deed of the 11th of *February* 1814, and of the recovery suffered in pursuance of it, of the deeds of the 4th and 5th *March* 1814, and of the will of the daughter of *T. M.*, but omitting altogether the deeds of the 9th and 10th *October* 1796; and it further stated, that *T. M.* was seised in fee of the premises. The opinion of counsel was, that the vendor had a good title, but that opinion would not have been given if the deeds of lease and release of the 9th and 10th *October* 1796, or those of the 25th and 26th *February* 1814 had been stated. The plaintiff afterwards being advised that his title was incomplete, paid a sum of money to *T. M.* the devisee in remainder, for a confirmation of his title. Held, first, that the recovery suffered by the daughter of *T. M.* was invalid, because at that time the legal estate for life was in *J. C.*, and she was only equitable tenant for life, with a legal re-

mainder in tail; and, therefore, that the title was bad.

Held, secondly, that upon these facts a jury were warranted in finding the defendant guilty of negligence, so as to make him liable in this action. *Ireson v. Pearman. Gow. one, 4s. M. 5 & G. 4.*

Page 739

49. Where a scheme for establishing a tontine was put forth, stating that the money subscribed was to be laid out at interest, and after some subscriptions had been paid to the directors, in whom the management of the concern was vested, but before any part of the money was laid out at interest, the directors resolved to abandon the project: Held, that such subscriber might in an action for money had and received, recover the whole of the money advanced by him, without the deduction of any part towards the payment of the expences incurred. *Nockells v. Crosby and Others, M. 5 & 6 G. 4.* 874

POOR.

By statute 55 G. 3. c. 137. s. 6. no churchwarden or overseer of the poor, either in his own name or in the name of any other person, shall supply *for his own profit* any goods, materials, or provisions for the use of any workhouse, or otherwise for the support or maintenance of the poor in any place for which he shall be appointed overseer, during the time he shall retain such appointment, nor shall be concerned directly or indirectly in supplying the same, or in any contract or contracts relating thereto, under the penalty of 100l. Held, that an overseer who supplied coals indirectly for the use of the poor, was not liable to the penalty, unless he did so after a view

them to his own profit.   Skinner v.
Buckee, T. 5 G. 4.   Page 6

POOR RATE.

See OVERSEER, 3.

By a statute of the 9th G. W. 3. the
poor of the town of Kingston-upon-
Hull are placed under the management of a corporation established by that act, and are to be
maintained by money, to be levied
" by taxation of every inhabitant,
and of all lands, houses, tithes impropriate, appropriation of tithes,
and all stocks and estates in the
said town in equal proportions, according to their respective worths
and values." Upon an appeal
against a rate made by virtue of
this act, it appeared that it omitted, first, persons not resident in
Hull, but having stock in trade
there which had produced a specified profit in the last year; secondly, a tenant of houses which
he underlet at a specified profit,
the undertenants being rated, but
excused from paying on account
of poverty; thirdly, owners and
part owners of ships registered at
Hull, and trading to and from that
port, and within the port at the
time when the rate was made.
Some of these persons were resident in Hull, others were not.
Some profits had been derived from
the ships in the preceding year,
but the appellants could not shew
the amount. Held, that the act
in question made all personal property rateable, whether the owner
were or were not resident in Hull,
and that consequently the first
and third classes of persons ought
to have been included in the rate,
and that it was not incumbent on
the appellants to shew the amount
of profit made by the ships, for this
it being established they were prom
VOL. III.

liable, they ought not to have
been altogether omitted; secondly,
that the tenant of houses underlet,
as before mentioned, was not liable
to be rated. The Hull Dock Company were rated at the full amount
of their profits, without first making any deduction for the poor-
rate: Held, that this was wrong,
that the "worth and value" could
only be the profits, minus the outgoings, and that, therefore, supposing other property to be rated
at a rack rent, the poor-rate should
have been calculated upon such a
sum as would, together with the
rate, make up the whole amount of
profits. The King v. The Hull
Dock Company, M. 5 G. 4.
Page 516

PRACTICE.

1. The court will not change the
venue in an action on an award.
Stanway v. Heslop, T. 5 G. 4.   9
2. Assumpsit for goods sold and delivered, and on the money counts.
Pleas, general issue, and the statute of limitations. Defendant
paid money into court generally:
Held, that such payment did not
take the case out of the statute.
Long v. Greville, T. 5 G. 4.   10
3. Where a defendant was by a
Judge's order allowed to go to
trial upon certain terms, upon payment to the plaintiff of a certain
sum of money and the costs incurred up to the date of the order,
and the plaintiff consented to the
trial proceeding on those terms
before the costs had been paid:
Held, that the defendant having
obtained a verdict, was bound to
pay those costs, and could not set
them off against those afterwards
taxed for him on and proview in
pinash v. Stamp, T. 5 G. 4.   105
4. Issue in a declaration served with
a copy of process by original was

3 P   eight

wards the cause, before it came on for trial, and all matters in difference were referred to an arbitrator who had power to examine the parties and call for books, &c.; and it was agreed that the costs should abide the event, the arbitrator having awarded to the plaintiff the sum of 1*l.* 19*s.*, a motion was made to allow the defendant his costs: Held, that this was not a case within the 48 *G.* 3. *c.* 46. *s.* 3., and that the defendant was not entitled to costs. *Keene* v. *Deable, M.* 5 *G.* 4. Page 491

15. Where the third proclamation was made at the door of the church of the parish of which the defendant was described to be in the writ, and in the bond upon which the action was brought, but where he did not reside at the time when the proclamation was made, the Court reversed the outlawry as for want of proclamations, and ordered bail to be taken to pay the condemnation money. *Rayer* v. *Cooke, M.* 5 *G.* 4. 529

16. Where an application is made to set off costs and damages in one action against those recovered in a cross action, an attorney has a lien on the judgment obtained by his client against the opposite party, to the extent of his costs of that cause only. *Stephens* v. *Weston and Griffiths, M.* 5 *G.* 4. 535

17. An ejectment brought in an inferior court on a lease executed and sealed on the premises which were within the jurisdiction of that court, may be removed into this court by certiorari, if there be any ground for believing that it cannot be impartially tried in the inferior court. *Patterson dem. Gradridge and Others* v. *Eades, M.* 5 *G.* 4. 550

18. The Court will not, before issue joined, entertain a motion to change the venue in an action on

a specialty. *Weatherby* v. *Goring, M.* 5 *G.* 4. Page 552

19. By the statute 13 *Car.* 2. *c.* 2. *s.* 3., upon an appearance for the defendant by attorney of the term wherein the process is returnable, unless the plaintiff declare before the end of the term then next following after appearance, judgment of non pros. for want of a declaration may be entered against him: Held, that the statute contemplated such an appearance as would entitle the plaintiff to declare; and, therefore, where a latitat against three defendants having issued, returnable on the last day of *Trinity* term, but only one of the defendants being served, an alias issued returnable on the last day of *Michaelmas* term, and one other of the defendants was served with a copy: in *Hilary* term following a pluries latitat issued, returnable on the last day of *Hilary* term, but which was not served on the third defendant, and another pluries issued returnable on the 19th of *May* in *Easter* term, a copy of which was served on the third defendant; an appearance was entered for all the defendants in *Easter* term, and the plaintiff not having declared in *Trinity* term, the defendant signed judgment of non-pros: Held, that such judgment was regular, within the stat. 13 *Car.* 2. *c.* 2. *s.* 3. *Inwood* v. *Mawley, M.* 5 *G.* 4. 553

20. A special case was stated for the opinion of the Court. The greater part of the statement was fictitious. The Court fined the attorney. *In the Matter of Elsam, an Attorney, M.* 5 *G.* 4. 597

21. Where a continuance was entered from *Trinity* to the first day of *Michaelmas* term, and matter arising during the interval, was pleaded before the first day of *Michaelmas* term by way of plea puis darrein

darrein continuance, the Court ordered the plea to be taken off the file. *The King* v. *Taylor*, H. 5 & 6 G. 4.   Page 612

22. The sheriff having taken goods in execution under a fi. fa., the proceeds of which are not sufficient to satisfy the plaintiff's claim, cannot against him retain any thing beyond the poundage allowed by the statute 29 *Eliz. c.* 4. *Buckle* v. *Bewes*, H. 5 & 6 G. 4.   688

23. The appointment of surveyors of highways under the 13 G. c. 78. cannot be removed into this court by certiorari. *The King* v. *The Justices of St. Alban's*, H. 5 & 6 G. 4.   698

24. The Court referred it to the master to take an account of the rents and profits of an estate received by the plaintiff, who was in possession by virtue of an elegit, and ordered that the plaintiff should give up possession if it appeared that all the monies due to him had been received. *Price* v. *Varney*, H. 5 & 6 G. 4.   733

25. In tort, a party suing out bailable process jointly against several, may declare separately against one of them. *Wilson* v. *Edwards*, H. 5 & 6 G. 4.   734

26. Where a defendant obtained time to plead on the terms of giving judgment of the term, and afterwards brought a writ of error, the Court quashed the writ. *Care* v. *Masey*, H. 5 & 6 G. 4.   Page 735

27. Where a party seeking to reverse an outlawry, does not appear in person, but by attorney, it must appear by affidavit that the attorney acts at the instance of the outlaw. *Plunkett* v. *Buchanan*, H. 5 & 6 G. 4.   736

28. In case against an attorney for negligence, it appeared that the plaintiff in *Hilary* term 4 G. 4., obtained final judgment against H.

who surrendered in discharge of his bail on the day preceding the essoign day of *Easter* term, but notice of the surrender was not given until two days afterwards. *H.* not having been charged in execution in *Easter* term, was superseded and discharged out of custody by a Judge of K. B.: Held, that the present action could not be maintained, for that *H.* was improperly superseded; inasmuch as the two terms allowed by the rule of court *Hilary* term 46 G. 3. for charging a prisoner in execution, are to be calculated from the time of giving notice of the surrender, which in this case was not done until after the legal commencement of *Easter* term: Held, secondly, that even if *H.* had been properly superseded, still the present defendant would not have been liable to an action for negligence, the meaning of the rule of Court being obscure. *Laidler* v. *Elliott*, H. 5 & 6 G. 4.   Page 738

PRESUMPTION,

See EVIDENCE, 20.

PRINCIPAL AND AGENT.

1. *A.* employed *B.*, his agent, to import goods from a foreign country. Upon the arrival of the goods, *B.*, who resided in *London*, transmitted to *A.*, who resided in the country, the invoice, but delivered the bill of lading to a warehouse-keeper, in order to get the goods entered and warehoused. In the warehouse-keeper's books they were described as the property of *B.* By the bill of lading the goods were to be delivered to the order of the shipper, or his assigns, and it was indorsed by the shipper in blank. *B.* had no authority from *A.* to sell the goods, but after they had been standing in his name in the warehouse-keeper's books

books nearly five months, B. sold them: Held, in an action of trover brought by A. against the purchasers, that upon these facts, the jury ought to have been directed that A. was entitled to recover, inasmuch as B. had no authority to sell, or, at least, it ought to have been submitted as a question of fact to the jury, whether A. by his conduct enabled B. to hold himself out to the world, as having the property, as well as the possession of the goods. *Dyer* v. *Pearson and Others*, T. 5 G. 4. Page 38

2. Where a foreign prince gave bonds, whereby he declared himself and his successors bound to every person who should, for the time being, be the holders of the bonds for the payment of the principal and interest in a certain manner: Held, that the property in those instruments passed by delivery, as the property in bank notes, exchequer bills, or bills of exchange payable to bearer; and that, consequently, an agent in whose hands such a bond was placed for a special purpose, might confer a good title by pledging it to a person who did not know that the party pledging was not the real owner. *Gorgier* v. *Mieville and Another*, T. 5 G. 4. 45

3. The master of a ship, which was injured by the perils of the sea, put into the *Mauritius*, and there abandoned the ship and cargo, which were afterwards sold under an order of the Vice Admiralty Court there, and the proceeds paid into that court. The cargo was not damaged or perishable, nor was there any pressing necessity for the sale of it. The owners of the cargo brought an action on the case against the owners of the ship for wrongfully selling the cargo, instead of carrying it to *London*, according to their contract, with a count in trover, and recovered a

general verdict for the value of the ship and freight, which was one-fifth of the value of the cargo. They also sent out a power of attorney to an agent at the *Mauritius*, to procure from the Vice Admiralty Court there, the proceeds of the sale which had been paid in. The agent demanded them, but they had been previously remitted to the High Court of Admiralty in this country. In an action for money had and received by the owners against the purchaser of the goods: Held, first, that the captain had not any authority to sell the cargo, although acting *bonâ fide*, and under the authority of the Vice Admiralty Court; secondly, that the recovery against the owners of the ship was no answer to the present action; thirdly, that the proceeds of the sale at the *Mauritius* not having been paid when demanded, the plaintiffs were in the same situation as if no such demand had been made, and therefore entitled to recover the value of the goods from the defendant. *Morris and Another* v. *Robinson*, T. 5 G. 4. Page 196

4. Certain bills of exchange, drawn upon and accepted by the *E. I.* Company in favor of *W. H.* in *India*, were afterwards indorsed to *D.* and *C.* by an agent for *W. H.*, under a supposed authority given by a power of attorney, which was seen and inspected by the acceptors; *D.* and *C.* indorsed the bill to *B.* and Co., their bankers, in order that the latter might, as their agents, present them for payment when due; *B.* and Co. put their names on the back of the bills, presented them for payment, and received the amount, which they soon after paid over to their principals. It was afterwards discovered, that the power of attorney given by *W. H.* did not authorise

3 P 3 his

his agent to indorse the bills, and the administrator of *W. H.*, in an action against the acceptors, recovered the amount of them. The acceptors then brought an action against *B.* and *Co.*, and declared, on a supposed undertaking by them, that they, as holders, were entitled to receive the amount of the bills. The jury found that the plaintiffs paid the bills on the faith of the power of attorney, and not of the indorsement by the defendants, and that the latter paid over the money before they had notice of the invalidity of the first indorsement: Held, that, under these circumstances, the plaintiffs could not recover against the defendants.

Semble, that an indorser does not implicitly warrant the validity of prior indorsements. *The East India Company* v. *Tritton and Others, T.* 5 *G.* 4.   Page 280

5. *A.* and Co. merchants at *Rio Janeiro,* consigned cottons to *B.* in this country for sale, and sent bills of lading, which shewed that the cottons were sent on account and risk of the consignors. *B.* employed *C.* and *D.*, brokers at *Liverpool,* to effect the sales, which they did; some at a credit of ten days, and bills at three months; others for cash in one month. *C.* and *D.* made large advances to *B.*, and received the proceeds of the cotton when due. Before that time *B.* had become bankrupt. In an action by *A.* and Co. against *C.* and *D.* for money had and received: Held, that the latter were not entitled to retain for the advances made by them to *B.*, for that he was a factor for sale only, and had no authority to pledge the goods, and that the plaintiffs were entitled to recover the net proceeds, deducting such sums only as *B.* could have retained. *A.* and Co.,

when they consigned the cottons to *B.*, requested him to make remittances in anticipation of sales: Held, secondly, that this request did not give *B.* any special authority to pledge the goods. *Queiroz and Others* v. *Trueman and Another, T.* 5 *G.* 4.   Page 342

6. An agent employed by a commercial house in *London* to collect debts in the country, delivered a parcel containing bank notes to a common carrier, to be forwarded to his principals in *London,* which parcel was lost. The carriers had given notice that they would not be accountable for parcels containing bank notes. The agent had no knowledge of such notice, but the principals had: Held, that it was their duty to have instructed their agent not to send bank notes by that carrier, and that the latter was not responsible. *Mayhew and Another* v. *Eames and Another, H.* 5 & 6 *G.* 4.   601

PROHIBITION.

A curate cannot have the benefit of a proceeding by monition for the recovery of a salary assigned by a bishop without the consent of the incumbent, the incumbent being resident on his benefice, and discharging the duties generally, but desirous of the assistance of a curate. *The King* v. *The Bishop of Peterborough, T.* 5 *G.* 4.   47

PROMOTIONS.   177

PUIS DARRIEN CONTINUANCE.

See PLEADING, 21.

RATE.

See INCLOSURE ACT, 1. OVERSEER, 3. POOR RATE.

RECEIPT.

See STAMP, 2.

REMOVAL, ORDER OF.

An order of removal was made, and suspended on the same day, by reason of the infirmity of the pauper. She lived three years afterwards, and no notice of the order of removal was served on the parish to which she was to be removed under the order, until after the death of the pauper: Held, that notice of the order not having been served within a reasonable time, the order of removal was a nullity. *The King* v. *The Inhabitants of Lampeter, M. 5 G. 4.*

Page 454

RULES OF COURT.

T. 5 G. 4. 176, 177

SEA.

See EVIDENCE 3.

SETTLEMENT — *By Apprenticeship.*

1. A pauper, settled in the parish of N. C., in the county of Nottingham, was, pursuant to an order of two justices of the county, bound apprentice by the churchwardens and overseers of that parish to *A.B.* of another parish, in a borough situate in the same county, but having justices who had exclusive jurisdiction therein. The indenture was allowed by the two county justices, but no notice was given to the overseers of the poor of the parish in the borough of the intention to bind such apprentice, nor did they or any of them attend before the county justices who allowed the indenture, and admit

such notice: Held, by three justices, *Abbott* C.J. dissentiente, that by 56 *G.* 3. *c.* 139. the indenture was void for want of such notice, and that the pauper did not gain any settlement by serving under it. *The King* v. *The Inhabitants of Newark-upon-Trent, T. 5 G. 4.*

Page 59

2. An infant bound himself apprentice for seven years, and served three of them; having then quarrelled with his master, the latter offered to sell him the remainder of his time for 6*d.* The infant paid the money, and went away, and bound himself to another master in another parish: Held, that the infant had no power to dissolve the first apprenticeship; the second binding was therefore invalid, and no settlement could be gained by service under it. *The King* v. *The Inhabitants of Wigston, M. 5 G. 4.*

484

3. Where a parish has united with others for the support of the poor according to the provisions of the 22 *G.* 3. *c.* 83., and a guardian has been appointed, the churchwardens and overseers may nevertheless bind poor children apprentices, and it is not necessary that the guardian should sign the indenture. *The King* v. *The Inhabitants of Lutterworth, M. 5 G. 4.*

487

SETTLEMENT — *By Hiring and Service.*

A. B., at ten years of age, went to *C. D.* for meat and clothes as long as he had a mind to stop; he was to do what he could, and what he was bid. *A. B.* remained two years with *C. D.* upon these terms: Held, that there was no yearly hiring, and therefore no settlement gained by the service. *The King* v. *Christ's Parish in York, M. 5 G. 4.*

459

SHIP OWNER.

The master of a ship, which was injured by the perils of the sea, put into the *Mauritius*, and there abandoned the ship and cargo, which were afterwards sold under an order of the Vice-Admiralty Court there, and the proceeds paid into that court. The cargo was not damaged or perishable, nor was there any pressing necessity for the sale of it. The owners of the cargo brought an action on the case against the owners of the ship, for wrongfully selling the cargo, instead of carrying it to *London* according to their contract, with a count in trover, and recovered a general verdict for the value of the ship and freight, which was one-fifth of the value of the cargo. They also sent out a power of attorney to an agent at the *Mauritius* to procure from the Vice-Admiralty Court there the proceeds of the sale, which had been paid in. The agent demanded them, but they had been previously remitted to the High Court of Admiralty in this country. In an action for money had and received by the owners against the purchaser of the goods: Held, first, that the captain had not any authority to sell the cargo, although acting *bonâ fide* and under the order of the Vice-Admiralty Court; secondly, that the recovery against the owners of the ship was no answer to the present action; thirdly, that the proceeds of the sale at the *Mauritius* not having been paid when demanded, the plaintiffs were in the same situation as if no such demand had been made, and therefore entitled to recover the value of the goods from the defendant. *Morris and Another* v. *Robinson*, T. 5 G. 4,

Page 196

STAMP.

1. *A.* entered into a written agreement with *B.* for the hire of a piece of land for the purpose of making bricks. *C.* afterwards made an offer in writing to let another piece of land to *A.* upon the terms contained in the agreement between him (*A.*) and *B.*, and at a subsequent time *A.* verbally accepted this offer. In an action by *C.* for a breach of some of the terms of this contract: Held, that the written offer made by *C.* was admissible in evidence without being stamped. *Drant* v. *Brown*, Executor of *Leggott*, H. 5 & 6 G. 4,

Page 665

2. In replevin defendant avowed for rent due upon a demise, at a certain fixed rent. Plea, that plaintiff did not hold under defendant at the rent mentioned in the avowry, and issue joined upon that fact. At the trial, the defendant, in order to prove the holding as alleged, tendered in evidence certain unstamped papers, the effect of which was, to shew that the plaintiff had paid rent at the rate mentioned in the avowry: Held, that these papers were inadmissible for want of stamps, inasmuch as they were in effect tendered to prove the payment of the rent; for if they did not prove the payment of the rent they would not support the issue, and would on that ground be inadmissible.

The defendant's steward proved that a lease had been executed by the defendant but not by the plaintiff, the terms of which had been reduced into writing by the assent of both parties, and he stated that to be the final agreement between the parties. The plaintiff, in order to negative this statement, tendered in evidence another unstamped paper, in the hand-writing of the defend-

defendant's steward, the effect of which was, to shew that it was subsequently proposed by him, that the plaintiff was to hold at a rent different from that mentioned in the lease; Held, that as this paper was not signed by the parties, it did not amount to an agreement or minute of an agreement, but to a proposal only, and, therefore, that it did not require a stamp, and was properly received in evidence. *Hawkins* v. *Warre*, H. 5 & 6 G. 4.

Page 690

STEWARD.

The lord of a manor may, by deed, grant the stewardship of the manor and of the courts thereto belonging, for the life of the grantee. A term of 500 years, created in 1712, was, upon a sale of the estate in 1785, assigned to attend the inheritance. Upon a subsequent sale in 1799, there was a general declaration in the conveyance, that all persons having outstanding terms should hold them in trust to attend the inheritances; but no particular term was specified: Held, that in support of the grant of the stewardship made in 1821, it was properly left to the jury to say whether they thought the term had been surrendered, and that they were justified in finding that it had: *Bartlett* v. *Downes*, H. 5 & 6 G. 4. 616

SUNDAY.

See VENDOR AND VENDEE, 5.

SUPERSEDEAS.

See PRACTICE, 28.

SURETY.

Where B. being indebted to A. procured E. to join with him in giving

a joint and several promissory note for the amount, and afterwards having become further indebted, and being pressed by A. for further security, by deed (reciting the debt, and that for a part a note had been given by him (B.) and C., and that A. having demanded payment of the debt, B. had requested him to accept a *further* security), assigned to A. all his household goods, &c. as a *further* security, with a proviso that he should not be deprived of the possession of the property assigned, until after three days' notice: Held, that this deed did not extinguish or suspend the remedy on the note, but that A. might, notwithstanding the deeds, sue C. at any time. *Twopenny* v. *Young*, T. 5 G. 4.　　Page 208

TITHES.

1. Where in case for not carrying away tithe corn, the plaintiff alleged that it was "lawfully and in due manner set out:" Held, that this allegation was satisfied, by proof that the tithe was set out according to an agreement between the parties, although it varied from the mode prescribed by the common law.

Whether the whole crop has been left on the ground for a reasonable time after the tithe has been set out, in order that the tithe owner may compare the tenth part with the other nine, is a question for the jury and not for the Court. *Facey* v. *Hurdom*, T. 5 G. 4.　　213

2. Where a private inclosure act (reciting that it was expedient that the tithes in the parish should be extinguished, and an adequate compensation should be made to the vicar,) enacted that the commissioners should, in a certain mode, ascertain what yearly sum the tithes were worth, and that there should

should be issuing and payable to the vicar out of the lands, each yearly sum, " free and clear of all rates, taxes, and deductions whatsoever." Held, that the vicar was not rateable to the poor in respect of the yearly sum so ascertained and paid to him. *Chatfield, Clerk, v. Ruston, H. 5 & 6 G. 4.*

TITLE DEEDS.

See VENDOR AND VENDEE, 4.

TRESPASS.

In trespass against two magistrates, for giving plaintiff's landlord possession of a farm as a deserted farm; they produced in evidence a record of their proceedings under that act, which set forth all such circumstances as were necessary to give them jurisdiction, and by which it appeared that they had pursued the directions of the statute: Held, that this was conclusive as an answer to the action. *Beston v. Carew and Another, H. 5 & 6 G. 4.*

TROVER.

1. A. employed B. his agent to import goods from a foreign country. Upon the arrival of the goods B., who resided in London, transmitted to A, who resided in the country the invoice, but delivered the bill of lading to a warehouse-keeper, in order to get the goods entered and warehoused. In the warehouse-keeper's books they were described as the property of B. By the bill of lading the goods were to be delivered to the order of the shipper or his assigns, and it was indorsed by the shipper in blank. B. had no authority from A. to sell

the goods, but after they had been standing in his name in the warehouse-keeper's books nearly five months, B. sold them: Held, in an action of trover brought by A. against the purchasers, that upon these facts the jury ought to have been directed that A. was entitled to recover, inasmuch as B. had no authority to sell, or at least that it ought to have been submitted as a question of fact to the jury, whether A. had by his conduct enabled B. to hold himself out to the world as having the property as well as the possession of the goods. *Dyer v. Pearson and Others, T. 5 G. 4.*

2. Plaintiff having contracted to purchase an estate of B., had the deeds of conveyance prepared at his own expence, and sent them to B. for execution. B. executed and gave them to a servant to be sent back; the servant delivered them to defendant, an attorney, who had a demand upon B. for business done in his profession. No directions were given to defendant to retain the deeds until the purchase money should be paid. Some necessary parties refused to execute the deeds, and plaintiff having abandoned the contract, demanded the deeds from the defendant, who refused to deliver them up, claiming to have a lien for his demand against B. In trover for deeds and stamped pieces of parchments: Held, that the plaintiff was entitled to recover the deeds, at all events, in a cancelled if not in an uncancelled state. *Littledale J. dubitante, Esdaile v. Oxenham, T. 5 G. 4.*

USURY.

1. When a person has two demands upon another, one arising out of a lawful contract, the other out of a contract

contract forbidden by law, and the debtor makes a payment which is not specifically appropriated by either party at the time of payment, the law will appropriate it to the debt recognized by law; and therefore where distinct sums of money were due, one for goods sold, the other for money lent on a usurious contract, and a payment was made which was not specifically appropriated to either debt by debtor or creditor, it was held that the law would afterwards appropriate such payment to the debt for goods sold. Where a bill of exchange was given for the principal money lent, and interest to accrue due on a usurious contract, and before the bill became due the lender advanced a further sum of money on the general credit of the borrower, which enabled the latter to pay the bill, it was held that the payment of the usurious interest was complete as soon as the bill was paid. *Wright and Another, Assignees, v. Laing, T. 5 G. 4.*

Page 165

2. *A. B.* and *C.* carried on the business of bankers in copartnership. *A.* advanced large sums of money to the concern, which he raised by selling out stock, and he took separate bonds for 18,000*l.* from *B.* and *C.*, for the replacing of 9000*l.* 3 per cent. consols by each, being their respective proportions of the stock sold by *A.* The stock not being replaced, *A.* brought actions, and recovered judgments on the bonds. *A.* afterwards retired from the concern, and at that time 20,000*l.* 3 per cent. consols was due to him; by the deed of dissolution *B.* and *C.* covenanted to replace it by four instalments, and that if they failed to do so, *A.* might resort to the judgments recovered on the bonds; and further, that he should have a lien on certain specified securities for that debt, and also as an indemnity against partnership debts which they covenanted to pay. One instalment was replaced when due, but *B.* and *C.* having failed to replace the second, a new agreement (not under seal) was entered into, whereby it was agreed that the transaction should be considered as a loan of money from the first, and that the sum produced by the sale of the 15,000*l.* 3 per cent. which remained due, which was 10,083*l.*, should be the debt, and be repaid at a future day with 5 per cent. interest. The value of 15,000*l.* 3 per cent. consols at the date of this last agreement was 8437*l.* Before any part of the 10,083*l.* was paid, *B.* and *C.* became bankrupts, and at the issuing of the commission, two out of the three remaining days fixed by the deed of dissolution for the re-transfer of stock had passed. Held, that the second agreement was void for usury, but that the deed of dissolution remained binding, and that *A.* might prove under the commission against *B.* and *C.* for the 15,000*l.* 3 per cent. consols, the value of the two instalments due before the bankruptcy, to be ascertained by the price of consols on the days when those sums respectively became due; the value of the third to be taken at the price of consols on the day when the commission issued, with a rebate for the interval between that day and the day fixed for the re-transfer of that instalment; and further, that *A.* still had the lien given by the deed. *A.* having paid certain old partnership debts after he left the concern: Held, secondly, that he might prove for those also. Whilst *A.* remained in the bank he received interest upon his advances without any deduction for property tax: Held, thirdly, that no deduction

duction was to be made, in respect
of that from the sum to be proved
by him, inasmuch as it did not appear that the bankrupts had accounted to government for the property tax on the monies so paid.
Parker v. Ramsbottom and Others,
T. 5 G. 4. Page 257

3. Where the lender of stock reserved to himself the dividends by
way of interest, and the option of
deciding at a future day whether
he would have the stock replaced,
or the sum produced by the sale of
it repaid, to him, in money with
5 per cent. interest: Held, that
this bargain was usurious, and that
it made no difference whether the
whole of the agreement was contained in one instrument, or whether the lender procured the execution of two instruments, by one
of which he might compel the replacing of the stock, by the other
the payment of the money and interest. *White and Another, Executors, v. Wright*, T. 5 G. 4. 273

4. Debt for money had and received.
Plea, general issue, and set off for
money lent, paid, &c. At the trial
it appeared that the plaintiffs *A.* and
Co. in *England* consigned goods
to the defendants, *B.* and Co. at
Gibraltar, to be sold on commission. *B.* and Co. as soon as
the bills of lading and invoices
were delivered to their agents in
London, advanced, through them,
to *A.* and Co. two-thirds of the invoice price of the goods, by bills at
ninety days; and for these advances
received interest at the rate of 6 per
cent., calculated from the date of
the bills, which was the usual rate of
interest at *Gibraltar*. In an action
for the proceeds of the goods:
Held, that this could not be considered as a loan of money in
England, and was not usurious, and
that the defendants were entitled to
set off the monies so advanced.

*Harvey and Others, Assignees, v.
Archbold and Others*, H. 5 & 6 G. 4.
Page 626
5. In an action brought to recover
penalties under the statute of usury,
it appeared that the contract was
made in one county and the money
paid in another. The venue was
laid in the county where the contract was made: Held, that it ought
to have been laid where the usurious
interest was received. *Pearson v.
M'Gowan*, H. 5 & 6 G. 4. 700

VARIANCE.

1. Where in an action to a false return to a *fieri facias*, the declaration
stated that the plaintiff, in *Trinity*
term 2 G. 4., by the judgment recovered, &c. " as appears by the
record," and the proof was of a
judgment in *Easter* term 3 G. 4.:
Held, that this was no variance;
for that the averment, " as appears
by the record," was surplusage, and
might be rejected, inasmuch as the
judgment was not the foundation
of, but mere inducement to the
action. *Stoddart v. Palmer*, T.
5 G. 4. 2
2. Declaration stated that plaintiff
was an attorney, and had been employed as vestry clerk in the parish
of *A.*, and that whilst he was such
vestry clerk, certain prosecutions
were carried on against *B.* for certain misdemeanors, and in furtherance of such proceedings, and to
bring the same to a successful issue,
certain sums of money belonging
to the parishioners were appropriated and applied to the discharge of the expenses incurred
on account of the said proceedings; yet defendant intending, &c.
to injure the plaintiff in his profession of an attorney, and to cause
him to be esteemed a fraudulent
practiser in his said profession, and
in his office as vestry clerk, and to
cause

cause it to be suspected that the plaintiff had fraudulently applied money belonging to the parishioners; on, &c., at, &c., falsely and maliciously published of and concerning the plaintiff, and of and concerning *the matters aforesaid, the libel, &c.* It appeared on the production of the libel at the trial, that the imputation was, that the plaintiff had applied the parish money in payment of the expences of the prosecution *after* it had terminated : Held, that this was no variance, because it did not alter the character of the libel, the fraud imputed to the plaintiff being the same whether the money was misapplied before or after the proceedings had terminated ; and that the allegation that the libel was published of and concerning *the matters aforesaid,* did not make it necessary to prove precisely that the libel did relate to every part of the matter previously stated. *May, Gent. one, &c. v. Brown, T. 5 G. 4.*
Page 113

9. Declaration for a libel stated that the plaintiff was an attorney, and that the defendant intending to injure him in his good name, and in his said profession of an attorney, published a libel of and concerning the plaintiff, and of and concerning him in his said profession. At the trial the plaintiff failed in proving that at the time of the publication of the libel he was an attorney : Held, that this was not a fatal variance between the allegation and the proof, the words of the libel being objectionable, although not used with reference to the professional character of the plaintiff. *Lewis v. Walter, T. 5 G. 4.*
138

8. Assumpsit, that in consideration that plaintiff would advance a sum of money to *A. B.,* defendant promised that provision should be

made for repaying the plaintiff. At the trial it appeared that the defendant had given to the plaintiff the guarantee stated in the declaration, and that the latter was a partner with two other persons in a banking house, and that the firm had advanced money and charged *A. B.* in account with the same : Held, that the averment in the declaration, that the plaintiff had advanced the money, was not supported by the proof, there being no evidence to shew that the money had been advanced to the plaintiff by the firm, and by him to *A. B. Garrett v. Handley, M. 5 G. 4.*
Page 462

5. Where a manufacturer had adopted a particular mark for his goods, in order to denote that they were manufactured by him : Held, that an action on the case was maintainable by him against another person, who adopted the same mark for the purpose of denoting that his goods were manufactured by the plaintiff, and who sold the goods so marked as and for goods manufactured by the plaintiff. The declaration stated that defendant sold the goods as and for goods manufactured by the plaintiff; it appeared in evidence that the person who bought the goods knew by whom they were manufactured, but that the defendant used the plaintiff's mark, and sold the goods so marked, in order that his customers might, and in fact they did, resell them as and for goods manufactured by the plaintiff: Held, that this evidence supported the declaration. *Sykes v. Sykes, M. 5 G. 4.*
541

VENDOR AND VENDEE.

1. Where goods of the value of 14l. were made to order, and remained in the possession of the vendor at the

the request of the vendee, with the exception of a small part which the latter took away : Held, that there was no acceptance of the residue of the goods within the Statute of Frauds, section 17. *Thompson v. Maceroni, T. 5 G. 4.*

Page 1

2. *A.* employed *B.,* his agent, to import goods from a foreign country. Upon the arrival of the goods *B.,* who resided in *London,* transmitted to *A.,* who resided in the country, the invoice, but delivered the bill of lading to a warehouse-keeper, in order to get the goods entered and warehoused. In the warehouse-keeper's books they were described as the property of *B.* By the bill of lading the goods were to be delivered to the order of the shipper or his assigns, and it was indorsed by the shipper in blank. *B.* had no authority from *A.* to sell the goods, but after they had been standing in his name in the warehouse-keeper's books nearly five months, *B.* sold them : Held, in an action of trover brought by *A.* against the purchasers, that upon these facts the jury ought to have been directed that *A.* was entitled to recover, inasmuch as *B.* had no authority to sell, or at least it ought to have been submitted as a question of fact to the jury, whether *A.* had by his conduct enabled *B.* to hold himself out to the world, as having the property, as well as the possession of the goods. *Dyer v. Pearson and Others, T. 5 G 4.* 38

3. The master of a ship, which was injured by the perils of the sea, put into the *Mauritius,* and there abandoned the ship and cargo, which were afterwards sold under an order of the Vice Admiralty Court there, and the proceeds paid into that court. The cargo was not damaged or perishable, nor was

there any pressing necessity for the sale of it. The owners of the cargo brought an action on the case against the owners of the ship for wrongfully selling the cargo, instead of carrying it to *London* according to their contract, with a count in trover, and recovered a general verdict for the value of the ship and freight, which was one-fifth of the value of the cargo. They also sent out a power of attorney to an agent at the *Mauritius,* to procure from the Vice Admiralty Court there, the proceeds of the sale which had been paid in. The agent demanded them, but they had been previously remitted to the High Court of Admiralty in this country. In an action for money had and received by the owners against the purchasers of the goods : Held, first, that the captain had not any authority to sell the cargo, although acting *bonâ fide* and under the authority of the Vice Admiralty Court ; secondly, that the recovery against the owners of the ship was no answer to the present action ; thirdly, that the proceeds of the sale at the *Mauritius* not having been paid when demanded, the plaintiffs were in the same situation as if no such demand had been made, and therefore entitled to recover the value of the goods from the defendant. *Morris and Another v. Robinson,* T. 5 G. 4.

Page 196

4. Plaintiff having contracted to purchase an estate of *B.*, had the deeds of conveyance prepared at his own expense, and sent them to *B.* for execution. *B.* executed and gave them to a servant to be sent back. The servant delivered them to defendant, an attorney, who had a demand of 100l. upon *B.* for business done in his profession. No directions were given to defendant to retain the deeds

until

until the purchase money should be paid. Some necessary parties refused to execute the deeds, and plaintiff having abandoned the contract, demanded the deeds from defendant, who refused to deliver them up, claiming to have a lien for his demand against B. In trover for deeds and stamped pieces of parchment: Held, that the plaintiff was entitled to recover the deeds at all events, in a cancelled, if not in an uncancelled state. *Littledale* J. dubitante. *Esdaile* v. *Oxenham, T. 5 G. 4.*

Page 225

5. *A.* not knowing that *B.* was a horse dealer, made a verbal bargain with him on a *Sunday* for the purchase of a horse. The price (which was above 10*l.*) was then specified, and *B.* warranted the horse to be sound. It was not delivered, however, until the following *Tuesday*, when the money was paid: Held, that there was not any complete contract until the delivery of the horse, and consequently that the contract was not void within the statute 29 *Car. 2. c. 7. s. 2.* But assuming it to be void, held, secondly, in an action for breach of the warranty, that the purchaser having no knowledge of the fact that the vendor was exercising his ordinary calling on the *Sunday*, had not been guilty of any breach of the law, and therefore was entitled to recover back the price of the horse. *Blossome* v. *Williams, T. 5 G. 4.* 232

6. A hogshead of wine in the warehouse of the *London* Dock Company was sold for 13*l.*, and a delivery order was given to the vendee. There was no contract in writing: Held, that the acceptance of the delivery order by the vendee

was not an actual acceptance of the wine within the statute of frauds. *Bentall and Others, Assignees,* v. *Burn, M. 5 G. 4.*

Page 423

7. It was agreed between the vendors and vendee of goods that the latter should pay 10*s.* per ton beyond the market price, which sum was to be applied in liquidation of an old debt due to one of the vendors. The payment of the goods was guaranteed by a third person, but the bargain between the parties was not communicated by the surety: Held, that that was a fraud on the surety, and rendered the guaranty void. *Pidcock and Others* v. *Bishop, H. 5 & 6 G. 4.* 605

8. Where the vendor of a public-house made pending the treaty, certain deceitful representations respecting the amount of the business done in the house, and the rent received for a part of the premises, whereby the plaintiff was induced to give a large sum for the premises: Held, that the latter might maintain an action on the case for the deceitful representations, although they were not noticed in the conveyance of the premises, or in a written memorandum of the bargain, which was drawn up after the representations were made. *Dobell* v. *Stevens, H. 5 & 6 G. 4.* 623

VENUE.

WILL.

WITNESS.

END OF THE THIRD VOLUME.

CPSIA information can be obtained
at www.ICGtesting.com
Printed in the USA
BVHW061851051118
532208BV00009B/186/P